492-2069
Gillie
Pauliette

Physiology of Behavior

PHYSIOLOGY OF BEHAVIOR

Neil R. Carlson
University of Massachusetts

Allyn and Bacon, Inc.
Boston   London   Sydney   Toronto

Library of Congress Cataloging in Publication Data

Carlson, Neil R.   1942-
    Physiology of behavior.

    Bibliography: p.
    Includes index.
    1.   Psychology, Physiological. I.   Title.
QP360.C35   152   76-49957

ISBN 0-205-05706-3

Fourth printing…July, 1978

ISBN 0-205-05930-9 (International)

This book is dedicated to the people closest to me: my wife, MARY, *my children,* KERSTIN *and* PAUL, *and my parents,* ALICE *and* FRITZ.

Contents

Contents

Preface

As my colleagues know, a competent physiological psychologist must know something of anatomy, physiology, biochemistry, pharmacology, and endocrinology—and have a good understanding of behavioral processes. Depending upon one's particular area of study, special competence in some of the biological subfields is necessary. Also, one cannot perform research without having the appropriate technical skills—surgical, histological, or electronic, for example.

The breadth of the field we call physiological psychology, and the extent to which this field relies on other disciplines, makes its study a rather daunting prospect for most students. Similarly, a prospective author is daunted by the task of writing a textbook that will provide students with a solid introduction to the field. If ambiguities or contradictory results are glossed over, students are misled, and an injustice is done to the many careful researchers who are trying to unravel the subtle complexities of physiology and behavior. On the other hand, a disservice is done to students, and to the field, by becoming enmeshed in the details of research that do not reveal anything about *process*, or the underlying physiological mechanisms that determine an organism's behavior.

I have attempted to steer clear of the pitfalls of oversimplification and I have tried to avoid following what appear to be blind alleys. This means that in some instances I have stated that we do not yet know which of two or more contradictory generalizations is true, and that in other instances I have not reported on experiments that have not advanced our understanding of physiological mechanisms of behavior.

This text is designed for serious students who are willing to work. In return for their effort, I have endeavored to write a book that will provide a solid foundation for further study in the area. Those students who will not take any subsequent courses in this or related areas should receive the satisfaction of a much better understanding of their own behavior. Also, they will have a greater appreciation for the forthcoming advances in medical practices related to various disorders that affect a person's perceptual processes or behavior. It was my wish, in writing this text, that a student who carefully reads this book will henceforth perceive human behavior in a new light.

Besides the effort to avoid oversimplifications and the snare of the arcane, I had several other goals in mind as I wrote this book. First, I attempted to describe the physiology of *human* behavior, insofar as possible. A rat is a good subject for the study of the physiological control of food intake. However, recent evidence shows that if we wish to understand the anatomy of the memory process in the human brain, we must study the human brain itself, or at least the brains of higher primates. We humans are able to learn and integrate information across sensory modalities in ways that most other animals cannot.

A second principle that has guided my writing is to leave no steps out of logical discourse. My teaching experience has taught me that an entire lecture can be wasted if the students do not understand all of the "obvious" conclusions of a given experiment before the next one is described. The problem for the instructor is that the puzzlement usually leads to feverish note-taking ("I'll get all the facts down so that I can figure out what they mean later"). And a roomful of busy, attentive students tends, unfortunately, to reinforce the lecturer for what he or she is doing. I am sure all my colleagues have been stopped cold by a student's question that shows a lack of understanding of details long since passed, and, even more alarming, quizzical looks on other students' faces, confirming that they, too, have the same question. Painful experiences such as these have taught me to examine all the logical steps between the discussion of one experiment and the next and to make sure that they are all explicitly stated.

A third principle, which is closely related to the second, is to provide the student with the background necessary for the understanding of a given set of experiments. In this regard, students are taught the nature of postsynaptic potentials and the decision-making process of integration, the mechanism of the liberation of transmitter substance, the biosynthesis of the neurotransmitters, and principles of neuropharmacology so that they can understand the use of the phenothiazines and butyrophenones in the treatment of schizophrenia. I have been careful to provide enough biological background to the various topics in this book so that a course in zoology or physiology need not be a prerequisite to understanding the content. However, students with such a background will find the reading easier, and they will probably get more out of it.

In this book I have emphasized the fact that physiological psychology is the study of the *physiological*, not merely *neural*, bases of behavior. We must not restrict our view of the organism to those parts above the neck; the rest of the body does more than move the head around. For example, unless we understand how the kidney works and how blood volume is monitored and maintained, we cannot understand the physiology of thirst, no matter how many brain lesions we produce, or how many neurons we record from, or how many areas we electrically stimulate.

During the past few years, the efforts of researchers have yielded some outstanding results that have significantly advanced our understanding of physiology and behavior. Some of these results have not yet been described and discussed in a textbook of physiological psychology. Also, we have gained new insights into the meaning of phenomena that have been known about for some time. Finally, some knowledge that has been regarded as commonplace by investigators in other fields has only recently been appreciated by physiological psychologists. A few examples discussed in this book are as follows:

Recycling of the membrane of the synaptic vesicles
Regulation of the extracellular fluid by glia, and its relationship to epilepsy
Visual processing (even in humans) independent of striate cortex
Contribution of the study of the apraxias to the understanding of the initiation and control of movement

Role of the basal ganglia in "slow ramp" movements and of the cerebellum in rapid movements

Organizational and activational effects of hormones on brain and behavior

Identification of receptors in the liver as significant determinants of hunger and satiety

Role of fat metabolism in obesity produced by VMH lesions

Tail pinch, dopaminergic systems, and recovery from the LH syndrome

Rise and fall of the subfornical organ as the location of receptors that mediate angiotensin-produced thirst

Nucleus circularis and control of ADH release

Lack of serious harm from sleep deprivation

Role of D sleep in learning

Mechanism underlying the cyclicity of S sleep and D sleep

Psychosurgery

Reward mechanisms, dopaminergic systems, and schizophrenia

Evaluation of the gate-control theory of pain

Analgesia produced by electrical brain stimulation

Opiate receptors and endogenous opiates of the brain

Importance of cross-modal transfer of information to the understanding of human memory

Disconnection syndromes in humans and animals

Reevaluation of the effects of temporal lobectomies in humans

Phosphorylation and the control of protein synthesis with regard to memory formation

Although I must take all the blame for the shortcomings of this book, I want to publicly thank students and colleagues for helping me by reading and criticizing early drafts of the manuscript, for suggesting references, and for letting me talk with them, trying out my ideas and conclusions. I want to express special thanks to John Donahoe, Robert Feldman, Kay Fite, Mark Friedman, Richard Gold, Bruce Rideout, Peter Rosenfeld, Nico Spinelli, Otfried Spreen, Leanna Standish, Richard Valcourt, George Wade, and David Walker. I also want to express my thanks to the people at Allyn and Bacon who provided so much encouragement and support: Frank Ruggirello, my editor; Allen Workman, who made many valuable suggestions about the book's organization and outline; and Sheryl Avruch, who improved my prose and otherwise caught my errors (almost all of them, I hope) and guided the book through the stages of production. To my wife Mary goes a special thank you for all she did to assist and encourage me, including (among many other things) a lot of help with the typing of the manuscript. I also want to thank Rhoda Drake for all the trips she made to the library for me. Finally, I want to thank the University of Massachusetts for supporting me on sabbatical leave, during which I wrote most of the book, and the University of Victoria, British Columbia, for generously providing me with office space and use of its library facilities during my stay there.

xiii

One of the most rewarding aspects of publication of this book would be the establishment of a dialogue with students and colleagues who read this book. I hope very much that you will write to me and tell me what you like and dislike about it. Please write to me at the Department of Psychology, Tobin Hall, University of Massachusetts, Amherst, Massachusetts 01002. I also hope that you will write to discuss issues I have raised in this book or some that I have not raised that you think I should have. I enjoyed writing this book even more than I thought I would, and the pleasure would be extended by receiving correspondence from you.

Neil R. Carlson

Introduction

1

BRAIN AND MIND

It is human nature to wish to understand and predict events that affect our lives, and it was long ago that our ancestors first looked inside the human body to see what makes it work. Of course, people recognized then that the interior of a human looked remarkably like that of an animal. They also recognized that humans and animals were distinctly different. Humans thought, planned, talked, made laws, and fought wars. Animals, on the other hand, could be useful to humans, providing them with commodities like food and clothing or providing them with amusement as pets. Animals could even be dangerous. They could not, however, threaten the supremacy of *Homo sapiens* as thinkers, talkers, and planners. If the insides of humans and animals were so similar, what accounted for human superiority? Were early humans confronted with this question?

Probably not. Long before our ancestors began trying to figure out how their bodies worked, they had undoubtedly concluded that there were souls or spirits inhabiting their bodies. The thinking part of their bodies would not be seen when a human body was cut open. Even if one were searching for anatomical explanations for human intellect, gross dissection of the body would not provide many clues. Our brains are not really disproportionately large in relation to the size of our bodies. Thus, the first people who peered into the human body did not find an organ whose appearance explained our uniqueness.

This is not to say that our ancesors did not correctly identify the head as the locus of thought and feelings; after all, the eyes and ears let sights and sounds into the head. Furthermore, head injuries produced singular effects: a blow to the head often resulted in confusion and disorientation, while more severe wounding could cause blindness, deafness, paralysis, or loss of memory. Thus, it appeared that our minds or souls lived in our heads. Apparently the head also had room for foreign spirits; skulls of primitive people have been found with carefully drilled holes in them, presumably to let these intruders out. However, general acceptance of our brains as the *basis*, and not just the *locus*, of our minds is a much more recent event.

It is a basic premise of physiological psychology that our minds are no more than the manifestations of functioning human brains. The mind does not *control* the brain; neither does the brain *control* the mind. Rather, the brain, in its operations, gives rise to the mind. Physiological psychologists have no answer to the mystery of self-awareness, that peculiarly private experience. If we are indeed machines, why are we conscious of our own existence? The fact that we cannot now answer this question does not mean that we must abandon the conviction that our behavior, our feelings, and our thoughts are no more than functions of our physiology. After all, a denial of the physiological basis of mind does not explain anything, either.

Along with human self-awareness comes a feeling of special insight into the control of our behavior. We feel that we are free to decide, to do as we want—in other words, we feel like we have free will. We distinguish between automatic, reflexive behaviors (sneezing, or jumping when startled, for example) and those that we *choose* to perform. Even when we find ourselves compulsively doing something we do not wish to do (smoking, or being too critical of others, or going out when we mean to study), we interpret these behaviors as resulting from failures of will: if we would just try harder, we could control our behavior. Even physiological psychologists feel that way.

The Unity of Consciousness

Human awareness also brings with it a feeling of unity of consciousness; each of us is a single individual, with a store of memories, needs, hopes, and feelings. Our personalities may have different aspects, and our tastes may change, but to each of us our mind appears to be a single entity. When we observe an object we do not experience the feel of it, the sound of it, and the sight of it as belonging to different objects. Neither do we experience our various sense modalities as providing separate awareness; we perceive them as different inputs to a single consciousness. And yet, as we shall see later (in chapter 18), this does not appear to be the case for most animals other than ourselves. Their minds (if the term *mind* can be applied to animals other than humans) are probably *not* unitary, since present evidence suggests that experiences gained by way of one sense modality do not easily modify experiences gained by way of another sense modality. A human would have no trouble recognizing, by touch, in the dark, objects previously seen but not felt. This is not, however, generally true for other animals.

Information about the environment is conveyed to the brain by sensory nerves, and it is analyzed there by various sensory systems. These systems occupy relatively distinct parts of the brain. This separation means, for example, that the identification of patterns of sound as words is accomplished by regions of the brain distinct from those that interpret a visual pattern as a representation of the person speaking these words. The integration of information received by different sensory modalities appears to be accomplished by means of interconnections between brain regions that perform these analyses. In effect, these interconnections unify our sensory awareness.

Two Minds in One: The Effects of Surgical Division of the Brain

The fact that awareness depends on specific connections within the brain is shown quite dramatically by the behavior of people whose brains have been surgically divided. The most important connection between the right and left hemispheres of the brain is provided by the *corpus callosum*. Besides conveying information, the corpus callosum occasionally transmits (in people with certain forms of epilepsy) a violent storm of neural impulses from one side of the brain to the other. In an attempt to control this disorder, the corpus callosum was severed surgically in several people whose epilepsy did not respond to medication (Bogen, Fisher, and Vogel, 1965). The results were generally quite successful, providing the patients with considerable relief. (See **FIGURE 1.1.**)

One might think that such an operation would disrupt a person's behavior in a clearly observable manner. Instead, these people appear quite normal, at least to the casual observer. Careful study is needed to reveal the fact that the cerebral hemispheres of these people, no longer able to interchange information, can independently perceive, think, act, and remember. In fact, as we shall see, the hemispheres can even engage in conflict.

Although the right and left sides of the brain operate indepen-

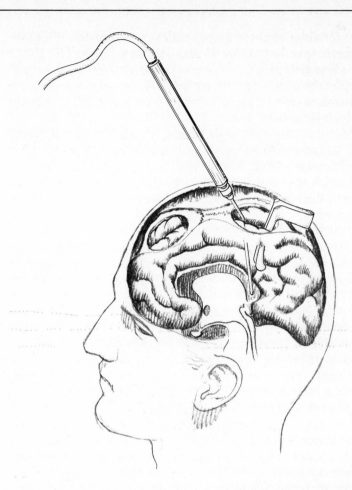

FIGURE 1.1   Schematic view of the surgical separation of the cerebral hemisphere produced by cutting the corpus callosum. (From Gazzaniga, M. S., *Fundamentals of Psychology.* New York: Academic Press, 1973.)

dently after the corpus callosum has been severed, the left hemisphere, because of its unique capabilities, dominates the person's behavior. Mechanisms located in the left hemisphere are responsible for the comprehension and production of speech. For example, damage to one region of the left hemisphere will impair a person's ability to comprehend the meaning of speech. Damage to another region will prevent normal speech, although the patient will still be able to understand spoken words. Destruction of the same regions of the right hemisphere will not produce these disabilities; people with damage to the right hemisphere can converse normally. (Contrary to popular belief, speech mechanisms are usually located in the left hemisphere whether a person is left- or right-handed. The right hemisphere is dominant for speech in only a small minority of the population.)

The fact that a person's verbal activities are normally controlled by one hemisphere accounts for the relatively minor change

seen in these activities after the corpus callosum is severed. This normal hemispheric speech dominance also accounts for the fact that a person with a bisected brain does not give the impression of possessing two independently operating hemispheres, since only one of them (the left) controls speech. The right hemisphere is not able to express itself verbally; it is mute.

Besides being mute, the right hemisphere is also an extremely poor reader. Because of this fact, one of the first things a person with a split brain learns is to hold a book with the right hand while reading. The muscles of the arms and legs are largely controlled by the opposite side of the brain. (The nerve fibers conveying the impulses from brain to muscle cross to the other side in lower parts of the brain and in the spinal cord and are thus not affected when the corpus callosum is severed.) This arrangement means that the right hemisphere controls the left hand. Since the right hemisphere is not able to comprehend the meaning of the words on a page being read by the left hemisphere, it will find reading to be a boring task. Therefore, a book held in the left hand (which is controlled by the right hemisphere) will be quickly put down. (See **FIGURE 1.2.**) Since the right hemisphere is able to enjoy and appreciate nonverbal visual stimuli, the left hand quite readily holds up interesting pictures so that they may be examined. Patients with a split brain are struck by this independence of the left side of their body; they note that the left arm seems to have a mind of its own.

Since verbal communication with a person whose brain has been bisected means communication with the left hemisphere only, an observer tends not to detect the presence of the right hemisphere, except in clear-cut cases where the left hand attempts to perform a task that contradicts the person's verbal behavior. In the laboratory, however, sensory information may be presented independently to the left and right hemispheres. These studies are described by Gazzaniga (1970). For example, a blindfolded patient can easily give the name of a simple object felt by the right hand. If an object is placed in the left hand, however, the patient cannot verbally identify it. (Sensory information from each hand is sent to the opposite hemisphere.) If the object is then placed among several others and the blindfold is removed, the patient is able to point to the appropriate object (with the left hand, of course). Thus, the right hemisphere is capable of perceiving and remembering, and it can also initiate hand and arm movements that demonstrate the perception and the memory.

Just as a given hemisphere controls, and receives sensory information from, the limbs on the other side of the body, so visual stimuli located to the left and right of the *fixation point* (the place the eyes are "looking at") are transmitted to the contralateral (opposite-side) hemisphere. If we look straight ahead, the left hemisphere

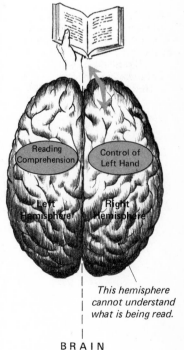

FIGURE 1.2 The right hemisphere is not interested in a book it cannot read.

sees objects to our right, and the right one sees objects to our left. Thus, the cerebral hemispheres of a patient with a split brain can be shown different visual stimuli. For example, if the word *fork* is shown just to the left hemisphere, the person can say "fork" or can select a fork from other objects with the right hand (but not the left hand, of course). If the words are simple enough, the right hemisphere, with its rudimentary language ability, can read words and select the appropriate objects. If asked to repeat the word, however, the patient reports seeing nothing.

COMMUNICATION BETWEEN TWO MINDS IN ONE HEAD. Although the hemispheres of a patient with a split brain can no longer communicate by means of the corpus callosum, they can sometimes convey messages to each other by different means. The right hemisphere hears whatever is spoken by the left hemisphere, of course, and understands much of what is being said. (The right hemisphere is therefore much more aware of the separate existence of another entity in the person's body.) In certain situations the right hemisphere can pass information on to the left. If a patient is confronted with a simple test requiring yes or no answers based upon visual stimuli, correct answers are often obtained even when the stimuli are shown to the right hemisphere. For example, the right hemisphere might be shown a patch of red. The patient is asked, "Was that red?" If the answer is yes, the patient just waits for the next item. Sometimes (half of the time, in fact) the patient first says no, shakes his or her head, and, frowning, says: "That's wrong. I meant yes." The right hemisphere perceives the stimulus and identifies it as being red. If it hears the left hemisphere cause the patient to answer yes to the question "Was that red?" it does not produce any response. If it hears an answer that contradicts what it saw, the right hemisphere initiates a head-shake and a frown, which tells the left hemisphere that the answer was incorrect, and the left hemisphere changes its answer.

It is quite clear that a person with a bisected brain possesses two minds. It would surely be quibbling to assert that there is no "mind" in the right hemisphere because it cannot talk to us. Each hemisphere can perceive and react to its own sensory input, and thus it appears likely that each hemisphere has its own consciousness. The left hemisphere will answer yes to the question "Are you conscious and aware of yourself?" but the right hemisphere cannot. The fact that the nonverbal hemisphere can appreciate the sight of an interesting picture (as shown by the fact that the patient will hold the picture in the left hand) argues for an independent consciousness. Even more compelling is the fact that the right brain can apparently become impatient with the ineptness of the left brain on a given task. On occasions when the patient was required to respond with the right hand to a stimulus seen by the right hemisphere, the left hand (controlled by the hemisphere that knows the answer) has been observed to push the right hand away in order to perform the task correctly.

The point of this discussion is that mind is the result of a functioning brain. The fact that disconnecting the hemispheres gives rise to two distinct minds—with different capacities, memories, and (probably) personalities—provides, I believe, the most persuasive proof that the unity of our conscious awareness is a product of the interconnections of various regions of the brain. In chapter 18 we shall see that different types of disconnections (within only one hemisphere) can similarly disrupt the unity of a person's sensory awareness, so that (for example) a person may hear a word and respond appropriately to it without being able to say what the word was.

THE BRAIN: ORGAN OF DECISION AND CONTROL

The brain receives information, makes decisions, and produces effects. People are most familiar with input of a sensory nature: vision, audition, touch. We are also familiar with the brain's output through the nerves controlling the muscles with which we move our bodies. But the brain also receives information other than that transmitted through the sensory nerves, and it controls more than the skeletal muscles.

Figure 1.3 schematically classifies the communication channels of the brain into inputs and outputs and further divides each of these classifications according to the medium used for the transmission— neural and nonneural. (See **FIGURE 1.3.**) The familiar neural (sensory) inputs will be discussed in chapters 8 and 9. The motor outputs (neural and nonneural) will be discussed in a general manner in chapter 10. Besides controlling the skeletal muscles, neural outputs of the brain also control muscles such as those of the gut, the heart, the urinary bladder, and the iris of the eye. The brain also controls the hormonal output of some glands by means of neural connection. For example, the *adrenal medulla* produces *epinephrine* (Adrenalin) in response to neural commands from the brain. Finally, the brain produces and secretes hormones of its own, which control the hormone output of the *anterior pituitary*, a gland attached to the base of the brain. The hormones of the anterior pituitary, in turn, affect many physiological systems of the body. Growth of the bones, sexual maturation, and regulation of the body's mineral balance are a few of the phenomena controlled by the brain through its influence on

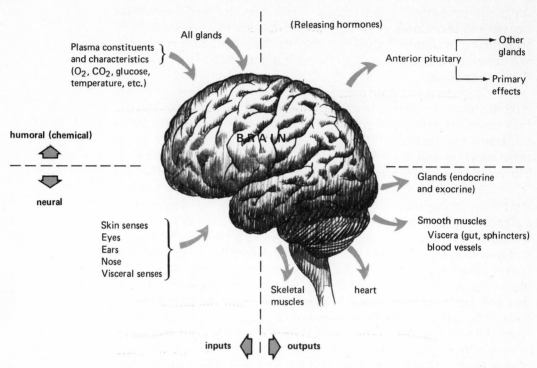

All glands

(Releasing hormones)

Plasma constituents
and characteristics
(O_2, CO_2, glucose,
temperature, etc.)

Anterior pituitary

Other
glands

Primary
effects

humoral (chemical)

B R A I N

neural

Glands (endocrine
and exocrine)

Smooth muscles
Viscera (gut, sphincters)
blood vessels

Skin senses
Eyes
Ears
Nose
Visceral senses

Skeletal
muscles

heart

inputs

outputs

FIGURE 1.3   Schematic representation of the communication channels between the brain and the rest of the body.

the hormonal output of the anterior pituitary.   Specific examples of the role of the nonneural outputs of the brain will be discussed in chapter 11 (sexual development and behavior), chapter 12 (hunger), and chapter 16 (emotion).

The final quadrant of Figure 1.3 represents the communication channel that is probably the least familiar: nonneural input to the brain.   The brain (and, therefore, the animal's behavior) is affected by many hormones, as will be discussed in chapters 11, 12, 13, and 16. The brain also responds to other nonneural inputs, such as body temperature, the amount of oxygen carried by the blood, and the concentration of the blood plasma.   Some of the nonneural, nonhormonal inputs to the brain will be considered in the chapters on hunger and thirst (chapters 12 and 13).

Before the physiological basis of behavior can be discussed, it will be necessary to have a basic understanding of the way the brain processes information.   Therefore, chapters 2, 3, 4, and 5 are concerned with those elements of the brain that transmit and process information: the neurons.   These chapters explain how neurons communicate and make decisions, and how information is transmitted into, out of, and within the brain.   The chemistry of neural communication is described, providing a basis for understanding how drugs affect behavior. Chapter 6 outlines the anatomy of the nervous system and introduces a few facts about the functions of some of its structures. In chapter 7 the research techniques of the neuroscientist are described and discussed, along with some of the limitations of these techniques.

Chapters 8 and 9 are concerned with sensory processes. Chapter 8 describes the way in which environmental events are translated into neural activity, and how the information thus represented is transmitted to the brain. Chapter 9 discusses the nature of the neural representation and the means by which it is analyzed by the brain. The motor (output) systems of the brain are described in chapter 10.

Chapters 11 through 20 outline the progress made by physiological psychologists in understanding the physiological basis of sexual behavior, hunger, thirst, sleep, emotional behavior, reward, mental disorder, pain, learning, and memory. In these chapters I have attempted to select the most important experiments and to integrate the information presented. By being as concrete and explicit as possible in my conclusions I hope to establish a conceptual framework that will facilitate your efforts to learn more about the physiological basis of behavior. New facts, standing in isolation, are difficult to learn and to remember. (You will certainly agree with this statement as you acquire the new vocabulary presented in the early chapters of this book. Nothing is more difficult to learn than a set of new names.) Once a conceptual framework is established, however, it is quite easy to digest new information. In some instances I have made logical jumps (when experimental data are not available) in order to tie some facts together. Subsequent research may prove the tentative conclusions to be incorrect, but your grasp of the conceptual framework will make it easy for you to correct the erroneous conclusions. Without the framework you would probably forget much of the information learned in a course in physiological psychology, and the results of the subsequent research might not mean anything at all to you.

SOME MECHANICAL DETAILS

A few words about the format of the book: I have tried to integrate text and illustrations as closely as possible. In my experience, one of the most annoying aspects of reading some books is not knowing when to look at an illustration. When reading complicated material, I often find that I look at the figure too soon, before I have read enough to understand it, or that I look at it too late and realize that I could have made more sense out of the text if I had just looked at the figure sooner. Furthermore, after looking at the illustration, I often find it difficult to return to the place where I stopped reading. Therefore, in this book you will find the figure reference in boldface (like this: **FIGURE 5.6**), which means "stop reading and look at the figure." I have placed these references in the locations I think will be optimal. If you look away from the text then, you will be assured that you will not be interrupting a line of reasoning in a crucial place and will not have to reread several sentences to get going again. Furthermore, the boldface will make it easier for you to find your place again. You will find sections like this: "Figure 6.1 shows an alligator and a human. The alligator is certainly laid out in a linear fashion—we can draw a straight line that starts between its eyes and continues down the center of its spinal cord. (See **FIGURE 6.1**.)" This particular example is a trivial one and will give you no problems no matter when you look at the figure. But in other cases the material is more complex, and you will have less trouble if you know what to look for before you stop reading and examine the illustration.

I hope that in reading this book you will come not only to learn more about the brain but also to appreciate it for the marvellous instrument it is. The brain is wonderfully complex, and perhaps the most remarkable thing of all is that we are able to use it to understand it.

SUGGESTED READINGS

Gazzaniga, M. F. *The Bisected Brain.* New York: Appleton, 1970. A fascinating description of the effects of disconnecting the cerebral hemispheres.

The Cells of the Nervous System

2

The body is made of living cells, and the nervous system is no exception to this rule. This chapter describes the cells of the nervous system and the special functions they perform.

CELLS OF THE CENTRAL NERVOUS SYSTEM

Neurons

The nerve cell, or neuron, is the information processing and transmitting element of both the central nervous system (brain and spinal cord) and the peripheral nervous system (nerves and other structures outside the central nervous system). Neurons can receive information about the environment. They can "argue" and reach decisions. They can produce muscular movements and glandular secretions. They can store information and retrieve it—even years later.

Before describing the particular characteristics of neurons, I will describe the structures and properties these cells have in common with other cells of the body. Not all structures will be mentioned; I will discuss only those that serve roles related to the unique characteristics of neurons.

STRUCTURES OF CELLS. Figure 2.1 illustrates a typical animal cell. (See **FIGURE 2.1**.) The *membrane* defines the boundary of the cell. It consists of a double layer of lipid (fatlike) molecules in which float various structures made of protein molecules. The membrane is an exceedingly complex structure; it is far more than a bag holding in the contents of the cell. It is an active part of the cell, keeping in some substances and keeping out others. It even uses up energy by actively extruding some substances and pulling others in. The membrane contains specialized molecules that detect substances outside the cell (such as hormones) and pass information about the presence of these substances to the interior of the cell. The membrane of the neuron is especially important in the transmission of information, and its characteristics will be discussed in more detail later.

The bulk of the cell consists of *cytoplasm*. Cytoplasm is complex and varies considerably across types of cells, but it can be most easily characterized as a jellylike, semiliquid substance, filling the space outlined by the membrane. Cytoplasm is not static and inert; it streams and flows.

Mitochondria are important in the energy cycle of the cell; many of the biochemical steps involved in the extraction of energy from the breakdown of glucose take place on the *cristae* of mitochondria. Highly active cells, then, contain a large proportion of mitochondria. These structures are shaped like oval beads and are formed of a double membrane. The inner membrane is wrinkled, and the

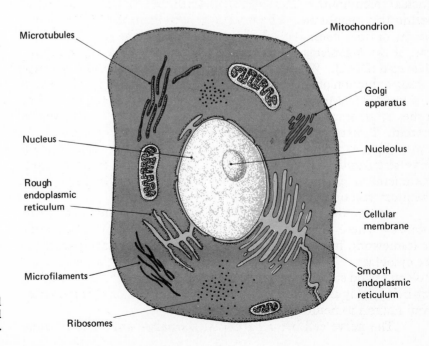

Microtubules

Mitochondrion

Golgi apparatus

Nucleus

Nucleolus

Rough endoplasmic reticulum

Cellular membrane

Microfilaments

Smooth endoplasmic reticulum

Ribosomes

FIGURE 2.1 The principal structures of a typical animal cell.

wrinkles make up a set of shelves (cristae) that fill the inside of the bead.

Endoplasmic reticulum appears in two forms: rough and smooth. Both types consist of membrane and are continuous with the outer membrane of the cell. It is thought that endoplasmic reticulum is concerned with transport of substances around the cytoplasm and provides channels for segregation of various molecules involved in different cellular processes. *Rough endoplasmic reticulum* may be differentiated from the smooth type in that it contains *ribosomes.* These structures, which are attached to the endoplasmic reticulum, are the sites for protein synthesis in the cell. The protein produced by the ribosomes attached to rough endoplasmic reticulum is destined to be transported out of the cell. For example, the hormone *insulin* (a protein) is manufactured there in certain cells of the pancreas. Unattached ribosomes are also distributed around the cytoplasm; the unattached variety is thought to produce protein for use within the cell.

The *Golgi apparatus* also consists of membrane. This structure serves as a wrapping or packaging agent. For example, secretory cells wrap their product in a membrane produced by the Golgi apparatus. When the cell secretes its products, the container migrates to the outer membrane of the cell, fuses with it, and bursts, spilling the product into the extracellular fluid.

The *nucleus* of the cell is round or oval and is covered by the nuclear membrane. The *nucleolus* and the *chromosomes* reside within this membrane. The nucleolus is concerned with the manufacture of ribosomes. The chromosomes contain the genetic information of the organism. They consist of long strands of *deoxyribonucleic acid* (DNA). When active, portions of the chromosomes (*genes*) cause production of another complex molecule, *messenger ribonucleic acid* (mRNA). Messenger RNA leaves the nuclear membrane and attaches to ribosomes, where it causes the production of a particular protein. Protein synthesis is an important function of cells, and this topic will be examined in greater detail later (in chapter 20). Proteins serve as *enzymes,* as well as providing structure, and enzymes direct the chemical processes of a cell by selectively facilitating specific chemical reactions.

Arranged throughout the cell are *microfilaments* and *microtubules.* These long, slender, hairlike structures serve as a matrix, or framework, into which are imbedded the various components of the cytoplasm. They also serve an active function in the transport of molecules and structures from place to place within the cell, and they apparently play an essential role in the communication of information from neuron to neuron.

The nerve cell has a particular specialty—information transmission and decision making. Some neurons have an additional talent: they can detect changes in the environment and transmit information about these changes to other neurons. Another kind of neuron produces hormones or hormonelike substances; these *neurosecretory cells* can deposit, into the bloodstream, chemical substances that may affect other cells within the brain or in other organs.

STRUCTURES OF NEURONS. Neurons come in many shapes and varieties, according to the specialized job they perform. They usually have, in one form or another, the following four structures or regions: (1) cell body, or soma; (2) dendrites; (3) axon; and (4) terminal buttons.

Cell Body (or Soma). The cell body (or soma) contains the nucleus and much of the machinery that provides for the life processes of the cell. (See **FIGURE 2.2**.) The soma is defined as the portion that contains the nucleus, and its shape varies considerably in different kinds of neurons.

Dendrites. *Dendron* is the Greek word for tree, and the dendrites of the neuron resemble nothing more closely than trees. (See **FIGURE 2.2**.) These dendrites vary in shape even more widely than do real trees; a glance at Figure 2.3 will give you an idea of the many forms they may take. (See **FIGURE 2.3**.) Neurons "converse" with one another, and the dendrites, along with the membrane of the soma, receive these neural messages. The messages from neuron to neuron pass across the *synapse*, a junction between *terminal buttons* (described below) of the transmitting cell and a portion of the somatic or dendritic membrane of the receiving cell.

FIGURE 2.2 The principal structures or regions of a neuron.

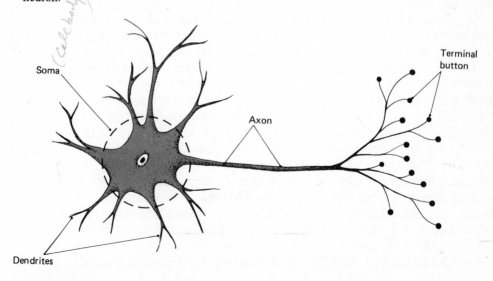

Synapses on dendrites of many neurons occur not on the branches or twigs but on little buds known as *dendritic spines*. Figure 2.4 illustrates a terminal button of the sending cell and a dendritic spine of the receiving cell. (See **FIGURE 2.4.**) Communication at a synapse is one way; a terminal button transmits messages to the listening cell but does not receive messages from it.

Synapses occur not only between terminal button and dendritic membrane, but also between terminal button and somatic membrane. There are no spines on the membrane of the soma; the terminal buttons just meet the smooth surface of the membrane. (See **FIGURE 2.5.**)

Axon. The dendritic and somatic membranes receive messages from other cells. The information is processed (chapters 3 and 4 describe this processing) and the resulting message, if any, is passed down the axon to another set of cells—the cells that *this* neuron transmits messages to.

The axon is a long, slender tube. (See **FIGURE 2.2.**) It carries information away from the cell body down to the terminal buttons. The message is electrical in nature, but it is not carried down the axon the way a message travels down a telephone wire. Just how it is transmitted will be described in chapter 3.

Axons and their branches come in different shapes, as do dendrites. There are three principal types of neurons, classified according to the way their axons and dendrites leave the soma.

The neuron depicted in Figure 2.2 is the most common type found in the central nervous system; it is *multipolar*. That is, the somatic membrane gives rise to one axon, but to the trunks of many dendritic trees.

Bipolar neurons give rise to one axon and one dendrite, at opposite ends of the soma. (See **FIGURE 2.6.**) These neurons are usually sensory in nature; that is, they are located out and away from the central nervous system. They convey visual, auditory, and vestibular (balance, from the inner ears) information in mammals. The dendrites of these cells receive information directly from special *receptor cells* (see chapter 8) about what is going on in the environment, and their axons pass this information along to other neurons back in the central nervous system (usually referred to as the *CNS*).

The third type of nerve cell is the *unipolar* neuron. It has only one stalk leaving the soma; this stalk then divides into two branches a short distance from the soma. (See **FIGURE 2.7.**) Both ends of these branches arborize (divide up like the branches of a tree—for some reason they arborize in Latin rather than dendrotize in Greek). The unipolar cell, like the bipolar cell, transmits information from the environment into the CNS. The distal arborizations (those away

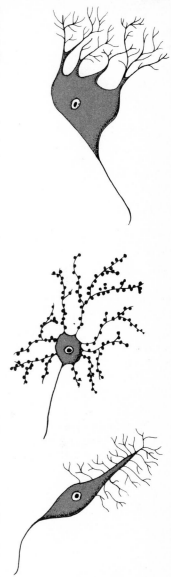

FIGURE 2.3 A sample of the variety of dendritic shapes found in various types of neurons.

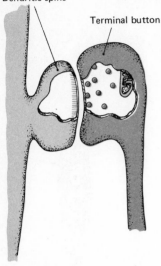

Dendritic spine

Terminal button

FIGURE 2.4 A synapse of a
terminal button on a dendritic
spine.

from the CNS) are dendrites; the proximal arborizations (those toward —actually, within—the CNS) end in terminal buttons. These unipolar neurons receive sensory information either from specialized receptor cells, as do bipolar neurons, or directly from the environment, thus serving as receptor cells themselves. The message does not pass across the somatic membrane of unipolar neurons, as it does in multipolar and bipolar neurons. The soma, in the case of unipolar neurons, serves principally as the factory that supplies the axon with what it needs to be alive and functioning. The soma of all types of neurons serves this role also, of course, but the somatic membrane of multipolar and bipolar neurons additionally participates in transmission of information and in the decision-making process.

Terminal Buttons. The axon divides and branches a number of times. At the end of each of the twigs is found a little knob called the terminal button. These buttons have a very special function; when a message is passed down the axon, the terminals of the transmitting cell secrete a chemical called a *transmitter substance.* This chemical (there are a variety of different transmitter substances in the CNS) is picked up by the receiving cell and produces an effect there. This effect will be a factor considered in the decision-making process of the receiving cell, and, depending on the decision made, information will (or will not) be sent down the axon of *that* cell. In chapter 4 the detailed structure of terminal buttons will be described, along with the rest of the structures that make up synapses.

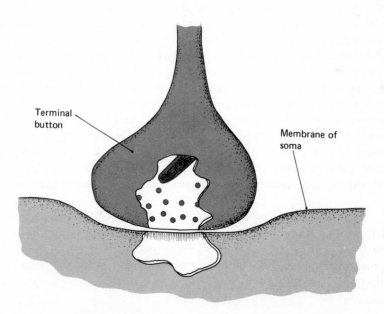

Terminal
button

Membrane of
soma

FIGURE 2.5 A synapse of a
terminal button on somatic
membrane.

Glia

The term *glia* means glue, and in a real sense the glial cell glues the CNS together. But glia do much more than that. Neurons lead a very sheltered existence; they are physically and chemically buffered from the rest of the body by the glial cells. These cells surround neurons and hold them in place; they are responsible for the transport of substances essential for metabolism from capillaries to the neurons, and for the transport of waste products from neurons to the capillaries; they insulate neurons from one another so that neural messages do not get scrambled; they regulate the chemical composition of the extracellular fluid; they even act as housekeepers, destroying and removing the carcasses of neurons that are killed by injury or that die as a result of "old age."

There are several types of glial cells, each of which plays a special role in the central nervous system.

ASTROCYTES (ASTROGLIA). Astrocyte means star cell, and this name accurately describes the shape of these cells. Astrocytes are rather large, as glia go, and provide physical and nutritional support to neurons. Together with microglia, they also clean up debris within the brain. Finally, they chemically buffer the extracellular fluid, but this function will be described further in chapter 3.

Transport of Metabolites. Some of the astrocyte's processes (the arms of the star) are wrapped around blood vessels; other processes are wrapped around parts of neurons, so that the somatic and dendritic membrane of neurons is completely surrounded by astrocytes. Nerve cells have very little direct access to the extracellular fluid surrounding capillaries; the astrocytes surround the capillaries, forming an exclusive compartment around the blood vessels, separated from the rest of the extracellular fluid in the CNS. Hence, neurons depend on astrocytes for transport of substances to and from the blood. This relationship is schematized in **FIGURE 2.8.** Astrocytes allow only certain substances to be exchanged between neurons and the extracellular fluid bathing them. The astrocytes around the capillaries thus form a *blood-brain barrier*, which will be discussed in more detail under a separate heading later in the chapter.

Support. Besides transporting substances between capillaries and neurons, astrocytes serve as the matrix that holds neurons in place. They also surround and isolate synapses, preventing the chemical messages passed between neurons (transmitter substances) from leaving the immediate vicinity. Thus, astrocytes provide each syn-

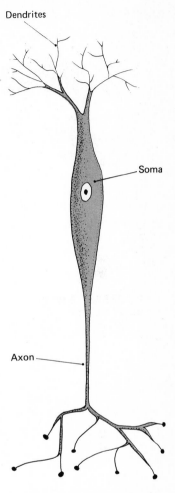

Dendrites

Soma

Axon

FIGURE 2.6   A bipolar neuron.

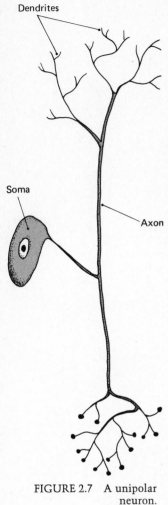

Dendrites

Soma

Axon

FIGURE 2.7 A unipolar neuron.

apse with an isolation booth, keeping the neurons' conversations private.

Housekeeping. Neurons occasionally die of "old age" (that means we do not know exactly why they die.) Others are killed by head injury, cerebrovascular accident (blood clot or rupturing of a blood vessel), or disease. Certain kinds of astrocytes (along with the microglia) then take up the task of cleaning away the debris. These cells are able to travel around the CNS; they extend and retract their processes (*pseudopodia,* or "false feet") and glide about the way amoebas do. They come in contact with pieces of debris, pushing themselves against and finally engulfing and digesting portions of the dead neurons. We call this process *phagocytosis,* and cells capable of doing this are called *phagocytes* (eating cells). If there is a considerable amount of injured tissue to be cleaned up, astrocytes will divide and produce enough new cells to do the task. Once the dead tissue is broken down, a framework of glial cells will be left to fill in the vacant area, and a specialized kind of astrocyte will form scar tissue, walling off the area.

MICROGLIA. Microglia are smaller than the other types of glia. They serve as phagocytes, along with the astrocytes.

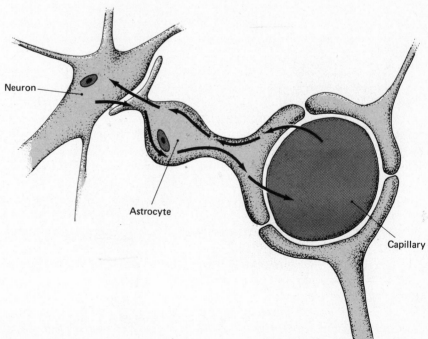

Neuron

Astrocyte

Capillary

FIGURE 2.8 A schematic representation of the transport of substances between neurons and the blood supply.

OLIGODENDROGLIA. These glial cells are residents of the CNS, and their principal function is to provide the *myelin sheath*, which insulates most axons from one another. (Some axons are not myelinated and lack this sheath.) Myelin is made of lipid (70–80 percent) and protein (20–30 percent). It is produced by the oligodendroglia in the form of a tube surrounding the axon. This tube does not form a continuous sheath, but consists of a series of segments, with a small portion of uncoated axon between the segments. This bare portion of axon is called a *node of Ranvier*, after its discoverer. The myelinated axon, then, resembles a string of elongated beads. (Actually, the beads are quite elongated, their length being approximately 80 times their width.)

A given oligodendroglial cell produces only one segment of myelin covering a given axon, but it may provide one segment for each of several different axons. During development of the CNS, oligodendroglia form processes shaped something like canoe paddles. Each of these paddle-shaped processes then wraps many times around a segment of an axon and, while doing so, produces layers of myelin. Each paddle, then, becomes a segment of an axon's myelin sheath. (See **FIGURE 2.9**.)

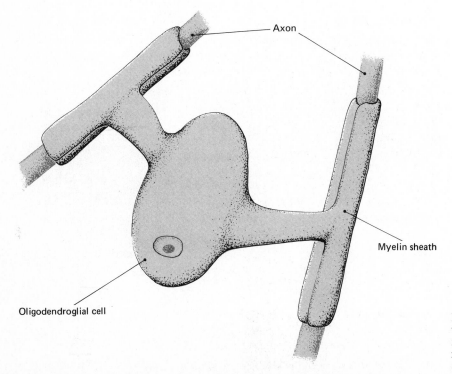

Axon

Myelin sheath

Oligodendroglial cell

FIGURE 2.9   The process by which the myelin sheath is formed on axons of the central nervous system by the oligodendroglia.

Unmyelinated axons of the CNS are not actually naked; they are also covered by oligodendroglia. However, in this case the glial cells do not manufacture myelin. The axons are covered in a different way, also. Instead of being wrapped in segments by the processes of the oligodendroglia, unmyelinated axons pass right through the cell bodies of the glial cells. (See **FIGURE 2.10.**) Each oligodendroglial cell provides support for several axons.

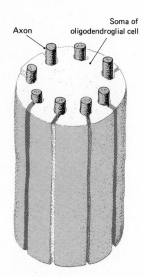

Axon

Soma of oligodendroglial cell

FIGURE 2.10 Support is provided for the unmyelinated axons of the central nervous system by the oligodendroglia.

Ependymal Cells

Ependymal cells are the third major type of cell found in the CNS. They form a membrane around the *ventricles* of the brain. The brain floats within the cranial cavity, in a bath of *cerebrospinal fluid.* This fluid also fills a series of interconnected chambers—the ventricles—within the brain. These liquid-filled spaces provide a sort of hydraulic cushion for the brain.

Cerebrospinal fluid is a clear liquid produced by a particular type of ependymal cell found in the *choroid plexus,* a mass of specialized tissue that protrudes into the ventricles. Cerebrospinal fluid is constantly being produced by the choroid plexus. The fluid flows through the ventricles (and their interconnecting ducts) and is reabsorbed into the blood supply after the journey through the chambers of the brain. In chapter 6 the anatomy of the system of ventricles, and flow of cerebrospinal fluid, is discussed in greater detail.

So far we have considered the principal cells of the CNS: neurons, glia, and ependymal cells. A few other types of cells also reside in the brain—cells which comprise the linings of arteries and veins, and, of course, the red and white blood cells within the blood vessels. There are also cells that form a set of membranes that surround the brain and spinal cord. This lining (the *meninges*) will be discussed in chapter 6.

CELLS OF THE PERIPHERAL NERVOUS SYSTEM

There are three principal types of cells in the peripheral nervous system: neurons (which have just been described), satellite cells, and Schwann cells.

Satellite Cells

The supportive function served by glia in the CNS is served by their counterparts in the peripheral nervous system (PNS), the *satellite cells.*

These cells provide physical support to the cell bodies of neurons located outside the central nervous system. Groups of neural cell bodies (excluding those found in sense organs) are located in three places in the PNS: (1) in the *ganglia* of *spinal nerves,* (2) in the ganglia of *cranial nerves,* and (3) in the ganglia of the *autonomic nervous system.* (Chapter 6 contains a description of these ganglia.) Ganglia are groups of nerve cell bodies that are located outside the CNS. They are covered with connective tissue and form discrete nodules. The neurons packed within these nodules are held in place by satellite cells.

Schwann Cells

Some kinds of oligodendroglia produce myelin in the CNS, and other kinds merely envelop a number of axons. In the peripheral nervous system the *Schwann cells* provide the same functions. Most axons in the PNS are myelinated. The myelin sheath occurs in segments, as it does in the CNS, and each segment consists of a single Schwann cell, wrapped many times around the axon. In the CNS the oligodendroglia grow a number of paddle-shaped processes that wrap around a number of axons. In the PNS a Schwann cell provides myelin for only one axon, and the entire cell—not merely a cellular process—surrounds the axon.

A rather crude way of visualizing the relationship of Schwann cells to an axon is to picture a series of fried eggs (the yolks of the eggs represent the nuclei of the Schwann cells) wrapped around a rope. (I find this analogy helpful, if unappetizing.) Figure 2.11 schematizes the process by which a Schwann cell wraps around an axon. (See **FIGURE 2.11.**)

Schwann cells also differ from their CNS counterparts, the oligodendroglia, in an important way. If damage occurs to a peripheral nerve (consisting of a bundle of many myelinated axons, all covered in a sheath of tough, elastic connective tissue), the Schwann cells aid in the digestion of the dead and dying axons. Then the Schwann cells arrange themselves in a series of cylinders, which act as guides for regrowth of the axons. The distal portions of the severed axons die, but the stump of each severed axon grows sprouts, which then grow in all directions. If one of these sprouts encounters a cylinder provided by a Schwann cell, that sprout will quickly grow through the tube (at a rate of up to 3 or 4 mm/day), while the other, nonproductive sprouts of that axon wither away. If the cut ends of the nerve are still located close enough to each other, the axons will reinnervate the muscles and sense organs they serve.

On the other hand, if the cut ends of the nerve are displaced, or if a section of the nerve is damaged beyond repair, the axons will

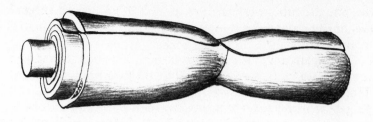

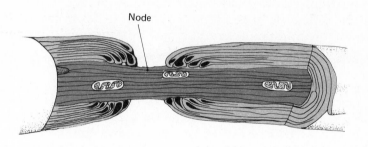

Node

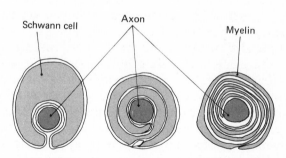

Schwann cell   Axon   Myelin

FIGURE 2.11   The process by
which the myelin sheath is
formed on axons of the
peripheral nervous system by
the Schwann cells.

not be able to find their way to the original sites of innervation.   In
such cases, neurosurgeons can sew the cut ends of the nerves together,
if not too much of the nerve has been damaged.   (Nerves are flexible
and can be stretched a bit.)   If too long a section has been lost, and if
the nerve was an important one (controlling hand muscles, for example), a piece of nerve of about the same size can be taken from
another part of the body.   Nerves overlap quite a bit in the area of
tissue they innervate.   Neurosurgeons have no trouble finding a
branch of a large leg muscle, for example, that the patient can lose
without ill effect.   The piece of nerve from the leg can then be
grafted to the damaged nerve in the arm.   The surgeon works under
a special microscope using the very precise technique of *microsurgery*.
The axons in the excised and transplanted piece of nerve die away, of

course, but the tubes produced by the Schwann cells then guide the sprouts of the damaged nerve and help them find their way back to the hand muscles.

Unfortunately, the glial cells of the CNS are not so cooperative as the supporting cells of the PNS. If axons in the brain or spinal cord are damaged, new sprouts will form, as in the PNS. However, the budding axons encounter scar tissue produced by the astrocytes, and they cannot penetrate this barrier. Even if they could get through, the axons would not reestablish their original connections without guidance similar to that provided by the Schwann cells of the PNS. Thus, the difference in the regenerative properties of the CNS and PNS results from differences in the characteristics of the supporting cells, not from differences in the neurons.

BLOOD-BRAIN BARRIER

The final topic to be discussed in this chapter is the *blood-brain barrier*. If a dye such as trypan blue is injected into the bloodstream, all tissues except the brain and spinal cord will be tinted blue. Careful microscopic examination will show that the dye left the capillaries but did not get past the astrocytes surrounding the blood vessels. However, if this same dye is injected into the ventricles of the brain, the blue color will spread throughout the CNS. These experiments demonstrate that the extracellular fluid within the brain is divided into two compartments: one bathes the neuron, and the other is restricted by the astrocytes to the area immediately surrounding the capillaries.

This blood-brain barrier is *selectively permeable*. Some substances can cross (permeate) this barrier; others cannot. The most recent evidence suggests that astrocytes play the largest role in determining which molecules are allowed to pass, but the cells making up the walls of the capillaries also contribute to the barrier.

The blood-brain barrier is not uniform throughout the nervous system. In several places the barrier is more permeable, allowing certain substances excluded elsewhere to cross relatively freely. For example, the *area postrema* of the lower portion of the brain is involved in the initiation of vomiting. The blood-brain barrier is somewhat weaker there, and hence this region is more sensitive to toxic substances in the blood. A poison that enters the circulatory system from the stomach can thus stimulate this area to initiate vomiting. Hopefully (from the organism's point of view), the poison can be expelled from the stomach before it causes too much damage.

It has been noted that the blood-brain barrier works, to a certain extent, both ways. (That is, there is also a *brain-blood barrier*.) Proteins present in the extracellular fluid of the brain cannot enter the blood supply, and hence are not recognized by the *immune system* as belonging to the body of the organism. Indeed, if the protein constituent of CNS myelin is injected into an animal's blood supply, antibodies are produced that destroy tissue in the central nervous system. The disease thus produced is called *experimental allergic encephalomyelitis* and resembles *multiple sclerosis* (Einstein, 1972). It is thought that multiple sclerosis results from virus-produced damage to the blood-brain barrier, which allows myelin protein to enter the blood supply. This invasion of a "foreign protein" mobilizes the immune system against CNS myelin. With the insulation gone, messages being carried by the axons are no longer kept separate, and the scrambling of messages results in sensory disorders and loss of muscular control. As the disease progresses, the axons themselves are destroyed.

SUGGESTED READINGS

DUNN, A. J. and BONDY, S. C. *Functional Chemistry of the Brain*. Flushing, N.Y.: SP Books, 1974. Distributed by Halstead Press, Division of John Wiley & Sons. This is an excellent, well-written book that contains material relevant to this chapter and to the next three chapters. I learned a lot from reading this book, and I recommend it highly.

DYSON, R. D. *Essentials of Cell Biology*. Boston: Allyn and Bacon, 1975. Information about cellular machinery in general (not specifically cells found in the nervous system) can be found in a cell biology text such as this one.

ECCLES, J. C. *The Understanding of the Brain*. New York: McGraw-Hill, 1973. This paperback book by the Nobel Prize–winning scientist Sir John Eccles includes material related to this chapter and to the following two as well. There is less detail than is found in Minckler's book concerning cellular anatomy, but this book is probably the better buy.

MINCKLER, J. *Introduction to Neuroscience*. St. Louis: Mosby, 1973. A good all-around introduction to cells of the nervous system can be found in chapters 8–11 (especially chapter 10).

SCHMIDT, R. F. (editor). *Fundamentals of Neurophysiology*. New York: Springer-Verlag, 1975. This is a somewhat more detailed (and more expensive) paperback. Like the Eccles volume, it also contains material related to subsequent chapters.

The Excitable Membrane: Membrane Potentials and the Transmission of Information

3

Chapter 2 described various types of cells that make up the nervous system, and noted that neurons constitute the decision-making elements of the CNS. The decision they make—based on the effects received from the terminal buttons of other cells—is whether or not the axon will send a message down to its terminal buttons. If this message is sent, the terminal buttons then "talk" to the cells on which they synapse.

The present chapter considers the nature of the message carried by the axon and the way in which this message is initiated and transmitted. The message is electrical in nature, but the axon does not carry it the way a wire transmits electrical current. Instead, the message is transmitted by means of complex changes in the membrane of the axon, which result in exchanges of various chemical constituents of the extracellular fluid and the fluid within the axon. These exchanges produce electrical currents.

Forces That Move Molecules

To understand the entire process, it is necessary first to examine some of the forces involved in propagation of information along the axon. I will describe a series of simple "experiments" that will make it easier for me to explain some much more complex experiments later.

DIFFUSION.   When a spoonful of sugar is carefully poured into a container of water, it settles to the bottom.   After a time, the sugar dissolves, but it remains close to the bottom of the container.   After a much longer time (probably several days), the molecules of sugar distribute themselves evenly throughout the water, even if no one stirs the liquid.   The process whereby molecules distribute themselves evenly throughout the medium in which they are dissolved is called *diffusion.*   The same process occurs with mixture of gases, and even (on a tremendously longer time scale) with solids.

Diffusion is characterized by movement of molecules down a *concentration gradient.*   Once the sugar dissolves, it is located in highest concentration at the bottom of the container.   The concentration of sugar molecules is the lowest at the top.   Thus, there is a gradient of concentration of sugar molecules, which goes from highest (at the bottom) to lowest (at the top).

When there are no forces or barriers to prevent it, molecules diffuse down their concentration gradient; that is, they travel from regions of high concentration to regions of low concentration.   Molecules are constantly in motion, and their rate of movement is proportional to the temperature.   Only at absolute zero (0° Kelvin = − 273.1° C = −459.6° F) do molecules cease their random movement. As they move about, they bump into one another, and the colliding molecules veer off in different directions.   The result of these collisions, in our example, is to produce a net movement of water molecules downward and of sugar molecules upward.   (Just as there is a concentration gradient for sugar molecules, so there is one for water molecules; initially, water is most concentrated at the top of the container, and least concentrated at the bottom.)

Imagine an experiment that could be performed in the absence of gravity (in a manned satellite orbiting the earth, for example).   This experiment uses a glass container with a barrier down the middle, separating the vessel into two equal chambers.   Suppose nylon mesh is used as a "barrier."   A 10-percent sugar solution is poured into the left side and a 5-percent sugar solution into the right.   Since the nylon mesh barrier is *permeable* to both sugar and water molecules (i.e., it lets them both pass through freely), the container soon has a 7.5-percent sugar solution on both sides.   This is merely another example of diffusion.   (See **FIGURE 3.1.**)

OSMOSIS.   Suppose, however, that we replace the barrier with a thin piece of uncoated cellophane.   (This experiment will not work with regular cellophane, which is coated to make it waterproof.)   Uncoated cellophane is not waterproof; it has pores large enough to allow water molecules to pass through.   The pores are too small, however, to permit passage of sugar molecules.   If we once more pour a 10-percent

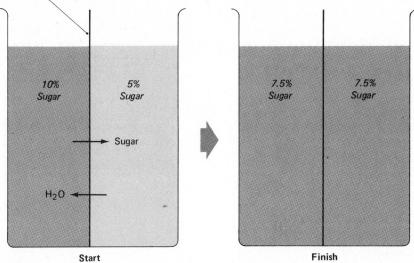

Nylon mesh barrier—water and sugar freely pass through

10%
Sugar

5%
Sugar

Sugar

H₂O

Start

7.5%
Sugar

7.5%
Sugar

Finish

FIGURE 3.1 Both water and sugar molecules readily diffuse through the nylon mesh barrier, moving down their concentration gradients.

sugar solution into the left compartment and a 5-percent solution into the right one we have again created concentration gradients for sugar and water molecules. But, since sugar molecules cannot pass through the cellophane membrane, there will be no movement of sugar.

However, the water can get through the barrier, and after a period of time there will be a 7.5-percent sugar solution on both sides of the barrier. (See **FIGURE 3.2.**) Another way of describing the process is to say that it started with a 95-percent "water solution" on the right and a 90-percent solution on the left. Water moved down its concentration gradient, reducing the concentration of water molecules on the right and increasing the concentration on the left until the concentrations on both sides were equal.

Note that although the concentrations are equal now, the volumes are not. The levels of liquid on each side of the cellophane are different. (See **FIGURE 3.2.**) That disparity causes no trouble in the gravity-free environment where this experiment is being conducted, but things would not be so simple on earth, as will soon be apparent.

The phenomenon just described is called *osmosis*; it is defined as diffusion through a semipermeable membrane.

HYDROSTATIC PRESSURE. Imagine performing another experiment with the container, again using the cellophane barrier. This time, however, we shall conduct the experiment on earth. We shall fill both chambers with pure water: 100 ml in the left one and 50 ml in

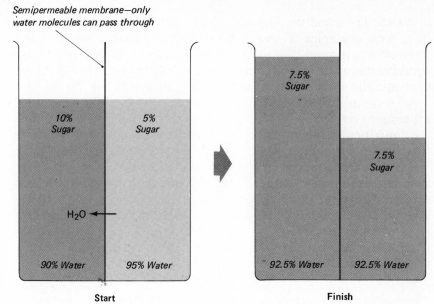

FIGURE 3.2 In the absence of gravity, water diffuses through the semipermeable membrane, moving down its concentration gradient. Osmotic equilibrium is thus achieved.

the right. Soon the right-hand container gains water and the left one loses it, until each side contains 75 ml. (See **FIGURE 3.3.**) Because we used pure water, osmosis is not observed. Instead, the water volumes become equal because of the effects of *hydrostatic pressure*, supplied by the force of gravity. We all know that water runs down-hill, so no one should be surprised by the results of this experiment.

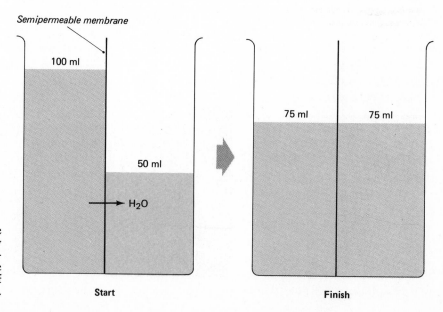

FIGURE 3.3 In the presence of gravity, water is forced by gravity across the semipermeable membrane until the level of liquid on both sides of the container is equal.

DYNAMIC EQUILIBRIUM: PUTTING THE FORCES TOGETHER. So far we have seen examples of two different forces (osmotic pressure and hydrostatic pressure) that bring a system from an initial state of *disequilibrium* to one of *equilibrium*. (*Libra* means balance, so a system is at equilibrium when there is an equal balance of forces.)

To complicate things just a bit, imagine performing the osmosis experiment on earth. We place equal volumes of sugar solution in the container, a 10-percent sugar solution in the left and a 5-percent solution in the right. Initially, only one force is present—osmotic pressure, causing water molecules to move from right to left. As soon as a difference in the height of the solution on each side begins to occur, however, hydrostatic pressure begins to push water from left to right. Eventually the forces reach a standoff, so that the movement of molecules going left and right is equal. (See **FIGURE 3.4.**) Equilibrium is reached, but it is the result of two equal and opposing disequilibriums; there is no hydrostatic or osmotic equilibrium.

DEVELOPMENT OF THE MEMBRANE POTENTIAL

The phenomena described in the previous section and the concept of the equilibrium of opposing forces can be related to the way neurons work. The membrane of the axon, like the uncoated cellophane barrier, is semipermeable, and it is part of a system normally at equilibrium. The extracellular and intracellular fluids are more compli-

FIGURE 3.4 Water moves from right to left, down its osmotic gradient, but as water accumulates on the left side of the container, hydrostatic pressure begins to cause a movement of water toward the right. Eventually a point of equilibrium is reached, and there is no net movement of water.

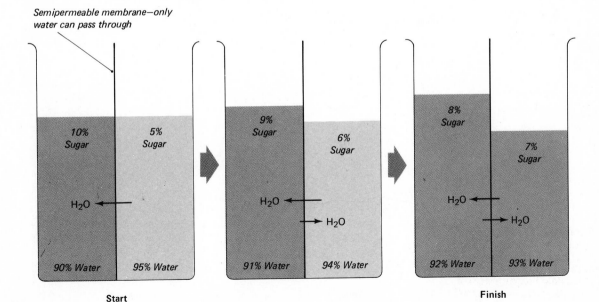

Semipermeable membrane—only water can pass through

Start

Finish

cated than sugar solutions, however, and it is not necessary to consider hydrostatic pressure in describing the transmission of information by the axon. *Electrostatic pressure* will take its place.

ELECTROSTATIC PRESSURE. Many substances split into two parts, each with an opposing electrical charge, when the substance is dissolved in water. We call substances with this property *electrolytes*; the charged particles into which they decompose are called *ions*. Ions have either a positive charge (*cation*) or a negative charge (*anion*). For example, many molecules of sodium chloride (NaCl, table salt) split into so-

FIGURE 3.5 Development of a membrane potential (hypothetical). The starting point is shown on the left. The upper right shows how an electrostatic charge would develop if potassium ions were allowed to move down their concentration gradient until osmotic equilibrium was achieved. This result could never occur. The lower right portion of the illustration shows how the osmotic and electrostatic pressures balance each other, just as hydrostatic and electrostatic equilibrium balanced in the example shown in Figure 3.4.

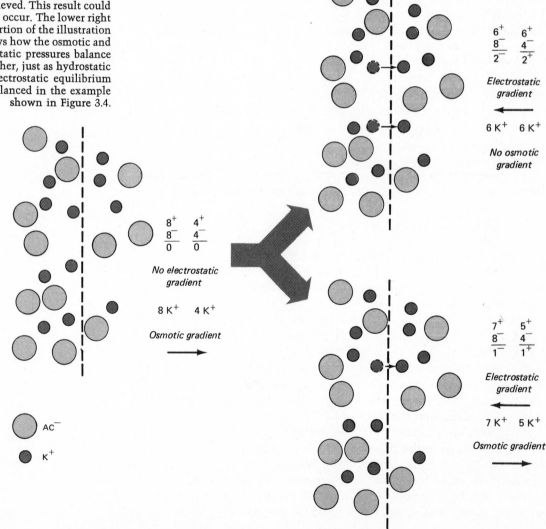

$$\frac{8^+}{8^-}\ \ \frac{4^+}{4^-}$$
$$\frac{}{0}\ \ \ \ \frac{}{0}$$

No electrostatic gradient

8 K$^+$ 4 K$^+$

Osmotic gradient →

$$\frac{6^+}{8^-}\ \ \frac{6^+}{4^-}$$
$$\frac{}{2^-}\ \ \ \frac{}{2^+}$$

Electrostatic gradient

←

6 K$^+$ 6 K$^+$

No osmotic gradient

$$\frac{7^+}{8^-}\ \ \frac{5^+}{4^-}$$
$$\frac{}{1^-}\ \ \ \frac{}{1^+}$$

Electrostatic gradient

←

7 K$^+$ 5 K$^+$

Osmotic gradient →

○ AC$^-$

● K$^+$

dium cations (Na^+) and chloride anions (Cl^-) when dissolved in water. (I find that the easiest way to keep the terms cation and anion straight is to think of the cation's plus sign as a cross, and remember the superstition of a black cat crossing your path. Stupid little mnemonic devices like this are the easiest to remember.)

As everyone has undoubtedly learned, particles with like charges repel each other (+ repels + and − repels −), but particles with different charges are attracted to each other (+ and − attract). The force exerted by this attraction or repulsion provides electrostatic pressure.

A HYPOTHETICAL EXAMPLE. We can produce an electrical charge by using our divided container and a solution of a chemical that splits into ions. We will put a concentrated solution of potassium acetate in the left compartment and a dilute solution on the right. If the membrane were permeable to both potassium (K^+) and acetate (AC^-) ions, the result would be a migration of both ions (and of water, also) down their concentration gradients. If only water could get through the membrane, we would be essentially repeating the last experiment we conducted with the sugar solutions.

Suppose, however, that the K^+ ions could pass through the pores in the membrane but that the acetate ions could not, because of their greater size. For the sake of simplicity, let us assume that we have started with 8 molecules of potassium acetate on the left and 4 molecules on the right. We will assume that all the molecules dissociate (split into ions), giving the result seen in **FIGURE 3.5, LEFT.** Since there is an equal number of anions and cations on each side of the membrane, there is no net electrical charge.

Osmotic equilibrium would demand an equal number of K^+ ions on each side of the membrane (remember, AC^- ions cannot cross the membrane). This would be accomplished by the movement of two K^+ ions down their concentration gradient, from left to right. This state is shown in the upper right drawing of Figure 3.5. If you count the ions, however, you will see that there are two extra anions on the left and two extra cations on the right. (See **FIGURE 3.5, UPPER RIGHT.**) The two K^+ ions that just crossed to the right would now be repelled by the excess positive charge on that side and attracted by the negative charge on the left. In other words, the *electrostatic gradient* for these ions goes from right to left. This means, of course, that the state of affairs illustrated in the upper right drawing would not occur. The electrostatic pressure that builds up as the K^+ ions go to the right opposes further migration of these ions down their concentration gradient. Just as there was a standoff in the previous experiment between osmotic and hydrostatic pressure, so there will be a standoff in this case between osmotic and electrostatic pressure. The actual outcome is illustrated in Figure 3.5, lower right. The drawing shows seven K^+ ions on the left, and five of them on the right. Thus the osmotic and electrostatic pressures balance each other. (See **FIGURE 3.5, LOWER RIGHT.**)

The Nernst Equation: What Causes the Axonal Membrane Potential?

Since the amount of osmotic pressure being exerted across a membrane depends upon the relative concentrations of the solutions on each side, it is possible to determine this pressure merely by measuring the relative concentrations. Furthermore, since the electrostatic and osmotic forces balance perfectly once the system has reached equilibrium, we then know the value of the electrical charge across the membrane. (If you know the value of one force, you know the value of an opposing force that balances it.)

The Nernst equation expresses this relationship:

$$V = k \log ([X_L]/[X_R])$$

where $V =$ voltage across the membrane (in millivolts, or $1/1000$ volt)

$k =$ a constant that depends on such experimental conditions as temperature (its sign depends on the charge of the ion in question)

$[X_L]$ and $[X_R] =$ the concentrations of the ion in question on the left and right of the membrane

If the ion is equally distributed on both sides of the membrane, $[X_L]/[X_R] = 1$, and since the logarithm of 1 is 0, the membrane voltage $= 0$. As the disparity between the concentrations of the ion increases, so does the membrane voltage.

The Nernst equation, then, allows us to answer this question: How much charge must there be across the membrane to counteract the osmotic pressure that results from the observed ionic imbalance?

Now let us look at the axon. The membrane of the axon is selectively permeable, allowing some but not all ions to cross; thus, there is a charge across the axonal membrane (membrane potential). Axons found in mammalian nervous systems are difficult to study; they are small, not easily isolated, and impossible to separate from their associated oligodendroglia or Schwann cells. Fortunately, nature has provided the squid with an axon of enormous (relatively speaking, that is) diameter. The *giant squid axon* (this is a giant axon of a squid, not the axon of a giant squid) is about 0.5 mm in diameter. That might not sound huge, but it is hundreds of times greater than the diameter of the largest mammalian axon.

The cations most important to axonal transmission of information are those of sodium (Na$^+$) and potassium (K$^+$). (The single plus sign indicates a single unit of positive charge.) The most important anions are those of chloride (Cl$^-$) and various protein anions (usually symbolized by A$^-$). The concentrations of these ions within the cytoplasm (more properly called axoplasm) of the giant squid axon and the concentration of these ions in the extracellular fluid (seawater) are given (in millimoles/liter) below:

Ion	External Concentration	Internal Concentration
Na$^+$	460	50
K$^+$	10	400
Cl$^-$	560	40
A$^-$	0	345

If we apply the Nernst equation to the various ions, we can see whether it is possible to predict the membrane potential from the distribution of ions on each side of the membrane.

Before doing any calculations, we should first examine the limitations of the Nernst equation. In order for it to give valid results, several conditions must be met. In other words, assumptions about the system are made that must be true if the equation is to work.

These assumptions are as follows:

1. *There are no forces other than electrostatic pressure counterbalancing the osmotic pressure.* If there are other forces, then osmotic and electrostatic pressures need not be equal, and knowing the osmotic pressure will not tell us the value of the electrostatic pressure.

2. *The ion in question is free to traverse the membrane.* If the ion cannot cross the barrier, unequal concentrations do not have to be opposed by electrostatic pressure; the membrane barrier is sufficient by itself. If the barrier were of glass, for example, the two solutions would not interact at all.

3. *The system has reached equilibrium.* The Nernst equation applies only after enough time has elapsed for all the forces to be balanced.

It is important to note that the form of the Nernst equation used here is simplified a bit and will work only for *monovalent ions,* that is, ones with a single positive or negative charge. Also, the sign of the result depends on whether we examine an anion or a cation.

Let's calculate what the membrane potential should be, given the extracellular and intracellular concentrations of the chloride ion.

The Nernst equation, again, is as follows:

$$V = k \log \left([X_o] / [X_i] \right)$$

where $[X_o]$ and $[X_i]$ refer to the concentrations of ion X outside and inside the axon.

At 20° C, and for an anion, $k = -58$, so we can solve the equation for Cl^- as follows:

$$V = -58 \log (560/40)$$

$$= -58 \log (14)$$

$$= -58(1.1461)$$

$$= -66.5 \text{ mV}$$

The membrane potential can be measured directly with a voltmeter, placing one wire inside the axon and another into the seawater bathing the axon. (See **FIGURE 3.6**.)

We would observe that the membrane potential was −70 mV, close to the voltage we predicted from the distribution of Cl^- using the Nernst equation. (Convention has the membrane potential expressed as inside relative to outside. A negative membrane potential means that the inside is charged negatively, the outside positively.)

The equation can be tried with the other ions. Before we even bother with A^- (the protein anions located exclusively within the cell) I will tell you that the membrane is impermeable to these large molecules; therefore, for this ion, assumption 2 of the Nernst equation is violated. The membrane, and not electrostatic pressure, holds the A^- ions in, so the Nernst equation should not be used here. You can see that osmotic pressure would tend to push A^- out, and so would electrostatic pressure; clearly, these forces do not oppose in the case of A^-. (See **FIGURE 3.7**.)

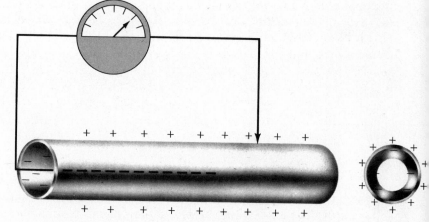

FIGURE 3.6 A schematic drawing of the method for recording the membrane potential of an axon.

Now let's try potassium. At 20° C, and for a cation, $k = 58$, so the equation is as follows:

$$V = k \log ([K_o^+]/[K_i^+])$$

$$= 58 \log (10/400)$$

$$= 58 \log (0.025)$$

$$= 58(-1.6)$$

$$= -93 \text{ mV}$$

The calculated voltage is somewhat greater than the charge that is actually observed (-70 mV). Either there is a certain amount of measurement error or something is wrong. The reason for the discrepancy will soon be apparent.

The calculations for the sodium ion are as follows:

$$V = k \log ([Na_o^+]/[Na_i^+])$$

$$= 58 \log (460/50)$$

$$= 58 \log (9.2)$$

$$= 58(0.96)$$

$$= 56 \text{ mV}$$

This voltage does not come anywhere near the actual membrane potential (-70 mV). Something is clearly wrong.

The measurements of ionic concentration and of the membrane potential are accurate. The Nernst equation is not in error; it has a solid foundation in the laws of thermodynamics. Therefore, one or more of its assumptions must have been violated.

Actually, the only assumption not violated is the last one; the system has indeed reached equilibrium. However, when we measure the permeability of the membrane to Na^+ ions, we find that it is very low; sodium ions pass through the membrane with great difficulty. Thus, assumption 2 (that the ion is free to cross the membrane) is violated. That does not appear to be all, however. Figure 3.7 shows that osmotic pressure would tend to drive Na^+ into the axon. So would electrostatic pressure since the outside is positively charged, and the inside is negatively charged. Look again at **FIGURE 3.7.**

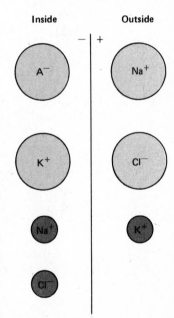

FIGURE 3.7 The relative concentration of some of the most important ions inside and outside the axon.

The Sodium-Potassium Pump

If there were an absolute barrier to Na^+ (as there is for A^-), it would never enter the axon. However, if a giant squid axon is placed in a dish of seawater containing some radioactive Na^+, is allowed to sit a while, and then is removed and washed off, the axon is found to be radioactive. This means that Na^+ from the seawater got into the axon. However, if we analyze the axoplasm for Na^+, we find that its concentration is unchanged. This indicates that as much sodium left the axon as came in.

It's easy to see how Na^+ got into the axon—it was pushed through a slightly leaky barrier by electrostatic and osmotic pressure. But what force pushed an equal number of sodium ions back outside?

Studies have shown that there is a pump in the membrane: the *sodium-potassium pump*. This mechanism forces sodium out of the cell and forces potassium in. Since the membrane resistance to Na^+ is quite high, most of it stays out. Since the membrane resistance to K^+ is quite low (about 1/100 that of Na^+), only a little extra potassium remains inside the cell; most goes back outside.

This pump uses energy; up to 40 percent of the neuron's energy expenditure goes into the sodium-potassium pump. If the axon is poisoned with DNP (dinitrophenol), a chemical that halts biochemical processes necessary for energy production in a cell, the pump stops, and Na^+ leaks into the cell. If the temperature is varied, the pump speeds up or slows down, thus altering the concentrations of Na^+ within the axon. Thus, there is good evidence that a metabolically active sodium-potassium pump exists in the cell membrane.

The effect of the sodium-potassium pump, then, is to produce a tremendous osmotic and electrostatic gradient for sodium; if the membrane barrier for sodium were to break down, Na^+ ions would rush into the axon. The pump also produces a slight excess of K^+ ions inside. The process is rather like trying to fill a leaky bucket, since most of the K^+ ions brought into the cell rush back outside. However, there is some membrane resistance to the flow of K^+, so that the pump is able to build up a slight osmotic gradient for potassium. If the barrier to K^+ were to fall completely, there would be a net movement of these ions out of the cell, and the membrane would become more charged than it is (there would be even more cations on the outside, and fewer inside).

We have seen that, because of the selective permeability of the membrane and because of the presence of the sodium-potassium pump, the membrane is electrically polarized or charged. The outside is charged positively, and the inside is charged negatively. A decrease in the resistance of the membrane to sodium, however, would allow a great number of Na^+ ions to enter the cell (lowering the membrane potential, whereas a decrease in the resistance of the membrane to potassium would *raise* the membrane potential, since K^+ ions would leave the cell.

THE ACTION POTENTIAL

Now that we understand the production of the membrane potential, we can examine its role in the transmission of information in the nervous system.   As we shall see, changes in membrane permeability of Na$^+$ and K$^+$ produce the electrical message carried down the axon.

Measurement of Changes in the Axonal Membrane Potential

First we shall examine the nature of the message.   To do this, we place an isolated squid axon in a dish of seawater and use an *oscilloscope* to record electrical events from the axon.   A more detailed description of this device can be found in chapter 7, but it will be sufficient to say here that an oscilloscope records voltages, as does a voltmeter, but also produces a record of changing voltages, graphing them as a function of time.   For example, Figure 3.8 shows a hypothetical curve drawn by an oscilloscope.   This is not a graph of a real phenomenon, but only a curve for illustrative purposes.   We can see that the voltage being recorded started at −100 mV, changed rapidly to −50 mV (in about 5 milliseconds, of 5/1000 of a second), and then more slowly changed back to −100 mV.   (See **FIGURE 3.8.**)

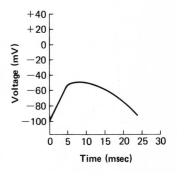

FIGURE 3.8   An example of a curve that could be traced by an oscilloscope.

We will attach the oscilloscope to the axon via two wires (more properly called *electrodes*), one recording the voltage on the outside, and one inserted into the axoplasm.   Since the resting potential of the axon is around −70 mV, the graph obtained (when the axon is not disturbed) is a straight horizontal line at −70 mV.   In addition, we will use another device—a shocker that will allow us to pass electrical current through the axonal membrane and thus artificially alter the membrane potential.   (See **FIGURE 3.9.**)   The shocker can pass posi-

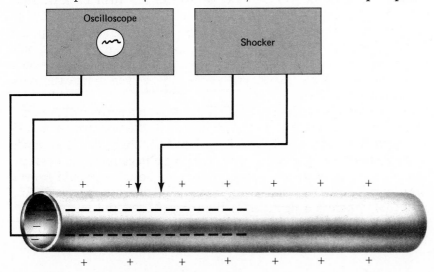

FIGURE 3.9   A schematic representation of the means by which an axon can be shocked while its membrane potential is being recorded.

tive or negative current through the electrode on the outside of the axon, thus raising the membrane potential in that region (making it more positive outside) or lowering it (making it less positive). Positive shocks, which increase the membrane potential, produce *hyperpolarization* (more polarization). Negative shocks, which decrease the membrane potential, produce *hypopolarization* (less polarization). To be consistent with other writers, I shall use the term *depolarization* instead of hypopolarization. This term is not really correct (depolarization literally means removal of polarization), but it is the term most generally used.

Triggering the Action Potential

Figure 3.10 shows a graph drawn by an oscilloscope monitoring the effects of a series of brief depolarizing and hyperpolarizing shocks to the axon. The graphs of the effects of these separate shocks are superimposed on the same drawing so that we can compare them. The shock intensity is labelled in arbitrary units from 1 to 5, 5 representing the highest intensity, + representing hyperpolarizing pulses, and − representing depolarizing pulses. (See **FIGURE 3.10**.)

As you can see, successively stronger hyperpolarizations (+ shocks) produce successively larger disturbances in the membrane potential. The changes in the membrane potential last considerably longer than the very brief shocks. The reasons for this phenomenon (having to do with the resistive and capacitive properties of the membrane and axoplasm) need not concern us here. Figure 3.10 also shows the effects of the depolarizing shocks. The results in this case are different; the effects of the low-intensity shocks (−1 to −3) mirror those of the hyperpolarizing shocks, but once the membrane potential reaches a certain point (approximately −60 mV for most axons), it suddenly breaks away and reverses itself (so that the outside becomes *negative*). Then the potential quickly returns to normal. The whole process takes about 2 milliseconds. (See **FIGURE 3.10**.)

This phenomenon, a very rapid reversal of the membrane potential, is called the *action potential*. It constitutes the message carried by the axon. The voltage level at which the membrane "breaks away" with an action potential is called the *threshold of excitation*. This process is what the decision made by the neuron is all about: whether or not to produce an action potential. The decision depends on whether the threshold of excitation is reached. Furthermore, the action potential is the event that initiates the release of transmitter substance from the terminal buttons, thus making them "talk" to the receiving cells.

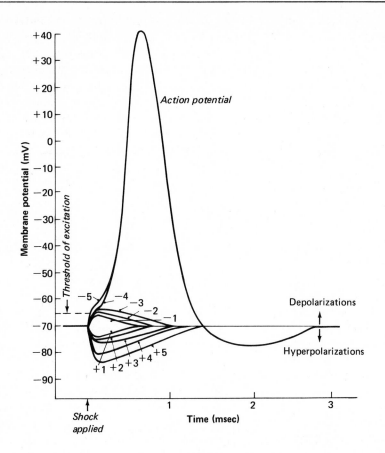

FIGURE 3.10 A schematic drawing of the results that would be seen on the oscilloscope screen if various shocks were delivered to the axon pictured in Figure 3.9.

Ionic Events during the Action Potential

Experiments have shown that the action potential results from a transient drop in the membrane resistance to Na^+ (allowing these ions to rush into the cell), immediately followed by a transient drop in the membrane resistance to K^+ (allowing these ions to rush out of the cell). It is time now to examine the evidence for these events.

EVIDENCE FOR THE INFLUX OF SODIUM. We have seen that an axon will become radioactive after being placed in a dish of seawater containing radioactive sodium. The rate of uptake of radioactivity is a measure of the amount of sodium that gets through the membrane in a given period of time. If this axon is now repeatedly stimulated to produce action potentials, we find that it becomes even more radioactive; the electrical activity of the axon has resulted in an increased influx of sodium. The concentration of sodium in the axoplasm has not changed, however. The sodium-potassium pump must have become more active in order to counteract the increased influx of sodium.

Perhaps the following analogy will help make clear why the radioactivity of the axon increases even though the intracellular Na^+ concentration remains the same. Suppose we have two beakers of water, a large one and a small one. If we repeatedly pour a little water from the large one into the small one, and then pour the same amount back, we do not increase the volume of water in the small beaker, but we gradually introduce more and more molecules of water from the large beaker into the small one. If we started with ink in the large beaker, the contents of the small beaker gradually becomes darker as we exchange a little bit of their contents. Similarly, radioactive sodium from the seawater mixes with the sodium in the axoplasm even though increased activity of the sodium-potassium pump keeps the amount of intracellular sodium at a constant level.

It appears, then, that sodium enters the axon during action potential; excess intracellular sodium is then removed by the sodium-potassium pump. A very clever set of experiments by Hodgkin, Huxley, and Katz (see Katz, 1966) revealed the time course of the sodium influx (and of the potassium efflux, or outflow, that immediately follows it) during the action potential.

THE SEQUENCE OF IONIC FLUXES. The process of ionic flow occurs in the following sequence:

1. As soon as the threshold of excitation is reached, the membrane barrier to sodium drops (actually, to ⅛ the normal value), and Na^+ comes rushing in, down its electrostatic and osmotic gradients. This produces a rapid change in the membrane potential, from -70 mV to $+50$ mV.

2. The membrane once again becomes resistant to the flow of sodium; the whole process of sodium influx lasts only about one millisecond.

3. The membrane now drops its resistance to potassium. This resistance was not extremely high to begin with, but now it is quite low. Since, at the peak of the action potential, the inside of the axon is now positively charged, K^+ ions are driven *out* of the cell, down the osmotic and electrostatic gradients. This efflux of cations causes the membrane potential to go back down again. As a matter of fact, it overshoots the usual value of the resting potential (-70 mV) and only gradually returns to normal. (See **FIGURE 3.11.**) If you will recall, the Nernst equation indicated that the membrane potential should be at -93 mV to account for the observed internal and external concentrations of K^+, thus showing that the sodium-potassium pump kept some excess potassium within the cell. With

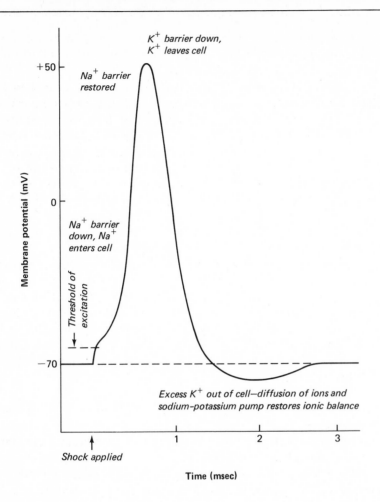

Membrane potential (mV)

K$^+$ barrier down,
K$^+$ leaves cell

+50

Na$^+$ barrier
restored

0

Na$^+$ barrier
down, Na$^+$
enters cell

Threshold of
excitation

−70

Excess K$^+$ out of cell—diffusion of ions and
sodium-potassium pump restores ionic balance

1   2   3

Shock applied

Time (msec)

FIGURE 3.11   The ionic fluxes
during the action potential.

the drop in the membrane resistance to K$^+$, this excess potassium can leak out and make the outside even more positive—the membrane becomes more polarized than usual.

4. Finally, the K$^+$ resistance of the membrane goes back up to its normal level, and the sodium-potassium pump removes the Na$^+$ ions that leaked in and retrieves the K$^+$ ions that leaked out.

How much ionic flow is there? When I say "sodium rushed in," I do not mean that the entire axoplasm becomes flooded with sodium. Because the drop in membrane resistance to sodium is so brief, and because diffusion over any appreciable distance takes some time, not too many Na$^+$ molecules flow in, and not too many K$^+$ molecules flow out. At the peak of the action potential, the layer of fluid immediately inside the axon is full of Na$^+$ ions that have just arrived; this is, indeed, enough to reverse the membrane potential. Not enough time has elapsed, however, for these ions to fill the entire axon. Before this event can take place, the Na$^+$ barrier goes up again, and K$^+$ starts flowing out. Experiments have shown that an action potential temporarily increases the number of Na$^+$ ions inside the giant squid axon by 1/300,000. The concentration just inside the membrane is high, but the total number of ions entering the cell is very small, relative to the number already there. On a short-term basis the sodium-potassium pump is not very important. The few Na$^+$ ions that leak in diffuse into the rest of the axoplasm, and the slight increase in Na$^+$ concentration is hardly noticeable. On a long-term basis, of course, the sodium-potassium pump is necessary, but it would take many action potentials to cause any serious gain of Na$^+$ within the cell.

The situation is different for the smallest unmyelinated axons in the mammalian CNS (approximately 0.1 micrometer, or 1/10,000 mm in diameter). These axons increase their intracellular Na$^+$ concentration by 10 percent when the axon fires, so to these fibers the sodium-potassium pump is important even on a short-term basis.

So far we have seen what produces the membrane potential and how changes in this potential, initiated by depolarization of the membrane to around −60 mV (the threshold of excitation), result in an action potential. Now let us examine the characteristics of the membrane that are responsible for selective permeability, and for the changes in permeability that produce the action potential.

Membrane Changes Responsible for the Ionic Fluxes

Although sodium molecules are smaller than potassium molecules, when these substances are dissolved in water their ions attract a number of molecules of water. These water molecules attach to the ions, forming a sort of bubble surrounding each of them. Sodium ions attract more water molecules, and hence the hydrated ("watered") Na$^+$ ions are larger than the hydrated K$^+$ ions. It has been suggested that the membrane is perforated by small pores. These hypothetical pores could account for the membrane's selective permeability; the smaller hydrated K$^+$ ions would pass through the pores more easily than the larger hydrated Na$^+$ ions.

If the existence of pores in the membrane can account for selective permeability, how can one account for the temporary decrease in permeabilities to Na$^+$ and K$^+$ during the action potential? It cannot just be that the pores open up more, or else the membrane resistances to K$^+$ and Na$^+$ would drop simultaneously. Remember, hydrated Na$^+$ ions are the larger of the two, and if the pores opened up enough to let these ions through, membrane resistance to the smaller K$^+$ ions would have to fall. Instead, the membrane resistance to Na$^+$

falls first and is followed by a fall in the K^+ resistance. Various theories have been proposed to account for this selective permeability, but no one can say with any assurance what the actual mechanism might be.

One hypothesis is rather intriguing, however, since it accounts for two phenomena—the selective fall in Na^+ resistance and the transitory nature of this fall. The drop in the membrane resistance to sodium is triggered by depolarization of the membrane, but if the Na^+ resistance were merely a function of the membrane potential, then there would be no way to explain why the Na^+ resistance reasserts itself while the membrane is still depolarized. The hypothesis suggests that there is a finite number of *sodium carriers* in the membrane. When triggered by depolarization of the membrane, these carriers transport sodium across the membrane. The sodium carriers remain on the inside of the membrane until the resting potential is restored. Then they move back to the outside of the membrane, ready to transport another cargo of Na^+ into the axoplasm. This hypothesis has yet to be proved, but it does account for the selectivity of the fall in the Na^+ resistance of the membrane and also for its transitory nature; there are only so many carriers, and they are not reset until the resting potential is restored.

We need not hypothesize carriers for the fall in K^+ resistance that follows the fall in Na^+ resistance. If the pores in the membrane open up a little wider, they will allow K^+ to pass through more freely without allowing the larger hydrated Na^+ ions through.

I would like to emphasize the following point again: the existence of pores and Na^+ carriers is hypothetical, and that means unproved. This may be how the membrane works, but much study and experimentation will be needed to elucidate these mechanisms.

PROPAGATION OF THE ACTION POTENTIAL

Conduction by Cable Properties

Now that we have a basic understanding of the membrane potential and production of the action potential, we can discuss the final topic of this chapter—movement of the message down the axon, or *propagation of the action potential*. To study this phenomenon, we shall again make use of the giant squid axon. A shocker will be attached to one electrode in the axoplasm and another on the outside of the membrane, at one end of the axon. An oscilloscope will be used to record membrane potentials. It will also be attached to two electrodes, one in the axoplasm and the other touching the outside of the axonal membrane. This external electrode is moveable, so that recordings can be made from any location along the surface of the axon. (See **FIGURE 3.12.**)

A subthreshold, depolarizing shock (too small to produce an action potential) is produced at one end of an axon, and the results are recorded at a point near the site of stimulation. This procedure is repeated, recording farther and farther down the axon. These shocks produce disturbances in the axon that diminish as the recording electrode moves farther away from the point of stimulation. (See **FIGURE 3.13.**) Note, however, that there is no noticeable delay in

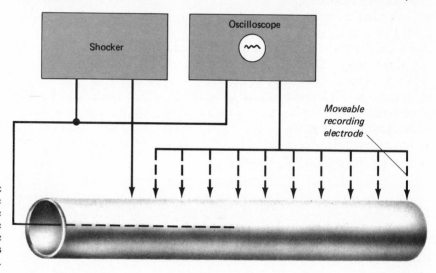

FIGURE 3.12   A schematic representation of the procedure by which shocks can be delivered to one end of the axon while recording the membrane potential various distances away.

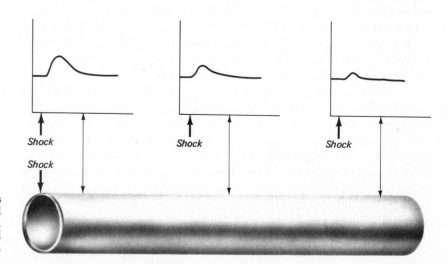

FIGURE 3.13   The results obtained when a subthreshold shock is applied to the axon. This demonstrates decremental conduction.

the onset of this disturbance; transmission is almost instantaneous. (See **FIGURE 3.13.**) This means that transmission of the subthreshold depolarization is *passive*. The axon is acting like a cable, carrying along the current started at one end. This property of the axon follows laws, discovered in the nineteenth century, concerning conduction of electricity along submarine telegraph cables laid along the ocean floor. Submarine cables degrade an electrical signal because of leakage of the insulator, resistance of the wire, and capacitance between the wire and the conductor (seawater) surrounding it. If you put a large pulse in at one end, you get, at the other end, a much smaller signal. Furthermore, the crispness of the pulse is lost; you get a slowly changing potential similar in shape to the disturbances we recorded from the axon. (Remember, the signal applied to the axon was a brief, sharp pulse.) We say that the transmission of subthreshold depolarizations follows the laws describing the *cable properties* of the axon. The axon is not doing anything different from what we would expect from a submarine cable. (Of course, the submarine cable has a much lower resistance and transmits this kind of electrical disturbance much farther than an axon could, but both of these conductors follow the same laws.) Since hyperpolarizations never elicit action potentials, these disturbances are also transmitted via the passive cable properties of an axon.

All-or-None Conduction of the Action Potential

Now let's produce a number of suprathreshold (above-threshold) depolarizing shocks to the end of the axon, and record at successively greater distances from the site of stimulation. This time we shall record an action potential, with a peak of around +50 mV, at each point along the axon. Conduction of the action potential is much slower than conduction of electrical disturbances transmitted via the passive cable properties of the axon, however. The action potential arrives later and later as we move the recording electrode away from the stimulating electrode. (See **FIGURE 3.14.**)

We have, by doing these two experiments, established a basic law of axonal transmission: the *all-or-none law*. This law states that you get an action potential or you do not; once it has been triggered, it is transmitted down the axon to its end. It always remains the same size, without growing or diminishing. I should note here that the axon will transmit an action potential in either direction, or even in both directions if you start one in the middle of its length. Since action potentials are started, in intact organisms, at one end only, the axon exclusively carries one-way traffic.

How is the action potential propagated? Since we know how

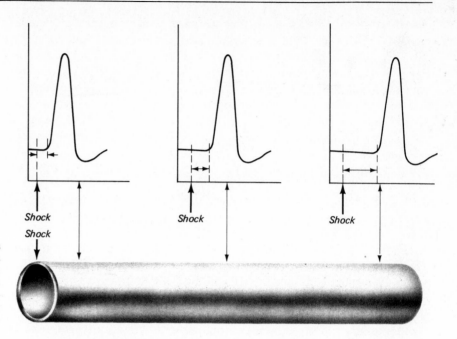

FIGURE 3.14 The results obtained when the axon is given a shock that is above the threshold of excitation. This demonstrates the non-decremental conduction of an action potential.

the action potential is triggered, and since we know about the passive cable properties of axons, it will be easy to explain this phenomenon. Consider, for sake of simplicity, that the axon is divided into segments. (See **FIGURE 3.15**.) We shall stimulate the segment at the left end, triggering an action potential there. This potential will spread, via passive cable properties, to the next segment. It may decline a bit in size, but it will still be large enough to depolarize the next segment above the threshold of excitation, so an action potential is triggered there. The action potential then is transmitted via passive cable properties of the axon to the next segment, and . . . well, I think you get the picture (**FIGURE 3.15**).

The naked axon is not really divided into segments; propagation of the action potential is a smooth, continuous process. If you think of the axon as being divided into infinitesimally small segments, you can describe a continuous process.

CONDUCTION IN MYELINATED AXONS. You will remember from the last chapter (I hope) that most axons are myelinated; segments of them are covered by a myelin sheath produced by the CNS oligodendroglia or the PNS Schwann cells. These segments are separated by portions of naked axon, the nodes of Ranvier. Myelinated axons are *really* segmented, and they transmit the action potential in the way I just described for the hypothetically segmented axon. Let us shock one end of a myelinated axon and then record the membrane po-

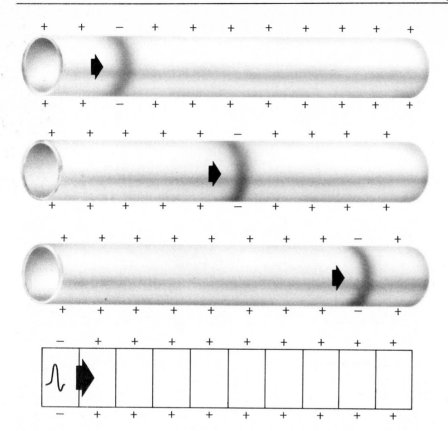

FIGURE 3.15 Propagation of an action potential down an unmyelinated axon.

tential at various places underneath the Schwann cell covering one segment. We shall record with extremely thin electrodes that can pierce the Schwann cell without significant damage (see chapter 7 for a description of these electrodes). The results are shown in Figure 3.16. (See **FIGURE 3.16.**) Note that the "action potential" gets smaller as it passes along the membrane wrapped by the Schwann cell. Why did I write "action potential" rather than action potential? Because the disturbance only looks like an action potential—it really is not one. If it were, we'd have to repeal the all-or-none law.

We do not have to repeal the law, however. The Schwann cell (and the oligodendroglia of the CNS) wraps very tightly around the axon, leaving no measureable extracellular fluid around it except at the nodes of Ranvier, where the axon is naked. If there is no extracellular fluid, there can be no inward flow of Na^+ when the resistance of the membrane to Na^+ drops. There is no extracellular sodium to get into the cell. Then how does the "action potential" travel along the axonal membrane covered by the myelin sheath? You guessed it—cable properties. The axon passively transmits the elec-

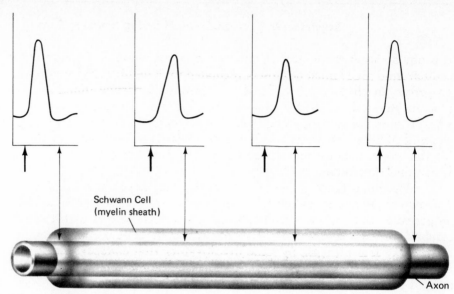

FIGURE 3.16 Propagation of
an action potential down a
myelinated axon.

trical disturbance resulting from the action potential down to the
next node of Ranvier. The disturbance gets smaller, but it is still
large enough at the next node to trigger an action potential there.
The action potential gets retriggered, or repeated, at each node of
Ranvier, and it is passed, via the cable properties of the axon, to the
next node.

What advantage is there to this kind of axon? There are two:
Saltatory conduction (from the Latin *saltare,* to dance), jumping from
node to node, is faster than the continuous conduction down an unmyelinated axon. The fastest myelinated axon can transmit action
potentials at a speed of 100 meters per second (that is around 224 miles
per hour). This increased speed of conduction occurs because the
transmission between the nodes is by means of the axon's cable
properties, and you will recall that this conduction is extremely fast.
A delay is introduced at each node, of course, as the action potential
builds up.

The second advantage to saltatory conduction is an economic
one. Energy must be expended by the sodium-potassium pump to get
rid of the excess sodium ions that leak into the axon during the action
potential. This pump is given work to do all along an unmyelinated
axon, because sodium leaks in everywhere. Since sodium can leak
into a myelinated axon only at the nodes of Ranvier, much less gets
in, and consequently much less has to be pumped out again. A myelinated fiber, therefore, does not need to expend as much energy to
maintain its sodium balance.

Regulation of Extracellular Fluid during Neural Activity

It is obvious that the concentration of the various ions in the extracellular fluid (ECF) must be closely regulated for a neuron to function properly. In chapter 2 I outlined the various supportive functions of astrocytes and mentioned that one of them is to aid in the regulation of ionic concentrations of the ECF. Studies have shown that glia will, if necessary, take up or liberate potassium ions, maintaining the proper balance for normal neuronal functioning (Henn, Haljämae, and Hamberger, 1972).

The importance of the electrolyte-regulating function of glia is shown in the disease called epilepsy. This disorder is characterized by periodic bouts of uncontrolled firing of neurons, especially in the *cerebral cortex* (a layer of neural tissue covering the largest portion of the brain). It is thought, by some investigators, that epilepsy results from a deficient potassium uptake mechanism in glial cells. The increased extracellular potassium increases the excitability of cerebral neurons (Tower, 1960). The disorder is treated with anticonvulsant drugs that depress neural conduction, probably by interfering with sodium conductivity of the membrane.

In this chapter we have seen how the membrane produces a resting potential, and how changes in its Na^+ and K^+ permeability result in an action potential. Finally, we have seen how the axon transmits this action potential down to the end. In the next chapter we will see how the neuron decides whether to "fire" the axon, and we will investigate the nature of the message transmitted by terminal buttons at the synapse.

SUGGESTED READINGS

DUNN, A. J., and BONDY, S. C. *Functional Chemistry of the Brain*. Flushing, N.Y.: SP Books, 1974. Distributed by Halstead Press, Division of John Wiley & Sons.

ECCLES, J. C. *The Understanding of the Brain*. New York: McGraw-Hill, 1973.

KATZ, B. *Nerve, Muscle, and Synapse*. New York: McGraw-Hill, 1966.

SCHMIDT, R. F. (editor). *Fundamentals of Neurophysiology*. New York: Springer-Verlag, 1975.

The books by Dunn and Bondy, Eccles, and Schmidt have already been recommended. Dunn and Bondy's text is best for its coverage of synaptic transmission and pharmacology, covered in the next two chapters. The books by Eccles and Schmidt have more detail about axonal conduction. The book by Katz is probably the easiest to understand; it is thorough and detailed, but it is written in an easy, informal style.

Neural Communication and the Decision-Making Process

4

In chapter 3 we learned how the characteristics of the axonal membrane result in a resting membrane potential and how a small decrease in this potential results in an action potential that is propagated down the axon. In this chapter we shall study (1) *synaptic transmission,* or the way in which terminal buttons send their messages across the synapse to the receiving cells; (2) *postsynaptic potentials,* or the response of the receiving cells to the transmitter substance released by the terminal buttons of the transmitting cells; and (3) the process of *integration,* by which a neuron decides whether or not to send an action potential down its axon. We shall also see how (4) *presynaptic inhibition* reduces the amount of transmitter substance released by a terminal button, and hence diminishes the message sent to the receiving cell.

SYNAPTIC TRANSMISSION

As we learned in chapter 2, neurons talk to other neurons by means of synapses, and the medium used for these one-sided conversations is the diffusion of transmitter substance across the gap between the terminal button and the membrane of the receiving cell. When a terminal button "talks," it causes a brief alteration in the membrane of the receiving cell. The net effect of these disturbances in the resting potential, occurring at the many synapses on the receiving cell, is what determines whether the cell fires its axon and talks to *its* receiving cells.

The topic of synaptic transmission will be divided into two parts: a description of the structure of synapses, and a discussion of the production, release, and deactivation of transmitter substances.

Structure of Synapses

Synapses are junctions between the terminal buttons at the ends of the axonal branches of one cell and (usually) somatic or dendritic membrane of another. Since a message is transmitted only one way, it makes sense to use different terms in referring to the two membranes on each side of the synapse; the membrane of the transmitting cell is the *presynaptic membrane*, and that of the receiving cell is the *postsynaptic membrane*. As shown in Figure 4.1, these membranes are separated by a small gap, variable from synapse to synapse, but usually around 200 Å wide. (See **FIGURE 4.1.**)

The space separating the presynaptic and postsynaptic membranes is referred to as the *synaptic cleft*. This region contains extra-

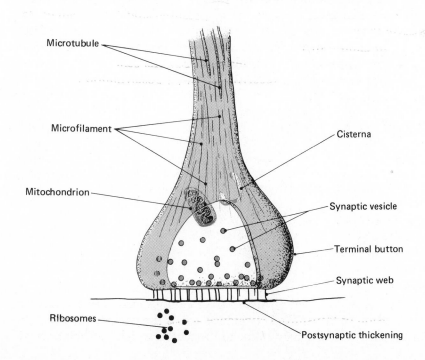

Microtubule

Microfilament

Mitochondrion

Ribosomes

Cisterna

Synaptic vesicle

Terminal button

Synaptic web

Postsynaptic thickening

FIGURE 4.1 Details of a synapse.

cellular fluid, through which the transmitter substance diffuses. For many years it was thought that the synaptic cleft was an open, fluid-filled space, but in recent years some photographs have shown the presence of numerous filaments joining the presynaptic and post-synaptic membranes. The function of this so-called *synaptic web* is not clear. It does appear to hold the presynaptic and postsynaptic membranes together. Brain tissue can be broken apart and homogenized (run through a blender), and synaptic knobs can be separated out by means of differential centrifugation. (This process allows us to isolate particles on the basis of their specific gravity; if a container filled with a suspension of heavy and light particles is spun in a centrifuge, the heavy particles will migrate toward the bottom. The same phenomenon drives the mercury to the bottom of a clinical thermometer as you "shake it," or swing it through an arc.) The terminal buttons of brain tissue subjected to such treatment appear in *synaptosomes* ("synapse bodies"), which usually include a piece of the postsynaptic membrane, suggesting that the synaptic web holds the membranes together. There is no evidence, however, that the synaptic web plays any role in the process of synaptic transmission.

As you may have noticed in Figure 4.1, there are two prominent structures in the cytoplasm of the terminal button—*mitochondria* and *synaptic vesicles*. You will recall from chapter 2 that many of the biochemical steps in the extraction of energy from glucose are located on the cristae of the mitochondria; hence, their presence near the terminal button suggests the presence of processes there that require energy.

Synaptic vesicles are small rounded objects; some are spheres and others are oval. They appear to be packages (the term *vesicle* means "little bladder") that contain transmitter substance. They are produced locally, in the cisternae. (See **FIGURE 4.1.**) Actually, as we shall see a little later, the cisternae are recycling plants rather than manufacturing plants. These structures do not make synaptic vesicles out of raw materials, but out of the membrane of old vesicles that have expelled their contents into the synaptic cleft.

Synaptic vesicles are also produced in the soma of the neuron. If a nerve is *ligated* (that just means "tied") with a bit of thread and later examined under the electron microscope, a collection of vesicles —along with a lot of other material—will be found on the *proximal* (closer to soma) side of the obstruction. These vesicles are presumably produced in the Golgi apparatus, the packaging plant of the cell, and are sent down to the terminals via *axoplasmic transport,* an active process involving movement of substances along microtubules that run the length of the axon.

Ribosomes are found around the cytoplasm of the receiving cell, near the postsynaptic membrane, but they are not found in the terminal buttons. Since proteins are made at the ribosomes, the fact that ribosomes are found near the postsynaptic membrane implies that protein synthesis is important for some aspect of the process of receiving messages from terminal buttons.

The microtubules and microfilaments that are found running down the length of the axon also travel through the terminal buttons. Just as axoplasmic transport is accomplished by these thin fibers, so they are thought to transport substances within the terminal buttons.

The postsynaptic membrane under the terminal button is somewhat thicker than the membrane elsewhere. Some synapses are characterized by thicker postsynaptic membranes than others, but it is not known whether these differences have any functional significance.

Mechanisms of Synaptic Transmission

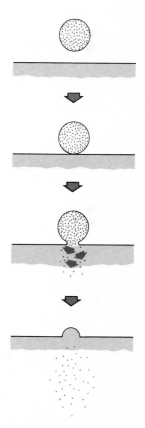

Transmitter substance is produced in the terminal buttons. Raw materials are sent down the axoplasm from the soma and are used to make transmitter substance. These materials may also be recycled; the breakdown products of the transmitter substance usually reenter the terminal button, to be used again. In some cases, as we'll see, the transmitter substance is retrieved intact and is used again.

RELEASE OF TRANSMITTER SUBSTANCE. The release of transmitter substance, and the recycling of the container, is a fascinating process. When the axon fires (propagates an action potential), a number of synaptic vesicles migrate to the presynaptic membrane, adhere to it, and then rupture, spilling their contents into the synaptic cleft. (See **FIGURE 4.2.**)

The evidence that synaptic vesicles contain transmitter substance and that they spill their contents into the synaptic cleft is quite strong. If an isolated frog nerve-muscle pair is poisoned with venom of the black widow spider, the muscle will contract vigorously for several minutes because the venom causes release of transmitter substance from the terminal buttons that synapse on the muscle fiber. (These synapses are actually called *neuromuscular junctions.*) If the terminal buttons are then examined under the microscope, synaptic vesicles are found to be lacking. The terminal buttons also appear to be larger, as though additions (from the expended vesicles) had been made to the membrane.

RECYCLING OF THE VESICULAR MEMBRANE. A study by Heuser and Reese (1973) has outlined the means by which the membrane used in synaptic vesicles appears to be recycled. As the synaptic vesicles fuse

FIGURE 4.2 The process by which synaptic vesicles release the transmitter substance into the synaptic cleft.

with the presynaptic membrane and burst open, the terminal button gets larger. At the point of junction between the axon and the terminal button, little buds of membrane pinch off into the cytoplasm (a process called *pinocytosis*) and migrate to the cisternae, where they fuse into a large, irregularly shaped structure. Then, pieces of membrane are broken off the cisternae and get filled with molecules of transmitter substance. (See **FIGURE 4.3.**)

Heuser and Reese performed an experiment using *horseradish peroxidase*. This substance, with such an improbable name, is very useful to neurochemists and neuroanatomists. It can be placed somewhere in the body and found later when the tissue of the animal is examined microscopically—there are specific stains that indicate its presence and whereabouts. If horseradish peroxidase is injected into the brain, none of it enters the terminal buttons unless their axons are stimulated to fire. Then the substance is found—first in vesicles in the cytoplasm near the shoulder of the terminal button, and then in the cisternae, and finally in vesicles near the presynaptic membrane (on their way to inject their contents into the synaptic cleft).

We have seen the cycle followed by the synaptic vesicles, but what force guides and moves them around? It has been found that the synaptic membrane vesicles are coated with a protein called *stenin*, and the presynaptic membrane with a protein called *neurin*. The microtubules that run through the cytoplasm are also coated with a substance like neurin, and they appear to be able to interact with the stenin on the membrane of the vesicles. The interaction between the microtubules and the stenin that coats the vesicles causes a ratchet-like action and propels the vesicles to the presynaptic membrane.

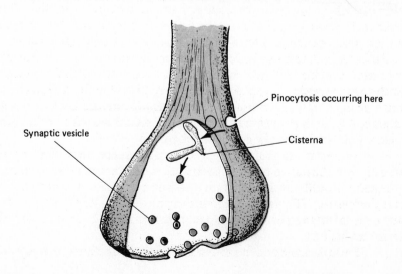

FIGURE 4.3   Recycling of the vesicular membrane

Synaptic vesicle

Pinocytosis occurring here

Cisterna

Once the vesicles are attached to the presynaptic membrane, the neurin on this membrane and the stenin on the vesicles interact in a similar way, rupturing the vesicles. Neurin and stenin appear to be very similar to *actin* and *myosin*, two proteins found in muscle. These substances interact in a ratchetlike arrangement, and provide the motive force of muscles.

As we shall see in chapter 10, actin and myosin are stimulated to exert the force in a muscular contraction by the entry of calcium into the cell. Similarly, the synaptic vesicles migrate to the presynaptic membrane and rupture only after calcium enters the terminals. (If the extracellular fluid is artificially depleted of calcium, the synapses can no longer function.) The entry of calcium into the terminal buttons (perhaps by means of temporary opening of "calcium pores") appears to be the event that initiates synaptic release of transmitter substance.

TERMINATION OF THE POSTSYNAPTIC POTENTIAL. We have examined the production and release of transmitter substance. I have already mentioned that the postsynaptic membrane is hypopolarized or hyperpolarized (depending on the nature of the synapse) by the transmitter substance. The change in the membrane potential is brief, however. If the presence of transmitter substance alters the membrane potential, what restores the situation to normal so quickly?

There are two answers, because there are two processes, *deactivation* of the transmitter substance and its *re-uptake* by the terminal button. Deactivation is accomplished by an enzyme that destroys the transmitter molecule. For example, transmission at the neuromuscular junction and at some synapses is via a chemical called *acetylcholine* (abbreviated ACh). Release of this chemical into the synaptic cleft causes a change in the postsynaptic membrane potential. This change is short-lived because the postsynaptic membrane contains an enzyme called *acetylcholinesterase* (mercifully referred to as AChE). AChE destroys ACh by cleaving it into *choline* and the *acetate* ion. Neither of these substances affects the electrical potential of the postsynaptic membrane, so as the ACh molecules are destroyed, the resting potential is restored. Acetylcholinesterase is an extremely energetic ACh destroyer; one molecule of AChE will chop apart more than 64,000 molecules of acetylcholine each second!

Re-uptake is the other process that keeps the effect of the transmitter substance brief. (Re-uptake seems to me to be redundant —uptake would say it just as well—but re-uptake has become the standard term.) This process is nothing more than an extremely rapid removal of transmitter substance from the synaptic cleft by the terminal button.

The postsynaptic membrane of synapses using this method

need not contain an enzyme to inactivate the transmitter; the synaptic vesicles of the terminal button squirt a little out, and the presynaptic membrane takes it back in, giving the postsynaptic membrane only a brief exposure to the transmitter substance.

POSTSYNAPTIC POTENTIALS

The brief depolarization or hyperpolarization produced in the postsynaptic membrane by the action of the transmitter substance is called a postsynaptic potential. Since depolarization brings the membrane of the cell closer to the threshold of excitation (the point at which an action potential will be elicited in the axon), and thus raises the probability of axonal firing, depolarizing effects of synaptic transmission are referred to as *excitatory postsynaptic potentials* (*EPSPs*). Hyperpolarizing postsynaptic potentials move the membrane potential away from the threshold of excitation and are hence referred to as *inhibitory postsynaptic potentials* (*IPSPs*). In a later section (Integration) we shall see how these effects, occurring at synapses on the somatic and dendritic membrane, determine whether or not the neuron fires, but in this section we shall concern ourselves with the mechanism whereby postsynaptic potentials are produced.

Transmitter substance has an effect on the membrane potential only at the synapses; if a little bit is injected into the extracellular fluid on a synapse-free region of a neuron, no postsynaptic potential is recorded. It appears that there must be special molecules attached to the postsynaptic membrane. These molecules (*receptor sites*) and the transmitter substance have an affinity for each other; when a molecule of the transmitter substance diffuses across the synaptic cleft, it meets one of these specialized molecules and attaches to it. Once it does, changes in permeability of the postsynaptic membranes are somehow initiated, and the result is a flow of ions through the membrane. This process is schematized in Figure 4.4. It is as though molecules of the transmitter substance acted as keys to unlock doors covering pores in the membrane. (See **FIGURE 4.4.**)

The illustration does not pretend to show how the mechanism actually works, since that is not known. It just serves as an easy way to picture how transmitter substances might increase membrane permeability.

Since the postsynaptic potentials can be either depolarizing (excitatory) or hyperpolarizing (inhibitory), the alterations in membrane permeability must be specific to particular species of ions. Let's review the ionic balance across the membrane before we examine the nature of these changes in permeability.

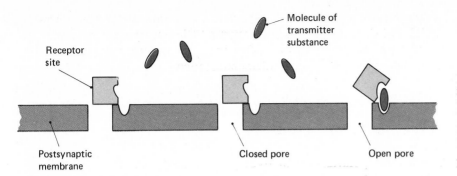

FIGURE 4.4 A possible way in which molecules of transmitter substance can alter the permeability of the postsynaptic membrane. (Adapted from Eccles, J. C., *The Understanding of the Brain.* New York: McGraw-Hill, 1973.)

There is a large electrostatic and osmotic gradient for sodium; this ion would rush in, depolarizing the membrane, if it were allowed to. There is a small osmotic gradient for potassium; it would flow out (hyperpolarizing the membrane) if it could. Osmotic and electrostatic pressures balance very nicely for the chloride ion. The membrane provides a bit of resistance to the flow of Cl^- ions, but since there is no chloride pump, the distribution of chloride is able to balance itself across the membrane. A decrease in the membrane resistance to chloride alone, then, would have no effect on the membrane potential. The protein anions within the cytoplasm are enormous in size, relative to the potassium, chloride, and sodium ions; there are no pores in the membrane wide enough to allow these ions to leak out.

Ionic Movements during EPSPs

Let us consider EPSPs first. They are depolarizations, so a positive ion must leak in, or perhaps a negative ion leaks out. (See **FIGURE 4.5.**) The only negative ion that could leak out would be chloride, but since the distribution of chloride is balanced at the resting potential, we have to reject this possibility; therefore, positive ions must leak in. The most likely candidate is sodium. If the membrane resistance to sodium were to drop, Na^+ would rush in (this happens, of course, in the action potential) and depolarization would occur. Experiments have shown this to be the case.

In fact, experiments have shown that the pores that open up in response to liberation of an excitatory transmitter allow two ions to flow through the membrane—sodium and potassium. Sodium is, of course, the most important one; an influx of Na^+ depolarizes the cell. As this occurs, however, it drives some K^+ out. Without this efflux of K^+ the EPSP would be even larger. One would think that if the pores were large enough to admit sodium, certainly chloride ions should get through also; after all, Cl^- ions are even a bit smaller

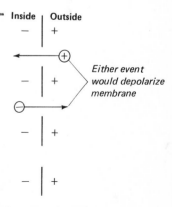

FIGURE 4.5 These ionic movements could depolarize the membrane.

than K$^+$ ions. However, it has been shown experimentally that chloride ions do not cross the membrane during the EPSP.

The most likely description of the pores is as follows: they are large enough to admit Na$^+$ and K$^+$ ions, but the walls of the pore contain a negative charge that repels the Cl$^-$ ion. These pores are shown schematically in Figure 4.6. Sodium ions are shown entering the cell through some pores, while potassium ions leave via some others. Chloride ions are repelled by the negative charge and hence cannot enter the channels. (See **FIGURE 4.6.**)

Ionic Movements during IPSPs

IPSPs are easier to describe. These potentials result from the temporary opening of pores large enough to admit potassium or chloride ions, but still too small to admit sodium ions. When these pores are opened by molecules of the transmitter substance, K$^+$ ions leave the cell, down their concentration gradient. This migration of ions hyperpolarizes the membrane potential and begins to attract some Cl$^-$ ions out of the cell. If it were not for the mobility of these chloride ions through the membrane, the IPSP would be even larger than is actually observed.

Thus, to account for the hyperpolarizing effects of the inhibitory transmitter substance, we only have to assume that the pores

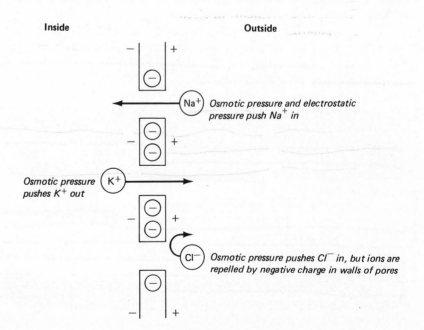

Inside   Outside

Na$^+$ Osmotic pressure and electrostatic pressure push Na$^+$ in

Osmotic pressure pushes K$^+$ out K$^+$

Cl$^-$ Osmotic pressure pushes Cl$^-$ in, but ions are repelled by negative charge in walls of pores

FIGURE 4.6 An EPSP results from an influx of sodium and an efflux of potassium.

that open up are just large enough to admit potassium and chloride ions, but not quite large enough to let sodium ions get through.

INTEGRATION

The only reason for studying postsynaptic potentials in such detail is that these potentials determine whether or not a cell sends a message down its axon. To illustrate integration, or the decision-making process of neurons, we can perform an experiment similar to one we did in chapter 3.

A giant squid axon is isolated in a dish of seawater and a recording electrode is placed on the membrane. Electrodes from two shockers are attached to the end of the axon; one delivers brief positive shocks to the outside of the membrane (hyperpolarizations) and the other delivers brief negative shocks (depolarizations). (See **FIGURE 4.7.**)

We know from chapter 3 that if the depolarizing shocks reach the axon's threshold of excitation, we will elicit an action potential. Subthreshold depolarizations, and all hyperpolarizations, will produce *graded potentials* that will be propagated down the axon according to its passive cable properties. (This sort of transmission is usually referred to as *decremental conduction*, as opposed to the *nondecremental* conduction of the action potential, which is transmitted without diminution, or decrement, in size.)

The depolarizing shocker (the *excitatory shocker*) is set at a level just barely sufficient to trigger an action potential. We will

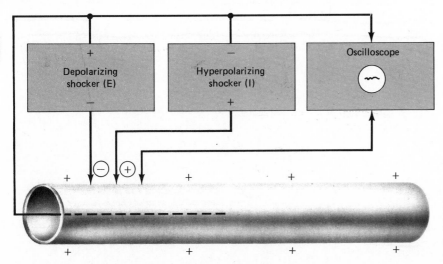

FIGURE 4.7 A schematic representation of the means by which an axon can be stimulated with both negative and positive shocks.

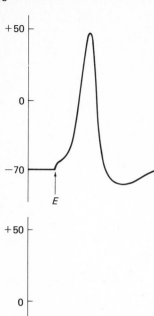

FIGURE 4.8   A depolarizing shock that normally produces an action potential can be inhibited by a previously produced hyperpolarizing shock.

find that, if we deliver a pulse from the hyperpolarizing shocker (*inhibitory shocker*) just before delivering an excitatory shock, we prevent the occurrence of the action potential. (That is to say, we *inhibit* the action potential.)   The inhibitory pulse increases the membrane potential, so that the effects of the excitatory pulse do not make it to the threshold of excitation.   (See **FIGURE 4.8.**)   Thus, we see how excitatory and inhibitory changes in the membrane potential can cancel each other.

Let us examine another phenomenon.   This time we administer a small, subthreshold, excitatory pulse.   Before the effects of this one are over, we shock the membrane again, and again, until eventually the axon fires.   (See **FIGURE 4.9.**)   The effects of closely spaced subthreshold excitations are cumulative; a number of small excitations can achieve the same result as a single large one.   This process is called *temporal summation,* that is, the addition of the effects of small excitations across time.

Let us demonstrate one more phenomenon.   If we simultaneously deliver excitatory shocks from two electrodes placed on the axonal membrane, the effects of these shocks are added together. Therefore, two subthreshold shocks can summate and trigger an action potential.   We call the addition of potential changes from shocks applied to various parts of the membrane *spatial summation*.

Of course, there are no electrodes on the axons of neurons in the intact animal.   There are, instead, terminal buttons arranged on the somatic and dendritic membrane of these cells, capable of producing EPSPs and IPSPs.   These postsynaptic potentials summate, in a process referred to as *integration*.   (Integration simply means addition.)

The membrane of dendrites and soma is not capable of producing an action potential; only an axon can do that.   The membrane potential at the axon hillock is what determines whether the axon fires.   This region, the junction between soma and axon, is capable of producing an action potential, and if it fires, an impulse is propagated down the axon.   EPSPs and IPSPs occurring at the synapses on the soma and dendrites are transmitted decrementally, according to the passive-cable properties of the neural membrane.   These postsynaptic potentials are integrated, and whenever the net result (at the axon hillock) exceeds the threshold of excitation, the axon fires. If many excitatory synapses on the cell fire at a high rate, the axon of the cell will also fire at a high rate.   If inhibitory synapses now begin firing, there will be a fall in the rate of production of action potentials.   The rate of a cell's firing, then, depends on the relative numbers of EPSPs and IPSPs occurring on its dendritic and somatic membrane.   In chapter 10 we shall see how choices are made by the

process of integration. Conflicts between very simple competing behaviors (reflexes) are resolved in favor of the one that is most able to
excite the appropriate motor neurons and most able to inhibit the ones
that produce the competing behaviors.

PRESYNAPTIC INHIBITION

So far I have been discussing only postsynaptic excitation or inhibition, occurring at *axosomatic* or *axodendritic* synapses. There is
another kind of synapse (*axoaxonic*), which consists of a junction
between a terminal button and an axon of another cell. I have left
discussion of this type of synapse until last, because it does not contribute to a process of integration, as do the axosomatic and axodendritic synapses. Axoaxonic synapses instead alter the amount
of transmitter substance liberated by the terminal buttons of the axon
they synapse with (but only if that axon itself fires).

   The release of transmitter substance by a terminal button is initiated by an action potential. Experiments have shown that the
amount released (and hence the size of the resulting PSP) depends on
the magnitude of the change in the membrane potential. Normally
this is a constant amount: from −70 mV to +50 mV, or a total
change of 120 mV. Furthermore, the transition in potential must be
rapid. A slow change in the membrane potential will not release
transmitter substance.

   Here, then, is how presynaptic inhibition works. The axon of
cell A fires, and its terminal button liberates transmitter substance,
which depolarizes the membrane of axon B. (See **FIGURE 4.10.**)
Please note that I said it produces depolarization, which at axosomatic
or axodendritic synapses would be called an EPSP. This depolarization does not bring the axonic membrane to its threshold of excitation
and is therefore conducted to the terminal button via passive cable
properties of the axon. Since the potential change is relatively slow
no transmitter substance is released by the terminal. If an action
potential is now sent down axon B, the membrane potential will
quickly shoot up to +50 mV and then drop back down. Since transmitter substance is liberated in proportion to the change in the membrane potential, less than the normal amount will be released. The
action potential is occurring in a less-than-normally polarized terminal, and thus the total change in the membrane potential will be
smaller than usual. (See **FIGURE 4.11.**)
   Axoaxonic synapses can obviously have an effect only if the
axon being inhibited is actually firing. These synapses might be

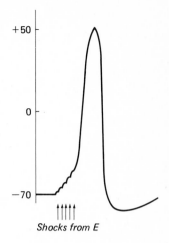

FIGURE 4.9 Temporal
summation can occur if
subthreshold depolarizations
are presented in rapid
succession.

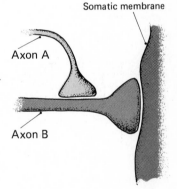

FIGURE 4.10 An axoaxonic
synapse.

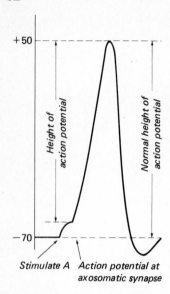

Height of action potential

Normal height of action potential

+50

−70

Stimulate A   Action potential at axosomatic synapse

FIGURE 4.11   Presynaptic inhibition.

useful in the following way: presynaptic inhibition on a particular input to a cell will reduce the responsiveness of that cell to only that kind of input; the cell will respond just as readily to its other inputs.

This chapter has described how cells communicate and how their one-way conversations determine the rate of axonal firing of the receiving cell. In the next chapter we shall examine the nature of the various transmitter substances and the effects of various drugs and biochemical agents on the functions of axonal transmission and synaptic communication.

SUGGESTED   READINGS

DUNN, A. J., and BONDY, S. C. *Functional Chemistry of the Brain.* Flushing, N.Y.: SP Books, 1974. Distributed by Halstead Press, Division of John Wiley & Sons. An excellent source of information about the mechanisms of synaptic transmission: release of transmitter substance, recycling of the vesicular membrane, etc.

ECCLES, J. C. *The Understanding of the Brain.* New York: McGraw-Hill, 1973.

KATZ, B. *Nerve, Muscle, and Synapse.* New York: McGraw-Hill, 1966.

SCHMIDT, R. F. (editor). *Fundamentals of Neurophysiology.* New York: Springer-Verlag, 1975.

These books by Eccles, Katz, and Schmidt provide more information about ionic fluxes and alterations in the postsynaptic membrane.

ECCLES, J. C. The Synapse. *Scientific American,* January, 1965. This article is available as a reprint in *Progress in Psychobiology* (introduction by R. F. Thompson). San Francisco: W. H. Freeman, 1976. This is a worthwhile volume; I shall recommend other articles from it in subsequent chapters.

Biochemistry and Pharmacology of Synaptic Transmission

5

As we have seen in chapters 3 and 4, the brain processes and transmits information through the movements of chemicals; synaptic transmission is accomplished by means of the extrusion of transmitter substance from the terminal buttons and its acceptance by receptor sites. This chapter will describe in more detail the biochemical processes involved in the synthesis, storage, release, and deactivation of transmitter substances, and it will show how various drugs interact with these processes.

THE VARIETY OF TRANSMITTER SUBSTANCES

As we saw in chapter 4, transmitter substances have two general effects on the postsynaptic membrane: depolarization (EPSP) or hyperpolarization (IPSP). One might suspect, then, that there would be two kinds of transmitter substances, inhibitory and excitatory. There are, instead, many more kinds of transmitter substances. Some are exclusively (so far as we know) excitatory or inhibitory, and some may produce either excitation or inhibition, depending on the nature of the postsynaptic receptor sites.

It is extremely difficult to prove that a given chemical serves as a transmitter substance; the evidence is quite good for six, and suggestive, but not at all conclusive, for several more. Table 5.1 provides a list of compounds that are suspected of being transmitter substances (the first six have the firmest status), along with their distribution in the nervous system and their hypothesized effects on postsynaptic cells. (See **TABLE 5.1.**)

One might reasonably wonder why Nature saw fit to provide the nervous system with so many transmitters (and I might note that most neurochemists suspect that further research will expand the list). There would appear to be at least three explanations for the diversity of transmitter substances: "historical accident," different types of postsynaptic potentials, and biochemical separation of functional systems.

1. *Historical accident.* Different functions of the nervous system developed at different times in our evolutionary history; earlier-evolving functions had a smaller set of biochemical mechanisms to choose from, whereas functions developing later could make use of a wider range of mechanisms that had evolved for other purposes. For example, there are two distinct components of the mammalian visual system. One component is made up of small, unmyelinated

TABLE 5.1 Probable Transmitter Substances

Probable Transmitter Substance	Location	Hypothesized Effect
Acetylcholine (ACh)	Brain, spinal cord, autonomic ganglia, target organs of the parasympathetic nervous system	Excitation in brain and autonomic ganglia, excitation or inhibition in target organs
Norepinephrine (NE)	Brain (see Figure 15.9), target organs of sympathetic nervous system	Inhibition in brain, excitation or inhibition in target organs
Dopamine (DA)	Brain (see Figure 15.8)	Inhibition
Serotonin (5-hydroxytryptamine, or 5-HT)	Brain	Inhibition
Gamma-amino butyric acid (GABA)	Brain (especially cerebral and cerebellar cortex)	Inhibition
Glycine	Spinal cord interneurons	Inhibition
Glutamic acid	Brain, spinal sensory neurons	Excitation
Aspartic acid	Spinal cord interneurons, brain (?)	Excitation
Taurine, serine, substance P	(?)	(?)

axons. This system is presumably of earlier evolutionary origin, since it anatomically resembles the visual system of lower vertebrates, and it is involved more with visual reflexes than with visual discrimination. The "newer" component consists of larger, myelinated fibers. Presumably, the older component evolved before the evolutionary development of large myelinated axons; functional systems were constructed out of the building blocks then available.

Similarly, we may make some guesses concerning the evolutionary "age" of various transmitter substances. *Glutamic acid* and *gamma-amino butyric acid (GABA)* are thought to be the oldest. They have direct excitatory (glutamic acid) and inhibitory (GABA) effects on axons, which suggests that they had a general modulating role even before the evolutionary development of specific receptor molecules. Cells have evolved a biochemical pathway called the *GABA shunt*. In the extraction of energy from glucose, the cell performs a complex series of biochemical reactions constituting the *Krebs citric acid cycle*. The GABA shunt consists of a series of reactions that take a metabolic "shortcut" across this cycle and, in so doing, extract slightly less energy from glucose. However, these reactions produce the compounds glutamic acid and GABA, which might then be used as neurotransmitters.

I should point out that we actually do not—and cannot—know when the various transmitter substances were evolved, not having been present at the time. It is interesting to make these speculations, however.

2. *Different types of postsynaptic potentials.* I have not discussed the time course of postsynaptic potentials, but have only described the direction of the change in the electrical charge across the neural membrane. Postsynaptic potentials can vary in duration from a few milliseconds up to a second or more. The duration of a PSP is, of course, a function of many things: amount of transmitter substance liberated, type and number of receptor sites, amount of deactivating enzyme present at the synapse, and rate of re-uptake at the terminal button, to name a few. Studies have shown that the time course of alteration of the postsynaptic membrane potential is also a function of the transmitter substance; some generally produce short-lived PSPs, whereas others produce a more prolonged effect. The nervous system undoubtedly uses these fast-acting and slow-acting synapses in different ways.

It has also been suggested that, besides triggering the PSPs themselves, transmitter substances might produce biochemical changes in the postsynaptic cells, causing long-term alterations in cell functioning. This is a very plausible hypothesis. As we shall see, some transmitter substances do more than cause conformational changes in the membrane and thus alter its permeability to the various ions; they produce their effects by triggering biochemical reactions within the cytoplasm of the postsynaptic cell. The biochemical changes within the cytoplasm might very well produce more (and longer-term) effects besides alterations in membrane permeability. As you might imagine, much attention has been paid to the possibility that these hypothetical changes are involved in the memory process. This hypothesis will be discussed in chapter 20.

3. *Biochemical separation of functional systems.* A third possible explanation exists for the occurrence of several different transmitter substances. By using a special transmitter throughout a system responsible for a given function, that system might be altered or modulated by neurohumoral substances affecting those synapses. (A *neurohumor* is a chemical secreted by a neuron; *humor* means "fluid.") As I noted earlier, there are many neurosecretory cells in the CNS; these cells might affect behavior of populations of cells by secreting, into the extracellular fluid, chemicals that modulate the effects of a given transmitter substance. In this way, a particular brain function might be selectively facilitated or inhibited.

This suggestion seems very likely, by virtue of the fact that there do seem to be anatomically distinct systems whose neurons use a particular transmitter substance, and which mediate a particular function. Because of this fact, neuropharmacologists have been able to administer drugs that affect the activity of certain types of neurons and thus produce relatively specific behavioral effects. It is unlikely that Nature devised the various systems so that neuropharmacologists could tinker with them and affect the organism's behavior; it is more likely that scientists are learning how to do some of the things neurosecretory cells are able to do. As we shall see in chapter 17, the *analgesic* (pain-relieving) effect of morphine occurs because this drug resembles a chemical produced by the brain itself. And, of course, we can even synthesize compounds that the body has not learned to make and affect these systems in novel ways.

TRANSMITTER SUBSTANCES

Having examined some reasons put forth for the variety of transmitter substances present in the nervous system, let us turn our attention to the nature and mode of action of the transmitters themselves. We know more about *acetylcholine* and *norepinephrine* than any other transmitters because one or the other of these two substances occurs exclusively in various parts of the peripheral nervous system. The accessibility of these peripheral neurons, and the fact that they are segregated as to type of transmitter, has made them the easiest to study. Conclusive evidence concerning transmitter substances residing within the CNS is much more difficult to come by, since the neurons not only are harder to get at, but they are also intermingled with neurons of other types.

Acetylcholine

DISTRIBUTION.   In vertebrates, acetylcholine (ACh) is the substance liberated at synapses on skeletal muscles (neuromuscular junctions). ACh is also the transmitter substance in the *ganglia* (collections of cell bodies and nerve terminals located outside the CNS) of the *autonomic nervous system*. The autonomic nervous system (described in more detail in chapter 6) is the part of the peripheral nervous system concerned with "vegetative functions"—control of the digestive system, heart rate, blood pressure, etc. Axons from *preganglionic* neurons whose cell bodies are located within the CNS enter the peripheral ganglia, where they synapse with the *postganglionic* neurons, whose axons then proceed to the target organ they innervate (heart, blood vessel, intestine, sphincter, etc.). Acetylcholine is used to transmit EPSPs from preganglionic to postganglionic neurons. The postganglionic neurons then affect their target organs by secreting either acetylcholine or norepinephrine. Figure 5.1 schematizes this relationship. (See **FIGURE 5.1.**)

SYNTHESIS AND DEACTIVATION.   Acetylcholine is produced by means of the following reaction:

$$\text{acetyl CoA} + \text{choline} \underset{}{\overset{\text{choline acetylase}}{\rightleftharpoons}} \text{ACh} + \text{CoA}$$

Coenzyme A (CoA) is a complex molecule, consisting in part of the vitamin *pantothenic acid*. CoA is a ubiquitously useful substance, taking part in many reactions in the body. All substances that enter the Krebs citric acid cycle, where they are metabolized to provide energy, are first converted to acetate and joined with CoA to form acetyl CoA. Similarly, in the synthesis of acetylcholine, CoA acts as a carrier for the acetate ion, which gets attached to choline to make acetylcholine (ACh). Acetyl CoA, then, is coenzyme A with its attached acetate ion. Choline, a substance derived from the breakdown of *lipids* (fatty substances), is taken into the neuron from general circulation. In the presence of the enzyme *choline acetylase*, the acetate ion is transferred from the CoA molecule to the choline molecule, yielding a molecule of ACh and one of plain old CoA.

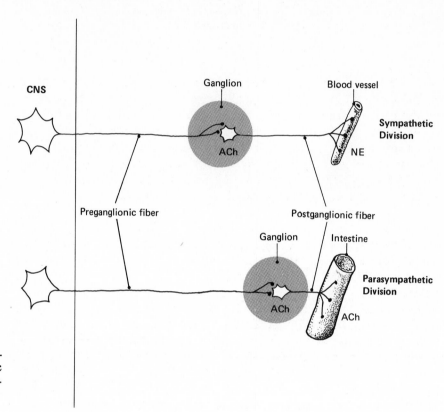

FIGURE 5.1 Neurotrans-
mitters in the autonomic
nervous system.

Without the enzyme choline acetylase the reaction would proceed too slowly to keep up with the expenditure of ACh in synaptic transmission. Enzymes consist of special protein molecules that act as catalysts; that is, they cause a chemical reaction to take place without becoming a part of the final product themselves (note that all enzymes' names end in *-ase*). Since cells contain the constituents necessary to synthesize nearly anything, the compounds they actually do produce depend mainly upon the particular enzymes present. There are, furthermore, enzymes that break molecules apart as well as put them together, so the enzymes present in a particular region of a cell determine which molecules are permitted to remain intact. In the case of the reversible reaction below, the relative concentrations of enzymes X and Y determine whether the complex substance AB, or its constituents, will predominate in the cell. Enzyme X makes A and B join together, while enzyme Y splits AB apart. (Energy may also be required to make the reactions proceed.)

$$A + B \underset{Y}{\overset{X}{\rightleftharpoons}} AB$$

When a substance is produced within a cell, its rate of synthesis is limited by some factors that prevent an excessive amount of production. In the synthesis of ACh, there is a more-than-sufficient quantity of acetyl CoA to combine with available choline, and adequate supplies of choline acetylase are present to catalyze the reaction. The rate of reaction, then, is limited by the amount of available choline. This means that, should a molecule of choline come by, it will be grabbed and will get an acetate ion clapped onto it.

It makes a great deal of sense to make choline the rate-limiting substance in the synthesis of acetylcholine. When ACh is liberated into the synaptic cleft, it is quickly split apart and thus destroyed by acetylcholinesterase (AChE) of the postsynaptic cell, as we saw in chapter 4. The choline, or most of it, is then taken up by the terminal button, to be reused in new molecules of ACh. An overabundance of acetyl CoA and choline acetylase means that the rate of ACh synthesis will depend mostly on the rate of the re-uptake of choline, subsequent to its use as part of a molecule of transmitter substance.

Sometimes excess ACh is produced—more than can be stored in the synaptic vesicles. For this reason, AChE is also present in the presynaptic cell. This AChE cannot destroy the ACh stored in the vesicles, but it can—and does—destroy any transmitter substance produced by the cell in excess of the capacity of the synaptic vesicles.

TYPES OF CHOLINERGIC RECEPTORS. Acetylcholine is, in general, an excitatory transmitter substance, but in some species it can also have inhibitory effects; the nature of the PSPs produced appear to depend upon the type of receptor molecule at the postsynaptic membrane. In the mammalian nervous system there appear to be two types of receptors (both mediating EPSPs), *muscarinic* and *nicotinic*. These receptors are so named because they are stimulated by the drugs *muscarine* and *nicotine*. The *cholinergic* receptors (those stimulated by ACh) of the autonomic ganglia and those of the neuromuscular junction are nicotinic. The cholinergic receptors of the target organs of the autonomic nervous system are muscarinic. Both types of cholinergic receptors are found in the CNS. The spinal cord contains nicotinic receptors. These receptors also predominate in the brain, but some muscarinic receptors are also found there. Figure 5.2 schematizes the distribution of nicotinic and muscarinic synapses, denoted by the letters *N* and *M*. (See **FIGURE 5.2.**)

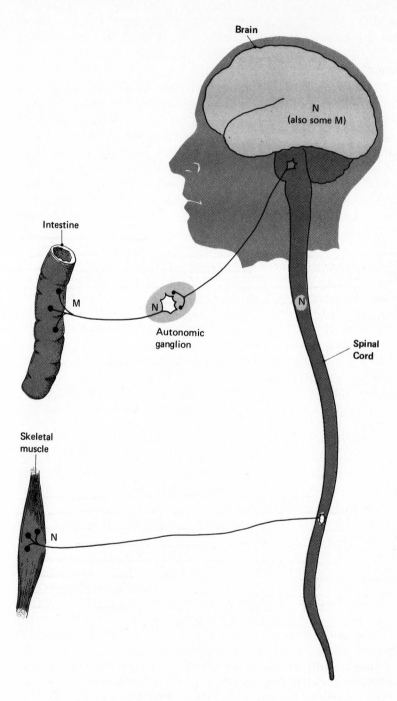

FIGURE 5.2 Relative distribution of nicotinic (N) and muscarinic (M) synapses.

DRUGS THAT AFFECT CHOLINERGIC SYNAPSES.   In order to outline the various kinds of drugs that might affect cholinergic synapses, let us examine the steps in the production and use of ACh.   As we have seen, ACh is produced from choline and acetate; its synthesis may be indirectly inhibited by the drug *hemicholinium*, which prevents the transport of choline across the cell membrane.   Since ACh is resynthesized from the choline taken up by the terminals, hemicholinium administration will result in rapid depletion of ACh in the nerve terminals.   Once produced and stored in synaptic vesicles, ACh is normally released into the synaptic cleft upon stimulation of the presynaptic axon.   The potent drug *botulinum toxin* (present in improperly preserved food infected with the microorganism *Clostridium botulinum*) prevents release of ACh, and thus selectively shuts off cholinergic synapses.   Venom of the black widow spider, on the other hand, causes the continuous release of ACh into the synaptic cleft.

Once ACh is liberated into the synaptic cleft, it must interact with functioning cholinergic receptors in order to produce a PSP. *False transmitters* can prevent ACh from activating the receptors; these substances occupy the receptor sites and prevent ACh from attaching to them, but they do not trigger the membrane events that normally produce PSPs.   Since the false transmitters are not destroyed by AChE, they remain in the receptor sites for a long time. Muscarinic synapses are blocked by plant alkaloids such as *atropine* (named after Atropos, one of the three Fates of Greek mythology, who cut the thread of life).   Nicotinic synapses are blocked by *d-tubocurarine*, the active ingredient of *curare*, a potent paralytic agent discovered by South American Indians.   This drug paralyzes skeletal muscles by blocking nicotinic receptors without affecting the brain, since it cannot cross the blood-brain barrier.   If not provided with artificial respiration, the fully conscious recipient of this drug dies of suffocation, not being able to breathe.

There are also excitatory compounds that attach to cholinergic receptors and induce postsynaptic potentials; examples of this kind of drug, muscarine and nicotine, have already been given.

Finally, after triggering the postsynaptic events that produce a PSP, ACh is normally deactivated by AChE (acetylcholinesterase). AChE can be temporarily inhibited by drugs such as *eserine*, or permanently inhibited by *diisopropylfluorophosphate* (happily called *DFP*).   These drugs, because they deactivate AChE, greatly potentiate the effects of cholinergic activity by prolonging the PSPs produced by ACh.   Many organophosphate insecticides work in this way; hence, the antidote for these poisons is atropine, which binds with and blocks cholinergic receptors in the brain, thus compensating for the excessively long PSPs produced by liberation of ACh at the synapse.

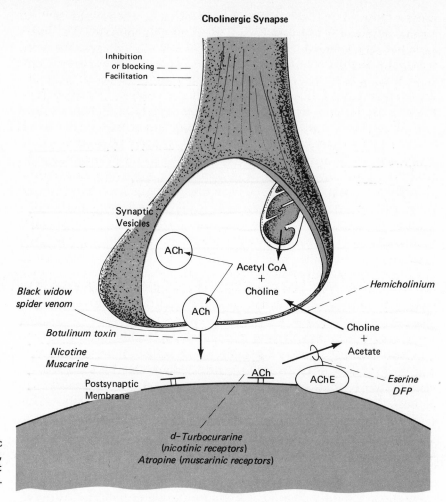

Cholinergic Synapse

Inhibition
or blocking — — —
Facilitation ————

Synaptic
Vesicles

ACh

Acetyl CoA
+
Choline

ACh

*Black widow
spider venom*

Hemicholinium

Choline
+
Acetate

Botulinum toxin — — —

*Nicotine
Muscarine* ———

ACh

ACh

AChE

*Eserine
DFP*

Postsynaptic
Membrane

*d–Turbocurarine
(nicotinic receptors)*
Atropine (muscarinic receptors)

FIGURE 5.3 A schematic
model of a cholinergic synapse,
along with some drugs that
affect it.

Figure 5.3 schematizes the sites of drug action at a cholinergic synapse. (See **FIGURE 5.3.**)

Norepinephrine

DISTRIBUTION.   Because of its presence in some postganglionic terminals of the autonomic nervous system (see Figure 5.1), norepinephrine has, along with ACh, received much experimental attention. I should note now that *Adrenalin* and *epinephrine* (and, of course, noradrenalin and norepinephrine) are synonymous. Epinephrine (Adrenalin) is produced by the medulla (central core) of the *adrenal glands*, small endocrine glands located above the kidneys (*ad renal* means "toward kidney" in Latin). In Greek, one would say *epi nephros* (upon the kidney); hence the term epinephrine. The latter term has been adopted by pharmacologists (probably because the word Adrenalin has been appropriated by a drug company as a proprietary name); therefore, to be consistent with general usage I'll call the transmitter substance norepinephrine (or more often, simply *NE*). Unfortunately, everyone still uses noradrenergic (or just adrenergic) for the adjective form; norepinephrinergic just never caught on.

Norepinephrine generally (but not always) appears to be inhibitory in effect on neurons of the CNS. At the target organs of the sympathetic nervous system it is usually excitatory. Hillarp, Thieme, and Torp (1962) discovered that when fish brain tissue was exposed to dry formaldehyde gas, noradrenergic neurons would fluoresce a bright yellow color when the tissue was examined under ultraviolet light. The development of this histofluorescence technique has made it possible to trace the precise circuitry of noradrenergic neurons in the brain. (See Figure 15.9.)

DRUGS THAT AFFECT NORADRENERGIC SYNAPSES. Noradrenergic synapses may be affected by drugs in a variety of ways. The amino acid *tyrosine* serves as the precursor for NE. Tyrosine is transformed into L-DOPA(L-3,4-dihydroxyphenylalanine) by action of the enzyme *tyrosine hydroxylase* (a hydroxyl group is added). DOPA then loses a carboxyl group through the activity of *DOPA decarboxylase* and becomes *dopamine*. Dopamine and norepinephrine are called *catecholamines*; as we'll see in the next section, dopamine itself is a neurotransmitter. Finally, dopamine gains a hydroxyl group via *dopamine-β-hydroxylase* and becomes norepinephrine. These reactions are shown in **FIGURE 5.4.**

The synthesis of NE may be blocked by administration of *α-methyl-para-tyrosine* (*AMPT*). This drug inhibits tyrosine hydroxylase and prevents the synthesis of DOPA, and thus of dopamine and NE. (See **FIGURE 5.4.**) Drugs that block the effects of other relevant biosynthetic enzymes have also been found, but AMPT is most often used experimentally.

Reserpine, a drug used extensively as a hypotensive (blood pressure–reducing) agent, decreases activity at NE synapses by indirectly preventing storage of NE in synaptic vesicles. Actually, reserpine makes the vesicular membrane "leaky," so that the neurotransmitter cannot be held inside. It escapes and is destroyed by MAO and COMT. *Amphetamine*, on the other hand, stimulates the release of NE (and dopamine, as well) into the synaptic cleft, and, furthermore, directly stimulates postsynaptic NE receptors, mimicking the effects of NE.

We saw that there are two types of cholinergic receptors. Simi-

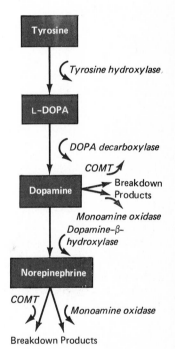

FIGURE 5.4 Biosynthesis of catecholamines.

larly, there are two types of adrenergic receptors, *alpha* and *beta*. Alpha receptors mediate smooth muscle contraction (such as that of the blood vessels, thus raising blood pressure when stimulated), whereas beta receptors increase heart muscle contractions and relax smooth muscles of the bronchi and intestines. Thus, adrenergic drugs are used in treatment of the symptoms of asthma, for example. Both alpha and beta receptors are stimulated by *isoproterenol*, but this drug most effectively stimulates beta receptors. Beta receptors are selectively blocked by *propanalol*, whereas *phentolamine* antagonizes alpha receptors.

The postsynaptic effects of NE are normally terminated by re-uptake of the transmitter by the terminals, rather than by enzymatic deactivation (as is the case with ACh). Drugs that affect the rate of re-uptake alter the properties of noradrenergic synapses. *Imipramine* acts as a potent inhibitor of re-uptake of NE (and also of another neurotransmitter, *serotonin*); hence, the PSPs produced at noradrenergic synapses are considerably facilitated. Imipramine and other drugs with similar effects have been used in the treatment of chronic depression, which appears to result from decreased activity in noradrenergic (and/or serotonergic) neurons. (Depression is a side effect that sometimes accompanies the use of such hypotensives as reserpine.) Conversely, manic activity seems to be due to increased noradrenergic activity. Manias have been successfully treated with lithium salts; lithium somehow increases the rate of re-uptake of NE by the terminal buttons, decreasing the duration of PSPs.

Monoamine oxidase (MAO) and *catechol-O-methyltransferase (COMT)* are enzymes that break down dopamine and norepinephrine, among other things. It is thought that MAO is used by catecholamine-producing cells to regulate the amounts of transmitter substance produced. The drug *pargyline* acts as an inhibitor of MAO; its administration therefore increases catecholamine production and liberation. Like imipramine, pargyline has been successfully used in the treatment of depression.

The discovery of a substance with a lethal affinity for noradrenergic (and also dopaminergic) neurons has provided neuroscientists with a very useful tool. The drug *6-hydroxydopamine (6-HD)* is taken up selectively by terminal buttons of these cells, and once the drug reaches a sufficient cytoplasmic concentration, it kills the cells. Although 6-HD crosses the blood-brain barrier quite slowly and is therefore not very useful in systemic administration, it can be injected directly into specific regions of the brain, where it selectively destroys the catecholaminergic cells. By observing the behavior of animals that now lack these neurons, one can attempt to infer their functions.

Figure 5.5 schematizes the sites of drug action at a noradrenergic synapse. (See **FIGURE 5.5.**)

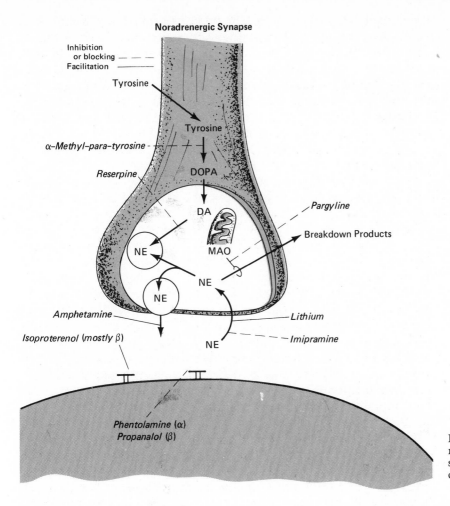

Noradrenergic Synapse

Inhibition
or blocking
Facilitation

Tyrosine

Tyrosine

α–Methyl-para-tyrosine

DOPA

Reserpine

DA

Pargyline

Breakdown Products

NE

MAO

NE

NE

Amphetamine

Lithium

Isoproterenol (mostly β)

Imipramine

NE

NE

Phentolamine (α)
Propanalol (β)

FIGURE 5.5   A schematic
model of a noradrenergic
synapse, along with some
drugs that affect it.

Dopamine

Like NE, dopamine appears to be inhibitory.   Development of a histofluorescence technique specific for dopamine has made it possible to
diagram its distribution in the CNS.   (See Figure 15.8.)   We have already seen the biosynthetic pathway for dopamine (*DA*) in Figure 5.4;
this transmitter is the immediate precursor of norepinephrine.   Like
NE, its synthesis is inhibited by AMPT; it is impossible to block dopamine synthesis without also affectng NE.   Many of the drugs that
affect NE synapses similarly affect dopaminergic synapses: reserpine
prevents storage of the transmitter in the synaptic vesicles, and amphetamine facilitates its release into the synaptic cleft.   Pargyline increases DA levels in the terminal button by inhibiting MAO.

However, some drugs have been found that selectively affect DA terminals. *Benztropine* inhibits the re-uptake of DA (like NE, DA is deactivated by re-uptake); hence, this drug facilitates the effects of dopaminergic activity. *Parkinson's disease* has been successfully treated with benztropine. This disease, characterized by tremors and progressive rigidity of the limbs, appears to result from degeneration of dopaminergic neurons in brain structures involved in movement—specifically, a pathway from the *substantia nigra* to the *caudate nucleus* (see chapter 10). The substantia nigra is so called because it is naturally stained black with *melanin,* the substance that gives color to skin. This compound is produced by the breakdown of dopamine. The DA neurons in this pathway normally inhibit cholinergic neurons, and the release of the cholinergic neurons from inhibition results in the patient's rigidity. Administration of benztropine facilitates the activity of the remaining dopaminergic neurons by interfering with DA re-uptake, and thus alleviates symptoms of the disease. Similarly, the disease has been treated with L-DOPA, the precursor of dopamine.

Dopamine has been implicated as a transmitter that might be involved in *schizophrenia*, a serious mental disorder (*psychosis*) characterized by disruption of normal, logical thought processes. *Chlorpromazine* and related compounds have been found to have a profound antipsychotic effect; independent of sedative effects, these drugs alleviate the symptoms of schizophrenia—enough to have dramatically reduced the hospital population of schizophrenics. The most important neuropharmacological effect of the antipsychotic drugs seems to be blockage of dopaminergic receptors in the brain. If *apomorphine*, which directly stimulates DA receptors, is given to schizophrenic patients whose symptoms have successfully been brought under control by one of the antipsychotic drugs, their symptoms return. As you might predict from the previous paragraph, a frequent side effect of the antipsychotic drugs is development of symptoms like those of Parkinson's disease. Fortunately, drugs are available that combine the antidopaminergic effect with an anticholinergic effect (thus suppressing activity of cholinergic neurons no longer inhibited by the DA cells). These drugs produce minimal parkinsonian symptoms. The role of dopamine in schizophrenia is described in fuller detail in chapter 17.

Figure 5.6 schematizes the sites of drug action at a dopaminergic synapse. (See **FIGURE 5.6.**)

Serotonin

The inhibitory transmitter serotonin (also called *5-hydroxytryptamine,* or *5-HT*) has received a considerable amount of experimental atten-

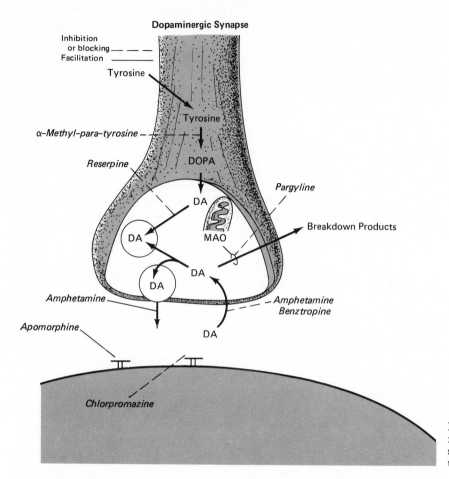

FIGURE 5.6   A schematic model of a dopaminergic synapse, along with some drugs that affect it.

tion.   It is produced by means of a biosynthetic pathway starting with the amino acid *tryptophan*.   Tryptophan receives a hydroxyl group via the enzyme *tryptophan hydroxylase* and becomes *5-hydroxytryptophan* (*5-HTP*).   The enzyme *aromatic amino acid decarboxylase* removes a carboxyl group from 5-HTP, and the result is 5-HT (serotonin).   Figure 5.7 illustrates these reactions.   (See **FIGURE 5.7.**)

The regional distribution of 5-HT in the CNS has been studied with the advent of specific staining techniques.   Serotonergic neurons in various hindbrain locations send axons to the spinal cord and into forebrain regions.

There are a number of pharmacological agents that affect serotonergic neurons.   *Para-chlorophenylalanine* (*PCPA*) inhibits the enzyme tryptophan hydroxylase, thus blocking the synthesis of 5-HT. Reserpine prevents vesicular storage of 5-HT (as well as norepineph-

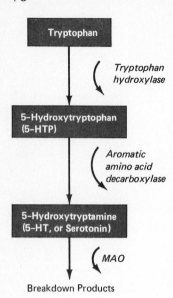

Tryptophan

Tryptophan hydroxylase

5-Hydroxytryptophan (5-HTP)

Aromatic amino acid decarboxylase

5-Hydroxytryptamine (5-HT, or Serotonin)

MAO

Breakdown Products

FIGURE 5.7 Biosynthesis of serotonin (5-HT).

rine); thus it deactivates these synapses. *Cinanserin* acts as a false transmitter; it binds to serotonergic receptors without stimulating them.

Facilitating drugs include *amitryptyline*, which blocks the re-uptake of 5-HT (which normally terminates the PSP), and iproniazid, which inhibits MAO, the enzyme that destroys excess 5-HT in the terminal buttons. Another strategy that has been used to increase the amount of brain 5-HT has been to inject the animal with the 5-HT precursor, 5-HTP. Adequate supplies of aromatic amino acid de-carboxylase, which convert the 5-HTP to 5-HT, are present in the brain.

The hallucinogen *lysergic acid diethylamide (LSD)* appears to exert its effects at serotonergic synapses, but not in a simple manner. LSD appears to block the effects of 5-HT, but other serotonin-blocking agents, such as *2-bromo LSD*, do not act as hallucinogens. The precise way that LSD works is not known.

Recent research on the role of serotonin-containing neurons in the CNS has been facilitated by the discovery of the substance *5,6-dihydroxytryptamine (5,6-DHT)*. This drug produces effects like that of 6-HD on NE and DA cells; it is selectively taken up by seroto-nergic cells and then it subsequently kills them. The sites of drug action at a serotonergic synapse are schematized in **FIGURE 5.8.**

Glutamic acid

Glutamic acid is found throughout the brain. Its precursor, *alpha-ketoglutaric acid*, is available in abundant quantities from the Krebs citric acid cycle. Chinese food also provides a lot of glutamic acid; MSG (monosodium glutamate) is the sodium salt of glutamic acid. Most investigators believe that it is a transmitter substance—indeed, it is probably the principal excitatory neurotransmitter in the brain—but evidence is still not conclusive. It appears that the postsynaptic effects of glutamic acid are terminated by re-uptake.

So far, only two drugs are known to specifically affect glutamic acid synapses: (1) an inhibitor, *glutamic acid diethyl ester*, which blocks glutamic acid receptors, and (2) a facilitator, *glutamic acid dimethyl ester*, which blocks re-uptake of glutamic acid by the termi-nal buttons.

GABA

Gamma-amino butyric acid is produced from glutamic acid by the action of *GAD (glutamic acid decarboxylase)*. GABA appears to be

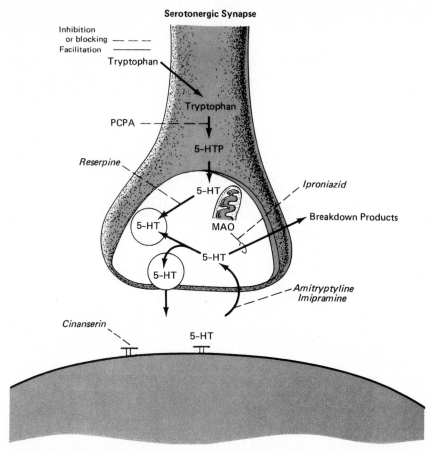

Serotonergic Synapse

Inhibition
or blocking — — —
Facilitation ————

Tryptophan

Tryptophan

PCPA —

5-HTP

Reserpine

5-HT

Iproniazid

5-HT

MAO

Breakdown Products

5-HT

5-HT

Amitryptyline
Imipramine

Cinanserin

5-HT

FIGURE 5.8 A schematic model of a serotonergic synapse, along with some drugs that affect it.

inhibitory, and it appears to have a widespread distribution throughout the *gray matter* (cellular areas) of the brain. GABA is also found in the *dorsal horn* of the spinal cord (see chapter 6).

Relatively few drugs have been discovered that specifically affect GABA. *Tetanus toxin* inhibits release of GABA into the synaptic cleft. *Picrotoxin* and (more specifically) *bicuculline* antagonize the effects of GABA on the receptor sites, whereas *muscimol* (a hallucinogen) stimulates these receptors. The postsynaptic effects of GABA appear to be terminated by re-uptake, but no compounds have been shown specifically to affect rate of uptake.

GABA has been implicated in a serious hereditary neurological disorder, Huntington's chorea. This disease is characterized by involuntary movements, depression, progressive mental deterioration, and, ultimately, death. It has been suggested (Perry, Hansen, and Kloster, 1973) that the disease results from degeneration of GABA cells in the *basal ganglia* (brain structures concerned with motor control—see chapters 6 and 10).

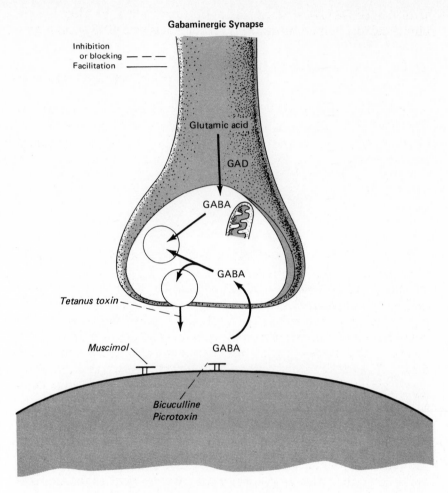

Gabaminergic Synapse

Inhibition or blocking — — —
Facilitation ———

Glutamic acid

GAD

GABA

GABA

Tetanus toxin

Muscimol

GABA

Bicuculline
Picrotoxin

FIGURE 5.9 A schematic model of a gabaminergic synapse, along with some drugs that affect it.

Figure 5.9 schematizes the sites of drug action at a gabaminergic synapse. (See **FIGURE 5.9.**)

Glycine

The amino acid *glycine* appears to be the inhibitory neurotransmitter in the spinal cord and possibly in lower portions of the brain. Little is known about its biosynthetic pathway; there are several possible routes, but not enough is known to decide how neurons produce glycine. Only two drugs affect the hypothesized glycine synapses with any degree of specificity; tetanus toxin inhibits glycine release (along with that of GABA), whereas the poison *strychnine*, by blocking glycine receptors (which mediate inhibition), acts as a CNS stimulant.

Other Suspected Transmitters

Other amino acids (*taurine, aspartic acid,* and *serine*) have been suspected of serving as neurotransmitters, as has *substance P* (a *polypeptide*, related structurally to the proteins). There also appears to be an amine (related to 5-HT) that is much more resistant to the effects of PCPA than is serotonin, but this transmitter has yet to be analyzed and identified.

MECHANISMS OF POSTSYNAPTIC ACTIVITY

The exact way in which transmitter substances alter the ionic permeability of postsynaptic neurons is not known. Some transmitters (e.g., ACh) appear to have a relatively direct effect on receptor molecules that determine the permeability characteristics of the membrane "pores." The mode of action of some other transmitters is much less direct. They involve activation of a substance known as *cyclic AMP.*

      Situated in the postsynaptic membrane of at least some dopaminergic and noradrenergic synapses (perhaps in all, but the evidence is lacking) are molecules of *adenyl cyclase,* attached to receptor molecules. When stimulated by the neurotransmitter, adenyl cyclase becomes active and produces, in the cytoplasm, *cyclic AMP* (*cyclic adenosine monophosphate*) from *ATP* (*adenosine triphosphate*). The cyclic AMP then acts as a cofactor for enzymes called *kinases;* these enzymes, becoming active in the presence of cyclic AMP, cause *phosphorylation* (addition of a phosphate group) of proteins in the postsynaptic membrane. Phosphorylation changes the physical configuration (bending and folding) of a protein. This process, then, could alter the shape of proteins responsible for the permeability properties of the membrane. Figure 5.10 illustrates this process. (See **FIGURE 5.10.**)

      Phosphorylation of proteins associated with the nucleus can also alter regulation of protein synthesis of the cell. (In fact, cyclic AMP–stimulated protein synthesis is the means by which some hormones, such as insulin, affect their target cells.) Thus, in investigations of the memory process, neuroscientists have recently given much attention to processes mediated by cyclic AMP.

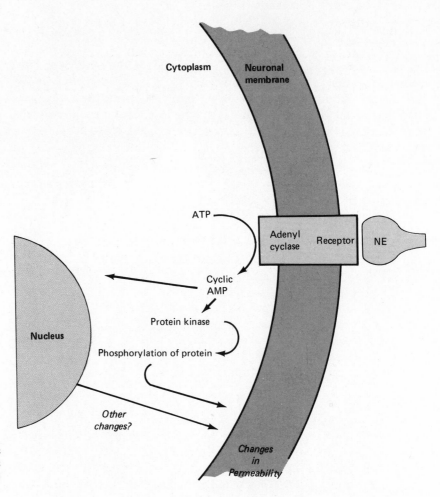

FIGURE 5.10 A schematic model of a postsynaptic membrane containing receptors that activate adenyl cyclase.

In this chapter I have described the substances that are thought to serve as neurotransmitters, and I have described the ways that drugs can selectively affect the production and activity of these substances. In later chapters we shall see how neuroscientists have used these pharmacological agents to try to discover how the brain controls behavior.

SUGGESTED READINGS

ALBERS, R. W., SIEGEL, G. J., KATZMAN, R., and AGRANOFF, B. W. (editors). *Basic Neurochemistry.* Boston: Little, Brown, 1972.

AXELROD, J. Neurotransmitters. *Scientific American,* June, 1974. This article is available as a reprint in *Progress in Psychobiology* (introductions by R. F. Thompson). San Francisco: W. H. Freeman, 1976.

COOPER, J. R., BLOOM, F. E., and ROTH, R. H. *The Biochemical Basis of Neuropharmacology.* New York: Oxford University Press, 1974.

DUNN, A. J., and BONDY, S. C. *Functional Chemistry of the Brain.* Flushing, N.Y.: SP Books, 1974. Distributed by Halstead Press, Division of John Wiley & Sons.

IVERSON, S. D., and IVERSON, L. L. *Behavioral Pharmacology.* New York: Oxford University Press, 1975.

The chapter by Axelrod is a good, easy-to-understand introduction to neurotransmitters. All of the books are excellent. The book by Dunn and Bondy covers a range of topics related to neurochemistry, including general brain metabolism as well as synaptic transmission. *Behavioral Pharmacology* (Iverson and Iverson) discusses the behavioral effects of psychoactive drugs in considerable detail. The authors also describe the behavioral and biochemical procedures used in psychopharmacological investigations. The text by Cooper, Bloom, and Roth is somewhat more advanced than the other books, and concentrates on the pharmacology of synapses. The book edited by Albers et al. contains chapters by different authors on a wide variety of topics related to neurochemistry. Most of the chapters are rather detailed.

Introduction to the Structure of the Nervous System

6

We have, so far, studied the structure and function of neurons and their supporting cells. We have seen how neurons communicate and reach decisions. Now it is time to begin discussion of some functional systems of the brain; that means it will be necessary, first, to become acquainted with the general structure of the nervous system.

In this chapter I shall make no attempt to present a course in neuroanatomy. I would rather present less material and have you learn nearly all of it than present a lot of material and have you try to figure out what is important enough to remember. I shall try to keep the number of terms introduced here to a minimum (as you will see, the minimum is still a pretty large number). In later chapters dealing with specific functional systems, I shall present more information concerning the relevant anatomy; you should have no trouble incorporating the new information into the general framework you will receive in this chapter. This scheme will permit me to distribute the anatomical details a bit more (minimizing the probability of neuroanatomical information overload) and will allow me to discuss structure and function together. Anatomy is always more interesting (and easier to learn) when it is presented in a functional context.

The nervous system consists of the brain and spinal cord, which make up the central nervous system (CNS), and the cranial nerves, spinal nerves, and peripheral ganglia, which constitute the peripheral nervous system (PNS). The central nervous system is encased in bone; the brain is covered by the skull, and the spinal cord resides within the *vertebral column.*

DIRECTIONS AND PLANES OF SECTION

When describing topographical features (hills, roads, rivers, etc.), we need to use terms denoting directions (e.g., the road goes north, and then turns to the east as it climbs the hill). Similarly, in describing structures of the nervous system and their interconnecting pathways, we must have available a set of words that define geographical relationships. We could use the terms *in front of, above, to the side of,* etc., but then different terms would have to be used in describing the same set of neural structures of animals like humans, who walk erect and whose spinal cord is oriented at right angles to the ground, and animals like the rat, whose spinal cord is normally parallel to the ground. To make it easier to describe anatomical directions, a standard set of terms has been adopted.

Directions in the nervous system are normally taken relative to the *neuraxis,* an imaginary line drawn through the spinal cord up to the front of the brain. For simplicity's sake, let us consider an animal with a straight neuraxis. Figure 6.1 shows an alligator and a human. This alligator is certainly laid out in a linear fashion—we can draw a straight line that starts between its eyes and continues down the center of its spinal cord. (See **FIGURE 6.1.**) The front end is *anterior,* and the tail is *posterior.* The terms *rostral* (toward the beak) and *caudal* (toward the tail) are also employed; I shall use these latter terms more often. The top of the head and the back are part of the *dorsal* surface, while the *ventral* surface faces the ground. (The spinal cord, then, is located in a position dorsal to the abdominal surface and ventral to the surface of the animal's back.) These directions are somewhat more complicated in the human, since the neuraxis takes a 90-degree bend. The front views of the alligator and the human illustrate the terms *lateral* and *medial,* toward the side and toward the midline, respectively. (See **FIGURE 6.1.**) When describing brain structures, the terms *superior* and *inferior* are often used. The superior structure is above (dorsal to) the inferior one.

To see what is in the nervous system, we have to cut it open; to be able to convey information about what we find, we slice it in a standard way. Figure 6.2 shows the nervous system of an alligator and that of a human. Again, let us first consider the alligator. We can slice the nervous system in three ways: (1) *transversely,* like a salami, giving us *cross sections,* or *transverse sections* or *frontal sec-*

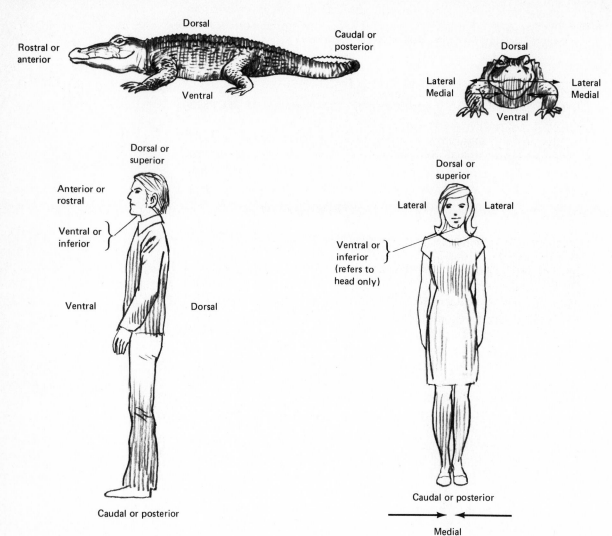

tions or *coronal sections*; (2) parallel to the ground, giving us *horizontal sections*; and (3) perpendicular to the ground and parallel to the neuraxis, giving us *sagittal sections*. It is unfortunate that so many terms are used to refer to the first plane of section; I shall try to use only two in the text—*frontal sections* through the brain and *cross sections* through the spinal cord. (See **FIGURE 6.2.**)

I should mention one section that you will encounter often in this text—the *midsagittal section*. If you sliced the brain down the middle, dividing it into its two symmetrical halves, you would have cut it through its *midsagittal plane*. If you then looked at one half

CNS of Alligator

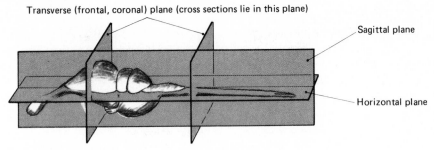

Transverse (frontal, coronal) plane (cross sections lie in this plane)

Sagittal plane

Horizontal plane

CNS of Human

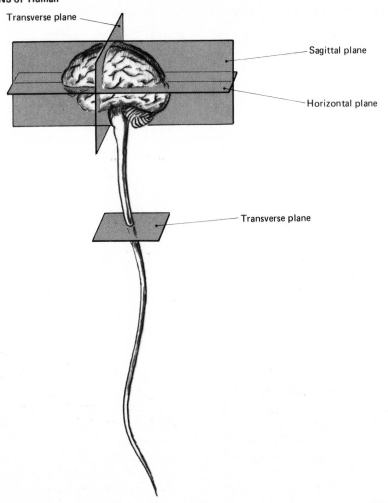

Transverse plane

Sagittal plane

Horizontal plane

Transverse plane

FIGURE 6.2   Planes of section as they relate to the central nervous system of an alligator and a human.

of the brain with its cut surface toward you, you would be getting a *midsagittal view*. You will see many of these views of the brain in this text.

GROSS FEATURES OF THE BRAIN

Figure 6.3 illustrates the relationship of the brain and spinal cord to the head and neck of a human. (See **FIGURE 6.3.**) The brain is a large mass of neurons, glia, and supporting cells. It is the most protected organ of the body, encased in a tough, bony skull and floating in a pool of *cerebrospinal fluid*. The brain receives a copious supply of blood and is chemically guarded by the blood-brain barrier.

Blood Supply

The brain receives aproximately 20 percent of the blood flow from the heart, and it receives this blood flow continuously. Other parts of the body (e.g., skeletal muscle, digestive system) receive varying quantities of blood, depending on their needs, relative to those of other regions. The brain, however, always receives its share. The brain cannot store its fuel (primarily glucose and keto acids), nor can it temporarily extract energy without oxygen as can the muscles; therefore, a consistent blood supply is essential. A one-second interruption of the blood flow to the brain uses up much of the dissolved oxygen; a six-second interruption produces unconsciousness. Irreversible damage occurs within a few minutes.

Circulation of blood in the body proceeds from arteries to arterioles to capillaries; the capillaries then drain into venules, which collect and become veins. The veins travel back to the heart, where the process begins again. Regional blood flow is controlled by smooth muscles in the walls of arteries and arterioles. Contraction of circular fibers constricts the arterioles and restricts blood flow; contraction of longitudinal fibers dilates the arterioles. The smooth muscles of the arterioles are controlled by nerve endings and by levels of various hormones. The arterioles of the brain, however, are not very responsive to changes in the general physiological state of the organism. Instead, increases in local levels of carbon dioxide cause dilation of the brain's blood vessels. Blood flow to various regions is thus regulated by local demand; an increased rate of metabolism produces excess carbon dioxide, which results in a corresponding increase in regional blood flow.

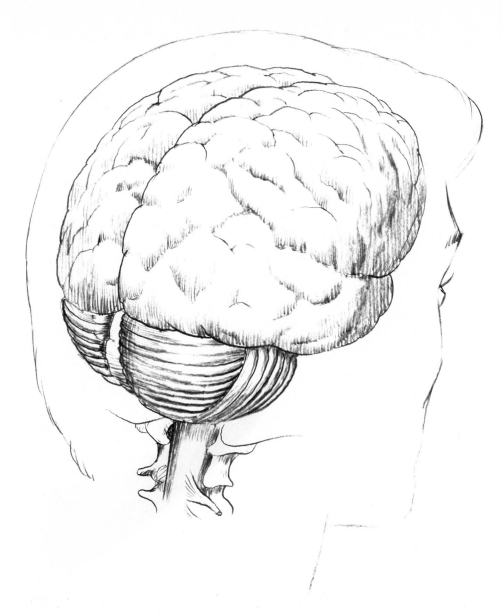

Figure 6.4 shows a bottom view of the brain and its major arterial supply. (The spinal cord has been cut off, as have the left half of the cerebellum and the left temporal lobe.) Two major sets of arteries serve the brain: the _vertebral arteries_ (drawn in black), which serve the caudal portion of the brain, and the _internal carotid arteries_ (drawn in white), which serve the rostral portions. (See **FIGURE 6.4.**) You can see that the blood supply is rather peculiar; major

FIGURE 6.3   The relationship of the brain and spinal cord to the head and neck.

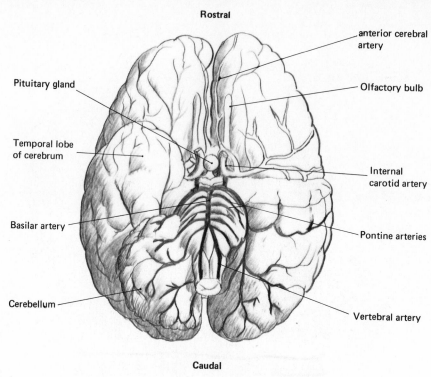

Rostral

anterior cerebral artery

Pituitary gland

Olfactory bulb

Temporal lobe of cerebrum

Internal carotid artery

Basilar artery

Pontine arteries

Cerebellum

Vertebral artery

Caudal

FIGURE 6.4   Arterial supply to the brain. (Adapted with permission from McGraw-Hill Book Co. from *The Human Nervous System*, 2nd edition, by Noback and Demarest. Copyright © 1975, by McGraw-Hill, Inc.)

arteries join together and then separate again. Normally, there is little mixing of blood from the rostral and caudal arterial supplies, or, in the case of the rostral supply, that of the right and left sides of the brain. If a blood vessel becomes occluded, however, blood flow can follow alternative routes, reducing the probability of loss of blood supply and subsequent destruction of brain tissue.

Venous drainage of the brain is shown in Figure 6.5. Major veins, like major arteries, are interconnected, so that blood in some veins can flow in either direction (shown by double-ended arrows), depending on intracerebral pressures in various parts of the brain. (See **FIGURE 6.5.**)

Meninges

The entire nervous system—brain, spinal cord, cranial and spinal nerves, and autonomic ganglia—is covered by tough connective tissue. The protective sheath around the brain and spinal cord is referred to as the *meninges*. The meninges consist of three layers, the inner two

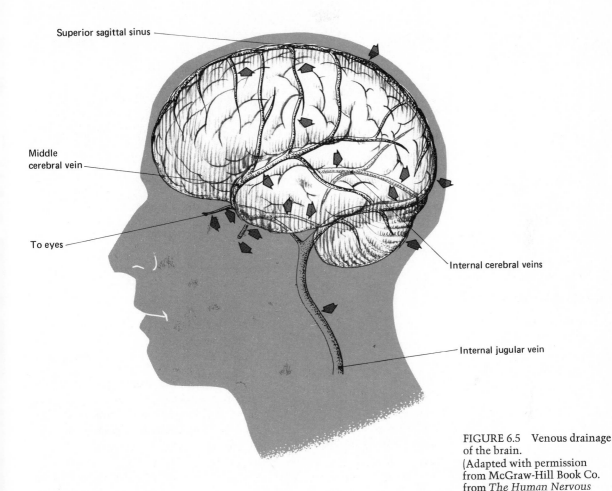

Superior sagittal sinus

Middle
cerebral vein

To eyes

Internal cerebral veins

Internal jugular vein

FIGURE 6.5   Venous drainage
of the brain.
(Adapted with permission
from McGraw-Hill Book Co.
from *The Human Nervous
System*, 2nd edition, by Noback
and Demarest. Copyright ©
1975, by McGraw-Hill, Inc.)

of which are shown in Figure 6.6.   The outer layer is thick, tough,
and unstretchable; its name, *dura mater*, means "hard mother" (and
I don't know why).   The middle layer (*arachnoid*—"spider-shaped,"
probably called so because of the weblike appearance of the *arachnoid
trabeculae* that protrude from it) is soft and spongy, and lies beneath
the dura mater.   Closely attached to the brain and spinal cord, and
following every surface convolution, is the *pia mater* ("soft mother").
The smaller surface blood vessels of the brain and spinal cord are
contained within this layer.   Between the pia mater and arachnoid
is a gap called the *subarachnoid space*.   This space is filled with cere-

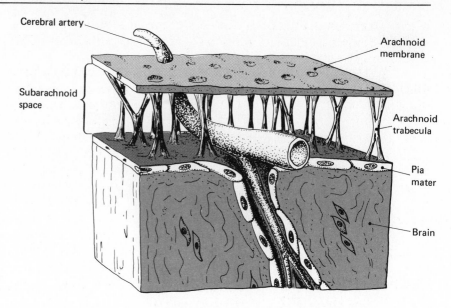

Cerebral artery

Arachnoid membrane

Subarachnoid space

Arachnoid trabecula

Pia mater

Brain

FIGURE 6.6 A schematic drawing of the arachnoid, subarachnoid space, and pia mater. (Adapted from Curtis, B. A., Jacobson, S., and Marcus, E. M. (editors), *An Introduction to the Neurosciences*. Philadelphia: W. B. Saunders, 1972.)

brospinal fluid (CSF), and through it pass large blood vessels. (See **FIGURE 6.6.**)

The peripheral nervous system is covered with two layers of meninges. The middle layer (arachnoid), with its associated pool of CSF, covers only the brain and spinal cord. Outside the CNS the outer and inner layers (dura mater and pia mater) fuse and form a sheath covering the spinal and cranial nerves and the autonomic ganglia.

Ventricular System and the Production of CSF

The brain is very soft and jellylike. The considerable weight of a human brain (approximately 1400 gm), along with its delicate construction, necessitates that it be protected from shock. A human brain cannot even support its own weight well; it is extremely difficult to remove and handle a fresh brain from a recently deceased human without damaging it.

The intact brain within a living human is, fortunately, well protected. It floats in the bath of cerebrospinal fluid contained within the meninges. Since the brain is completely immersed in liquid, its net weight is reduced to approximately 80 gm, and pressure on the base of the brain is therefore considerably diminished. The cerebrospinal fluid surrounding the brain and spinal cord also reduces the shock to the CNS that would be caused by sudden head movement. Painful headaches accompany head movements after clinical removal of the cerebrospinal fluid prior to special X-ray tests; these headaches attest to the value of CSF as a shock-absorbing medium. (Fresh CSF is subsequently produced, and the headaches disappear.)

The brain contains a series of hollow, interconnected chambers filled with cerebrospinal fluid. These chambers are connected with the subarachnoid space via small openings (*foramena*), and they are also continuous with the narrow, tubelike *central canal* of the spinal cord. Figure 6.7 consists of drawings of two views of the human brain, with the ventricular system shaded in. (See **FIGURE 6.7.**) The largest chamber is the *lateral ventricle*, with its *anterior horn, body, posterior horn,* and *inferior horn*. There are actually two lateral ventricles, as is shown in the bottom drawing, but only the one nearer the viewer is represented in the sagittal view of the upper drawing. The lateral ventricles are connected, via the *foramen of Monroe,* to the *third ventricle*. The third ventricle is located at the midline of the brain; it is a single structure, and its walls divide the local region of the brain into symmetrical halves. A bridge of neural tissue (*massa intermedia*) crosses through the middle of the third ventricle. The *cerebral aqueduct,* a long tube, connects the third ventricle to the *fourth ventricle,* which, at its caudal end, connects with the central canal of the spinal cord. (There is no first or second ventricle.) (See **FIGURE 6.7.**)

Cerebrospinal fluid is manufactured by the meninges; a special vascular structure of the pia mater (*choroid plexus*) protrudes into each of the ventricles and produces CSF from blood plasma. CSF is continuously produced; the total volume is approximately 125 ml, and the half-life of CSF (the time it takes for half of the CSF present in the ventricular system to be replaced by fresh CSF) is about 3 hours, so several times this amount is produced by the choroid plexus each day. The continuous production of CSF means that there must be a mechanism for its removal; Figure 6.8 illustrates the production, circulation, and reabsorption of cerebrospinal fluid. (See **FIGURE 6.8.**)

The illustration shows a midsagittal view of the central nervous system, so the lateral ventricles, located on each side of the brain, cannot be shown. (To visualize the lateral ventricles, refer to the uppermost drawing of Figure 6.7, and visually "superimpose" the third ventricles of this figure on Figure 6.8. The massa intermedia serves as a convenient reference point.) (See **FIGURES 6.7** and **6.8.**) CSF is produced by the choroid plexus of the lateral ventricles, and it flows through the foramen of Monroe into the third ventricle. Additional CSF is produced in this ventricle and then flows through the cerebral aqueduct to the fourth ventricle, where still more CSF is produced. CSF leaves the fourth ventricle via the *foramen of Magendie* and the *foramina of Luschka* (laterally located—not shown in Figure 6.8) and collects in the subarachnoid space surrounding the brain. All CSF

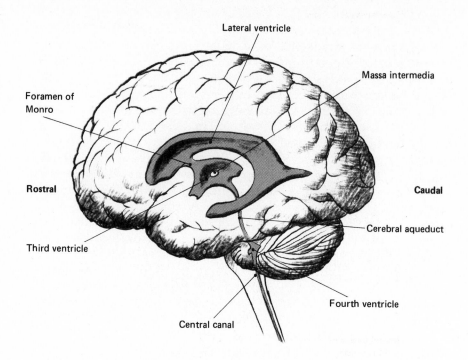

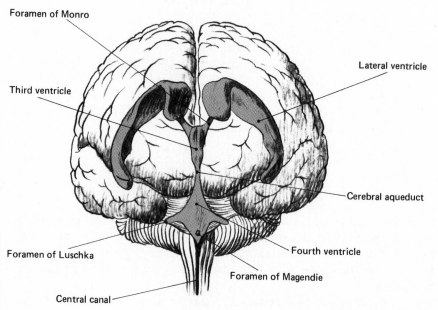

FIGURE 6.7   The ventricular system of the brain. (Adapted with permission from McGraw-Hill Book Co. from *The Human Nervous System*, 2nd edition, by Noback and Demarest. Copyright © 1975, by McGraw-Hill, Inc.)

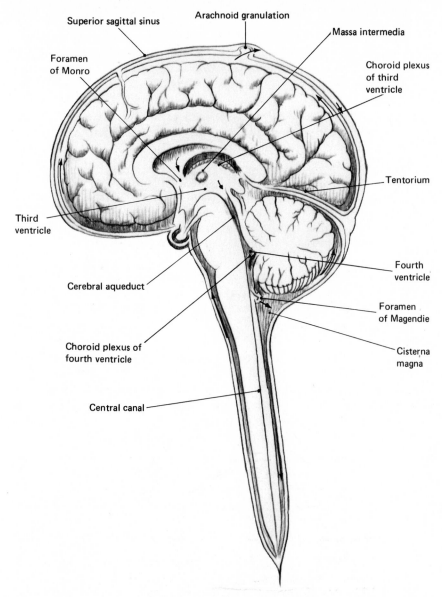

Superior sagittal sinus

Arachnoid granulation

Massa intermedia

Foramen of Monro

Choroid plexus of third ventricle

Tentorium

Third ventricle

Cerebral aqueduct

Fourth ventricle

Foramen of Magendie

Choroid plexus of fourth ventricle

Cisterna magna

Central canal

FIGURE 6.8   Circulation of cerebrospinal fluid through the ventricular system. (Adapted with permission from McGraw-Hill Book Co. from *The Human Nervous System*, 2nd edition, by Noback and Demarest. Copyright © 1975, by McGraw-Hill, Inc.)

thus flows into the subarachnoid space around the central nervous system where it is reabsorbed into the blood supply through the *arachnoid granulations*. The arachnoid granulations protrude into the *superior sagittal sinus*, which eventually drains into the veins serving the brain.

Figure 6.8 also illustrates a fold of dura mater, the *tentorium*, which separates the cerebellum from the overlying cerebrum. (See

FIGURE 6.8.) This tough sheet of connective tissue extends to the top of the brainstem, leaving an opening (*tentorial notch*) through which the brainstem passes. Prizefighters (unless they are extremely good and quit early enough) usually receive a good many blows to the head. This repeated jarring of the brain often causes bruising of the brainstem against the edge of the tentorium; the result of this assault is one of the causes of the "punch-drunk" syndrome.

The meninges, skull, and vertebral column encase the CNS in a rigid container of fixed volume. This fact means that any growth in the mass of the brain must result in displacement of the fluid contents of the container. Hence, growth of a brain tumor, depending on its location, will often result in deformation of the walls of the ventricular system, as the invading mass takes up volume previously occupied by CSF. (It is quite fortunate that these hollow ventricles exist; the only other fluid-filled spaces are the blood vessels, which would be constricted by a growing tumor if there were no ventricles in the brain.) To diagnose and locate brain tumors, clinicians often take X-ray photographs of the ventricular system. (Air or a *radiopaque dye* must be injected to make the ventricular system visible.) By comparing the *ventriculogram* thus obtained with normal ones, a radiologist can determine the location and extent of tumors within the brain.

Occasionally the flow of CSF is interrupted at some point in its route of passage. For example, the cerebral aqueduct may be blocked by a tumor. This occlusion results in greatly increased pressure within the ventricles, since the choroid plexus continues to produce CSF. The walls of the ventricles then expand and produce a condition known as *hydrocephalus* (literally, "water-head"). If the obstruction remains, and if nothing is done to reverse the increased intracerebral pressure, blood vessels will be occluded, and permanent —perhaps fatal—brain damage will occur. The *optic nerves*, serving the eyes, are covered with meningeal layers, including the inelastic dura mater. Increased intracerebral pressure is thus transmitted through the contents of the optic nerve the way water pressure can be transmitted through a hose. The pressure will cause the *optic disk* (attachment of the optic nerve to the eye) to bulge forward into the fluid cavity of the eye. The state of the optic disk, which can be seen at the back of the eye by looking through the pupil, is used as a clinical sign in the diagnosis of hydrocephalus.

ANATOMICAL SUBDIVISIONS OF THE BRAIN

The brain is usually divided into *forebrain, midbrain,* and *hindbrain.* These major divisions are further subdivided; Table 6.1 presents these subdivisions, along with the principal structures found in each region. (See **TABLE 6.1.**)

TABLE 6.1   Anatomical Subdivisions of the Brain

Major Division	Subdivision	Principal Structures
Forebrain	Telencephalon	Cerebral cortex Basal ganglia Limbic system
	Diencephalon	Thalamus Hypothalamus
Midbrain	Mesencephalon	Tectum Tegmentum
Hindbrain	Metencephalon	Cerebellum Pons
	Myelencephalon	Medulla oblongata

Telencephalon

The "end brain" includes the *cerebral cortex*, covering the surface of the cerebral hemispheres, the *basal ganglia*, and the *limbic system*. The latter two sets of structures are located, principally, within the deep or *subcortical* portions of the brain.

CEREBRAL CORTEX.   Cortex means "bark," and the cerebral cortex surrounds the cerebral hemispheres like the bark of a tree. In humans the cortex is greatly convoluted; these convolutions, consisting of *sulci* (small grooves), *fissures* (large grooves), and *gyri* (bulges between adjacent sulci or fissures), greatly enlarge the surface area of the cortex, as compared with a similarly sized smooth brain. A human brain contains approximately 20 square feet of cortical area—larger than the surface of the average office desk. The amount of cerebral cortex, relative to the size of the rest of the brain, correlates well with phylogenetic development; higher animals have more cortex.

The surface of the cerebral hemispheres is divided into five lobes. Four of these lobes (*frontal, parietal, temporal,* and *occipital*) are visible on the lateral surface and are shown in Figure 6.9. (See **FIGURE 6.9.**)

The midsagittal view in Figure 6.10 shows the *limbic lobe* and lets us see the inner surface of the other four lobes. (See **FIGURE 6.10.**) Also note the *corpus callosum*. This is the largest *commissure* in the brain; it consists of white matter (myelinated axons) connecting the two hemispheres of the brain. (See **FIGURE 6.10.**)

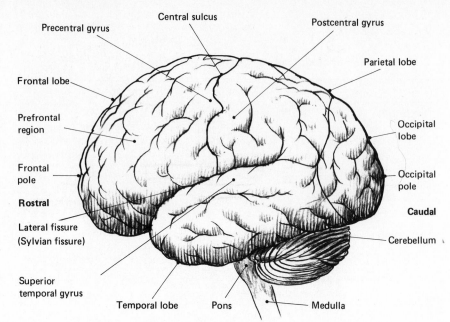

FIGURE 6.9 A lateral view of the human brain.

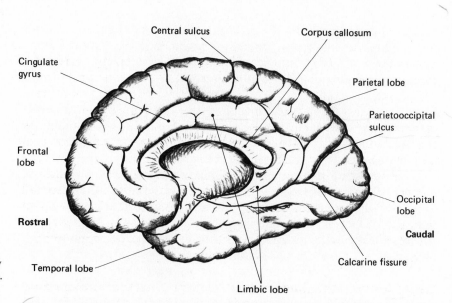

FIGURE 6.10 Midsagittal view of the human brain.

The frontal, parietal, temporal, and occipital lobes consist of neocortex—the most recently evolved neural tissue. The limbic lobe consists of limbic cortex (often called paleocortex) and is a part of the limbic system, which includes a number of interconnected subcortical brain structures.

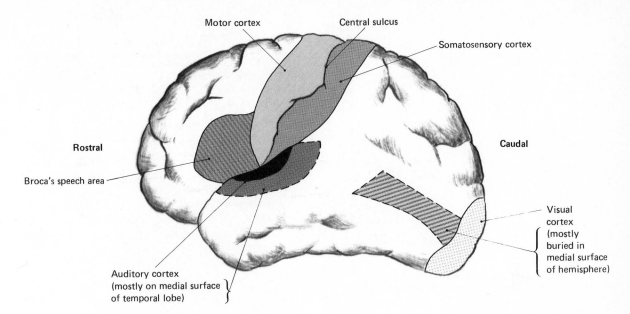

FIGURE 6.11 A schematic lateral view of the human brain showing some of the important cortical areas. Only the more prominent sulci and gyri are shown.

There are several neocortical regions that have special functions. Some of these areas are shown in Figure 6.11. *Sensory areas* receive primary sensory information from the receptors for audition, vision, somatosenses (touch, pressure, temperature, etc.), and taste. *Motor cortex* contains neurons that participate in the control of movement. Other regions are associated with higher functions; for example, damage to *Broca's speech area* in the frontal lobe leads to an inability to speak. (See **FIGURE 6.11.**)

As we shall subsequently see in later chapters, the terms *motor*, *sensory*, and *association* are misleading. Motor cortex (often referred to today as motor-sensory cortex) contains neurons that receive direct inputs from the ascending sensory system. Somatosensory cortex, on the other hand, contains neurons that join the descending motor fiber pathways (as does much of association cortex).

LIMBIC SYSTEM.   The limbic system consists of a set of interconnected structures including limbic cortex, *hippocampal formation* (usually referred to as *hippocampus*), *amygdaloid complex* (usually called *amygdala*), *septum, anterior thalamus*, and *mammillary body*. (The latter two structures are part of the diencephalon, not the telencephalon, but they are generally considered to be part of the limbic system.) Figure 6.12 illustrates these structures and their interconnec-

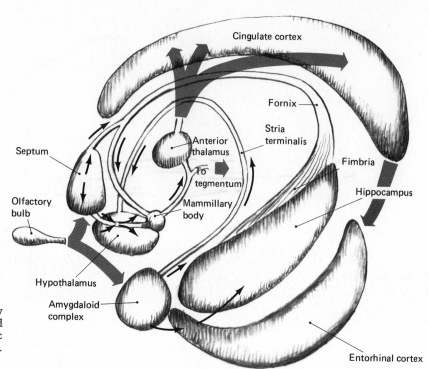

FIGURE 6.12 A very schematic, simplified representation of the limbic system.

tions. (See **FIGURE 6.12.**) The limbic system is involved in emotional behavior, motivation, and (perhaps) memory; it will be discussed in more detail in later chapters.

BASAL GANGLIA. The basal ganglia (*amygdala, globus pallidus, caudate nucleus,* and *putamen*) are shown in Figure 6.13. (See **FIGURE 6.13.**) The basal ganglia are concerned with motor control and constitute a major portion of the extrapyramidal motor system (described in more detail in chapter 10). Parkinson's disease, for example, is characterized by degeneration of dopaminergic cells that send axons to the caudate nucleus.

The basal ganglia also play a role in emotional behavior; destruction of portions of the amygdala (which shares membership in the limbic system and basal ganglia) often produces taming of normally aggressive animals. Recently, neurosurgeons have surgically removed amygdalas of pathologically violent humans in an attempt to control their aggressive outbursts. (These operations will be described in chapter 16.)

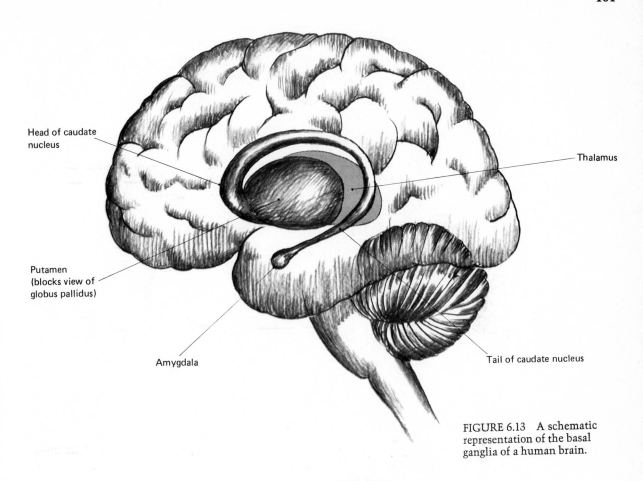

Head of caudate
nucleus

Thalamus

Putamen
(blocks view of
globus pallidus)

Amygdala

Tail of caudate nucleus

FIGURE 6.13 A schematic
representation of the basal
ganglia of a human brain.

Diencephalon

The diencephalon is the most rostral portion of the brainstem. (See **FIGURE 6.14.**) The two most important structures of the "interbrain" are the thalamus and hypothalamus.

THALAMUS.   The thalamus is located in the dorsal part of the diencephalon. It is a large, two-lobed structure, whose sides are connected by the massa intermedia, which pierces the middle of the third ventricle. (See **FIGURE 6.15.**) (The massa intermedia is probably not a very important structure, since the brains of some apparently normal people have been observed to lack this bridge of tissue.)

The majority of neural input to the cerebral cortex is received from the thalamus; indeed, much of the cortical surface can be divided into regions receiving *projections* from specific parts of the

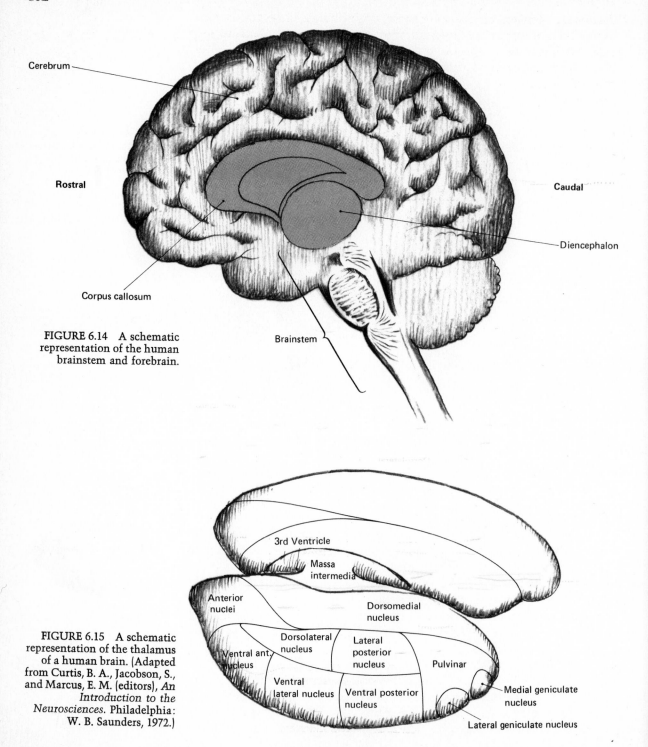

Cerebrum

Rostral

Caudal

Diencephalon

Corpus callosum

FIGURE 6.14 A schematic representation of the human brainstem and forebrain.

Brainstem

3rd Ventricle

Massa intermedia

Anterior nuclei

Dorsomedial nucleus

FIGURE 6.15 A schematic representation of the thalamus of a human brain. (Adapted from Curtis, B. A., Jacobson, S., and Marcus, E. M. (editors), *An Introduction to the Neurosciences*. Philadelphia: W. B. Saunders, 1972.)

Dorsolateral nucleus

Lateral posterior nucleus

Ventral ant. nucleus

Ventral lateral nucleus

Ventral posterior nucleus

Pulvinar

Medial geniculate nucleus

Lateral geniculate nucleus

thalamus. (*Projection fibers* are those sets of axons, from cell bodies located in one region of the brain, that synapse on other neurons located within another specific region.) The thalamus can be divided into a number of *nuclei* (discrete clumpings of a large number of neurons of similar shape). Some of these nuclei (*sensory relay nuclei*) receive sensory information from terminals of incoming axons. The neurons in these nuclei then relay the sensory information to specific sensory projection areas of the cortex. For example, the *lateral geniculate nucleus* projects to visual cortex, the *medial geniculate nucleus* projects to auditory cortex, and the *ventral posterior nuclei* project to somatosensory cortex. (See **FIGURE 6.16.**)

Other thalamic nuclei project to specific regions of cortex, but they do not relay primary sensory information. For example, the

FIGURE 6.16 A schematic representation of the thalamus, along with some of the principal inputs and outputs of the various thalamic regions. Besides these inputs and outputs, there are many interconnections among the various thalamic regions.

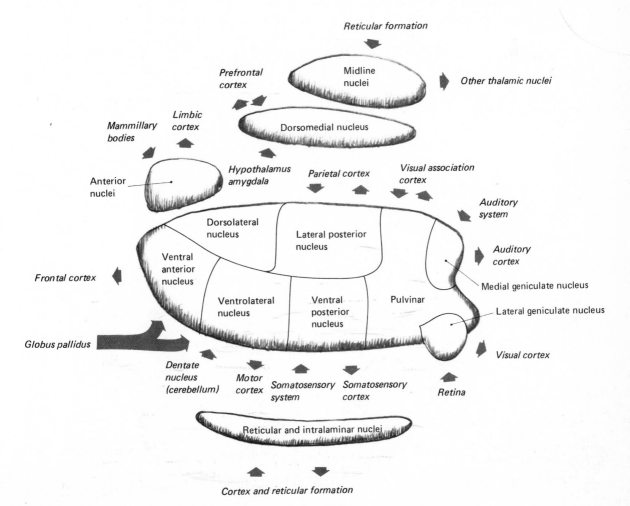

ventrolateral nucleus projects to motor cortex, the *dorsomedial nucleus* projects to prefrontal cortex, the *pulvinar* projects to parietal cortex, and the *anterior nuclei* project to limbic cortex. Other thalamic nuclei (e.g., *midline* and *reticular* nuclei) project diffusely to widespread regions of cortex and to other thalamic nuclei. (See **FIGURE 6.16.**)

HYPOTHALAMUS.   The hypothalamus lies at the base of the brain. Although it is a relatively small structure, it is of considerable importance in control of the autonomic nervous system, in reflex integration, in control of the endocrine system, and in organization of behaviors related to survival of the species. (One often refers to the hypothalamus as controlling the four F's: fighting, feeding, fleeing, and mating.)

The hypothalamus is situated on both sides of the inferior portion of the third ventricle. As its name implies, this structure is located beneath the thalamus (not immediately beneath it; the *subthalamus*—concerned with motor control—is located between the thalamus and the hypothalamus). The hypothalamus is a very complex structure. It contains many nuclei and fiber tracts; Figure 6.17 indicates its location and size. Note that the pituitary gland is attached to the base of the hypothalamus via the *pituitary stalk*. (See **FIGURE 6.17.**) The role of the hypothalamus in control of the four F's will be considered in several chapters later in the book (chapters 11, 12, 13, 16), along with more detailed descriptions of its anatomy.

Mesencephalon

The mesencephalon, or *midbrain*, is the portion of the brainstem just caudal to the diencephalon. It is usually divided into parts: the dorsal *tectum* and the ventral *tegmentum*.

TECTUM.   The principal structures of the tectum ("roof") are the *superior colliculi* and *inferior colliculi* (collectively referred to as the *corpora quadrigemina*, or "bodies of four twins"). Figure 6.18 illustrates a dorsal and ventral view of the brainstem, with the overlying cerebrum and cerebellum removed. The four bumps on the dorsal surface are the superior and inferior colliculi (a colliculus is a "small hill"). (See **FIGURE 6.18.**) The inferior colliculi are a part of the auditory system. As you will see in chapter 9, all fibers conveying auditory information pass through the inferior colliculi on the way to the medial geniculate nucleus and auditory cortex; many of them also synapse there. The superior colliculi are part of the visual system. In mammals, however, they are not the most important part. Mam-

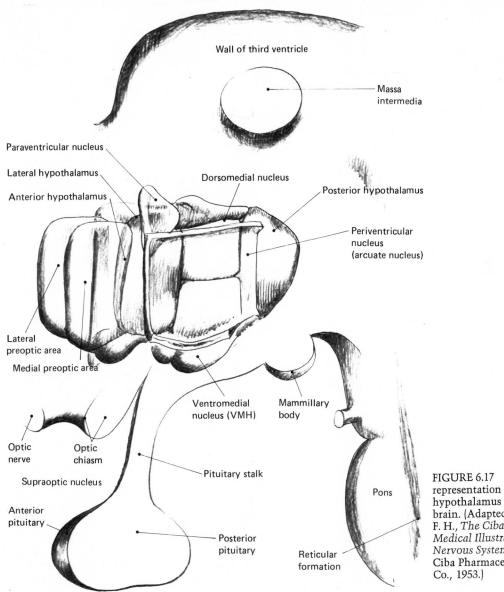

FIGURE 6.17 A schematic representation of the hypothalamus of the human brain. (Adapted from Netter, F. H., *The Ciba Collection of Medical Illustrations*. Vol. 1, *Nervous System*. Summit, N.J.: Ciba Pharmaceutical Products Co., 1953.)

mals have evolved an addition to the collicular system (the sole visual system in lower vertebrates): the direct retino-geniculate-visual cortex system. The superior colliculi have been left, however, with a role in vision—principally in visual reflexes and reactions to moving stimuli, although recent evidence suggests that the perceptual capacities of the tectum have been underestimated.

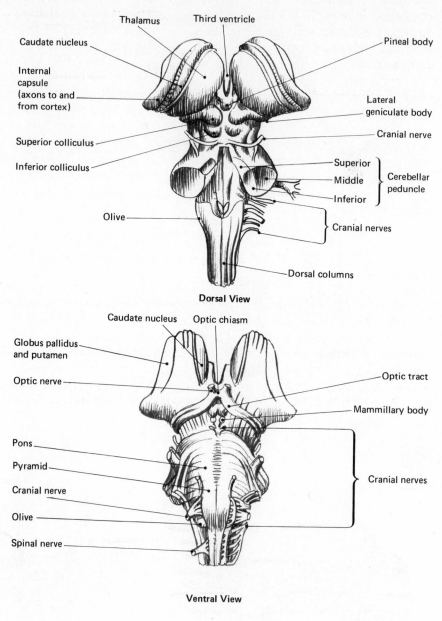

FIGURE 6.18   Two views of the human brainstem. (Adapted with permission from McGraw-Hill Book Co. from *The Human Nervous System*, 2nd edition, by Noback and Demarest. Copyright © 1975, by McGraw-Hill, Inc., and Curtis, B. A., Jacobson, S., and Marcus, E. M. (editors), *An Introduction to the Neurosciences*. Philadelphia: W. B. Saunders, 1972.)

TEGMENTUM.   The tegmentum consists principally of the rostral end of the *reticular formation*, several nuclei controlling eye movements, and the *red nucleus* and *substantia nigra* (parts of the extrapyramidal motor system).

RETICULAR FORMATION. The reticular formation is a large structure consisting of numerous (over ninety in all) nuclei. It is also characterized by a diffuse, interconnected network of neurons with complex dendritic and axonal processes. (Indeed, *reticulum* means "little net"; early anatomists were struck by the netlike appearance of the reticular formation.) The reticular formation (*rf*) occupies the central core of the brainstem, from the lower border of the medulla to the upper border of the midbrain. (Most neuroscientists consider the reticular and midline nuclei of the thalamus to be a functional extension of the reticular formation.) The rf receives sensory information by means of various pathways, and projects fibers to cortex, thalamus, and spinal cord. It plays a role in sleep and arousal, selective attention, muscle tonus, and control of various vital reflexes. Some of these functions will be described more fully in later chapters.

Metencephalon

CEREBELLUM. The *cerebellum* ("little brain") is like a miniature version of the cerebrum. It is covered by *cerebellar cortex* and has a set of *deep cerebellar nuclei* that project to cerebellar cortex just as the thalamic nuclei project to cerebral cortex. Figure 6.19 shows two views of the brainstem: one with the cerebellum attached and the other with the cerebellum dissected away, to illustrate the superior, middle, and inferior *cerebellar peduncles*, bundles of white matter that connect the cerebellum to the brainstem. (See **FIGURE 6.19.**)

FIGURE 6.19 A schematic representation of the human brainstem, showing how the cerebellum connects with this region. (Adapted from Curtis, B. A., Jacobson, S., and Marcus, E. M. (editors), *An Introduction to the Neurosciences*. Philadelphia: W. B. Saunders, 1972.)

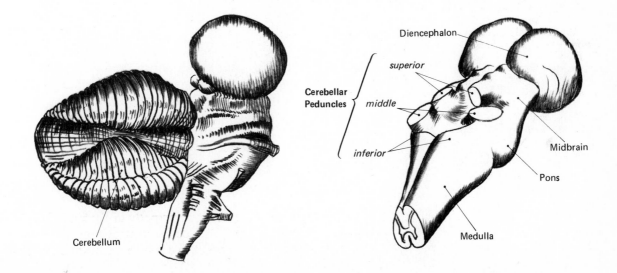

Cerebellum

Cerebellar Peduncles
superior
middle
inferior

Diencephalon
Midbrain
Pons
Medulla

Without the cerebellum it would be impossible to stand, walk, or perform any coordinated movements. (A virtuoso pianist or other performing musician probably owes much to his or her cerebellum.) The cerebellum receives visual, auditory, vestibular, and somatosensory information, and it also receives information about individual muscular movements being directed by the brain. The cerebellum integrates this information and modifies the motor outflow, exerting a coordinating and smoothing effect on the movements. Cerebellar damage results in jerky, poorly coordinated, exaggerated movements; extensive cerebellar damage makes it impossible even to stand.

PONS. The *pons*, a rather large bulge in the brainstem, lies immediately ventral to the cerebellum. Refer back to **FIGURE 6.18.** The pons contains, in its core, a portion of the reticular formation, including some nuclei that appear to be important in sleep and arousal. Several cranial nerve nuclei, serving the head and facial region, are located in the pons.

Myelencephalon

MEDULLA. The *medulla oblongata* (usually just called the *medulla*) is the most caudal portion of the brainstem; its lower border is the rostral end of the spinal cord. The medulla contains part of the reticular formation, including nuclei that control vital functions such as regulation of the cardiovascular system, respiration, and skeletal muscle tonus. Several cranial nerve nuclei are also located there.

SPINAL CORD

The spinal cord is a roughly cylindrical structure, containing a bulge in its lower middle region and gradually tapering to a point in the lower back region. The principal function of the spinal cord is to distribute motor fibers to the effectors of the body (glands and muscles) and to collect somatosensory information to be passed on to the brain. The spinal cord also has a certain degree of autonomy from the brain; various reflexive control circuits (some of which are described in chapter 10) are located there.

The spinal cord is protected by the vertebral column, which is composed of twenty-four individual vertebrae of the *cervical, thoracic,* and *lumbar* regions, and the fused vertebrae making up the *sacral* and *coccygeal* portions of the column. Figure 6.20 illustrates the divisions and structures of the spinal cord and vertebral column. Note that the spinal cord is only about ⅔ as long as the vertebral column; the rest of the space is filled by a mass of *spinal roots* composing the *cauda equina* ("mare's tail"). (See **FIGURE 6.20.**)

Early in embryological development the vertebral column and spinal cord are of the same length. As development progresses, the

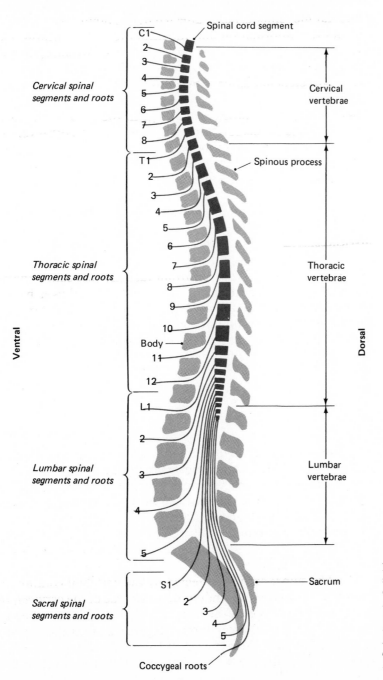

FIGURE 6.20 A sagittal section through the spinal column, showing the attachments of the spinal roots. (Adapted from Noback, C. R., and Demarest, R. J., *The Nervous System: Introduction and Review.* New York: McGraw-Hill, 1972.)

vertebral column grows faster than does the spinal cord. This differential growth rate causes the spinal roots to be displaced downward; the most caudal roots travel the farthest before they emerge through the intervertebral foramena and thus compose the cauda equina. To produce the *caudal block* sometimes used in childbirth, a local anesthetic can be injected into the CSF contained within the dural sac surrounding the cauda equina.

Small bundles of fibers (*fila*) emerge from the spinal cord in two straight lines along its dorsolateral and ventrolateral surfaces. Groups of these fila fuse together and become the thirty-one paired sets of *dorsal* and *ventral roots*. These roots, in turn, join together as they pass through openings between the vertebrae (*intervertebral foramena*) and become the thirty-one pairs of spinal nerves. Figure 6.21 illustrates the appearance of the vertebral column and of individual vertebrae. A cross section of the spinal column taken between two adjacent vertebrae shows the junction of the dorsal and ventral roots in the intervertebral foramena. (See **FIGURE 6.21.**)

The spinal cord, like the brain, consists of white matter and gray matter. Unlike the brain, its white matter (consisting of ascending and descending bundles of myelinated axons) is on the outside; the gray matter (mostly cell bodies and short, unmyelinated axons) is on the inside. Figure 6.22 shows a cross section through the spinal cord. Ascending tracts are shown in dark gray; descending tracts, in light gray. (See **FIGURE 6.22.**) The ascending (sensory) tracts will be described in a section on somatosenses in chapter 9. Similarly, the descending (motor) tracts will be described in chapter 10.

PERIPHERAL NERVOUS SYSTEM

The brain and spinal cord communicate with skeletal muscles and sensory systems of the rest of the body via the cranial and spinal nerves. Glands, smooth muscles, and cardiac muscle are regulated by the autonomic nervous system, consisting of offshoots of spinal and cranial nerves and the associated autonomic ganglia.

Spinal Nerves

The spinal nerves begin at the junction of the dorsal and ventral roots of the spinal cord. The nerves leave the vertebral column and travel, branching repeatedly as they go, to the muscles or sensory receptors they innervate. Branches of spinal nerves often follow blood vessels, especially those branches that innervate skeletal muscles. Figure

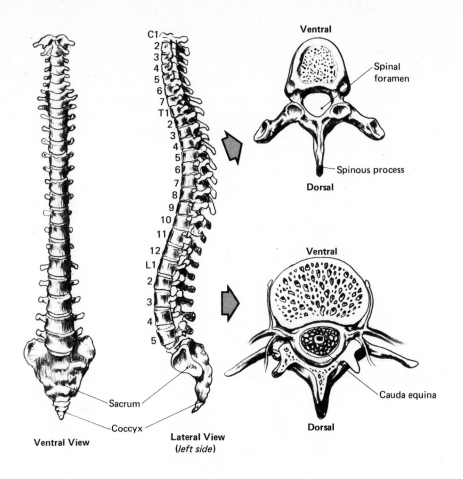

Ventral

Spinal foramen

Spinous process

Dorsal

Ventral

Cauda equina

Dorsal

C1
2
3
4
5
6
7
T1
2
3
4
5
6
7
8
9
10
11
12
L1
2
3
4
5

Sacrum

Coccyx

Ventral View

Lateral View
(*left side*)

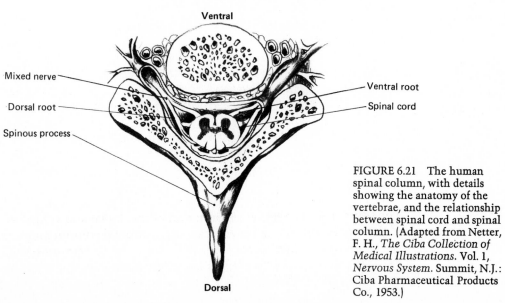

Ventral

Mixed nerve

Dorsal root

Spinous process

Ventral root

Spinal cord

Dorsal

FIGURE 6.21   The human spinal column, with details showing the anatomy of the vertebrae, and the relationship between spinal cord and spinal column. (Adapted from Netter, F. H., *The Ciba Collection of Medical Illustrations.* Vol. 1, *Nervous System.* Summit, N.J.: Ciba Pharmaceutical Products Co., 1953.)

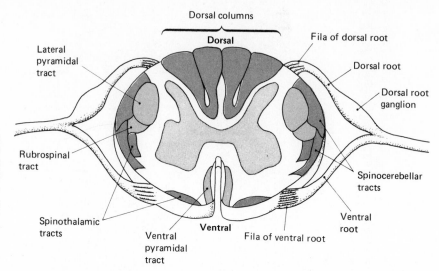

FIGURE 6.22 A schematic cross section through the spinal cord, showing the principal ascending (sensory) and descending (motor) tracts. (Adapted from Netter, F. H., *The Ciba Collection of Medical Illustrations*. Vol. 1, *Nervous System*. Summit, N.J.: Ciba Pharmaceutical Products Co., 1953.)

6.23 shows a dorsal view of a human with a few branches of the spinal nerves. Note that the spinal nerves of the thoracic region follow spaces between the ribs. These *intercostal nerves* (*costa* means "rib") are paralleled by the intercostal arteries and veins. (See **FIGURE 6.23.**) Note also that some of the spinal nerves fuse together and then divide again; the fusions are referred to as *plexuses* (braids).

Figure 6.24 illustrates the pathways by which sensory information enters the spinal cord and motor information leaves it. (See **FIGURE 6.24.**) First let us consider afferent (incoming) fibers. The cell bodies of all nerve fibers bringing sensory information into the brain and spinal cord are located outside the central nervous system (with the sole exception of the visual system; the retina of the eye is considered to be a part of the brain). The cell bodies that give rise to the axons afferent to the spinal cord reside in the *dorsal root ganglia*, rounded swellings of the dorsal root. The afferent neurons are of the unipolar type (described in chapter 2). The axonal stalk divides close to the cell body; it sends one limb into the spinal cord and the other limb out to the sensory organ. Note that the dorsal root is completely sensory in nature; all its fibers are afferent to the spinal cord. (See **FIGURE 6.24.**)

Cell bodies that give rise to the ventral root are located within the gray matter of the spinal cord, in either the *ventral horn* or the *intermediate horn*. The axons of these multipolar neurons leave the spinal cord via a ventral root, which joins a dorsal root to make a spinal nerve (often referred to as a *mixed nerve* because it carries both sensory and motor fibers). (See **FIGURE 6.24.**)

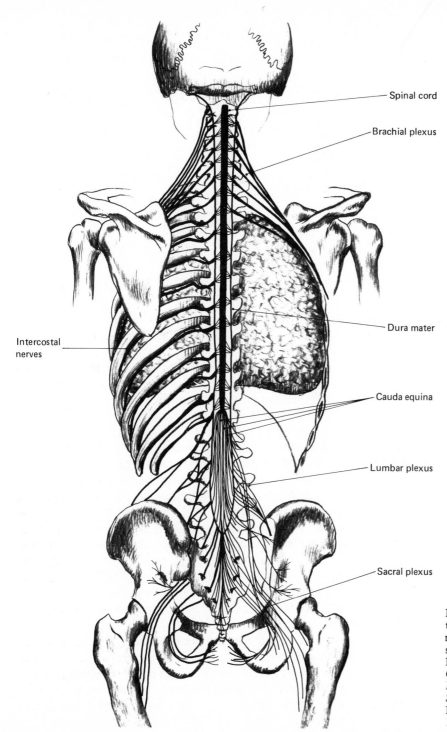

Spinal cord

Brachial plexus

Dura mater

Intercostal nerves

Cauda equina

Lumbar plexus

Sacral plexus

FIGURE 6.23   A dorsal view of the human body, showing the routes travelled by the principal spinal nerves. (Adapted from Netter, F. H., *The Ciba Collection of Medical Illustrations.* Vol. 1, *Nervous System.* Summit, N.J.: Ciba Pharmaceutical Products Co., 1953.)

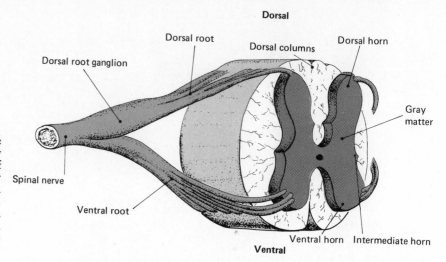

FIGURE 6.24 A section of the spinal cord, schematically illustrating the attachment of the spinal roots and their merging into the spinal nerve. (Adapted from Gross, C. M. (editor), *Gray's Anatomy*. Philadelphia: Lea and Febiger, 1966.)

Cranial Nerves

Twelve pairs of nerves leave the ventral surface of the brain. These cranial nerves serve sensory and motor functions of the head and neck region. (One of them, the *tenth*, or *vagus nerve*, serves autonomic functions of organs in the thoracic and abdominal cavities.) Figure 6.25 presents a view of the base of the brain and illustrates the cranial nerves and the structures they serve. Note that efferent (motor) fibers are shown in dark gray and that afferent (sensory) fibers are shown in light gray. (See **FIGURE 6.25.**)

As I mentioned in the previous section, cell bodies of nerve fibers afferent to the brain and spinal cord (except for the visual system) are located outside the CNS. Somatosensory information (and also gustation, or taste) is received, via the cranial nerves, from unipolar neurons whose cell bodies reside in *cranial nerve ganglia* (structures similar to the dorsal root ganglia of the spinal cord). (See **FIGURE 6.25.**) Auditory, vestibular, and visual information is received via fibers of bipolar neurons (described in chapter 2). Olfactory information is received via a complex system; the olfactory bulbs, at the ends of the olfactory nerves, contain a considerable amount of neural circuitry. The cell bodies that give rise to the olfactory nerve fibers are of the multipolar type. The various sensory receptors will be described in chapter 8; the corresponding neural pathways will be found in chapter 9.

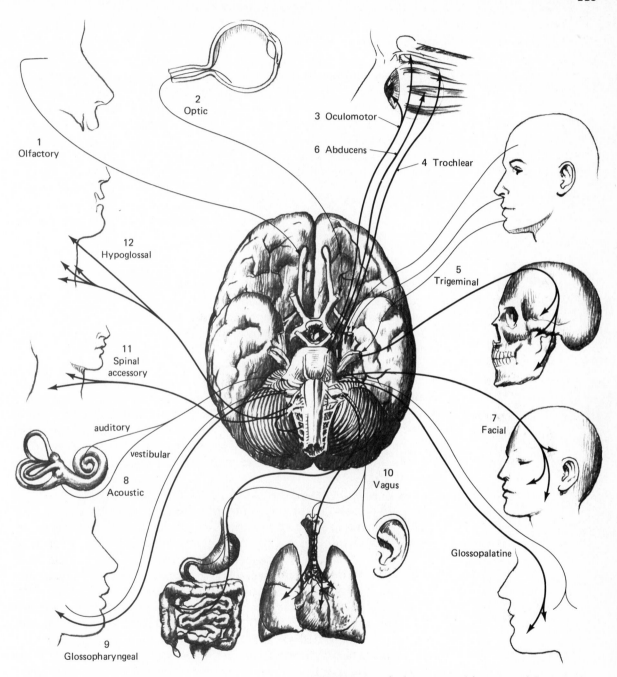

1
Olfactory

2
Optic

3 Oculomotor

6 Abducens

4 Trochlear

5
Trigeminal

12
Hypoglossal

11
Spinal
accessory

7
Facial

auditory

vestibular

8
Acoustic

10
Vagus

Glossopalatine

9
Glossopharyngeal

FIGURE 6.25 The locations and functions of the cranial nerves. (Adapted from Netter, F. H., *The Ciba Collection of Medical Illustrations.* Vol. 1, *Nervous System.* Summit, N.J.: Ciba Pharmaceutical Products Co., 1953.)

AUTONOMIC NERVOUS SYSTEM

The autonomic nervous system (ANS) is concerned with regulation of smooth muscle, cardiac muscle, and glands. Smooth muscle is found in the skin (associated with hair follicles), in blood vessels, in the eye (controlling pupil size and accommodation of the lens), and in the wall and sphincters of the gut, gall bladder, and urinary bladder. Merely describing the organs innervated by the autonomic nervous system suggests the function of this system: regulation of "vegetative processes" in the body. The ANS consists of two anatomically separate systems, the *sympathetic* and *parasympathetic* divisions.

Sympathetic Division of the ANS

The sympathetic division is most active when catabolic processes (i.e., those involved with expenditure of energy from reserves stored in the body) are required. For example, increased blood flow to skeletal muscles, secretion of epinephrine (resulting in increased heart rate and a rise in blood sugar level), and *piloerection* (erection of fur in mammals who have it and production of "goose bumps" in humans) are some effects mediated by the sympathetic nervous system during excitement. The cell bodies of sympathetic motor neurons are located in the intermediate horn of the gray matter of the thoracic and lumbar regions of the spinal cord. The fibers of these neurons exit via the ventral roots. After joining the spinal nerves, the fibers branch off and pass, via *white rami*, into *spinal sympathetic ganglia*. Figure 6.26 shows the relationship of these ganglia to the spinal nerves and the spinal cord. Note that the various spinal sympathetic ganglia are connected to the neighboring ganglia above and below, and thus form the *sympathetic chain*. (See **FIGURE 6.26.**)

All sympathetic motor fibers enter the ganglia of the sympathetic chain, but not all of them synapse there. Some leave the ganglia (for example, those which enter the *splanchnic* nerve) and travel to one of the sympathetic ganglia (for example, the *inferior mesenteric ganglion*) located away from the spinal cord, among the internal organs. There they synapse on *postganglionic neurons*, which in turn send axons to the target organs (e.g., intestine, stomach, kidney). (See **FIGURE 6.27, TOP.**) Other fibers synapse in ganglia of the sympathetic chain; the fibers of the postganglionic neurons, in this case, follow one of two pathways to their target organs: (1) Postganglionic fibers to the skin, and its blood vessels, sweat glands, and hair follicles, follow the *gray rami* back to the spinal nerves, and then travel to the periphery. (White rami contain myelinated fibers; the

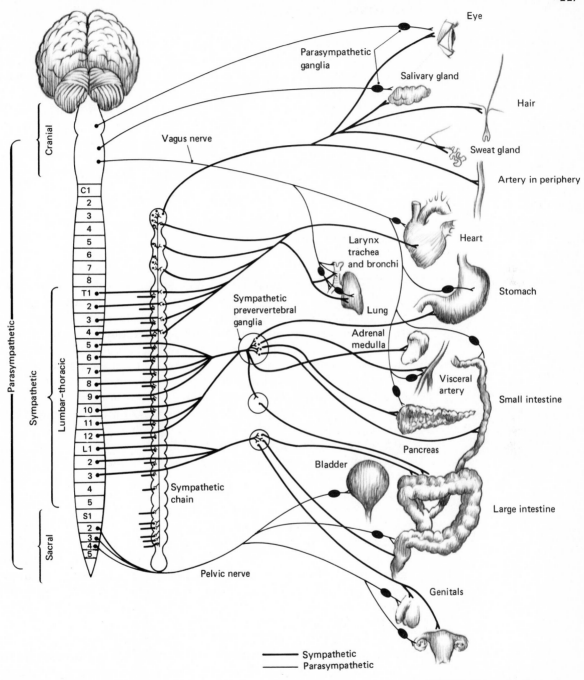

Eye

Parasympathetic
ganglia

Salivary gland

Hair

Sweat gland

Artery in periphery

Cranial

Vagus nerve

C1
2
3
4
5
6
7
8
T1
2
3
4
5
6
7
8
9
10
11
12
L1
2
3
4
5
S1
2
3
4
5

Larynx
trachea
and bronchi

Heart

Sympathetic
preververtebral
ganglia

Lung

Stomach

Adrenal
medulla

Visceral
artery

Small intestine

Parasympathetic

Sympathetic

Lumbar–thoracic

Pancreas

Bladder

Large intestine

Sympathetic
chain

Sacral

Pelvic nerve

Genitals

——— Sympathetic
———— Parasympathetic

FIGURE 6.26   A schematic
overview of the autonomic
nervous system and the target
organs it serves.

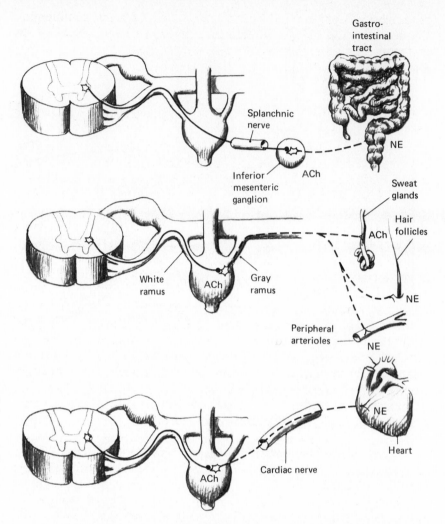

FIGURE 6.27 Pathways followed by efferents of the sympathetic nervous system. (Adapted from Netter, F. H., *The Ciba Collection of Medical Illustrations.* Vol. 1, *Nervous System.* Summit, N.J.: Ciba Pharmaceutical Products Co., 1953.)

postganglionic fibers that pass through the gray rami are unmyelinated, and hence are gray in appearance.) (See **FIGURE 6.27, MIDDLE.**) (2) Postganglionic fibers to various internal organs (e.g., heart, bronchi, large internal blood vessels, target organs within the head) leave the ganglia of the sympathetic chain via a nerve (e.g., one of the *cardiac* or *pulmonary nerves*) and travel directly to the target organ. (See **FIGURE 6.27, BOTTOM.**)

All synapses within the sympathetic ganglia are cholinergic; the terminals on the target organs, belonging to the postganglionic fibers, are adrenergic. The exception to this rule is provided by the sweat glands, innervated by cholinergic terminals. (The transmitter substances are represented in the previous illustrations by ACh or NE.) The medulla of the adrenal gland is innervated directly by preganglionic sympathetic fibers (whose terminals are cholinergic). The secretory cells of the adrenal medulla may be thought of as the postganglionic cells; they are, of course, adrenergic, secreting epinephrine and norepinephrine.

Parasympathetic Division of the ANS

The parasympathetic part of the autonomic nervous system is concerned with effects supporting *anabolic* activities (those concerned with increases in the body's supply of stored energy). The anabolic and catabolic processes of the body together make up its *metabolism*. Such effects as salivation, gastric and intestinal motility, secretion of digestive juices, and increased blood flow to the gastrointestinal system are mediated by the parasympathetic division of the ANS.

Cell bodies that give rise to preganglionic nerve fibers are located in two regions: the nuclei of the cranial nerves and the intermediate horn of the gray matter in the sacral region of the spinal cord. Thus, the parasympathetic division of the ANS has often been referred to as the *craniosacral* system. Figure 6.28 illustrates the parasympathetic division and shows the pathways followed by the preganglionic and postganglionic fibers. Parasympathetic ganglia are located in the immediate vicinity of the target organs; the postganglionic fibers are therefore relatively short. (See **FIGURE 6.28**.) The terminals of both preganglionic and postganglionic neurons are cholinergic (as indicated by ACh in the illustration).

Division of the autonomic nervous system into sympathetic and parasympathetic can be done easily on the basis of anatomy, but I should emphasize that these systems function together in a cooperative fashion. For example, if a man sits resting on a hot day, digesting his meal, parasympathetic activity increases the blood flow to the gastrointestinal system, stimulates motility of the stomach and gut, and increases secretion of digestive juices. At the same time, sympathetic fibers produce sweating. Perhaps the man and a particularly attractive female friend catch sight of each other; sympathetic activity dilates their pupils and increases their heart rate and rate of respiration. The man's parasympathetic activity results (perhaps, depending on the nature of their prior associations) in penile erection. We can see, from this example, that the two branches of the autonomic nervous system have very specific effects, and one branch can dominate in a given organ while the other branch exerts its effect in a different organ. (There *are* general effects, however. If the people in my example subsequently engage in sexual behavior, the man's parasympathetic activity, which is producing his erection and contin-

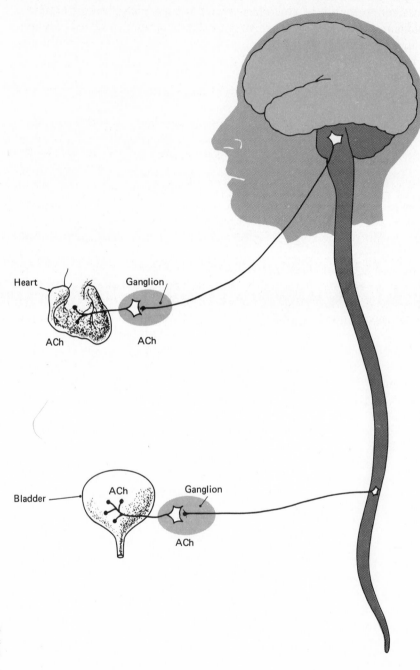

FIGURE 6.28   Pathways
followed by efferents of the
parasympathetic nervous
system.

uing to aid in the digestion of his food, will suddenly be replaced by massive sympathetic activity—with accompanying loss of erection, cold clammy sweat, cessation of the digestive process, rapid heart rate, shallow, rapid breathing, and secretion of epinephrine—should one of their spouses surprise them.)

SUGGESTED READINGS

CARPENTER, M. B. *Core Text of Neuroanatomy.* Baltimore: Williams & Wilkins, 1972.

NETTER, F. H. *The Ciba Collection of Medical Illustrations.* Vol. 1, *Nervous System.* Summit N.J.: Ciba Pharmaceutical Products Co., 1953.

NOBACK, C. R., and DEMAREST, R. J. *The Nervous System: Introduction and Review.* New York: McGraw-Hill, 1972.

The nervous system is exceedingly intricate; I am sure you do not have to be told that after reading this chapter. The nervous system is also beautiful when it is rendered by a good artist. The drawings in these three books are indeed beautiful—especially the full-color plates in Netter's volume. The books by Car-

penter and by Noback and Demarest are more informative, however.

CROSBY, E. C., HUMPHREY, T., and LAUER, E. W. *Correlative Anatomy of the Nervous System.* New York: Macmillan, 1962.

TRUEX, R. C., and CARPENTER, M. B. *Human Neuroanatomy,* ed. 6. Baltimore: Williams & Wilkins, 1969.

The first three books are useful for learning neuroanatomy; these latter two are for reference once you have studied one of the books from the first list. The amount of detail contained in the book by Crosby, Humphrey, and Lauer and in the one by Truex and Carpenter makes them heavy going for the beginner.

Research Methods of Physiological Psychology

7

Study of the biological basis of behavior involves the efforts of scientists in many disciplines: physiology, neuroanatomy, biochemistry, psychology, endocrinology, and histology, to name but a few. To pursue a project of research in physiological psychology requires competence in many experimental techniques. Since contradictory results are often obtained by the use of different procedures, one must be very familiar with the advantages and limitations of the various methods employed, so that the truth can be arrived at. Scientific investigation entails a process of asking questions of Nature. The method used frames the question, and often we receive a puzzling answer, only to realize later that we were not asking the question we thought we were.

The experimental methods used by physiological psychologists include neuroanatomical techniques, ablation, electrical recording, electrical stimulation, and chemical techniques. The boundaries of these categories are not distinct; for example, electrical stimulation and recording techniques can be used to obtain anatomical information.

NEUROANATOMICAL TECHNIQUES

Histological Procedures

The gross anatomy of the brain was described long ago, and everything that could be identified was given a name. Early anatomists named most brain structures according to their similarity to commonplace objects: amygdala, or "almond-shaped object"; hippocampus, or "seahorse"; genu, or "knee"; cortex, or "bark"; pons, or "bridge"; uncus, or "hook"—to give a few examples. More recent names tend to be duller: for example, the *nucleus ventralis medialis thalami, pars magnocellularis* (this clever name means "large-celled part of the ventral medial nucleus of the thalamus").

Detailed anatomical information about the brain has been obtained through use of various histological, or tissue-preparing, techniques. As we have seen, the brain consists of many billions of neurons and glial cells, the nerve cells forming distinct nuclei and fiber bundles. We cannot possibly see any cellular detail by gross examination of the brain. Even a microscope is useless without *fixation* and *staining* of the neural tissue.

FIXATION. If we hope to study the tissue in the form it had at the time of the organism's death, we must destroy the *autolytic* (literally, "self-dissolving") *enzymes*, which will otherwise turn the tissue into amorphous mush. The tissue must also be preserved to prevent its decomposition by bacteria or molds. To achieve both of these objectives, the neural tissue is placed in a *fixative.* The most commonly used fixative is *formalin*, an aqueous solution of *formaldehyde*, a gas. Formalin halts autolysis, hardens the very soft and fragile brain, and kills any microorganisms that might destroy it. There are other fixatives—various combinations of acids (such as picric acid), alcohols, and metallic salts, for example—but formalin preserves and hardens well, penetrates the tissue rapidly, and is very cheap and easy to obtain, so this substance is almost always the one chosen to fix brain tissue.

Often the fixation process is given a head start by *perfusion* of the cerebral vascular system with the fixative. Almost always, the brain is at least perfused with a saline solution. The following procedure is used: The animal whose brain is to be studied is killed with an overdose of a general anesthetic (usually *ether* or *sodium pentobarbital*). The thoracic cavity is opened, and the *right atrium* (one of the chambers of the heart) is cut open. A needle is inserted into the heart, or a cannula (small metal tube) is inserted into the large artery (the *aorta*) leaving the heart, and the animal's blood is replaced with a salt solution; the blood leaves via the cut in the atrium. (The animal's brain is perfused because better histological results are obtained when there is no blood present in the tissue.) Often the vascular system is then perfused with formalin, in order to speed up the process of fixation. The head is removed, the skull is opened, and the brain is removed and placed in a jar containing the fixative. (Brain removal—or perhaps I should say removal of an *intact* brain— takes a bit of practice. The brain is exceedingly delicate.)

Once the brain has been fixed, it is necessary to slice it into thin sections and to stain various cellular structures in order to see anatomical details. Some procedures require that the tissue be stained before being sliced, but the techniques most commonly used by physiological psychologists call for sectioning first, and then staining. Therefore, I shall describe the procedures in that order.

SECTIONING.   In order to slice (or *section)* neural tissue, a *microtome* is commonly used. A microtome (literally, "that which slices small") is an instrument capable of slicing tissue into very thin sections. Sections prepared for examination under a light microscope are typically 10 μm to 80 μm in thickness; those prepared for the electron microscope are generally cut at less than 1 μm. (A *micrometer,* abbreviated μm, is 1/1000 of a millimeter.) Electron microscopy will be considered separately in a later section.

A microtome must contain three parts: a knife, a platform on which to mount the tissue, and a mechanism that advances the knife (or the platform) the correct amount after each slice, so that another section can be cut. Figure 7.1 shows two commonly used microtomes. The one on the left is a *sliding microtome.* The knife holder slides forward on an oiled rail and takes a section off the top of the tissue on the platform. The platform automatically rises by a predetermined amount as the knife and holder are pushed back. (See **FIGURE 7.1, LEFT.**) To operate the *rotary microtome* shown on the right, you simply turn the wheel. The tissue platform moves up and down relative to the vertically mounted knife. The tissue is cut as it descends, and the platform is automatically advanced on the upstroke, moving the tissue into position for the next slice. (See **FIGURE 7.1, RIGHT.**)

Slicing brain tissue is not quite so simple as it might at first appear. As I mentioned, raw neural tissue is very soft. Fixation by immersion in formalin will harden the brain (to the texture of cheese, but without its characteristic stickiness). Either of two techniques can be used to make the tissue hard enough to cut thinly: *freezing* or *embedding.*

Freezing is conceptually the easier. The tissue can be chilled with blasts of compressed carbon dioxide, with dry ice (solid carbon dioxide), or with various kinds of refrigeration units. A particular type of microtome (a *cryostat)* operates within the confines of a freezer. Often the brain is first soaked in a sucrose (table sugar) solution; this procedure minimizes tissue damage by preventing the formation of large ice crystals as the brain freezes. The temperature of the brain must be carefully regulated; if the block is too cold, the tissue will shatter into little fragments. If it is too warm, a layer of tissue will be torn off rather than sliced off. Frozen sections can be cut with either sliding or rotary microtomes.

FIGURE 7.1 *Left:* Sliding microtome. *Right:* Rotary microtome.

The brain can be embedded in materials that are of sliceable consistency at room temperature. (That has to be pretty consistent, for some substances. The laboratory can be brought to a halt if the air-conditioning fails on a hot day.) The usual materials for embedding are *paraffin* and *nitrocellulose*. Paraffin comes in various grades, according to the room temperature at which it can best be sliced. The brain is first soaked in a solvent for paraffin (such as *xylene*) and then soaked in successively stronger solutions of paraffin (in an oven kept at a temperature just above the melting point for paraffin). Then the brain is placed in a small container of liquid paraffin, which is allowed to cool and harden. The entire block is sliced, the paraffin providing physical support for the tissue. A rotary microtome is used for cutting paraffin-embedded sections. It is fascinating to watch the cutting of these sections; as the knife passes through the block, it warms it slightly so that the sections get glued together, end to end. (See **FIGURE 7.2.**) It is immensely gratifying, after having spent a lot of time preparing the tissue, to see the sections emerge in a beautiful ribbon.

The brain can also be embodied in nitrocellulose. This compound, produced from the reaction of nitric acid with cellulose, is sometimes referred to as *gun cotton*. (Cotton can serve as the source of cellulose fibers.) In past years, histological technicians had to make sure they kept their gun cotton wet, because once it dried out, the

FIGURE 7.2 A "ribbon" being formed as a paraffin-embedded brain is sectioned on a rotary microtome.

vibration of even a footstep in the lab might cause the nitrocellulose to blow up. Today we usually purchase a commercial product that will not explode upon impact.

The brain is infiltrated with successively more concentrated solutions of nitrocellulose. The embedding medium is hardened into a block by the action of chloroform vapor. The block, along with its enclosed brain tissue, attains the consistency of soft cheese rind (again, without any stickiness). The block is usually cut on a sliding microtome.

Plastics can be used for embedding tissue, but this procedure is reserved for preparation of sections for the electron microscope.

After the tissue is cut, it is usually mounted on glass microscope slides with an agent such as *albumin* (protein extracted from egg whites). The slide is dried and heated, and the albumin becomes insoluble, cementing the tissue sections to the glass. The tissue can then be stained, the entire slide being put into the various chemical solutions. (Some staining procedures require that the individual sections be stained first, and then mounted onto slides—a much more tedious process.) The stained and mounted sections are then covered with a *mounting medium* and a very thin glass coverslip is placed over the sections. The mounting medium (which is very thick and resinous) gradually dries out, thus keeping the coverslip in position.

STAINING.   If you looked at an unstained section of brain tissue under a microscope, you would be able to see (especially if the tissue were kept wet) the outlines of some large cellular masses and the more prominent fiber bundles.   But no fine detail would be revealed.   The study of microscopic neuroanatomy requires special *histological stains*.   There are basically three types of stains used for neural tissue: those which reveal cell bodies by interacting with contents of the cytoplasm, those which selectively color myelin sheaths, and those which stain the cell membrane (entire cell, or just the axons).

   Cell-body Stains.   Cell-body stains give color to the *Nissl substance* contained in the cytoplasm, thus outlining cell bodies.   In the late nineteenth century, Franz Nissl, a German neurologist, discovered that *methylene blue*, an *aniline dye* (derived from the distillation of coal tar), would stain cell bodies of brain tissue.   The material that takes up the dye consists of RNA, DNA, and *nucleoproteins*, located in the nucleus and scattered, in the form of granules, in the cytoplasm.   Many dyes can be used to stain cell bodies, but the most frequently used are methylene blue and *cresyl violet*.   The dyes, by the way, were not developed for histological purposes; they were manufactured for use in dyeing cloth.

   The discovery of cell-body stains (also called Nissl stains) made it possible to identify nuclear masses in the brain.   Figure 7.3 shows a frontal section of a cat brain stained with Nissl stain (cresyl violet).   Note that it is possible to observe fiber bundles by their lighter appearance; they do not take up the stain.   (See **FIGURE 7.3.**)   The

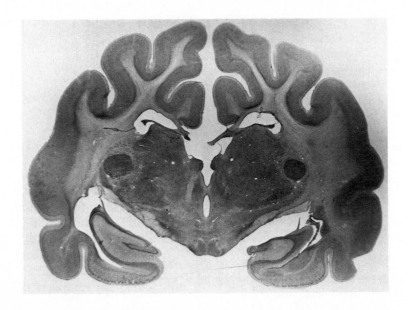

FIGURE 7.3   A frontal section of a cat brain, stained with a Nissl stain (cresyl violet). (Histological material courtesy of Mary Carlson.)

stain is not selective for *neural* cell bodies. All cells are stained, neurons and glia alike. It is up to the experimenter to determine which is which—by size, shape, and location.

Myelin Stains. Myelin stains color myelin sheaths. These stains (such as the *Weil* method, which employs *hematoxylin,* a dye extracted from *logwood*) make it possible to identify fiber bundles. (What is light in Figure 7.3 is dark in Figure 7.4.) However, pathways of single fibers cannot be traced. There is simply too much intermingling of the individual fibers. (See **FIGURE 7.4.**)

Membrane Stains. Membrane stains contain salts of various heavy metals (silver, uranium, osmium, etc.) that interact with the somatic, dendritic, and axonal membrane. The *Golgi-Cox stain* (which uses silver) is, for some mysterious reason, highly selective, staining only a fraction of the neurons in a given region. (Why this happens is not known, and the selectivity undoubtedly gives a biased view of the neurons that populate a given region.) The selective staining makes it possible, however, to observe the processes and arborizations of individual neurons and to trace details of synaptic interconnections. Figure 7.5 shows the appearance of individual neurons of the cerebral cortex stained by a new modification of the Golgi-Cox stain. Note the individual neurons and their intercon-

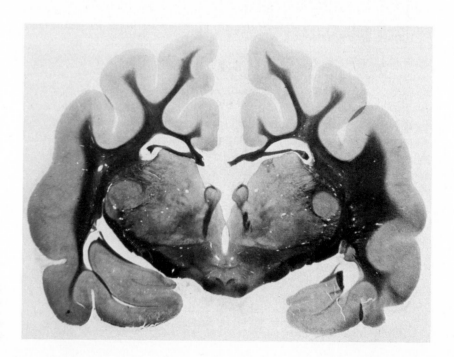

FIGURE 7.4 A frontal section of a cat brain, stained with a myelin stain (Weil method). (Histological material courtesy of Mary Carlson.)

necting processes. The large cells in the center are oligodendroglia, providing myelin sheaths for the bundles of fibers running horizontally. (See **FIGURE 7.5.**)

Degenerating-axon Stains. A special variant of the cell membrane stain was devised by Walle Nauta and Paul Gygax in the middle of this century. The Nauta-Gygax stain (which uses silver) identifies axons that are dying and are in the process of being destroyed by phagocytes. This stain might seem too esoteric to be of any practical use, but as we shall see, most of the detailed information we now possess concerning the interconnections of various neural structures has been obtained by the use of this method.

FIGURE 7.5 A section of cortex of a cat brain, stained by the Golgi-Cox method, as modified by D. N. Spinelli and J. K. Lane. Unlike previous versions of the Golgi-Cox method, this one stains neural processes right to the outer edge of the cortex. (Histological material courtesy of D. N. Spinelli and J. K. Lane.)

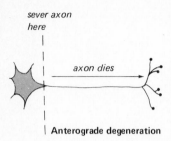

sever axon
here

axon dies

Anterograde degeneration

FIGURE 7.6   Anterograde
degeneration.

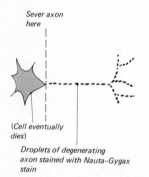

Sever axon
here

(Cell eventually
dies)

Droplets of degenerating
axon stained with Nauta-Gygax
stain

FIGURE 7.7   A schematic
representation of the
appearance of a degenerating
axon as shown by the Nauta-
Gygax stain.

Degeneration Studies

ANTEROGRADE DEGENERATION.   If a cell body is destroyed, or if the axon is cut, the distal portion of the axon quickly dies and disintegrates.   This process is called *anterograde degeneration*.   (See **FIGURE 7.6.**)   The Nauta stain will identify these degenerating axons as trails of black droplets.   (See **FIGURE 7.7.**)

A photograph of the actual appearance of such degenerating fibers is shown in **FIGURE 7.8**; note the trails of droplets leaving the large horizontal fiber bundle.   Let us suppose we want to trace the efferent fibers of neurons in nucleus A of Figure 7.9.   A myelin stain would be useless, since the fibers we are interested in are entangled among those belonging to neurons of the other nuclei.   (See **FIGURE 7.9.**)   However, if we destroy the cells in nucleus A (I shall explain how in a later section) the efferents will degenerate.   (So will the afferents—fibers entering the nucleus to synapse there, but I shall discuss that complication later.)   If we destroy nucleus A in the living animal, wait about eight days for degeneration to become well established, and then kill the animal, we will have a brain with a set of specially labelled axons.   The degenerating axons belong to cells of nucleus A.   We use the Nauta-Gygax stain to identify these axons and observe results like those of **FIGURE 7.10.**   The Nauta-

FIGURE 7.8   A portion of a
mouse brain. Degenerating
axons as revealed by the Nauta-
Gygax method are shown
emerging from a large fiber
bundle. (Histological material
courtesy of Leanna Standish.)

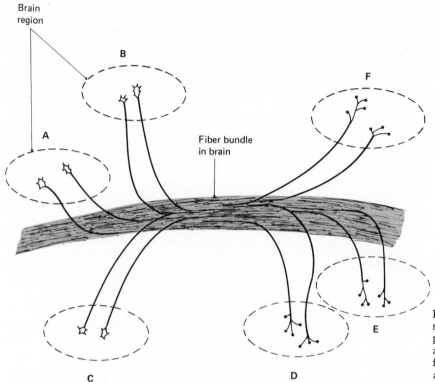

Brain region

B

F

A

Fiber bundle
in brain

C

D

E

FIGURE 7.9 A highly
schematic representation of the
problem encountered in
attempting to trace efferent
fibers from one structure to
another.

Gygax stain has recently been supplemented by the Fink-Heimer stain
(developed in Nauta's laboratory at MIT). These two stains permit
us to see degenerating axons, as well as their terminal buttons. Much
of the knowledge we now have of the detailed connections of the
brain was obtained through such combinations of local tissue destruction and the tracing of the degenerating axons.

RETROGRADE DEGENERATION. When an axon of a neuron in the central nervous system is cut, the fiber gradually degenerates back toward
the cell body, which itself subsequently dies. (See **FIGURE 7.11.**)
This process, called *retrograde degeneration*, is gradual, because the
cell body is alive until the end, supplying nutrients for the truncated
axon. In the periphery, the axon can regenerate if the Schwann cells
are able to reestablish a sheath for the damaged fibers to grow through.
Oligodendroglia of the CNS lack this property, so the axon eventually
dies. If the severed axon is one of several branches attached to the
principal fiber of a neuron, the degeneration process may halt at a
junction point and proceed no farther. (See **FIGURE 7.12.**)

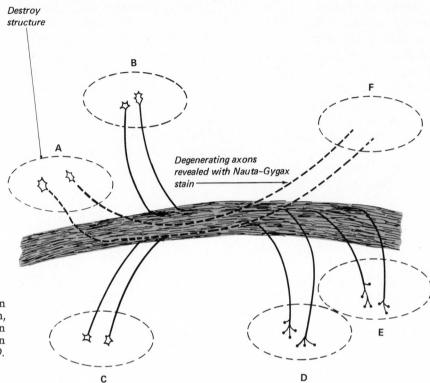

FIGURE 7.10 The application of anterograde degeneration, shown by a degenerating axon stain, to the problem shown in Figure 7.9.

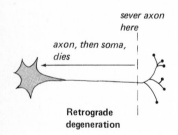

FIGURE 7.11 Retrograde degeneration.

During retrograde degeneration, part of the axon (at any given time) will be intact, a small part will be in the process of degenerating, and the rest will be completely destroyed. Only the actively degenerating portion will be stained by the Nauta-Gygax method, so this procedure will not identify pathways undergoing retrograde degeneration. However, Nissl stains can be used to locate the cells that give rise to these fibers. Consider the illustration in Figure 7.13. We would like to know which subcortical nuclei project to a given cortical region. (See **FIGURE 7.13.**) We could, of course, destroy nuclei, one by one, and look for anterograde degeneration via the Nauta technique. It is more difficult, however, to make precisely localized subcortical lesions; moreover, we would have to destroy, in separate animals, every subcortical region that might project to that area. To be certain, we would have to produce hundreds of lesions, in every portion of the brain.

Instead, we could destroy the cortical area we are interested in and let the animal live for a long period of time (on the order of six weeks for a rodent—longer for mammals with larger brains). Then, once we were sure of the death of the neurons whose axons formerly projected to that area, we would kill the animal and prepare cell-stained sections. We would then look for the regions with missing neurons; specifically, we would seek areas of *gliosis*, i.e., places where the degenerated neurons had been replaced by glial cells. Figure 7.14 shows a nucleus of the thalamus of a mouse containing normal neurons (top) and the same nucleus (in another animal, of course) after retrograde degeneration (bottom). Note that the normal neurons are much larger than the glial cells that replace them. (See **FIGURE 7.14.**) Thus, anterograde degeneration and the Nauta or Fink-Heimer stain can tell us where the efferents of a structure go, and retrograde degeneration and a Nissl stain can tell us where the afferents of a brain region come from.

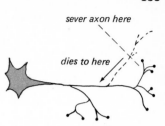

FIGURE 7.12 Incomplete retrograde degeneration, observed when only one branch of an axon is severed. In this case the cell body does not die.

Electron Microscopy

The light microscope is limited in its ability to resolve extremely small details. Because of the nature of light itself, magnification of more than approximately 1500 times does not add any detail. In order to see such small anatomical structures as synaptic vesicles and details

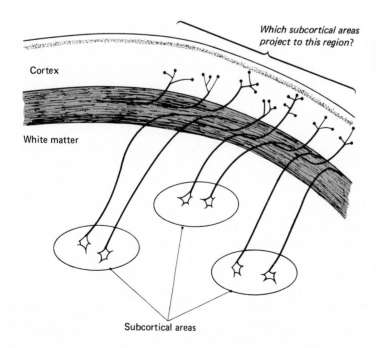

FIGURE 7.13 A highly schematic representation of the problem encountered in attempting to ascertain which subcortical areas project to a given region of cortex.

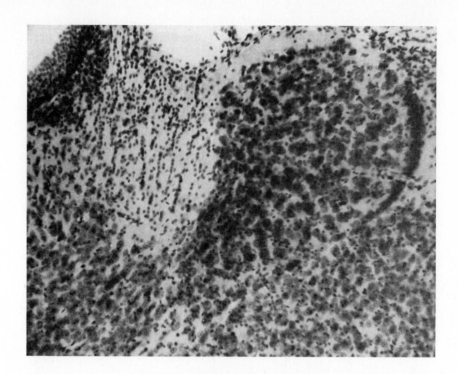

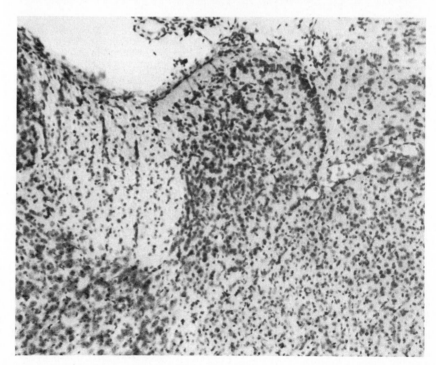

FIGURE 7.14 The appearance of a normal thalamic nucleus (*top*) and the appearance of the same nucleus after retrograde degeneration (*bottom*), produced by ablating the cortical area to which this nucleus projects.

of cell organelles it is necessary to use an electron microscope. A beam of electrons, smaller than the photons that constitute visible light, is passed through the tissue to be examined. (The tissue must first be coated with a substance that produces detailed variations in the resistance to the passage of electrons, much like staining for light microscopy, causing various portions of the tissue to absorb light.) A shadow of the tissue is then cast upon a sheet of photographic film, which is exposed by the electrons. Electron micrographs produced in this way can provide information about structural details on the order of a few angstrom units.

ABLATION OF NEURAL TISSUE

In order to perform degeneration studies we must be able to destroy a particular region of the brain. It is very easy to do so if we can see the tissue to be destroyed. To produce cortical *ablations* (literally, a "carrying away," although generally the term is also used when the damaged tissue is left in place), we anesthetize the animal, cut the scalp, remove a portion of the skull, and destroy the desired amount of cortical tissue. Almost always, a suction device is used to *aspirate* the brain tissue. The dura mater is cut away and a glass pipette is placed on the surface of the brain. A vacuum pump attached to the pipette sucks up the brain as if it were jelly. The pipette also removes blood, which is highly toxic to the brain when it is outside of the blood vessels. It is quite easy, with practice, to aspirate away the cortical gray matter, stopping at the underlying layer of white matter, which has a much tougher consistency. A *cautery* (instrument with a heated point) can also be used to destroy regions of cortex, but the extent of the damage is more difficult to control.

Stereotaxic Surgery

Most experimentally produced *brain lesions* are produced by means of *stereotaxic surgery*. (The terms *lesion* and *ablation* are used interchangeably in physiological psychology.) Stereotaxis literally means "solid arrangement"; more specifically, it refers to the ability to locate objects in space. If an experiment calls for destruction of a subcortical brain structure, one cannot merely slice the brain open and aspirate the appropriate area, since a tremendous amount of damage to other structures would result from such a procedure. It is much better, instead, to insert a fine electrically insulated wire into the brain and kill the region of tissue around the wire's exposed tip by means of electricity. To do so, however, we have to know where to put the wire.

Stereotaxic surgery requires two things: (1) a device that will hold the animal's head in place and move the wire (or some other attachment) through measured distances in all three axes of space (*stereotaxic apparatus*) and (2) a *stereotaxic atlas*, or series of maps, of the brain. I shall describe the atlas, first.

THE STEREOTAXIC ATLAS. No two brains of animals of a given species are completely identical, but there is enough similarity between different individuals (especially if one uses genetically homogeneous inbred strains of animals) to predict the location of a given brain structure, relative to external features of the head. For instance, a given thalamic nucleus of a rat might be so many millimeters ventral, anterior, and lateral to a point formed by the junction of several bones of the skull. Figure 7.15 shows two views of a rat skull: a drawing of the dorsal surface and, beneath it, a midsagittal view. (See **FIGURE 7.15.**) The junction of the *coronal* and *sagittal sutures* (seams between adjacent bones of the skull) is labelled *bregma*. If the animal's skull is oriented as shown in the illustration, a given region of the brain occupies a fairly constant location in space, relative to bregma. Not all atlases use bregma as the reference point, but this reference is the easiest to describe.

A stereotaxic atlas contains pages that correspond to frontal sections taken at various distances anterior and posterior to bregma. For example, the page shown in Figure 7.16 is identified as being 0.6 mm anterior to bregma. If we wanted to place the tip of a wire in the structure labelled F (the fornix), we would have to drill a hole through the skull 0.6 mm anterior to bregma (because the structure shows up on the 0.6 mm page) and 1.0 mm lateral to the midline. (See **FIGURE 7.15** and **FIGURE 7.16.**) The electrode would be lowered through the hole until the tip was 7.0 mm lower than the skull height at bregma. (See **FIGURE 7.16.**) Thus, by finding a neural structure (which we cannot see in our animal) on one of the pages of a stereotaxic atlas, we can determine the structure's location relative to bregma (which we can see). I should note that, because of variations in different strains and ages of animals, the atlas gives only an approximate location. It is always necessary to try out a new set of coordinates, perform histology on the animal's brain to see where you really placed the lesion, correct the numbers, and try again.

There are human stereotaxic atlases, by the way. Usually multiple landmarks are used, including X-ray ventriculograms (see chapter 6), and the location of the wire (or other device) inserted into the brain is verified by taking X-rays before producing a brain lesion.

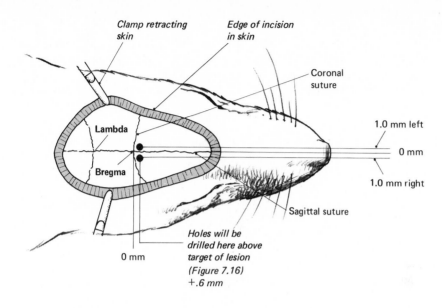

Clamp retracting skin

Edge of incision in skin

Coronal suture

Lambda

Bregma

1.0 mm left

0 mm

1.0 mm right

Sagittal suture

0 mm

Holes will be drilled here above target of lesion (Figure 7.16) +.6 mm

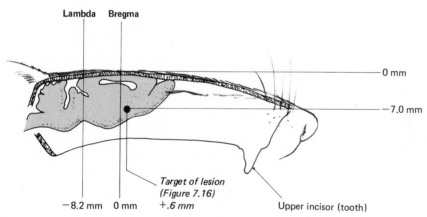

Lambda   Bregma

0 mm

−7.0 mm

Target of lesion (Figure 7.16) +.6 mm

−8.2 mm   0 mm

Upper incisor (tooth)

FIGURE 7.15 Relationship of the skull sutures to the brain of a rat.

THE STEREOTAXIC APPARATUS. The principle for operation of the stereotaxic apparatus is quite simple. There is a headholder that orients the animal's skull in the proper direction, a holder for the electrode, and a calibrated mechanism that moves the electrode holder in measured distances along the three axes: anterior-posterior, dorsal-ventral, and lateral-medial. Figure 7.17 illustrates a stereotaxic apparatus designed for small animals; various headholders can be used to outfit this device for such diverse species as rats, mice, hamsters, pigeons, and turtles. (See **FIGURE 7.17.**)

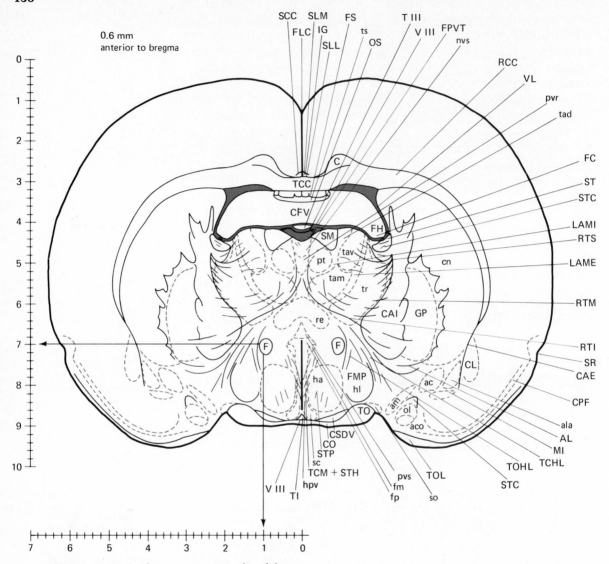

FIGURE 7.16   A page from a stereotaxic atlas of the rat brain. The scale on the side and bottom of the figure has been modified in order to be consistent with my description of bregma as a reference point. (From König, J. F. R., and Klippel, R. A., *The Rat Brain: A Stereotaxic Atlas of the Forebrain and Lower Parts of the Brain Stem.* Copyright © 1963 by the Williams & Wilkins Co., Baltimore.)

Once the stereotaxic coordinates have been obtained, the animal is anesthetized and placed in the apparatus, and the scalp is cut open.   The skull is exposed and the electrode is placed with its tip on bregma.   The location of bregma is measured along each of the axes, and the electrode is moved the proper distance along the anterior-posterior and lateral-medial axes to a point just above the target. A hole is drilled through the skull just below the electrode, and the electrode is then lowered into the brain by the proper amount. A lesion (described in the next section) is produced, the electrode is raised, the wound is sewed together, and the animal is taken out of the stereotaxic apparatus. (Usually a given brain structure is destroyed *bilaterally,* one lesion on each side of the brain. Destruction of only one side of many structures that are not specifically sensory or motor in nature will produce little or no behavioral effect—the function can, in many cases, be carried out very nicely by the remaining side.)

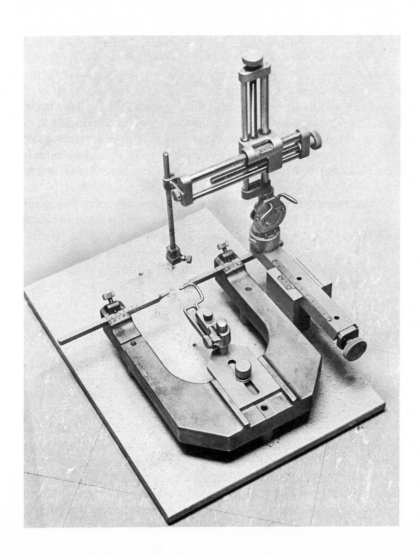

FIGURE 7.17 A stereotaxic apparatus for performing brain surgery on rats.

Lesion Production

Subcortical brain lesions are usually produced by passing electrical current through a wire of stainless steel or platinum, electrically insulated except for a portion of the tip. The wire is stereotaxically guided so that the end of it is in the appropriate location, and the *lesion maker* is turned on. Two kinds of electrical current can be used. Direct current (d.c.) produces lesions by initiating chemical reactions whose products destroy the cells in the vicinity of the electrode tip (Gold, 1975). *Radiofrequency* (RF) lesion makers produce alternating current of a very high frequency. This current does not stimulate neural tissue, nor does it produce chemical reactions. It destroys cells with heat, produced by the passage of the current through the tissue, which offers electrical resistance. Radiofrequency lesions have a distinct advantage—no metal ions are left in the damaged tissue. When d.c. lesions are produced, some of the electrode is left behind. Ions of metal are chemically eroded from the electrode by means of *electrolysis,* the same process used for plating objects with metal. It would appear to be more prudent to make radiofrequency lesions and thus avoid possible long-term effects produced by metal deposition.

Behavioral Studies

I have already discussed one of the reasons for producing brain lesions —the tracing of neuroanatomical pathways. Brain lesions can also be produced in an attempt to identify the function of a particular region of the brain. The rationale for lesion studies is that the function of an area of the brain is inferred from the behavioral capacity missing from an animal's repertoire after destruction of that area. To take a trivial example: if an animal can no longer see after a brain lesion, the area destroyed was probably involved in vision.

We must be very careful in interpreting the effects of brain lesions, however. For example, how did we ascertain that the operated animal was blind? Did it bump into objects, or fail to run through a maze toward the light that signals the location of food, or no longer constrict its pupils to light? An animal could bump into objects as a result of deficits in motor coordination, or it could have lost memory for a maze problem, or it could see quite well but could have lost visual reflexes. The experimenter must be clever enough to ask the right question, especially when studying complex processes such as hunger, attention, or memory. Even when studying simpler processes, people can be fooled. For years it was thought that the laboratory rat was blind. Think about it: how would you test to see whether a rat could see? Remember, they have *vibrissae* (whiskers), which can be used to detect a wall before bumping into it, or the edge of a table before walking off it. The animals can also follow odor trails around the room.

The interpretation of lesion studies is also complicated by the fact that all regions of the brain are interconnected, and no one part does any one thing. When a nucleus is destroyed, the lesion may also sever axons passing through the area. If a structure normally inhibits another, the observed changes in behavior might really be a function of disinhibition of that second structure. Yet another complication was pointed out by Illis (1963), who noted that brain lesions produced temporary degenerative changes in synapses in the vicinity of the lesion. These effects lasted for at least two weeks. Very often we see a partial recovery of function some time after production of a brain lesion. It is impossible to say whether this recovery results from a "taking over" of the function of the damaged structure by some other brain region or from repair of the temporarily injured synapses. In later chapters we shall see numerous examples of the difficulty of deducing the role of a brain region from the behavior of an animal lacking that region. I should note that, these problems notwithstanding, the lesion technique is the most frequently used experimental method of the physiological psychologist.

I should also note that histological evaluation must be made of each animal's brain lesion. Brain lesions often miss the mark, and it is necessary to verify the precise location of the lesions after testing the animals behaviorally. Nothing gladdens an experimenter's heart more than finding that the one animal in the study whose behavior was not consistent with that of the other animals (or with the experimenter's hypothesis) actually had a brain lesion in the wrong location. Now this animal's data can be thrown out! (All too often, though, it is one of the "good" animals that has the bad lesion.)

RECORDINGS OF THE BRAIN'S ELECTRICAL ACTIVITY

Rationale

Axons produce action potentials, and terminal buttons elicit post-synaptic potentials. These electrical events can be recorded (as we have already seen), and perhaps regional changes in electrical activity might indicate the functions of the area being recorded from, during, for example, stimulus presentations, or decision making, or motor activities. The rationale seems sound, but, as we shall see, electrical recordings of neural activity, especially of those electrical events that might be correlated with complex behaviors, are very difficult to interpret.

Recordings can be made chronically, over an extended period of time after the animal recovers from surgery, or for a relatively short period of time, during which the animal is kept anesthetized. Acute recordings, made while the animal is anesthetized, are usually restricted to studies of sensory pathways or (in conjunction with electrical stimulation of the brain) to investigations of anatomical pathways in the brain (to be described later.) Acute recordings seldom involve behavioral observations, since the behavioral capacity of an anesthetized animal is, at best, limited.

Chronic electrodes can be implanted in the brain with the aid of a stereotaxic apparatus, and an electrical socket, attached to the electrode, can be cemented to the animal's skull (with an acrylic plastic used for making dental plates). Then, after recovery from surgery, the animal can be "plugged in" to the recording system. (See **FIGURE 7.18.**)

Electrical recordings can be taken through very small electrodes that detect the activity of one (or just a few) neurons, or large electrodes that respond to the electrical activity of large populations of neurons can be used. The electrical signal detected by the electrode is quite small and must be *amplified*. A biological amplifier works just like the amplifiers in a stereo system, converting the weak signals recorded at the brain (similar in magnitude to the signals from a phonograph cartridge) into stronger ones, large enough to be displayed on the appropriate device. (The analogy with the sound system even applies here; recordings of the activity of single neurons are often played through loudspeakers, as we shall see.) Output devices vary considerably. Their basic purpose is to convert the raw data (ampli-

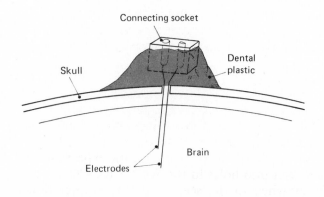

FIGURE 7.18 A schematic representation of the means by which electrodes can be chronically implanted in an animal's brain.

fied electrical signals from the brain) into a form we can perceive—
usually a visual display.

Electrodes

MICROELECTRODES. *Microelectrodes* have a very fine tip, small
enough to be able to record the electrical activity of individual neurons. (We usually refer to this process as *single-unit* recording, a unit
referring to a single neuron.) Microelectrodes can be constructed of
metal or of glass tubes. Metal electrodes are sharpened by electrolytic
etching in an acid solution. Current is passed through a fine wire as it
is moved in and out of the solution. The tip erodes away, leaving
a very fine, sharp point. The wire (usually of tungsten or stainless
steel) is then insulated with a special varnish. The very end of the
tip is so sharp that it does not retain insulation and thus can record
electrical signals.

Electrodes can also be constructed of fine glass tubes. Glass
has an interesting property: if a hollow tube of glass is heated until
it is soft, and if the ends are pulled apart, the softened glass will
stretch into a very fine filament. This filament, no matter how thin,
will still have a hole running through it. To construct glass microelectrodes, one heats the middle of a length of capillary tubing (glass
with an outside diameter of approximately 1 mm) and then pulls
the ends sharply apart. The glass tube is drawn out finer and finer,
until the tube snaps apart. The result is two *micropipettes,* as shown
in **FIGURE 7.19.** (These devices are usually produced with the aid
of a special machine, called a *micropipette puller.*) Glass will not conduct electricity, so the micropipette is filled with a conducting liquid,
such as a solution of potassium chloride. Glass micropipettes were
used to provide the data concerning axonal conduction and synaptic
transmission, described in earlier chapters of this book.

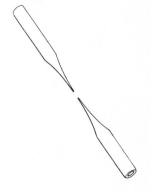

FIGURE 7.19 The production
of two micropipettes from a
single piece of fine glass tubing.

MACROELECTRODES. *Macroelectrodes,* which record the activity of a
very large number of neurons, are not nearly so difficult to make or
to use. They can be constructed from a variety of materials: stainless
steel or platinum wires, insulated except for the tip (these can be
inserted into the brain or placed on top of it); small balls of metal
attached to wires, which can be placed on the exposed cortex; screws
that can be driven into holes in the skull; flat disks of silver or gold
that can be attached to the scalp with an electrically conductive
paste (used for recordings taken from the human head); or thin, un-
insulated platinum wires that can be inserted into the scalp (again,
for human recordings).

Macroelectrodes do not detect the activity of individual neurons; rather, the records obtained with these devices represent the slow potentials (EPSPs and IPSPs) of many thousands—or millions—of cells in the area of the electrode. Recordings taken from the scalp, especially, represent the electrical activity of an enormous number of neurons.

Amplifiers

The main function of amplifiers used for electrical recording is to increase the amplitude of the signal obtained from the electrode. Another function is to *filter* the input, that is, to amplify selectively only a certain set of frequencies. For example, if we wanted to record unit activity with a microelectrode, we would set the filtration controls on the amplifier so that only high frequencies would be amplified. Thus, we would see the occurrence of action potentials, but low-frequency signals would not be seen. On the other hand, we would want to amplify only lower frequencies (approximately 2–50 Hz) when recording the summed slow potentials from a larger area of the brain. Figure 7.20 illustrates this filtration process—a composite signal, containing unit activity along with slow potentials, is shown on the left, with the selectively filtered signals shown on the right. (See **FIGURE 7.20.**) (A microelectrode is capable of recording slow potentials as well as units. If we were interested only in slow potentials, however, we would make a macroelectrode rather than take the trouble to make a microelectrode.)

Output Devices

We obviously cannot directly observe the electrical activity from an amplifier; just as a sound system is useless without speakers or headphones, so a biological amplifier is useless without an output device.

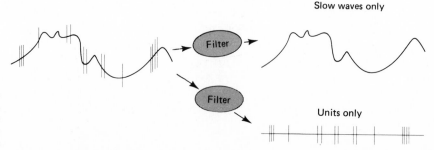

FIGURE 7.20 The separation of a composite signal, containing both slow waves and action potentials, into two separate signals.

I shall describe three output devices: oscilloscopes, ink-writing oscillographs, and computers.

OSCILLOSCOPE. In chapter 3 I described the basic principle of an oscilloscope—the plotting of electrical potentials as a function of time. The display unit of an oscilloscope is demonstrated in **FIGURE 7.21.** This *cathode-ray tube* contains an *electron gun*, which emits a focussed stream of electrons toward the face of the tube. A special surface on the inside of the glass converts some of the energy of the electrons into a visible spot of light. Electrons are negatively charged and are thus attracted to positively charged objects and repelled by negatively charged ones. The plates arranged above and below the electron beam, and on each side, can be electrically charged, thus directing the beam to various places on the face of the tube. The dot can thus be moved independently by the *horizontal* and *vertical deflection plates.* (See **FIGURE 7.21.**) (If you have ever played with one of the new electronic games, or used an Etch-a-Sketch, you will know what I mean. One knob can move the dot up and down while the other moves it left or right—these movements are independent of each other.)

  The horizontal deflection plates are usually attached to a timing circuit, which sweeps the beam from left to right at a constant speed. Simultaneously, the output of the biological amplifier moves the beam up and down. We thus obtain a graph of electrical activity as a function of time.

  To illustrate the use of an oscilloscope for the recording of unit activity, consider the experiment outlined in **FIGURE 7.22.** A light is flashed in front of the cat, and, at the same time, the dot on the oscilloscope is started across the screen. (We say that we "trigger the sweep.") Let's say that we are recording from a cell in visual cortex that responds to a light flash by giving a burst of action potentials. The record of this event will be seen on the face of the oscil-

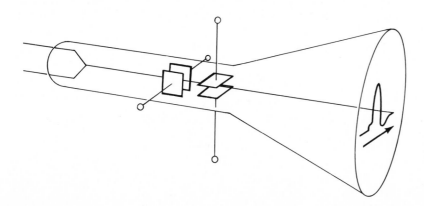

FIGURE 7.21 A schematic and simplified representation of the cathode-ray tube from an oscilloscope.

loscope as vertical lines superimposed on a horizontal one (if the beam is moved slowly). If the beam is moved rapidly, we will see the shapes of the individual action potentials. (See **FIGURE 7.22.**) You might wonder how the illustrated display can be seen—after all, the display consists of a moving dot, and I have shown a continuous line. Most oscilloscope screens exhibit *persistence,* however. As the dot moves, it leaves a trace of its pathway behind, which slowly fades away.

When recording single-unit activity, the investigator usually also attaches the output of the amplifier to a loudspeaker. When a microelectrode is lowered through the brain, it is necessary to stop a bit before the optimal recording point, to allow the brain tissue, which has been pushed down a little by the progress of the electrode, to spring back up. If the electrode goes down too far, there is a very high probability that the cell will become injured or killed by the electrode as the tissue moves up. Therefore, it is necessary to detect the firing of a cell as soon as possible, so that the progress of the electrode can be stopped in time. Our ears are much more efficient than our eyes in extracting the faint signal of a firing neuron from the random background noise. You can hear the ticking, snapping sound of unit activity from the speaker long before its presence can be visually detected on the face of the oscilloscope. Our auditory system really does a superb job of extracting signal from noise.

Oscilloscopes are also ideal for the display of *evoked potentials.*

FIGURE 7.22 A schematic representation of the means by which the responses of single units to a flash of light can be recorded.

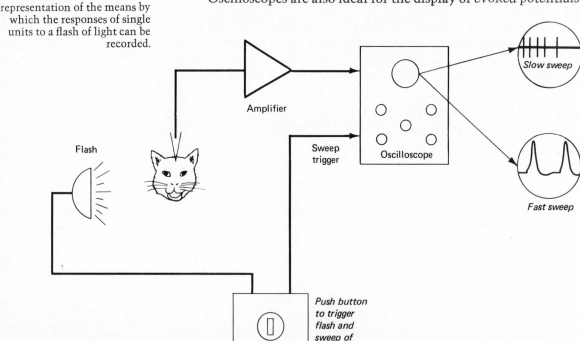

When a stimulus is presented to an organism, a series of electrical events is initiated at the receptor organ. This activity is conducted into the brain and propagates through various neural pathways in the brain. If an electrode is placed in or near these pathways, it is possible to record the electrical activity evoked by the stimulus. For example, one might place a scalp electrode on the back of a person's head and present a flash of light, while simultaneously triggering the sweep of an oscilloscope. Figure 7.23 shows such an experiment, along with the evoked potential from visual cortex, recorded through the skull and scalp. (See **FIGURE 7.23.**)

INK-WRITING OSCILLOGRAPH. Oscilloscopes are most useful in the display of phasic activity, such as an evoked potential, which occurs during a relatively brief period of time. If neural activity is continuously recorded and displayed on an oscilloscope screen, it will be seen as a series of successive sweeps of the beam, thus presenting a rather confusing picture. A much better device for such a purpose is the *ink-writing oscillograph* (often called a polygraph).

The time base of the polygraph is provided by a mechanism that moves a very long strip of paper past a series of pens. The pens are, essentially, the pointers of large voltmeters, moving up and down in response to the electrical signal sent to them by the biological amplifiers. Figure 7.24 illustrates a record of electrical activity recorded from electrodes attached to various locations on a person's scalp. (See **FIGURE 7.24.**) Such records are called *electroencephalograms* (*EEGs*), or "writings of electricity from the head." They can be used to diagnose epilepsy or brain tumors, or to study various stages of sleep and wakefulness, which are associated with characteristic patterns of electrical activity. This last phenomenon will be described in

FIGURE 7.23 A schematic representation of the means by which evoked potentials in response to a flash of light can be recorded from the scalp of a human head.

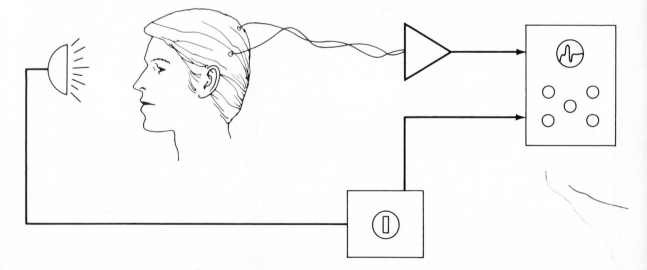

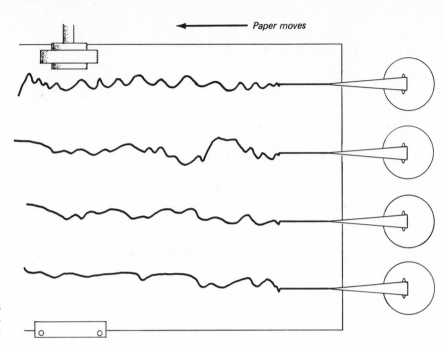

Paper moves

FIGURE 7.24 A record from an ink-writing oscillograph (polygraph).

more detail in chapter 14. I should note that many modern polygraphs do not use ink; they print electrostatically, or with heated pens on specially treated paper. Nevertheless, their principle of operation is the same.

COMPUTER. Finally, a computer can be used as an output device. A computer can convert the *analog signal* (one that can continuously vary, like the EEG) received from the biological amplifier into a series of numbers (*digital values*). Figure 7.25 illustrates how a series of digital values can represent an evoked potential. Each point represents the voltage of the continuous analog signal at an instant of time. (Each point is one millisecond apart.) The values were stored in a computer and were later displayed on the screen of an oscilloscope. (See **FIGURE 7.25.**)

A computer can do more than display the data, furthermore; it can perform many kinds of analyses. For example, it can compute the *latencies* (time intervals) between stimulus and the onset of an evoked potential, or it can count the number of action potentials elicited by a stimulus. One of the most common functions of a computer is the averaging of a series of individual evoked potentials.

Figure 7.26 shows a series of evoked potentials recorded from rat visual cortex, in response to a flash of light. Notice that these

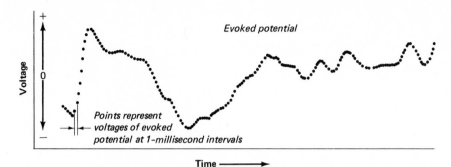

FIGURE 7.25 An evoked potential as represented by a display of points digitized by and stored in a computer.

evoked potentials generally resemble one another, but do not look identical. (See **FIGURE 7.26.**) The individual waves were digitized by a computer, the series of numbers thus obtained were added together, and the total was divided by the number of sweeps (four sweeps, in this case). The resulting numbers describe the average wave, shown at the bottom. The individual variations of the single sweeps, which represent "noise," or other brain activity not related to the light flash, are "averaged out" by this process. Usually, many more than four waves are averaged together, and the result is even smoother than is shown in this example. (See **FIGURE 7.26.**)

The averaging technique is extremely useful in extracting a signal from the ongoing electrical activity of the brain. The average of several hundred sweeps will often reveal that a brain structure is receiving previously unsuspected sensory information. There are dangers, however. Figure 7.27 shows a series of (imaginary) evoked potentials, each of which has a single, sharp-peaked wave occurring at various times. Note, however, that the average curve has a broad, gentle wave and thus resembles none of the individual evoked potentials. The averaging process gives a very poor representation of discrete events that have any variability in time of occurrence. (See **FIGURE 7.27.**) One must guard against such possibilities by examining individual waves, as well as the averages.

Behavioral Studies

The usefulness of electrical recording in the study of sensory pathways should be obvious. In these studies we know when the electrical signals are elicited at the receptors, and we look for subsequent neural events. We can even study motor systems in a similar manner. The recorded electrical activity is stored (on magnetic tape, or in a computer memory) and when a movement is made the records are averaged *backward* in time from the onset of the movement, to look for

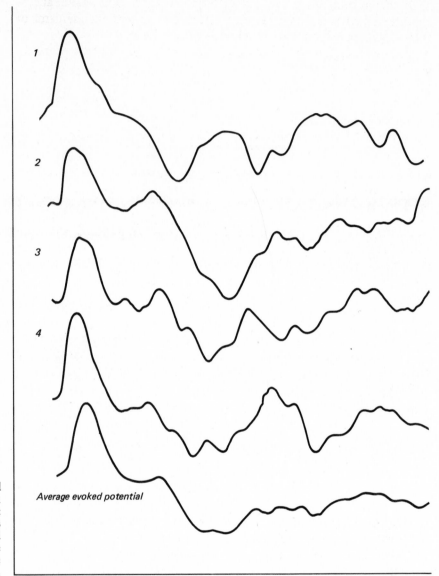

1

2

3

4

Average evoked potential

FIGURE 7.26 Evoked potentials in response to a flash of light, recorded from rat visual cortex. The top curves are individual evoked potentials; the bottom curve represents the average of the individual curves.

potentials that were present before the movement.

Other studies might involve the correlation of continuously recorded electrical activity in various brain structures with the on-going behavior of the animal. Stages of sleep and activity, feeding, and other "spontaneous behaviors" can be observed, or the animals can be trained in some task or subjected to diverse situations in order to observe the response of various brain structures. If we find that a brain region becomes more active after an animal is deprived of access to water, perhaps that region has something to do with mechanisms of thirst. The problems associated with use of electrical recordings will be discussed in later chapters dealing with particular physiological and behavioral processes.

ELECTRICAL STIMULATION OF THE BRAIN

Neural activity can be elicited by electrical stimulation. In chapter 3, I described the way in which action potentials could be produced by delivering electrical pulses to an axon. Various neural structures can also be stimulated through electrodes inserted into the brain; the stimulation experiment, like the recording experiment, can be either acute or chronic.

Identification of Neural Connections

One of the most clear-cut uses of electrical stimulation is demonstrated in neuroanatomical studies. If stimulation delivered through an electrode in structure A produces an evoked potential recorded from an electrode in structure B, then the structures must be connected. Details of their interconnections—directness of the pathway, diffuseness of connections, etc.—can also be inferred from the record obtained. (See **FIGURE 7.28.**)

Electrical Stimulation during Neurosurgery

One of the more interesting uses of electrical stimulation of the brain was developed by Wilder Penfield (see Penfield and Jasper, 1954) in the treatment of *focal epilepsy.* This disease is characterized by a localized region of neural tissue that periodically irritates surrounding areas, triggering an epileptic seizure (wild, sustained firing of cerebral neurons, resulting in some degree of behavioral disruption, often including convulsions). If severe cases of focal epilepsy do not respond to medication, surgical excision of the focus is necessary. But how can the focus be identified?

Prior to the onset of a seizure, many patients report the experience of an *aura.* Auras are diverse in nature; some people describe odors, some say that everything appears bright and shimmering, and others report a sense of fear and dread. Since the auras probably

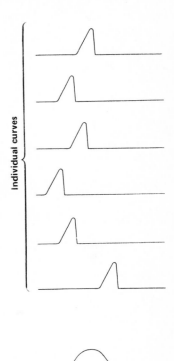

FIGURE 7.27 A fallacy introduced by the averaging process. The average curve at the bottom contains a broad, low rise, whereas the individual curves each contain a sharp peak, which occurs at variable times.

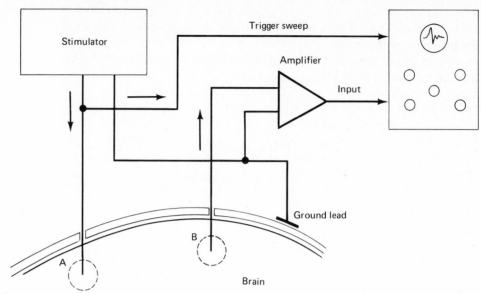

FIGURE 7.28   A schematic representation of the means by which one area of the brain can be stimulated while recording in another area. This procedure permits inferences to be made concerning the nature of the neural connections between these areas.

resulted from stimulation of the brain tissue surrounding the focus, Penfield reasoned that he might identify this area by electrically stimulating various parts of the brain in the unanesthetized patient. The electrode locations that would produce the aura would identify the focus.

Patients undergoing open-head surgery first have their head shaved. Then a local anesthetic is administered to the scalp along the line that will be followed by the incision. The scalp is cut all the way around, and the skull under the cut is sawed through. The top of the skull can then be removed (like the top of a soft-boiled egg, if you'll excuse the analogy). The dura mater is then cut and folded back, and the naked brain is thus available to the surgeon.

Penfield touched the tip of a metal electrode to various parts of the brain and noted the effects on the patient's behavior. For example, stimulation of motor cortex produced movement, and stimulation of auditory cortex elicited reports of the presence of buzzing noises. If all went well, an aura was produced, and the appropriate region was removed. The dura was sewn back together and the top of the skull was replaced.

Besides giving the patients relief from their epileptic attacks, the procedure provided Penfield with a lot of interesting data. As he stimulated various parts of the brain, he noted the effect and placed a sterile piece of paper, on which was written a number, on the point stimulated. After the operation he could compare the recorded notes with a photograph of the patient's brain, showing the location of the points of stimulation.

Behavioral Studies

Stimulation of the brain of an unanesthetized, freely moving animal often produces behavioral changes. For example, hypothalamic stimulation can elicit such behaviors as feeding, drinking, grooming, attack, or escape, which suggests that the hypothalamus is involved in the control of these behaviors. Stimulation of the caudate nucleus often halts ongoing behavior, suggesting that this structure is involved in motor inhibition. Brain stimulation can serve as a stimulus for a learned task or can even serve as a rewarding or punishing event. These latter two phenomena are described in chapter 17.

There are problems in the interpretation of the results of electrical stimulation of the brain. An electrical stimulus (usually a series of pulses) can never duplicate the natural neural processes that go on in the brain. The normal interplay of spatial and temporal patterns of excitation and inhibition is destroyed by the artificial stimulation of an area. It would almost be like attaching a rope to the arms of the members of an orchestra and then shaking all the ropes simultaneously to see what they can play. (Sometimes, in fact, local stimulation is used to produce a "temporary lesion"—the region is put out of commission by the meaningless artificial stimulation.) The surprising thing is that stimulation so often *does* produce orderly changes in behavior.

CHEMICAL TECHNIQUES

In this section I shall discuss various histochemical and pharmacological techniques that have been developed to help elucidate brain mechanisms.

Identification of Transmitter Substances

A few structures (e.g., autonomic ganglia) contain only one transmitter substance, which makes its identification relatively easy (with the stress on *relatively*, not *easy*). In the brain, identifying the transmitter substance is more difficult. The principal methods used to identify a neurotransmitter are the use of staining techniques for the transmitter, recording of postsynaptic potentials after *iontophoretic* application of the transmitter into the vicinity of the cell, and localization of transmitter-destroying enzymes.

As we saw in chapter 5, exposure of fresh brain sections to formaldehyde gas results in chemical reactions that cause monoamine-containing cells (i.e., those containing dopamine, norepineph-rine, or serotonin) to fluoresce a bright green or yellow color when the tissue is examined under a special microscope that uses ultra-violet light. Anatomical pathways of neurons containing dopamine, norepinephrine, and serotonin have thus been discovered. Confirma-tion of these results, and the tentative identification of other trans-mitters whose presence cannot be visualized by histofluorescence techniques, has been obtained through use of iontophoresis. A *dou-ble-barrelled micropipette* is prepared, one pipette inside the other. The longer (inner) pipette is inserted into a neuron, and records are made of its membrane potential. The shorter pipette is filled with an ionized form of the neurotransmitter to be tested. Very small amounts of the neurotransmitter can be ejected from the pipette by passing electrical current through it; the charged molecules are car-ried with the electrical current out through the tip of the micropipette. (See **FIGURE 7.29.**) If applications of this neurotransmitter, and not of others, produce PSPs, it suggests that the postsynaptic membrane contains receptors for this substance. (By inference, the local terminal buttons also use this chemical to transmit synaptic information.)

Sometimes neurotransmitters are located indirectly. Acetyl-choline is normally deactivated by acetylcholinesterase. Although ACh cannot be identified by staining, AChE can. The presence of AChE in a cell, then, suggests that the terminals synapsing upon it secrete this neurotransmitter.

Stimulation or Inhibition of Particular Transmitters

In chapter 5 I described various chemicals that mimic a particular transmitter, facilitate its production and/or release, prevent its re-lease, block the postsynaptic receptors, or prevent the destruction or re-uptake of the transmitter. Thus, these substances can be used to observe the behavioral effects of stimulation or inhibition of a particular neurotransmitter. For example, depletion of serotonin by PCPA produces insomnia (at least temporarily), and thus suggests the involvement of this transmitter in sleep.

Particular kinds of synapses can be inhibited or stimulated by injection of various pharmacological agents directly into parts of the brain. This can even be done chronically; a *cannula* (small metal tube) can be placed in an animal's brain, and a fitting, attached to the cannula, can be cemented to the skull. At a later date a flexible tube can be connected to the fitting, and a chemical can be injected into the brain. (See **FIGURE 7.30.**) Other methods have been de-

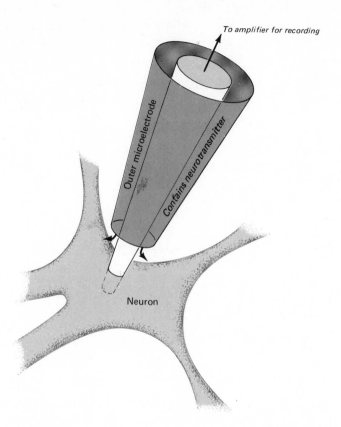

FIGURE 7.29 Iontophoresis. Molecules of a neuro-transmitter are carried out of the outer pipette by an electric current. Intracellular recordings are made by means of the inner pipette to determine whether the neuron responds to the neurotransmitter.

vised to permit the introduction of a powdered chemical into a specific brain region.

Radioactive Tracers

DETERMINATION OF RATE OF CHEMICAL REACTIONS. Radioactive chemicals are very useful in the analysis of brain functions. They can be used to determine the rate of incorporation of a given substance in various chemical reactions ("turnover rate") or to label particular neurons.

    If we wanted to determine the relative rates of protein synthesis in various neural structures, for example, we could inject an animal with a measured amount of radioactive amino acids (which are used as building blocks for protein). After waiting for a period of time, we would kill the animal and dissect the brain. The amount of radioactivity in a given portion of brain tissue would provide an index of

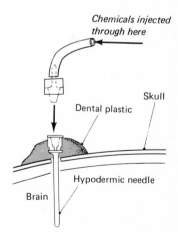

FIGURE 7.30 A chronic intracranial cannula. Chemicals can be infused into the brain through this device.

the amount of radioactive amino acid that had been incorporated into protein, and hence a measure of the rate of protein synthesis since the injection.

DETERMINATION OF SITE OF ACTION OF A BEHAVIORALLY EFFECTIVE CHEMICAL. Suppose we were interested in finding out where *testosterone* (a male sex hormone) is taken up in the brain. The fact that testosterone can affect behavior suggests that some brain cells selectively take up this hormone. We could inject an animal with radioactive testosterone, wait a while, kill the animal, slice its brain, and mount the sections on microscope slides. In the dark, we could coat the sections with a *photographic emulsion* (the substance found on photographic film). After waiting a while, we would develop the emulsion on the slides, just as we would develop some film. If the radioactive testosterone were taken up selectively by any neurons, the concentration of the radioactive substance would cause local exposure of the photographic emulsion. (Radiation will expose film, just as light will. Film will be ruined if it goes through an airport X-ray machine, unless it is shielded in metal containers.) Thus, one can look for black spots, betraying the presence of concentrations of radioactive testosterone. This procedure (called *autoradiography,* roughly translated as "writing with one's own radiation") can be used for locating the sites of action of a number of behaviorally active chemicals.

There are two restrictions in the use of autoradiography, however. The compound must be obtainable in radioactive form, and the substance must produce its effect in an intact form, and not break down rapidly. Very misleading results might be obtained if the substance breaks down and only one of the resulting products produces the change in behavior. If the radioactive molecule remains attached to the active portion, the results will be useful. If the "behaviorally inert" portion retains the radioactive molecule, the results of autoradiography will be meaningless. (See **FIGURE 7.31.**) The problem is that all too often the identity of the effective molecule is not known.

This chapter has barely skimmed the surface of the techniques available to students of brain functions. However, you have been introduced to the major types of research methods used, and you should have no trouble understanding the particular experiments I shall describe in later chapters of this book. Hopefully, you have also learned enough so that you will be able to understand the rationale behind most experimental procedures you might read about in scientific journals or other books.

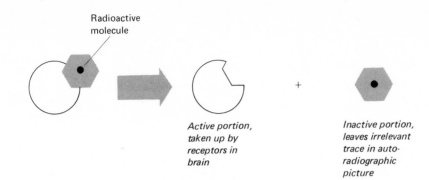

Radioactive molecule

Active portion, taken up by receptors in brain

Inactive portion, leaves irrelevant trace in auto-radiographic picture

+

FIGURE 7.31   A possible source of error in auto-radiographic tracer studies.

SUGGESTED READINGS

SKINNER, J. E. *Neuroscience: A Laboratory Manual.* Philadelphia: Saunders, 1971.

WEBSTER, W. G. *Principles of Research Methodology in Physiological Psychology.* New York: Harper & Row, 1975.

These are "how to do it" manuals designed for laboratory courses in physiological psychology. Webster's book emphasizes "experiments" that can be done as laboratory projects, whereas Skinner's book emphasizes technique. Skinner's book also includes a valuable stereotaxic atlas of the rat brain and excellent guides for the dissection of cow and sheep brains. Both books contain a list of references pertaining to particular investigative techniques.

SLOTNICK, B. M., and LEONARD, C. M. *A Stereotaxic Atlas of the Albino Mouse Forebrain.* Rockville, Md.: Public Health Service, 1975. (U.S. Government Printing Office Stock Number 017-024-00491-0.)

KÖNIG, J. F. R., and KLIPPEL, R. A. *The Rat Brain: A Stereotaxic Atlas of the Forebrain and Lower Parts of the Brain Stem.* Baltimore: Williams & Wilkins, 1963.

PELLIGRINO, L. J., and CUSHMAN, A. J. *A Stereotaxic Atlas of the Rat Brain.* New York: Appleton-Century-Crofts, 1967.

SNIDER, R. S., and NIEMER, W. T. *A Stereotaxic Atlas of the Cat Brain.* Chicago: University of Chicago Press, 1961.

These stereotaxic atlases (arranged in order of brain size) are the standard references for investigators who use these species. Of the two rat brain atlases, König and Klippel's is more useful for studying neuroanatomy, whereas Pelligrino and Cushman's atlas is more useful as a guide for stereotaxic surgery.

Receptor Organs and the Transduction of Sensory Information

8

In order for us to experience the world, there must be changes in patterns of neural activity in our brains that correspond to physical events in the environment. The real world surrounds us, but our perception of it takes place within our head. The topic of this chapter will be the process by which environmental change affects neural firing (*sensory transduction*); in this chapter and in chapter 9 we shall study the subsequent anatomical pathways followed by sensory information and the nature of *sensory coding* in the brain.

We receive information about the environment from our sensory receptors. Stimuli impinge on the receptors and, through various processes, alter their electrical characteristics. These electrical changes (called either receptor potentials or generator potentials—the distinction will be made shortly) modify the pattern of firing in axons leading into the CNS. In this chapter I shall describe the anatomy and location of the various receptors, and shall summarize what is known or hypothesized about the nature of sensory transduction.

RECEPTOR AND GENERATOR POTENTIALS. There are two basic types of receptor cells. One kind has an axon and communicates with other neurons by means of normal synaptic transmission. Sensory events affecting these cells produce *generator potentials*. These potentials are similar in function to postsynaptic potentials; they raise or lower the probability that the axon of the sensory neuron will fire (or, more descriptively, they raise or lower the axon's rate of firing). The other type of receptor cell does not have an axon and does not produce action potentials. This receptor sustains slow potential changes (*receptor potentials*) when stimulated by sensory events. Receptor potentials are transmitted, either electrically or chemically, to neurons with axons capable of producing action potentials. The receptor potential thus alters the rate of firing of these latter neurons. The basic distinction, then, is between receptor cells that have axons (and are true neurons) and those that do not. Figure 8.1 illustrates the process of transduction of sensory information into neural firing. (See **FIGURE 8.1**.)

THE SENSORY MODALITIES. It is often said that there are five senses: sight, hearing, smell, taste, and touch. Actually, we have more than five senses. The problem is that people do not agree on just how many more. Certainly, sensory physiologists agree that we should add the vestibular senses; the inner ear provides us with information about orientation and angular acceleration (changes in speed of rotation) of the head, as well as auditory information. Vestibular information is very important; we use it to maintain our balance. However, we are not "aware" of it as we are of vision or olfaction, for example, so it is easy to see why vestibular sensation was left off the list (which was drawn up long before there were any scientific investigations on sensory systems). Furthermore, receptors for vestibular information are not visible unless one dissects the region of the inner ear, and the receptors are always functioning; we cannot turn them off the way we can close our eyes. If something is constantly present, we tend not to notice it.

The sense of "touch" also includes several kinds of information. The *somatosenses* (a much better word than touch) include sensitivity to pressure, touch, warmth, cold, skin vibration, limb position and movement, and pain. There is no disagreement about the fact that we can detect these stimuli; the issue is whether or not they are detected by separate senses. As we shall see in the discussion of somatosenses in this chapter, we do not even know which receptors are responsible for some of these sensations.

The rest of this chapter will be divided into seven sections, covering the transduction of visual, auditory, vestibular, cutaneous, kinesthetic/organic, gustatory, and olfactory information. Each section will describe (1) the nature of the stimulus that excites the receptors; (2) anatomy of the receptor organ, including a discussion of ways in which the stimulus is modified by the sensory apparatus or organ; (3) anatomy of the receptor cells; (4) the process of transduc-

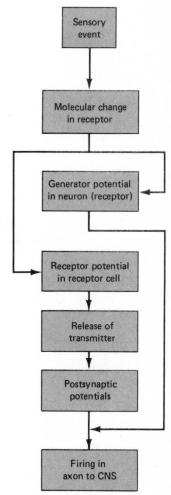

FIGURE 8.1 A schematic representation of the way in which physical stimuli are transduced into neural activity.

tion of physical energy into patterns of neural activity; (5) the route followed by the sensory information through the peripheral nervous system; and (6) the role of efferents from the CNS to the sense organ and its receptors.

VISION

The Stimulus

As we all know, we must have light in order to make use of our eyes. Light, for humans, is a narrow band of the electromagnetic spectrum. Electromagnetic radiation with a wavelength of between 380 and 760 nm (nanometer, or one-billionth of a meter) is visible to us. (See **FIGURE 8.2.**) Other animals can sense different ranges of electromagnetic radiation. A rattlesnake, for example, can use infrared radiation in detecting its prey; it can thus locate warm-blooded animals in the dark. The range of wavelengths we call light is that part of a continuum which we humans can see.

Anatomy of the Eye

The eyes are suspended in the *orbits*. They are moved by six muscles attached to the outer coat of the eye (*sclera*). Normally, we cannot look behind our eyeballs and see these muscles because of the presence of the *conjunctiva*. These mucous membranes line the eyelid and fold back to attach to the eye (thus preventing a contact lens that has slipped off the cornea from "falling behind the eye"). Figure 8.3 illustrates the external and internal anatomy of the eye. (See **FIGURE 8.3.**)

The outer layer of the eye, the sclera, is opaque, not permitting entry of light. The *cornea,* however, is transparent and admits light. The amount of light entering the eye is regulated by the size of the *pupil,* formed by the opening in the *iris,* which consists of a ring of muscles situated behind the cornea. The iris contains two bands of muscles, the *dilator* (whose contraction enlarges the pupil) and the *sphincter* (whose contraction reduces it). The sphincter is innervated by cholinergic fibers of the parasympathetic nervous system; cholinergic blockers (for example, belladonna alkaloids such as atropine) thus produce pupillary dilation by relaxing the sphincter of the iris. In fact, *belladonna* received its name from this effect. Belladonna means "beautiful lady" and was used in ancient times to enhance a woman's sex appeal. (Dilated pupils often indicate interest, and

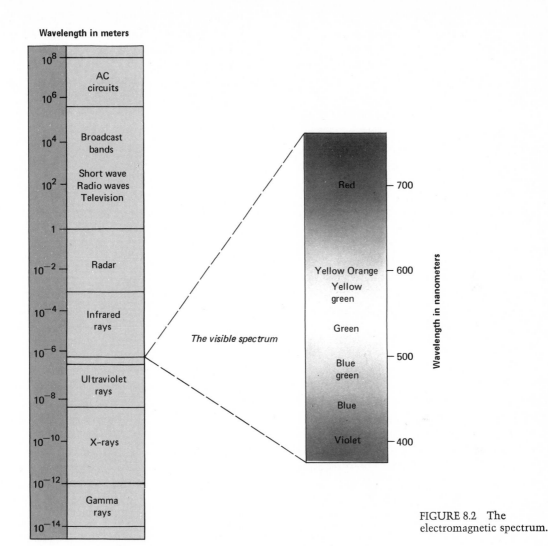

FIGURE 8.2 The electromagnetic spectrum.

there is, to almost any man, nothing more attractive than a woman who finds him interesting.)

The lens is situated immediately behind the iris. It consists of a series of transparent (naturally) onionlike layers. Its shape can be altered by contraction of the *ciliary muscles*. Normally, because of the tension of elastic fibers that suspend the lens, the lens is relatively flat (and thus is focussed on distant objects). When the ciliary muscles contract, tension is taken off these fibers, and the lens springs back to its normally rounded shape. The lens can, therefore, focus images of near or distant objects on the *retina*, the light-receptive surface on the back of the eye.

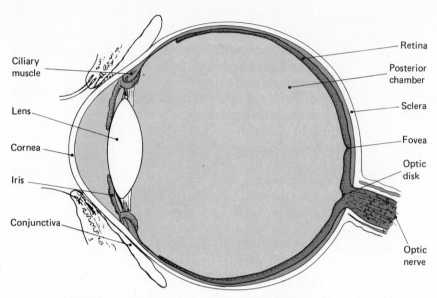

Ciliary
muscle

Lens

Cornea

Iris

Conjunctiva

Retina

Posterior
chamber

Sclera

Fovea

Optic
disk

Optic
nerve

FIGURE 8.3   The human eye.

Light then passes through the fluid-filled *posterior chamber* of the eye and falls on the retina. In the retina are located the receptor cells, the *rods* and *cones.* Cones, which mediate color vision and provide vision of the highest acuity (ability to detect fine details), are most densely packed at the back of the eye and thin out toward the periphery. The *fovea,* or central region of the retina, which mediates our most detailed and accurate vision, contains only cones. Rods, on the other hand, are most numerous in the periphery. Rods are incapable of detecting colors, but are more sensitive to light. In a very dimly lighted room we use our rod vision; therefore, we are color blind, and we cannot see very well at the center of our visual field (because there are no rods in the fovea). You have probably noticed, while out on a dark night, that looking directly at a dim, distant light (that is, placing the image of the light on the fovea) causes it to disappear.

Another feature of the retina is the *optic disk,* where the axons conveying visual information gather together and leave the eye via the optic nerve. The optic disk produces a *blind spot* because no receptors are located there. We do not normally perceive our blind spots, but their presence can be demonstrated. If you have not found your blind spot before, you might want to try the exercise described in **FIGURE 8.4.**

Close examination of the retina shows that it consists of several layers of neuron cell bodies, their axons and dendrites, and the receptors themselves. Figure 8.5 illustrates a cross section through the retina, which is usually divided into three main layers, the *photoreceptive layer,* the *bipolar cell layer,* and the *ganglion cell layer.*

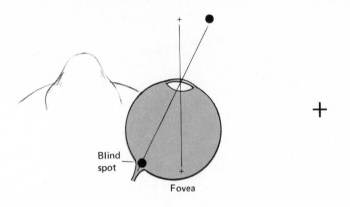

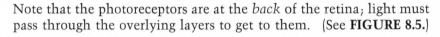

FIGURE 8.4 FIGURE 8.4 A test for the blind spot. With the left eye closed, look at the + with the right eye and move the page back and forth. At about 20 cm the black circle disappears from the visual field because it falls on the blind spot.

Note that the photoreceptors are at the *back* of the retina; light must pass through the overlying layers to get to them. (See **FIGURE 8.5.**)

Anatomy of the Photoreceptors

Figure 8.6 shows a drawing, reconstructed from electron micrographs, of a single rod and cone of a frog. Note that each photoreceptor contains a layered outer segment, connected by a cilium to the inner segments. The oil droplet does not occur in mammalian retinas. (See **FIGURE 8.6.**) Figure 8.7 shows, in greater detail, the outer segments of the rods and cones. Although outer segments of both receptors are layered (the layers are called *lamellae*), there is a basic difference. Rods contain free-floating disks, whereas the lamellae of the cones consist of one continuous folded membrane. (See **FIGURE 8.7.**) According to studies by Young (1970), new protein is perpetually produced by the receptor cells to replace that which gets worn out. Rods continuously shed old disks off the end, while new replacement disks are produced at the base of the outer segment. Cones, however, do not produce new folds. The tapered shape of the outer segment is apparently determined by development. The outer lamellae are produced early in fetal life, whereas inner ones are produced later. As the cones grow, the segments they produce are correspondingly larger. At the base of the outer segments the cones produce new protein, which migrates outward and becomes incorporated into the lamellae.

Transduction of Visual Information

Light can be conceived of as electromagnetic radiation or as particles of energy (*photons*). This fact bothers many people who prefer a unified view of the world, but physicists have learned to live with

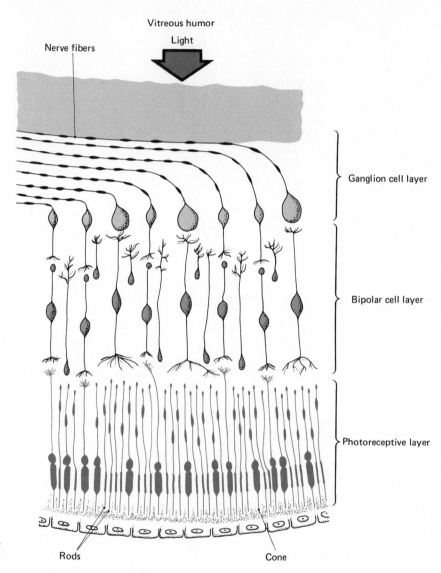

FIGURE 8.5   A section through the retina.

these contradictory theories—both of which appear to be correct. The photon is the stimulus that excites a receptive cell of the retina, and it appears that rods are able to detect the presence of only one photon, the minimum quantity of light that can exist.   Our photoreceptors, then, are exquisitely sensitive detectors of light.

The first step in the process of transduction of light is chemical, and it involves a special chemical, or *photopigment*.   Photopigments

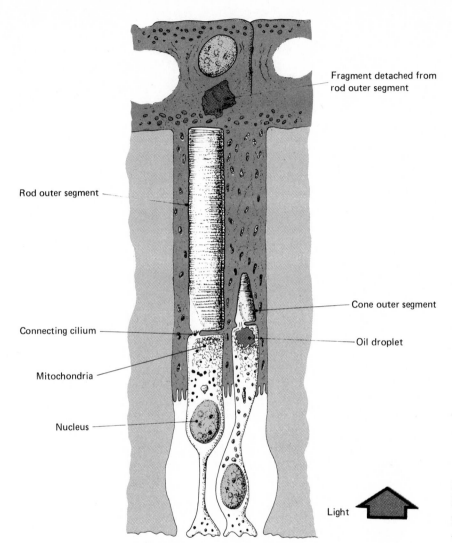

Fragment detached from
rod outer segment

Rod outer segment

Cone outer segment

Connecting cilium

Oil droplet

Mitochondria

Nucleus

Light

FIGURE 8.6 Photoreceptors.
(Redrawn from Young, R. W.,
Visual cells. Copyright © 1970
by Scientific American, Inc.
All rights reserved.)

consist of two parts, *opsin* (a protein) and *retinal* (a smaller molecule, derived from vitamin A). There are several forms of opsin; let us consider the photopigment of human rods, *rhodopsin*, which consists of *rod opsin* plus retinal.

Retinal is synthesized from *retinol* (vitamin A). (This is why carrots, rich in retinol, are said to be good for your eyesight.) Retinal is a molecule with a long chain that is capable of bending at a specific point. The straight-chained form of retinal is called *all-trans-retinal*; the form with a bend is called *ll-cis-retinal*. The bent form, 11-*cis*-retinal, is the only naturally occurring form of retinal capable

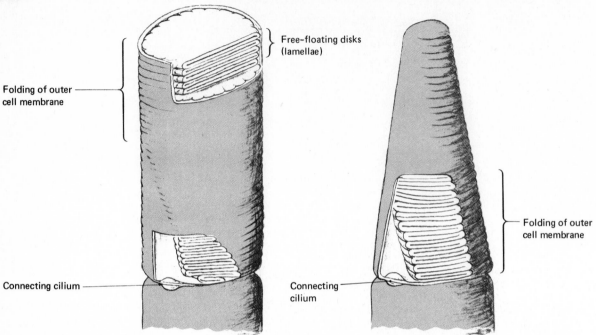

Free-floating disks (lamellae)

Folding of outer cell membrane

Folding of outer cell membrane

Connecting cilium

Connecting cilium

FIGURE 8.7 Details of photoreceptors. (Redrawn from Young, R. W., Visual cells. Copyright © 1970 by Scientific American, Inc. All rights reserved.)

of attaching to rod opsin to form rhodopsin. The 11-*cis*-form of retinal, moreover, is very unstable; it can exist only in the dark. When a molecule of rhodopsin is exposed to light (i.e., absorbs a photon), the bend in the retinal chain straightens out, and the retinal assumes the all-*trans* form. Since rod opsin cannot remain attached to all-*trans*-retinal, the rhodopsin breaks into its two constituents. This fission somehow affects the permeability of the membrane of the rod, and subsequent changes in ionic fluxes produce a receptor potential. The precise mechanism is unknown; it has been suggested that rod opsin, now dissociated from the retinal, attaches itself to the membrane of the rod or to one of its lamellae and causes a decrease in membrane permeability. The resulting hyperpolarization constitutes the receptor potential (Wald, 1968; Hagins, Penn, and Yoshikami, 1970). Since 11-*cis*-retinal is continuously being re-formed in the eye, the magnitude of the receptor potential produced by a rod depends upon the intensity of light to which it is exposed.

In primates, four different opsins (rod opsin and three kinds of cone opsins) join with retinal to produce four different photopigments. Each of these compounds most readily absorbs light of a particular wavelength. A given cone contains only one of the three cone photopigments; the various cones are thus maximally sensitive to either red, green, or blue light. The visual system uses information from these three types of cones to produce color vision.

Origin of the Optic Nerve

The ganglion cell layer of the retina gives rise to fibers of the optic nerve (the second cranial nerve). Figure 8.8 is a schematic drawing of a primate retina. (See **FIGURE 8.8.**) The photoreceptors synapse with the bipolar cells—rods with *rod bipolar cells* and cones with

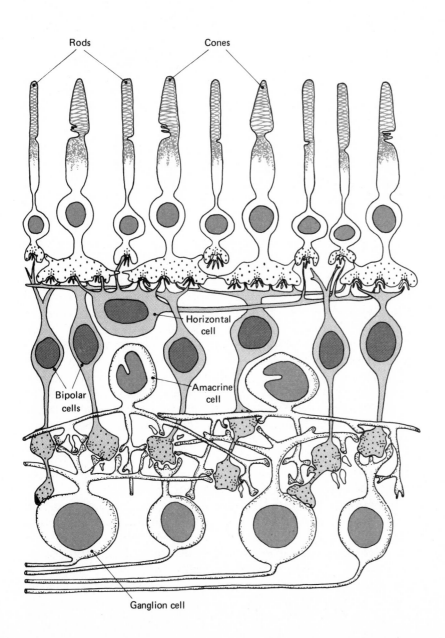

Rods   Cones

Horizontal cell

Bipolar cells

Amacrine cell

Ganglion cell

FIGURE 8.8   Details of retinal circuitry. (Redrawn by permission of the Royal Society and the authors from Dowling, J. E., and Boycott, B. B., *Proceedings of the Royal Society* (London), 1966, Series B, *166*, 80–111.)

midget bipolar or *flat bipolar cells.* The *horizontal cells* receive synapses from a number of photoreceptors, and themselves synapse upon bipolar cells. As we shall see in chapter 9, the horizontal cells play an important role in the analysis of visual information. The distal (away from photoreceptor) ends of the bipolar cells are interconnected via the *amacrine cells.* Finally, the ganglion cells, receiving information from the bipolar cells, send axons toward the optic disk and give rise to the optic nerve. (See **FIGURE 8.8.**)

Efferent Control from the CNS

As we have seen, the amount of light falling on the retina is controlled by the size of the pupillary aperture, which depends on the degree of contraction of the sphincter and dilator muscles of the iris. Pupillary size depends on two factors. The first factor is the degree of arousal of the organism; if sympathetic activity dominates, the pupils will dilate, whereas parasympathetic activity produces constriction. The second factor is the amount of light falling on the retina. Increases or decreases in the level of illumination produce corresponding pupillary constriction or dilation. Exposure to extremely bright light will produce reflexive squinting, which further reduces the size of the aperture.

Shape of the lens is also controlled by the brain, to focus the image of near or distant objects on the retina. This accommodation for distance is normally integrated with convergence of the eyes. When we look at a near object, the eyes turn inward so that the two images of the object fall on corresponding portions of the retinas. As we shall see later, this leads to stimulation of corresponding cells in visual cortex on both sides of the brain, producing a fused image. Convergence of the eyes and accommodation of the lens normally occur together, so that the object on which the eyes are focussed is also the object on which the eyes converge. If you hold a pencil in front of you and focus on distant objects, you see two blurry pencils. If you then focus on the pencil, you get two blurry views of the background.

Control of eye movement is a very complicated process; as we study the process, we realize that it takes a very sophisticated computer to accomplish what our brain does in moving the eyes. When the brain commands skeletal muscles to pick up a weight, it relies on sensory feedback to determine whether the arms in fact moved; perhaps the weight is too heavy to lift. The eyes, on the other hand, are free to move, and when the brain sends signals to the six muscles controlling eye movement, it "assumes" that the eye does as it is told. Sensory organs within the eye muscles signal information concerning muscle length back to the brain (Davson, 1972), but it is not yet clear what the brain does with this information. The process by which the brain controls eye movements is schematized in Figure 8.9. (See **FIGURE 8.9.**)

The lack of feedback from the eye can be demonstrated easily. We all perceive the world to be fixed in one place; if we shift our gaze, we experience a constant environment being scanned by moving eyes. However, the retinas themselves do not have enough information to make this decision. A moving world and a moving eyeball produce the same changes in the retinal image. The brain has access to the commands it gave to the eye muscles, however, and if changes in retinal image correspond with changes in the commands to the eye muscles, we perceive the world as being stationary.

Suppose the retinal image of the world changed while the commands to the eye muscles were constant: we would perceive movement. Try this experiment: Cover your left eye with your left

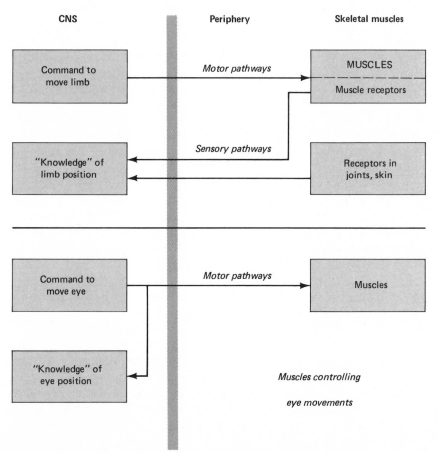

FIGURE 8.9 Interpretation of movement depends upon signals to the eye muscles rather than upon proprioceptive feedback.

hand. Look down a bit and to the left. Now touch the right side of the upper eyelid of your right eye and push against your eyeball. The eye will move, and as it does, it will appear to you that the world is also moving. The brain detected movement of the image on the retina, but there were no commands to move the muscles; ergo, the world moved. Fortunately, there is more to our brains than that. Other parts of the brain are carrying out the experiment, and they say, "No, the world just looks as though it is moving; the finger is moving the eye."

The opposite experiment has been performed—the eyes were held in place while the brain commanded their movement (Hammond, Merton, and Sutton, 1956). Since it is difficult to hold on to an eyeball without damaging it, Merton's eye muscles were injected with curare (which, you will recall, blocks nicotinic cholinergic synapses, and hence paralyzes the muscles). Merton then "willed" an upward movement of his eyes. Signals went to the appropriate eye muscles. Other brain structures were informed that the eyes had moved (but, of course, they had not). The retinal image did not change, even though the eye muscles were commanded to move; therefore, the system concluded that the world had moved up. Every time the subject "willed" a movement of the eyes, he perceived a corresponding movement of the world precisely following his gaze.

Besides CNS control of eye movement, pupil size, and accommodation of the lens, there appears to be a much more subtle control of retinal information. Spinelli, Pribram, and Weingarten (1965) found that auditory clicks produced electrical activity in the optic nerve. The responses ceased when the nerve was cut between the brain and the recording electrode. Thus, there appear to be efferent fibers from brain to retina. Cragg (1962) confirmed studies from the late nineteenth century that found nerve terminals, among the amacrine cells, at the ends of axons coming from the vicinity of the optic disk. These, presumably, are terminals of the efferent fibers whose presence was demonstrated by Spinelli and his coworkers. The role of these fibers in visual functioning is not known.

AUDITION

The Stimulus

We hear sounds, which are normally transmitted via rapid successive condensations and rarefactions of air. If an object vibrates at the proper frequency (between approximately 20 and 15,000 times per second), the pressure changes it induces in the air will, if the object is near enough, ultimately stimulate receptive cells in our ears. We can also stimulate these receptors by placing a vibrating object against the bones of the head, bypassing air conduction altogether.

Anatomy of the Ear

Figure 8.10 shows a section through the ear and auditory canal, and illustrates the apparatus of the middle and inner ear. (See **FIGURE 8.10.**) Sound is funnelled via the *pinna* (external ear) through the *external auditory canal* to the *tympanic membrane* (eardrum), which vibrates with the sound. We are not very good at moving our ears, but by orienting our heads, we can modify the sound that finally reaches the receptors. A muscle in the tympanic membrane (*tensor tympani*) can alter the membrane's tension and thus control the amount of sound that is permitted to pass through to the middle ear.

FIGURE 8.10 The auditory apparatus. (Adapted from Gulick, W. L., *Hearing: Physiology and Psychophysics.* New York: Oxford University Press, 1971.)

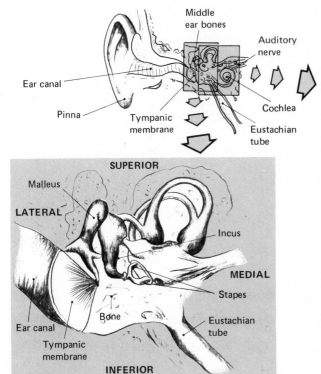

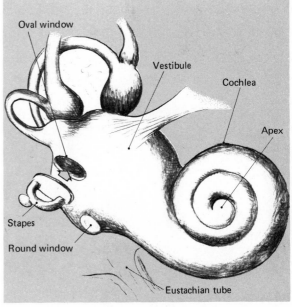

The *ossicles,* bones of the middle ear, are set into vibration by the tympanic membrane. The *malleus* (hammer) connects with the tympanic membrane and transmits vibrations via the *incus* (anvil) and *stapes* (stirrup) to the cochlea, the inner ear structure containing the receptors. The baseplate of the stapes presses against the membrane behind the *oval window,* the opening in the bony process surrounding the cochlea. (See **FIGURE 8.10.**) The *stapedius muscle,* when contracted, directs the baseplate of the stapes away from its normal point of attachment to the oval window, and hence dampens the vibration passed on to the receptive cells.

The *cochlea* is filled with fluid; this means that sounds transmitted through the air must be transferred into a liquid medium. This process normally is very inefficient—99.9 percent of the energy of airborne sound would be reflected away if the air impinged directly against the oval window of the cochlea. (If you have ever swum underwater, you have probably noted how quiet it is there; most of the sound arising in the air is reflected off the surface of the water.) The chain of ossicles serves as an extremely efficient means of energy transmission. The bones provide mechanical advantage, the baseplate of the stapes making smaller, but more forceful, excursions against the oval window than the tympanic membrane makes against the malleus.

The name cochlea comes from the Greek word *kokhlos,* or land snail. It is indeed snail-shaped, consisting of two and three-quarters turns of a gradually tapering cylinder. The cochlea is divided longitudinally into three sections, as shown in **FIGURE 8.11.** The auditory receptors are called *hair cells,* and they are anchored, via rodlike *Deiters' cells,* to the *basilar membrane.* The cilia of the hair cells pass through the *reticular membrane* and their ends attach to the fairly rigid *tectorial membrane,* which projects overhead like a shelf. (The

FIGURE 8.11 The organ of Corti. (Adapted from Gulick, W. L., *Hearing: Physiology and Psychophysics.* New York: Oxford University Press, 1971.)

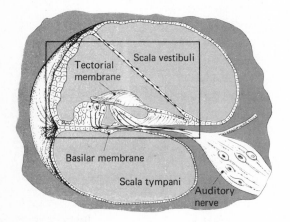

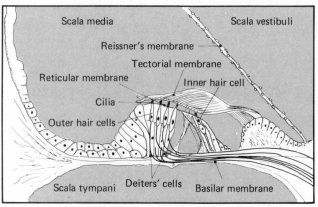

entire structure, including the basilar membrane, hair cells, and tectorial membrane, is referred to as the *organ of Corti*.) See **FIGURE 8.11.** Sonic vibrations cause movement of the basilar membrane relative to the tectorial membrane, and the resultant stretch exerted on the cilia of the hair cells produces the receptor potential.

If the cochlea were a closed system, no vibration would be transmitted via the oval window, since liquids are essentially incompressible. However, there is a membrane-covered opening, the *round window*, which allows the fluid contents of the cochlea to move back and forth. The baseplate of the stapes presses against the oval window, which increases the hydrostatic pressure within the *vestibule*, a chamber to which the cochlea is attached. The *scala vestibuli* (literally, the stairway of the vestibule) connects with the vestibule and conducts the pressure around the turns of the cochlea. Some portion of the basilar membrane vibrates with the sound waves, transmitting the waves of pressure changes into the *scala tympani*. Pressure changes in the scala tympani are transmitted to the membrane of the round window, which moves in and out in a manner opposite to movements of the oval window. The top drawing of Figure 8.12 shows the cochlea straightened out. A sound wave is deforming the basilar membrane. The middle drawing shows the continuity of the fluid within the scala vestibuli and the scala tympani. (See **FIGURE 8.12.**)

FIGURE 8.12 Deformation of the basilar membrane causes a shearing force to be exerted on the cilia of the auditory hair cells. (Adapted from von Békésy, G., The ear. *Scientific American*, August, 1957, and from Gulick, W. L., *Hearing: Physiology and Psychophysics*. New York: Oxford University Press, 1971.)

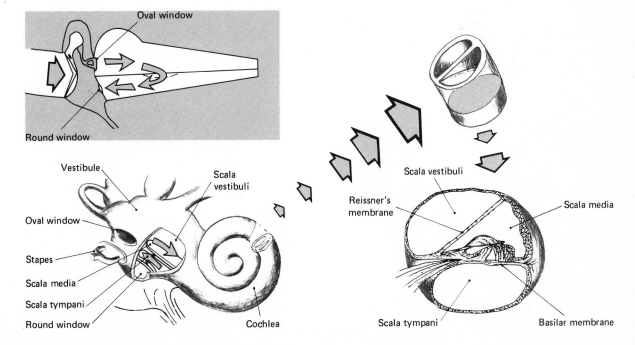

Anatomy of the Auditory Hair Cells

There are two types of auditory receptors, *inner* and *outer* hair cells, lying on the inside and outside of the cochlear coils. In the human cochlea, there are 3400 inner hair cells and 12,000 outer hair cells. Figure 8.13 illustrates the two types of cells and their supporting Deiters' cells. (See **FIGURE 8.13.**) These cells synapse with nerve terminals that pass through the *neural channels*. The left side of Figure 8.14 (drawn from a photograph taken by means of a scanning electron microscope) illustrates the rows of cilia on the inner and outer hair cells. The right side of the same figure shows the cilia of a single outer hair cell; note the characteristic M shape (or W shape, depending on your point of view) taken by the cilia. (See **FIGURE 8.14.**)

Transduction of Auditory Information

Although the process by which the organ of Corti converts mechanical energy into neural activity has received intense study, we still do not know how this process occurs. George von Békésy, in a lifetime of brilliant studies on cochleas of various animals, from human cadavers to elephants, found that the vibratory energy exerted on the oval window resulted in deformations in the shape of the basilar

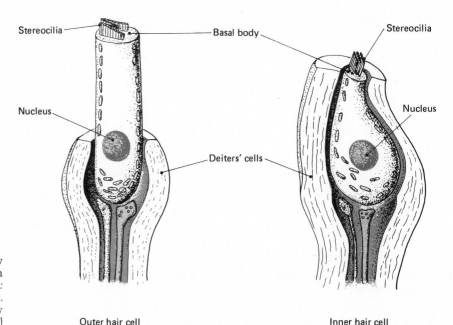

FIGURE 8.13 The auditory hair cells. (Adapted from Gulick, W. L., *Hearing: Physiology and Psychophysics.* New York: Oxford University Press, 1971.)

Outer hair cell

Inner hair cell

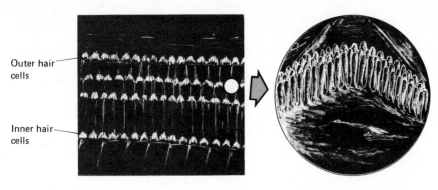

Outer hair cells

Inner hair cells

FIGURE 8.14 The appearance of the cilia of the inner and outer hair cells. (Adapted from Angelborg, A. R., and Engström, H., The normal organ of Corti. In *Basic Mechanisms in Hearing*, edited by A. R. Møeller. New York: Academic Press, 1973.)

membrane called "traveling waves." These deformations occur at different portions of the membrane, depending upon the frequency of the stimulus. The physics of the production of these waves is too complicated to be presented here (anyway, I take it on faith, myself). It suffices to say that, because of resonances of the cochlear spirals, and because of the physical properties of the basilar membrane, low-frequency sounds cause a maximum deformation at the apical end of the basilar membrane, whereas high-frequency sounds cause the end nearest the oval window to bend.

As the basilar membrane bends, it produces a shearing force on the stiff cilia of the hair cells, which is thus transmitted to the *cuticular plate* anchoring the base of the cilia to the top of the hair cells. Somehow, the shearing force produces a receptor potential. Many suggestions have been made concerning the means by which the shearing results in a receptor potential, but the evidence (which I shall now review) is still inconclusive.

In 1930, Wever and Bray discovered that if one amplified signals from a cat's *cochlear nerve,* and passed these signals through a loudspeaker, the cat's ear served as a very good microphone. One could talk into the cat's ear and hear one's voice over the loudspeaker. Wever and Bray were not recording nerve action potentials; these so-called *microphonics* could be recorded directly from the cochlea even in animals whose cochlear nerves had been previously cut and whose auditory fibers had subsequently degenerated. Thus, the electrical signal came from the organ of Corti itself. Once the blood supply to the inner ear was cut off, the *cochlear potential* (the more usual term for the cochlear microphonics) disappeared within a few hours.

It is generally (but not universally) assumed that the cochlear potential represents a summed recording of the receptor potentials of individual hair cells. Many different transducer mechanisms have been suggested; I will describe one of them (from Gulick, 1971), which I find appealing. Figure 8.15 shows a cross section through a coil of the cochlea. There are two (and probably three) kinds of liquid within the cochlea; the scala vestibuli and scala tympani contain *perilymph*, while the scala media contains *endolymph*. The region immediately surrounding the bodies of the hair cells contains *cortilymph*, thought to be different from the endolymph of the scala media (Angelborg and Engström, 1973). The interior of the hair cells is negative (by 20 to 70 mV) relative to the fluid that bathes them; furthermore, there is a potential difference between perilymph and endolymph, the endolymph being 50 to 80 mV positive to the perilymph. (See **FIGURE 8.15**.) Although there are large differences in the potassium ion content of perilymph and endolymph, it appears that this ionic difference is not the cause of the electrical potential difference; experimental manipulations of K^+ concentrations of the perilymph and endolymph have not led to corresponding changes in electrical charge (Eldredge and Miller, 1971).

Close microscopic examination of the hair cells shows that there is a bare spot in the cuticular plate; just below this bare spot is the basal body of the hair cell, and just above it is a small pore, approximately 1.5 μm in diameter (Hawkins, 1965). (See **FIGURE 8.16**.) A considerable amount of Golgi apparatus and a large number of mitochondria and granules are located around the basal body,

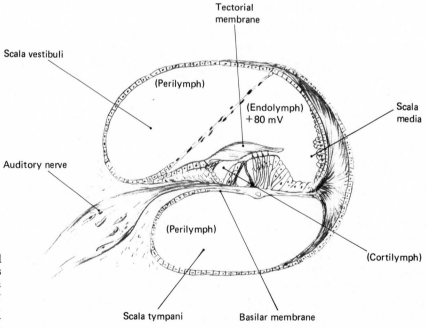

FIGURE 8.15 The electrical charges in the various regions of the cochlea. (Adapted from Gulick, W. L., *Hearing: Physiology and Psychophysics.* New York: Oxford University Press, 1971.)

Tectorial membrane

Scala vestibuli

(Perilymph)

(Endolymph) +80 mV

Scala media

Auditory nerve

(Perilymph)

(Cortilymph)

Scala tympani

Basilar membrane

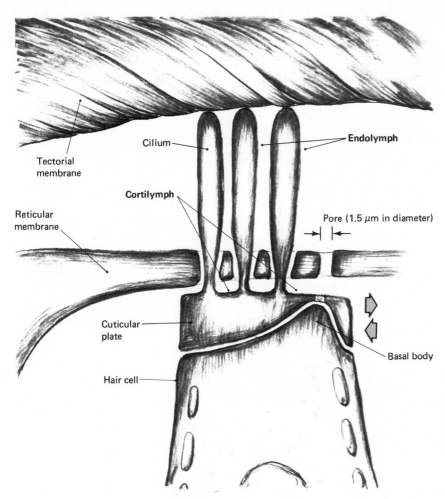

Tectorial membrane

Cilium

Endolymph

Cortilymph

Reticular membrane

Pore (1.5 μm in diameter)

Cuticular plate

Basal body

Hair cell

FIGURE 8.16 A shearing force on the cilia causes movement of the cuticular plate, and an ensuing movement of ions might be the event that produces the auditory generator potential. (Adapted from Gulick, W. L., *Hearing: Physiology and Psychophysics.* New York: Oxford University Press, 1971.)

which has led to the suggestion (Engström, Ades, and Hawkins, 1965) that the basal body might be the excitable portion of the hair cell. When the basilar membrane deforms and causes the cilia to be pulled, the cuticular plate moves relative to the basal body. This alters exposure of the membrane of the basal body to the endolymph that enters through the pore in the reticular membrane. Changes in ionic composition of the fluid bathing the basal body thus alter its membrane potential. (Alternatively, the basal body may be electrically stimulated by a flow of current through the pore and opening in the cuticular plate.) The potential changes are then propagated toward the base of the hair cell and alter flow of transmitter substance to the dendrites of afferent neurons of the cochlea. (See **FIGURE 8.16.**)

Origin of the Auditory Nerve

The afferent fibers of the cochlear nerve (a branch of the *auditory nerve,* or eighth cranial nerve) are produced by bipolar cells that reside in the *spiral ganglion*. The reason for this ganglion's name is made clear in Figure 8.17, which shows the scala media (*not* the entire cochlea) with its associated neural structures. Note that the spiral ganglion is not one structure, but consists of numerous bunches of nerve fibers, each containing a small nodule. The cell bodies of the bipolar sensory neurons reside within these nodules. (See **FIGURE 8.17.**)

Figure 8.18 shows a diagram of the synaptic connections of inner and outer hair cells. Note that there are both afferent and efferent connections; the cochlear nerve contains both incoming and outgoing fibers. (See **FIGURE 8.18.**) The appearance of vesicles within the efferent nerve terminals, and within the cytoplasm of the hair cells in the vicinity of the afferent nerve endings, suggests that information is transmitted chemically. The transmitter substance that conveys sensory information from the hair cells to the dendrites of the cochlear nerve neuron has not been identified (Fex, 1972); efferent transmission (which is inhibitory in nature) appears to be cholinergic (Fex, 1973).

Approximately 95 percent of the afferent cochlear nerve fibers synapse with the inner hair cells, on a one receptor–one neuron basis (Spoendlin, 1973). The other 5 percent of the sensory fibers synapse with the outer hair cells, on a ten receptor–one neuron basis. Thus, although the inner hair cells represent only 22 percent of the total number of receptive cells, they appear to be of primary importance in transmission of auditory information to the CNS.

FIGURE 8.17   The spiral ganglion and the cochlear nerve. (Adapted from Gulick, W. L., *Hearing: Physiology and Psychophysics.* New York: Oxford University Press, 1971.)

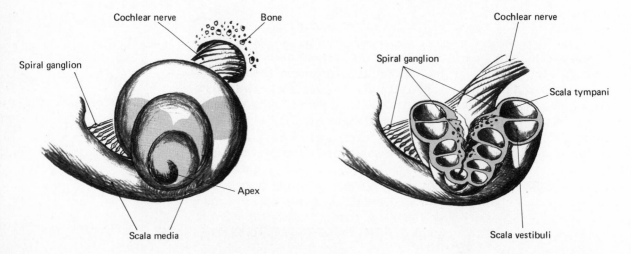

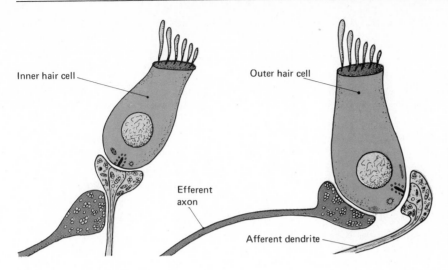

Inner hair cell

Outer hair cell

Efferent axon

Afferent dendrite

FIGURE 8.18   Details of the synaptic connections of the auditory hair cells. (Adapted from Spoendlin, H., The innervation of the cochlear receptor. In *Basic Mechanisms in Hearing*, edited by A. R. Møeller. New York: Academic Press, 1973.)

Efferent Control from the CNS

In describing the muscles of the middle ear, the stapedius and tensor tympani, I also described their function in protective reflexes acting to reduce the probability of hair cell damage upon exposure to loud noise.   This is about all the control we humans have over the nature of vibrations reaching the oval window (other than turning our head or putting our fingers in our ears).   There is some evidence that the size of the external auditory canal and the elasticity of its walls can be altered slightly by the contraction of surrounding muscles, but the effects of these modifications are minor.   Other mammals (e.g., cat, rabbit) have horn-shaped ears that can be independently turned toward the source of the sound.

As I noted in the previous section, the hair cells receive a considerable number of efferent terminals, which are inhibitory in effect. The efferent terminals synapse directly upon the outer hair cells and upon the dendrites to which the inner hair cells direct their sensory information.   (Refer back to **FIGURE 8.18.**)   The cell bodies of the efferent fibers are located in the *superior olivary nuclei* of the medulla. Approximately 500 efferent axons leave the nucleus on each side of the brain; 400 travel to the *contralateral* (other side) cochlea, and 100 go to the *ipsilateral* (same side) cochlea.

The precise role of these fibers is not known.   Some investigators have suggested that they play a role in selective attention; others propose that they are involved in the sharpening of frequency-specific information from the hair cells.

Finally, an autonomic efferent system to the cochlea has been discovered (Spoendlin and Lichtensteiger, 1966; Spoendlin, 1973). The termination of these noradrenergic sympathetic fibers has not been found yet, and their role is completely unknown.

VESTIBULAR SYSTEM

The Stimuli

The vestibular system has two components: the *vestibular sacs* and the *semicircular canals.* They represent two of the three components of the bony labyrinths. (We just studied the other component, the cochlea.) As we shall see, the vestibular sacs respond to the force of gravity and inform the brain about the head's orientation. The semicircular canals respond to angular acceleration; they detect changes in rotation of the head, but not steady rotation. They also respond (but rather weakly) to position or linear acceleration.

Anatomy of the Vestibular Apparatus

Figure 8.19 shows the bony labyrinths: the cochlea, the semicircular canals, and the two vestibular sacs—the *utricle* and the *saccule.* (See **FIGURE 8.19.**) The semicircular canals will be considered first.

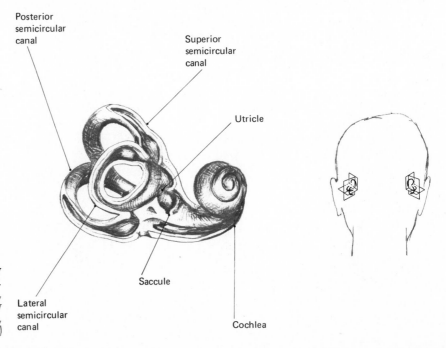

FIGURE 8.19 The bony labyrinths of the inner ear. (Adapted from Geldard, F. A., *The Human Senses,* ed. 2. New York: John Wiley & Sons, 1972.)

Posterior semicircular canal

Superior semicircular canal

Utricle

Saccule

Lateral semicircular canal

Cochlea

The semicircular canals approximate the three major planes of the head: sagittal, transverse, and horizontal. Each canal responds maximally to angular acceleration in its plane. A horizontal section of one semicircular canal is represented schematically in Figure 8.20. The enlargement (*ampulla*) contains the *crista*, the organ containing the sensory receptors. (See **FIGURE 8.20.**) The crista consists of a large number of hair cells, whose cilia are embedded in a gelatinous mass called the *cupula*. The semicircular canal consists of a membranous canal floating within a bony one; the membranous canal contains endolymph and floats within perilymph. The crista consists of a gelatinous mass that blocks part of the ampulla.

In order to explain the effects of angular acceleration on the semicircular canals, I shall first describe an "experiment." If we place a glass of water on the exact center of a turntable, and then start the turntable spinning, the water in the glass will, at first, remain stationary (the glass will be moving with respect to the water it contains). Eventually, however, the water will begin rotating with the container. If we then shut the turntable off, the water will continue spinning for a while because of its inertia.

The semicircular canals operate on the same principle. The endolymph within these canals, like the water in the glass, resists movement when the head begins to rotate. This inertial resistance pushes the endolymph against the cupula, causing it to bend until the fluid begins to move at the same speed as the head. If the head rotation is then stopped, the endolymph, still circulating through the canal, pushes the cupula the other way. Angular acceleration is thus translated into bending of the crista, which exerts a shearing force on the cilia of the hair cells. This process was directly observed by Steinhausen (1931), who injected a drop of oil in the par-

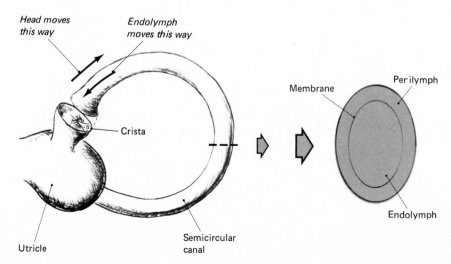

Head moves this way

Endolymph moves this way

Crista

Utricle

Semicircular canal

Membrane

Perilymph

Endolymph

FIGURE 8.20 A horizontal section through one semicircular canal.

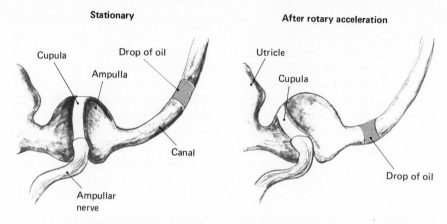

FIGURE 8.21   A diagram of Steinhausen's demonstration that movement of the endolymph causes displacement of the cupula. (Adapted from Dohlman, G., *Proceedings of the Royal Society of Medicine*, 1935, 28, 1371–1380.)

tially dissected semicircular canal of a pike (a fish with a large and easily accessible vestibular apparatus).   Figure 8.21 shows the effects of rotation of the semicircular canal in a clockwise direction; the endolymph resists the rotation and pushes the cupula to the right. (See **FIGURE 8.21.**)

The vestibular sacs (utricle and saccule) work very differently. These organs are roughly circular in shape, and each contains a patch of receptive tissue (on the "floor" of the utricle and on the "wall" of the saccule, when the head is in an upright position).   The receptive tissue, like that of the semicircular canals and cochlea, contains hair cells.   The cilia of these receptors are embedded in an overlying gelatinous mass, which contains something rather unusual—*otoconia*, small crystals of calcium carbonate.   (See **FIGURE 8.22.**)   The weight of the crystals causes the gelatinous mass to shift in position as the orientation of the head changes.   Thus, movement produces a shearing force on the cilia of the receptive hair cells.

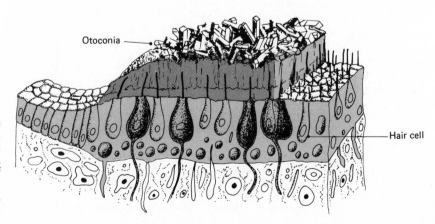

FIGURE 8.22   The receptive tissue of the utricle and saccule. (Adapted from Iurato, S., Light microscope features. In *Submicroscopic Structure of the Inner Ear*, edited by S. Iurato. Oxford: Pergamon Press, 1967.)

Anatomy of the Receptor Cells

The hair cells of the semicircular canal and vestibular sacs are very similar in morphology. There are two types of cells, appearing in both organs, as shown in **FIGURE 8.23.** The *type I* hair cell is embedded in a dendritic process (called a *calyx*) similar in shape to an egg cup. Transmission appears to be chemically mediated across slight indentations, indicated by the small arrows in the drawing. (See **FIGURE 8.23.**) Efferent terminals (apparently cholinergic) synapse on the outside of the calyx, but not on the type I hair cell itself. *Type II* hair cells are not surrounded by a calyx; they synapse with both afferent and efferent terminals. As the figure indicates, hair cells of both types may synapse with branches of the same dendrite. (See **FIGURE 8.23.**)

Each hair cell contains one long *kinocilium* and several *stereocilia,* which decrease in size away from the kinocilium. These cilia are rooted in a cuticular plate. A basal body underlies the kinocilium (indeed, the bare patch above the basal body of the auditory hair cell represents a vestigial kinocilium; during embryological development the auditory receptors possess kinocilia, which later degenerate, leaving the patch). It has been suggested (Flock, 1965; Wërsall, Flock, and Lundquist, 1965) that the orientation of the cilia gives the receptor maximal sensitivity to shearing force in one direction—namely, across the stereocilia, toward the kinocilium. (See **FIGURE 8.23.**)

The hair cells of the crista are all oriented in one direction,

FIGURE 8.23   The two types of vestibular hair cells. (Adapted from Ades, H. W., and Engström, H., Form and innervation in the vestibular epithelia. In *The Role of the Vestibular Organs in the Exploration of Space,* edited by A. Graybill. U.S. Naval School of Medicine: NASA SP-77, 1965.)

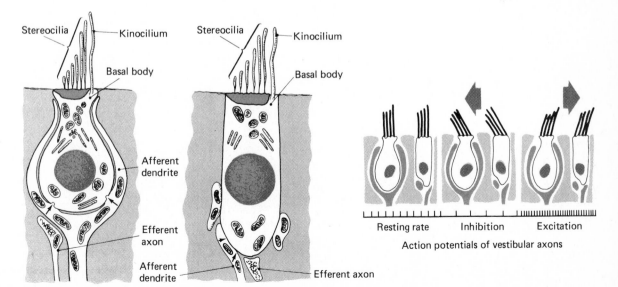

Stereocilia — Kinocilium

Basal body

Afferent dendrite

Efferent axon

Afferent dendrite

Stereocilia — Kinocilium

Basal body

Efferent axon

Resting rate   Inhibition   Excitation

Action potentials of vestibular axons

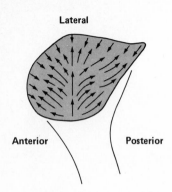

Lateral

Anterior   Posterior

FIGURE 8.24 Hair cells in different regions of the utricle are sensitive to shearing forces in different directions. (Adapted from Flock, Å., *Journal of Cell Biology,* 1964, 22, 413–431.)

and they are thus sensitive to movement of the cupula in one direction. When head rotation causes the cupula to bend toward the utricle, the hair cells are stimulated, which produces an increased firing rate of associated afferent neurons in the *vestibular nerve.* Bending of the cupula in the opposite direction produces a slight decrease in firing rate. Thus, the semicircular canals of the right and left ear together provide information about the magnitude and direction of angular rotation of the head. (See **FIGURE 8.23.**)

The hair cells of the utricle and saccule are oriented in various directions; thus, different groups of hair cells signal different angles of head tilt. (See **FIGURE 8.24.**)

Transduction of Vestibular Information

As we saw in previous sections, the hair cells of the vestibular apparatus apparently produce a receptor potential in response to a shearing force across the cilia, and they pass this information on to the afferent neurons by means of chemical transmission. It is not known how the shearing force produces a receptor potential; it seems likely that the transduction mechanisms of vestibular and auditory hair cells are similar (one can also record microphonics in response to vestibular stimulation).

Origin of the Vestibular Nerve

The vestibular and cochlear nerves constitute the two branches of the eighth cranial nerve (auditory nerve). The bipolar cell bodies that give rise to the afferent fibers of the vestibular nerve are contained in the *vestibular ganglion,* which appears as a nodule on the vestibular nerve. Efferent fibers arise from cell bodies in the *fastigial nucleus* of the cerebellum and the *vestibular nuclei* of the medulla.

Efferent Control from the CNS

The efferent fibers of the vestibular nerve appear to exert an inhibitory effect on the firing rate of the afferent neurons. Activity of these efferents changes during tactile stimulation, somatic movement, and eye movements (Goldberg and Fernandez, 1975), but the role of modulation of receptor activity by the CNS is completely unknown.

SKIN SENSES

The somatosenses are usually divided into two groupings: (1) the skin senses (cutaneous senses) and (2) kinesthesia and organic sensitivity. I shall discuss the skin senses in this section.

The Stimuli

At least three qualities of sensation are received by the skin: pressure, temperature, and pain. This is the minimal number; many investigators class cold and warmth sensitivity separately and distinguish between touch and pressure, for example. The classical method for determining which sensory qualities are detected has been to make a 20 × 20 mm grid on the skin (with a rubber stamp) and test each square separately for sensitivity to various kinds of stimuli produced by pins, hot or cold probes, or fine hairs. Studies such as this indicate that not all squares are sensitive to all stimuli. One square might be sensitive to cold and pain, another to touch alone, another to warmth, touch, and pain, etc. The results suggest that there are independent systems mediating sensitivity to various stimuli. Furthermore, if the squares of skin are stimulated with a small electric spark, the same stimulus gives rise to different sensations in different squares (Bishop, 1943).

I shall divide cutaneous sensation into the three broadest categories—pressure, temperature, and pain—and shall discuss thermoreceptors, mechanoreceptors, and pain receptors (some call them *nociceptors*—"hurt" receptors).

The stimulus that excites thermoreceptors is obvious: temperature (chiefly changes in temperature). Pressure receptors are stimulated by mechanical deformation of the skin. Again, these receptors respond best to changes; mechanoreceptors quickly adapt to constant stimuli of moderate intensity. The stimulus that excites pain receptors has not yet been specified. Pain seems to be elicited by a variety of procedures that produce tissue damage. These procedures might produce a common effect, which then stimulates pain receptors in a similar way, or a variety of mechanisms might transduce the stimuli that cause pain. To further complicate the story, pain can be aroused via almost any sensory modality, if the stimulus is intense enough. This section, however, will deal only with cutaneous pain.

Anatomy of the Skin and Its Receptive Organs

The skin is a complex and vital organ of the body—one that we tend to take for granted. We cannot survive without it; extensive skin burns are fatal. Our cells, which must be bathed by a warm fluid, are protected from the hostile environment by the skin's outer layers. The skin participates in thermoregulation by producing sweat, thus cooling the body, or by restricting its circulation of blood, thus conserving heat. Its appearance varies widely across the body, from mucous membrane to hairy skin to the smooth, hairless skin of the palms and on the soles of the feet.

Skin consists of subcutaneous tissue, dermis, and epidermis, and contains various receptors scattered throughout these layers. Figure 8.25 shows a section through hairy and *glabrous* skin (smooth, hairless skin, such as that of our fingertips and palms). Note that hairy skin is innervated by one type of encapsulated nerve endings, the *Iggo corpuscles*, and by unencapsulated (free) nerve endings. The free nerve endings include the *dermal plexus* (which is shared by hairy and glabrous skin), the basketwork of nerve endings around the hair follicle, and the free nerve endings that terminate around the emergence of the hair from the skin. (See **FIGURE 8.25.**)

Glabrous skin, however, contains both free nerve endings and axons that terminate within specialized end organs. Over the years, investigators have described a large number of cutaneous receptors, but subsequent research has shown many of them to be *artefacts* of the staining process used to reveal the microscopic structure of the skin. (Artefact means "made by art"—hence artificially introduced, not normally existing in the tissue.) Other specialized end organs have been shown to be variants of a single form, changing shape as a function of age. Sinclair (1967) suggests that there are really only four organized endings found in glabrous skin.

Pacinian corpuscles are the largest sensory end organs in the body. They are found in glabrous skin, external genitalia, mammary glands, and various internal organs. These receptors consist of series of onionlike layers wrapped around the terminal of a myelinated fiber. (See **FIGURE 8.25.**) They are especially sensitive to touch, their axons giving a burst of responses when the capsule is moved relative to the fiber. The inside of the corpuscle is filled with a viscous substance that offers some resistance to the movement of the nerve ending inside. This construction gives the Pacinian corpuscle peculiar response characteristics, as we shall see later.

Meissner's corpuscles are smaller than Pacinian corpuscles. They are found in the papillae, which are small elevations of the dermis that project up into the epidermis. These end organs are innervated by several axons, unlike the Pacinian corpuscles, each of which contains a single nerve fiber. (See **FIGURE 8.25.**)

Merkel's disks are found in the same locations as Meissner's corpuscles. The disks are single, flattened epithelial cells, each lying in close proximity to the terminal branches of an axon. (See **FIGURE 8.25.**)

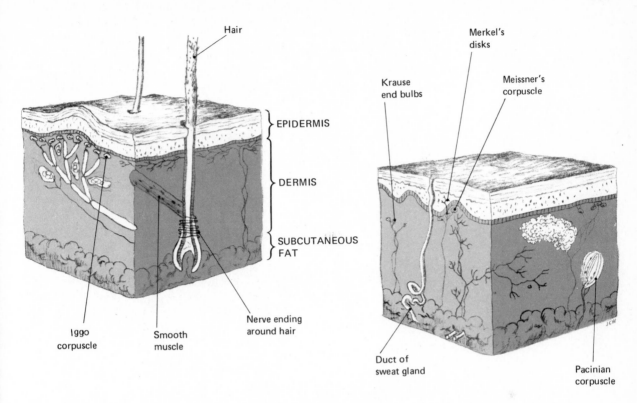

Hair

Merkel's disks

Krause end bulbs

Meissner's corpuscle

EPIDERMIS

DERMIS

SUBCUTANEOUS FAT

Iggo corpuscle

Smooth muscle

Nerve ending around hair

Duct of sweat gland

Pacinian corpuscle

FIGURE 8.25   Schematic sections through hairy and glabrous (smooth) skin.

Krause end bulbs are found in *mucocutaneous zones*—the junctions between mucous membrane and dry skin, such as the edge of the lips, eyelids, glans penis, and clitoris. They consist of loops of unmyelinated fibers similar in appearance to balls of yarn. Each end bulb represents two to six fibers. (See **FIGURE 8.25.**)

Transduction of Cutaneous Stimulation

Many unsuccessful attempts have been made to relate receptor type to sensory quality. It would seem logical to assign a particular function to a particular receptor—and many texts still do—but there does not appear to be a consistent relationship between stimulus and receptive end organ. Hairy skin, for example, contains only free nerve endings and Iggo corpuscles, but it can detect the same sensory qualities as glabrous skin, with all of its specialized terminal structures. (The sensitivities of these areas differ considerably, of course.)   Furthermore, affected areas of the skin of people afflicted with *psoriasis* (a congenital skin disease) show gross changes in sensory innervation without accompanying changes in cutaneous sensitivity.

TEMPERATURE. Thermal receptors are difficult to study, since changes in temperature alter metabolic activity, and also rate of axonal firing, of a variety of cells. For example, a receptor that responds to pressure might produce varying amounts of activity in response to the same mechanical stimulus, depending upon the temperature. Nevertheless, investigators have recently identified cold receptors as being small myelinated axons that branch into unmyelinated fibers in the upper layer of the dermis (Hensel, 1974). Warmth receptors have not been anatomically identified, and so far, the transduction of temperature changes into rate of axonal firing has not been explained.

An ingenious experiment by Bazett, McGlone, Williams, and Lufkin (1932) showed long ago that receptors for warmth and cold lie at different depths in the skin. The investigators lifted the prepuce (foreskin) of uncircumsized males with dull fish hooks. They applied thermal stimuli on one side of the folded skin and recorded the rate at which the temperature changes were transmitted through the skin by placing small temperature sensors on the opposite side. They then correlated these observations with verbal reports of warmth and coolness. The investigators concluded that cold receptors were close to the skin and that warmth receptors were located deeper in the tissue. (This experiment shows the extremities to which scientists will go to obtain information—pun intended.)

PRESSURE. Pressure sensitivity appears to be related to movement of the skin. The skin is sensitive only to deformation, or bending, and not to pressure exerted evenly across its surface. For example, if you dipped your finger into a pool of mercury, pressure would be exerted on all portions of your skin below the surface of the liquid. Nevertheless, you would feel only a ring of sensation, at the air/mercury junction. This is the only part of the skin that is bent, and it is here that skin receptors are stimulated. (Since mercury is quite poisonous if it enters a break in the skin, please do not try this demonstration—just imagine it.)

Mechanical pressure appears to be transduced by a variety of receptors, both encapsulated and unencapsulated. The best-studied one is the Pacinian corpuscle. This organ responds to bending, relative to the axon that enters it. If the onionlike layers are dissected away (Loewenstein and Rathkamp, 1958), this receptor still responds to bending of the naked axon; thus, the transducer is the terminal itself. The generator potential that is produced is proportional to the degree of bending. If the threshold of excitation is exceeded, an action potential is produced at the first node of Ranvier. Loewenstein and Mendelson (1965) have shown that the layers of the corpuscle alter the mechanical characteristics of the organ, so that the axon responds briefly when the intact organ is bent and again when it is released.

We do not know how bending of the tip of the nerve ending in a Pacinian corpuscle produces a generator potential. Presumably, the bending changes membrane permeability, and the resulting flow of the ions across the membrane alters its potential. It is tempting to speculate that membrane "pores" are somehow enlarged as a result of this bending and stretching of the membrane. It is not known whether other mechanoreceptors operate on the principle followed by the ending within the Pacinian corpuscles. Most investigators assume that they do, and that the encapsulated endings serve only to modify the physical stimulus transduced by a portion of the neuron itself.

A special form of mechanoreception is produced by the bending of a hair. As was seen in Figure 8.25, there is a basketlike nerve ending around the base of the hair, and there are also free nerve endings near the location where the hair emerges from the skin. The basketlike endings seem to be less sensitive to hair movement. Stetson (1923) glued the hair to the skin at its point of emergence, so that movement of the hair stimulated only the deeper nerve endings. (To visualize this, picture the hair as an oar. The glue made the skin stiff and served as an oarlock; movement of the hair "rowed" the base of it through the underlying layers of skin.) Under these conditions, the hair could be moved quite a bit before giving rise to sensation. Conversely, an artificial hair glued to the skin worked as well as a real one (as far as tactile sensitivity goes), suggesting that normal sensitivity to touch in hairy areas is mediated by free nerve endings near the surface.

PAIN. The story of pain is quite different from that of temperature and pressure; the analysis of this sensation is extremely difficult. It is obvious that our awareness of pain and our emotional reaction to it depend on central factors. We can, for example, have a tooth removed painlessly while under hypnosis, which has no effect on stimulation of pain fibers. I shall deal with pain in greater detail in a later chapter on reward and punishment (chapter 17); here I shall consider only the peripheral aspects of pain.

Most investigators identify pain reception with the networks of free nerve endings in the skin. Pain appears to be produced by a variety of procedures that produce tissue damage. Most investigators believe that the damage leads to an increase in some extracellular substance that stimulates pain fibers. Many substances can be injected into the skin to produce pain, and a variety of them have been proposed as candidates for the role of chemical mediator of pain. (The usual procedure for testing chemically mediated pain nowadays is to produce a blister with *cantharides*—spanish fly—and then to pick off the top of the blister and treat the raw skin with the chemical to be tested.) A good relationship between intensity of pain and concentration of the potassium ion has been observed (Keele, 1966). This is of significance because tissue damage produces an extracellular increase in K^+ concentration. Other investigators have noted that pain is also produced by a low pH level (acidic solution), and by histamine, acetylcholine, and serotonin (Sinclair, 1967). The chemical mediator has not yet been identified; the nature of the substance, when identified, should suggest the means of sensory transduction. (There could, of course, be more than one mediator.)

Route of Somatosensory Fibers to the CNS

Somatosensory fibers enter the CNS via spinal and cranial (principally the *trigeminal*, or fifth) nerves. The cell bodies of these unipolar neurons are located in the dorsal root ganglia and cranial nerve ganglia.

Efferent Control from the CNS

There do not appear to be any efferent mechanisms that specifically alter responsiveness of cutaneous receptors. Changes in peripheral blood flow, sweating, and piloerection could, of course, alter the firing patterns of receptors to the appropriate stimuli, and touching and feeling an object obviously involve motor mechanisms as much as sensory mechanisms. There are, however, no direct efferents to the receptors themselves, in contrast to what we have seen in the case of other sense modalities.

KINESTHESIA AND ORGANIC SENSITIVITY

We are aware of the position and movement of limbs of our body, and we certainly can detect when our intestines are swollen with gas, or when a kidney stone passes through a ureter. And we know when our bladders are full. Kinesthesia (literally, "movement sensation") generally refers to appreciation of both movement and position of the limbs, whereas organic sensitivity refers to feelings received from internal organs.

The Stimuli

Stretch receptors in skeletal muscles report changes in muscle length to the CNS, and stretch receptors in tendons measure the force being exerted by the muscles. Receptors within joints between adjacent bones respond to the magnitude and direction of limb movement. The muscle length detectors (sensory endings on the *intrafusal muscle fibers*) do not give rise to conscious sensations; their information is used in motor control systems. These receptors will be discussed separately in chapter 10. Organic sensitivity is provided via receptors in the linings of muscles, outer layers of the gastrointestinal system and other internal organs, and linings of the abdominal and thoracic cavities. Many of these tissues are sensitive only to stretch and do not report sensations when cut, burned, or crushed. In addition, the stomach and esophagus are responsive to heat and cold and to some chemicals.

Anatomy of the Organs and Their Receptive Cells

A schematic view of a skeletal muscle is shown in **FIGURE 8.26.** Four kinds of information are received by muscle and tendon afferents.

    1. The sensory endings on the intrafusal muscle fibers signal muscle length.

FIGURE 8.26   A skeletal muscle and its sense receptors. (Adapted from Bloom and Fawcett, *A Textbook of Histology*. Philadelphia: W. B. Saunders, 1968.)

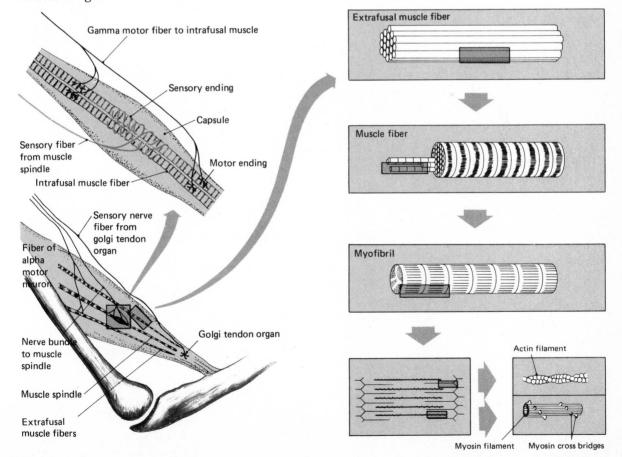

2. The sensory endings within the *Golgi tendon organ* at the muscle/tendon junction respond to tension exerted by the muscle on the tendon.

3. The membranous covering of the muscle (*fascia*) contains Pacinian corpuscles. These receptors apparently signal deep pressure exerted upon muscles, which can be felt even if the overlying cutaneous receptors are anesthetized or denervated.

4. Throughout the muscle and its overlying fascia are distributed free nerve endings, which generally follow the blood supply. These receptors presumably signal pain that accompanies prolonged exertion or muscle cramps.

The tissue that lines the joints contains free nerve endings and encapsulated receptors, such as Pacinian corpuscles. The encapsulated endings presumably mediate sensitivity to joint movement and position, while stimulation of the free nerve endings produces pain (such as that which accompanies arthritis).

Pacinian corpuscles and free nerve endings are also found in the outer layers of various internal organs and give rise to organic sensations.

Transduction of Kinesthetic and Organic Information

The mechanoreceptors and pain receptors are similar to those found in the skin; presumably, they transduce sensory information in similar ways.

Route of Kinesthetic and Organic Afferent Fibers to the CNS

The cell bodies of the receptors reside within the dorsal root ganglia or cranial nerve ganglia. Kinesthetic fibers are carried in the same nerves that convey motor fibers to the skeletal muscles. Organic sensitivity, however, is conveyed over fibers that travel with efferents of the autonomic nervous system and thus pass (without synapsing) through the autonomic ganglia on their way to the CNS. In general, pain is conveyed via afferents that accompany sympathetic fibers, whereas nonpainful stimuli are transmitted via nerves containing parasympathetic afferents.

Efferent Control from the CNS

The kinesthetic receptors described in this section respond to the effects of CNS motor outflow (by definition), and organic sensitivity is modified by activity of the gastrointestinal system, for example. There does not appear to be any direct control of these receptors by efferent fibers. The role of CNS feedback in the intrafusal muscle fiber system is described in chapter 10.

GUSTATION

So far, we have been studying stimuli with physical energy: thermal, photic, or kinetic. The stimuli received by the last two senses to be studied, gustation and olfaction, do not, in any obvious way, transmit energy to the receptors.

The Stimuli

For a substance to be tasted, molecules of it must dissolve in the saliva and stimulate the taste receptors on the tongue. Tastes of different substances vary, but much less than we generally realize. There are only four qualities of taste: bitter, sour, sweet, and salty. Much of the flavor of good steak depends on its odor; to an *anosmic* person (lacking the sense of smell) or to a person whose nostrils are stopped up, an onion tastes like an apple, a steak like salty cardboard.

Anatomy of the Taste Buds and Gustatory Cells

The tongue, palate, pharynx, and larynx contain approximately 10,000 taste buds. Most of these receptive organs are arranged around *papillae*, small protuberances of the tongue. Papillae are surrounded by moatlike trenches that serve to trap saliva. The taste buds (approximately 200 of them, for the larger papillae) surround the trenches, and their pores open into them. Figure 8.27 shows a cross section through a taste bud opening into a trench in the tongue. (See **FIGURE 8.27.**)

Individual papillae can be examined by placing a small glass tube over them and applying gentle suction, turning them inside out (von Békésy, 1964). Von Békésy found that electrical or chemical stimulation produced only a single sensation, and he concluded that each papilla is specific for one of the four taste qualities. However, Bealer and Smith (1975) later found that one-third of the papillae tested produced responses to stimuli of all four taste qualities.

Taste receptor cells are not neurons; they are specialized cells that synapse with dendrites of sensory neurons. The receptor cells possess hairlike processes that project through the pores of the taste

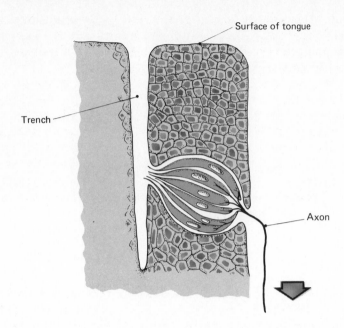

Surface of tongue

Trench

Axon

FIGURE 8.27 A taste bud. (Adapted from Woodworth, R. S., *Psychology*, ed. 4, New York: Holt, 1940.)

bud into the trench adjacent to the papilla. It was previously thought that there were two types of cells in the taste buds, receptors and *sustentacular* (supporting) *cells*, but it has been shown that the various shapes of cells represent different portions of the life process of a receptor cell. Gustatory receptors have a life-span of only ten days. They quickly wear out, being directly exposed to a rather hostile environment. As they degenerate, they are replaced by newly developed cells; the dendrite of the sensory fiber is somehow passed on to the new cell (Beidler, 1970). The presence of vesicles within the cytoplasm of the receptor cell around the synaptic region suggests that transmission at this synapse is by chemical means.

Transduction of Gustatory Information

It seems most likely that transduction of taste is accomplished by means of a process similar to chemical transmission at synapses: some characteristic of the stimulus molecule is "recognized" by the receptor, and it produces changes in membrane permeability and subsequent receptor potentials. Attempts have been made to specify the molecular characteristics that stimulate different types of receptors, thus determining taste.

Acids, in general, are sour. The lower the pH, the more sour the taste. To taste salty, a substance must ionize. Salty substances contain such metallic cations as Na^+, K^+, and Li^+, with a halogen or other small anion (Cl^-, Br^-, SO_4^{--}, NO_3^-, etc.). As the salt molecules begin to get larger, they begin to taste bitter (e.g., sodium acetate). Bitter substances are difficult to characterize. They tend to be large molecules and to contain nitrogen. Various alkaloids (e.g., quinine) impart a bitter taste. Sweet substances tend to be moderately large, nonionizing, organic molecules. Like the salts, as they grow larger, they tend to elicit sensations of bitterness along with sweetness (e.g., saccharine). Dzendolet (1968) has suggested a common characteristic of sweet substances, a molecular arrangement that makes them hydrogen ion acceptors. Removal of hydrogen ions from the receptor sites presumably stimulates the sensation of sweetness.

Obviously, since we do not understand precisely which molecular structures are associated with taste qualities, we are a long way from understanding the mechanism of transduction of gustatory stimuli.

Route of Gustatory Fibers to the Brain

The cell bodies that give rise to afferent fibers are located in the ganglia of the seventh (facial), ninth (glossopharyngeal), and tenth (vagus) nerve. Taste buds on the anterior two-thirds of the tongue synapse with fibers of the *chorda tympani,* a division of the facial nerve. (This nerve passes through the middle ear, and can be recorded from or stimulated electrically. Recordings have even been taken from this nerve during the course of human ear operations.) Fibers of the glossopharyngeal nerve serve the posterior third of the tongue, while branches of the vagus nerve innervate the pharynx and larynx.

Efferent Control from the CNS

Some investigators suspect that there might be efferent synapses on taste receptors, but these suggestions are quite tentative (Murray and Murray, 1970). There is no evidence for a mechanism of efferent control of taste receptors.

OLFACTION

The Stimulus

It is easy to give a superficial description of the stimulus for odor—molecules of those substances that are volatile (i.e., that evaporate at a reasonable temperature) and can dissolve in the mucus that coats the olfactory epithelium. A more specific description is a different matter. As we shall see, it is much more difficult to explain, on a molecular basis, why different substances have different odors.

Anatomy of the Olfactory Apparatus

Our olfactory receptors reside within two patches of mucous membrane (*olfactory epithelium*), each having an area of about one square inch. The olfactory epithelium is located at the top of the nasal cavity as shown in **FIGURE 8.28.** Air entering the nostrils is swept upward (especially when we sniff at an odor) by action of the *turbinate bones* and reaches the sensory receptors.

The *olfactory bulb*, an enlargement on the end of the olfactory (first cranial) nerve, lies at the base of the brain, just above the bony *cribriform plate*. The olfactory receptors communicate with the ol-

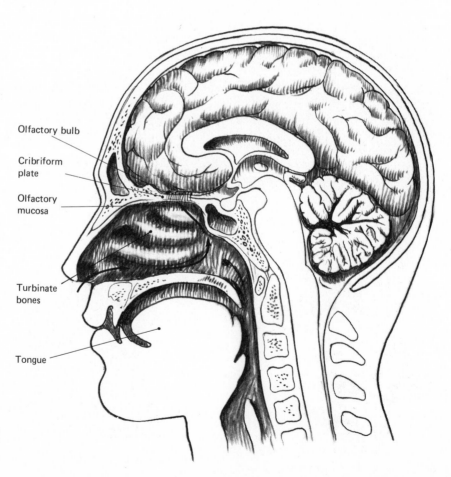

Olfactory bulb

Cribriform plate

Olfactory mucosa

Turbinate bones

Tongue

FIGURE 8.28 A schematic representation of the olfactory bulb and olfactory mucosa.

factory bulbs via groups of axons that pass through the numerous small holes in the cribriform plate. Afferent fibers from the trigeminal nerve also terminate here, in the form of free nerve endings, and presumably mediate pain in response to noxious chemical stimulation.

Anatomy of the Olfactory Receptors

Figure 8.29 illustrates a group of olfactory receptors, along with the sustentacular cells that support them. (See **FIGURE 8.29.**) The receptors are cell bodies of neurons, and they give rise to the axons that pass through the cribriform plate to the olfactory bulb. The receptors possess numerous cilia, which project from the surface of the mucosa. It is assumed that primary reception of the odor molecules takes place on these cilia.

Transduction of Olfactory Information

The means by which odor molecules produce generator potentials is a complete mystery. Apparently, there are receptor sites on the cilia that are stimulated by odor molecules. Figure 8.30 shows the relative size of a cross section through an olfactory cilium and of a camphor molecule, indicated by a dot. We can see that the process of trans-

FIGURE 8.29   The olfactory receptors. (Adapted from de Lorenzo, A. J., Studies on the ultrastructure and histophysiology of all membranes, nerve fibers, and synaptic junctions in chemoreceptors. In *Olfaction and Taste*, edited by Y. Zotterman. New York: Macmillan, 1963.)

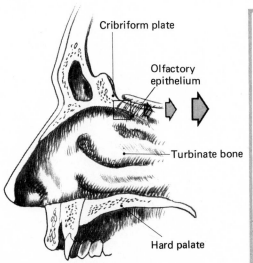

Cribriform plate

Olfactory epithelium

Turbinate bone

Hard palate

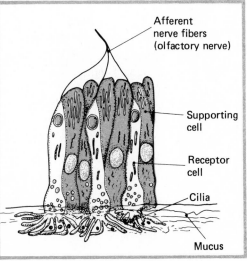

Afferent nerve fibers (olfactory nerve)

Supporting cell

Receptor cell

Cilia

Mucus

Cross section of olfactory cilium

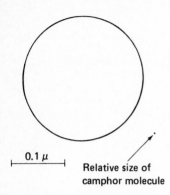

0.1 μ

Relative size of camphor molecule

FIGURE 8.30 Relative sizes of the cross section through an olfactory cilium and a camphor molecule.

duction must be quite subtle, involving molecular events. (See **FIGURE 8.30.**) Information is propagated down the cilia to the cell body, and ultimately to the axon, where generator potentials are translated into altered rates of firing. Information transfer down the cilia might be electrical, or it might even be mechanical. Cilia are known to be motile (e.g., the cilia of cells lining the respiratory tracts, the cilia and flagella of bacteria and sperm cells) and their motility and stiffness vary as a function of changes in ionic concentrations.

Origin of Olfactory Nerve Fibers

The axons of the olfactory receptors do not enter the olfactory nerve. Instead, they synapse with the dendrites of *mitral cells* in the olfactory bulbs, in the complex axonic and dendritic arborizations called *olfactory glomeruli*. The axons of the mitral cells then enter the olfactory nerve. Some axons synapse in the brain, whereas others cross the brain, enter the other olfactory nerve, and synapse in the contralateral olfactory bulb.

The olfactory bulbs are much more than bumps on the olfactory nerves. They contain a considerable amount of neural circuitry and receive efferent fibers from the brain. A good deal of sensory integration undoubtedly takes place in the olfactory bulb. The nature of this integration, however, is not known.

Efferent Control from the CNS

Efferent fibers from several locations in the brain enter the olfactory bulbs. The synapses of these fibers appear to be inhibitory, but their role in the processing of olfactory information is a mystery.

The brain also controls the effects of olfactory stimuli in a more obvious way: we can sniff the air, maximizing the exposure of our olfactory epithelium to the odor molecules, or we can pinch our nostrils and breathe through the mouth, thus producing minimal olfactory stimulation.

SUGGESTED READINGS

GELDARD, F. A. *The Human Senses*, ed. 2. New York: John Wiley & Sons, 1972.

UTTAL, R. W. *The Psychobiology of Sensory Coding.* New York: Harper & Row, 1973.

These two references cover all the senses. Geldard's book contains more information about *psychophysics* (the study of the relationship between physical events and sensation), whereas Uttal emphasizes neural coding. If you read these two books, you will become well versed in sensory psychology and sensory physiology.

DAVSON, H. *The Physiology of the Eye*, ed. 3. New York: Academic Press, 1972.

GULICK, W. L. *Hearing: Physiology and Psychophysics.* New York: Oxford University Press, 1971.

These books contain more detailed information about the eye and the ear. Gulick's book contains excellent illustrations (some of which served as models for figures in this chapter).

Sensory Coding

9

In the previous chapter we saw how environmental events produce generator or receptor potentials, with subsequent changes in firing rates of afferent neurons of the spinal and cranial nerves. In this chapter I shall describe how various features of the environment—for example, shape, color, and brightness of visual forms, pitch and loudness of sounds—are coded into particular spatial and temporal patterns of neural firing, and how this coded information is transmitted to the cortex.

The concept of *sensory coding* deserves some discussion. A code consists of a set of rules whereby information may be transformed from one set of symbols into another. The different forms a message takes as it gets translated by various coding rules need not resemble each other. Spatial differences in the original messages may be represented by temporal differences, temporal differences by spatial ones. Graphs, such as the ones I used in chapters 3 and 4, represent the use of spatial coding to portray a variety of dimensions; a graph of the action potential uses two spatial dimensions to represent (a) the electrical charge across the membrane and (b) time. As long as we know the rules of the transformations (and these are given by the labels on the axes), we can reconstruct the event represented by the graph.

To illustrate further: a written message might be given to the first of several people standing in a line. That person could read the message in Spanish to the second, who would say it in English to the third, who would convey it via semaphore signals to the fourth, who might tell the fifth person, "The message is Hamlet's soliloquy." Up to the fourth person, the representation of the message was transformed in reasonably simple ways. Transmission between the fourth and fifth person did not resemble previous transmissions; the coding used here relied on the fact that the fourth and fifth people were each familiar with Hamlet's soliloquy. As we shall see, it is possible that some elements of the sensory system "learn" frequently perceived stimulus complexes; the subsequent presence of these stimuli can then be represented more simply, by the activity of these elements.

At the level of the receptor, sensory events can be represented in a graded manner. The cochlear microphonic, for example, encodes auditory information perfectly, with all its nuances. A single axon, on the other hand, has a one-letter alphabet available to it. It can transmit an action potential or it can remain silent. In order to transmit information more complicated than presence or absence of a given stimulus, the axon must use the only available dimension, time. Intensity of stimulation, for instance, can be encoded by rate of neural firing.

When we consider a large number of neurons, we can see another way in which information can be encoded. Stimulus intensity, transformed into a temporal code (rate of firing) by a single neuron, can be represented spatially by a number of neurons. For example, if receptors were individually tuned to respond selectively to particular intensities of the stimulus, we would be able to determine the magnitude of the sensory event by noting the location of the active receptor. The nervous system thus has available to it only these two basic formats in which to represent information: *spatial coding* and *temporal coding*. Spatial coding is often referred to as *line-specific coding*; activity of a given line (chain of neurons from the receptor organ to the brain) represents a particular intensity, quality, or location of the stimulus.

Temporal codes can be much more complicated than rate. Any complex message capable of being put into words can be transmitted via Morse code, for instance. And most computers communicate with remote instruments such as teletypewriters and display consoles, and even other computers, by means of temporal pulse codes transmitted on a single line. These mechanical devices use patterns of pulses, rather than mere rate, to represent information. The pulses represent successive *bits* (binary digits) of information, which in turn represent numbers or letters. For example, if the letter B is represented by the *bit pattern* 00110001, we could just as well signal the zeros and ones with the absence and presence of electrical pulses at the appropriate times. The pattern 00110001 would be transmitted as a short pause (two units long), two pulses, a longer pause (three units long), and another pulse. Of course, the receiving device would have to know when the message started, and it would need some kind of clock to measure the interval between pulses to determine how many missing pulses (zeros) there were.

The nervous system might use temporal codes of similar complexity to represent sensory information. And spatial codes could be much more complex than "which neuron is firing?"; the stimulus could be represented by patterns of activity across many thousands of neurons. Perkel and Bullock (1968) list a number of ways in which the nervous system could code sensory information. They call these *"candidate neural codes."* If we find that some complex aspect of neuronal firing is related to a stimulus dimension, we have not necessarily identified a neural code. The relationship could be an *epiphenomenon,* spuriously introduced by the process of producing the real code.

The only way to find out whether a candidate code is actually one used by the nervous system is to see whether it conveys information that ultimately affects the behavior of the organism. The following analogy should make this point clear. It has been observed that porpoises and other marine mammals can produce a huge repertoire of complex sounds. Are these sounds used for communication? Do they encode information? Studies performed on a single porpoise could not answer these questions; they could do no more than establish "candidate codes." We might find that particular sounds were associated with feeding, or play, or frustration, etc. But unless we established that these sounds subsequently affected the behavior of other porpoises, we would not have shown them to be a means of communication. Similarly, what a given neuron, or group of neurons, says in response to stimulus changes does not provide enough information to establish a neural code. We must also show that other neurons are "listening" to that message. As you might imagine, very few neural codes have been established in such a way.

Another problem we encounter when we consider sensory coding is the identification of the ultimate destination of the information. Where does the message go? For simple organisms, or for simple reflex activity in more complex organisms, we can follow the message right out to the effectors. The stimulus elicits activity in a chain of neurons beginning at a set of receptors and ending at a set of effectors. Very often, however, the stimulus produces no immediate effect on behavior, but instead results in some unobservable internal changes that manifest themselves in behavior much later. Obviously, we have now entered the domain of memory. But where, anatomically, did we enter that domain? And what neurons are responsible for our *experience* of this stimulus? Most scientists investigating the transmission of sensory information would consider their task complete when they had described the nature of the message as it appears in sensory cortex. As Uttal puts it:

> ... there really is no requirement for any decoding of the message at its destination. We certainly do not know what aspects of neural action are identifiable ... with experience, but it seems almost certain that all that is required is that there *exist* some representation of the pattern at some appropriately high level of the nervous system. (Uttal, 1973, p. 208)

Uttal's position seems reasonable. Obviously, the human nervous system gives rise to conscious experience, but since we have no idea how to explain this very private phenomenon, we must, by default, identify experience of a stimulus with its cortical representation. We must be careful not to seek for a decoder that looks at this representation and interprets the pattern. If we do so, we commit the error of looking for a *homunculus*, a "little man" who resides in our heads, looking at, and interpreting, the activity of cortical neurons the way we might look at a display panel of some piece of complex machinery. Experience must be recognized as an emergent property of the nervous system. Arrival of coded sensory information— somewhere in the brain—*is* the experience itself.

With this discussion concluded, let us move to something more concrete—a description of the ascending sensory pathways and a summary of the sensory codes that have been identified so far. Most of these codes express relationships between stimulus parameters and neural events; therefore, they must still be regarded as candidate codes.

VISION

Spatial Representation in the Ascending Visual Pathway

The best word to describe the first level of analysis of the retinal image would be mosaic. Literally, a *mosaic* is a picture consisting of a large number of discrete elements—bits of glass or ceramic, for example. The lens of the eye casts an image of the environment on the retinal photoreceptors, and these receptors each code their small portion of the image by responding at a rate that is related to local photic intensity. The photoreceptors are not connected to the ganglion cells (whose axons transmit visual information over the optic nerves) on a one-to-one basis. At the periphery of the retina, many individual receptors (mostly rods) converge on a single ganglion cell. Foveal vision is more direct, with a ganglion cell receiving information from only one or a few cones. These receptor-to-axon relationships accord very well with the fact that our foveal (central) vision is most acute, and our peripheral vision much less precise. In a sense, the pieces constituting the matrix get larger as one goes from fovea to periphery, and the image transmitted to the brain becomes correspondingly cruder.

The retina also contains a considerable amount of circuitry that encodes the visual information in a more complex way. The ganglion cells do more than signal local light intensity, as the photoreceptors do. The activity of these cells is modified by complex spatial and temporal aspects of the visual stimulus. Before we examine the nature of this level of coding, however, we should become acquainted with the anatomy of the ascending visual system.

The route from optic nerve to cortex is the simplest pathway of all the sense modalities. The axons of the retinal ganglion cells ascend via the optic nerves (which become the optic tracts as they enter the brain) to the lateral geniculate nucleus of the thalamus. The terminals of these axons synapse on cells of the lateral geniculate nucleus, which in turn send their axons via the *optic radiations* to visual cortex, that region surrounding the *calcarine fissure* (*calcarine,* "spur-shaped") at the most posterior region of the cerebrum.

Ignoring for a moment the complexities of coding that take place in the retina, we find that the visual system maintains the spatial code seen on the retinal mosaic all the way up to visual cortex. There is a *retinotopic* representation on the cortex. That is, a given region of the retina excites a given set of cells in visual cortex, and adjacent retinal regions excite adjacent cortical areas. This topographic representation appears to be a real sensory code. If a two-dimensional array of electrodes is placed over human visual cortex, the person will report "seeing" geometric shapes that correspond to the pattern of electrodes stimulated (Dobelle, Mladejovsky, and Girvin, 1974). This study was carried out on peripherally blinded people to ascertain the feasibility of providing visual prostheses. (A *prosthesis,* literally "addition," is an artificial device made to take the place of a missing or damaged part of the body.) Unfortunately, long-term electrical stimulation results in tissue damage and this fact rules out the use of such man-made replacement parts in the immediate future. Some other way will have to be found to stimulate cortical neurons. Further evidence for the reality of the spatial code on the surface of the cortex comes from the fact that damage to restricted regions of visual cortex produces specific blindness for corresponding portions of the visual receptive field. (It is interesting to note that the brain "fills in" these *scotomas* the way it fills in the blind spot caused by the exit of the optic nerve from the eye. People are often not aware of small scotomas until they are carefully tested for.)

The retinal surface is not represented on visual cortex in a linear fashion; the picture is much distorted. It is as if you printed a picture on a sheet of rubber and stretched it in various directions. The center of the sheet is stretched the most—foveal vision, with its great acuity, takes up approximately 25 percent of visual cortex.

Let us now examine the ascending visual system in more detail. Figure 9.1 illustrates a diagrammatic view of the human brain as observed from below. The optic nerves join together at the base of the brain to form the *optic chiasm* (*khiasma*, "cross"). There, axons from ganglion cells serving the inner halves of the retina (the nasal sides) cross through the chiasm and ascend to the lateral geniculate nucleus of the opposite side of the brain. (See **FIGURE 9.1.**) The lens inverts the image of the world projected on the retina (and similarly reverses left and right). Therefore, the *decussation* (crossing) of axons representing the nasal retinal fields results in a separate representation of each half of the visual field, divided vertically, in the lateral geniculate nucleus of the opposite side of the brain. (See **FIGURE 9.1.**) Each lateral geniculate nucleus then projects in a straightforward manner to the ipsilateral visual cortex; as a matter of fact, the lateral geniculate nuclei are the only subcortical afferents of primary visual cortex of primates. Since there is a considerable amount of overlap in the visual fields of our eyes, this means that many cortical regions receive information about the same point in the visual field from both eyes.

Besides the retino-geniculate-visual cortex system just described, there is another one, involving the superior colliculi. Some fibers in the optic tracts *bifurcate* (fork into two branches), sending axons via the *retinotectal tract* to the superior colliculus. *Secondary visual cortex*, which surrounds primary visual cortex, receives visual information by means of a system of fibers from the superior colliculi to posterior thalamus to cortex. Furthermore, both primary and secondary visual cortex send axons back to the lateral geniculate and to the superior colliculi.

Coding of Intensity

The eye is a remarkably sensitive organ, responding to an incredible range of stimulus intensity. The smallest stimulus that can be detected is much less than one-millionth the intensity of the brightest light to which the eye can be exposed without damage. Obviously, then, this range of brightness cannot be faithfully represented by neural firing rate. A neuron cannot vary its firing rate by a factor of more than a million. The upper limit of most neurons is less than 1000 impulses per second. One-millionth that rate would be one

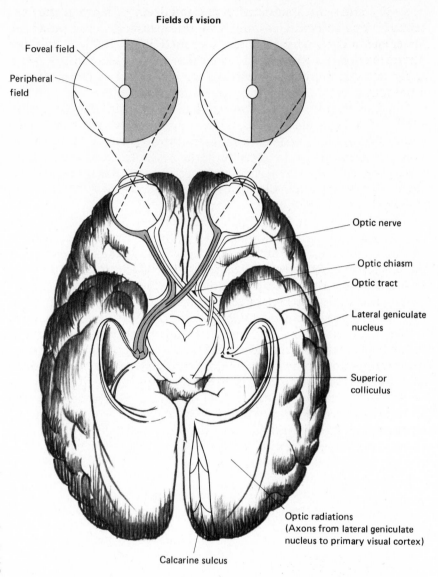

Fields of vision

Foveal field

Peripheral field

Optic nerve

Optic chiasm

Optic tract

Lateral geniculate nucleus

Superior colliculus

Optic radiations (Axons from lateral geniculate nucleus to primary visual cortex)

Calcarine sulcus

FIGURE 9.1 The primary visual pathways. (Adapted with permission from McGraw-Hill Book Co. from *The Human Nervous System*, 2nd edition, by Noback and Demarest. Copyright © 1975, by McGraw-Hill, Inc.)

action potential every 1⅔ minutes—a rate so slow as to be meaningless. Therefore, photic intensity must be represented in a *nonlinear* fashion by firing rate. Figure 9.2 illustrates the relationship between light intensity and the amplitude of the generator potential produced by the photoreceptive cells in the eye of the *Limulus* (horseshoe crab). You can easily see that the curve in this figure is not at all linear: changes in intensity of the light stimulus at the upper end of the scale produce hardly any alterations in the amplitude of the generator potential. The receptors are much more sensitive to changes at the lower end of the brightness scale. (See **FIGURE 9.2.**) This nonlinear responsiveness represents a compression of information. A large range of stimulus intensity is represented by a smaller range of amplitude.

The range of intensity information in the primate eye (and in the eye of most other mammals) is extended by the existence of two types of receptors. Rods can detect light at levels of brightness too dim for cones to respond to. Intensity is thus represented by the firing rate of two populations of receptors. For the visual system, then, spatial (line-specific) coding, as well as temporal coding (rate), is used to represent intensity.

As one passes from the photoreceptors to the ganglion cell layer of the retina, one finds that few cells respond in a simple way to the amount of light falling on a small portion of the retina. A small percentage of cells respond in a simple fashion to overall brightness, but most cells respond to particular *features* of the retinal image (DeValois, 1965). Psychologically, absolute brightness (except at the extremes of the range) is not an important variable. We tend to adapt to the overall level of illumination and judge various portions of the visual field as to their relative brightness. A white piece of paper seen in dim light appears to us to be brighter than a piece of gray paper seen in brighter light, even though the intensity of light being reflected from the gray paper might be greater. We should not be surprised that most cells of our visual system generally exhibit a similar disregard for overall brightness.

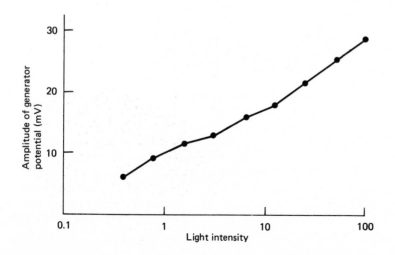

FIGURE 9.2 The relationship between light intensity and the generator potential in the eye of the horseshoe crab. (Adapted from Fuortes, M. G. F., *American Journal of Ophthalmology*, 1958, 46, 210–223.)

Receptive Fields and Feature Detection

I have described the fact that spatial relationships of the retinal mosaic are maintained in the lateral geniculate nucleus and visual cortex. The representation is not in the form of simple dots. Research has shown that individual cells respond to more complex features of the retinal image. The portion of the visual field to which a given cell responds is defined as the cell's *receptive field*. The identification of a cell's receptive field is accomplished by a procedure called *mapping*. The animal is anesthetized and a screen is placed in front of it. Recordings of action potentials are taken from single neurons while a small spot is moved around on the screen. (Sometimes a small spot of light is shone directly on the retina.) The receptive field is defined as the area of the screen (or retina) in which the stimulus elicits a response from the cell. Response merely means change in rate of firing; information is coded just as well by a decreased rate of firing as it is by an increased rate.

RECEPTIVE FIELDS IN THE RETINA. Kuffler (1953), recording from ganglion cells in the retina of the cat, first discovered the basic type of receptive field that has been shown to exist in the mammalian retina. He found that the receptive field consists of a roughly circular center, surrounded by a ring. In his experiments, cells responded in opposite manner to the two regions. A spot of light presented to the central field produced a burst of unit activity. When the spot was presented to the surrounding field, no response was detected, but the cell fired vigorously for a while when the spot of light was turned off. The cell thus responded in a center-on, surround-off manner. Subsequent investigations (e.g., Rodieck and Stone, 1965a) have also identified cells that give a contrary center-off, surround-on response. Simultaneous presentation of a stimulus to both center and surround gives no response; the cells, therefore, serve to compare the brightness of the center spot with its surround, giving the greatest response when the contrast is maximal. Rodieck and Stone (1965b) also found these cells to be very responsive to movement through the receptive field. A white spot on a dark background or a dark spot on a white background gave similar results.

It is possible to construct a neural model that can account for contrast-sensitive cells. Before I describe such a model, I should say a few words about modeling. In the case of many neurophysiological or perceptual phenomena, it is possible to take pencil in hand and draw a "wiring diagram" of neurons that will "account for" the phenomenon. Especially if we postulate only known properties for our neurons, we are tempted to conclude that, since the model works, the nervous system must be wired that way. Obviously, this conclusion is unwarranted, and such models are useless unless they suggest experiments that can be performed with live organisms. If we find out that a given neural model constructed to account for phenomenon A also should give rise to phenomenon B, we can then try to ascertain whether phenomenon B takes place in an actual nervous system. These models serve another purpose in this text: they illustrate how complex properties of the nervous system can emerge from simple elements.

With that caution, let me present a neural model for the contrast-sensitive ganglion cells. First I shall define the symbols I will be using; they will remain consistent throughout the book. Cell bodies of unipolar or bipolar neurons will be represented symbolically as circles; a concave-sided polygon will represent a multipolar neuron. (See **FIGURE 9.3.**) Excitatory synapses will be represented by filled circles at the end of the axon, while open circles will signify inhibitory synapses. (See **FIGURE 9.3.**) If needed to prevent ambiguity, arrows will indicate the normal direction of propagation of information, in the form of either action potentials or dendritic graded potentials.

Figure 9.4 shows how two kinds of bipolar cells might converge upon a single ganglion cell to produce an ensemble constituting a receptive field, with a center-surround sensitive to contrast. (See **FIGURE 9.4.**) All receptors are of the same type. They produce receptor potentials in response to light and hence excite the associated bipolar cells. Considering a given ganglion cell and its receptive field: the bipolar cell excites its associated ganglion cell when stimulated by its photoreceptor(s). This would represent a center-on response. When a photoreceptor in the periphery of the receptive field of the ganglion cell is stimulated, inhibition (mediated by the horizontal cells) lowers the rate of firing of the bipolar cell and thus produces a surround-off response. Note that an individual photoreceptor can serve as the center of one receptive field and participate in the surround of another. In this example, a spot of light in the center of the field would raise the rate of firing of the ganglion cell, whereas light applied to the surrounding area would slow it down. Intermediate amounts of light applied to the two fields simultaneously would produce intermediate rates, depending on the degree of contrast. We do not actually know for certain whether this coding of contrast is accomplished by these means in the retina, but I think this model makes it easier to see that such a level of analysis can be made by the actual cells of the retina, shown in **FIGURE 9.5.**

CODING OF FEATURES IN THE RETINA OF THE FROG.   The retina of some nonmammalian vertebrates, and that of some mammals, performs a much more complex analysis of visual information than the one we have just seen. In a classic study, Lettvin, Maturana, McCullock, and

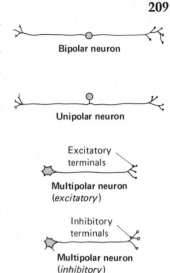

FIGURE 9.3   Conventions that will be used to represent synaptic connections in this text.

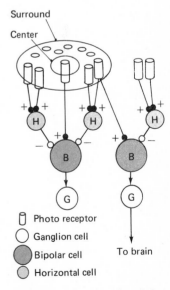

FIGURE 9.4   A neural model that can account for the existence of a ganglion cell with a center-on, surround-off response.

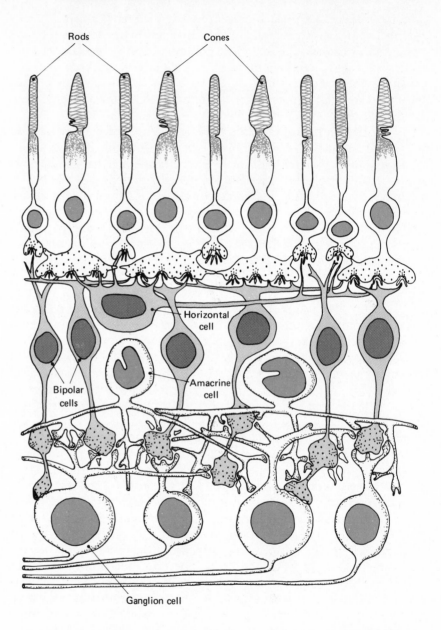

Rods

Cones

Horizontal
cell

Bipolar
cells

Amacrine
cell

Ganglion cell

FIGURE 9.5   Details of retinal circuitry. (Redrawn by permission of the Royal Society and the authors from Dowling, J. E., and Boycott, B. B., *Proceedings of the Royal Society (London)*, 1966, Series B, 166, 80–111.)

Pitts (1959) studied "what the frog's eye tells the frog's brain." They found that the frog's eye tells the brain quite a lot. The authors first noted that the frog's eyes seem to be concerned principally with movement. If you have ever tried to feed a captured frog, you have undoubtedly noticed that the animal will not eat insects offered to it unless they are moving. You must either provide the animal with living insects or jiggle a dead bug or a bit of meat on a thread in front of the frog. Furthermore, a frog does not appear to analyze the scene in front of him; he jumps to the darkest location in the visual field if disturbed. As Lettvin and his colleague note, that is a safe strategy; since the frog is at home on land or in water, it does not matter where his jump takes him. Dark places are usually safer than bright ones.

The investigators presented a variety of different visual stimuli to the frog as they recorded single-unit activity in the optic nerve. They placed a 14-inch-diameter aluminum hemisphere around the frog's head and moved stimuli around the visual field by means of a magnet held in back of the dome. (See **FIGURE 9.6**.) They found several types of cells, which responded best to complex aspects of the image on the retina. One of these cells responded best to a curved, dark edge moving into its receptive field. The stimulus that produced maximum excitation of the cell was a small spot, and movement (especially irregular movement) enhanced the response. Cells of this type produced a sustained train of impulses as a small dark spot moved into the receptive field, and they continued to fire as long as the spot remained there. When the illumination was turned off (even for a fraction of a second), the cell ceased its firing, and it did not respond again to the spot when the light was turned on again. The cell "forgets" a spot once it disappears for a while. A pattern of dots moved *as a whole* had no effect on this type of cell, even if one of the dots moved through the receptive field. However, if a dot within the receptive field moved relative to the other dots, the cell responded vigorously.

We are forced to the conclusion that this type of cell is a "bug detector." The strength of this conviction is only enhanced by the following demonstration: Lettvin and his colleagues placed a photograph of the frog's natural habitat in front of the frog. They placed a small dot on the photograph and moved it into the receptive field of a "bug detector." The cell responded beautifully. However, movement of the entire photograph—with or without the dot attached to it—had no effect at all. The demonstration does not, of course, *prove* that the frog uses cells of this type to detect bugs (and the animal may require, in addition, other kinds of information before it strikes), but it is difficult to imagine that these cells are not used for this purpose.

CODING OF FEATURES IN THE MAMMALIAN VISUAL CORTEX. Compared with mammals, frogs are relatively simple animals, and their visual requirements seem to be well served by units such as the "bug detector." Primates, however, which use their visual systems to extract all kinds of information, do not appear to rely on wired-in analy-

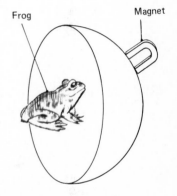

Frog

Magnet

FIGURE 9.6 The apparatus used by Lettvin and his colleagues to study visual coding in the frog.

sis at the retinal level. We do not find any evidence of complex feature detection in the retina or lateral geniculate nucleus, but recordings from cells in the visual cortex show that such analysis occurs there.

It is a difficult and tedious process to investigate feature detection performed by cells of the visual cortex. Once a microelectrode has been inserted into the brain, there is a finite amount of time in which to search for the optimal stimulus. Slight movement of the brain tissue relative to the electrode can cause the neuron being recorded from to become lost, and physical contact between electrode and cell can kill the neuron. Therefore, one has to start hunting quickly for the "best" stimulus. The fact that it is impossible to try out every possible shape, moving in all possible directions within all parts of the visual field, means that the best stimulus found for that cell is merely the best one that has been tried. The stimulus finally chosen might bear a very poor resemblance to the real "best stimulus."

Bearing this in mind, let us examine the pioneering work of David Hubel and Torsten Wiesel of Harvard University. They (Hubel and Wiesel, 1965) have identified cells responding to lines that may send their information to another cell, which then detects line orientations over a large area of the visual field. These complex cells, in turn, send their pooled information to hypercomplex cells, which respond to particular angles of intersecting lines and to specific movement. Our perception of the world appears to be gained, in part, by a process of feature detection of line segments and angles. A triangle would be represented by cells responding to the three angles and the line segments between them. This information would be somewhat redundant—you need not specify the lines once you have specified the angles and their locations—and this redundancy might account for the fact that we see both objects in Figure 9.7 as triangles, even though the lower illustration is incomplete. (See **FIGURE 9.7.**) The cortical cells that code for the three angles are presumably enough to give rise to the perception of a triangle.

Not all investigators agree with the interpretation Hubel and Wiesel place on their data. Spinelli and Barrett (1969) used a special computer-assisted technique to identify receptive fields of cortical neurons. They placed a round black spot on a white screen and moved the spot by means of a magnet attached to a computer-driven device behind the screen. The spot could be moved throughout the entire area of the screen by means of a series of fifty sequential horizontal or vertical sweeps. (See **FIGURE 9.8.**) The stimulus spot was moved in a series of small discrete steps (fifty per line), and the computer recorded the number of action potentials produced while the stimulus was in each of the 2500 positions. The

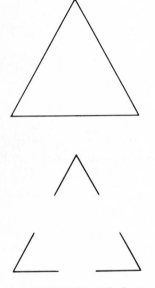

FIGURE 9.7 The brain interprets both of these figures as triangles.

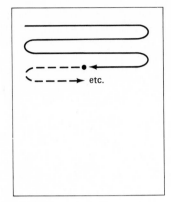

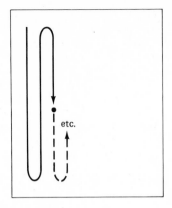

FIGURE 9.8 The horizontal and vertical scanning procedure used by Spinelli and his coworkers.

receptive field of the neuron recorded from was displayed by the computer on the face of an oscilloscope. Each of the stimulus positions was represented by a corresponding location on the oscilloscope screen; if the number of action potentials recorded from the cell exceeded some criterion number while the stimulus was in a given position, a dot was displayed in the corresponding position on the oscilloscope. Figure 9.9 illustrates a typical receptive field of a visual cortical cell mapped by this technique. This cell has an inhibitory center with an excitatory surround. There are differences between the two plots, which were made by means of horizontal (upper figure) and vertical (lower figure) movements of the dot, indicating that the cell has some directional sensitivity. (See **FIGURE 9.9.**) Unlike Hubel and Wiesel, Spinelli and Barrett found a substantial number of cells with simple circular receptive fields, similar to those usually recorded from retinal ganglion cells. Other cortical cells had quite large, diffuse fields, responding equally to stimulation over a wide area.

THE PLASTICITY OF THE VISUAL SYSTEM. In 1971, Hirsch and Spinelli reported an astonishing discovery—visual experience could modify the receptive fields of neurons in the visual cortex of a cat. Hirsch and Spinelli raised kittens in the dark from birth. At three weeks of age the kittens were fitted with a special pair of goggles that presented a separate visual pattern to each eye. One eye was presented with a view of three horizontal bars; the other eye saw three vertical bars. A photograph of one of these kittens is shown in Figure 9.10. (The kittens spent only a part of each day wearing the goggles; most of their time was spent—goggle-less—in the dark. See **FIGURE 9.10.**) When the cats were ten to twelve weeks of age, the receptive fields of cortical neurons were determined by the previously described computer technique. Figure 9.11 presents some plots of receptive

Stimulus movement

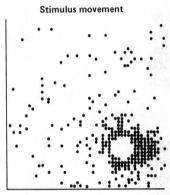

Horizontal

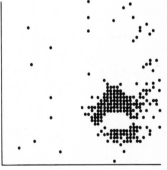

Vertical

FIGURE 9.9 Receptive fields of single neurons as revealed by Spinelli's scanning method. (From Spinelli, D. N., *Experimental Neurology*, 1967, *19*, 291–315.)

FIGURE 9.10 A kitten wearing the training goggles from one of Spinelli's experiments. The horizontal and vertical stripes on the outside of the goggles are for identification purposes only; the actual stimuli are contained within the goggles and are illuminated by transparent openings at the sides (out of which the kitten cannot see). The cardboard cone prevents the kitten from dislodging the goggles.

fields; note the vertically oriented and horizontally oriented visual fields. (See **FIGURE 9.11.**) It is interesting that the specifically oriented receptive fields were produced by stimulation of the eye that had been exposed to bars of the appropriate orientation. That is, receptive fields of neurons responding to the horizontally stimulated eye were found to be horizontal in their orientation; similarly, the vertically stimulated eye produced vertical receptive fields. Also, contrary to what is seen in normally reared kittens, the authors found no cells with binocular receptive fields. (The training procedure prevented stimuli from ever being binocularly perceived.)

In a later study, Spinelli, Hirsch, Phelps, and Metzler (1972) examined the receptive fields of the same cats that were used in the 1971 study, allowing the animals a period of exposure, without the goggles, to a normal visual environment. The results were quite striking: compared with the earlier study, the receptive fields were much more similar to those of normally reared cats. Cells with disk-shaped receptive fields were found, as were cells that responded binocularly. The emergence of these cells seemed to be related to experience; cats whose eyes showed the best degree of convergence (and, hence, the most effective binocular vision) showed the most binocularly responsive cells. The authors still found cells with horizontally or vertically oriented receptive fields; if anything, the fields were even more sharply defined. Again, the elongated receptive fields were elicited only by stimulation of the appropriate eye.

Spinelli and his colleagues suggest that the visual system contains a substantial number of cells that are not "committed" to analysis of any particular features. As a result of exposure to various kinds of visual stimuli, cells begin to respond to prevalent features. Once a cell becomes committed to a feature ("learns" to respond to it as a result of changes in synaptic connections with other cells), it remains committed. This scheme, if true, would permit the ultimate degree of flexibility, allowing the visual system to make most efficient use of feature detection mechanisms appropriate to a given animal's visual environment.

FIGURE 9.11 The receptive fields of single cortical neurons recorded from a cat that had worn goggles such as those shown in Figure 9.10. (From Hirsch, H. V. B., and Spinelli, D. N., *Experimental Brain Research*, 1971, 12, 509–527.)

VISUAL PROCESSING INDEPENDENT OF PRIMARY VISUAL CORTEX. It has generally been believed that the visual system works in a serial manner. That is, visual information goes from retina to primary visual cortex to secondary visual cortex, to (as we shall see) third-order visual cortex. As the information is transmitted from one region to another, successively more complicated analyses are performed. The outcome of one level of analysis presumably serves as the raw material for the succeeding level. However, there is evidence to suggest that the scheme is more complicated than this. It has been found that removal of primary visual cortex in monkeys does not prevent the animals from subsequently making discriminations based on color or pattern, *so long as secondary visual cortex was spared* (Pasik, Pasik, and Schilder, 1969; Schilder, Pasik, and Pasik, 1972). Since removal of primary visual cortex produces complete retrograde degeneration in the lateral geniculate nuclei, this means that the retinotectal pathway must be mediating these functions.

Even in humans with lesions of primary visual cortex, careful testing has shown that the *scotomas* (or blind regions, corresponding to the damaged areas of cortex) are not absolute. Weiskrantz, Warrington, Sanders, and Marshall (1974) found that a person could detect differences between various stimuli (such as X and O) presented to his blind region when he was forced to make a choice among alternatives. The patient reported no "awareness" of stimuli presented there, but was nevertheless able to respond correctly.

VISUAL FUNCTIONS OF THE TEMPORAL LOBE. Cortical regions besides primary and secondary visual cortex appear to participate in the analysis of visual information. In primates, temporal cortex appears to be involved in the recognition of visual stimuli. Klüver and Bucy (1939) observed an interesting change in the behavior of monkeys whose temporal lobes had been excised. The operated animals became hypersexual (which is saying a lot, for a monkey), less aggressive, and considerably less able to discriminate ordinary objects visually. The visual deficit (called "psychic blindness" by Klüver and Bucy) was characterized by a disruption of visual recognition and was later shown to be a result of cortical damage. The changes in emotional behavior appeared to be produced by removal of subcortical structures. The monkeys exhibited a considerable amount of "oral investigation"; they mouthed objects in their environment. Apparently, this increased oral behavior was secondary to the visual deficit. When the monkey was given a tray containing a mixture of food (raisins, nuts, etc.) along with hardware of similar size (nuts and bolts), it picked up each object and placed it in its mouth. If the object was a piece of hardware, the monkey returned it to the tray; if it was food, the monkey ate it. The monkeys could otherwise see quite well. They could get around the environment without bumping into things and could accurately pick up small objects with their fingers.

Recording studies have confirmed the importance of temporal cortex in the complex analysis of visual information. Cells there tend to respond to complex visual stimuli. Gross, Rocha-Miranda, and Bender (1972) found a particularly interesting cell, which gave its best response to a drawing of a monkey's hand; other stimuli produced a response whose magnitude depended on the degree of similarity (as judged by the experimenters) to a monkey's hand. It would be impossible, without presenting all possible stimuli, to demonstrate that a neuron in temporal cortex served as a "hand detector," but the results of investigations like this one suggest that temporal cortex (which receives visual information relayed from visual cortex) participates in higher-level visual analysis. This region of cortex will be discussed again in chapter 18; as we shall see, it appears to play a special role in visual memory.

Color Vision

Various theories of color vision have been proposed for many years—long before it was possible to disprove or validate them by physiological means. In 1807, Thomas Young suggested that color vision could be accounted for by the presence of three visual receptors, each sensitive to a single color. This theory was suggested by the fact that, for the human observer, any color can be reproduced by mixing various quantities of three colors judiciously selected from different points along the spectrum. (Actually, if you accept some restrictions, you can choose any three colors, so long as any one cannot be produced by mixing the other two. We may ignore that nicety, since, as we shall see, Nature chose three colors judiciously.)

I want to emphasize the point that I am referring to *color* mixing, not pigment mixing. In combining pigments, we find that yellow and blue paint mix to make green. Color mixing refers to the addition of two or more light sources. If we shine a beam of red light and a beam of bluish green light together on a white screen, we will see yellow light. If we mix yellow and blue light, we get white light.

The concept of primary colors has been with us for a long time, and it appears to have some psychological validity. Humans have long regarded yellow, blue, red, and green as primary colors. All other colors can be described as mixtures of these primaries. One can speak of a bluish green or yellowish green, and orange appears to have both red and yellow qualities. Purple resembles both red and blue. But we would never describe yellow as anything but yellow; a slightly longer wavelength starts looking reddish, while a slightly shorter wavelength starts looking greenish. Similarly, we see green, blue, and red as primary. The psychological reality of these four colors has suggested that representation of these colors in the visual system provides the primary information for the perception of color.

COLOR CODING IN THE RETINA. Two theories of color vision predominated prior to the definitive physiological studies. The earliest theory maintained that there were three kinds of color receptors, responding maximally to red, blue, or green light. Other theories, taking into account the primariness of yellow, suggested that there were instead two kinds of color receptors, each of which represented a pair of complementary colors in opponent fashion. The two receptors (red-green and blue-yellow) would produce excitation in response to one of the colors, and inhibition in response to the other. Both types of theory also suggested that there was another class of receptors (rods) responding only to light intensity, in a color-blind manner.

Physiological investigations of retinal photoreceptors in higher primates have ruled in favor of the three-cone theory. Study has been made of the absorption characteristics of single cones isolated from the primate retina. The results show that a given receptor preferentially absorbs light of one of three wavelengths, giving strong evidence for the analysis of color by three different kinds of color receptors. (See **FIGURE 9.12.**) Even more direct proof has been obtained from electrophysiological investigations. Recordings of generator potentials have been taken from single cones in the retina of the carp (a

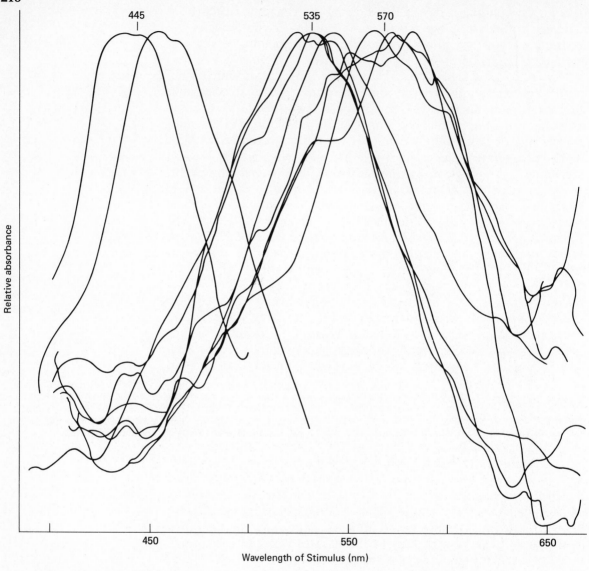

445   535   570

450   550   650

Relative absorbance

Wavelength of Stimulus (nm)

FIGURE 9.12 Absorption characteristics of single cones isolated from the primate retina. (From Marks, W. B., Dobelle, W. H., and MacNichol, E. F., *Science*, 13 March 1964, *143*, 1181–1183. Copyright 1964 by the American Association for the Advancement of Science.)

fish) in response to brief pulses of light of varying wavelength. The receptors fell into three types, as represented in **FIGURE 9.13.**

A fascinating phenomenon occurs in the neural circuitry of the retina between the cones and ganglion cells; the three-color code gets translated into an opponent-color system. Daw (1968) found that most receptive fields of color-sensitive ganglion cells are arranged in a center-surround fashion. For example, the cell might give an on-response to red and an off-response to green in the center, and the opposite set of responses in the surround. Furthermore, Gouras (1968)

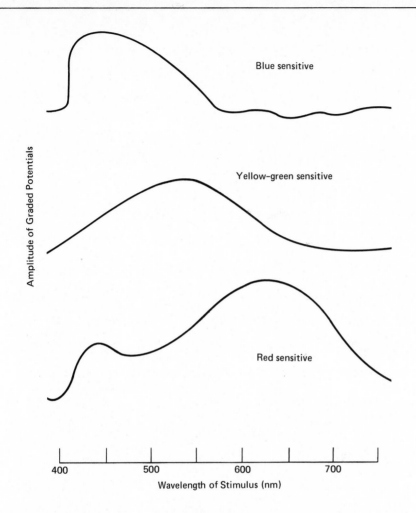

Blue sensitive

Yellow–green sensitive

Red sensitive

Amplitude of Graded Potentials

400   500   600   700

Wavelength of Stimulus (nm)

FIGURE 9.13 Generator potentials from single color-sensitive cones in the retina of the carp. (Redrawn from Tomita, T., Kaneko, A., Murakami, M., and Pautler, E., *Vision Research*, 1967, 7, 519–537.)

has found a few ganglion cells that respond best to only one color. These cells also act as center-surround contrast detectors for different intensities of light of that color.

COLOR CODING IN THE LATERAL GENICULATE NUCLEUS.   At the level of the lateral geniculate nucleus, primate color vision appears to be entirely coded by cells that respond in opponent fashion to complimentary colors.   DeValois, Abramov, and Jacobs (1966), recording action potentials from lateral geniculate neurons, found two major types of opponent cells: red-green detectors and blue-yellow detectors. Each of these categories could be subdivided into two more categories, depending on the type of response seen.   Letting G, R, Y, and B stand for green, red, yellow, and blue, and letting $+$ and $-$ represent excitation and inhibition, there were four types of opponent cells: $+R -G$,

FIGURE 9.14 Responses recorded from single neurons in the lateral geniculate nucleus. These neurons appear to encode color in an opponent process. (From DeValois, R. L., Abramov, I., and Jacobs, G. H., *Journal of the Optical Society of America*, 1966, 56, 966–977.)

$-R +G$, $+Y -B$, and $-Y +B$. These four types of opponent cells are shown in Figure 9.14, which represents frequency of unit firing as a function of wavelength of the stimulus. (See **FIGURE 9.14.**)

COLOR CODING IN CORTEX. The nature of sensory coding for color in the visual cortex is uncertain. Investigators have found cells that

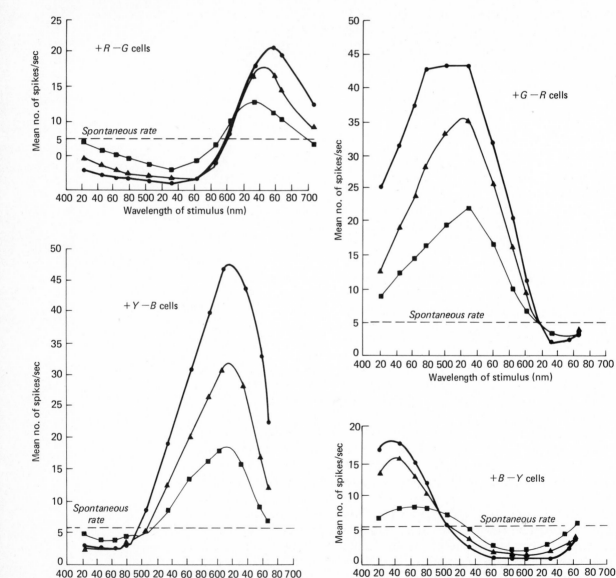

selectively respond to one of three colors, so there seems to be a reemergence of the three-color code seen at the level of the receptor, along with cells showing opponent-type responses (Motokawa, Taira, and Okuda, 1962). Andersen, Buchmann, and Lennox-Buchthal (1962) found cortical cells that responded best to light of particular wavelengths, but the best wavelengths were spread across the entire spectrum. The cells did not cluster into three groups. According to Gouras and Krüger (1975), the study of color coding in cortical neurons is complicated by the fact that a given cell responds to form as well as to color, and only careful quantitative study will identify the chromatic information conveyed by these "multi-duty detectors."

AUDITION

We have seen that the visual system maintains a spatial representation of the retinal surface, with additional levels of feature extraction. As we shall see, points on the basilar membrane are similarly represented by locations on the surface of auditory cortex. Let us first examine the anatomy of ascending auditory information.

The Ascending Auditory Pathways

The anatomy of the auditory system is more complicated than that of the visual system. Rather than give a detailed verbal description of the pathways, I shall refer you to **FIGURE 9.15.** Note that fibers enter the cochlear nuclei of the medulla, and most of them cross to the other side of the brain at the level of the pons. From there they go through the *lateral lemniscus* (a large bundle of axons) to the inferior colliculus, medial geniculate nucleus, and, finally, to auditory cortex. As you can see, there are many synapses along the way to complicate the story. And auditory information is relayed to the cerebellum and reticular formation as well. (See **FIGURE 9.15.**)

If we unrolled the basilar membrane into a flat strip and followed afferent fibers serving successive points along its length, we would reach successive points along the surface of auditory cortex, the basal end being represented most medially, the apical end most laterally. Since, as we shall see, various parts of the basilar membrane respond best to particular frequencies of sound, this point-to-point relationship between cortex and basilar membrane is referred to as *tonotopic representation* (*tonos,* "tone"; *topos,* "place").

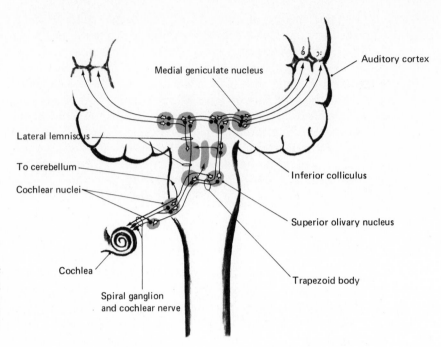

FIGURE 9.15 The pathway of
the auditory system. (Adapted
from Noback, C. R., *The
Human Nervous System*. New
York: McGraw-Hill, 1967.)

Frequency Detection

CODING BY LOCATION ON THE BASILAR MEMBRANE.   The psychological
dimension of *pitch* best corresponds to the physical dimension of
frequency of the sound stimulus.   Pitch can be affected somewhat
by other factors (loud tones have a slightly higher pitch than softer
ones of the same frequency), but for the purposes of our discussion I
shall equate pitch with frequency.   The work of von Békésy has
shown us that, because of the mechanical construction of the cochlea
and basilar membrane, there is a relationship between the location of
maximum deformation of the basilar membrane and frequency of
the stimulus.   Figure 9.16 illustrates the amount of deformation along
the length of the basilar membrane produced by stimulation with
tones of various frequencies.   Note that higher frequencies produce
more displacement at the basal end of the membrane (closest to the
stapes).   (See **FIGURE 9.16.**)

This spatial coding of frequency on the basilar membrane is
more than just a candidate code.   The antibiotic drugs *kanamycin*
and *neomycin* produce degeneration of the auditory hair cells (and
also, incidentally, vestibular hair cells).   Damage to auditory hair
cells begins at the basal end of the cochlea and progresses toward the
apical end; this can be verified by killing experimental animals after

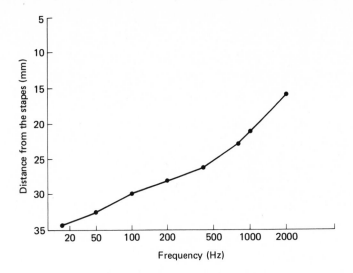

FIGURE 9.16 Encoding of pitch by location of maximum deformation of the basilar membrane. (From von Békésy, G., *Journal of the Acoustical Society of America*, 1949, 21, 233–245.)

treating them with the antibiotic for varying amounts of time. Longer exposures to the drug are associated with increased progress of hair cell damage down the basilar membrane. The progressive death of hair cells very nicely parallels a progressive hearing loss; the highest frequencies are the first to go, and the lowest are the last (Stebbins, Miller, Johnsson, and Hawkins, 1969).

Evidence from a variety of experiments has shown that although the basilar membrane codes for frequency along its length, the coding is not very specific. A given frequency causes a large region of the basilar membrane to be deformed. However, people can detect changes in frequency of only 2 or 3 Hz. It is difficult to understand how such precise pitch determinations can be made by an organ with such a broad tuning characteristic. Recordings made from single auditory nerve fibers also show a very precise degree of frequency tuning—better than would be predicted by the broad area of the basilar membrane that is deformed by a particular frequency. Figure 9.17 shows the frequency response of sixteen auditory nerve fibers. Note that each fiber is represented by a V-shaped curve. (See **FIGURE 9.17.**) The data were collected as follows: a fiber was located with a microelectrode, and tones of various frequencies and intensities were presented to the ear. For each cell, points were plotted that corresponded to the least intense tone that gave a response at a given frequency. The V shapes indicate that as the intensity goes up (as shown by points higher on the vertical axis), a given fiber responds to a wider range of frequencies. At low intensity levels, the frequency specificity of a given fiber is very good.

Some process that sharpens the frequency tuning character-

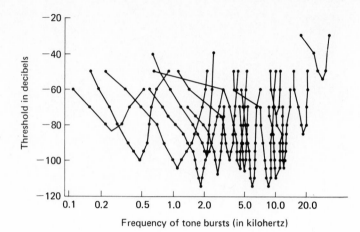

FIGURE 9.17 "Tuning curves" of single auditory nerve fibers. (From Kiang, N. Y.-S., *Acta oto-laryngologica*, 1965, 59, 186–200.)

istics of the auditory nerve fibers must take place on the basilar membrane. A mechanism that might account for this process is *lateral inhibition*. This concept has gained wide acceptance as an explanation for contrast enhancement, and it has been directly observed in the compound eye of the horseshoe crab (Hartline and Ratliff, 1958). If a single *ommatidium* (individual element of the compound eye)— let us call it O_1—is stimulated with light, the surrounding ommatidia become less sensitive to light; they are inhibited by O_1. The inhibition is propagated in all directions away from O_1, the closest receptors beng inhibited the most. The amount of inhibition produced by an ommatidium, furthermore, is proportional to the amount of light falling on it. Let us see how this process sharpens responsiveness to contrast. First have a glance at **FIGURE 9.18.** If we allow 100 units of light to fall on O_1 and 70 units on O_2 (located to the right of O_1), the cells will mutually inhibit each other. O_1, however, being stimulated by a greater amount of light, will inhibit O_2 more than this cell will inhibit O_1. As the responsiveness of O_2 to light decreases, this ommatidium will consequently inhibit O_1 still less. O_1 will respond more and inhibit O_2 even more. Eventually an equilibrium will be achieved, with O_2 responding at a rate far below that of O_1. (The entire process actually takes place very rapidly.) (See **FIGURE 9.18.**) The net effect of the process of lateral inhibition in the eye of *Limulus* is to exaggerate the response of the receptor getting the most light, relative to the response of its neighbors.

Lateral inhibition has been suggested as a mechanism that would increase the sharpness of frequency tuning of the hair cells along the basilar membrane. The cells receiving the greatest stimulation would inhibit their neighbors more than they would be inhibited by their neighbors, so only the most-stimulated units would

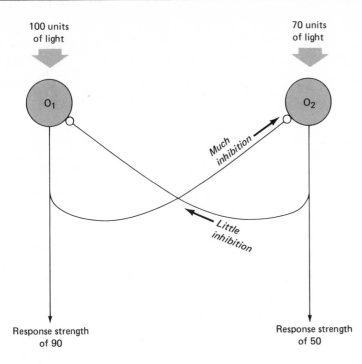

FIGURE 9.18   A schematic representation of the process of lateral inhibition.

respond.   Physiological evidence for such a tuning mechanism has not yet been obtained.

Frequency discrimination appears to be as sharp at the level of the auditory nerve as it is anywhere in the auditory system.   Single-unit recordings have provided no evidence for any additional tuning mechanisms at higher levels; Figure 9.19 illustrates frequency-intensity responses of a number of units recorded from the cochlear nerve, trapezoid body, inferior colliculus, and medial geniculate nucleus. (See **FIGURE 9.19.**)

TEMPORAL CODING OF PITCH.   We have seen that frequency is nicely coded for in a spatial manner on the basilar membrane.   However, the lowest frequencies do not appear to be accounted for in this manner. Kiang (1965), whose data were presented in Figure 9.17, was unable to find any cells responding best to frequencies of less than 200 Hz. How, then, can low frequencies be distinguished?   It appears that lower frequencies are encoded by neural firing that is synchronized to the movements of the apical end of the basilar membrane.   The neurons fire in time with the sonic vibrations.

Good evidence for frequency coding by synchronized firing of the auditory hair cells is provided by a study by Miller and Taylor (1948).   These investigators presented *white noise* (sound containing

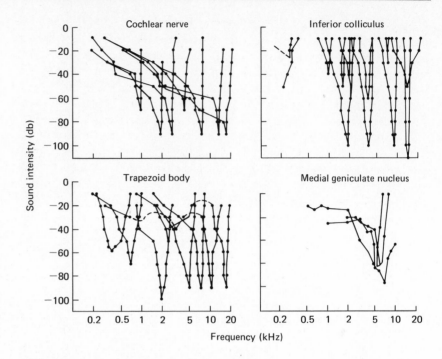

FIGURE 9.19 "Tuning curves" recorded at various levels of the auditory pathways. (From Katsuki, Y., Neural mechanism of auditory sensation in cats. In Rosenblith, W. A., *Sensory Communication*. Copyright 1961 by MIT Press, Cambridge, Mass.)

all frequencies, similar to the hissing sound you hear between FM radio stations, or the sound you hear on a vacant TV channel) to human observers. When they rapidly switched the white noise on and off, the observers reported that they heard a tone corresponding to the frequency of pulsation. The white noise, containing all frequencies, stimulated the entire length of the basilar membrane, so the frequency that was detected could not be coded by place. The auditory system, therefore, can detect pitch coded by synchronous firing of auditory nerve fibers.

Auditory nerve fibers also show a phenomenon called *phase locking,* even to rather high (5000 Hz) frequencies. Phase locking describes the tendency for a cell to fire only at a particular portion of the repetitive cycle of vibration of the basilar membrane. This phenomenon is illustrated in Figure 9.20. Vibration of the basilar membrane is represented by the wavy line at the top. The output of a cell that perfectly follows every wave is shown on line B. (See **FIGURE 9.20.**) Lines C and D show how other cells might not respond at the frequency of the stimulus all the time, but when they fire they tend to fire during the same portion of the cycle. (See **FIGURE 9.20.**) This phenomenon is demonstrated by the auditory system, as was shown by Rose, Brugge, Anderson, and Hind (1967). The graphs shown in Figure 9.21 are *frequency histograms.* Note the regularity of the distributions. (See **FIGURE 9.21.**) The horizontal axes represent time between two successive action potentials. To construct

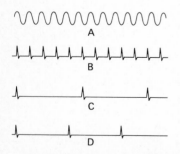

FIGURE 9.20 A schematic representation of the process of phase locking.

such plots, we find an active fiber and turn on the stimulus. We start a clock as soon as an action potential is recorded, and stop it when we detect another one. We then note the time, reset the clock, and see how long it takes for another action potential to occur. (Of course, being poor mortals, we engage the services of a high-speed computer to do the timing and recording for us.) After we have recorded and timed for a while we will have a series of numbers— inter-spike intervals. We note that there seem to be clusters of numbers; for a cell stimulated with a 1000-Hz tone, the inter-spike intervals tend to be 1, 2, 3, 4 (etc.) milliseconds. We find very few at 1.5 or 2.5, etc. When we plot the number of times we observe a given interval, we see these clusters of times in the figure. Note, especially, the graph for the 1000-Hz tone, with its regular clusters at even 1-millisecond intervals. (See **FIGURE 9.21.**) The cells clearly

FIGURE 9.21 Evidence that individual auditory fibers show phase locking to pure tones. (From Rose, J. E., Brugge, J. F., Anderson, D. J., and Hind, J. E., *Journal of Neurophysiology,* 1967, *30,* 769–793.)

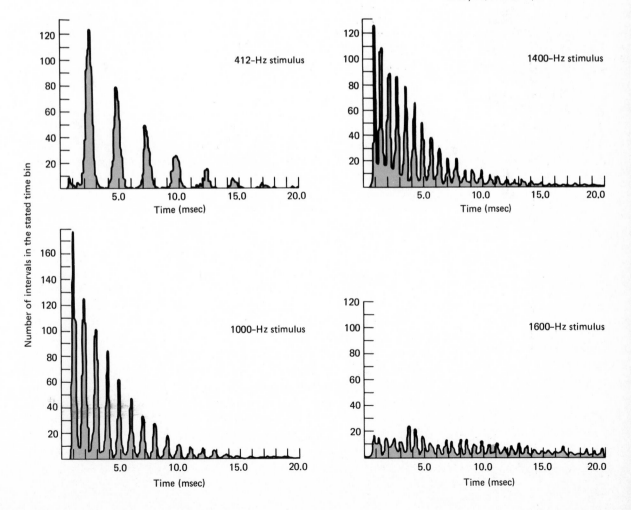

"lock on" to a portion of the wave of vibration, even if they do not always fire at the same constant rate.

Earlier theories of frequency coding suggested that even very high frequencies could be encoded by a *volley principle* (Wever, 1949). These theories suggested, in the absence of physiological data, that cells would phase lock to the stimulus in the manner demonstrated by Rose, Brugge, Anderson, and Hind. Figure 9.22 illustrates how the firing of a number of fibers, phase-locked to the stimulus but firing at a much lower rate, could be "summed" to produce the frequency of the stimulus. (See **FIGURE 9.22.**) This theory, therefore, gets around the fact that cells cannot fire at rates much above 1000 impulses per second. However, the bottom line, entitled "Fibers *a–e* combined," is rather bothersome. Combined by whom or what? (See **FIGURE 9.22.**) Unless a cell somewhere in the brain can fire at the rate shown on the bottom line, it is difficult to see how the information represented by the various fibers can be integrated. Why, then, do auditory neurons show this phase locking to high frequency stimuli? As we shall see in a later section, it is quite likely that this phenomenon is used by the auditory system in localizing the source of a sound.

Coding of Intensity

We noted that the visual system compresses the intensity range of light. This compression occurs even more in the auditory system. Wilska (1935) glued a small wooden rod to a volunteer's tympanic membrane (temporarily, of course). He made the rod vibrate longi-

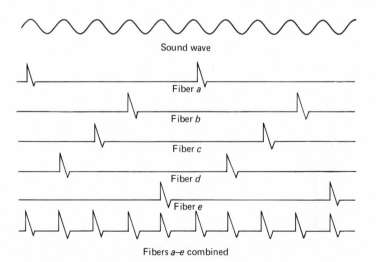

Sound wave

Fiber *a*

Fiber *b*

Fiber *c*

Fiber *d*

Fiber *e*

Fibers *a–e* combined

FIGURE 9.22 Wever's volley theory. But what combines fibers *a–e*? (Adapted from Wever, E. G., *Theory of Hearing.* New York: John Wiley & Sons, 1949.)

tudinally by means of an electromagnetic coil that could be energized with alternating current. The frequency and intensity of the current could be varied, which consequently changed the loudness and pitch of the stimulus to the subject. Wilska observed the rod under a microscope and measured the distance it moved in vibration. This movement was related to the amount of electrical current used, so that he could calculate the extremely minute vibrations that were too small to detect under the microscope. The astonishing result was that, in order for the subject to detect a sound, the eardrum need be vibrated a distance of less than the diameter of a hydrogen atom! This means that, in very quiet environments, a young, healthy ear is limited in its ability to detect sounds in the air by the masking noise of blood rushing through the cranial blood vessels, not by the sensitivity of the auditory system itself. A more recent study using modern measuring instruments (Tonndorf and Khanna, 1968) has shown that Wilska's measurements might even be on the conservative side.

The range of sounds to which the ear can respond is (I hesitate to say it) somewhere on the order of 100 trillion to one (Uttal, 1973). Such a phenomenal range is subject to great compression. Figure 9.23 shows the relationship between intensity of the stimulus and the size of the evoked potentials recorded at the cochlear nucleus. (See **FIGURE 9.23.**)

CODING OF INTENSITY IN THE BRAIN.   Coding of intensity seems to be rather constant throughout the auditory system. Response curves to various click intensities recorded at the inferior colliculus, medial geniculate nucleus, white matter containing axons to cortex, and auditory cortex are presented in Figure 9.24. Note that the curves appear quite similar. (The scale on the horizontal axis is nonlinear,

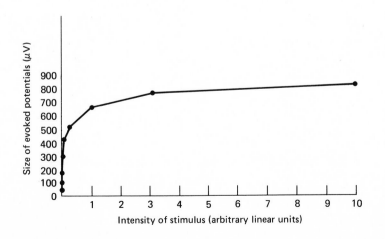

FIGURE 9.23   The relationship between size of evoked potentials recorded from the cochlear nucleus and intensity of the stimulus. (Data, redrawn on a linear scale, are from Saunders, J. C., Cochlear nucleus and auditory cortex correlates of a click stimulus-intensity discrimination in cats. *Journal of Comparative and Physiological Psychology*, 1970, 72, 8–16. Copyright 1970 by the American Psychological Association. Used by permission.)

and represents a different range of stimulus intensity, so the curves shown here do not resemble the one shown in the previous graph). (See **FIGURE 9.24.**)

We noted earlier that frequency is spatially coded on the surface of auditory cortex. Tunturi (1952) found that intensity is also spatially coded at this level—by vertical distance from the cortical surface. Tunturi placed electrodes at various locations on and in a dog's auditory cortex, and recorded evoked potentials to sound. He then stimulated the animal's ear with various frequencies and intensities. His plots of the most effective stimuli are shown in Figure 9.25. Note that the surface was most effectively stimulated by tones of lower intensity, whereas deeper locations required louder tones. (See **FIGURE 9.25.**) Low-frequency tones (below 100 Hz) are not represented; detection of these frequencies is presumably mediated by subcortical regions of the brain.

Auditory cortex appears to be unnecessary for frequency or intensity discriminations. If auditory cortex (primary and various secondary auditory areas surrounding it) is removed, a cat can still discriminate among tones of differing frequencies. What is lost is the ability to discriminate more complex characteristics of auditory information. For example, the cats cannot discriminate among different three-note "tunes" (Diamond and Neff, 1957).

Feature Detection in the Auditory System

So far I have discussed coding of only pitch and loudness. The auditory system responds to other qualities of sonic stimuli besides these

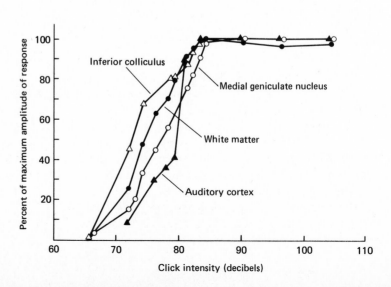

FIGURE 9.24 Magnitude of the evoked response to various click intensities recorded at different locations in the auditory system. (From Etholm, B., *Acta oto-laryngologica*, 1969, 67, 319–325.)

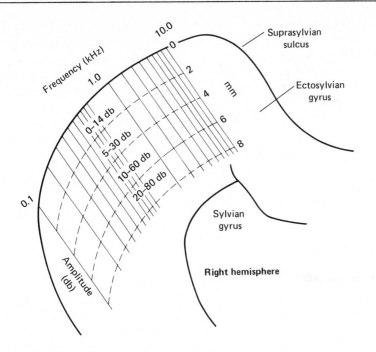

FIGURE 9.25 Coding of intensity and frequency of auditory stimuli by location in auditory cortex. (From Tunturi, A. R., *American Journal of Physiology*, 1952, *168*, 712–727.)

two, however. For example, our ears are very good at locating the source of sound in a lateral dimension. We cannot tell whether a sound is in back or in front of us, but we are very good at determining whether it is to the right or left of us. (To discriminate front from back, we merely turn our heads, transforming the discrimination into a left-right decision.) There are two separate physiological mechanisms used to detect sound sources; we use *phase differences* for low frequencies (less than approximately 3000 Hz) and intensity differences for higher frequencies. Stevens and Newman (1936) found that localization is worst at approximately 3000 Hz, presumably because both mechanisms are rather inefficient at that frequency.

LOCALIZATION BY MEANS OF PHASE DIFFERENCES. Phase differences refer to the simultaneous arrival, at each ear, of different portions of the oscillating sound wave. If we assume a speed of 700 miles per hour for the propagation of sound through the air (the actual value depends on temperature, barometric pressure, and humidity), adjacent cycles of a 1000-Hz tone are 12.3 inches apart. Thus, if there are auditory neurons that are phase-locked to the stimulus (and we have seen that there are), a tone presented by a sound source closer to one ear than the other would produce an asynchrony in the firing patterns of the two ears. Comparing the auditory neurons of the left and right ears, we would find that impulses occurred at slightly different times.

The effects of a single click are easier to visualize than those of a continuous tone. If the sound pressure wave from a click reaches one ear sooner, it initiates action potentials before they can occur in the other auditory system. Studies have shown that the human ear can detect these differences down to a fraction of a millisecond (Wallach, Newman, and Rosenzweig, 1949).

An ingenious neural model to account for such fine temporal discriminations was presented by Licklider (1959). He proposed the model shown in Figure 9.26. If we assume that the neurons that receive synaptic input will fire only if the incoming signals are nearly simultaneous, then the middle one of these cells will fire only if the sound (a click, for simplicity) reaches the ears simultaneously; the two incoming impulses will travel the same distance and converge on the cell in the middle. (See **FIGURE 9.26.**) If the stimulus reaches the right ear first, a cell toward the left will fire, because the signal on the right-ear line gets a head start on the left-ear line, and the two signals converge toward the left. (See **FIGURE 9.26.**) The model is attractive because it is so simple, but there is no evidence that the auditory system actually contains such a circuit.

LOCALIZATION BY MEANS OF INTENSITY DIFFRENCES. The other localization mechanism relies upon the differences in intensity of sound pressure received by the ears. At high frequencies it is more difficult to detect phase differences in the stimulus, but intensity differences become greater. Low frequencies pass more easily through objects than do high frequencies; you can easily demonstrate this by comparing the frequencies of outside sounds you hear when a window is open with those you hear when the window is shut. Shrill noises become quieter with the window closed, but the rumble of trucks is much less affected. Similarly, if a high-frequency sound is pre-

FIGURE 9.26 Licklider's model of the means by which the auditory system can detect which ear receives the sound first. (Adapted from Roederer, J. G., *Introduction to the Physics and Psychophysics of Music.* New York: Springer-Verlag, 1973.)

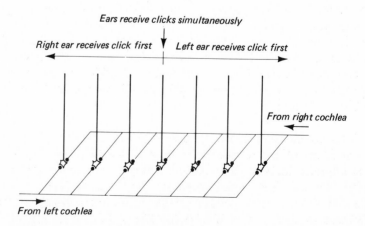

Ears receive clicks simultaneously

Right ear receives click first   *Left ear receives click first*

From right cochlea

From left cochlea

sented from the right, the head casts a "sonic shadow" on the left ear, producing an intensity difference.

ECHO SUPPRESSION. Whenever we are confronted with a sound within a building, or even outside (unless we are standing on a feature-less plain), we are confronted with multiple echoes. However, unless the echo is very pronounced and of sufficiently long delay, we hear only one sound, the first to reach our ears. Etholm (1969) has observed a physiological mechanism that might possibly account for this "echo suppression." He found that if two closely spaced clicks were presented to the ear, the evoked response to the second would be con-siderably diminished. Thus, the first sharp, transient sound to arrive appears to suppress sounds that immediately follow it. A steady sound (much less important than transients for such things as speech detection) presumably would not produce such an effect.

DETECTION OF OTHER FEATURES. The auditory system also detects other features, but the mechanisms are not nearly so well defined. Various studies (Whitfield and Evans, 1965; Goldstein, Hall, and But-terfield, 1968) have found cells responding only to onset or offset of a sound (or both), and to changes in pitch or intensity (sometimes only to changes in one direction). These results accord with the fact that changing stimuli attract our attention better than do steady ones. Data are scanty so far, so we have no real conception of the coding mechanism used, or even of precisely what features are coded.

VESTIBULAR SYSTEM

Vestibular stimulation does not produce any readily definable sen-sation; certain low-frequency stimulation of the vestibular sacs can produce nausea, and stimulation of the semicircular canals can pro-duce dizziness and rhythmic eye movements (*nystagmus*). How-ever, there is no primary sensation, as there is for audition and vision, for example. Therefore, discussion of the vestibular system will be restricted to a description of its neural pathways and the results of vestibular stimulation.

THE VESTIBULAR PATHWAYS. Figure 9.27 illustrates the afferent and efferent fibers of the vestibular system. (See **FIGURE 9.27.**) Most of the afferent fibers of the vestibular nerve synapse within the four *vestibular nuclei*, but some fibers travel to the cerebellum. Neurons of the vestibular nuclei send their axons to the cerebellum, spinal cord, medulla, and pons. (See **FIGURE 9.27.**) There also appear to be

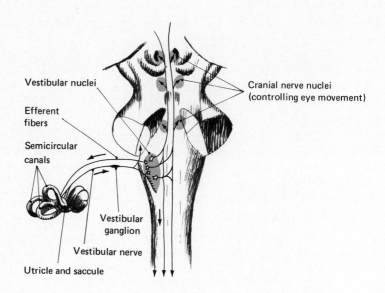

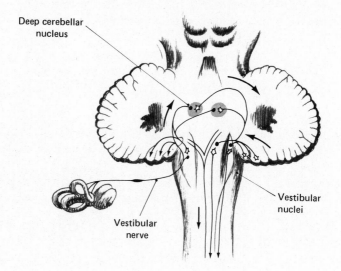

FIGURE 9.27 The pathways
followed by neurons in the
vestibular system.
(Adapted with permission
from McGraw-Hill Book Co.
from *The Human Nervous
System*, 2nd edition, by Noback
and Demarest. Copyright ©
1975, by McGraw-Hill, Inc.)

vestibular projections to temporal cortex, but the precise pathways have not been determined. Most investigators believe that the cortical projections are responsible for feelings of dizziness, and that the activity of projections to the lower brainstem can produce nausea and vomiting. Projections to nuclei controlling neck muscles are clearly involved in maintaining an upright position of the head.

Perhaps the most interesting connections are those to the cranial nerve nuclei (third, fourth, and sixth) controlling the eye muscles. As we walk or—especially—run, the head is jarred quite a bit. The vestibular system exerts direct control on eye movement, to compensate for the sudden head movements. This process maintains a fairly steady retinal image. Test this reflex yourself: look at a distant object and hit yourself on the side of the head. Note that your image of the world jumps a bit, but not too much. People who have suffered vestibular damage, and who lack this reflex, have great difficulty seeing anything while walking or running. Everything becomes a blur of movement.

SOMATOSENSES

In the last chapter I classified the somatosenses into two categories: (1) cutaneous sensitivity and (2) kinesthesia and organic sensitivity. In this chapter I shall consider only cutaneous sensitivity; a discussion of kinesthesia will be left for chapter 10. Too little is known about coding of organic sensitivity to warrant discussion here.

Cutaneous Pathways

There are several distinct neural pathways followed by cutaneous sensory information. Two will be described here. One (the *lemniscal system*) conveys precisely localized information from touch receptors. The other (*spinothalamic system*) carries pain and temperature sensation, which is less precisely localized.

LEMNISCAL PATHWAYS. The lemniscal pathways are outlined in **FIGURE 9.28.** Almost all of the fibers convey information to the contralateral hemisphere. The first-order neuron has a very long axon. In the case of spinal afferents, the axon of the unipolar cell (whose soma is located in a dorsal root ganglion) ascends through the dorsal columns to the cuneate or gracile nucleus of the medulla. (The destination depends on the location of the receptor—upper regions of the body send fibers to the cuneate nucleus, lower regions to the gracile nucleus.) (See **FIGURE 9.28.**) These axons are the longest nerve fibers of the body; a touch receptor in the big toe is on one end of a single axon stretching all the way to the medulla. Fibers of the second-order neurons decussate (cross to the other side of the brain) and travel via the *medial lemniscus* (a large fiber bundle) to the ventral posterior nuclei of the thalamus. The neurons synapse there, and third-order neurons project to somatosensory cortex (postcentral gyrus of the parietal lobe).

Most touch receptors rostral to the ears send information via the trigeminal, facial, and vagus nerves. We shall consider the major pathway, from the trigeminal nerve. This pathway is almost a

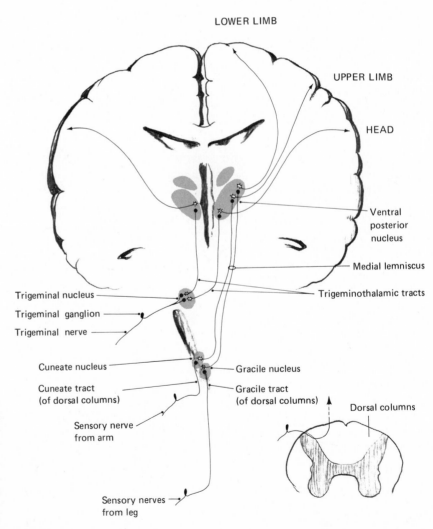

FIGURE 9.28 The pathways followed by neurons that mediate fine touch and pressure, and feedback from the muscles and joint receptors. (Adapted from Noback, C. R., and Demarest, R. J., *The Nervous System: Introduction and Review.* New York: McGraw-Hill, 1972.)

LOWER LIMB

UPPER LIMB

HEAD

Ventral posterior nucleus

Medial lemniscus

Trigeminothalamic tracts

Trigeminal nucleus

Trigeminal ganglion

Trigeminal nerve

Cuneate nucleus

Gracile nucleus

Cuneate tract (of dorsal columns)

Gracile tract (of dorsal columns)

Dorsal columns

Sensory nerve from arm

Sensory nerves from leg

replica of the dorsal column pathway.   Most second-order neurons decussate and travel via the *trigeminal lemniscus* (parallel to the medial lemniscus) to the ventral posterior nuclei.   The third-order fibers project to somatosensory cortex.   (See **FIGURE 9.28.**)

SPINOTHALAMIC AND RETICULOTHALAMIC PATHWAYS.   Figure 9.29 illustrates the spinothalamic and reticulothalamic systems, which carry information about temperature and pain.   (See **FIGURE 9.29.**) (Pain will be discussed separately in chapter 17.)   The afferent fibers synapse as soon as they enter the central nervous system, either in the dorsal horn of the spinal cord or in the *trigeminal nucleus.*

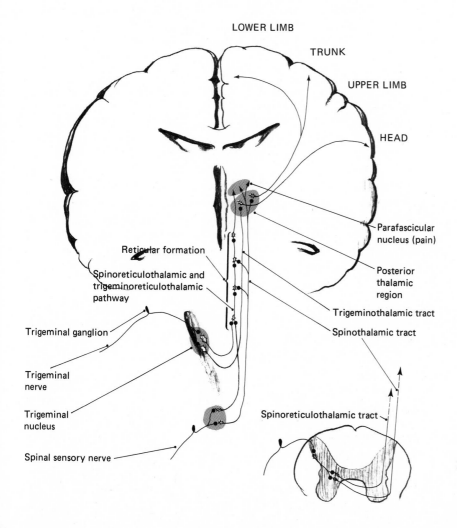

LOWER LIMB

TRUNK

UPPER LIMB

HEAD

Parafascicular nucleus (pain)

Reticular formation

Spinoreticulothalamic and trigeminoreticulothalamic pathway

Posterior thalamic region

Trigeminothalamic tract

Spinothalamic tract

Trigeminal ganglion

Trigeminal nerve

Trigeminal nucleus

Spinal sensory nerve

Spinoreticulothalamic tract

FIGURE 9.29   The pathways followed by neurons that mediate diffuse touch and pressure, temperature, and pain. (Adapted from Noback, C. R., and Demarest, R. J., *The Nervous System: Introduction and Review.* New York: McGraw-Hill, 1972.)

Second-order neurons decussate immediately; some ascend via the spinothalamic (or trigeminothalamic) tracts directly to the ventral posterior nuclei of the thalamus. Others follow a diffuse, polysynaptic pathway through the reticular formation. Note that the spinothalamic tract also gives off collaterals to the reticular formation as it passes by. (See **FIGURE 9.29.**) From the thalamus, most third-order fibers conveying pain and temperature information project to *secondary somatosensory cortex.*

SOMATOSENSORY CORTEX.   Figure 9.30 shows a lateral view of a monkey brain, with a drawing vaguely resembling two monkeys. (See **FIGURE 9.30.**) These drawings (animunculi—they would be called homunculi if drawn on a human brain) roughly indicate which parts of the body project to which areas of primary and secondary somatosensory cortex. Note that an inordinate amount of cortical tissue is given to representation of fingers and lips, corresponding to the greater tactile sensitivity of these regions. (See **FIGURE 9.30.**)

Neural Coding of Somatosensory Information

CODING OF TACTILE STIMULI.   Coding of location of a stimulus on the body surface is accomplished by means of spatial coding—the *somatotopic representation* illustrated in the previous figure. Single units of the somatosensory system can be recorded from, and their receptive

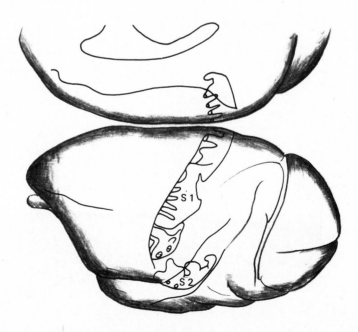

FIGURE 9.30   Sensory animunculi, indicating the regions of the body that project to particular areas of somatosensory cortex. (Adapted from Woolsey, C. N., Organization of somatic sensory and motor areas of the cerebral cortex. In *Biological and Biochemical Bases of Behavior,* edited by H. F. Harlow and C. N. Woolsey. Madison: University of Wisconsin Press, 1958.)

fields can be determined by stimulating the skin with the appropriate stimulus and noting the size and location of the area from which responses are elicited. In general, the larger myelinated fibers of the lemniscal system, serving touch and fine pressure, respond to a relatively small area of skin. Unmyelinated fibers and the smaller myelinated fibers have larger receptive fields and are part of the spinothalamic system, responding to temperature changes or pain-eliciting stimuli. The receptive fields, when measured by the response of cortical neurons, appear to have characteristics similar to retinal ganglion cells; there is a central region of skin that produces excitation, and a surrounding region that produces inhibition (Mountcastle and Powell, 1959). This phenomenon is presumably produced by lateral inhibitory mechanisms within the central nervous system, and it supposedly increases fineness of localization.

The range of stimulus energy transduced by the cutaneous receptors is a very small fraction of the range detected by the auditory and visual systems. The absolute level of stimulus intensity required to stimulate the cutaneous receptors, furthermore, is on the order of millions of times higher. Compression of the range of stimulus intensity occurs at the level of some cutaneous receptors; others transduce energy linearly. Figure 9.31 illustrates the response of a neuron in the ventral posterior area of the thalamus as a function of stimulus intensity (amount of skin indentation produced by a small probe) applied to a single touch receptor in hairy skin of a monkey. Note that changes in stimulus intensity produce less change in response at higher levels than at lower levels. (See **FIGURE 9.31.**)

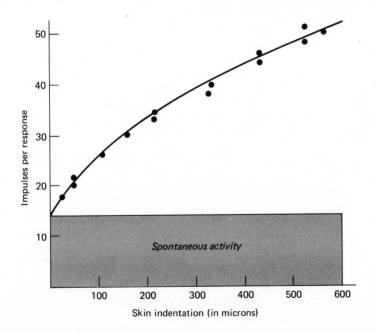

FIGURE 9.31 Response of a single neuron in ventral posterior thalamus as a function of skin indentation produced by a small probe. The neuron is responding to information from a single touch receptor in hairy skin of a monkey. (Redrawn from Mountcastle, V. B., The problem of sensing and the neural coding of sensory events. In *The Neurosciences*, edited by G. Quarton, T. Melnechuk, and F. O. Schmitt. New York: Rockefeller University Press, 1967.)

However, receptors in glabrous skin appear to transduce tactile stimuli in a linear manner, as is shown in Figure 9.32. In this experiment, recordings were taken directly from a myelinated axon serving tactile receptors in glabrous skin at the base of a monkey's thumb. (See **FIGURE 9.32.**)

In all cases, intensity appears to be coded in a linear fashion past the level of the receptor. Mountcastle (1967) summarized a number of experiments that showed a linear relationship between firing rate of the peripheral afferent fiber and all subsequent levels of the somatosensory system. Even estimations of stimulus intensity by humans were related to receptor stimulation in a linear fashion. Figure 9.33 shows perceived intensity as a function of stimulus intensity (amount of skin deformation from a small probe placed on the distal pad—fingerprint portion—of the middle finger). Note that the relationship is a nearly straight line. (See **FIGURE 9.33.**)

ADAPTATION. It has been known for a long time that a moderate, constant stimulus applied to the skin fails to produce any sensation after it has been present for a while. We not only ignore the pressure of a wristwatch, but we cannot feel it at all if we keep our arm still (assuming that the band is not painfully tight). Physiological studies have shown that the reason for the lack of sensation is absence of receptor firing; the receptors adapt to a constant stimulus.

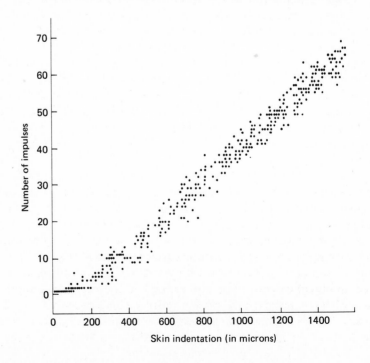

FIGURE 9.32 Response of a single axon served by pressure-sensitive receptors in the base of the thumb of a monkey. (Redrawn from Mountcastle, V. B., The problem of sensing and the neural coding of sensory events. In *The Neurosciences*, edited by G. Quarton, T. Melnechuk, and F. O. Schmitt. New York: Rockefeller University Press, 1967.)

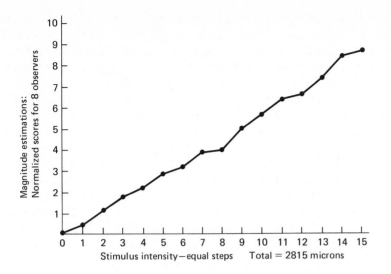

FIGURE 9.33 Estimated magnitude of intensity of tactile stimuli presented to the finger of human subjects. (Redrawn from Mountcastle, V. B., The problem of sensing and the neural coding of sensory events. In *The Neurosciences*, edited by G. Quarton, T. Melnechuk, and F. O. Schmitt. New York: Rockefeller University Press, 1967.)

This adaptation is not a result of any "fatigue" of physical or chemical processes within the receptor. Adaptation can be explained as a function of the mechanical construction of the receptors and their relationship to skin and (in some cases) end organs. As we saw in chapter 8, the fibers of Pacinian corpuscles respond once when the receptor is bent and again when it is released, because of the way the nerve ending "floats" within the viscous interior of the corpuscle. Therefore, these receptors adapt almost immediately to a constant stimulus. Most other fibers adapt less quickly. Nafe and Wagoner (1941) recorded the sensations reported by human subjects as a stimulus weight gradually moved downward as it deformed the skin. Pressure was reported until the weight finally stopped moving. When the weight was increased, pressure was reported until downward movement stopped again. Pressure sensations were also briefly recorded when the weight was removed while the surface of the skin regained its normal shape.

RESPONSIVENESS TO MOVING STIMULI. A moderate, constant, non-damaging stimulus is rarely of any importance to an organism, so this adaptation mechanism is useful. Our cutaneous senses are used much more often to analyze shapes and textures of stimulus objects moving with respect to the surface of the skin. Sometimes the object itself moves, but more often we do the moving ourselves. If I placed an object in your palm and asked you to keep your hand still, you would have a great deal of difficulty recognizing the object by touch alone. If you were permitted to move your hand, you would manipulate the object, letting its surface slide across your palm and the pads of your fingers. You would be able to describe its three-dimensional shape, hardness, texture, slipperiness, etc. (Obviously your motor system must cooperate, and you need kinesthetic sensation from your muscles and joints, besides the cutaneous information.) If you squeeze the object and feel a lot of well-localized pressure in return, it is hard. If you feel a less intense, more diffuse pressure in return, it is soft. If it produces vibrations as it moves over the ridges on your fingers, it is rough. If very little effort is needed to move the object while pressing it against your skin, it is slippery. If it does not produce vibrations as it moves across your skin, but moves in a jerky fashion, and if it takes effort to remove your fingers from its surface, it is sticky.

Mountcastle (1967) describes the results of experiments he and his colleagues performed in the investigation of movement-sensitive receptors. The investigators found that the receptors in glabrous skin could be divided into two types according to their sensitivity to vibration. Figure 9.34 illustrates the minimum amplitude on a sine-wave stimulus (vibrating the surface of the skin) necessary to produce a sensation in human subjects. As the frequency increases from 1 to 40 Hz, the stimulus amplitude needed for sensation steadily decreases. After 40 Hz, the decrease follows a very different function. (See **FIGURE 9.34.**) These results strongly suggest that two types

FIGURE 9.34 Amplitude of the sine-wave stimulus at psychophysical threshold (the point at which it could barely be felt) as a function of frequency of the stimulus. (Redrawn from Mountcastle, V. B., The problem of sensing and the neural coding of sensory events. In *The Neurosciences*, edited by G. Quarton, T. Melnechuk, and F. O. Schmitt. New York: Rockefeller University Press, 1967.)

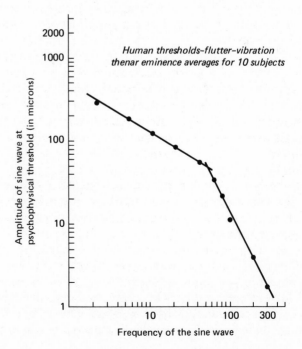

of receptors respond to different frequency ranges. Physiological studies by Mountcastle and his colleagues indicated that low-frequency detection was performed by quickly adapting mechanoreceptors in the surface of the skin. Higher frequencies were detected by Pacinian corpuscles located in deeper tissue.

These investigators also studied the nature of neural coding for frequency. The signal from the low-frequency receptors was represented faithfully up to the level of the cortex. However, high-frequency signals from the Pacinian corpuscles, while still represented in the thalamus and thalamocortical fibers, were not observed in somatosensory cortex. Uttal (1973) suggests that it is likely that frequency, represented by rate of unit firing in the thalamus, becomes coded in a spatial manner at the level of the cortex. Frequency of vibration, perhaps, is coded by firing of different sets of cortical neurons.

DETECTION OF COOLNESS AND WARMTH. Thermal sensation is a very complicated process, and not much is known about coding of temperature at higher levels of the CNS. Coolness and warmth, as we saw in the last chapter, are detected by different receptors. The responses of these two types of receptors combine to provide thermal sensations. There is a temperature level that, for a particular region of skin, will produce a sensation of temperature neutrality—neither warmth nor coolness is reported. This neutral point is not an absolute value but depends on the prior history of thermal stimulation of that area. If the temperature of a region of skin is raised by a few degrees, the initial feeling of warmth is replaced by one of neutrality. If the skin temperature is lowered to its initial value, it now feels cool. Thus, increases in temperature lower the sensitivity of warmth receptors and raise sensitivity of cold receptors. The converse holds for decreases in skin temperature. This adaptation to ambient temperature can be easily demonstrated by placing one hand in a bucket of warm water and the other in a bucket of cool water until some adaptation has taken place. Simultaneous immersion of both hands in water of intermediate temperature leads to a peculiar sensation: the water feels warm to one hand and cool to the other.

The necessity for the central nervous system to combine information from warmth and cold receptors is further underscored by data of Hensel and Kenshalo, illustrated in Figure 9.35. Average firing rates of warmth- and cold-sensitive fibers is shown as a function of temperature. Note that each of the curves successively rises and falls with an increase in temperature. (See **FIGURE 9.35.**) Thus, firing rate of either system does not reliably encode temperature; cold receptors, for example, fire at the same rate at 17° C as they do at 34° C. (See **FIGURE 9.35.**) Thus, the brain must use information

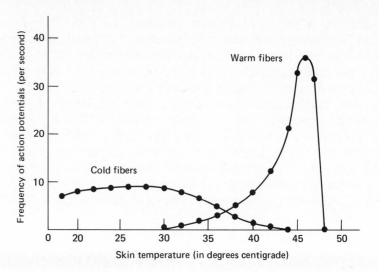

FIGURE 9.35 Since a given neuron responds at the same rate to two different temperatures, our perception of temperature depends on input from more than one type of neuron. (From Hensel, H., and Kenshalo, D. R., Warm receptors in the nasal region of cats. *Journal of Physiology (London),* 1969, *204,* 99–112. Reprinted by permission of Cambridge University Press.)

from both populations of receptors in determining temperature (Hensel, 1974).

GUSTATION

The Neural Pathway for Taste

No diagram is presented for the ascending gustatory pathway because its presence might be misleading; it would imply that we know more about the anatomy of the gustatory system than we really do. Taste fibers, arriving via various complicated pathways through the eighth, ninth, and tenth cranial nerves, synapse in the *solitary nucleus* of the medulla. The second-order neurons decussate and somehow arrive at the ventral posterior region of the thalamus. Thalamic neurons project to an imperfectly defined region of parietal cortex, probably the inferior portion of the somatosensory area.

Neural Coding of Taste

Although peripheral nerve responses to gustatory stimuli have been well studied, little work has been done on central coding of the taste qualities. In general, a given fiber is sensitive to all four taste qualities, but it responds best to one of them. This suggests that taste-quality judgments must depend upon central analysis of the pattern of information on many different neurons, as is the case for the two types of temperature receptors. A study by Doetsch, Ganchrow, Nelson, and Erickson (1969) revealed that cells in the solitary nucleus of the medulla exhibited the same multiquality sensitivity to taste that is shown by peripheral fibers. Although the investigators were able to record thalamic and cortical responses to electrical stimulation of the peripheral nerves for taste, they could not detect any response in these areas to normal gustatory stimuli. Other investigators recorded multiple-unit activity in the thalamus in response to taste (Frommer, 1961), but no success has been achieved within the cortex. The nature of central coding of gustation, then, is still completely unknown.

OLFACTION

The Neural Pathways for Odor

The complexity of the olfactory bulb, and the interconnections of these structures via fibers passing through the anterior commissure, was discussed in chapter 8. The mitral cells in the olfactory bulb give rise to the afferent fibers of the olfactory nerve, and the fibers are distributed, via the olfactory tracts, to many regions of the brain. These axons terminate in limbic cortex at the base of the brain; there is no primary olfactory projection through the thalamus to neocortex, as there is for the other senses. Most of the subcortical structures of the limbic system also receive olfactory input; this fact undoubtedly is related to the importance of odors in the regulation of hormonal systems and of species-typical behaviors (including the four F's) of many species of mammals.

Coding of Odor Quality

Although there have been many attempts to identify odor primaries corresponding to the sweet, sour, bitter, and salty qualities of taste, we still cannot say with any certainty how odor quality is encoded. Needless to say, since peripheral coding mechanisms have not been identified, nothing is known about coding at more central levels.

The concept of primary olfactory qualities has been prevalent for quite some time—partly because of the fact that it is easier to conceive of the coding of the overwhelming number of discriminable odors by a few primary dimensions than by a myriad of different types of receptors. After all, new substances with new odors are synthesized every year, and it would be unreasonable to expect that we evolved specific receptors for all the odors yet to be experienced.

Two other pieces of information suggest that odors may be sorted out according to some classification scheme. Some people have very specific anosmias; they cannot detect certain odors. This fact would suggest that there are various receptor types, and that these people lack one or more kinds of these specific receptors. The second piece of data is that we humans seem to be able to reach some agreements about the similarities of odors. Classifications such as fruity, pinelike, and musky make sense to most of us, and we are willing to say that there is more similarity between the odors of pine oil and cedar oil than between skunk and the smell of limes. More weight is given to these similarities by the fact that adaptation to one odor (i.e., loss of sensitivity after constant stimulation) produces a corresponding adaptation to similar odors (Moncrieff, 1956).

Recordings taken from single olfactory receptors have not helped to classify "odor primaries," unfortunately. In a discussion of their attempt to determine what the frog's nose tells the frog's brain, Lettvin and Gesteland (1965) point out that they were completely unable to find any specific classes of olfactory fibers that coded for odor qualities. Unlike the small number of different types of visual fibers of the frog reported by Lettvin and his colleagues in 1959, the olfactory fibers defied such classification. A given fiber would be found to respond differentially to various odor molecules, being excited by some, inhibited by others, and unaffected by still others. Its neighbor would have a different, idiosyncratic response. Coding of olfactory information into "odor primaries," if they indeed exist, must result from a complex interaction of various receptors.

STEREOSPECIFIC THEORY. How does one begin to construct a set of possible odor primaries in order to develop a theory of olfaction? Amoore tried to do so by means of a literature search. He looked through the chemical literature and noted that the terms used by chemists to describe the odor of a compound could be divided into seven classifications: camphoraceous, ethereal, floral, musky, pepperminty, pungent, and putrid. Amoore went on to examine the three-dimensional structures of the various molecules, to see if there could be any way to classify them according to shape. His conclusion was that the "primary odors" could be characterized by seven different molecular configurations, recognized by receptive sites of similar shapes, two of which are shown in Figure 9.36. (See **FIGURE 9.36.**)

Amoore constructed plastic models of the molecules and receptors. Then he attempted, by several means, to correlate the "goodness-of-fit" of the molecular models and receptor models with observers' judgments of the similarities of the odors the models repre-

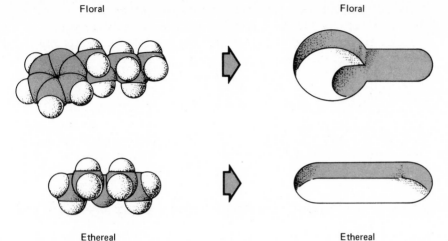

Floral

Floral

Ethereal

Ethereal

FIGURE 9.36 Examples of the molecular shape of two odorous substances, along with their hypothesized receptors. (Adapted from Amoore, J. E., *Molecular Basis of Odor.* Springfield, Ill.: Charles C Thomas, 1970.)

sented. In other words, were odors whose molecules fit the receptor model well judged more similar than odors whose molecules fit the receptor model poorly? Unfortunately, the relationship was not particularly good. Amoore then abandoned his model of the hypothesized receptor sites and concentrated on the molecular models themselves. He had much more success with this procedure. Three-dimensional similarity (judged by a shape-recognizing computer that "looked at" the molecular models with a television camera) correlated very well with observers' ratings of odor similarity. Thus, there appears to be supporting evidence for the suggestion that there are primary odors, and that the molecular configuration determines a substance's smell. We still do not know what the nature of the receptors might be. (See Amoore, 1970, for a review of his studies.)

Gas Chromatograph Theory. Another theory of olfaction has been proposed by Mozell (1970), who suggests that the olfactory system might work like a gas chromatograph. This analytical instrument consists of a column or small tube filled with an *adsorbent* powder (to *adsorb* means "to stick to"). The unknown gas is passed through the adsorbent medium, and the distance a substance passes as it is being adsorbed serves as an index of its chemical composition. Mozell recorded electrical potentials to odor from nerve branches serving different portions of the olfactory mucosa of the frog. He found that different substances produced different spatial patterns of activity, as evidenced by differences in the activity of the two nerve branches. When the substance was wafted across the olfactory mucosa in the opposite direction, the spatial pattern of activity reversed. Furthermore, there seemed to be similarities between chromatographic analyses of the odor molecules used and the pattern of activity seen across the frog's olfactory mucosa. This intriguing hypothesis certainly warrants further investigation.

SUGGESTED READINGS

GELDARD, F. A. *The Human Senses*, ed. 2. New York: John Wiley & Sons, 1972.

UTTAL, R. W. *The Psychobiology of Sensory Coding*. New York: Harper & Row, 1973.

    Uttal's book is most directly related to this chapter.

HUBEL, D. H. The visual cortex of the brain. *Scientific American*, November, 1963.

MacNICHOL, E. F. Three-pigment color vision. *Scientific American*, December, 1964.

NOTON, D., and STARK, L. Eye movements and visual perception. *Scientific American*, June, 1971.

PETTIGREW, J. D. The neurophysiology of binocular vision. *Scientific American*, August, 1972.

    The above four articles are included in *Progress in Psychobiology* (introductions by R. F. Thompson). San Francisco: W. H. Freeman, 1976.

Glands, Muscles, and the Control of Movement

10

So far, much has been said about neural communication and the transduction of sensory information and its transmission into the brain. All these processes would be useless without some means of interacting with the environment. There is no selective advantage in having sensory systems unless the organism can utilize the information thus provided by taking some physical action. To interact with the environment we need *effectors*. The name effector was appropriately chosen, since it refers to cells that are located at the distal end of peripheral efferent nerve fibers and that produce physical effects as a result of neural stimulation. We possess two types of effectors: muscle fibers and secretory cells. In this chapter I shall describe the principles of glandular secretion and muscular contraction. I shall then discuss the control of these effects, first on a simpler level by reflexive mechanisms and then on a more complex, integrative level by the motor systems of the brain.

GLANDS

Almost all glands, both *endocrine* and *exocrine*, are controlled by the brain. There are a few exceptions; for example, the *parathyroids*, which regulate calcium metabolism, respond directly to the calcium level of the blood. However, most other glands either receive direct neural control or are controlled by a series of events initiated by the *hypothalamic hormones.*

Exocrine Glands

Exocrine (literally, "outside-secreting") glands are those which have a duct, through which the gland's products are secreted. For example, the lachrymal glands secrete tears through a duct to the inner surface of the eyelid; the liver and pancreas secrete digestive juices into the intestine; the seminal vesicles and prostate secrete fluids into the male genitourinary system; and the sweat glands and sebaceous glands secrete sweat and oil to the surface of the skin. All of the innervated exocrine glands are controlled by the autonomic nervous system. The salivary glands, for example, receive postganglionic fibers of both the parasympathetic and the sympathetic divisions. The parasympathetic division, active during such anabolic processes as digestion, produces a copious secretion of thin, watery saliva. Stimulation of the sympathetic division also results in secretion, but of a smaller quantity of thick, viscous saliva. (This is why the inside of your mouth feels sticky during periods of fright or extreme excitement.)

Some exocrine glands store their secretions and release them in response to neural stimulation. The liver, for example, secretes bile, the amount of secretion being under control of both neural and hormonal factors. The bile is stored in the gallbladder and is retained there so long as the *sphincter of Oddi* is constricted. This sphincter (composed of *smooth muscle,* to be described later) relaxes and muscles in the wall of the gallbladder contract upon neural stimulation received via the vagus nerve, thus allowing the stored bile to be secreted into the digestive system. (See **FIGURE 10.1.**)

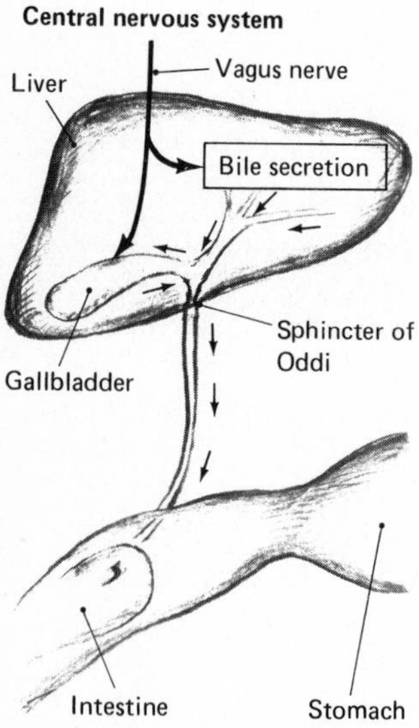

FIGURE 10.1 Example of an exocrine gland controlled by the central nervous system.

Endocrine Glands

Endocrine (or "inside-secreting") glands secrete their products into the extracellular fluid surrounding capillaries; thus, the hormones they produce enter the blood. These glands do not store hormones in containers like the gallbladder; instead, the hormones are stored inside vesicles in the cytoplasm of hormone-producing cells. When stimulated to do so, the hormones are secreted by means of a process very similar to the liberation of transmitter substance by nerve terminals.

Usually, the stimuli that trigger the release of the hormone also increase its rate of production.

As we saw in chapter 1, the brain communicates with the effectors of the body by neural and nonneural means. Much of the endocrine system is controlled by the hypothalamic hormones produced in the brain. There is a small but very crucial vascular system (the *hypothalamic-hypophyseal portal system*) that interconnects the hypothalamus and *anterior pituitary gland (adenohypophysis)*. Arterioles of the hypothalamus branch into capillaries and then drain into small veins that travel to the anterior pituitary, where they branch into another set of capillaries. Therefore, substances that enter the hypothalamic capillaries of this system travel directly to the anterior pituitary before they are diluted in the large volume of blood in the vascular system. (See **FIGURE 10.2.**) A small portal system

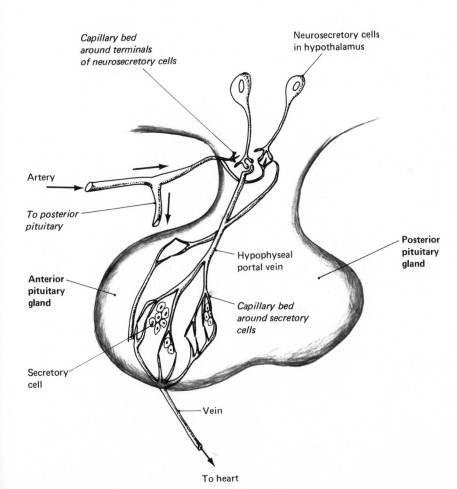

FIGURE 10.2   The pituitary gland, showing the portal blood supply. Hypothalamic hormones are released by the neurosecretory cells in the capillaries of the hypothalamus, near its junction with the pituitary stalk. (Adapted from Crosby, E. C., Humphrey, T., and Lauer, E. W., *Correlative Anatomy of the Nervous System.* New York: Macmillan, 1962.)

going in the opposite direction, from anterior pituitary to hypothalamus, has been discovered. This system undoubtedly provides the hypothalamus with information concerning the release of pituitary hormones.

The hypothalamus produces a number of *releasing* and *inhibiting hormones*. These substances are released by neurosecretory cells into the extracellular fluid around the hypothalamic capillaries of the portal system. The cell bodies of these specialized neurons reside within various hypothalamic nuclei. (See **FIGURE 10.2.**)

The hypothalamic hormones regulate the synthesis and release of the anterior pituitary hormones. Most of these hormones (the *trophic* hormones) produce indirect effects; they stimulate the production and release of hormones in other endocrine glands. Two of them, *prolactin* and *somatotrophic hormone* (*growth hormone*), produce direct effects. The behavioral effects of many of these hormones will be discussed later; the sex hormones in chapter 11, insulin in chapter 12, and aldosterone and the kidney hormones in chapter 13.

The anterior pituitary hormones are proteins; they stimulate their *target cells* by interacting with receptors on the surface of these cells, in a manner very similar to the interaction between transmitter substance and receptor site. The acceptance of a hormone molecule by a receptor on the target cell initiates the appropriate changes in the cell. Most of these changes appear to be mediated by the adenyl cyclase–cyclic AMP process, which also mediates the postsynaptic effects of norepinephrine and dopamine (chapter 5).

Steroid hormones, produced by the adrenal cortex and gonads, are composed of very small molecules and have no difficulty in entering the target cells. They attach to substances in the nucleus and direct the machinery of the cell to alter its protein production.

The hypothalamus also produces the hormones of the *posterior pituitary* (*neurohypophysis*). These hormones (*oxytocin*, which stimulates ejection of milk and uterine contractions at the time of childbirth, and *antidiuretic hormone*, which regulates urine output by the kidney) are produced by cell bodies in the hypothalamus. The hormones travel in vesicles down through the axoplasm, where they collect in the terminals within the posterior pituitary. When an axon fires, the hormone contained within the terminals is liberated and enters the circulatory system.

The adrenal medulla, also controlled neurally, closely resembles a sympathetic ganglion. It is innervated by preganglionic fibers, and its secretory cells are analogous to postganglionic sympathetic neurons. These cells secrete epinephrine and a little norepinephrine when they are neurally stimulated. Secretions of the adrenal medulla function chiefly as an adjunct to the direct neural effects of sympathetic activity; for example, epinephrine increases heart rate and constricts peripheral blood vessels. This gland also stimulates a function that cannot be mediated neurally—an increase in the conversion of *glycogen* ("animal starch") into glucose within skeletal muscle cells, increasing the energy available to them.

MUSCLES

Mammals have three types of muscles: skeletal muscle (often called *striated muscle* because of its bands and stripes), cardiac muscle, and smooth muscle (so called because it lacks striations).

SKELETAL MUSCLE. Skeletal muscles are usually attached to bone at each end and move the bones relative to each other. (Exceptions include eye muscles and some abdominal muscles, attached to bone at one end only.) Muscles are fastened to bones via tendons, very strong bands of connective tissue. Some are very short, others quite long. Most of the muscles that move our fingers, for example, are located in the upper forearm, and they communicate with the fingers via tendons that are many inches long. Several different classes of movement can be accomplished by the skeletal muscles, but I shall refer principally to only two of them: *flexion* and *extension*. Contraction of a *flexor* muscle produces flexion, a drawing in of a limb, opposed to extension. *Extensor* muscles are the so-called *antigravity muscles* —the ones we use to stand up. Picture a four-legged animal. Lifting of a paw would be described as flexion; putting it back down would be extension. I should note that we sometimes talk about "flexing" our muscles. This is an incorrect use of the term. Muscles *contract*; limbs *flex*. When a weight lifter exhibits his arm muscles, he is simultaneously contracting the flexors and extensors of that limb.

SMOOTH MUSCLE. There are two types of smooth muscle, both of which are controlled by the autonomic nervous system. *Multiunit smooth muscles* are found, for example, in larger arteries, around hair follicles (where they produce piloerection), and in the eye (controlling lens adjustment and pupillary dilation). This type of smooth muscle is normally inactive, but it will contract in response to neural stimulation or to certain hormones. *Single-unit smooth muscle* normally contracts in a rhythmic fashion. Some of these cells spontaneously produce *pacemaker potentials* (we could regard them as self-initiated EPSPs). These slow potentials elicit action potentials, which are propagated by adjacent smooth muscle fibers, resulting in a wave of muscular contraction. The efferent nerve supply (and various hormones) modulates the rhythmic rate, increasing or decreasing it, instead of eliciting the individual contractions. Single-unit smooth muscles are found chiefly in the gastrointestinal system, uterus, and small blood vessels.

CARDIAC MUSCLE.   Finally, there is cardiac muscle, the location of which is specified by its name.   This type of muscle looks somewhat like striated muscle, but acts like single-unit smooth muscle.   The heart beats regularly, even if it is denervated.   Neural activity and, again, certain hormones serve to modulate heart rate.   A group of cells in the *pacemaker* of the heart are rhythmically active and initiate contractions of cardiac muscle.

Anatomy of Skeletal Muscle

The detailed structure of a skeletal muscle is shown in **FIGURE 10.3.** As you can see from this illustration (which is highly schematic and omits many details for clarity), there are two types of muscle fibers, served by three kinds of nerve endings.   The *extrafusal muscle fibers* are served by the axons of the *alpha motor neurons*.   These fibers are responsible for the force produced by a muscle when it contracts. The *intrafusal muscle fibers* are served by two axons, one afferent and one efferent.   The afferent ending is found in the central region (*capsule*) of the intrafusal muscle fiber.   This ending is a mechanoreceptor, sensitive to forces applied to the ends of the intrafusal muscle fiber.   There is more than one type of afferent ending, but for simplicity only one kind is shown here.   The efferent to this muscle fiber can cause the fiber to contract; this contraction, however, contributes an insignificant amount of mechanical force to the muscle as a whole.   The only function of contraction of the intrafusal muscle fiber, as we shall see, is to modify the sensitivity of the fiber's afferent ending to stretch.

Note that a single myelinated axon of an alpha motor neuron serves several muscle fibers.   (See **FIGURE 10.3.**)   In primates, the number of muscle fibers served by a single axon varies considerably, from as few as a dozen in muscles controlling the fingers or eyes to many hundreds in large muscles of the leg.   An alpha motor neuron, its axon, and associated extrafusal muscle fibers constitute an entity known as a *motor unit.*

A single muscle fiber can, in turn, be divided into a number of *myofibrils*, which consist of overlapping strands of *actin* and *myosin*. Note the small protrusions on the myosin filaments; these structures (*myosin cross bridges*) are the motile elements that interact with the actin filaments and produce muscular contractions.   (See **FIGURE 10.3.**)

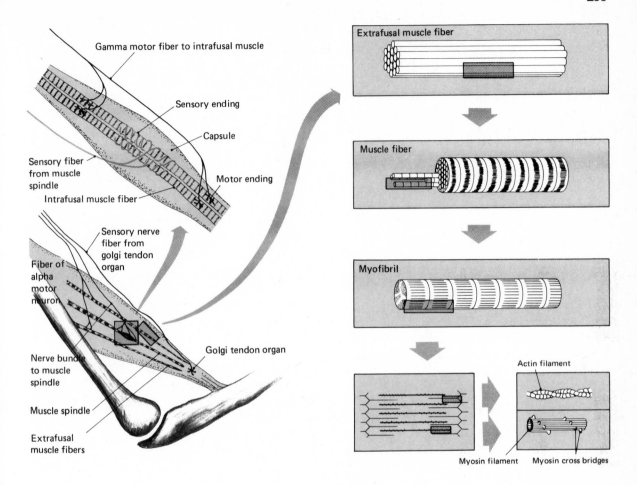

Figure 10.3 labels: Gamma motor fiber to intrafusal muscle; Sensory ending; Capsule; Sensory fiber from muscle spindle; Motor ending; Intrafusal muscle fiber; Sensory nerve fiber from golgi tendon organ; Fiber of alpha motor neuron; Nerve bundle to muscle spindle; Muscle spindle; Extrafusal muscle fibers; Golgi tendon organ; Extrafusal muscle fiber; Muscle fiber; Myofibril; Actin filament; Myosin filament; Myosin cross bridges

FIGURE 10.3 Anatomy of striated (skeletal) muscle. (Adapted from Bloom and Fawcett, *A Textbook of Histology*. Philadelphia: W. B. Saunders, 1968.)

Neuromuscular Junctions

The synapse between an efferent nerve terminal and the membrane of a muscle fiber is called a *neuromuscular junction.* The nerve terminals synapse on *motor end plates,* located in grooves along the surface of the muscle fibers. When an axon fires, acetylcholine is liberated by the terminals and produces a depolarization of the post-synaptic membrane (*end plate potential,* or *EPP*). The end plate potential is much larger than a corresponding EPSP in the central nervous system; an EPP *always* causes the normal, healthy muscle fiber to fire. The membrane of the muscle fiber propagates an action potential along its length, thus inducing a contraction, or *twitch,* of the muscle fiber.

The muscle fiber twitch is just as much an all-or-none phe-nomenon as the action potential of the axon. Thus, elicitation of an action potential in an alpha motor neuron *guarantees* the contraction of the muscle fibers that are a part of this motor unit. The last place where decisions can be made in the nervous system is at the level of the motor neuron. There, excitatory and inhibitory nerve terminals can produce their conflicting effects, but nothing can prevent the contraction of all the muscle fibers of a motor unit once the motor neuron fires. Sherrington, the great pioneering neurophysiologist, thus referred to the *lower motor neuron* of the spinal cord and cranial nerve nuclei as the site of the *final common pathway* of the decision-making process.

As the action potential, triggered by the EPP produced by release of ACh from the nerve terminal, propagates along the muscle fiber, it increases membrane permeability to Na^+ and K^+, a process normally associated with transmission of a nerve impulse. In addition, the membrane becomes more permeable to the calcium ion, and the entry of this ion activates the myosin cross bridges, thus causing the muscle twitch. Active membrane transport (i.e., a *calcium pump*) gets rid of the intracellular calcium and terminates the contraction.

Physical Basis of Muscular Contraction

The entry of Ca^{++} into the cytoplasm of a muscle fiber triggers a series of events that results in movement of the myosin cross bridges. These protrusions alternately attach to the actin strands, bend in one direction, detach themselves, bend back, reattach to the actin, etc. The cross bridges thus "row" along the actin filaments. Figure 10.4 illustrates the "rowing" sequence, and it shows how this sequence results in shortening of the muscle fiber. (See **FIGURE 10.4.**)

A single impulse of a motor neuron will produce a single muscle fiber twitch. The physical effects of the twitch will last considerably longer than will the action potential because of the elasticity of the muscle and the time required to rid the cell of calcium. Figure 10.5 shows how the physical effects of a series of action potentials can overlap, causing a sustained contraction by the muscle fiber. (A single motor unit in a leg muscle of a cat can raise a 100-gm weight, which attests to the remarkable strength of the contractile mechanism.) (See **FIGURE 10.5.**)

As you know quite well, muscular contraction is not an all-or-none phenomenon, as are the twitches of the constituent muscle fibers. Obviously, strength of muscular contraction is determined by the average rate of firing of the various motor units. If, at a given moment, many units are firing, the contraction will be forceful. If few are firing, the contraction will be weak.

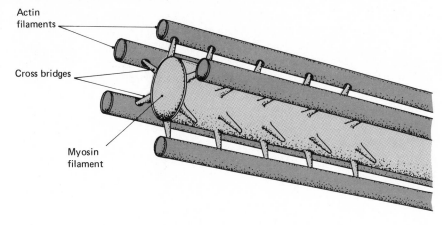

Actin filaments

Cross bridges

Myosin filament

FIGURE 10.4   The mechanism by which muscles contract. The myosin cross bridges perform "rowing" movements, which cause the actin and myosin filaments to move relative to each other. (Adapted from Anthony, C. P., and Kolthoff, N. J., *Textbook of Anatomy and Physiology*, ed. 8. St. Louis: C. V. Mosby, 1971.)

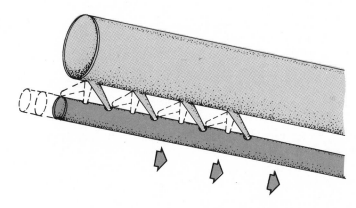

Sensory Feedback from the Muscles

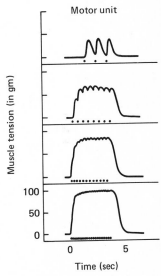

Motor unit

Muscle tension (in gm)

Time (sec)

FIGURE 10.5   A rapid succession of action potentials can cause a muscle fiber to produce a sustained contraction. Each dot represents an individual action potential. (Adapted from Devanandan, M. S., Eccles, R. M., and Westerman, R. A., *Journal of Physiology (London)*, 1965, *178*, 359–367.)

The intrafusal muscle fibers contain sensory endings sensitive to stretch. These fibers (they are often referred to as *muscle spindles*) are arranged in parallel with the extrafusal muscle fibers. Therefore, they are stretched when the muscle lengthens and are relaxed when it shortens. Thus, even though these afferents are *stretch receptors*, they are actually *muscle-length detectors*. This distinction is important, as we shall see. Stretch receptors are also located within the tendons; this system is referred to as the *Golgi tendon organ*. Here, we see receptors that detect stretch exerted by the muscle, via its tendons, on the bones to which the muscle is attached. The stretch receptors of the Golgi tendon organ encode degree of stretch by rate of firing. It does not matter how long the muscle is—only how hard it is pulling. The receptors of the muscle spindle, on the other hand, detect muscle length, not tension.

Figure 10.6 shows the response of afferents of the muscle spindles and Golgi tendon organ to various types of movements. Figure 10.6A shows the effects of passive lengthening of the muscle, the kind of movement that would be seen, for example, if your forearm, held in a completely relaxed fashion, were slowly lowered by someone who was supporting it. The rate of firing of one type of muscle spindle afferent increases (MS$_1$), while the activity of the afferent of the Golgi tendon organ (GTO) remains unchanged. (See **FIGURE 10.6A.**) Figure 10.6B shows the same results if the arm were dropped quickly; note that this time MS$_2$ (the second type of muscle spindle afferent) fires a rapid burst of impulses. This fiber, then, signals rapid changes in muscle length. (See **FIGURE 10.6B.**) Figure 10.6C shows what would happen if a weight were suddenly dropped into

FIGURE 10.6 Effects of arm movements on the firing of muscle and tendon afferents. (A) Slow passive extension of the arm. (B) Rapid extension of the arm. (C) Addition of a weight to an arm held in a horizontal position. MS$_1$ and MS$_2$ are two types of muscle spindles; GTO is an afferent fiber from the Golgi tendon organ.

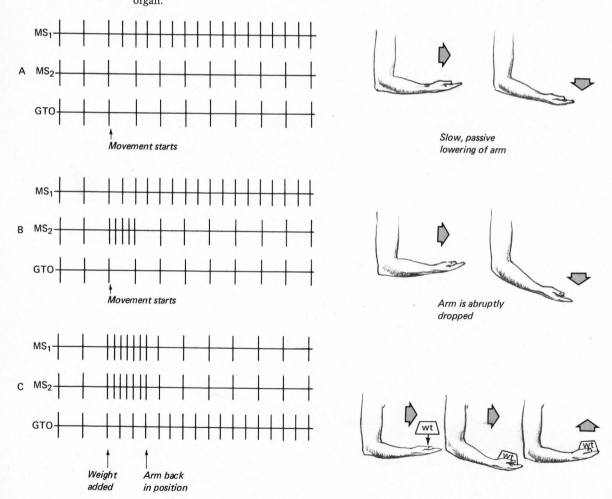

your hand while your forearm was held parallel to the ground. MS_1 and MS_2 (especially MS_2, which responds to rate of change in muscle length) will briefly fire, because your arm will lower briefly and then come back to the original position. GTO, monitoring strength of contraction, fires in proportion to the stress on the muscle, so it continues to fire, even after the original position of the arm is restored. (See **FIGURE 10.6C.**) I might note that, because of *Archimedes' principle*, which describes how force can be increased or decreased by means of levers, your *biceps* muscle must exert a force of 280 lb to support a weight of 40 lb carried in your hand. (See **FIGURE 10.7.**)

REFLEX CONTROL OF MOVEMENT

The Monosynaptic Stretch Reflex

It is easy to demonstrate the activity of the simplest functional neural pathway in the body. Sit on a surface high enough to allow your legs to dangle freely and have someone lightly tap your *patellar tendon* just below the kneecap. In response to this light tap your leg will kick forward. (I am sure few of you will bother with this demonstration, since you are quite familiar with it; most physical examinations include a test of the *patellar reflex*.) The time interval between the tendon tap and the start of the leg extension is about 50 msec. That interval is too short for the involvement of cortex—it would take considerably longer for sensory information to be relayed to cortex and motor information to be relayed back. For example, if a person

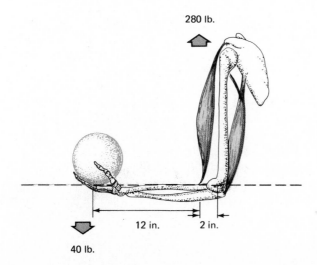

280 lb.

12 in.　2 in.

40 lb.

FIGURE 10.7 The force exerted by most muscles is considerably greater than the weight supported by the limb.

is asked to respond as fast as possible to a light flash by producing a muscular movement, the interval between the stimulus and the start of the movement will be several times greater than the time required for the patellar reflex. The patellar reflex occurs in response to a brief, quick stretch to the muscle (the tendon serves only to transmit the stretch), which causes sensory information to be sent to the spinal cord. Almost immediately, motor impulses are "reflected" back to the muscle—hence the term *reflex.*

Obviously, the patellar reflex as such has no utility; no selective advantage is bestowed upon animals that kick a limb when a tendon is tapped. If a more natural stimulus is applied, however, the utility of this mechanism becomes apparent. Figure 10.8 reproduces part of a previous figure, showing the effects of placing a weight in a person's hand. However, this time I have included a piece of the spinal cord, with its roots, to show the neural circuit that composes the *monosynaptic stretch reflex.* First follow the circuit: starting at the muscle spindle, afferent impulses follow the fiber to the gray matter of the spinal cord. The terminals synapse on an alpha motor neuron innervating the extrafusal muscle fibers of the same muscle. Only one synapse is encountered along the route from receptor to effector—hence the term *monosynaptic.* (See **FIGURE 10.8.**)

Now consider the sequence of events. The alpha motor neurons (and their associated muscle fibers) must fire at some constant rate to keep the limb in a constant position, as shown in the left-hand figure. When the weight is increased, the forearm begins to move down. This movement lengthens the muscle and increases the firing rate of the muscle spindle afferents. Since the afferent fibers synapse on the alpha motor neurons (and produce EPSPs), the firing rate of the motor neurons increases. Hence, the muscle contracts and pulls the weight up. (See **FIGURE 10.8.**)

The monosynaptic stretch reflex is probably most important in initiating the movement to restore the limb to the original position. The brain then uses information it receives from the muscle spindles to set a new firing level of the motor neurons, keeping the limb in the correct position. If the spindle afferent did not synapse with the alpha motor neuron, but only sent information to the brain, there would be a great lag between increased weight and the start of the muscle activity to restore limb position. The weight would probably be dropped. The reflex works in the opposite direction, also. When we pick up a weight that is lighter than we expect, the sudden muscle shortening quickly reduces activity of the spindle afferent and removes excitatory activity from the alpha motor neurons, slowing the rate of contraction. Otherwise, we would probably throw the weight into the air.

Another very significant role played by the monosynaptic stretch reflex is its control of posture. In order to stand, we humans

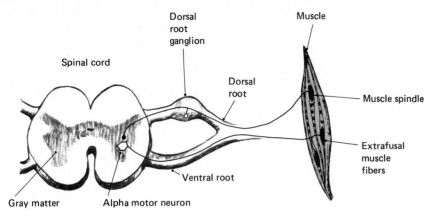

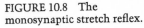

FIGURE 10.8 The monosynaptic stretch reflex.

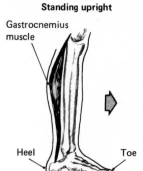

Standing upright

Gastrocnemius muscle

Heel

Toe

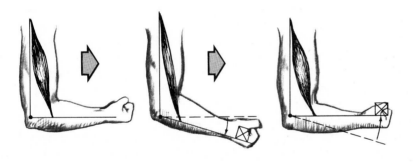

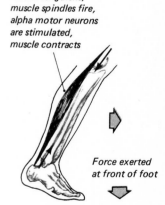

Leaning forward

Muscle lengthens, muscle spindles fire, alpha motor neurons are stimulated, muscle contracts

Force exerted at front of foot

must keep our center of gravity above our feet, or we will fall. As we stand, we tend to oscillate back and forth, and from side to side. Our vestibular sacs and our visual system play a very significant role in the maintenance of posture. These systems are aided, however, by the activity of the monosynaptic stretch reflex. For example, consider what happens when a person begins to lean forward. The large calf muscle (*gastrocnemius*) is stretched, and this stretching elicits compensatory muscular contraction that pushes the toes down, thus restoring upright posture. (See **FIGURE 10.9.**)

Polysynaptic Reflex Pathways

Before I begin to discuss some more complicated reflexes, I should mention the fact that the simple circuit diagrams used here (including the one you just looked at in Figure 10.8) are quite fallacious. Many neurons participate in even the simplest reflex, but, for simplicity's sake, only a single chain of neurons is drawn. You should bear in mind that each neuron shown in the diagrams represents

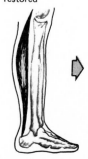

Upright posture restored

FIGURE 10.9 The role of the monosynaptic stretch reflex in postural control.

hundreds or thousands of neurons, each axon synapsing on many neurons, and each neuron receiving synapses from many different axons. The multiple branching of axons represents *divergence* of information and the multiple input on a single neuron represents *convergence* of information. These processes are shown in **FIGURE 10.10.** The diagram of a reflex would be awfully untidy if I tried to represent the amount of divergence and convergence that really occurs.

As we previously saw, the afferent fibers from the Golgi tendon organs serve as detectors of muscle stretch. There are two populations of GTO afferents, with different sensitivities to stretch. The more sensitive afferents tell the brain how hard the muscle is pulling. The less sensitive ones have an additional function. Their terminals synapse on spinal cord *interneurons* (neurons that reside entirely within the gray matter of the spinal cord and serve to interconnect other spinal neurons). These interneurons synapse, in turn, on the alpha motor neurons serving the same muscle. The interneurons liberate glycine, and hence produce IPSPs on the motor neurons. (See **FIGURE 10.11.**) The function of this *polysynaptic* reflex pathway (specifically, it is *disynaptic,* since two synapses are involved) is to decrease the strength of muscular contraction when there is danger of damage to the tendons or bones to which the muscles are attached. Weight lifters can lift heavier weights if their tendon organs are deactivated with injections of a local anesthetic, but they run the risk of pulling the tendon away from the bone, or even breaking the bone.

The discovery of the inhibitory tendon organ reflex provided the first real evidence of neural inhibition, long before the synaptic mechanisms were understood. A *decerebrate* cat (one whose brain stem has been cut through) exhibits a phenomenon known as *decerebrate rigidity.* This rigidity results from excitation originating

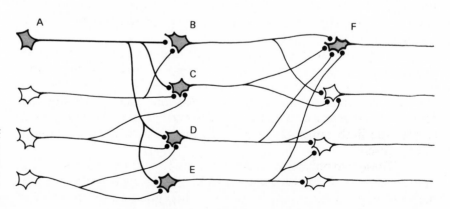

FIGURE 10.10   Examples of divergence (neuron A synapses with neurons B, C, D, and E) and convergence (neurons B, C, D, and E synapse with neuron F).

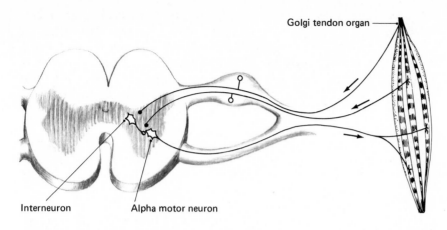

Golgi tendon organ

Interneuron   Alpha motor neuron

FIGURE 10.11   Input from the Golgi tendon organ can cause IPSPs to occur on the alpha motor neuron.

in the caudal reticular formation, which greatly facilitates all stretch reflexes, especially of extensor muscles. (In a later section we shall see how this facilitation is accomplished.) Rostral to the brainstem transection is an inhibitory region of the reticular formation, which normally counterbalances the excitatory one. If you attempt to flex the outstretched leg of a decerebrate cat, you will meet with increasing resistance, which suddenly melts away, allowing the limb to flex. It almost feels as though you were closing the blade of a pocket-knife— hence the term *clasp-knife reflex*. The sudden release is, of course, mediated by activation of the tendon organ reflex.

The monosynaptic stretch reflex is not quite so simple as it might first appear. Muscles are arranged in opposing pairs. The *agonist* moves the limb in the direction being studied, and since muscles cannot push back, the *antagonist* muscle is necessary to move the limb back in the opposite direction. (*Agōn* means "contest"; hence the terms agonist and antagonist.) Consider this fact, then: when a stretch reflex is elicited in the agonist, it contracts quickly, thus causing the antagonist to lengthen. It would appear, then, that the antagonist is presented with a stimulus that should elicit *its* stretch reflex. And yet the antagonist relaxes instead. Let's see why.

Afferents of the muscle spindles, besides sending terminals to the alpha motor neuron and to the brain, also synapse on inhibitory interneurons, which, in turn, synapse on alpha motor neurons serving the antagonistic muscle. (See **FIGURE 10.12.**) This means that a stretch reflex excites the agonist and inhibits the antagonist, so that the limb can move in the direction controlled by the stimulated muscle.

These two polysynaptic reflexes are only a small fraction of the many that have been discovered so far. For example, reflex flexion of one forelimb produces extension of the other one, and even involves

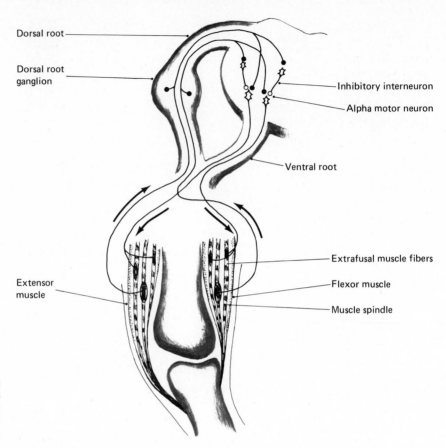

Dorsal root

Dorsal root ganglion

Inhibitory interneuron

Alpha motor neuron

Ventral root

Extrafusal muscle fibers

Flexor muscle

Extensor muscle

Muscle spindle

FIGURE 10.12 Firing of the muscle spindle causes excitation on the alpha motor neuron of the agonist, and inhibition on the antagonist.

the hindlimbs. But let us now examine the role of the fourth nerve fiber to the muscle—the efferent to the intrafusal muscle fiber.

The Gamma Motor System

The muscle spindles are very sensitive to changes in muscle length; they will increase their rate of firing when the muscle is lengthened by a very small amount. The interesting thing is that this detection mechanism is adjustable. Remember that the ends of the intrafusal muscle fiber can be contracted by activity of the associated efferent fiber; rate of firing determines the degree of contraction. When the muscle spindles are relaxed, they are relatively insensitive to stretch. If, however, they are being stimulated at a high rate by their efferents, they are very sensitive to changes in muscle length. This property of adjustable sensitivity simplifies the role of the brain in controlling movements.

We already saw that the spindle afferents help maintain limb position even when the load carried by the limb is altered. Efferent control of the muscle spindles permits these muscle-length detectors to assist in changes in limb position, as well. Consider a single muscle spindle. When its efferent fiber is completely silent, the spindle is completely relaxed and extended. As the firing rate of the fiber increases, the spindle gets shorter and shorter. If, simultaneously, the rest of the entire muscle also gets shorter, there will be no stretch on the nuclear bag region, and the afferent fiber will not respond. However, if the muscle spindle contracts faster than does the muscle as a whole, there will be a considerable amount of afferent activity.

The motor system makes use of this phenomenon in the following way: When commands from the brain are issued to move a limb, both the alpha motor neurons and the *gamma motor neurons* (the cell bodies that send efferent axons to the muscle spindles) are activated. The alpha motor neurons start the muscle contracting. If there is little resistance, both the extrafusal and the intrafusal fibers will contract at approximately the same rate, and little activity will be seen from the spindle afferents. However, if resistance is met, these fibers will fire and thus cause reflexive strengthening of the contraction. The brain thus makes use of the gamma motor system in moving the limbs. By establishing a rate of firing in the *gamma motor system*, the brain determines the length of the muscle spindles and thus, indirectly, the length of the entire muscle.

It was formerly thought that only the gamma motor neurons were activated to initiate movements, and that the alpha motor neurons were stimulated solely by the spindle afferents. However, Vallbo (1971) put small electrodes into his own peripheral nerves and found that contraction of the muscle (as shown by its electrical activity, recorded in the *electromyogram*) always preceded activity of the spindle afferent. Thus, the alpha motor neurons must have been activated directly by the brain, because the movement started before the afferent impulses were observed. (See **FIGURE 10.13.**)

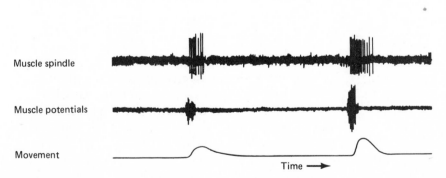

FIGURE 10.13 Evidence that the muscle begins moving before the muscle spindle begins firing proves that the alpha motor neurons directly initiate the movement. (From Vallbo, Å. B., Muscle spindle response at the outset of isometric voluntary contractions in man: Time difference between fusimotor and skeletomotor effects. *Journal of Physiology (London)*, 1971, *218*, 405–431. Used by permission of Cambridge University Press.)

Muscle spindle

Muscle potentials

Movement

Time ⟶

It is the gamma motor system, furthermore, that is largely responsible for *muscle tone*. Even when we are resting, there is a certain amount of muscular activity. (This phenomenon is probably necessary for the health of our muscles. If a peripheral nerve is cut, the muscle it serves will atrophy—wither away. Direct electrical stimulation of the muscle prevents this effect.) The rate of firing of the gamma motor neurons largely determines the degree of muscle tone. You can excite the gamma motor system yourself, and demonstrate its effects, by performing the *Jendrassic maneuver*. Have a friend test your patellar reflex and note its strength. Now clasp your fingers together in front of you and pull your hands in opposite directions, forcefully. While you are doing this, have your friend again test your patellar reflex. It should be more forceful now. The increased gamma motor activity to your arms "spills over" to the gamma motor neurons serving your leg muscles, in an example of divergence of information. The increased gamma motor activity enhances your patellar reflex. There are other ways, also, to increase gamma motor activity. One of the best is to walk over rough terrain in the dark. Your stretch reflexes are at a peak sensitivity, then.

Recurrent Collaterals

Figure 10.14 shows a more detailed view of an alpha motor neuron. Before its axon leaves the gray matter of the spinal cord, it sends off a collateral fiber. This fiber (called a *recurrent collateral*) branches, and the terminals synapse on inhibitory interneurons. These interneurons (called *Renshaw cells*) synapse on the same alpha motor neurons whose recurrent collateral stimulated them. (See **FIGURE 10.14.**) Thus, after an alpha motor neuron fires, it receives some self-initiated inhibition. (The IPSPs produced by Renshaw cells are quite long-lived—up to ½ sec.) This means that once the alpha motor neuron fires, it is difficult to get it to fire again for a period of time.

This phenomenon of *recurrent inhibition* accomplishes a useful purpose: the rotation of effort among the various motor units of a muscle. A weak muscular contraction requires a low rate of activity of the muscle fibers; during any given time interval, few of the fibers contract. This same effect could be accomplished by having a few fibers fire rapidly, or by having all fibers fire slowly. If the same small number of motor units fired repeatedly, however, they would quickly become fatigued. Since each motor unit follows a cycle of sensitivity—inhibition, followed by gradual recovery—a steady low level of excitation of all the neurons will cause each one to fire only in the sensitive portion of its cycle. Thus, the muscular

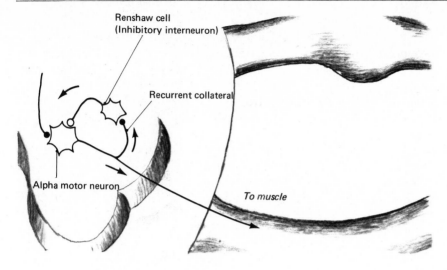

FIGURE 10.14   Recurrent inhibition.

effort is distributed among all the motor units, giving each one a period of rest. A more forceful contraction is produced by increased stimulation of the motor neurons, causing them to fire earlier in their cycle of sensitivity.

Complex Reflex Mechanisms

Reflex mechanisms can take care of many complex functions. Even if the spinal cord is severed from the brain, a female dog can become pregnant, carry her litter to term, and deliver the pups. In males, penile erection and ejaculation can be stimulated even after the spinal cord is cut. Humans with spinal cord damage have thus become fathers by means of artificial insemination.

The brain, as well as the spinal cord, participates in reflexes. A very high level of reflex integration can be demonstrated in a very nimble animal, the cat. If a cat's head is pushed down, the animal will flex its forelimbs and extend its hindlimbs. (See **FIGURE 10.15.**) The cat's body posture will also be changed when the head turns right or left, or rotates. These *tonic neck reflexes* combine with vestibular reflexes to produce the *righting reflex.* Figure 10.16 illustrates what happens when a cat is held upside down and dropped. First the head begins to return to its normal orientation (vestibular reflexes) and then the body follows the head (tonic neck reflexes). The mechanisms go together very nicely so that the cat invariably lands on its feet. (See **FIGURE 10.16.**)

Many afferents of muscle spindles and cutaneous receptors travel to motor cortex, and it is apparent that they can initiate or

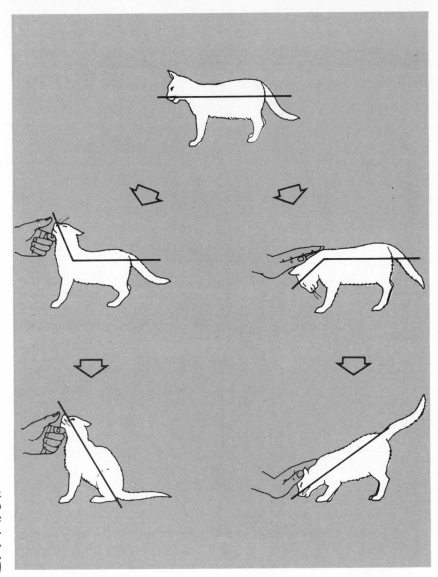

FIGURE 10.15 The tonic neck reflexes cause the cat's body to respond to movements of the head. (Adapted from Elliot, H. C., *Textbook of Neuroanatomy*, Philadelphia: J. B. Lippincott, 1963.)

facilitate reflex motor activity via this pathway. For example, Asanuma and Rosén (1972) and Rosén and Asanuma (1972) stimulated and recorded from discrete regions in motor cortex of monkeys. They found a reciprocal afferent and efferent organization in these cortical regions. For example, if stimulation of a locus on motor cortex produced thumb flexion, the same area was maximally sensitive to cutaneous stimulation of the ball of the thumb. Loci that produced thumb extension when stimulated appeared to be most responsive to touch along the back of the thumb. This organization, therefore, would appear to reinforce a movement that resulted in the touching of an object, and might, as Eccles (1973) notes, be responsible for a baby's grasp when an object is placed in its hand.

CENTRAL MOTOR CONTROL

So far I have been describing "automatic" motor control—something that is "involuntary," for the most part. I put these words in quotes because, although we all realize that there is a difference between such "involuntary" movements as the patellar reflex and such "voluntary" movements as I am making in moving my pen to write this, there is no way to define strictly either of these terms. The word voluntary comes from the Latin *voluntas*—"will." If we take a mechanistic view of the body, we must reject the notion of will; the body is a machine, and all effects must have causes. If we postulate free will, then there would be effects not determined by causes. But we cannot throw away the concept of "voluntary." We can get rid of the term by substituting some euphemism or other, but until we know much more than we do about the mechanisms of the brain, we are going to be stuck with that fuzzily defined term.

Motor cortex can be defined in various ways. Anatomically, it can be shown that some areas contribute to descending motor systems. Damage to motor functions can be observed after destruction of various cortical regions. Or, electrodes can be placed on various parts of cortex to determine which areas produce movements when electrically stimulated. The "classical" motor cortex is the precentral gyrus, but movements can be elicited from many other cortical regions. The "motor homunculus" of Figure 10.17 is drawn over "primary motor cortex" and represents the regions of the body that move in response to local electrical stimulation. (See **FIGURE 10.17.**) Just as cutaneous receptors from the fingers and lips project to a disproportionately large area of somatosensory cortex, a correspondingly large area of motor cortex elicits movements in our most precisely controlled structures—digits, lips, tongue, and vocal apparatus.

Only recently, it has been shown that another area of cortex is

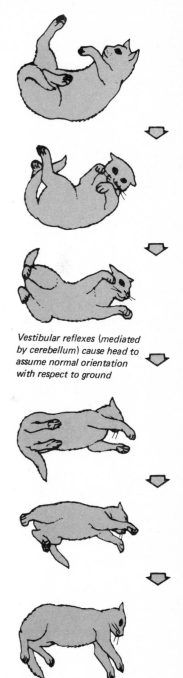

Vestibular reflexes (mediated by cerebellum) cause head to assume normal orientation with respect to ground

Tonic neck reflexes cause body to follow head

FIGURE 10.16   The righting reflex. Vestibular reflexes cause the cat's head to right first, and tonic neck reflexes cause the body to follow the cat's head. (Adapted from Marey, M., *Comptes Rendus des Séances de L'Académie des Sciences,* 1894, *119,* 714–721.)

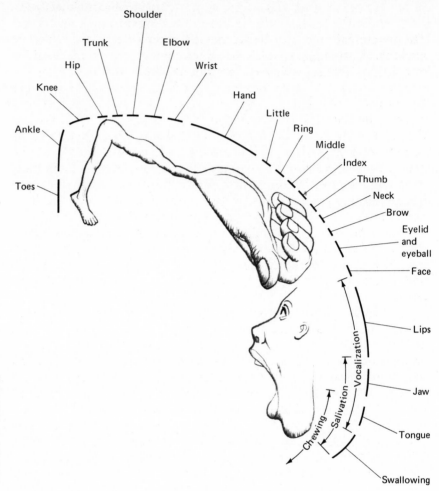

FIGURE 10.17 A motor homunculus. Stimulation of various regions of motor cortex causes movement in muscles of various parts of the body. (Adapted from Penfield, W., and Rasmussen, T., *The Cerebral Cortex of Man*. New York: Macmillan, 1950.)

involved in movement. Glickstein and his colleagues have discovered a neural circuit from secondary visual cortex to pons to cerebellum (Glickstein, King, and Stein, 1971; Glickstein and Stein, 1973; Gibson, Baker, Stein, and Glickstein, 1974). The authors suggest that secondary visual cortex "organizes responses to moving targets and relays such information to the cerebellum" (Gibson et al., 1974). Movement (or modification of movement) would then result from cerebellar activity. Thus, sensory cortex has a direct output to motor systems not mediated by "motor" cortex. And, as we shall see, cells of "somatosensory" cortex contribute a considerable portion of the descending motor fibers of cortex. Therefore, a rigid distinction between sensory and motor areas of cortex is not valid.

The Pyramidal Motor System

The pyramidal motor system generally receives a disproportionate amount of attention in discussions of motor control mechanisms in mammals, considering its importance. The pyramidal motor system consists of a long, monosynaptic pathway from cortex to motor neurons (or interneurons) of the cranial nerve nuclei and ventral horn of the spinal cord. In humans, most of the fibers decussate at the level of the medulla; a variable number of fibers (averaging 20 percent in humans) descend through the ipsilateral spinal cord. However, most of these fibers eventually decussate in the spinal cord near their level of termination. Collateral fibers are also sent to ventrolateral thalamus, red nucleus, pontine nuclei, inferior olive, and reticular formation. The system is schematically illustrated in **FIGURE 10.18.** It should be noted that, although the precentral gyrus is usually called "primary motor cortex," its cells contribute only about one-third of the descending fibers. The other fibers arise from cells of the postcentral gyrus (the somatosensory area), frontal cortex, and temporal cortex.

Just as we do not know the location of the brain regions that "experience" stimuli, we do not know where "voluntary" movements originate. (We could say that they originate at the sense receptors, because our behavior is a function of sensory stimuli, in both the recent and distant past, but that would be begging the question.) It is clear that "voluntary" movements are *not* initiated in the precentral gyrus. Electrical stimulation of this area initiates irresistible movements in human patients, but the patients invariably report that the stimulation elicited the movement itself, and not a desire to move. We do not know the starting point of motor systems any more than we know the ending point of sensory systems. There is some evidence that the "associational" areas of cortex participate in the initiation of movements. Damage to these areas in humans leads to movements that are well integrated but robotlike in character, lacking purpose or direction (Crosby, Humphrey and Lauer, 1962). However, these results do not rule out the possible participation of subcortical areas of the brain in the control of these "voluntary" movements. As we shall see, subcortical control appears to be quite important.

INITIATION VERSUS CONTROL OF MOVEMENT: THE APRAXIAS. The evidence that most directly implicates association cortex in the initiation of voluntary movements is provided by study of the *apraxias*—inabilities to perform certain types of movements after lesions of cerebral cortex. As Geschwind (1975) points out, some of these disorders can be viewed as deficits of understanding.

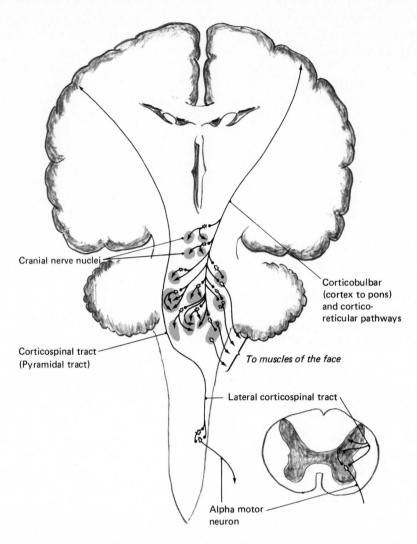

Cranial nerve nuclei

Corticobulbar
(cortex to pons)
and cortico-
reticular pathways

Corticospinal tract
(Pyramidal tract)

To muscles of the face

Lateral corticospinal tract

Alpha motor
neuron

FIGURE 10.18 Pathway of the pyramidal motor system. Note the complex interconnections with various subcortical motor nuclei.
(Adapted with permission from McGraw-Hill Book Co. from *The Human Nervous System*, 2nd edition, by Noback and Demarest. Copyright © 1975, by McGraw-Hill, Inc.)

In order for a movement to be performed in response to spoken commands, the sounds must be analyzed for meaning and the results of this analysis must be forwarded to brain mechanisms involved in producing the appropriate movements. Speech is analyzed for meaning by a region of auditory association cortex located on the left temporal lobe. (This region will be discussed in more detail in chapter 18.)

Certain brain lesions (produced by tumors or by cerebrovascular accident) can disrupt connections between this auditory association cortex and motor cortex of the frontal lobe. Therefore, motor mechanisms controlled by the frontal lobes cannot be activated by speech. However, the temporal lobes contain many motor neurons that project to the extrapyramidal motor system—especially the parts controlling postural changes and movements of the proximal musculature, as opposed to the distal musculature of the forearms and hands. When a patient with such lesions is asked to "assume a boxer's stance," he readily does so. When asked to "jab with your hand," he remains immobile. Similarly, he will not wave his hand in response to verbal commands, but he will readily nod his head if asked to do so.

This syndrome can best be explained in the following way: The meaning of the verbal message is decoded by auditory association cortex of the left temporal lobe. If the motor neurons of the temporal lobe are able to initiate the commanded movement, the patient responds appropriately. If the movement requires the participation of frontal cortical mechanisms, the patient does not respond. The fact that he is able to make movements of the distal musculature is shown by the fact that he can wave back if someone waves at him, and that he can handle objects appropriately if they are given to him. Therefore, this form of apraxia does not appear to result from damage to motor mechanisms, but rather to result from interrupted communication between mechanisms that initiate movements and those that control them.

THE PYRAMIDAL SYSTEM IN EVOLUTIONARY PERSPECTIVE. The pyramidal motor system is not essential to movement—not even to many well-integrated, skilled behaviors. In humans, the "pyramidal tract syndrome"—that is, the deficits following damage to these structures—characteristically includes *paresis* (partial paralysis), spasticity, depression of cutaneous reflexes, and exaggeration of stretch reflexes. However, it appears that much of the deficit that is seen actually results from damage to other motor systems adjacent to the pyramidal system. Instead, the principal motor effects appear to be decreased muscle strength (particularly in the flexors of the hands), impaired dexterity of the hands and fingers, and increased reaction time in response to visual stimuli (Brooks and Stoney, 1971). Clearly, an individual could survive quite well without this system. This is not to say that the pyramidal motor system is not needed by our species; to the contrary, our evolution was shaped by the fact that we, as a group, are able to perform precise, fine movements with our hands and fingers. A clumsy individual human will survive, but our species would not have attained its present status if all humans had been clumsy.

It is commonly said that the pyramidal system is a recent evolutionary development and reaches its ultimate development in *Homo sapiens.* (We humans tend to think that *everything* reaches its ultimate development in our species.) However, Towe (1973) notes that analogous systems can be found in birds, and he argues that the pyramidal system was first seen in some common ancestor to mammals and birds and is thus very old, phylogenetically. He also notes that humans do not possess an inordinate number of pyramidal tract fibers, relative to body size; as a matter of fact, a mouse has fifty times more pyramidal tract fibers per kilogram of body weight than does a human. And some individual chimps and seals have a greater absolute number of pyramidal fibers than do some individual humans, even though the humans outweigh them. As Towe puts it, ". . . from the present perspective on his pyramidal tract, man shows up as just another mammal" (1973).

In an analysis of the comparative anatomy of the pyramidal tract, Heffner and Masterton (1975) concluded that two measurements were best correlated with a species' digital dexterity: depth of penetration of pyramidal fibers down the spinal cord (caudally), and depth of penetration of these fibers into the spinal gray matter (ventrally). Other measures, such as number or sizes of fibers in the pyramidal tract, bore poor relationship to dexterity. It is fairly easy to interpret the significance of the correlation between dexterity and depth of penetration (ventrally) into the gray matter of the spinal cord. The farther these fibers penetrate, the closer their terminal buttons are to the spinal motor neurons controlling the muscles. More dorsal terminations represent indirect control of the motor neurons through interneurons. It is not clear why depth of penetration into caudal regions of the spinal cord is related to dexterity; perhaps, as Heffner and Masterton suggest, dexterity of the hand and finger muscles requires better control over competing influences, arising from lower levels of the spinal cord, on the motor neurons controlling these muscles. In any event, their data seem to confirm the importance of the pyramidal system in control of fine movements of the fingers and hands.

ACTIVITY OF PYRAMIDAL TRACT NEURONS DURING MOVEMENT. Evarts (1965, 1968b, 1969) has recorded the activity of single neurons in the precentral gyrus of monkeys trained to move a lever back and forth by means of wrist flexions and extensions. Movements made in the correct amount of time resulted in the delivery of a bit of grape juice, a favored beverage for monkeys. The force needed to move the lever could be controlled by the experimenter. Figure 10.19 shows the experimental preparation as well as the relationship between lever movement and the firing of a cortical neuron. Note that the firing of this neuron is nicely related to the movement, the rate increasing during flexion. (See **FIGURE 10.19.**) Evarts also found that the firing rate of pyramidal tract neurons was generally related to the force of a movement, but not to its extent.

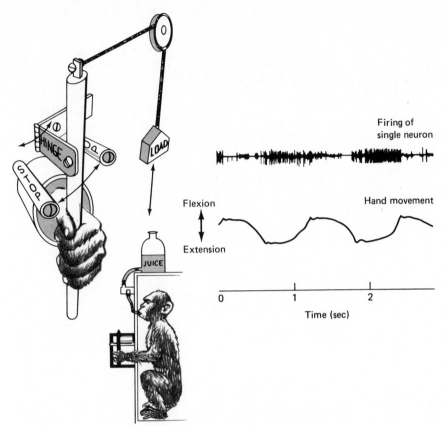

Firing of single neuron

Flexion

Extension

Hand movement

0 1 2

Time (sec)

FIGURE 10.19 The relationship between firing of single neurons in motor cortex and hand movement. The single unit records are redrawn from the original data and are therefore only approximate representations. (Redrawn from Evarts, E. V., Relation of pyramidal tract activity to force exerted during voluntary movement. *Journal of Neurophysiology*, 1968b, *31*, 14–27.)

THE PYRAMIDAL MOTOR SYSTEM AND VOLUNTARY MOVEMENT. We cannot conclude that the relationship between cell discharge and movement observed by Evarts proves that the cell thus initiates the movement (a point made by Evarts himself). Fetz (1973) found that neural activity of most cells he recorded from in motor cortex correlated well with contraction of proximal limb muscles (closest to the trunk). One might assume that electrical stimulation of the same sites would stimulate these muscles. However, such stimulation resulted in contraction of the *distal* limb muscles. Furthermore, stimulation of the appropriate sites in human precentral gyrus will produce facial movements, but Ward, Ojeman, and Calvin (1973) were unable to find many cells that fired in relation to "voluntary" movements of the same muscles.

Another study also suggests that the participation of the pyramidal system is of minor importance in the initiation of movement (Towe and Zimmerman, 1973). Muscular contractions can easily be elicited through cortical stimulation. Towe and Zimmerman found that transection of the pyramidal tracts had no effect on the threshold (i.e., weakest electrical shock capable of producing movements) or latency of movement (time between shock and onset of movement). And long ago, Lloyd (1941) showed that stimulation of the pyramidal tract produced movement only after a series of successive shocks, which contrasts with the fact that a single shock to cortex is sufficient to produce movement. Thus, cortically elicited movement does not appear to be mediated primarily via the corticospinal tract of the pyramidal motor system.

THE PYRAMIDAL SYSTEM AND CONTROL OF TACTUALLY GUIDED MOVEMENT. H. Kornhuber has described a proposed set of brain mechanisms that can account for the control of voluntary movements. (I must emphasize that the proposal attempts to account for *control* of voluntary movements, and not their *initiation*, which is an entirely different matter.) His explanation of control of rapid and slow "ramp movements" will be described in the next section.

Kornhuber (1974) suggests that the role of motor cortex and the pyramidal system is to regulate movements that require guidance from somatosensory information. Anatomically, the most common type of sensory input to neurons of motor cortex is from the somatosenses; indeed, somatosensory input is the only direct input to motor cortex. All others are via multisynaptic pathways (Pandya and Kuypers, 1969). Furthermore, finger movements, which require the highest degree of control from tactual feedback, are represented by the largest amount of cortical area (as we saw in Figure 10.17). It is important to bear in mind that the most important movements of our hands and fingers are those that manipulate objects; hence, we require accurate (and rapid) somatosensory feedback. Perhaps the most compelling evidence comes from lesion studies; animals lose their ability to react to somatosensory input, but not to input from other sense modalities, after destruction of motor cortex (Bard, 1938; Denny-Brown, 1960).

Evarts (1974) has provided electrophysiological evidence that nicely supports Kornhuber's suggestion that the neurons of motor cortex mediate tactual control of hand and finger movements. Using the apparatus shown in Figure 10.19, Evarts trained monkeys to produce a hand movement to a flash of a light or to a tactual stimulus delivered by means of the handle they were holding. Pyramidal tract neurons in motor cortex began firing 100 milliseconds after a visual stimulus, but responded in as brief an interval as 25 milliseconds to a tactual stimulus. Evarts' data provide further evidence for the preferential access of somatosensory input to these neurons, and thus lend support to Kornhuber's suggestion.

The Extrapyramidal Motor System

The term *extrapyramidal* was poorly chosen. It means "other than pyramidal" and suggests a subservient role. The pyramidal tracts are easily seen during gross examination of the brain and were hence described much earlier than were the complicated, diffuse, polysynaptic pathways of the extrapyramidal motor system.

Until fairly recently, much more was known about the anatomy of the extrapyramidal motor system than about its function. A supportive role was typically assigned to it; one often read that the pyramidal motor system initiates movements, while the extrapyramidal motor system smoothes out the movements and produces postural adjustments that support these movements. Portions of the extrapyramidal system do indeed appear to be involved in the smoothing-out of movements and in postural adjustments. However, the fact that well-integrated "voluntary" movements can occur after pyramidal tract sections would suggest that the extrapyramidal system is intimately involved in the initiation of movements as well.

The extrapyramidal system includes cortex and subcortical structures from forebrain to hindbrain. The telencephalic subcortical structures include parts of the basal ganglia—the caudate nucleus and putamen together constituting the *neostriatum* ("new grooved structure") and the globus pallidus constituting the *paleostriatum* ("old grooved structure"). The amygdala, although anatomically a part of the basal ganglia, is not functionally a part of the extrapyramidal motor system. Other parts of this system include various thalamic nuclei (ventral lateral, ventral anterior, and midline nuclei), subthalamic nucleus, red nucleus and substantia nigra of the pons, and portions of the brainstem reticular formation. The cerebellum plays a crucial role in integration and control of this system.

BASAL GANGLIA. The interconnections of the cortex and basal ganglia are very complex. Figure 10.20 illustrates a very schematic and simplified view of the interconnections. Note that there are opportunities for feedback and integration of information at all levels of the system. In particular, note the loop indicated by the shaded arrows, which will be discussed shortly. (See **FIGURE 10.20**.)

The basal ganglia appear to be principally related to facilitation and inhibition of motor sequences. For example, the globus pallidus appears to be facilitatory in nature. Destruction of this structure, which is the only part of the basal ganglia that directly projects to lower motor structures, results in a severe decrease in motor activities; the subject remains passive and immobile. Stimulation of the globus pallidus, on the other hand, facilitates reflex movements or those artificially elicited by cortical stimulation. The

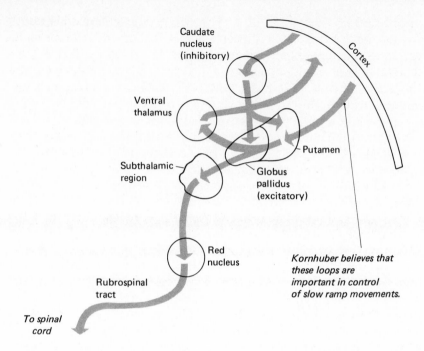

FIGURE 10.20 Some interconnections of basal ganglia. Note the loop that Kornhuber believes is involved in initiation of slow movements. Also note that the red nucleus provides the major motor output of the basal ganglia.

caudate nucleus, which receives motor information from cortex and feeds information back to cortex via the thalamic nuclei, appears to be involved in suppression of motor activity. Its stimulation will often cause an animal to cease its ongoing behavior, whereas destruction will lead to hyperactivity, such as the *obstinate progression* seen in cats with lesions of the caudate nucleus. A cat with such a lesion will pace incessantly, like a little robot. If it encounters a wall, it will continue to exhibit walking movements with its head against the wall (if the floor is slippery enough to permit its paws to slide backwards). Complex movements like these do not appear to be "programmed" in the basal ganglia; the sequences of muscular movements involved in locomotion appear to be organized elsewhere. However, the basal ganglia seem to have control over the starting and stopping of these activities. Humans with damage to the basal ganglia can usually walk, but they have difficulty in starting and stopping the locomotor sequence.

Tonic motor activities are also controlled by the basal ganglia. Parkinson's disease, which was discussed in chapter 5, results from damage to the dopaminergic neurons connecting the substantia nigra and neostriatum. The disease is characterized by muscular tremor, as well as difficulty in the initiation of movements. Patients with Parkinson's disease have difficulty in holding their hands still, but once they begin to manipulate something, the tremor disappears. I once heard of a very skillful surgeon who suffered from this *resting tremor* characteristic of Parkinson's disease. When he held his hands at his sides, they shook violently. However, once he picked up a scalpel, he was as steady as a rock. Nevertheless, I shudder at the thought of a patient succumbing to the anesthetic just after getting a glimpse of the trembling surgeon standing by the table.

The red nucleus (also called *nucleus ruber,* for those who prefer the Latin) appears to be an important link in the flow of information from cortex to motor neuron. As we saw, section of the pyramidal tracts does not prevent "voluntary" movement of even the distal limbs. However, subsequent damage to the *corticorubrospinal* system (cortex to red nucleus to spinal cord) leads to a complete loss of movement of distal limb muscles. The two systems appear to cooperate, for the loss of movement is not seen after sections of the rubrospinal tract alone (Eldred and Buchwald, 1967).

There are also *reticulospinal* fibers; portions of the brainstem reticular formation play a role in control of the gamma motor system. The control appears to be mostly tonic (long-lasting), as opposed to phasic (brief). Activity of many reticulospinal fibers is modified by cutaneous pressure from all over the body, suggesting that this system plays a role in maintenance of posture (Wolstencroft, 1964). As we saw in a previous section, there appears to be, in the caudal portion of the brainstem reticular formation, a region that facilitates extensor reflexes (and produces some flexor inhibition). There is another, more rostral region, that inhibits these effects. Decerebrate rigidity results from the sole influnce of the caudal, extensor-facilitating region. In humans, similar injury produces extension in the legs but flexion in the arms. Thus, we could really call the caudal region an antigravity-facilitating area. The flexors, rather than the extensors, of our arms are antigravity muscles, since we walk on two limbs. You have probably seen brain-damaged people, who hold their hands, curled at the wrists and fingers, by their shoulders. This is a manifestation of flexor-facilitation—and probably a corresponding extensor-inhibition—of the muscles of the upper limbs.

THE BASAL GANGLIA AS A GENERATOR OF "SLOW RAMP" MOVEMENTS. Kornhuber (1974) points out that damage to the basal ganglia disrupts a patient's ability to perform slow, smooth movements. The rapid movements made by the eyes are not impaired by such damage, however. (As we shall see, we cannot move our eyes slowly, unless we are tracking a slowly moving object.) The motor deficits that occur can be those of *release* (e.g., rigidity or uncontrollable writhing movements after damage to the caudate nucleus or putamen) or of *deficiency* (akinesia, or the inability to move, after damage to the globus pallidus or ventral thalamus). He suggests, therefore, that the basal ganglia participate in the control of these movements.

DeLong (1974) has obtained electrophysiological evidence in support of Kornhuber's suggestion. He recorded the activity of single neurons in the putamen during execution of both rapid and slow movements of a monkey's hand. A majority of the units preferentially responded before and during slow, rather than fast, movements.

CEREBELLUM. The cerebellum plays a very important role in motor control. It performs three major functions:

1. It interacts with the brainstem reticular formation in its control of the gamma motor system, receiving kinesthetic input and information from the vestibular nuclei.

2. It receives vestibular information and exerts control over the postural muscles through *cerebellovestibulospinal pathways.*

3. The newest part of the cerebellum (*neocerebellum*) is intimately involved in the execution of rapid, skilled movements.

Figure 10.21 shows a view of the surface of the cerebellum and illustrates the three regions associated with these three roles. (See **FIGURE 10.21.**)

THE CEREBELLUM AS A PROGRAMMER OF RAPID MOVEMENTS. The last of the three roles, control of rapid skilled movement, is the most interesting. Humans are able to perform motions that are complexes of many individual joint movements without "paying attention" to each component. For example, if you hold your arm out straight in front of you, it is possible for you to move it rapidly so that your hand describes a circle. Try this, and move your arm as rapidly as you can. You will note that in doing so, you engage not only the muscles of your arm, shoulder, and neck, but also those of your trunk and (especially if you stand) your legs. A phenomenal number

FIGURE 10.21 A schematic representation of the cerebellar cortex. (Adapted with permission from McGraw-Hill Book Co. from *The Human Nervous System*, 2nd edition, by Noback and Demarest. Copyright © 1975, by McGraw-Hill, Inc.)

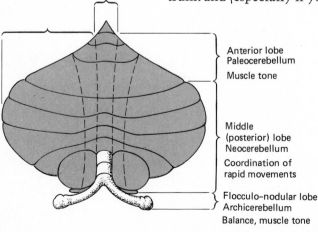

Vermis

Anterior lobe
Paleocerebellum
Muscle tone

Middle
(posterior) lobe
Neocerebellum
Coordination of
rapid movements

Flocculo-nodular lobe
Archicerebellum
Balance, muscle tone

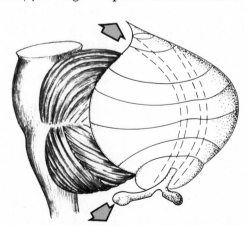

of muscles are called into action, and at precisely the correct time. Just considering the arm movement alone, various muscles must begin and end their contractions at precisely the correct time in order to produce a smooth motion. (After all, a single muscle cannot produce a circular motion at the end of the arm.) I find that I can perform this movement more than forty times in 10 seconds; this means that it takes less than 250 msec for each circular motion. The fastest pathway from muscle receptor to cortex to muscle would take on the order of 100 msec. This means that the movement cannot be controlled by sensory feedback—by the time the brain registered information about the whereabouts of the limb, and corrective information reached the muscles, almost one-half of the circle would have been completed. The fact that I had to practice a bit before I could even successfully count the movements suggests that feedback is not particularly prominent in this system.

Other examples of complex movements too fast for feedback correction abound. Almost any skilled *ballistic* (literally, "throwing") movement qualifies. Once you begin to swing a bat or a golf club, or throw a ball, you are "committed" to that movement. Midcourse corrections are exceedingly difficult. Instead, you observe the results and try again.

Figure 10.22 shows some of the inputs and outputs of the cerebellum. You will see that this structure not only receives information about what the muscles and limbs are doing, but also finds out what they are about to do, since it monitors information on its way down to the motor neurons. (See **FIGURE 10.22.**) Similarly, it sends fibers to various motor nuclei, thus modifying the commands received by the muscles. (See **FIGURE 10.22.**)

The nature of cerebellar control of skilled motor activity can best be seen by the effects of unilateral neocerebellar lesions in humans. People with such damage can produce skilled movements normally, on the unaffected side of the body. They can move the limbs on the affected side, but complex motions are made joint by joint. A patient once said, "The movements of my left arm are done subconsciously, but I have to think out each movement of the right (affected) arm. I come to a dead stop in turning and have to think before I start again" (Holmes, 1939).

Kornhuber has collected data that indicate that cerebellar cortex controls the initiation of rapid stepwise movements while the deep cerebellar nuclei are involved in stopping and holding after these movements. Control of eye movements is unique in that we are unable to move them slowly when scanning a stationary scene. Instead, our eyes make *saccades,* fast, jerky movements from place to place. The *duration,* and not the speed, of a saccade is what determines the size of an eye movement, since the motor neurons

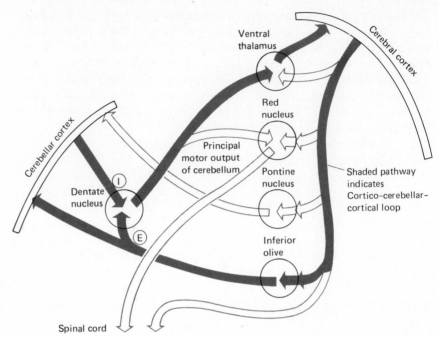

Ventral
thalamus

Red
nucleus

Principal
motor output
of cerebellum

Pontine
nucleus

Shaded pathway
indicates
Cortico-cerebellar-
cortical loop

Cerebral cortex

Cerebellar cortex

Dentate
nucleus

I

E

Inferior
olive

Spinal cord

FIGURE 10.22 The
relationship between the
cerebellum and motor systems.
Note the loop that Kornhuber
believes is involved with
control of rapidly executed
movements. Many details are
omitted, such as the sensory
input to the cerebellum.

controlling the eye muscles fire at the maximal rate during a saccade, regardless of its size. Cerebellar damage disrupts control of these movements; the eyes continue to move in a stepwise manner, but a number of irregular movements are required before the eyes reach the target (Kornhuber, 1974). Thus, the deficit is one of timing of brief intervals. Smooth occular pursuit of a slowly moving object is not impaired, however, by these lesions.

The same type of deficit can be seen during rapid limb movements; damage to cerebellar cortex impairs a patient's ability to aim a rapid hand movement at some point in space, although the movement can accurately be performed if it is done slowly.

In contrast to the timing function exhibited by cerebellar cortex, Kornhuber argues that the deep cerebellar nuclei are involved with stopping and holding. Lesions of the deep cerebellar nuclei result in an uncontrollable tremor when an attempt is made to fix the gaze; these tremors disappear when the eyes are closed (Aschoff, Conrad, and Kornhuber, 1970). Similarly, these lesions result in a rapid, oscillating tremor at the end of an aimed movement of the arm, although the ballistic movement itself is accurately performed (Kornhuber, 1974).

In summary, we have much to learn about where voluntary movements begin. However, a picture of the brain mechanisms that control fast and slow voluntary movements is beginning to emerge. The following movement summarizes Kornhuber's conclusions: Move your finger from a point a foot or so in front of your face up to the tip of your nose, as rapidly as you can. Cerebellar cortex is involved in timing the fast ballistic movement, whereas the deep cerebellar nuclei participate in stopping the motion. The basal ganglia then control a slow ramp motion that is terminated by tactual feedback from your finger touching your nose.

SUGGESTED READINGS

KORNHUBER, H. H. Cerebral cortex, cerebellum, and basal ganglia: An introduction to their motor functions. In *The Neurosciences: Third Study Program*, edited by F. O. Schmitt and F. G. Worden. Cambridge: MIT Press, 1974. I highly recommend this chapter of Kornhuber's. However, it is not particularly easy reading. I would suggest that you first read the *Scientific American* chapters before tackling this one. There are many other excellent articles in *The Neurosciences*, including several pertaining to motor control. Considering its size (1107 pages) and the high quality of the contributions, I would classify it as an excellent buy.

VANDER, A. J., SHERMAN, J. H., and LUCIANO, D. S. *Human Physiology: The Mechanisms of Body Function,* ed. 2. New York: McGraw-Hill, 1975. This book con-tains excellent descriptions of muscles and glands. It is very well written, thorough, and up-to-date.

EVARTS, E. V. Brain mechanisms in movement. *Scientific American*, July, 1973.

EVERT, J. P. The neural basis of visually guided behavior. *Scientific American*, March, 1974.

LLINÁS, R. R. The cortex of the cerebellum. *Scientific American*, January, 1975.

MERTON, P. A. How we control the contraction of our muscles. *Scientific American*, May, 1972.

These articles by Evarts, Evert, Llinás, and Merton are included in *Progress in Psychobiology* (introductions by R. F. Thompson). San Francisco: W. H. Freeman, 1976.

Sexual Development
and Behavior

11

The subject of this chapter is important to almost all of us. The
topics of other chapters might (I hope) be interesting, but discussion
of these topics is not capable of evoking the kinds of emotional reactions that may accompany discussions of sexual development and
sexual behavior. We all have our individual beliefs concerning
what constitutes appropriate and inappropriate sexual behavior and
what behaviors and interests should or should not be associated
with a person's gender. The discussion of sexual behavior in this
chapter will be biological, not ethical, and I shall make no attempt
to consider the varieties of human sexual practices, except as they
relate to physiological mechanisms. For example, researchers have
discovered no obvious neural or endocrinological mechanisms that
might account for such phenomena as pederasty, voyeurism, or necro-
philia. At the present time, such paraphilias (literally, "abnormal
loves") can probably be accounted for better by general psychological
theories than by specific physiological functions; these phenomena
will not be discussed here. On the other hand, there may be some
predisposing physiological bases for such psychosexual phenomena
as homosexuality, and evidence concerning these phenomena will be
reviewed.

   All behavior is a function of physiology, but the biological-
behavioral link is probably more obvious for sexual behavior than for

any other. First of all, sexual behavior depends upon morphology; an individual's behavior is certainly controlled to a large degree by the possession of male or female genitals. Second, a person's sexual desire is affected by his or her own sex hormones. For example, a castrated man, lacking male sex hormones, will eventually lose interest in sexual activity unless he is given pills containing hormones similar to those formerly produced by his own testes. Finally, sexual behavior is very strongly influenced by learning; it is possible for a person to adopt a sex role different from the one normally associated with his or her hormones and sex organs.

Sex hormones have a dual role in the control of sexual behavior. They have an *organizational* effect, shaping the ultimate development of a person's sexual organs and brain. Exposure to certain sex hormones before the fetus is born will *organize* the developing cells so that they will later develop into male or female sex organs (or, if the hormonal exposure is abnormal, the cells may develop into something in between the male and female forms). Furthermore, the developing brain is affected by exposure to hormones before birth; a man's brain is not precisely the same as that of a woman, at least in the way in which it responds to sex hormones. Because of the organizational effects of hormones, the physical (neural or genital) and hormonal determinants of sexual behavior cannot be studied separately.

The second role of sex hormones is their *activational* effect. For example, male hormones are necessary if a man is to produce sperms and experience a normal sex drive. However, male hormones will not have the same effects on a woman. She cannot produce sperms, since she does not have testes. Neither will male sex hormones induce in her a desire to assume a masculine role in sexual activity. Since her body (including her brain) was *organized* as a female, the *activational* effects of sex hormones are different from those seen in a man.

In this chapter, then, I shall discuss sexual development and the organizational control exerted by hormones. I shall also consider the activational effects of hormones—the role these chemicals play in our day-to-day behavior. Finally, I shall discuss evidence concerning the neural bases of our sexual behavior, and the way in which hormones interact with these neural circuits.

SEXUAL DEVELOPMENT

Humans and other mammals are *sexually dimorphic*; we come in two forms, male and female. I doubt that any of us need reminders

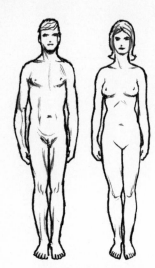

FIGURE 11.1 Sexual dimorphism. Note the differences between a male and a female.

of the essential differences, but they are, nonetheless, shown in **FIGURE 11.1.** Besides noting the differences in the genitalia, one can observe that males are generally larger, broader in the shoulders, and narrower in the hips, and that the patterns of facial, pubic, and chest hair are different. Furthermore, females have larger breasts. The internal and external genitalia are formed during intrauterine development; genitals begin to grow and secondary sex characteristics begin to develop in response to gonadal hormones secreted at the time of puberty.

Determination of Sex

All cells of the body (other than *gametes*—sperms or ova) contain twenty-three pairs of chromosomes, including a pair of sex chromosomes. The genetic information that programs the development of a human is contained in the DNA constituting these chromosomes, and the identity of the sex chromosomes determines that individual's sex. There are two types of sex chromosomes, X and Y. All humans, male and female, possess at least one X chromosome. The additional possession of a Y chromosome causes the individual to develop into a male.

CELL DIVISION AND THE PRODUCTION OF GAMETES. It is possible to observe the twenty-three pairs of human chromosomes. Epithelial cells are scraped from the mucous membrane on the inside of the cheek and then placed in a culture medium that supports their growth and division. During cell division (*mitosis*) the chromosomes must be duplicated so that the daughter cells (that is what they are called, regardless of the sex of the donor) each have the entire complement of genetic material. This process is shown schematically in Figure 11.2. (For simplicity's sake, only two pairs of chromosomes, rather than twenty-three, are shown.) (See **FIGURE 11.2**). Once cellular division is established, the culture is treated with *colchicine*, a drug that halts the process in the phase shown in part C of Figure 11.2. The drug dissolves the *spindle fibers* that pull the chromosomes apart. (See **FIGURE 11.2 C.**)

The dividing cells now contain a double set of twenty-three pairs of chromosomes in the nucleus, straightened out and easy to see. The cells are then squashed so as to flatten the chromosomes, and the genetic material is stained. Then the many cells are searched until one is found in which all the chromosomes can readily be seen. A photograph is taken, and the pictures of the chromosomes are cut out and rearranged according to size. Figure 11.3 illustrates a set of human chromosomes prepared in this way, before and after rearrangement.

Remember, we can see twice as many chromosomes as the cell normally contains, since the process of cell division was arrested just before each member of a duplicated chromosome, joined near the center, would normally separate and travel to each of the daughter cells. (See **FIGURE 11.3.**) The *karyotype* (literally, "nucleus mark") shown in this figure is that of a male, since we can see a Y chromosome.

In the production of gametes (ova and sperms—*gamein* means "to marry"), cells divide in a different way. During *meiosis* the members of the pairs of chromosomes separate, each member of a pair going to one of the daughter cells. (See **FIGURE 11.4.**) Each gamete contains one member of each of the twenty-three pairs of chromosomes, but the particular member of each pair is "selected" by a random process. If we tossed a coin twenty-three times, we would obtain one of 8,388,608 different sequences. Since the segregation of the chromosome pairs is as random (apparently) as the coin toss, a person can produce 8,388,608 different kinds of gametes. Since it takes the combination of two gametes to produce another human, a single couple could produce 8,388,608 × 8,388,608, or something like 703,-687,441,776,000 different children. Genetically identical siblings could be conceived at different times, but the probability is not very high.

FERTILIZATION AND THE DETERMINATION OF SEX. In the production of a new organism, a single sperm unites with a single ovum, and the genetic material contained in each of these gametes combines.

If we consider only the sex chromosomes, there are two kinds of sperms, X-bearing and Y-bearing. Females, with their XX complement, produce only X-bearing ova. Thus, since males, with their XY complement, produce both X-bearing and Y-bearing sperms, the sex of the offspring is determined by the sex chromosome contained in the sperm that fertilizes the ovum. (See **FIGURE 11.5.**)

Genetic sex, defined as female by the XX complement and as male by the XY complement, normally initiates a series of events that results in a reproductively competent organism, bearing the appropriate morphology and exhibiting the appropriate sexual behavior. Let us consider some of the details of that process.

Development of Genital Dimorphism

TISSUE DIFFERENTIATION. Specific locations (genes) on the chromosomes express themselves by means of a process (described in detail in chapter 20) that results in protein synthesis. The proteins thus produced act as structural elements of the cell, or as enzymes, controlling biosynthetic processes. Since all the cells of the developing embryo

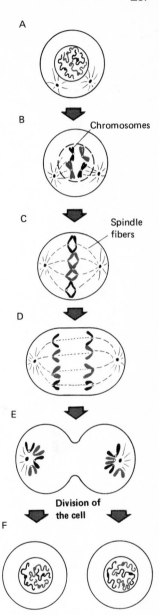

FIGURE 11.2 Mitosis, the process by which a somatic cell replicates itself. (From G. H. Orians, *The Study of Life*. Boston: Allyn and Bacon, Inc., 1973.)

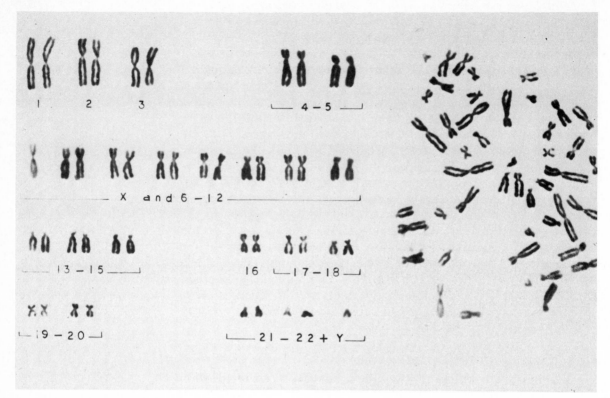

FIGURE 11.3   A karyotype of a cell whose division was arrested in metaphase (phase C of Figure 11.2). From Money, J., and Ehrhardt, A., *Man and Woman, Boy and Girl.* Copyright © 1973 by The Johns Hopkins University Press, Baltimore, Maryland. By permission.)

contain the same genetic information, an additional mechanism must account for *tissue differentiation:* some cells become liver cells, others become bone cells, others become neurons.   The expression of most genes in a given cell is repressed by special proteins.   The interaction of these proteins with substances in the cytoplasm determines whether a given gene (or set of genes) will be active.   Therefore, it is ultimately the cytoplasmic contents of a given cell that determine the nature of genetic expression within that cell.   As we shall see, the presence of particular hormones at critical stages of development can affect the process of differentiation, and hence the ultimate form the organism will take.

The process of cellular differentiation is still largely mysterious, although it is the subject of a considerable amount of research effort. In the process of successive cell divisions starting with a single fertilized ovum, there must be some unequal divisions of the cytoplasmic contents, or an external stimulus (such as a hormone) must alter the contents of some, but not all, cells.   If all the daughter cells of successive mitotic divisions received (and retained) the same cytoplasmic

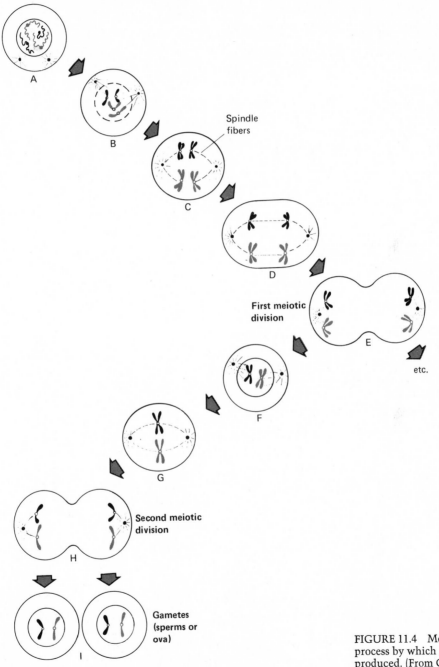

Spindle fibers

First meiotic division

etc.

Second meiotic division

Gametes (sperms or ova)

FIGURE 11.4   Meiosis, the process by which gametes are produced. (From G. H. Orians, *The Study of Life*. Boston: Allyn and Bacon, Inc., 1973.)

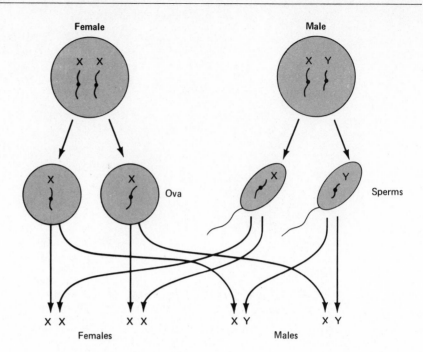

Female   Male

Ova

Sperms

Females   Males

FIGURE 11.5   The sex of the offspring depends on whether the sperm cell carries an X or a Y chromosome.

material, as well as the same genetic material, then how could the tissue differentiate? Instead of an embryo, there would be an amorphous mass of identical cells.

Once differentiation has begun, cells are influenced by their neighbors. At early stages of development it is possible to transplant a small piece of tissue to different parts of the organism and observe that the transplanted cells, and their daughter cells, will assume the form appropriate to their location. Thus, it is evident that cells can affect each other's protein synthesis; studies have shown that this interaction is transmitted by means of exchanges of secretions via the extracellular fluid and through contact among cells.

HORMONAL CONTROL OF SEXUAL DIFFERENTIATION.   Figure 11.6 shows the precursors of sex organs, both male and female. At this stage of development the fetus is bisexual. The precursor of the internal female sex organs is called the *Müllerian system*; the *Wolffian system* is the precursor of the male sex organs. A pair of sex glands (the *primordial*, or "first begun" gonads) is capable of developing into either ovaries or testes. (See **FIGURE 11.6.**) At this stage of development (7 to 8 weeks of fetal life) the sex chromosomes cause the cortex of the primordial gonads to develop into ovaries or its medulla into testes.

Once the gonads are differentiated, these organs control the rest of the development of the internal and external genitalia. If, at this point, the gonads are removed (as you might expect, this is an

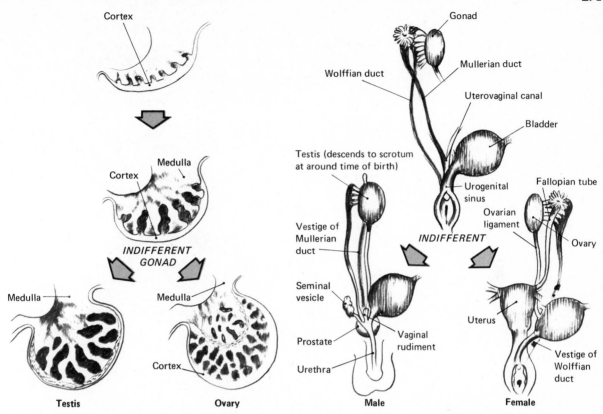

Cortex

Cortex · Medulla

INDIFFERENT GONAD

Medulla

Medulla

Cortex

Testis

Ovary

Wolffian duct

Gonad

Mullerian duct

Uterovaginal canal

Bladder

Testis (descends to scrotum at around time of birth)

Urogenital sinus

INDIFFERENT

Fallopian tube

Ovarian ligament

Ovary

Vestige of Mullerian duct

Seminal vesicle

Prostate

Urethra

Vaginal rudiment

Uterus

Vestige of Wolffian duct

Male

Female

FIGURE 11.6 Development of internal sex organs. (Adapted from Burns, R. K. In *Analysis of Development*, edited by B. H. Willier, P. A. Weiss, and V. Hamberger. Philadelphia: Saunders, 1955, and from Corning, H. K., *Lehrbuch der Entwicklungsgeschichte des Menschen*. Munich: J. F. Bergman, 1921.)

exceedingly delicate operation), the organism will be born female in appearance, with uterus, vagina, labia, and clitoris—regardless of genetic sex. A male is produced only if the fetus contains functioning —that is, hormone-secreting—testes. A female is produced otherwise, even if the ovaries are removed. Speaking metaphorically, Nature's impulse is to produce a female, and she will fail to do so only if stimulated, with the appropriate hormones, to produce a male.

During the stage of development of the internal genitalia, the testes of the developing fetus appear to produce a hormone, *Müllerian-inhibiting substance*, which causes the regression (disappearance) of the female internal genitalia. The testes also secrete *androgens* ("male producers"), which stimulate development of the male internal sex organs. Jost (1958) has shown that the effects of the Müllerian-inhibiting substance are local. If one testis is removed from a developing rabbit fetus, the Müllerian system (female) on that side will develop, and the Wolffian system will fail to develop. On the other side, which contains an intact testis, the Wolffian system will develop into the internal male genitalia, while the Müllerian system will regress.

The external genitalia develop from indifferent, bipotential primordia, which are capable of assuming either male or female form. Figure 11.7 illustrates this process; note that the principal analogous structures are penis/clitoris, urethral tube of the penis/labia minora, and scrotum/labia majora. (See **FIGURE 11.7**.) Without hormonal

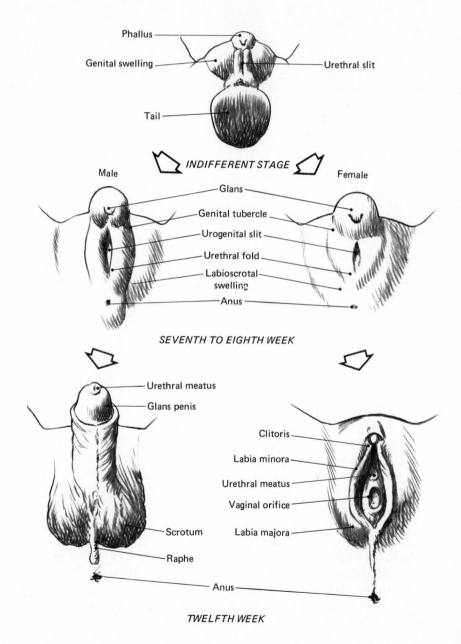

FIGURE 11.7 Development of the external genitalia. (Adapted from Spaulding, M. H. In *Contributions to Embryology*, Vol. 13. Washington, D.C.: Carnegie Institution of Washington, 1921.)

stimulation, the external genitalia will become female, regardless of chromosomal sex. However, the presence of androgens will result in masculine development. Thus, even though one of Jost's unilaterally castrated rabbits had female internal genitalia on one side, the external genitalia were male. The androgens secreted by the single testis were sufficient to stimulate masculinization of the external genitalia, even though the effects of Müllerian-inhibiting substance on the internal genitalia were local.

I should note that the ovaries of a developing female do not secrete "Wolffian-inhibiting substance." In fact, the Wolffian system does not disappear—it can still be found in grown women. Without androgens, however, the Wolffian system fails to develop, and it remains about as small as it was in the fetus.

HORMONAL CONTROL OF SEXUAL MATURATION. Secondary sex characteristics do not appear until the onset of puberty. If the genitals are hidden from view, the sex of a prepubescent child can only be guessed at. At puberty, however, the gonads are stimulated, by the anterior pituitary hormones, to produce their hormones. The pituitary gland produces two hormones (*gonadotrophins*) that stimulate the gonads, *follicle-stimulating hormone (FSH)* and *luteinizing hormone (LH)*. These hormones are named for effects produced in the female (*follicle* production and its subsequent *luteinization*—to be described later), but these same hormones are produced in the male, and they affect the production of sperm and testosterone in the testes. One can transplant an ovary into a male, for example, and observe that "male" FSH and LH work perfectly well (Bermant and Davidson, 1974). However, the ovary does not cycle (we shall soon see why).

In response to the gonadotrophic hormones the ovaries chiefly produce *estrogens* (a generic term for a series of related hormones) and the testes chiefly produce *testosterone* (an androgen). Both glands also produce a small amount of the hormones of the opposite sex. Both estrogens and testosterone initiate closure of the *epiphyses* (growing portions of the bones) and thus halt skeletal growth. Furthermore, estrogens cause breast development, changes in the deposition of body fat, and maturation of the female genitalia. Testosterone stimulates growth of facial, axillary (underarm), and pubic hair, lowers the voice, alters the hairline on the head (sometimes culminating in baldness in later life), stimulates muscular development, and causes genital growth. This description leaves out two of the female secondary sex characteristics: axillary and pubic hair. These are not produced by estrogens, but rather by *androstenedione (AD)*, a "male" sex hormone (androgen) produced by the adrenal glands. Even a prepubertally castrated male (eunuch) will grow axillary and pubic hair, in response to his own androstenedione.

The bipotentiality of many of the secondary sex characteristics remains throughout life. An adult male treated with an estrogen (to control an androgen-dependent tumor, for example) will grow breasts. Facial hair will become finer and softer. His voice will remain low, since the enlargement of the larynx is permanent. A woman receiving high levels of androgen (usually from a tumor that secretes AD) will grow a beard, and her voice will become lower (permanently, unfortunately).

A number of pathological conditions can prevent the normal development of an individual into male or female. Such people (or animals) are called *hermaphrodites* (from the mythical bisexual offspring of Hermes and Aphrodite). Originally, hermaphroditism referred to the ability to be reproductively competent as both a male and a female (seen in some animals, but not in mammals), but the term has been extended to individuals with ambiguous genital structure, internally and/or externally (Money and Ehrhardt, 1972). Nature's experiments in the production of such individuals have added much to our knowledge of the biological bases of differences in the behavior of human males and females.

As we have seen in this section, Nature would, but for the presence of the Y chromosome (in causing the testes to develop from the primordial sex organ), produce a female body. As we shall see in the next section, there is at least some degree of sexual dimorphism in the brain. Without prenatal secretion of androgens from the testes, the brain will be born "female."

Effects of Prenatal Sex Hormones on the Brain

The most clear-cut evidence for sex differences in brain function is seen in the control of the pituitary gland by the hypothalamic releasing hormones. The output of gonadotrophic hormones by the anterior pituitary gland is cyclic in females. In males it is relatively constant. (There are, in males, changes in response to stress or environmental stimuli, but there is no regular cyclicity in secretion.)

ORGANIZATIONAL EFFECTS OF ANDROGENS ON GONADOTROPHIN RELEASE. The cyclicity of the female is the "normal" condition. If newly born male rats are castrated, they can be stimulated to produce the pituitary gonadotrophins in a cyclic manner, as a female does (Pfeiffer, 1936). (I should note that rats are born at an early stage of development. Their sexual differentiation is still incomplete at birth, so that postnatal castration in rats is equivalent to intrauterine castration in many other mammalian species.) On the other hand, if a female rat is ovariectomized and given a testicular transplant at birth, she becomes "masculinized" and fails to show cycles in FSH- and LH-releasing hormones.

What accounts for the cyclicity in gonadotrophin release that characterizes the female pituitary gland? The gland itself is clearly not responsible; if a male pituitary is transplanted into a female, or a female pituitary into a male, the result will be gonadotrophin release characteristic of the sex of the animal receiving the transplant. The transplanted organ will cycle in a female body, but not in a male body (Harris and Jacobsohn, 1951–1952; Martinez and Bittner, 1956). Furthermore, a pituitary gland transplanted into a female will cycle only if it is placed close enough to the hypothalamus to allow revascularization (i.e., re-growth of blood vessels from hypothalamus to pituitary). Thus, the cyclicity of gonadotrophin secretion must be a result of cyclic release of the hypothalamic releasing hormones.

A number of studies have shown that *androgenization* (masculinization by means of androgens) of the hypothalamus and of the external genitalia can occur only during a critical period (Goy, Phoenix, and Young, 1962; Gorski, 1971). By administering androgens at different times, it is possible to produce noncycling females with female genitalia, or females with male genitalia whose brains regulate gonadotrophins in the normal (i.e., cyclic) female way. Furthermore, the degree of masculinization depends on the amount of androgen administered. It is interesting to note that small doses do not delay the onset of cycling in females; instead, the cycles end prematurely (Napoli and Gerall, 1970). Arai and Gorski (1968) have also shown that the masculinization of the hypothalamus takes only a few hours; a single injection of testosterone that was deactivated 6 hours later with a substance that inhibits the effects of androgens still caused the hypothalamus to convert to the male type.

Since the anterior pituitary gland is controlled by the hypothalamus, the evidence for differences in hypothalamic function is quite strong. Furthermore, Szentagothai, Flerko, Mess, and Halasz (1965) and Halasz (1968) have shown that other brain regions are not necessary for cyclic gonadotrophin release. They isolated an "island" of hypothalamic tissue around the pituitary stalk, cutting all around the border of this area with a stereotaxically mounted knife. As long as the preoptic area was included in the island, the female rats ovulated cyclically, indicating a cyclic release of gonadotrophin. The fact that androgens initiate changes in hypothalamic function does not in itself prove that these hormones directly affect the brain. Testosterone could be causing production of some other substance, which in turn acts on the hypothalamus. However, Nadler (1968) has shown that brain implants of testosterone, in amounts too small to produce a masculinizing effect if placed elsewhere in the body, suppressed later cyclicity in females. Thus, the evidence for direct interaction between testosterone and the developing brain appears quite good.

Besides removing androgens by surgical castration, the gonado-trophin release of males can be made to cycle by early administration of *androgen antagonists*, substances that suppress the effects of androgen. Small doses of progesterone counteract androgenization (Kincl and Maqueo, 1965), apparently by competing with cellular uptake of androgens (Stern and Eisenfeld, 1971). Other substances, such as barbiturates and inhibitors of protein synthesis (such as *puromycin*) also prevent masculinization (Gorski, 1971). The protein synthesis inhibitors probably block the *effects* of androgens rather than prevent their uptake by the cells. Remember, steroid hormones are taken directly into the nucleus of the cell, where they affect the machinery controlling protein synthesis (chapter 10). If protein synthesis is suppressed, the organizational effects of androgens in changing neural structure cannot be accomplished.

In order to understand how male and female brains might differ in their control of gonadotrophin release, we will first have to understand something about hormonal control of the menstrual cycle. Since surges of gonadotrophin release are not seen in an ovariecto-mized female, the sequence does not appear to rely on some intrinsic cyclicity of gonadotrophin release, but rather on the interaction between hypothalamus, anterior pituitary gland, and ovaries.

CONTROL OF THE MENSTRUAL CYCLE. A menstrual cycle (or *estrus cycle,* in sub-primate mammals) begins with the growth of ovarian follicles, small spheres of epithelial cells surrounding ova. The follicles grow in response to FSH secretion by the pituitary gland, and they begin to secrete estrogens. The estrogens, in turn, stimulate the hypothalamus to cause the production and release of a surge of LH by the anterior pituitary. Evidence for the stimulating effects of estrogens on hypothalamically induced LH release comes from studies (Barraclough, 1966; Everett and Nichols, 1968) showing that estrogen injections will advance the time of ovulation (i.e., cause an earlier surge of LH), and that electrical stimulation of portions of the hypothalamus produces the same effect.

In response to the LH surge, one of the ovarian follicles will rupture, releasing the ovum. The ruptured follicle, under the continued influence of LH, becomes a *corpus luteum* ("yellow body"), which produces progesterone. This steroid hormone (a *gestagen,* or pregnancy-promoting hormone) prepares the lining of the uterus for implantation of the ovum, should it be fertilized by a sperm. Meanwhile, the ovum, which is ruptured out into the abdominal cavity, enters one of the fallopian tubes and begins its progress down toward the uterus. (The ovum is directed into the fallopian tube by the "rowing" action of the ciliated cells around the opening. This process works remarkably well; if a woman lacks a right ovary and a left fallopian tube, her ova will nevertheless find their way across the abdominal cavity and into the fallopian tube.) If an ovum meets sperm cells during its travels down the fallopian tube and becomes fertilized, it will begin to divide, and several days later it will attach itself to the uterine wall.

If the ovum is not fertilized, or if it is fertilized too late for it to develop sufficiently by the time it gets to the uterus, or if implantation is prevented by the presence of an *intrauterine device* (*IUD*), the estrogen and progesterone levels will fall, and the lining of the walls of the uterus will slough off. Menstruation will commence. (See **FIGURE 11.8.**)

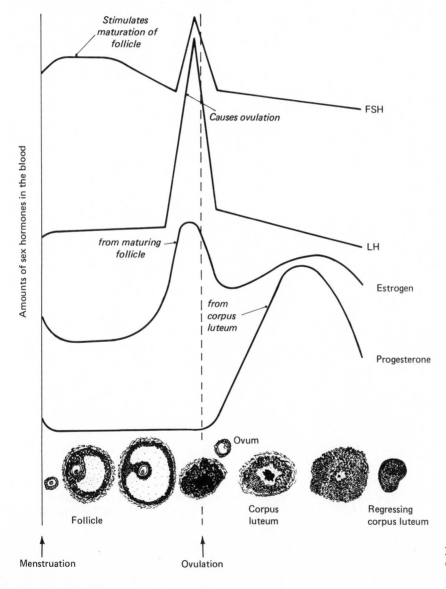

FIGURE 11.8 The menstrual cycle.

SEX DIFFERENCES IN THE PREOPTIC AREA OF THE HYPOTHALAMUS. Now, what might be the basis of the difference in male and female brains, with respect to gonadotrophin release? It appears to be relatively simple—the *preoptic area* of the male (androgenized) hypothalamus does not respond to estrogens by stimulating LH release. The estrogens produced by a developing follicle cannot trigger an LH surge. (See **FIGURE 11.9.**)

An experiment by Barraclough (1966) illustrates this effect beautifully. Stimulation of two regions of the hypothalamus will induce LH release, and hence ovulation, in a normal female rat. The *arcuate nucleus* of the basal hypothalamus contains the cell bodies of the neurosecretory cells that produce and release gonadotrophin-releasing hormones, and the preoptic region contains the cells that are stimulated by estrogen and that, in turn, stimulate the neurosecretory cells in the arcuate nucleus. (See **FIGURE 11.10.**) Figure 11.11 shows the results of Barraclough's study. Filled ovals mark the location of electrode tips that produced ovulation; open ovals show the location of unsuccessful sites. Look at the left illustration, and note that electrodes in both the preoptic area and the arcuate nucleus elicited ovulation. (See **FIGURE 11.11.**)

If a female rat is androgenized just after birth she will *not* ovulate in response to electrical stimulation anywhere in the brain. Nor, for that matter, will she ovulate in response to LH injections. However, the ovaries of these rats contain a large number of follicles, and Barraclough reasoned that perhaps the abnormally high level of

FIGURE 11.9 Neuroendocrine control of the menstrual cycle.

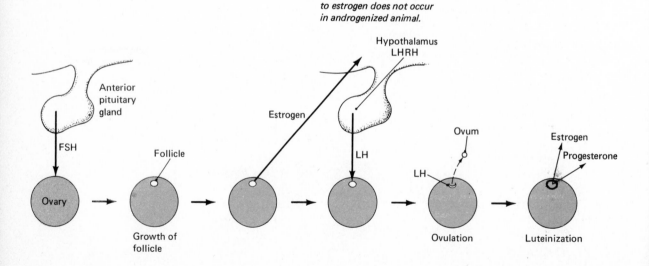

estrogen from these follicles prevented normal anterior pituitary functioning. He gave these androgenized female rats a single injection of progesterone, which temporarily brought the animals to *proestrus* (a state similar to the early part of the menstrual cycle). These progesterone-treated rats did not subsequently ovulate; instead, they returned later to the constant high-estrogen condition. However, if the brain was electrically stimulated during this temporary phase of proestrus, ovulation could be induced. This fact means that, even in the androgenized female rat: (a) when estrogen levels are not abnormally high, the anterior pituitary gland can be stimulated to secrete LH, and (b) the ovarian follicle can respond normally to this LH surge by ovulating. However, the only electrode locations that could trigger this ovulation were those in the arcuate nucleus. Stimulation of the preoptic area had no effect; compare the left and right illustrations of **FIGURE 11.11.**

These results suggest very strongly that the male-female difference in gonadotrophin release resides in the preoptic area, which is normally sensitive to estrogen. Electrical stimulation of this region does not cause LH release in a masculinized brain, even though the neurosecretory cells (in the arcuate nucleus) that release gonadotrophin-releasing hormones are still quite functional.

These experiments leave little doubt that androgens can alter the characteristics of the brain. As we shall see, the sexual behavior of female sub-primate mammals is dependent on the estrous cycle, and hence the sexual behavior of a female rat with an androgenized hypothalamus is quite different from that of a normal animal. However, the same invariant relationship is not seen between the sexual behavior and menstrual cycle of primates. In the next section I shall describe the sexual behavior of mammals with estrous and menstrual cycles, and in later sections I shall relate these behaviors to neural and hormonal processes. We shall also see that there is good evidence that the behavior of human females can be affected by organizational effects of androgens. Presumably, these behavioral differences reflect structural differences within the brain, but we lack direct evidence.

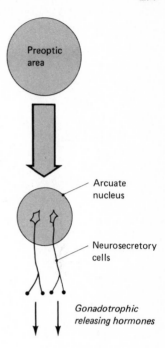

FIGURE 11.10 Relationships among the preoptic area, arcuate nucleus, and pituitary gland.

SEXUAL BEHAVIOR

Sexual Behavior in the Male

In order for fertilization to occur, a male mammal must ejaculate sperm-containing semen in the female's vagina. Most male mammals are ready and willing to do so at nearly any season of the year, depending on the receptivity of the female. Other *seasonal breeders* like the

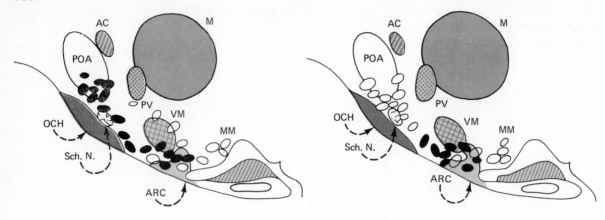

Normal female rat   Androgenized female rat

FIGURE 11.11 Electrical stimulation of the preoptic area results in release of LH only if the animal has not received androgens early in life. (Redrawn from Barraclough, C. A., *Recent Progress in Hormone Research*, 1966, 22, 503–539.)

deer will be sexually active only at certain times of the year; during the off-season their testes regress and produce almost no testosterone.

Male sexual behavior is quite varied, although the essential features of *intromission* (entry of the penis into the female's vagina), pelvic thrusting (rhythmic movement of the hindquarters, causing genital friction), and ejaculation are characteristic of all male mammals. (Humans, of course, have invented all kinds of copulatory and noncopulatory sexual behavior. For example, the pelvic movements leading to ejaculation may be performed by the woman, and sex play can lead to orgasm without intromission.)

Of all the laboratory animals, the sexual behavior of rats has been studied the most. When a male rat encounters a receptive female, he will, after spending some time nuzzling her and sniffing and licking her genitals, mount her and engage in pelvic thrusting. He will mount her several times, achieving intromission on most of the mountings. After eight to fifteen intromissions approximately one minute apart (each lasting only about one-quarter of a second) the male will ejaculate. At the time of ejaculation he shows a deep pelvic thrust and arches backward. The copulatory behavior of a mouse is similar, and even more dramatic. During the final intromission the male takes all four feet off the floor, climbing completely on top of the female. When he ejaculates he quivers and falls sideways to the ground. (Sometimes he takes the female with him.)

The male rat (along with many other male mammals) is most responsive to females who are "in heat." An ovariectomized female will be ignored, but an injection of estrogen will increase her sex appeal (and also change her behavior toward the male). As we shall see later, the stimuli that arouse his sexual interest are largely olfactory in nature, although visible changes, such as the swollen sex skin of a female monkey, also affect sex appeal.

Following ejaculation, the male refrains from sexual activity for a period of time (minutes, in a rat). Most mammals will return to copulate again, and again, showing a longer pause after each ejaculation. An interesting phenomenon can be demonstrated in some mammals. If the male, after finally becoming "exhausted" by repeated copulation with the same female, is presented with a new female, he begins to respond quickly—often as fast as he did with his initial contact with the first female. Successive introductions of new females can keep up his performance for prolonged periods of time. (The phenomenon, also seen in roosters, has been called the *Coolidge effect.* The following story is reputed to be true, but I cannot vouch for that fact. If it isn't true, it ought to be. Calvin Coolidge and his wife were touring a farm, when Mrs. Coolidge asked the farmer whether the continuous and vigorous sexual activity among the flock of hens was really the work of just one rooster. The reply was yes. "You might point that out to Mr. Coolidge," she said. Calvin Coolidge then asked the farmer whether a different hen was involved each time. The answer, again, was yes. "You might point that out to Mrs. Coolidge.")

The Coolidge effect is pronounced in the ram (male sheep). If a ram is given a new female after each ejaculation, he keeps up his performance (ejaculations in less than 2 minutes) with at least twelve different ewes. The experimenters, rather than the ram, got tired of shuffling sheep around (Bermant and Davidson, 1974). Figure 11.12 shows the striking difference in latency to ejaculate after reintroduction of the same female (upper curve) as opposed to introduction of new females (lower curve). (See **FIGURE 11.12.**) Beamer, Bermant, and Clegg (1969) tried to fool the rams by putting different clothing (coats and face masks) on the same female. The males were not fooled. They apparently smelled the same ewe, despite her varied disguise.

These phenomena—a renewal of interest in sexual behavior on introduction of a new female and a good memory for females already copulated with—are undoubtedly useful for species in which a single male inseminates all the members of his harem. He thus gets around to all of his females. Other mammalian species with approximately equal numbers of reproductively active males and females are less likely to show these phenomena.

Sexual Behavior in the Female

The mammalian female is generally described as being the passive participant in copulation. Although it is true that, in many species, her role during mounting and intromission itself is merely to assume a posture that exposes her genitals to the male (*lordosis* response),

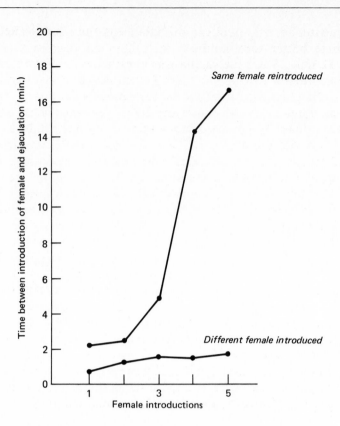

FIGURE 11.12 An example of the "Coolidge effect." (From Beamer, W., Bermant, G., and Clegg, M., *Animal Behaviour*, 1969, 17, 706–711.)

move the tail away (if she has one), and stand rigidly enough to support the weight of the male, her behavior in initiating copulation is often very active. Certainly if copulation with a nonestrous subprimate is attempted, she will either actively flee or rebuff the male. When in a receptive state, she will often approach the male, nuzzle him, sniff his genitals, and show behaviors characteristic of her species (quick, short, hopping movements in rats, for example). And a human female, depending on her social history, might take very active measures to arouse a male's interest in sexual activity with her.

An ingenious set of experiments by Bermant (1961a, 1961b) tested the preferred rate of sexual contact of female rats. Males normally pause for a while after intromissions, and for a longer time after intromissions that culminate in ejaculations. What about the females? Would they also, given a choice, delay sexual contact in a similar fashion? Bermant provided female rats with a lever they could press to produce a male rat. After a mount (regardless of whether it resulted in intromission) the male was removed. As shown in Figure 11.13, the females quickly pressed the lever after the male was removed following a mount (without intromission), paused a bit more after an intromission (without ejaculation), and waited the longest time before summoning a male after an ejaculation. (See **FIGURE 11.13.**) When the vagina was anesthetized, the female rats would continue requesting a male after a brief pause; they still discriminated among mounts, intromissions, and ejaculations, however, pausing the longest after the male ejaculated. When the penis was anesthetized (making it impossible for males to find the vaginal opening and achieve intromission), the female rats requested the presence of a male after very short intervals (Bermant and Westbrook, 1966). Thus it appears that male and female rats "prefer" about the same frequency of sexual contact, and their behavior is similarly regulated by genital stimulation. What superficially looked like passivity in the female really reflected a congruence in sexual appetite with that of the male.

Hormonal Control of Sexual Behavior

There are protein and steroid sex hormones. The protein hormones, LH, FSH, prolactin, and oxytocin, which are produced by the pituitary gland, do not appear to play an important role in the control of sexual behavior. Prolactin is necessary for milk production (and also plays a role in the luteinization of the ovarian follicle, in rodents). Oxytocin is important in parturition (it facilitates contractions of the uterus)

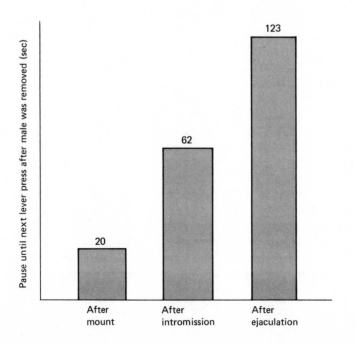

FIGURE 11.13 Time until lever press by the female rat after mounts, intromissions, and ejaculations. (Data from Bermant, G., *Science*, 1961a, *133*, 1771–1773.)

and milk ejection, and it might play a role in male and female orgasm. However, neither of these hormones is necessary for sexual behavior of higher mammals. In contrast, the hypothalamic releasing hormone for LH (*luteinizing hormone-releasing hormone* or *LHRH*) appears to play a significant role in the sexual receptivity of female rats. Pfaff (1973) found that LHRH increased receptivity of estrogen-treated rats. The ovaries and pituitary glands of these animals had been removed, so the effect appeared to be a direct one of the releasing hormone on the brain.

The sex steroids are of paramount importance. We have already seen the necessity of androgens in the masculinization of a fetus, and of androgens and estrogens in sexual maturation and normal sexual functioning. In this section we shall see how these hormones regulate behavior with their *organizational* and *activational* effects.

First, let us examine the metabolic pathways for the sex steroids. As indicated in Figure 11.14, the precursor for biosynthesis of steroid hormones is cholesterol. The appropriate enzymes can produce from cholesterol the entire complement of sex steroids. (See **FIGURE 11.14.**) All of these hormones are produced in both males and females, but the various steroids are produced in different amounts. The adrenal glands mainly produce such steroids as corticosterone and aldosterone, but they also produce sex hormones; androstenedione, for example, is responsible for a woman's pubic and

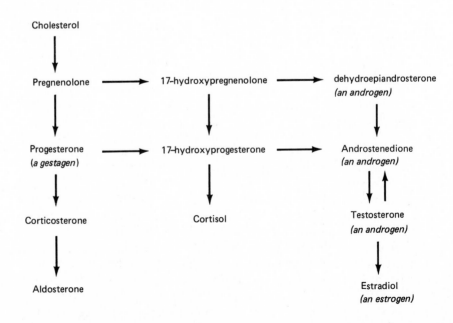

FIGURE 11.14 Biosynthesis of sex steroids.

axillary hair. The testes produce androgens (mainly testosterone), but they also make a little estradiol. Note that the ovaries are obliged to produce testosterone in making estradiol. (See **FIGURE 11.14.**) The blood testosterone level of women is approximately one-tenth that of men.

ORGANIZATIONAL EFFECTS OF SEX HORMONES. A myth that should be dispelled immediately is that men and women would exchange their behavioral roles if their hormonal balances were reversed (subject, of course, to anatomical differences). Nothing of this sort would happen. A loss of testosterone, and its replacement with estrogen, would alter a man's body (as we have seen), but he would not become a woman. He would despise his enlarging breasts. He would also regret his loss of potency, but would not become interested in female sexual behavior. Homosexuality will *not* be produced in a normal adult male by removal of testosterone and the administration of estrogen. Similarly, a woman will not lose her sexual interest in men and want to engage in sexual activity with other women as a result of testosterone treatment. She will not even lose her libido (even though men might be turned off by her beard and husky voice). In fact, she might become even more interested in sex than she was before.

The fact that sex hormones affect males and females in different ways can be attributed to the organizational effects of androgens during fetal development. You will remember that without androgens, Nature makes a female. The same is true for the behavior subsequently expressed in adulthood; prenatal androgens predispose the organisms to male behavior (regardless of genetic sex), whereas their lack predisposes toward female behavior. (I say "predispose," because we can only make probability statements about subsequent behavior. The effects of learning, as we shall see, can reverse the prenatal organizational effects of androgens, especially in humans.)

Rats are the animal of choice in studies of the organizational effects of sex steroids on later behavior, since their "critical period" with respect to sensitivity to androgens does not end until some time after birth. The critical period ends prenatally in most other animals (including humans). An adult female rat, previously treated with a single dose of testosterone just after birth, will (if her ovaries are intact) actively repulse the advances of a male rat. However, this female rat will show some mounting behavior if presented with an estrous female. Almost all normal female rats will show some mounting behavior, so this fact is not particularly striking. There is some increase in mounting, relative to normal females, but what is most significant is the lack of receptivity to the male's advances (Money and Ehrhardt, 1972). Ovariectomy followed by testosterone treatment will produce an increase in a female rat's mounting behavior, but this effect is substantially greater if the rat was androgenized at birth (Harris and Levine, 1965).

It seems most likely that the effects of early androgenization are produced in the brain, but one cannot overlook the fact that early testosterone treatment also produces clitoral enlargement; the role of altered sensory feedback from this organ might very well play a role in the female's mounting behavior (Beach, 1968; Swanson, 1971).

Masculinization in male rats can be prevented by castration just after birth, or by injections of substances that suppress androgens. The postnatally castrated male rat will show no sexual interest later in life unless hormones are administered. If he is injected with an estrogen followed by progesterone (the treatment that induces estrus in a female), he will exhibit female sexual behavior in response to a normal male rat (Grady, Phoenix, and Young, 1965). A normally androgenized male would be far less likely to respond in this way to injections of female hormones. If the neonatally castrated male rat is given testosterone at adulthood, instead, he will act pretty much like a normal female who receives such an injection. He will exhibit some mounting, but not nearly so much as seen in a normal male (Whalen, 1964). A male rat androgenized normally after birth but castrated in adulthood will show quite normal sexual behavior in response to testosterone injections. Thus, early androgenization is essential for normal male sexual behavior later in life, which occurs in response to the adult's own testicular secretion of testosterone. These effects are summarized in Table 11.1. Note that the rats' gonads were removed immediately after birth, so all effects are produced by the experimentally administered hormones. (See **TABLE 11.1.**)

What about humans? Are we exempt from the hormonal rules that govern the sexual behavior of other mammals? As we shall see, there is good evidence for effects of prenatal androgenization on morphology and behavior in humans. There is also good evidence for partial reversal of the behavioral effects as a result of learning. A person's gender identity and gender role (i.e., self-perceived identity as a male or female, and its expression in behavior and outward appearance) can be contrary to genetic sex, or contrary to the hormonal exposure of the developing brain.

If a female human fetus is treated with androgens, she will be born with varying degrees of clitoral hypertrophy (enlargement in size), and perhaps with some degree of labial fusion. (Remember, the scrotum and labia majora develop from the same primordia.) Such effects were seen in the cases of eleven girls whose mothers received a (now-obsolete) synthetic progestin in order to prevent miscarriage (Money and Ehrhardt, 1972). Unfortunately, the progestin sometimes

TABLE 11.1. Organizational and Activational Effects of Sex Hormones on the Sexual Behavior of Rats Gonad-ectomized Immediately after Birth

Sex	Hormones at Birth	Hormones at Adulthood	Sexual Behavior
Male	Estrogen or no hormone treatment	Progesterone + estrogen	Female
		Testosterone	None*
		None	None
	Testosterone	Progesterone + estrogen	None*
		Testosterone	Male
		None	None
Female	Estrogen or no hormone treatment	Progesterone + estrogen	Female
		Testosterone	None*
		None	None
	Testosterone	Progesterone + estrogen	None*
		Testosterone	Male
		None	None

* These treatments may produce weak effects but are ignored here for the sake of clarity.

had androgenizing effects, as was subsequently discovered.   The clitoral hypertrophy and labial fusion were corrected surgically after birth.   (The same syndrome can be observed in girls whose adrenal glands secrete abnormal amounts of androgens—the *adrenogenital syndrome.)*   The girls were raised and dressed as girls, and their gender identity was female.   However, they all were particularly tomboyish, preferring toy trucks and guns to dolls.   They preferred baseball to quiet games such as playing house.   (Goy, 1970, observed similar malelike behavior in female monkeys who were prenatally androgen-ized.)   The girls did not dislike wearing dresses on special occasions, but they mostly preferred slacks or shorts.   No special differences were seen in their childhood sex play, but since such behavior—in both males and females—is strongly suppressed in our society, one could hardly expect otherwise.   Most of the girls were much more inter-ested in careers than in marriage, but almost all foresaw, in a matter-of-fact way, future marriage and maternity.   At the time their report was written, Money and Ehrhardt noted that only a few of the girls had reached adolescence, but romantic interests appeared to emerge later in the prenatally androgenized girls.   No evidence of lesbianism was seen.

It should be noted that the behavior of none of these girls was "abnormal."   Many girls prefer toy trucks and cars to dolls, and slacks to dresses.   What would not be expected, however, is so much male-like interest from all members of a group of normal girls.   There seems to be no doubt that, in humans, prenatal androgens affect later behavior.

It was also found that the prenatal progestin treatment appeared to result in higher I.Q. scores. Before anyone concludes that males, with their normal androgenization, must therefore be more intelligent than females, it should be noted that male fetuses whose mothers were treated with progestin also showed increased I.Q. scores. Thus, the apparent increase in intelligence (if that is what it is) results from some special property of the synthetic progestin that is not present in androgens of the male fetus.

Prenatal estrogen does not appear to be any more important in producing a female human than it is in producing a female in other mammalian species. Humans with only one X chromosome will develop what is called Turner's syndrome. Because of the missing X chromosome, these people will not develop ovaries, and hence no estrogen will be produced. Nevertheless, these women will become just as "feminine" as normal XX females; unlike androgenized females, those with Turner's syndrome cannot be distinguished from normal females in behavior. (Some individuals with Turner's syndrome show mental retardation, so one cannot say that there are *no* deleterious effects other than the lack of ovaries.)

What about the male? Nature has performed the equivalent of the prenatal castration experiment (Money and Ehrhardt, 1972). Some males are insensitive to androgen (*androgenic insensitivity syndrome*—one of the more aptly named disorders). Thus, even though the primordial sex organs become testes, the testosterone they produce fails to masculinize the body. There is a rudimentary uterus and a very shallow vagina. The lack of female internal sex organs may be explained by the effects of Müllerian-inhibiting substance produced by the testes. (This syndrome, incidentally, provides further evidence for the distinction between Müllerian-inhibiting substance and testicular androgens.)

If an individual with this syndrome is raised as a girl, all is well. At puberty the body will become feminized by the small amounts of estrogen produced by the testes. (In the normal male, this estrogen is counteracted by the far greater amounts of testosterone.) At adulthood the individual will function sexually as a woman (surgical enlargement of the vagina may be necessary). Women with this syndrome report average libidos, including a normal frequency of orgasm in intercourse with a male. Homosexuality has not been reported. (We must define homosexuality carefully here. Chromosomally, copulation with a male would constitute "homosexuality," but since these people are morphologically and behaviorally female, homosexuality would entail sexual relations with a woman.)

The success of testicular estrogen in producing a female body is attested to in Figure 11.15; this woman, believe it or not, is genetically a male! (See **FIGURE 11.15**.) I think this photograph points out why it would be a tragedy to raise such an individual as a male.

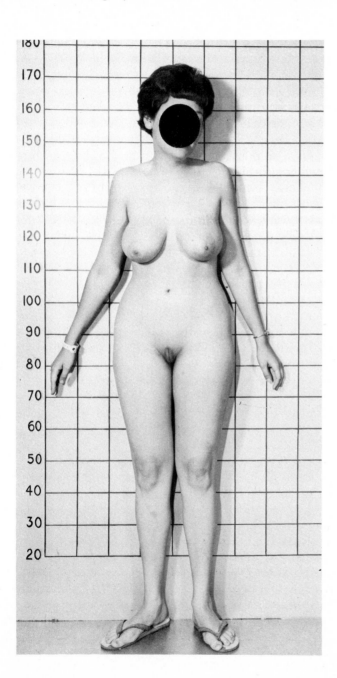

FIGURE 11.15 A genetic male displaying the androgenic insensitivity syndrome. The absence of pubic hair can be explained by the person's insensitivity to androstenedione (AD). (From Money, J., and Ehrhardt, A. A., *Man and Woman, Boy and Girl*. Copyright © 1973 by The Johns Hopkins University Press, Baltimore, Maryland. By permission.)

Testosterone treatment at puberty would be ineffective; all that could be done would be to remove the breasts surgically. The voice would remain high, and no beard would grow. As a matter of fact, the woman in the figure lacks pubic hair because of an insensitivity to AD, which normally stimulates its growth.

The picture that emerges is this: prenatal androgens are necessary for production of a male body and a male brain, with its subsequent propensity for typically masculine behavior. As seen in the case of the prenatally androgenized genetic females, however, this process is not absolute. If raised as a female, a partially androgenized girl will have more than the normal amount of masculine interests, but she will nevertheless perceive herself as female.

The power of a human's upbringing to contradict the effects of complete, natural, prenatal androgenization is seen in the following case (Money and Ehrhardt, 1972.) Identical twin boys were born to a couple and were raised normally until seven months of age, at which time one of the boys suffered accidental removal of his penis (a surgeon carelessly removed far too much tissue during an attempted circumcision). The cautery (a device that cuts tissue by means of electric current) was adjusted too high, and instead of removing the foreskin, the current burned off the entire penis. After a period of agonized indecision, the boy was (at seventeen months) subsequently raised as a girl. The first stage of plastic surgery, in creating a vagina, was performed. (The child will be given estrogen at puberty, and the final stages of surgery will be completed.) The child almost immediately responded to being treated as a girl, manifesting many behaviors typical of girls. She is neat and tidy (as opposed to her rather messy twin brother) and models her behavior on that of her mother. Since the two children are genetically identical, their differences in behavior must be attributed to the powerful effects of differential treatment of children who are perceived as boys or girls.

ACTIVATIONAL EFFECTS OF SEX HORMONES IN FEMALES. So far, we have seen more similarities than differences in the general role of sex hormones on morphological and behavioral development of various mammalian species. In adulthood, however, the sex steroids have somewhat different effects in higher and lower mammals. The most obvious difference is between females who have menstrual cycles and those who have estrous cycles.

The menstrual and estrous cycles are somewhat similar, in that they are characterized by similar interactions between pituitary gonadotrophins and estrogen and progesterone from the ovarian follicle (which subsequently becomes a corpus luteum). The cycle of the female rat, like that of the woman, is characterized by follicular estrogen, which stimulates an LH surge, followed by a minor secondary estrogen rise and an increase in progesterone level. Unlike the primate, the female rat will accept the male only at one stage of her cycle, near the time of ovulation. The hormones that are most important in controlling her sexual receptivity are estrogen and progesterone. Powers (1970) found that the duration of estrus depended principally upon the amount of estrogen, but that a high level of receptivity required that estrogen and progesterone both be present. In mammals who ovulate in response to mating (rabbits and cats, for example) an estrogen alone is necessary. In fact, in such animals, progesterone will have an inhibiting effect on mating behavior if it is given to an ovariectomized, estrogen-treated female just prior to mating tests (Young, 1961).

The sexual behavior of primates is not regulated in this way by the ovarian hormones. That is not to say that there are no hormonal effects, however. Female monkeys are more sexually receptive during mid-cycle (around the time of ovulation). Furthermore, the swelling of the skin around their genitals (*sex skin*) and the altered odor of the vaginal secretions combine to make them more attractive to males. In fact, the substance that produces this odor was identified by Michael, Keverne, and Bonsall (1971) as a mixture of short-chain fatty acids. The substances could be duplicated synthetically, and when they were applied to ovariectomized females, the animals became more interesting to males.

Many women report preferences for intercourse during different portions of the menstrual cycle, but no strong cyclicity in sexual desire can be generalized to all women. The *nature* of a woman's sexual desire does appear to be affected by the menstrual cycle, however. Money and Ehrhardt (1972) reviewed the work of other investigators and noted that at the menstrual period women report a desire to be more aggressive—to capture and contain the penis. During the ovulatory phase, they tend toward feelings of submissiveness and passivity. These general tendencies, obviously, can be obscured by an individual woman's sexual preferences.

The fact that female primates do not show the cyclic changes in sexual receptivity that characterize mammals with estrous cycles suggests that their receptivity is not particularly dependent on estrogen. Indeed, this appears to be the case. Ovariectomy (carried out all too often in the course of hysterectomy) does not abolish a woman's libido. (Nor does menopause, Nature's own "ovariectomy.") However, vaginal dryness and other physiological changes will occur, unless estrogen therapy is instituted. The other ovarian hormone, progesterone, might have an inhibitory effect on sexual desire (Grant and Mears, 1967; Kane, 1968). For this reason, some women report that a decrease in sexual desire accompanies the use of birth control pills (many of which contain some form of synthetic progestin). For many women, however, the release from the fear of pregnancy facilitates sexual desire much more than any direct suppressive effects of progestins.

Another difference between women and animals with estrous cycles is indicated by their contrasting reactions to androgens. You will recall that testosterone produces a small increase in malelike mounting behavior in female rats, even if they were not androgenized early in life. Androgens do not, however, stimulate male sexual behavior in women. On the contrary, these hormones appear to increase heterosexual desire. Removal of the adrenal gland (which secretes an androgen—androstenedione—in both men and women) appears to decrease libido in women, even though ovariectomy does not (Waxenberg, Drellich, and Sutherland, 1959). However, the adrenalectomies were performed during the later stages of terminal cancer, so it is difficult to draw definitive conclusions.

The results of research with monkeys appear to support the role of androstenedione as a "female libido hormone." Everitt and Herbert (1969) found that dexamethasone, a synthetic corticosteroid that causes a decrease in the blood levels of AD, produced a decline in sexual receptivity of female monkeys. Testosterone injections restored their behavior.

ACTIVATIONAL EFFECTS OF SEX HORMONES IN MALES. Men and male rats (and other mammals, for that matter) appear to resemble each other in their responsiveness to testosterone. With normal levels they are potent and fertile; without testosterone they become sterile (very quickly) and then impotent. Much emphasis has been placed on man's "emancipation from hormones." It is often said that humans, with their "high degree of corticalization" do not require hormones for sexual performance. These statements are not supported by the facts, however; they appear to result more from the typically human desire to see ourselves as not quite so dependent on our "biology" as other animals.

The decline in copulatory ability after castration varies considerably among individuals, even of the same species. Most rats cease to copulate within a few weeks, but some retain this ability for up to five months (Davidson, 1966b). Since the average life-span of a rat is a little over two years, this performance compares favorably with that of castrated humans, taking the different life-spans into account. As reported by Money and Ehrhardt (1972), some men lose potency immediately, whereas others show a slow, gradual decline over the years. The fact that the changes follow loss of testosterone is shown by the rapid return of libido and potency after administration of the male hormone.

There are individual fluctuations in testosterone level, as was nicely demonstrated by a researcher who was stationed on a remote island (Anonymous, 1970). Just before he left for visits to London (and to female company) his beard began growing faster. Anticipation of sexual activity stimulated testosterone production. Similarly, stress (during wartime) can lower testosterone levels (Rose, Bourne, Poe, Mougey, Collins, and Mason, 1969). It is difficult, however, to obtain a relationship between testosterone level and sexual behavior. Male sexual behavior appears to be essentially an all-or-none phenomenon; a given male will exhibit a particular level of behavior if he has sufficient testosterone (usually considerably less than the amount normally present in his blood). Extra testosterone has little effect on his sexual behavior (Young, 1961; Bermant and Davidson, 1974).

Homosexuality

It is impossible to say for certain why some people become homosexual while others become heterosexual. Homosexual behavior (male and female) has been seen in almost all mammalian species that have been studied. Homosexual episodes are often seen in humans (generally males) who are essentially heterosexual. In some societies, homosexual behavior is the norm during adolescence, followed by marriage and a normal heterosexual relationship (Money and Ehrhardt, 1972). However, some people become exclusively homosexual in desire and practice (*obligative*, as opposed to *facultative*, homosexuality). It is this condition which has received considerable study.

There is no doubt about the ability of the organizational effects of androgens to "bias" the later sexual proclivities of animals. Female rats, androgenized just after birth, will be much more likely to mount other receptive females (although it takes testosterone administration during adulthood, as we have seen, to demonstrate this altered sexual preference). Similarly, neonatally castrated male rats can be made to act like females if they are given estrogen and progesterone treatment as adults.

More subtle effects can be seen, also. Clemens (1971) found that the probability of malelike mounting was highest in female rats that shared their mother's uterus with several brothers; fewer brothers resulted in less male sexual behavior. Presumably, the females were partially androgenized by their brothers' testosterone. Since most humans do not have any company in the uterus, this factor apparently is not of much importance in human female homosexuality. (An androgen-secreting adrenal tumor in the mother would appear to be potentially a more important factor.)

There are also factors that might suppress the degree of androgenization of male fetuses. Ward (1972) put pregnant rats under stressful conditions (a bright light). The stress increased the mothers' corticosteroids, which presumably suppressed androgen production in the male fetuses. The male rats born to the stressed mothers had smaller external genitalia as adults and were deficient in their male sexual behavior. They were also more responsive to treatment with estrogen and progesterone, showing more lordosis than is seen in a normal male given these hormones.

It is impossible to say whether results such as those of Ward (or other investigators, who showed that androgenization could be prevented by maternal administration of barbiturates or inhibitors of protein synthesis) are relevant to human homosexuality. The fact remains that genetic males and females, androgenized or not, can be successfully raised as members of either sex (with plastic surgery early in life and hormonal administration later, if necessary). These people will typically be attracted to members of the sex opposite to that of their upbringing; the most important factor in their development is that both parents unambiguously treat them as male or female and provide them with a suitable image upon which to model their own sexual identity (Money and Ehrhardt, 1972).

Neural Mechanisms Controlling Sexual Behavior

SPINAL MECHANISMS. Genital stimulation can elicit sexual movements and postures in female cats and rats even after transection of the spinal cord below the brain (Beach, 1967; Hart 1969). Thus, at least some elements of sexual behavior are organized at the level of the spinal cord. These reflex activities apparently are controlled by brain mechanisms, being normally inhibited at times other than the peak of the estrous cycle. The inhibitory control can be removed by hypothalamic lesions in rats (Law and Meagher, 1958) or in guinea pigs (Goy and Phoenix, 1963); these animals exhibit lordosis during all phases of the estrous cycle.

The neocortex has also been implicated in inhibitory control of the spinal sexual reflexes. Cortical ablation (Beach, 1944) and chemical depression (Clemens, Wallen, and Gorski, 1967) have been shown to enhance lordosis in female rats. Cortical removal or chemical depression of cortex was effective only in the presence of estrogen; without estrogen the animals were unresponsive. These results mean that there appear to be subcortical circuits sensitive to estrogen that must be activated in order for lordosis to occur; these estrogen-sensitive circuits act to remove brain inhibition upon the spinal mechanisms mediating lordosis.

Whalen, Neubauer, and Gorzalka (1975) have obtained data that cast doubt on the conclusion that the neocortex is involved in inhibition of spinally mediated lordosis. These investigators observed, as Clemens, Wallen, and Gorski did, that chemical depression of the neocortex facilitated lordosis. However, Whalen and his colleagues also found that this enhancement could be eliminated by removing the adrenal glands or by chemically blocking their hormone release. They argued that the chemical depression, a stressful situation, stimulated the adrenal glands to increase their hormone output. One of the hormones secreted by the adrenal glands—progesterone—then facilitated the effects of estrogen. As we saw in the previous section, receptivity of female rodents is controlled by the joint action of estrogen and progesterone. These findings are summarized in **FIGURE 11.16.**

The reflex mechanisms responsible for control of penile erection and ejaculation are located in the spinal cord of the male animal. Hart (1967a) severed the spinal cords of dogs and observed not only erection and ejaculation, but also the characteristic pelvic thrusting, leg kicking, and arching back. A refractory period of 5 to 30 minutes followed ejaculations, during which time the animal was unresponsive. This contrasts with sexual behavior in the intact dog, which typically shows a pause of more than 30 minutes before sexual activity is resumed. Thus, the spinal cord is ready for more before the brain is.

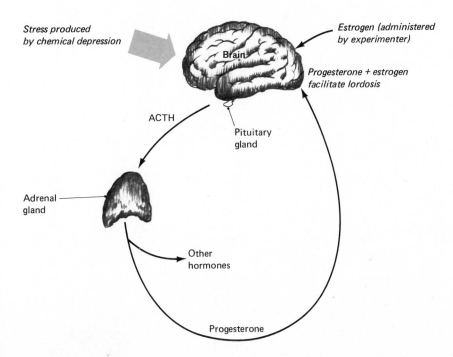

FIGURE 11.16 A schematic representation of the experiment by Whalen et al. (1975).

Hart obtained another piece of evidence for cerebral inhibition of spinal sexual reflexes; intense ejaculatory reactions, easily obtained by means of mechanical stimulation of the penis of a dog with a spinal transection, cannot be produced in a normal dog unless a receptive bitch is present. The odor and sight of a receptive female apparently disinhibit the cerebral mechanisms that normally prevent the expression of the intense ejaculatory response.

Emission of semen, as we have seen, is produced by a spinal reflex. Humans with spinal damage occasionally produce an erection and ejaculate. However, they do not experience an orgasm as a result, and they will be unaware of the erection and ejaculation unless they see it happening. They do, however, occasionally experience a "phantom erection" along with an orgasm, despite penile quiescence (Money, 1960; Comarr, 1970).

Brain Mechanisms. Penile erection and emission of semen appear to be controlled by different mechanisms. Herberg (1963) found that electrical stimulation of the *medial forebrain bundle* (a fiber system running in a rostral-caudal direction through the lateral hypothalamus) resulted in slow emission of semen, without penile erection, in rats. The electrical stimulation was also reinforcing; the rats would press a lever to turn on the current. The nature of the reinforcing effect is unclear. One cannot assume that the rats pressed the lever because the emission was reinforcing (as an orgasm might be), since rats will press a lever for electrical stimulation of other hypothalamic areas even when such stimulation does not result in emission (see chapter 17).

The neural circuitry involved in male sexual responses in the squirrel monkey was studied by MacLean and his coworkers. Locations were found all through the central nervous system, from the frontal lobe to the medulla, where electrical stimulation would produce erection and ejaculation. Many locations in the limbic system also give positive results; the investigators found locations where stimulation would produce signs of fear followed by an erection (as an apparent rebound phenomenon) when the stimulation was turned off. (In monkeys, penile erection is often used as a threat gesture, so the occurrence of a penile erection does not necessarily indicate that the brain region being stimulated is involved in sexual arousal.) The major neural system involved in penile erection appears to travel from the dorsomedial nucleus of the thalamus (which communicates with prefrontal cortex) to the hypothalamus to the ventral tegmentum to the anterior medulla (MacLean, Dua, and Denniston, 1963; Dua and MacLean, 1964).

Increases in male sexual behavior can be produced by stimulation in the vicinity of the preoptic area of the hypothalamus in rats

(Van Dis and Larsson, 1971). Such results could occur from direct facilitatory effects of the region on sexual behavior, or perhaps the stimulation could be disrupting inhibitory effects normally produced by that area (remember, electrical stimulation does not merely enhance the normal function of the neural tissue around the electrode tip). It appears more likely that the effects result from stimulation rather than disruption, since large preoptic lesions abolish sexual behavior in male rats (Heimer and Larsson, 1966, 1967). Testosterone therapy is ineffective in restoring this behavior. Female lordosis is not abolished by these lesions, but is instead facilitated. Powers and Valenstein (1972) found that female rats with preoptic lesions required less estrogen to show lordosis and were receptive for more days than were normal rats. It is interesting to note that the occasional mounting behavior seen in normal females, however, disappears after lesions of the preoptic region (Singer, 1968). According to Heimer and Larsson, female lordosis can be disrupted by brain lesions, but the critical region appears to be within the anterior hypothalamus just caudal to the preoptic area.

Hypothalamic lesions (ventromedial area) have even been produced in humans, in order to decrease the activity of male sex offenders (Roeder and Müller, 1969). The operations appear to suppress all forms of sexual behavior.

Destruction of tissue caudal to the hypothalamus facilitates male sexual activity (Heimer and Larsson, 1964; Goodman, Jansen, and Dewsbury, 1971). These lesions probably enhance male sexual behavior by interrupting hypothalamic inhibition normally exerted on more caudal mechanisms. However, the disinhibitory effects of cortical lesions on female sexual behavior are not seen in the behavior of males; large neocortical lesions (especially damage to frontal cortex) disrupt copulatory behavior of male rats (Larsson, 1964). This disparity in the role of cortex in males and females can probably be accounted for by the fact that the physical role of the male is more complicated and requires more motor control. Furthermore, whereas female receptivity (of mammals with estrous cycles) depends principally on her hormonal condition, the sexual excitement of the male depends principally on the sight and smell of a receptive female (Bermant and Taylor, 1969). His arousal, then, requires a higher degree of analysis of sensory information.

The temporal lobes of the brain appear to play a role in the modulation of sexual arousal, and in its direction toward an appropriate goal object. We have already seen (in chapter 9) that temporal cortex plays a role in the visual identification of the significance of objects. (Monkeys with temporal lobe damage can "see" objects; they can orient in space quite normally and can pick up small objects. They cannot, however, visually discriminate nuts and bolts from raisins and other small pieces of food. They must put everything into the mouth first, rejecting inedible objects and chewing and swallowing the edible ones.) Temporal lobe damage appears to impair an animal's ability to choose an appropriate sex object; male cats with these brain lesions have been reported to attempt copulation with everything in sight—the experimenter, a teddy bear, furniture—everything remotely mountable (Schreiner and Kling, 1956; Green, Clemente, and DeGroot, 1957). However, one must interpret such results carefully; repeated sexual testing of a normal male cat with receptive female cats in one particular room appears to lead to the association of that room with copulation. Such cats, on subsequent testing in that room, often attempt copulation with everything in sight.

In humans, temporal lobe dysfunctions are often correlated with decreased sex drives. For example, focal epilepsy (brain seizures that originate from localized, irritative lesions) of the temporal lobes is sometimes associated with impotence (Hierons and Saunders, 1966). Surgical removal of the affected tissue sometimes leads to hypersexuality (Blumer, 1970). Temporal lobe dysfunction is also occasionally found in people with bizarre fetishes. A particularly striking example was that of a man with a safety pin fetish. He suffered from a compulsion to gaze at a safety pin, and the staring would then trigger a seizure. After the seizure he would often dress in his wife's clothing. Surgery corrected the epilepsy, and along with it went the sexual aberrations (Mitchell, Falconer, and Hill, 1954). A similar case was reported by Hunter, Logue, and McMenemy (1963). Surgical removal of a patient's diseased temporal lobe eliminated his prior epilepsy and transvestitism.

Kolarsky, Freund, Machek, and Polak (1967) examined the cases of men with sexual disorders and found a good relationship between the disorders and actual or presumptive temporal lobe damage, especially if the damage occurred early in life.

It is difficult to provide a clear and concise summary of the results of study of brain mechanisms involved in sexual behavior. It is safe to say that the spinal cord contains the circuitry necessary for the basic sexual reflexes: lordosis, erection, ejaculation, pelvic thrusting, etc. The brain (especially the hypothalamus) regulates these reflexes, removing them from inhibitory control under the appropriate circumstances. The temporal lobe appears to be particularly important in the analysis of what circumstances are appropriate.

The limbic system plays an important role in the regulation of sexual behavior, but it is impossible, without much more study, to assess just what the role is. For example, a lesion in a particular portion of the limbic system might increase sexual behavior not by affecting circuitry directly involved in copulatory behavior, but by decreasing the expression of some state (fear, for example) that normally competes with the expression of sexual behavior.

All that can be said about the hypothalamus is that it is very important; more precise statements about circuitry cannot yet be made. The preoptic and ventromedial areas seem to be important in expression of male-type sexual behavior in both males and females. The anterior hypothalamus seems to be necessary for lordosis, whereas the preoptic area appears to play an inhibitory role. The existence of inhibitory effects mediated by the hypothalamus is also shown by the fact that lesions caudal to this area produce hypersexuality.

Finally, we saw that frontal cortex is important for male, but not female, sexual behavior in rodents, presumably because the mechanical aspects of the male role are more complex. In higher mammals, one would expect cortical damage to disrupt the sexual behavior of both males and females.

Neuroendocrine Control of Sexual Behavior

The final section of this chapter will consider the role of the nervous system in mediation of the behavioral effects of sex hormones.

The spinal cord contains the first level of control of sexual behavior. As we saw earlier, male and female sexual behavior can be elicited by genital stimulation from animals whose spinal cords have been severed. In a series of studies, Hart (1976b, 1968, 1969, 1970) found that hormones had no effect on sexual reflexes in female rats and dogs. Males of these species, however, were stimulated by testosterone; this hormone appeared to have direct effects on the spinal cord and/or peripheral portions of the sexual reflexes. It appears that the neural effects of androgens are not restricted to the brain.

We saw in the previous section that lesions of anterior hypothalamus and preoptic area depress female and male sexual behavior, respectively (Heimer and Larsson, 1966/1967; Singer, 1968). The effects of these lesions are not reversed by hormonal administration; thus these areas either contain the hormone-sensitive cells or are involved in mediating the effects of hormonal stimulation of neurons located elsewhere.

Investigators have implanted small portions of sex hormones directly into the brain. Estrogen implants in the hypothalamus will restore sexual behavior of ovariectomized cats and rats (Harris and Michael, 1964; Lisk, 1962). It appears that the anterior hypothalamus, at least in rats, is most responsive, but since there is always some spread of the hormone through adjacent tissue, it is not possible to ascertain the precise location of the estrogen-receptive cells. Progesterone, which, as we have seen, facilitates female sexual behavior if given subsequent to estrogen treatment, appears to exert its effects elsewhere. Rose, Claybough, Clemens, and Gorski (1971) found that progesterone implants in the midbrain reticular formation, but not in the hypothalamus, stimulated sexual behavior of ovariectomized, estrogen-primed female rats. The investigators implanted *cannulas* (small metal tubes) in the rats' brain and cemented these tubes to their skull to serve as guides for smaller cannulas. The smaller cannulas, containing progesterone, could then be placed into the larger, permanently attached ones, and thus into the brains of the animals, long after recovery from the effects of surgery. Progesterone implants in the midbrain reticular formation produced a stimulating effect within fifteen minutes.

Autoradiography studies have also shown (in the guinea pig) that neurons in the hypothalamus have a special affinity for progesterone (Sar and Stumpf, 1973). Furthermore, Wade, Harding, and Feder (1973) found that radioactive progesterone was taken up by cells of the midbrain, hypothalamus, cerebral cortex, and hippocampus of rats, hamsters, and guinea pigs. These investigators noted, furthermore, that the rate of uptake of progesterone appeared to be related to the species differences in the behavioral effectiveness of this hormone.

In males castrated after puberty, testosterone appears to be most effective when implanted in the anterior hypothalamus (Davidson, 1966a; Lisk, 1967; Johnston and Davidson, 1972). Again, diffusion of the hormone makes it impossible to localize precisely the regions that respond to its presence.

SUGGESTED READINGS

BERMANT, G., and DAVIDSON, J. M. *Biological Bases of Sexual Behavior.* New York: Harper & Row, 1974.

MONEY, J., and EHRHARDT, A. A. *Man and Woman, Boy and Girl.* Baltimore: The Johns Hopkins University Press, 1972.

It is particularly easy to prepare a list of suggested readings for this chapter. These two books are extremely well written and contain a wealth of information. Bermant and Davidson concentrate more on information from animal research, whereas Money and Ehrhardt emphasize human sexual development and behavior. If you are interested in the topic of this chapter, I would suggest that you obtain both volumes. The books are available in paperback.

Regulation and the Control of Food Intake

12

"The constancy of the internal milieu is a necessary condition for a free life" is the way Claude Bernard put it, back in the late nineteenth century. This famous quote very succinctly states what organisms must do if they intend to roam about in environments hostile to the living cells that comprise them (i.e., live a "free life")—they must regulate the internal fluid that bathes their cells (the so-called interstitial fluid).

Our cells require very precise control of their environment. The evolutionary process has not produced "tougher" cells; instead, it has produced the means by which the cells' environment can be regulated. The proper concentration of solutes is necessary, or the cells will lose water and shrink or gain water and swell as a result of osmosis. Nutrients and oxygen must be available, along with the proper hormones necessary for the entry of these substances into the cell, and waste products from the cell must not be allowed to accumulate. Temperature must be kept within a very small range, especially for proper functioning of nerve cells.

Single-celled organisms living in the ocean are, obviously, not able to regulate characteristics of their "extracellular fluid," the sea itself. It is possible for these organisms to change their buoyancy and thus ascend or descend to regions with a more favorable temperature or oxygen content, and some can swim a limited distance, but the existence of these organisms relies on the fact that their environment remains relatively constant. If it changes radically, they die; or in some cases they assume an inactive form until favorable conditions return.

As our single-celled ancestors evolved into more complex, multicellular organisms, they began to require regulatory mechanisms. Cells in the interior of their bodies could not rely on the process of diffusion to bring them nutrients and remove waste products. The animals evolved digestive, respiratory, circulatory, and excretory systems to facilitate the exchange of materials with the environment. Eventually, land-dwelling mammals evolved. Unlike sea-dwellers, who only have to seek sources of food, these animals must locate sources of water and periodically ingest it to prevent dehydration. And, unlike their *poikilothermic* ("varied-heat" or, more colloquially, "cold-blooded") counterparts, mammals have evolved mechanisms by which they may regulate their temperature by generating heat or losing it to the environment as required. These *homoiotherms* can therefore venture into regions far removed in temperature from their 37°–38° C interiors. Poikilotherms, on the other hand, must hibernate in cold weather, since their metabolic rates can fall so low that the animals cannot even move. In hot, sunny weather these animals must hide in the shade or immerse themselves in water.

The topic of this chapter and the next will be the means by which we mammals regulate our extracellular fluid by controlling our food and water intake. Judging from the number of articles in scientific journals, regulation (especially of feeding) is one of the most intensely studied problems in physiological psychology. There are several reasons for such interest. First, regulation is of primary importance to life; other functions (sexual behavior, for example) cannot be carried out unless our interstitial fluid is kept constant. Understanding the physiological mechanisms that control regulatory behaviors might give us insight into other processes—sensory mechanisms, motor mechanisms, learning—that were probably evolved, in large part, to provide a regular supply of food and water as the organisms ventured into environments of increasing complexity and variability. There is a reasonably good relationship between an animal's sensory and motor capacities and learning ability and the way in which it obtains its food. This fact does not mean that a species evolved mechanisms *in order to* get at a new source of food; it means, instead, that a selective advantage, in terms of additional sources of food, accrued to an animal that was capable of seeing better, or remembering better, or becoming more agile. A better understanding of the control of regulatory behavior might, then, assist investigation of mechanisms that underlie other behaviors.

The Regulatory Process

A regulatory mechanism is necessary whenever a system requires constancy of some substance in the face of varying availability and/or utilization of that substance. A regulatory mechanism consists of four essentials: a substance (or characteristic such as temperature) to be regulated, usually referred to as a *system variable*; a *set point*, or "optimal value" around which that system variable is regulated; a *detector* that is sensitive to deviations of the system variable above or below the set point; and a *correctional mechanism* capable of restoring the system variable to the set point.

A good example of a regulatory system is a room whose temperature is controlled by a thermostatically regulated heater, as illustrated in Figure 12.1. The system variable is air temperature of the room, and the detector for this variable is a thermostat. This device can be adjusted so that contacts of a switch will be closed when the temperature falls below a preset value (the set point). Closure of the switch contacts engages the correctional mechanism (the heating coils). (See **FIGURE 12.1.**)

If the rooms cools below the set point of the thermostat, the heater is turned on, which warms the room. The rise in room temperature causes the thermostat to turn the heater off. The effects initiated by the thermostat thus feed back to the thermostat and cause it to stop the correctional mechanism it started. This process is an example of *negative feedback,* and it is an essential characteristic of regulatory systems.

The term *feedback* should be self-explanatory; it refers to the consequences of an action affecting the factors that initiate that action.

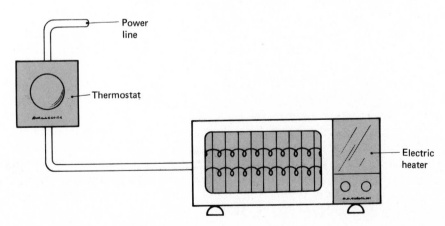

FIGURE 12.1 An example of a regulatory system.

The rise in temperature produced by switch contact closure acts upon the thermostat to open the contacts (turn the switch off) again. The feedback is described as *negative* because the consequences (temperature rise) of the action (turning on the heater) oppose the action (turning the heater off again).

Regulation of Intake: An Overview

O'Kelly, in a review of the problem of water regulation (O'Kelly, 1963), constructed a diagram that outlines the regulatory process in an organism's intake of food and water. (See **FIGURE 12.2**.) Living beings are *open systems*; they exchange energy and matter with their environment. Hence, there are input and output arrows shown above the box labelled *system variables*. Water, for example, is gained by ingestion and lost by excretion by the kidneys and sweat glands, and through the lungs. System variables are monitored by the detectors, which initiate correction internally or by means of behavior. Internal regulation includes such activities as the secretion of hormones that regulate the balance of various minerals, such as potassium and calcium. Behavioral regulation requires the animal to act. The box labelled *discrimination and orientation* implies a mechansm whereby the animal acts differentially toward environmental stimuli previously associated with the substance that is needed. (See **FIGURE 12.2**.) Ultimately, the animal ingests the substance required and thus alters the system variables. O'Kelly has included another box, labelled *satiety*, which interacts with the correctional mechanism. (See **FIGURE 12.2**.) The satiety mechanism serves to turn off corrective behavior even before the system variables, which are responsible for the initiation of ingestive behavior, are returned to the set point.

Why do we need a satiety mechanism? The reason lies in the physiology of our digestive system. Let us suppose (for the sake of argument) that we get hungry when some characteristics of our internal environment (for example, in the blood, interstitial fluid, cellular contents, or fat deposits) signal lowered energy stores. We begin to eat. But what makes us stop? Clearly, we do not work like the room-heating system I outlined. We do not continue eating until the energy stores of our cells are replenished, since it takes around four hours to digest a meal. We must possess a mechanism that says, "Stop—this meal, when digested and assimilated, will provide enough nutrition to restore things, eventually." The fact that we stop eating before a significant amount of food is digested makes it necessary to postulate a satiety mechanism.

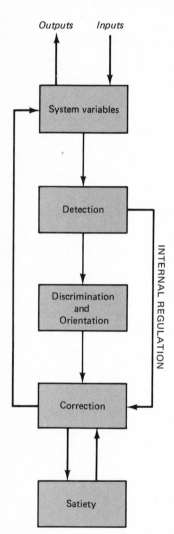

FIGURE 12.2 O'Kelly's model of regulation. (From O'Kelly, L. I., *Annual Review of Psychology*, 1963, *14*, 57–92.)

EXPERIMENTAL ANALYSIS OF THE REGULATION
OF INTAKE

How does one go about studying the physiological bases of regulation of intake? To put it most succinctly, one must find out what is regulated (and what the set point is), locate the detectors, and find out how the brain controls the initiation and suppression of ingestive behavior in response to signals from these detectors. Then one also has to find the way in which the satiety mechanism operates.

As you can imagine, the procedure is not nearly so simple as I have just outlined. Many sets of detectors monitor the system variables, and many different system variables appear to be implicated in ingestive behavior. Satiety has many sources, from several kinds of detectors. And the whole process may be overridden; even after a big dinner most people will eat a tasty dessert.

To find out whether a given variable (e.g., amount of glucose in the blood) is a factor in regulation of intake, one can experimentally alter this variable and observe the effects of such alteration on ingestive behavior. To search for detectors, one can change the value of the system variable in the vicinity of these hypothesized detectors and see whether ingestive behavior is altered. For example, if injections of water in a particular region of the brain caused a previously thirsty animal to cease drinking, the results would suggest that there were detectors sensitive to concentration of the interstitial fluid in that part of the brain. Finally, to locate brain mechanisms controlling ingestive behavior, one can perform brain lesion or brain stimulation studies, or locally block or stimulate particular types of synapses.

In this chapter and the next we shall see examples of a variety of ingenious experiments designed to isolate the critical variables and physiological mechanisms controlling intake. As we shall see, our ingestive behavior is affected by the sight, taste, odor, and texture of food, and the amount of food received in the stomach. The most important factor, however, is the quantity of nutrients stored in the cells of the body. For many years, physiological psychologists have assumed that detectors that measure the amount of stored nutrients are located within the brain. As we shall see, however, the most recent evidence suggests that it is the liver, not the brain, that monitors the store of nutrients. The detectors located in the brain do not appear to be responsible for control of feeding, but instead control hormonal secretion, which alters the availability of stored nutrients. The detectors in the brain are therefore part of the process O'Kelly calls "internal regulation."

In order to understand the newly found evidence concerning the control of food intake, we must first examine the processes of digestion, assimilation, and metabolism. Recent evidence, especially, has shown that it is essential that we understand how food is digested and absorbed, and how the body alternately stores and breaks down its energy supply.

The Digestive Process

First, look at an overall drawing of the digestive system. (See **FIGURE 12.3.**) Digestion begins in the mouth. We use our teeth to break down the food into pieces small enough to swallow safely and, in so doing, mix the food with saliva. The saliva serves several functions. It lubricates dry food and adds a digestive enzyme that begins the process of breaking down starches into sugars. Saliva also dissolves

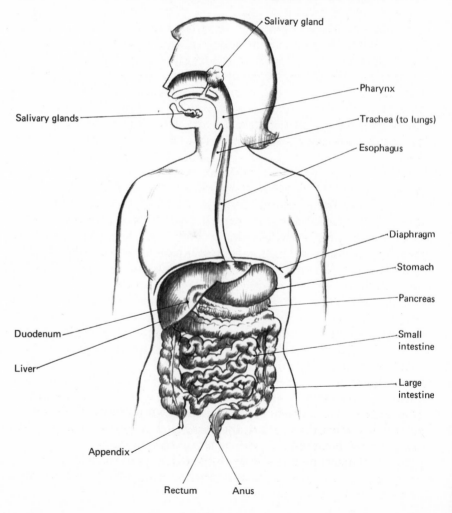

FIGURE 12.3 The digestive system.

molecules of the food so that the taste buds can be stimulated. Besides stimulating taste receptors, of course, the food stimulates olfactory receptors. Odor molecules enter the nose even before we begin to eat.

Swallowing involves a very complex set of reflexes that are voluntarily initiated but that are automatically controlled by the brain. Once the food is swallowed, it is propelled by waves of contractions of the circular smooth muscles of the esophagus down to the stomach.

The stomach, in response to both the bulk and the chemical nature of the food it receives, begins to secrete hydrochloric acid and the enzyme *pepsin.* Hydrochloric acid breaks the food into small particles, and pepsin breaks *peptide bonds,* thus beginning the process of breaking proteins in the food into their constituent amino acids. The stomach also becomes very active, churning the food around so that it becomes well mixed with digestive juices.

Gastric secretion and motility are controlled by several factors. The stomach is innervated by branches of the autonomic nervous system, and efferent fibers in these nerves provide one source of control. By this means, gastric secretion is stimulated by the sight and odor of food. Once food is in the stomach, stretch receptors and *chemoreceptors* (i.e., receptors sensitive to various chemicals) in the wall of the stomach trigger reflex activation (via the brain) of further gastric secretion.

The stomach empties into the *duodenum,* the upper portion (approximately 8 to 11 inches long) of the small intestine. (*Duodeni* means "twelve"; the duodenum is approximately twelve fingerwidths long.) The rate of gastric emptying is controlled by the composition of the foodstuffs received by the duodenum. The most important factors monitored by receptors in the duodenum are the amount of fat and the concentration of electrolytes. The presence of fats in the duodenum causes it to secrete a hormone (the chemical nature of which is still unidentified) called *enterogastrone.* This hormone is a potent inhibitor of gastric motility and thus makes the stomach empty its contents more slowly, allowing time for digestion in the duodenum.

The pancreas, which is located below the stomach, communicates with the duodenum by means of the pancreatic duct. (The pancreas, as we shall see, also produces two hormones, insulin and glucagon, and thus qualifies as an endocrine gland as well as an exocrine gland.) Pancreatic enzymes break down proteins, lipids, starch, and nucleic acids, thus continuing the digestive process. The pancreas also secretes bicarbonate, which neutralizes stomach acid. As the products of digestion begin to be absorbed into the bloodstream, and as the acid is neutralized by the bicarbonate, the stomach empties more foodstuff into the duodenum.

Digestive juices from the stomach and pancreas do a good job of breaking down proteins into amino acids, and starches and complex sugars into simple sugars. These water-soluble nutrients enter the capillaries of the intestinal *villi*, fingerlike structures that protrude into the intestine. (See **FIGURE 12.4.**) These capillaries drain into veins that travel directly to the liver. The veins branch into another set of capillaries within the liver; thus, the nutrients extracted from a meal reach the liver via the *hepatic portal system* before reaching any other portion of the body. (See **FIGURE 12.5.**)

Unlike the water-soluble nutrients, fats remain in fairly large droplets and cannot be absorbed to any extent without the presence of *bile*. The liver produces bile, and this substance breaks down the lipid droplets into very small particles—a process called *emulsification*. Milk, for example, is an emulsion, containing very fine particles of butterfat suspended in water. (In fact, the word emulsion comes

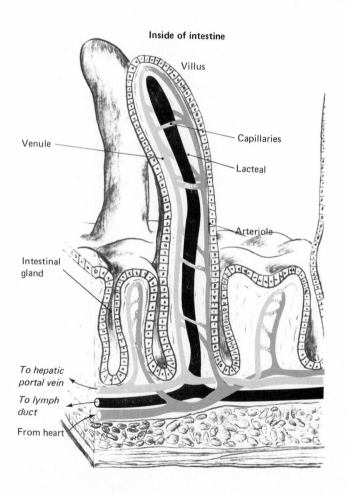

FIGURE 12.4 Intestinal villi. (Adapted from Vander, A. J., Sherman, J. H., and Luciano, D. S., *Human Physiology: The Mechanisms of Body Function*, ed. 2. New York: McGraw-Hill, 1975.)

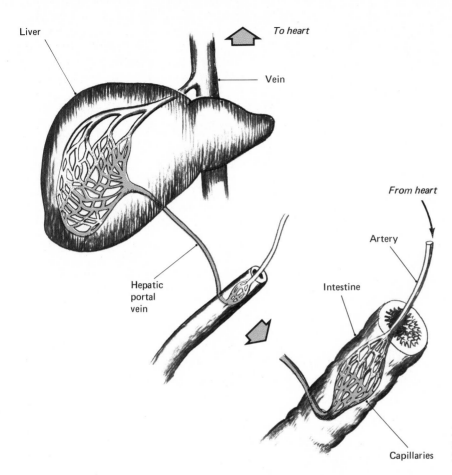

Liver

To heart

Vein

From heart

Artery

Intestine

Hepatic
portal
vein

Capillaries

FIGURE 12.5 A schematic
representation of the hepatic
portal blood supply.

from the Latin word *mulgēre*, which means "to milk.") Emulsified
fats can be absorbed into the *lacteals* located within the villi; the lacteals communicate with the lymphatic system, which then brings the
fats to a duct that empties into veins in the neck.

The meal passes through the small intestine, where most of the
available nutrients are absorbed. The residue enters the large intestine. Hardly any nutrients are absorbed in the large intestine, but a
considerable amount of water and electrolytes is reabsorbed. (This
reabsorption is extremely important. Cholera kills people by producing severe diarrhea, which results in the loss of fluids and electrolytes
through the feces.) The intestinal bacteria live mainly on undigested
cellulose. They produce some vitamins (especially *vitamin K*, important in the clotting of blood) that are absorbed into the body. Note
that I said "into the body." The contents of the digestive tract are not,

strictly speaking, within the body. If we are reduced, topologically, to our simplest form, we find that we are doughnut-shaped. The gastro-intestinal tract is the hole in the doughnut.

Storage and Utilization of Nutrients

The metabolic processes of the body are beautifully interrelated. At different times, the processes cooperate to produce (1) the *absorptive phase* (which occurs while a meal is being absorbed from the intestine) and (2) the *fasting phase* (which occurs after the nutrients have been absorbed, and which usually leads to hunger and ingestion of the next meal). As we shall see, the factors that cause metabolism to enter the fasting phase are the ones that also induce hunger; hence, we must understand metabolic processes if we are to understand the physio-logical control of food intake.

Energy can be obtained from the breakdown of various sub-stances.

1. Glucose can enter the *Krebs citric acid cycle* and be oxidized to carbon dioxide and water, liberating energy.

2. *Glycogen* (which we might call "animal starch") can be broken down (in the liver) to glucose, which can then be oxidized, or it can be broken down (in muscles) to *lactate* and *pyruvate,* yielding energy.

3. Lactate and pyruvate (from the muscles) themselves can enter the Krebs cycle and yield energy as they are oxidized to yield carbon dioxide and water.

4. Amino acids can be *deaminated* (NH_2 is removed) to pro-duce *keto acids.* The keto acids can be broken down to produce carbon dioxide and water, liberating energy in the process. The waste nitro-gen is converted, in most mammals, to *urea,* which is excreted by the kidneys.

5. Fats can be broken down to produce *fatty acids* and keto acids, which can be metabolized to carbon dioxide and water, again yielding energy.

These processes are summarized in **FIGURE 12.6.**

ABSORPTIVE PHASE. Figure 12.7 contains a simplified outline of the absorptive phase of metabolism. The numbers on the figure corre-spond to the list on page 331. This phase occurs while food is present in the gastrointestinal system. The absorptive phase is characterized by the following:

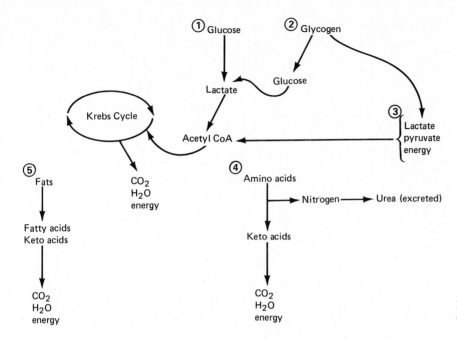

FIGURE 12.6 A schematic overview of metabolism.

1. Use of glucose as the primary energy source
2. Conversion of glucose into glycogen within the liver and muscles for storage
3. Synthesis of proteins from amino acids, as needed by cells (especially in the muscles)
4. Conversion of amino acids to keto acids, which are then used by the liver for energy, or are converted into fats
5. Conversion of glucose into fats
6. Storage of fats in *adipose tissue* (layers of body fat)

As you can see, the dominant characteristic of the absorptive phase is the storage of nutrients. Glucose is the principal fuel for metabolism. (See **FIGURE 12.7.**)

There are, as we have just seen, two primary sources of stored energy, glycogen and fats. Note that fats can be absorbed directly or synthesized from glucose or amino acids. Usually, only a small amount of protein needs to be synthesized, and the excess amino acids go into fat storage. If there is excess glucose, above the amount directly metabolized or put into storage in the form of glycogen, the remainder will be stored as fat. Thus, we can become fat even on a fat-free diet, if we eat high-calorie meals. The production of fat is an efficient way to store energy; a gram of fat contains 2¼ times the energy of a gram of amino acid or glucose.

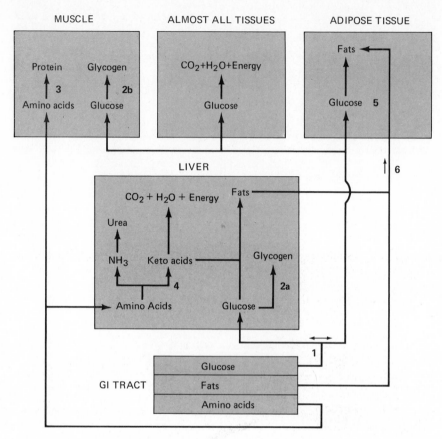

FIGURE 12.7 Metabolism during the absorptive phase. (Adapted from Vander, A. J., Sherman, J. H., and Luciano, D. S., *Human Physiology: The Mechanisms of Body Function*, ed. 2. New York: McGraw-Hill, 1975.)

FASTING PHASE. While a meal is being absorbed from the intestine, we live mainly on the glucose entering the blood supply. Once the food is absorbed, however, our cells must receive sources of energy elsewhere. Figure 12.8 shows the metabolic pathways during the fasting (or postabsorptive) phase. Again, the numbers below correspond to the numbers in the illustration.

1. Most body tissues use fatty acids and keto acids as sources of energy. It is commonly believed that the sole source of energy for the brain is glucose; this is not true, since the brain can quite readily metabolize keto acids. These substances come from fats stored in adipose tissue.

2. The liver has a special metabolic pathway. This organ transforms fatty acids to ketone bodies (a form of keto acid). These keto acids, which cannot be metabolized by the liver, enter the blood supply and are used as a further source of energy by other tissues.

3. Muscles break down glycogen to produce lactate and pyruvate. The reaction yields energy.

4. Lactate and pyruvate enter the blood supply and are converted, in the liver, to glucose.

5. Fats are broken down, in adipose tissue, to glycerol, which is converted by the liver into glucose.

6. During prolonged fasting, muscle protein may be broken down to amino acids, which are subsequently deaminated and converted into glucose by the liver.

7. The major utilization of glucose (which, as we can see, comes from several sources) is by the brain. (See **FIGURE 12.8.**)

To summarize: During fasting, muscles use glycogen for energy, and most other tissue (except the brain) uses fatty acids, derived from fats stored in adipose tissue. The brain uses only keto acids and glucose, which are derived (a) from fats, (b) from the lactate and pyruvate produced by the muscles during their utilization of glycogen, and, if necessary, (c) from the breakdown of protein. The fasting phase is characterized by the conversion of stored nutrients into use-

FIGURE 12.8 Metabolism during the fasting phase. (Adapted from Vander, A. J., Sherman, J. H., and Luciano, D. S., *Human Physiology: The Mechanisms of Body Function*, ed. 2. New York: McGraw-Hill, 1975.)

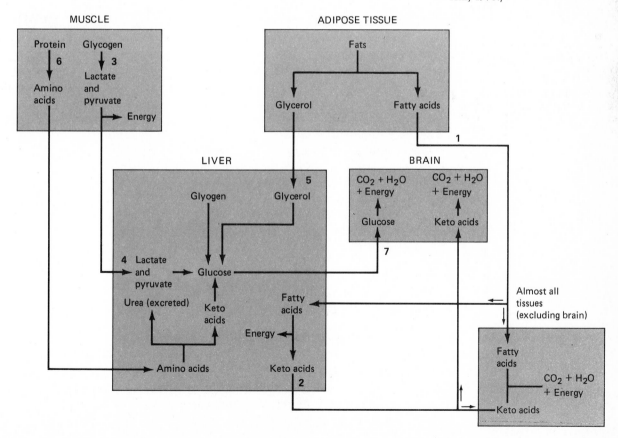

able forms: glucose (for the brain only), keto acids (for all of the body except the liver), and fatty acids (for all of the body except the brain).

Control of Metabolism

As we have just seen, the metabolic pathways followed during fasting and during absorption of nutrients are very different. There obviously must be mechanisms that control these metabolic pathways. As we shall see, this control is effected by the nervous system and by four hormones.

INSULIN AND THE ABSORPTIVE PHASE.   The absorptive phase of metabolism is produced primarily by the effects of insulin. Insulin is one of the two hormones secreted by the *islet cells* of the pancreas in its role as an endocrine gland. Insulin is a vital hormone. If the pancreas loses the ability to produce insulin, the disease *diabetes mellitus* results. Severe diabetes, if not treated with injections of insulin, can result in death. The lack of insulin results in a very high blood level of glucose, primarily because glucose cannot enter the cells of the body (except for cells of the nervous system and liver, which do not depend on insulin).

Deprived of glucose, the other cells rely principally on fats for energy. The glucose is passed through the kidneys and, in the process, causes a loss of sodium. If severe enough, the mineral loss can lead to low blood pressure, reduced blood flow, and, ultimately, death. Diabetes mellitus literally means "passing through of honey," because the urine of an untreated diabetic tastes sweet. (The diagnosis of this disease, fortunately, can be accomplished by chemical procedures, and no longer relies on the sense of taste.) The presence of sugar in the urine led an observant physician to note, several hundred years ago, that diabetes could be diagnosed, at least in men, by noting whether a person's shoes attracted flies.

Insulin has many metabolic effects, as shown in Figure 12.9.

1. Insulin facilitates the entry of glucose into the cell. Without insulin, body tissue cannot readily utilize glucose in metabolic processes. The nervous system and liver are exceptions; they can use glucose independent of insulin.

2. Insulin increases the conversion of glucose to glycogen.

3. The conversion of glucose into fats is increased, and the build-up of fat storage is thus facilitated.

4. The transport of amino acids into cells is facilitated, thus permitting protein synthesis to occur.

These four major effects of insulin are summarized in **FIGURE 12.9.**

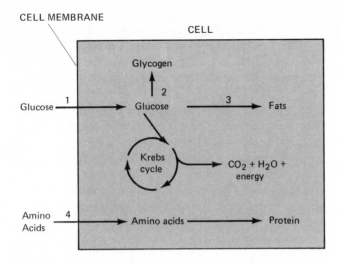

FIGURE 12.9 Effects of insulin on metabolism. (Adapted from Vander, A. J., Sherman, J. H., and Luciano, D. S., *Human Physiology: The Mechanisms of Body Function*, ed. 2. New York: McGraw-Hill, 1975.)

Insulin thus facilitates the metabolic pathways involved in the absorptive phase of metabolism: storage of nutrients and utilization of glucose.

CONTROL OF INSULIN SECRETION.   Three factors control insulin secretion. The first is the level of glucose in the blood. In a nice negative feedback system, the release of insulin is facilitated by high levels of glucose, and it is inhibited by low levels. During the absorptive phase, glucose is received from the intestines via the hepatic portal blood supply. This rise in blood glucose stimulates insulin secretion by directly affecting the pancreas. If the blood glucose level falls too far, insulin secretion is inhibited. Since no glucose is received from the intestines durng the fasting phase, there is a very low level of insulin secretion. Therefore, the set point and detectors for one means of control of blood glucose level are located in the pancreas. A rise in the level of amino acids also stimulates insulin secretion. This mechanism makes sense, since insulin facilitates entry of amino acids into the cells of the body.

The pancreas can also be stimulated by activity of its efferent nerve supply to produce insulin. The brain, therefore, has some control over blood sugar level.

FACTORS PRODUCING THE FASTING PHASE.   The fasting phase of metabolism is produced by several factors.

1. A low blood level of insulin makes it difficult for blood glucose to enter cells. Since the nervous system does not require insulin for utilization of glucose, much of the blood glucose during the fasting phase is available to the brain.

2. Four different factors stimulate the liver to convert other substances into glucose. These factors are (a) *glucagon*, the other hormone produced by the pancreas; (b) *epinephrine*, the principal hormone of the adrenal medulla; (c) *somatotrophic hormone*, also called *growth hormone*, produced by the anterior pituitary gland; and (d) activity of sympathetic fibers innervating the liver.

3. These same three hormones (and, additionally, the sympathetic fibers innervating adipose tissue) facilitate the breakdown of fats, making them available for use as energy-yielding material.

4. Epinephrine facilitates the breakdown of muscle glycogen to glucose.

5. Two factors, glucagon and activity of the sympathetic fibers innervating the liver, facilitate the breakdown of liver glycogen to glucose.

CONTROL OF FACTORS PRODUCING THE FASTING PHASE. Secretion of glucagon, like that of insulin, is controlled directly by the blood glucose level, but in the opposite way. The release of glucagon is facilitated by low blood glucose levels and inhibited by high levels. Furthermore, like insulin (and this time in the *same* direction), both glucagon and growth hormone are secreted in response to high levels of amino acids in the blood. The significance of this fact will soon be explained.

Epinephrine and growth hormone are secreted in response to a low blood glucose level. This effect is mediated by the central nervous system. Naturally, the other factor producing the fasting state, activity of the sympathetic fibers innervating liver and adipose tissue, is also controlled by the CNS. The location of detectors involved in the control of these factors will be discussed later.

I should now explain the significance of the fact that high levels of blood sugar stimulate only insulin release, but high levels of amino acids stimulate release of insulin, glucagon, and growth hormone. Suppose an animal eats a high-protein, low-carbohydrate meal. The amino acids trigger insulin release. Insulin facilitates cellular uptake of amino acids, so the body makes use of this nutrient. But insulin also facilitates cellular uptake of glucose and inhibits its synthesis. If no glucose were received from the intestine (as is the case for a high-protein, low-carbohydrate meal), the blood sugar level would fall drastically and endanger brain metabolism. The glucagon and growth hormone secreted in response to the high levels of amino acids help keep the blood sugar level up, so that the brain can continue to receive its fuel. (A summary is provided in **FIGURE 12.10.**)

We can see that the main factor that normally determines whether the body is in the fasting or absorptive phase is glucose (and secondarily, amino acids). If blood glucose levels (or amino acid levels) are being kept down by insulin (since new nutrients are con-

HIGH–PROTEIN, LOW–CARBOHYDRATE MEAL

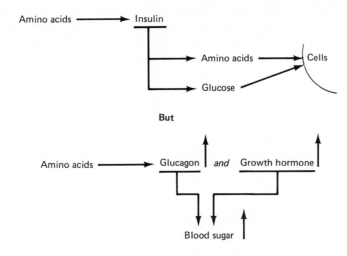

FIGURE 12.10 Metabolic effects of a meal high in protein and low in carbohydrates.

stantly being received by the intestines), metabolism is in the absorptive phase. If blood glucose levels must be kept up by glucagon, growth hormone, and epinephrine, metabolism is in the fasting phase. Since an animal does not require food during the absorptive phase, but should start looking for a meal when the fasting phase begins, one would suspect that the mechanisms that control these phases might also be those which trigger hunger and satiety.

Patterns of Food Intake

Most mammals feed periodically. They consume their food in meals. Perhaps a study of patterns of food intake will provide some insights into the control of ingestive behavior. If an animal such as a rat is given free access to food (that is to say, food is available *ad libitum*), the size of a given meal does not appear to be related to the time since the previous meal. However, the amount eaten at a given meal seems to determine the length of time an animal will wait until the subsequent meal; the larger the meal, the longer the pause in eating (Le Magnen, 1971). The significance of these observations might not be immediately apparent. Let us look at Le Magnen's conclusions.

First of all, the factors that start a meal do not appear to be the ones that stop it. One could predict that an animal would need more food if a long time has elapsed since the last meal, and less food if a short time has elapsed. But the duration of a meal, once started, appears to be independent of the time since the previous meal; the amount eaten appears to be relatively independent of need. This suggests that factors such as taste or amount of food (if any) already present in the stomach—and *not primarily need*—determine how much is eaten. However, if a large meal is eaten, an animal waits a long time before eating again. So the *onset* of a meal is determined by need. From these conclusions, we would expect that changes in an animal's expenditure of energy (changes in room temperature or exercise) would affect the frequency of meals, but not their size.

Le Magnen's conclusions are important for two reasons. First, we have a suggestion that we should look for different physiological mechanisms underlying the initiation and the suppression of eating. Second, we must look carefully at any study that purports to detect changes in ingestive behavior in a single meal, since changes in meal frequency, not meal size, appear to be the means by which an animal regulates its intake.

Perhaps this fact explains why so many people have trouble controlling their body weight. We eat three times a day, by social convention. This fact means that we cannot regulate intake by varying the time interval between meals, so we must adjust meal size. But if, in humans, meal size is not well related to need (as Le Magnen has shown to be true for rats), we might have difficulty in regulating our intake. Let us compare our pattern of food intake with the behavior of a predator such as a wolf. (Many years ago, hunting tribes of *Homo sapiens* probably resembled the wolf in their feeding habits.) Let us assume the wolf gorges itself on a kill. The wolves share the kill and devour everything, unless there is more than the animals' stomachs will hold. If the meal was large, the animals do not hunt again for a relatively long time. If each animal received only a small share, they hunt again very soon. What they do *not* do is hunt every few hours and then eat a small or large meal, depending on how hungry they are. Meal size, then, depends on the size of the kill, whereas the onset of feeding behavior depends on some central factors related to tissue need.

There is good evidence in support of Le Magnen's conclusion that meal frequency, not meal size, is what is normally regulated. If rats are placed on a food-deprivation schedule, having a one-hour access to food only once every 24 hours, the animals begin to lose weight. The meal size during the one-hour access to food increases slowly; apparently the animals have to learn to increase their intake during this hour (Lawrence and Mason, 1955). The difficulty these animals have in increasing their meal size suggests that they normally regulate intake by means of meal frequency and not size. Of course, with access to food occurring only once a day, they cannot regulate intake in the normal way.

Furthermore, if a dog is given a single meal each day, the size of the meal is unaffected by a prior intravenous (IV) injection (i.e., an injection directly into a vein) of enough glucose to supply it with 100 percent of its daily caloric needs (Janowitz, Hanson, and Grossman, 1949). By feeding the animal once a day, the investigators established that a meal would begin at a given time. Even though the animal had already received all the calories it needed from the injection of glucose, the availability of glucose for metabolism did not prevent ingestion of a normal-sized meal. Thus, the amount of food eaten did not appear to be controlled very well by tissue need.

If an animal's expenditure of energy changes, the animal must alter food intake accordingly, or it will gain or lose weight. Kissileff (1971) found that animals placed in a cold environment (which required a higher rate of energy expenditure to keep warm) increased their daily caloric intake by eating more often. Meal size remained constant.

Under special conditions animals will, however, increase meal size when their diet is diluted. Snowden (1969) produced chronic fistulas in rats by implanting a tube through which liquids could be injected into the mouth (*intraoral fistula*) or into the stomach (*intragastric fistula*). (See **FIGURE 12.11**.) The rats were trained to press a lever, which operated a valve that dispensed a small amount of liquid food through the fistula. Rates with both kinds of fistulas increased their intake in response to dilution of the diet. The increase in this case was in meal size rather than in the number of meals taken in a day. Except for abnormal situations such as this one, animals tend to regulate intake principally by means of meal frequency.

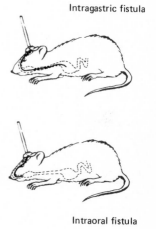

Intragastric fistula

Intraoral fistula

FIGURE 12.11 Intraoral and intragastric fistulas.

The Gastric Theory of Hunger and Satiety

The earliest attempts to explain regulation of food intake were based upon the observation that the sensation of hunger is generally identified as discomfort in the abdominal region. Cannon and Washburn (1912) found that "hunger pangs" were associated with contractions of an empty stomach. Washburn swallowed a balloon attached to the end of a flexible tube. The balloon was partially inflated, so that gastric contractions would increase the pressure within the balloon. Washburn's reports of hunger pangs generally coincided with gastric contractions. Observations such as these, and the fact that injections of glucose decrease gastric contractions, led Carlson (1916) to suggest that intake was regulated by feedback from the stomach.

As we shall see, the stomach does play a role in the regulation of food intake. However, if we consider a diagram such as the one in Figure 12.12, it should be apparent why peripheral factors, such as feedback received from the stomach, cannot adequately regulate food intake. The diagram is simple; there are inputs (food) and outputs

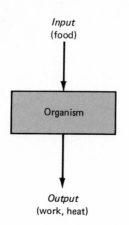

Input
(food)

Organism

Output
(work, heat)

FIGURE 12.12   Input must
equal output if the organism
is to maintain a constant
weight.

(work performed, heat produced—not what is anatomically suggested by the location of the arrow, opposite the end that receives the food). (See **FIGURE 12.12.**)   Let us assume that the body's supply of stored energy is regulated.   The inputs and outputs must be exactly equal (at least, on a long-term basis) or there will be a loss or gain.   Thus, if there are changes in the rate of energy expenditure, there must be corresponding changes in intake.   Peripheral factors, such as feedback from a full or empty stomach, cannot monitor changes in storage resulting from changes in energy expenditure.   Therefore, if the input-output equation is to be balanced, there must be measurement of some factors related to the amount of nutritive material within the body.

CENTRAL SYSTEM VARIABLES CONTROLLING FOOD INTAKE: THE THEORIES

There are three principal sources of energy: glucose, lipids (fats), and amino acids.   Hence, these substances have all been suggested as being factors monitored in the control of feeding.

Glucostatic Theory

It has been suggested that glucose, a nutrient vital to the brain, might be the most important system variable regulated by alterations in the intake of food.   It has been known for a long time that a fall in blood glucose (produced by an injection of insulin) leads to hunger (Morgan and Morgan, 1940), whereas injections of epinephrine or glucagon, which raise blood sugar level, produce satiety (Mayer, 1956).   The suggestion was made that low blood glucose levels meant hunger, whereas high blood glucose levels meant satiety.

This hypothesis was soon modified.   Patients suffering from untreated diabetes have an extremely high blood sugar level, and yet these people are usually very hungry.   If blood glucose is the system variable being measured and regulated, then the diabetics should not be hungry.   However, despite the fact that the blood glucose level is high, the cells of the body are not able to use the glucose.   Without insulin, glucose cannot enter the cells to be metabolized.   Thus, the body is in the fasting phase despite high blood glucose levels.

This consideration led Jean Mayer (1956) to hypothesize that the relevant system variable is the degree to which glucose can be utilized, not the mere amount of glucose present in the blood.   When one samples the arterial and venous blood of an untreated diabetic, one finds that the glucose levels in arterial and venous blood are almost identical. This "low A-V difference" means that the organs did not extract any significant amount of glucose from their arterial blood supply.

Eating is also produced by injections of *2-deoxy-D-glucose,* or *2-DG* (Smith and Epstein, 1969). This substance is similar to glucose in its molecular shape, but it cannot be metabolized. Injections of 2-DG block glucose metabolism and therefore reduce the availability of glucose to the body without lowering the blood sugar level. The fact that injections of 2-DG into the ventricles of the brain result in hunger (Miselis and Epstein, 1970) suggests that there are central glucoreceptors that control feeding.

SEARCH FOR BRAIN GLUCORECEPTORS. If glucose availability provides an important signal for the regulation of food intake, where are the receptors located? As I have noted, the nervous system is insensitive to the effects of insulin on glucose metabolism. The nervous system can utilize glucose even in the complete absence of insulin. Thus, although there is some electrophysiological evidence for hypothalamic neurons that respond to glucose (Desiraju, Banerjee, and Anand, 1968), one would not expect them to respond to glucose *availability*. The availability of glucose (to tissue other than that of the nervous system and liver) depends upon insulin, and if cells of the brain are unresponsive to the effects of insulin on glucose metabolism, then how can these cells monitor glucose availability?

Mayer (1955) has suggested that there are neurons in the hypothalamus that *are* sensitive to the effects of insulin. These cells thus act like other cells of the body; they metabolize glucose only when insulin is present. Presumably, their firing rate depends on their level of metabolism, thus coding for glucose availability. The evidence for the existence of these receptors, and their possible significance in regulation of intake, is given below. As we shall see, the evidence is not at all compelling.

In 1949, Brecher and Waxler discovered that injections of *gold thioglucose (GTG)* into mice resulted in gross overeating and consequent obesity. The animals looked like little tennis balls with a head, tail, and feet. It was found that the gold thioglucose apparently became concentrated in the vicinity of the *ventromedial nucleus* of the hypothalamus. (The location of this and other hypothalamic structures will be given later.) The gold component of the chemical, which is toxic, then killed the cells. It was hypothesized that this region (usually referred to as the *VMH*) contained glucoreceptors that became active when glucose availability was high. Satiety, then, would result from this activity. GTG thus destroyed the satiety mechanism by damaging the brain region containing these receptors.

The fact that GTG damaged the VMH suggested to many investigators that cells there had a special affinity for glucose. In support of this notion, it was found that neither gold thio*malate* nor gold thio*galactose* produced this localized brain damage; only gold thio*glucose* did (Mayer and Marshall, 1956). Furthermore, some studies have suggested that the VMH glucoreceptors might be responsive to the effects of insulin (unlike other neurons). Diabetic mice do not develop hypothalamic lesions when injected with GTG (presumably because their cells need insulin in order to utilize glucose), but these mice will develop VMH lesions when they are given an injection of insulin along with the GTG (Debons and Likuski, 1968). Insulin also produces this effect when injected directly into the hypothalamus (Debons, Krimsky, and From, 1970).

The significance of these results is questionable, however. Arees, Veltman, and Mayer (1969) observed that the GTG damages the hypothalamus indirectly by destroying capillaries in the vicinity of the ventromedial nucleus. Furthermore, Caffyn (1972) found that other poisons that do not contain glucose, but damage capillaries, also produce VMH lesions and an ensuing obesity. We must conclude that it is possible that there are brain glucoreceptors, but that so far there is not good evidence for their sensitivity to the effects of insulin. Without insulin sensitivity, these receptors cannot monitor glucose availability.

Besides the hypothesized VMH glucoreceptors, which might have a role in signalling satiety, it has been suggested that there are glucoreceptors in the lateral region of the hypothalamus that respond to *decreased* glucose. These receptors would not be damaged by GTG injections. Even after VMH lesions a rat will increase its food intake in response to the fall in blood glucose level caused by insulin injections. Early studies reported that this response is lost after lesions of the lateral hypothalamus (Epstein and Teitelbaum, 1967), perhaps because the glucoreceptors were destroyed. However, these lateral hypothalamic glucoreceptors (if they indeed exist) are not very important in normal regulation of food intake.

Blass and Kraly (1974) destroyed a fiber system of the lateral hypothalamus, which eliminated the response to 2-DG. That is, *glucoprivation* (depriving the cells of glucose) did not increase the animals' food intake. If a fall in the blood glucose level is an important system variable in the regulation of food intake, then rats with this type of brain lesion should have difficulty with such regulation. However, they did not. The animals ate more when given a diluted liquid diet, and they ate less of a concentrated diet. They regulated their food intake in response to changes in room temperature that produced alterations in their expenditure of energy. When body weight was temporarily raised by forced feeding (through a stomach tube) or lowered by starvation, the animals altered their food intake appropriately when given food *ad libitum,* and their weight returned to normal. By every measure, their regulation of food intake was normal, even though they no longer responded to lowered glucose availability produced by injections of 2-DG.

In a subsequent study, Stricker, Friedman, and Zigmond (1975) found that rats with lesions of the lateral hypothalamus would respond (with an increase in food intake) to gradually increasing doses of insulin. Single large doses of insulin apparently produce too much stress for these animals to cope with; large doses of insulin usually are lethal to rats with these brain lesions. These results cast a strong doubt on the importance of brain glucoreceptors in the regulation of food intake. As we shall see, the important receptors (and these do not seem to be simply *glucose* receptors) appear to be located in the liver.

Lipostatic Theory

As we saw earlier, calories that are ingested in excess of tissue need will be converted to fat, regardless of whether the calories are ingested in the form of fats, carbohydrates, or protein. And during fasting, the body's reserves of fat are broken down and used as a source of energy. Hence, it seems quite plausible that the amount of fat deposits might be involved in long-term regulation of food intake. (Fats are a form of lipid; hence the term *lipostatic* theory.) There is good evidence that this is the case; fat deposits do appear to be regulated. However, attempts to identify the system variables involved (e.g., amount of fatty acids in the blood) have not met with much success. This might be expected, since a factor involved in long-term regulation might be very poorly related to an animal's ingestive behavior on a short-term basis.

EVIDENCE FOR THE REGULATION OF FAT DEPOSITS. First, let us examine the evidence that the amount of body fat is regulated. Liebelt, Bordelon, and Liebelt (1973) have described a number of studies they have performed concerning the regulation of adipose tissue. They found that the body's total amount of fat appears to be regulated. When a piece of adipose tissue was transplanted from one mouse into another, the transplanted tissue normally withered away. However, when the experimenters first removed some of the adipose tissue belonging to the recipient animal, the transplants "took." In other words, when the total amount of fat tissue in the recipient mouse was surgically reduced, an implant grew—presumably in response to mechanisms encouraging growth of such tissue. Furthermore, when mice were treated with GTG, and consequently became *hyperphagic* (i.e., they ate in excessive amounts), they accepted a graft of adipose tissue while they were gaining weight (as though the VMH lesion had raised the "adipose tissue set point").

Another piece of evidence for regulation of body fat is that animals forced to eat—and to become fat—will reduce their food intake until their weight returns to normal levels (Hoebel and Teitelbaum, 1966; Steffens, 1975). Since excessive weight is carried mainly as body fat, perhaps adipose tissue gives rise to a satiety signal when the amount of tissue exceeds some set point. The evidence for mechanisms that regulate storage of fat seems, therefore, quite good.

SYSTEM VARIABLES IN REGULATION OF ADIPOSE TISSUE. The nature of the factors (presumably humoral) that facilitate or inhibit growth of fat tissue is not known. Possibly these factors also affect food intake. The factors cannot, however, entirely account for body weight regulation, as shown by the following studies.

It is possible to join together the skin of a pair of rats. This preparation (*parabiosis,* which means roughly "two like parts living together") might be termed an artificial Siamese twin operation. (See **FIGURE 12.13.**) The animals share a small amount of blood circulation—not enough to exchange significant amounts of nutrients, but enough to allow hormones and other humoral factors produced in one rat to affect the other. For example, when one member of a parabiotic preparation is made diabetic, it survives, because it receives insulin from its partner (Finerty, 1952).

Hervey (1959) and Fleming (1969) studied the effects of VMH lesions on parabiotic rats. They produced the lesion (by means of stereotaxic surgery) in one member of the pair. The animal with the VMH lesion became fat. However, the other rat did not. (In Hervey's study the animals without lesions lost weight, whereas in Fleming's study they maintained their normal weight.) We know from the studies of Liebelt and his coworkers that the fat deposits of the hyperphagic animal are growing, presumably in response to some humoral substance that encourages growth of adipose tissue. The intact members of the pair, however, do not respond to this fat-encouraging substance by increasing their food intake. Either the fat-encouraging substance does not affect appetite or it is opposed by some other humoral substance. (We shall encounter this fat-encouraging substance again, when we examine the reasons that VMH lesions produce hyperphagia and obesity.)

The fact that Hervey's intact rats lost weight while Fleming's rats maintained theirs can probably be accounted for by differences in the schedules of food availability. An additional experiment by Fleming confirms the suggestion that there is also a humoral factor

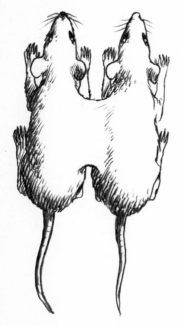

FIGURE 12.13 The parabiotic preparation, which interconnects some of the animals' blood supplies.

that suppresses intake. He allowed the members of a parabiotic pair of rats (both without lesions) to eat at different times. If one rat was fed 2 hours before the other, there was a decrease in food intake of the animal who ate last. These results suggest the release of an appetite-suppressing factor during the absorptive phase, which is probably what caused Hervey's normal rats to lose weight.

The lipostatic hypothesis remains an open issue. Liebelt's work clearly shows that fat tissue is regulated by some factors (probably humoral). The fact that removal of fat will reinstate hyperphagia in animals with VMH lesions who had previously reached a stable weight suggests that feedback from adipose tissue can affect satiety mechanisms. The nature of this feedback is completely unknown.

Aminostatic Theory

We obtain amino acids from the breakdown of proteins that we eat. We use these amino acids as a source of energy and in the synthesis of our own protein. Many amino acids can be synthesized in our bodies, but some (the *essential amino acids*) cannot, and these must be obtained from our diet. Since proteins are constructed by our cells during the absorptive phase of metabolism, and since amino acids cannot be stored from one meal to the next (amino acids not used for protein synthesis are used for energy or are converted into fat), ingestion of a meal that is deficient in some essential amino acids will result in decreased protein synthesis. Protein is therefore an essential component of our diet—especially high-quality protein, containing all the essential amino acids.

Assimilation of a meal rich in amino acids is very satiating, despite the fact that it results in a rather low blood glucose level (Mellinkoff, Frankland, Boyel, and Greipel, 1956). The large amount of amino acids being absorbed stimulates insulin release, which causes amino acids (but also glucose) to enter the cells. Glucagon and growth hormone, which are also secreted, keep the blood glucose level high enough to nourish the brain, but there is still a certain amount of *hypoglycemia* (low level of blood glucose). The satiating effect of amino acids is capitalized on by high-protein reducing diets.

These observations led Mellinkoff to hypothesize that blood level of amino acids was the system variable that regulated food intake. There is no doubt about amino acids playing a role in feeding behavior. If an animal is deprived of one or more essential amino acids, its food intake will gradually decrease until the missing amino acids are put back into the diet. As we shall see in chapter 13, in a section on specific hungers, animals learn to select foods that contain particular substances (such as vitamins, minerals, and essential amino acids) their bodies require. Regulation of these substances does not require a specific detector for each substance—only the ability to associate "feeling sick" or "feeling well" with ingestion of food with a particular flavor.

There is some evidence that argues against (but does not absolutely rule out) the existence of brain amino acid receptors that are important to food intake. Untreated diabetics have a high blood level of amino acids, along with a high glucose level, and they are nevertheless hungry. (Of course, there could be amino acid receptors that measure *utilization*, which requires the presence of insulin.) More significantly, various liver diseases (such as hepatitis) result in a severely depressed appetite despite a low level of amino acid in the blood (but adequate supplies of insulin—Kassil, Ugolev, and Chernigovskii, 1970). As we shall see shortly, there is evidence for detectors that monitor a factor related to amino acids—but they are located in the liver and not in the brain.

From Mouth to Large Intestine: Factors That Influence Food Intake

So far we have seen that food intake cannot be regulated by signals arising from an empty stomach; there must be a monitoring of some system variables located within the body. On a long-term basis, it seems plausible that some factor related to deposits of fat in adipose tissue is regulated, but the evidence is still scanty. There appear to be brain glucoreceptors, but convincing evidence that they respond to glucose is lacking. Glucoreceptors that respond to glucoprivation may exist in the lateral hypothalamus, but feeding in response to a sudden and dramatic fall in blood glucose level (the glucoprivic response) is not necessary for normal regulation of body weight and appears to be part of an emergency system. Thus, our search for detection mechanisms in the brain has not been very successful. And we have no evidence for a satiety mechanism that terminates a meal before the food is digested and assimilated. Let us therefore turn our attention to the progress of a meal from mouth to large intestine and look at the evidence concerning the effects of the various ingestive, digestive, and assimilative mechanisms on subsequent food intake.

Head Factors

The head contains several sets of receptors that play a role in food intake. We respond to the sight, odor, taste, and texture of food, and we can monitor the amount of food that is swallowed. As we saw in chapter 8, flavor is jointly determined by the odor and taste of a food. Only in rare cases (ingestion of a pure sugar or saccharine solution, for example) are the taste buds alone stimulated.

For many animals, olfaction plays a large role in locating food. In rats, for example, more electrical activity is recorded from the olfactory bulbs (in response to an odor associated with food) when the animal is hungry. When it is satiated, less activity is seen. Furthermore, this differential response is *not* seen for olfactory stimuli not associated with food (Giachetti, 1970). And olfaction plays a very significant role in judging the suitability of a given substance as a source of food; we will avoid eating food that smells rotten or rancid.

As we saw earlier, regulation requires the existence of negative feedback. In early stages of the ingestion of a meal, however, *positive feedback* is seen. That is, the consequences of ingestion of a palatable food lead to *increased* intake. We are all aware of the fact that we feel the hungriest as we begin to eat, and that *hors d'oeuvres* served just before a meal (often appropriately called appetizers) increase our interest in the main course. An even clearer example of positive feedback is seen in sexual activity. A person's sex drive, which might lead to contact with a partner, is increased, not reduced, by such contact. Increased sexual activities with the partner lead to more arousal and more activity. Ultimately, negative feedback may be applied by an orgasm, or by some other factors (reluctance to actually engage in intercourse, for example), but the fact is quite clear that early stages are characterized by positive feedback.

The role of positive feedback from "head factors" (often called *oropharyngeal factors,* but this term excludes the olfactory and visual systems) is clearly seen in the fact that an animal will press a lever for a longer time if the lever causes delivery of food into the mouth as opposed to delivery into the stomach. As we shall soon see, there are satiety factors that are activated by the delivery of food into the stomach. Intragastric feeding activates only negative feedback, whereas intraoral feeding activates the positive "head factors," which override the gastric (and other) satiety factors for a while.

This is not to say that head factors are only excitatory upon eating. Negative feedback is also aroused, but more slowly. When an animal is *esophagotomized,* head factors can be studied independently. In this preparation the esophagus is severed, and the cut ends are brought out through incisions in the skin. (See **FIGURE 12.14.**) When an esophagotomized animal eats, the food that is swallowed falls to the ground or is collected through a tube placed into the open end of the esophagus (we call this procedure *sham eating*). An esophagotomized animal will not eat indefinitely; a somewhat larger-than-normal meal is swallowed, and the animal stops eating (Janowitz and Grossman, 1949). This study thus demonstrates the existence of head factors involved in satiety. The fact that the animal soon returns to

FIGURE 12.14
Esophagotomy.

eat again indicates that these satiety factors are short-lived and normally must be superseded by satiety factors (gastric and duodenal ones, for example) farther down the digestive tract.

The head factors involved in satiety are even specific to taste. (I suppose we all have had the experience of not being able to "touch another bite" of a particular food we just ate to excess, but of being able, nevertheless, to eat some dessert.) Rats also demonstrate this phenomenon. If they are given four different flavors of food (actually the same food with different flavors added to it) in succession at a given meal, they will eat more than they normally do if given only one of them (Le Magnen, 1956). The animals will eat up to 270 percent of their normal intake, attesting to the power of the positive feedback, before it is counteracted by flavor-specific satiety (and by the increasing satiety produced by an enormously full stomach).

Gastric Factors

We have already seen that regulation of food intake cannot be accounted for solely by "hunger pangs" originating in the stomach. However, satiety signals appear to occur when food is received by the stomach. As we saw, a hungry rat will press a lever for intragastric delivery of food and will consume less than would be taken orally. The only plausible explanation for the cessation of lever pressing is inhibition from gastric and/or duodenal satiety signals.

When liquid food or a saline solution is injected into a rat's stomach, the animal subsequently eats less than normal (Berkun, Kessen, and Miller, 1952). The food injections produce more satiety than do the saline injections, suggesting that there are detectors for the presence of nutrients, as well as bulk, in the stomach. Janowitz and Hollander (1953) showed that food intake could be suppressed by inflating a balloon placed in the stomach. A much smaller volume of food was necessary to produce the same inhibitory effects, again suggesting the existence of gastric chemoreceptors as well as stretch receptors. Unit activity in afferent nerve fibers from the stomach has provided evidence for the existence of separate receptors for glucose and for amino acids (Sharma and Nasset, 1962).

The stomach is not essential for normal regulation of intake, however. It is not even necessary for feelings of hunger. Humans whose stomachs have been removed (because of cancer or the presence of large ulcers) still periodically get hungry (Ingelfinger, 1944). These people eat frequent, small meals, because of the absence of a stomach. In fact, a large meal causes nausea and discomfort, a factor that might be quite significant (as we shall soon see).

In summary, the stomach appears to be able to provide information to the brain about the presence of bulk or various nutrients. This information does not, however, appear to play a crucial role in regulation of intake.

Duodenal Factors

The entry of food into the duodenum triggers neurally and hormonally mediated reflex inhibition of gastric motility. The hormonal inhibition is accomplished principally by the secretion of enterogastrone; the motility of an isolated stomach pouch is suppressed upon the entry of food into the duodenum, even though the isolated pouch has no nerve supply (Robins and Boyd, 1923). (See **FIGURE 12.15.**)

Enterogastrone is secreted only when the stomach contains enough food so that some of it enters the duodenum. This hormone, then, would appear to be a good candidate for a role in production of satiety. You will recall that people who lack a stomach become satiated very quickly; in fact, a large meal is actually aversive. Perhaps this satiety, produced by the immediate entry of food into the duodenum, is mediated by enterogastrone. In fact, Schally, Redding, Lucien, and Meyer (1967) found that injections of enterogastrone suppressed subsequent food intake of mice that had been deprived of food for 17 hours.

More recently, Campbell and Davis (1974a, 1974b) found that injections of glucose (but not control injections of urea) into the duodenum suppressed subsequent food intake. The glucose concentration was at levels encountered by the duodenum in the course of digestion of a normal meal, so the results suggest the presence of duodenal glucose receptors that contribute to satiety.

The evidence so far suggests quite strongly that the duodenum plays a role in satiety. Whether this satiety is mediated via afferents from the duodenum to the brain (which are known to exist) or whether the satiety is produced by enterogastrone (or whether both mechanisms operate) is not yet clear.

Liver Factors

The role of the liver in control of food intake is only recently being appreciated. Studies in the past few years have shown that besides being a biochemical factory of crucial importance in metabolism, the liver also appears to be the source of both hunger and satiety signals. Mauricio Russek is the scientist most responsible for the recent attention paid to the role of the liver in regulation of food intake (Russek, 1971, contains a summary of his work up to that time). He

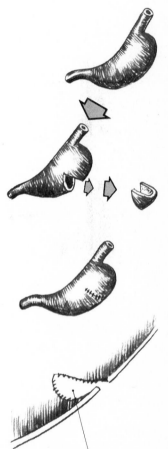

Inside of isolated gastric pouch can be observed through opening in abdominal wall.

FIGURE 12.15 When food is put into the duodenum, gastric contractions cease even in an isolated pouch that contains no nerve supply.

first noted that although intravenous (IV) injections of glucose were relatively ineffective in reducing food intake, *intraperitoneal* (IP) injections (that is, into the abdominal cavity) were quite effective in producing satiety. This observation certainly does not favor the hypothesis that brain glucoreceptors are important in food regulation. An IV injection of glucose raises the blood sugar considerably, whereas an IP injection raises it very little. Most of the glucose injected into the abdominal cavity is taken up by the liver and stored as glycogen. The fact that the glucose injected IP probably got no farther than the liver, but nevertheless produced satiety, suggested to Russek that the liver might contain receptors sensitive to glucose.

Russek then attached two chronic cannulas in a dog, one in the hepatic portal vein (the system carrying blood from the intestines to the liver) and another in the jugular vein. An injection of glucose into the portal vein produced long-lasting satiety, whereas a similar injection into the jugular vein had no effect on food intake. The satiating effect of intraportal glucose injections was eliminated by blocking neural transmission through the vagus nerve, which conveys information from the liver to the brain. The lack of effects produced by control injections of saline suggested that the liver contained receptors sensitive to glucose.

In 1969, Niijima obtained electrophysiological evidence for receptors in the liver that responded in a linear fashion to glucose concentration, high rates of activity being associated with *low* glucose concentration. The receptors did not respond to sodium chloride or to other sugars, but did respond to a sugar (*3-O-methylglucose*) that cannot be metabolized. This sugar, fortunately for Russek's hypothesis, also caused satiety when injected IP. The suppression of intake could not possibly be produced by stimulation of brain glucoreceptors sensitive to the rate of utilization of glucose, since 3-O-methylglucose cannot be utilized. Furthermore, Schmitt (1973) found that intraportal infusion of glucose affected the firing rate of neurons in the hypothalamus, providing excellent evidence that the liver receptors relay information to the brain.

LIVER RECEPTORS AND THE CONTROL OF FEEDING. The role of the liver in production of satiety in response to absorption of nutrients from the intestine is quite clear. These receptors might also account for the onset of hunger, since they are the first to "know" that no more food is being absorbed. These receptors fire at a high rate when the amount of nutrients in the portal blood supply is low, and this neural activity, transmitted to the brain, might stimulate food intake. The fact that liver denervation causes a prolonged decrease in food intake (15 to 45 percent of normal) suggests that the liver receptors might indeed be involved in hunger. Liver diseases such as hepatitis might cause lack of appetite because the organ is temporarily "denervated"; its receptors are not firing very much despite a low level of nutrients. Furthermore, Novin, VanderWeele, and Rezek (1973) found that intraportal injections of 2-DG (which suppresses glucose metabolism) led to *immediate* large (over 200 percent) increases in food intake. The latency between injection and feeding was short indeed; the animals usually began to eat during the injection.

You will recall that Le Magnen found a correlation between meal size and onset of the next meal, in animals fed *ad libitum*. The liver receptors can very nicely explain this relationship. Meal size, regulated by a number of factors (including palatability), determines how much food is received by the stomach and determines how long the body will be in the absorptive phase; a large meal takes longer to digest and assimilate. Therefore, if the next meal is begun when the liver receptors tell the brain that the absorptive phase is over, one would observe a good relationship between meal size and the time until the onset of the next meal.

The role of the liver receptors in hunger, and in the maintenance of later stages of satiety (i.e., while nutrients are being absorbed from the intestine), is straightforward. Early satiety can be accounted for by head factors, gastric factors, and duodenal factors. But Russek has even suggested a mechanism by which the liver might also be involved in early satiety. He suggests that the presence of food in the stomach triggers secretion of epinephine and glucagon and causes the sympathetic efferents of the liver to increase their activity. All these reflex mechanisms (elicited by afferent signals from stomach—or perhaps duodenum—to brain) would cause a breakdown of liver glycogen into glucose. This glucose would lower the firing rate of the liver receptors and suppress the "hunger signal" from the liver. However, let us suppose that (because of prior starvation or increased energy expenditure) there were low supplies of glycogen in the liver. Then the reflexes triggered by food in the stomach would be relatively ineffective in causing the synthesis of glucose in the liver. The animal would consequently eat a larger meal.

Russek cites evidence for all the links in this logical chain (I will not cite all of the individual studies).

1. The blood sugar level rises very quickly after the start of a meal.

2. Stimulation of the hepatic nerve causes breakdown of glycogen into glucose (*glycogenolysis*).

3. Electrical stimulation of the ventromedial nucleus of the hypothalamus (which receives information from receptors in the stomach) results in liver glycogenolysis.

4. The amount of glucose released by the liver depends on its prior glycogen storage.

These results are all consistent with Russek's suggestion that the liver can respond to gastric factors and cause suppression of food intake.

In a recent study, Novin, Sanderson, and VanderWeele (1974) found that glucose injections into the duodenum suppressed feeding only when the animal was allowed access to food *ad libitum*. When the animal was maintained, on a 22-hour food-deprivation schedule, duodenal administration had no effect on intake during the 2-hour access to food. These results support Russek's hypothesis. An animal with food available *ad libitum* would presumably have more glycogen stored in the liver. A reflex stimulation of glycogenolysis would inhibit intake. However, an animal on a food-deprivation schedule would have little stored glycogen, and the presence of glucose in the duodenum could not result in satiety mediated through liver glycogenolysis. Furthermore, the appetite-suppressing effect of duodenal glucose injections was eliminated by cutting the vagus nerve. This fact suggests that the effect is not mediated via enterogastrone released by the duodenum. It is likely that enterogastrone release is a separate mechanism and is triggered by nutrients (such as fats).

Novin and his colleagues observed just the opposite effect in the efficacy of small amounts of glucose injected into the hepatic portal vein; that is, intraportal glucose did not suppress appetite in the free-feeding condition, but did so in the deprivation condition. The authors suggested that there was already a fairly large amount of carbohydrate available under the free-feeding condition, and the amount of extra glucose received from the injection was too small to produce a noticeable effect.

A very significant study provides evidence that feeding is controlled by liver receptors, whereas metabolic adjustment to a low availability of nutrients (secretion of epinephrine, which causes glycogen to be converted to glucose) is controlled by brain receptors. Friedman, Rowland, Saller, and Stricker (1976) injected rats with insulin, making them hypoglycemic, and then administered injections of several different nutrients. Injections of the sugars glucose, *fructose,* or *mannose* all produced satiety; they blocked the eating that normally follows injections of insulin. Since fructose *cannot* cross the blood-brain barrier, the brain should have been "hungry." And yet the animals did *not* eat. Injections of a keto acid (ketone body) that can be used by the brain but *not* by the liver, did not abolish the feeding response. The animals' brains were "satiated" by the keto acid; nevertheless, the rats ate. Apparently the "hungry" liver stimulated the feeding.

It is significant that fructose produced satiety in rats with a low blood glucose level. Fructose can be metabolized in the Krebs cycle, and it is not first converted to glucose. This fact means that the liver receptors are not *glucose* receptors, but appear to monitor metabolic rate, as determined by the availability of nutrients.

Friedman and his colleagues found contrary evidence when they examined the effects of these metabolic fuels on the output of adrenal epinephrine in response to the low blood sugar level produced by insulin injections. Keto acids and glucose, fuels the brain can use, abolished the epinephrine response. Fructose, which does not enter the brain, had no effect. Therefore, brain receptors apparently control the release of epinephrine in response to metabolic need. Like the liver receptors, the brain receptors appear to monitor metabolic rate, and not just glucose level, since they respond to keto acids as well as to glucose.

The results of this study are summarized in **FIGURE 12.16.**

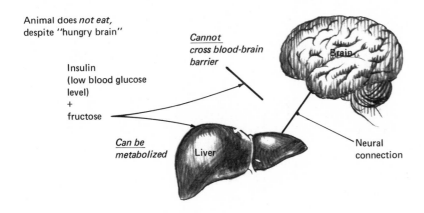

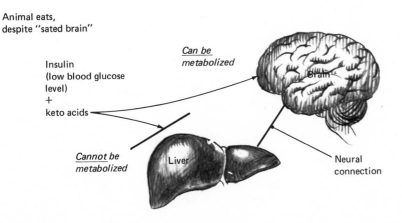

FIGURE 12.16 Summary of the experiment by Friedman, Rowland, Saller, and Stricker (1976).

CONCLUSIONS CONCERNING THE NATURE OF THE SYSTEM VARIABLES AND DETECTORS

It really is not necessary for me to say that the control of food intake is extremely complex; I am sure that you are convinced of that fact. The onset of a meal appears to occur in response to a decrease in the amount of nutrients being received from the digestive tract.

Head factors (sight, smell, taste, texture, feedback from swallowing) determine the palatability of a food, and, if the food is readily accepted, engage a positive feedback mechanism that is later overridden by negative feedback, or satiety. Some satiety signals originate from head factors (as is shown in sham-feeding experiments), but gastric and duodenal factors seem more important. There are several different satiety factors originating from the digestive system. Gastric distention causes neural inhibition of intake, but this factor appears to operate only at levels of distention higher than those normally encountered. Gastric chemoreceptors have been shown to exist, but it is not known whether they play a role in satiety, since some food very quickly enters the duodenum, and this entry is known to produce satiety. The duodenal chemoreceptors produce satiety signals, apparently by stimulating liver glycogenolysis and perhaps by more direct means, and this part of the intestine releases enterogastrone, which also reduces food intake. Finally, the liver, with its receptors, responds to the presence of nutrients in the blood received via the hepatic portal system, and it suppresses eating until the meal is digested and absorbed.

The work of Liebelt, who showed that total body fat is regulated, and that of Hervey and Fleming, who demonstrated the presence of a satiety factor in the blood, suggest that lipids appear to be important in long-term food regulation. How this factor interacts with the onset or cessation of a meal is unknown.

Finally, I should mention the importance of social factors and of learning. I said little about these factors because we do not know much at all about their physiological bases. Our ingestion of three meals a day, at regular times, probably defeats some of our regulatory mechanisms, which seem to have better control over the interval between meals than over the size of a meal. And our habit of following a meal with another course of increased palatability (dessert) raises our caloric intake above what we need. (You will recall that a rat, successively given four flavors of the same diet, will eat much more than it would normally take of only one of them.) And, as we all know, social factors are important. Even a chicken, satiated by a large meal, will begin to eat again if it sees another chicken eating nearby.

Brain Mechanisms Involved in Food Intake

I have described our current knowledge of the system variables involved in hunger and satiety, and the nature and location of the detectors that monitor these variables. Now it is time to turn to neural mechanisms that underlie the process of eating itself. Traditionally, research emphasis has focussed on a ventromedial hypothalamic "satiety center" and on a lateral hypothalamic "feeding center." As we shall see, these notions are being abandoned as a result of more recent evidence.

ANATOMY OF THE HYPOTHALAMUS. The hypothalamus is of major importance in the regulation of food intake. Since this section will describe the results of physiological manipulations of hypothalamic nuclei and associated fiber systems, a brief introduction to the anatomy of the hypothalamus is in order. (A schematic diagram of the hypothalamus was presented in Figure 6.17, on page 105.)

The hypothalamus, which lies at the base of the brain, can be divided into three zones along the lateral-medial axis. The *periventricular region* surrounds the third ventricle. The cells of this area are generally small. One part of this region (the *arcuate nucleus*) contains many neurosecretory cells involved in control of the pituitary gland. The second zone, the *medial region*, contains most of the hypothalamic nuclei, including the *supraoptic* and *paraventricular nuclei* (which, among other things, are involved in control of the posterior pituitary gland), the *ventromedial nucleus* (important in mechanisms of satiety), and the *dorsomedial nucleus*. The *lateral region*, through which pass the fibers of the *medial forebrain bundle*, is characterized by a diffuse organization of cell bodies and axons.

Rostrally, the hypothalamus is bounded by the *preoptic region;* there are pairs of *medial* and *lateral preoptic nuclei*. Some people consider the preoptic region to be a part of the hypothalamus, although these two brain regions have different embryological origins. The *mammillary bodies* are located at the caudal, ventral end of the hypothalamus. Within these bulges are located several sets of nuclei, the most prominent being the *lateral* and *medial mammillary nuclei*.

I shall not say too much, at this point, about the fiber connections of the hypothalamus, since an extensive description would not be of much use in discussing what we presently know about the role of the hypothalamus in food intake. For present purposes, we should realize that the various hypothalamic nuclei are intricately interconnected, and that the hypothalamus receives information from motor systems and from olfactory, gustatory, visual, and somatosensory systems. It also receives input from extensive areas of the limbic system, which is involved in motivation and emotional expression. The hypothalamus sends fibers to many parts of the brain, including thalamus, cortex, and motor systems. The most visible fiber tracts are the medial forebrain bundle (which connects the hypothalamus with midbrain structures), the *fornix* (which interconnects hippocampus, septum, and hypothalamus), and an efferent system that divides into the *mammillothalamic* and *mammillotegmental tracts* (connecting the mammillary bodies of the hypothalamus with the anterior thalamus and the tegmentum).

THE VENTROMEDIAL HYPOTHALAMIC SYNDROME. Tumors in the hypothalamic–pituitary stalk region were long ago shown to be associated with extreme obesity and, often, with genital atrophy. It was later shown that the genital atrophy resulted from loss of gonadotrophin secretion, but the obesity was independent of hormonal changes. The overeating and weight gain could be produced by lesions in the region of the ventromedial nucleus of the hypothalamus —the VMH (Hetherington and Ranson, 1939). (As we shall see, it is the *region* of the VMH, and not the nuclei themselves, that is involved in this syndrome.)

The VMH obesity syndrome seems to follow two stages (Brobeck, Tepperman, and Long, 1943). During the *dynamic phase* (a period of hyperphagia and weight gain lasting 4 to 12 weeks) the rats eat avidly, but as their weight increases, their motivation for food decreases (Miller, Bailey, and Stevenson, 1950). They become less willing to work for food or to tolerate aversive stimuli presented along with the food. Given a choice between food plus footshock and nothing, they will take nothing.

As the animals enter the *static phase* of the VMH obesity syndrome, they begin to eat less food, and their weight stabilizes. At this point the animals are very *finicky*; they will not eat food that is adulterated with quinine or diluted with cellulose. Only good-tasting food is consumed, and then only if it is easily available.

Some people have suggested that VMH lesions produce obesity solely by enhancing the palatability of the food; the food tastes so good to the animals that they just cannot stop eating. However, brain lesions in other areas cause similar enhancements in the appetitive value of food without producing obesity (Beatty and Schwartzbaum, 1968). Furthermore, rats with VMH lesions will overeat (by pressing a lever) even if the food is injected into the stomach and thus cannot be tasted (McGinty, Epstein, and Teitelbaum, 1965).

The fact of VMH obesity, along with the observation that the region contains cells that might be directly sensitive to glucose levels and to stimulation of chemoreceptors and stretch receptors in the digestive tract, has led to suggestions that the VMH might be a "satiety center." Electrical stimulation of the VMH has been shown to produce a cessation of eating, further suggesting that the normal role of this region is to inhibit food intake (Wyrwicka and Dobrzecka, 1960). However, no strong conclusions can be drawn from the effects of VMH stimulation. Such stimulation has been shown to be aversive (Krasne, 1962); an animal will work to turn the electrical current off. The aversive effects might just be incompatible with eating. (Suppose, for example, that someone applied an electric shock to your big toe during a meal. The fact that you stopped eating would not implicate your toe in satiety mechanisms.)

Two findings have cast doubt on the role of the VMH as a satiety *center*. It now appears that the lesion destroys fibers that travel in a rostral-caudal direction along the dorsal border of the nucleus. Lesions restricted to the VMH were shown to be ineffective in producing hyperphagia and obesity (Gold, 1973). Furthermore, Kapatos and Gold (1973) showed that electrolytic lesions or knife cuts placed along the *ventral noradrenergic bundle* (*VNA*) produced obesity. The lesions did not have to be bilaterally symmetrical to produce hyperphagia; that is, obesity occurred after a unilateral cut of the VNA at the level of the ventromedial nuclei along with a unilateral lesion, on the other side of the brain, in the VNA at the level of the midbrain. These results strongly suggest that it is the VNA destruction which produces the obesity. The asymmetrical lesions each cut half of the fibers, at different levels along the neuraxis.

Figure 12.17 shows a schematic map of the noradrenergic system mapped by the formaldehyde-histofluorescence technique. The effective lesions interrupted ascending fibers from cell bodies of the medulla and pons. (See **FIGURE 12.17.**) These fibers arise from areas

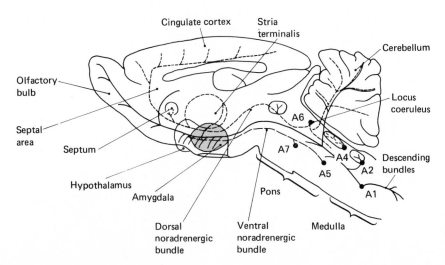

FIGURE 12.17 A map of the noradrenergic neurons of the rat brain. (Adapted from Livett, B. G., *British Medical Bulletin*, 1973, 29, 93–99, modified from Ungerstedt, V., *Acta Physiologica Scandinavica*, 1971, Suppl. 367.)

that receive afferent information over the autonomic nerves (Ungerstedt, 1971) and could thus be conveying satiety-related information to other brain regions.

Another piece of information that has confused the simple notion that the VMH is a "satiety center" is the observation by Powley and Opsahl (1974) that vagotomy (severing the vagus nerves) eliminated the obesity produced by VMH lesions. Powley and Opsahl produced VMH lesions in rats and permitted them to get fat. The vagus nerves were then severed. The animals decreased food intake until their body weight reached normal levels. The data are shown in **FIGURE 12.18.** The authors also found that vagotomy did not abolish the increased preference for a very palatable high-fat diet ("finickiness") that accompanies VMH lesions. The vagus nerve, therefore, is not involved in finickiness, but must be intact in order for the VMH obesity syndrome to occur.

A possible explanation for Powley and Opsahl's results is that the VMH lesions (which destroyed the ventral noradrenergic bundle) produced a vagally mediated increase in secretion of insulin. Chronic administration of insulin produces overeating and obesity (MacKay, Calloway, and Barnes, 1940), and VMH lesions result in increased blood levels of insulin (Frohman and Bernardis, 1968). However, the fact that hyperphagia is seen in diabetic rats with VMH lesions (Vilberg and Beatty, 1975) rules out this explanation. A diabetic rat cannot, by definition, be eating because of elevated blood levels of insulin.

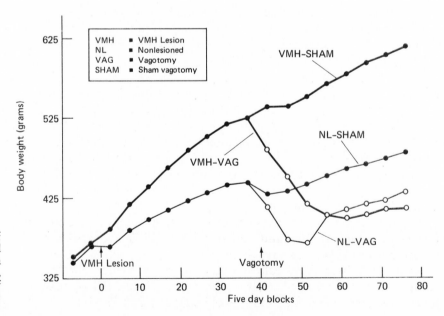

FIGURE 12.18 Effects of vagotomy on obesity produced by VMH lesions. (From Powley, T. L., and Opsahl, C. A., *American Journal of Physiology*, 1974, 226, 25–33.)

Powley and Keesey (1970) made an observation that suggests that the slow recovery of ingestive behavior might not depend on time, but on a gradual reduction in body weight to a new set point. They noted that animals recovered from LH lesions (from previous studies) were able to regulate their weight, albeit at a lower level than normal. They produced LH lesions in two groups of animals, a normally fed group and a group that had been starved down to a weight lower than the weight that recovered LH animals usually attained. Their results are shown in Figure 12.19. Note that the prestarved animals immediately began to eat and in fact gained a little weight. (See **FIGURE 12.19.**) The lesioned animals previously fed *ad libitum* were aphagic until their weight fell to the level at which they eventually stabilized (**FIGURE 12.19**).

These results suggest that somehow the set point for body weight is altered by LH lesions. At least, the threshold of hunger mechanisms appears to be raised; a stronger signal (perhaps lipostatic factors?) is needed to elicit eating. The stages of recovery might, therefore, only reflect the time it takes to lose weight. As we shall see, however, there is a simpler explanation for the entire LH syndrome.

I noted earlier that animals with LH lesions exhibit sensory and motor deficits. In fact, some studies indicate that aphagia and adipsia can be produced by damage to neural systems that have generally been characterized as sensory or motor in function. It appears that the *nigrostriatal bundle,* a collection of dopaminergic fibers from the substantia nigra to caudate nucleus (a part of the extrapyramidal motor system), plays an activating role in feeding behavior (and also

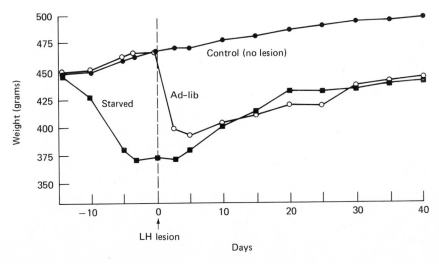

FIGURE 12.19 Effects of preoperative starvation on the LH syndrome. (From Powley, T. L., and Keesey, R. E., *Journal of Comparative and Physiological Psychology,* 1970, 70, 25–36.)

in other behaviors). This fiber bundle is usually damaged by LH lesions that produce aphagia. Electrolytic lesions of the substantia nigra and chemical destruction of the nigrostriatal fibers with 6-hydroxydopamine (6-HD) result in aphagia, adipsia, and decreases in movement (Ungerstedt, 1971). Other studies have shown that these lesions produce long-lasting finickiness, drinking only during meals, and other symptoms seen in animals with LH lesions (Fibiger, Zis, and McGeer, 1973). Furthermore, other lesions (such as those of the globus pallidus, another part of the extrapyramidal motor system) that produce adipsia and aphagia (Morgane, 1961) lower the concentration of dopamine in the caudate nucleus (Anden, Fuxe, Hamberger, and Hokfelt, 1966). The nigrostriatal dopaminergic system thus appears to be very important in feeding behavior and in other motor deficits seen after LH lesions.

In the previous section I mentioned the rather incredible fact that mild tail pinch will cause a satiated rat to begin eating. Antelman, Rowland, and Fisher (1976) have shown that such tail pinch can reverse the effects of lesions of the lateral hypothalamus or the nigrostriatal dopamine system on eating. When their tails were gently pinched, the aphagic animals would begin to eat. If they were stimulated often enough, a large proportion of these animals would eat sufficient amounts of food to "nurse themselves" to recovery.

In a series of experiments, Antelman, Szechtman, Chin, and Fisher (1976) demonstrated that eating induced by tail pinch results from stimulation of dopaminergic fibers. The effect was blocked by dopaminergic antagonists but not by noradrenergic antagonists. The authors have suggested that the nigrostriatal dopamine system not be considered a "feeding system," since, in the presence of appropriate goal objects, tail pinch (or electrical shock delivered to the tail) can elicit a variety of other behaviors, such as copulation or aggression (Caggiula, 1972). Perhaps the nigrostriatal dopaminergic system plays a role in the attention to stimuli related to these behaviors or in the arousal of motor systems necessary for their performance.

Yet another piece of evidence against the concept of an "LH feeding center" comes from a study by Zeigler and Karten (1974), who noted that a large number of ascending sensory fibers of the trigeminal system (which mediates somatosensory information from the head and neck region) pass through the brain in the vicinity of the lateral hypothalamus. The authors made lesions in various locations along the trigeminal lemniscus (which projects, you will recall, to the ventral posterior area of the thalamus). The lesions (which did not damage the hypothalamus) produced a period of adipsia and aphagia, followed by recovery. The animals subsequently regulated their weight at a new (lower) level. Perhaps the activity of the trigeminal system provides tonic stimulation similar to that produced by pinching the tail. The loss of this tonic input decreases the activity of the dopaminergic system.

So—does the lateral hypothalamus play any role in hunger, or does it just happen to be located near fibers of some important sensory and motor systems involved in a variety of behaviors? We do not yet have good answers to that question. The answers, when they come, will undoubtedly show that the process is extremely complex and involves many different mechanisms. The hypothalamus itself surely plays some role in hunger, but we certainly must abandon our concepts of feeding centers and satiety centers, that, in reciprocal fashion, determine when an animal eats.

SUGGESTED READINGS

BALAGURA, S. *Hunger: A Biopsychological Analysis.* New York: Basic Books, 1973.

FRIEDMAN, M. I., and STRICKER, E. M. The physiological psychology of hunger: A physiological perspective. *Psychological Review*, 1976 (in press).

NOVIN, D., WYRWICKA, W., and BRAY, G. A. (editors) *Hunger: Basic Mechanisms and Clinical Implications.* New York: Raven Press, 1976.

RUSSEK, M. Hepatic receptors and the neurophysiological mechanisms controlling feeding behavior. In *Neurosciences Research*, Vol. 4, edited by S. Ehrenpreis. New York: Academic Press, 1971.

The volume edited by Novin et al. contains the most up-to-date summary of the field that is available, written by the most prominent investigators in research on hunger and feeding. The article by Friedman and Stricker gives a new perspective to the field, emphasizing general metabolic factors rather than the concept of dual hunger and satiety mechanisms of the hypothalamus.

Thirst and the Control of Mineral Intake

13

As we saw in the introduction to the previous chapter, mammals have evolved regulatory mechanisms to maintain the constancy of their extracellular fluid. The regulation of the intake of nutrients is an extremely complex process, involving several different mechanisms. As we shall see in this chapter, much more is known about regulation of the water and mineral content of the extracellular fluid.

It was necessary, in chapter 12, to describe the ingestion, absorption, and assimilation of food, as well as the general metabolic processes by which nutrients are stored and utilized. Similarly, I shall describe the physiological processes that control water and sodium balance in the body. Fortunately, these processes are much simpler than the ones involved in regulation of nutrients. I shall restrict my discussion to water and sodium balance, since these substances are most important in water intake, the behavioral process we are interested in. I shall not discuss the specific regulation of minerals other than sodium. In the final section I shall, however, describe the process by which an animal can compensate for various deficiencies (of minerals, vitamins, specific amino acids, etc.) by altering its intake of various foodstuffs.

PHYSIOLOGICAL REGULATION OF WATER AND SODIUM BALANCE

Fluid Compartments of the Body

The fluid surrounding the cells of the body (the interstitial fluid) is approximately *iso-osmotic* with a 0.87 percent solution of sodium chloride. In other words, if extracellular fluid were placed on one side of a semipermeable membrane (which allowed water, but not other molecules, to pass through) and 0.87 percent NaCl solution were placed on the other, there would be no osmotic gradient and no net migration of water. Interstitial fluid is a protein-free *filtrate* of blood plasma; it is "squeezed" out of the porous capillaries by the action of blood pressure.

Two forces are involved in the formation (and, as we shall see, circulation) of interstitial fluid: hydrostatic pressure and osmotic pressure. Hydrostatic pressure, in a "typical capillary," is equal to approximately 35 mm Hg at the arterial end, and gradually decreases to approximately 15 mm Hg at the venous end. (The unit of measurement for hydrostatic pressure is the mm Hg—the amount of pressure that will lift a column of mercury one millimeter.) There is extra room in the interstitial space for more fluid, so a "back pressure" to the flow of fluid out of the capillaries is negligible (in normal circumstances). If this process were to go unchecked, of course, all of the fluid would leave the vascular system and enter the interstitial space. This does not happen because the hydrostatic pressure is opposed by osmotic pressure.

As water is squeezed out of the capillaries, so are most of the substances that are dissolved in it. The exception is protein; the walls of the capillaries are impermeable to these large molecules, so they remain in the plasma. The presence of proteins in the plasma, but not in the interstitial fluid, means that there will be a concentration difference, and hence a difference in osmotic pressure, between the two fluid compartments. There will thus be an osmotic pressure gradient tending to force the interstitial fluid back into the capillaries. This force has been calculated to be equal to a hydrostatic pressure of 25 mm Hg.

Figure 13.1 illustrates the process of plasma filtration. At the arterial end of the capillary an outward hydrostatic pressure of 35 mm Hg is opposed by an inward osmotic pressure of only 25 mm Hg, so plasma flows out. At the venous end the hydrostatic pressure has decreased to 15 mm Hg, so there is now a net *inward* pressure of 10 mm Hg. The outward flow (at the start of the capillary) and the inward flow (at the end) perfectly balance. (See **FIGURE 13.1.**)

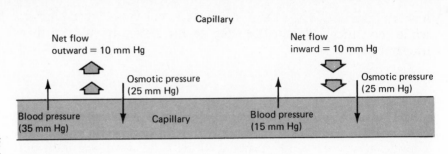

FIGURE 13.1 Filtration of plasma and the ensuing circulation of interstitial fluid.

Since this process is characterized by a balance of opposing forces, changes in one of the forces will result in a change in the balance of fluids. If, for example, the barrier to protein provided by the walls of the capillaries were eliminated, protein would be filtered out with the plasma, and the differences in the osmotic pressure of the two fluid compartments would decrease. There would then be a net flow of fluid from the blood plasma into the interstitial fluid, since the hydrostatic pressure would be unopposed. If you would like, you can demonstrate this process. Place your thumb on a hard surface, and hit it sharply with a hammer. You will note a rapid increase in the size of your thumb, resulting from leakage of protein through the damaged capillaries and a subsequent accumulation of interstitial fluid. (My publisher advises me to inform you that this suggested "demonstration" should not really be tried.)

There is a very close balance between the osmotic pressure of the extracellular fluid and that of the intracellular fluid. Increases in extracellular water will cause cells to swell, as they absorb water, which is travelling down its concentration gradient. Removal of water from the extracellular fluid, on the other hand, causes cells to lose water.

The relative sizes of the fluid compartments of the body are shown in Figure 13.2. Note that 67 percent of the body water is intracellular and that approximately 80 percent of the extracellular fluid is interstitial. The balance of the extracellular fluid, blood plasma, constitutes the smallest fluid compartment, only approximately 7 percent of total body water. (See **FIGURE 13.2**.)

As we have seen, the fluid compartments of the body are closely interrelated. Changes in the characteristics of one will cause changes in the others. And the total volume of two of these compartments, the blood plasma and intracellular fluid, must be closely regulated. A fair amount of interstitial fluid—so long as it is *isotonic* and does not alter the other fluid compartments—can accumulate without immediate harm. Too much or too little fluid in the blood plasma,

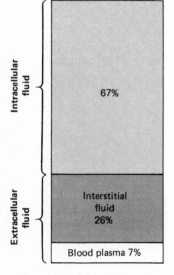

FIGURE 13.2 Relative size of the fluid compartments of the body.

however, can lead to heart failure or a disastrous fall in blood pressure, while too much or too little fluid in the cells can damage them irreparably.

Regulatory Mechanisms

Under most conditions we drink more water than our body needs, and the excess is excreted by the kidneys. Similarly, we ingest more sodium than we need, and the kidneys get rid of the surplus. Let us examine the way the kidneys handle these regulatory processes.

The anatomy of the kidney is shown in Figure 13.3. This organ consists of a large number (approximately one million in the human) of individual functional units called *nephrons*. Each of these nephrons extracts urine from the blood and carries the urine, via collecting ducts, to the ureter. The ureters, in turn, connect the kidneys to the urinary bladder. (See **FIGURE 13.3.**) During urination, the *urethra* passes the urine to the outside of the body. For our purposes, urine is outside the body once it reaches the bladder. Our society has developed customs pertaining to the release of urine from the bladder, but these customs have nothing to do with water regulation.

Production of urine begins in the glomerulus. Protein-free plasma is filtered from the capillaries and enters *Bowman's capsule.* (See **FIGURE 13.3.**) If this fluid were then passed out, unaltered, to the bladder, we would urinate ourselves to death in short order. Each day approximately 45 gallons of water (180 liters) is filtered into Bowman's capsule, so it should be quite obvious that most of the fluid reenters the capillaries somewhere.

As a matter of fact, approximately 99 percent of the water filtered by the glomeruli is subsequently reabsorbed. Other substances are also conserved; over 99 percent of the sodium and 100 percent of the glucose are reabsorbed. Reabsorption occurs in the renal tubules (renal means "of the kidney") and collecting ducts, and it may occur by means of active or passive processes. Sodium is reabsorbed by means of an active process, for example. A pump in the renal tubules is capable of reabsorbing sodium against its concentration gradient. The negatively charged chloride ion passively follows the positively charged sodium ion, so the net result is that salt is retained by the body.

This active reabsorption of sodium is the event that is responsible for the passive reabsorption of water from the renal tubules and collecting ducts. As NaCl accumulates in the interstitial fluid surrounding the renal tubules and collecting ducts, an osmotic gradient develops. If permitted to, water will travel down its concentration

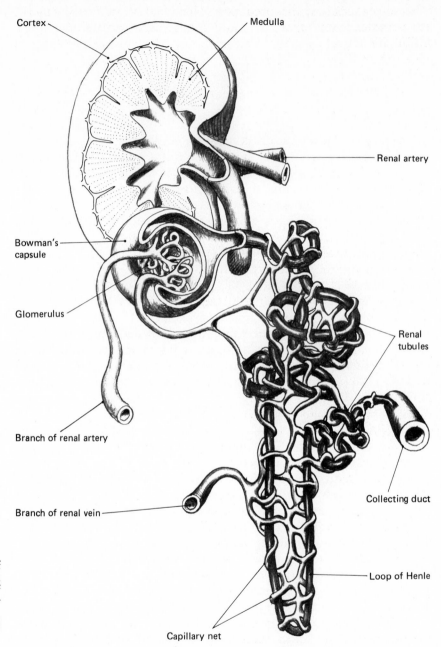

Cortex

Medulla

Renal artery

Bowman's capsule

Glomerulus

Renal tubules

Branch of renal artery

Collecting duct

Branch of renal vein

Loop of Henle

Capillary net

FIGURE 13.3 Anatomy of the kidney and nephron. (From Orians, G. H., *The Study of Life*. Copyright © 1973 by Allyn and Bacon, Inc., Boston, Massachusetts.)

gradient and thus re-enter the interstitial space. (The reabsorbed sodium and water will then enter the capillaries once again.)

Other substances are excreted, of course. Urea, the waste product from metabolism of amino acids, is excreted by passive means.

This substance is not regulated in the blood, but is carried away by the excess water that is excreted. Many foreign substances, such as penicillin, are actively *secreted* by the kidney. That is, independent of glomerular filtration, some substances are transported across the walls of the renal tubules and are deposited into the urine.

The two renal processes that we are interested in are (1) the active reabsorption of sodium and (2) the passive reabsorption of water, which depends on this transport of sodium. Control of water and sodium balance is achieved by (1) altering the rate of sodium transport and (2) varying the permeability of the walls of the distal tubules and collecting ducts. If these parts of the nephrons are permeable to water, it is reabsorbed. If their permeability to water goes down, a large amount of water is excreted in the urine. The dependency of water reabsorption tells us something else; unless sodium is actively reabsorbed, water cannot be retained by the body. Sodium deficits, then, will result in loss of water by the body. This fact explains why water balance cannot be discussed independently of sodium balance (and it explains why one must ingest salt in a hot climate when working—and sweating away salt—in order to prevent dehydration).

Now that we know how the kidney regulates sodium and water excretion (and I use the word "know" very loosely—I have not done justice to this marvelous organ in my brief description of its functions), we must turn our attention to the factors that control sodium reabsorption and the permeability of the distal tubules and collecting ducts.

The rate of sodium reabsorption is controlled by *aldosterone*, a hormone secreted by the adrenal cortex. Aldersterone stimulates reabsorption; therefore, its absence will result in a loss of sodium. A person with damaged adrenal glands will ingest large quantities of salt in an attempt to maintain a normal sodium balance. This *sodium appetite* seems to be innate; a young boy with faulty adrenal glands ate great amounts of salt each day. His parents were concerned, and his physician had him hospitalized. Unfortunately, he was denied access to salt while in the hospital, and, very shortly, he died.

Now that we know that aldosterone levels control sodium reabsorption, we must ask what controls aldosterone. The answer is somewhat complicated. Two factors—increased activity of the sympathetic fibers to the kidney and a fall in renal blood flow (we shall see shortly why these factors are significant)—result in secretion of the hormone *renin* by the *juxtaglomerular cells* (JG cells) of the kidney. Renin enters the blood supply and converts a substance called *angiotensinogen* into *angiotensin*. (There are two forms of the latter, angiotensin I and angiotensin II, but I shall ignore this fact for the sake of simplicity.) Angiotensin has several effects, one of which is to

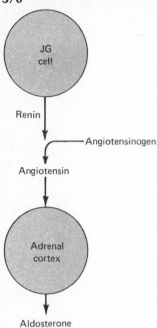

FIGURE 13.4   Control of aldosterone secretion by the kidney.

stimulate the adrenal cortex to produce aldosterone.   Therefore, a reduction in renal blood flow or increased activity of the sympathetic afferents of the kidney causes sodium to be retained by the body. (See **FIGURE 13.4.**)   The significance of this system will be explained shortly.

Water reabsorption, as we have seen, requires (1) that sodium be reabsorbed (so that the interstitial fluid around the renal tubules and collecting ducts contains a hypertonic salt solution) and (2) that the walls of the renal tubules and collecting ducts be permeable to water.   The permeability of these structures is controlled by a secretion of the posterior pituitary gland: *antidiuretic hormone*, or *ADH*. This hormone is actually produced by neurons in the supraoptic nucleus of the hypothalamus and transported, in vesicles, down through the axoplasm of these neurons.   ADH collects in the posterior pituitary gland and is released by neural stimulation.   (See **FIGURE 13.5.**)

The importance of ADH in the reabsorption of water is demonstrated by the disease produced by the lack of this hormone—*diabetes insipidus* (or "a not-tasty passing through"—the urine of a person with diabetes insipidus has very little taste, since it is so dilute).   You will

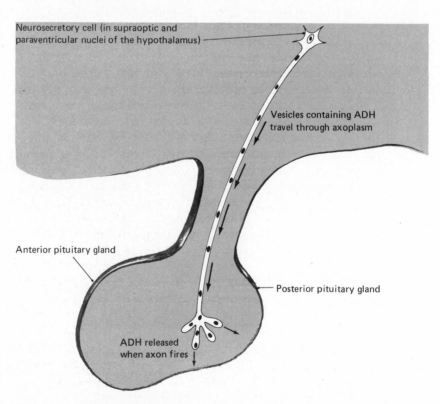

FIGURE 13.5   The posterior pituitary gland and ADH release.

recall that 180 liters of fluid is filtered through the glomeruli each day. Approximately 155 liters is reabsorbed by the proximal tubules (which are always permeable to water, regardless of the presence or absence of ADH). This leaves 25 liters. Lacking ADH, a person with diabetes insipidus will excrete these 25 liters. Having to pass over 6.5 gallons of urine each day (and, of course, having to drink an equal volume of water) makes it necessary to stay pretty close to a bathroom and a source of water. Injections of ADH increase the permeability of the distal tubules and collecting ducts to water and allow it to be reabsorbed. A normal excretion rate (approximately 1.5 liters, or under 2 quarts per day) is restored.

To summarize, sodium retention is regulated by aldosterone, which in turn is released in response to angiotensin. (Aldosterone release is also controlled by plasma potassium, but we shall ignore this factor.) Angiotensin is produced by secretion of renin by the kidneys, in response to neural stimulation or to decreased renal blood flow. Control of water retention is simpler; the level of activity of the neurosecretory cells in the supraoptic nucleus of the hypothalamus determines how much ADH is released, which in turn determines how much water is reabsorbed.

Detectors

Let us consider events that would produce disturbances in the body's water and salt balance, and then see what detection mechanisms might respond to these disturbances and what the appropriate correctional mechanisms should be. Let us suppose a person with diarrhea loses a considerable amount of body fluid. The fluid loss would be approximately isotonic, so the body's store of water and salt would be equally depleted. From which compartment(s) would the fluid loss come? The cells would not be affected so long as the concentration of the interstitial fluid remained the same. The loss of fluid, then, is in the extracellular compartment—the plasma and interstitial fluid. This loss of fluid from the extracellular compartments is called *hypovolemia*. (The term literally refers to a loss of *blood* volume, but since the two extracellular compartments are so intimately tied together, most people use the term hypovolemia to refer to loss of fluid from both extracellular compartments.) Loss of a small amount of interstitial fluid is not serious, but loss of plasma volume can have dire effects. To operate normally, the heart must have an adequate return of venous blood. Since the heart fills with blood passively, there must be an adequate amount of venous blood pressure. As venous blood pressure falls, because of the fluid loss, the output of the heart drops, which causes a further reduction in blood pressure.

Various compensatory mechanisms serve to raise the blood pressure (especially venous blood pressure). These include a restriction of blood flow to such organs as the kidney and constriction of smooth muscles in the walls of the veins. These mechanisms are highly effective if the fluid loss is not too great. But the venous blood pressure still remains lower than normal.

The *left atrium* of the heart, a chamber that passively fills with blood as a result of the force exerted by venous blood pressure, contains stretch receptors. These receptors fire at a rate proportional to the expansion of the left atrium; hence, they are *baroreceptors*, detecting changes in venous blood pressure. A fall in venous blood pressure triggers, by reflex mechanisms, an increased secretion of ADH and a release of renin by the kidney. The ADH secretion results in retention of water, whereas the secretion of renin (and subsequent production of angiotensin and release of aldosterone) results in retention of sodium. Furthermore, the decreased renal blood flow (a mechanism the body uses to maintain blood pressure) itself causes renin secretion. (See **FIGURE 13.6.**)

Therefore, loss of extracellular fluid results in the activation of mechanisms that conserve the body's supply of sodium and water. These mechanisms obviously cannot restore the volume of fluid lost; that requires ingestive mechanisms, which will be discussed shortly.

There is evidence for another set of detectors, besides those that monitor venous pressure and renal blood flow. Suppose an ani-

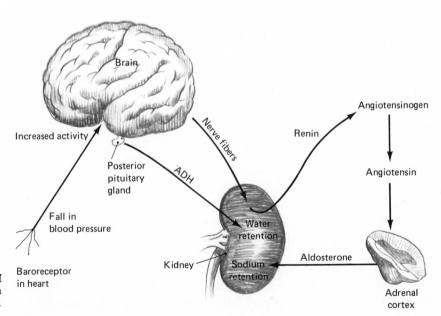

FIGURE 13.6   Control of ADH secretion by baroreceptors in the left atrium of the heart.

mal were given an injection of a hypertonic saline solution (i.e., a solution of sodium chloride more concentrated than body fluid). Sodium cannot enter cells (because of the Na^+ barrier and the sodium-potassium pump), so water leaves the cells, going down its concentration gradient. There is, therefore, an expansion of extracellular fluid volume, including the blood plasma. The hypervolemia stimulates the baroreceptors in the left atrium and inhibits the secretion of renin. As a result, water and sodium are excreted, and extracellular volume returns to normal. But what about the cells, which lost water? If the volume of intracellular fluid is to be restored, water must be ingested. The baroreceptors and detectors in the kidney are satisfied once the excess sodium (and accompanying water, borrowed from the intracellular fluid) is excreted. Therefore, other receptors must respond to cellular volume. I shall discuss the evidence for these detectors in the next section.

THIRST

Just as the extracellular and intracellular fluid compartments can be depleted independently, leaving the other compartment at near-normal values, thirst can be produced independently by depletion of either of these compartments.

Extracellular Thirst

As we saw in the previous section, a loss of extracellular fluid, produced by diarrhea, initiates correctional mechanisms that minimize further loss of water and sodium through the kidneys. As we shall see, this hypovolemia also produces thirst.

The easiest way to produce hypovolemia in experimental animals is to inject *colloids* into the peritoneal (abdominal) cavity (Fitzsimons, 1961). Colloids are gluelike substances made up of large molecules that cannot traverse cell membranes. Thus, they stay in the peritoneal cavity, and, because of osmotic pressure, extracellular fluid is drawn into the abdomen. Within an hour, the urine volume drops as a result of the mechanisms described in the previous section. At the same time, the animal begins to drink and continues to do so until the volume of fluid stolen from the extracellular fluid is replaced.

Fitzsimons injected a colloid (*polyethylene glycol*) in rats and then drained the fluid from the peritoneal cavity, getting rid of the colloid, along with the water and sodium it drew from the extracellular fluid. He allowed the rats to recover for a day or two, with food and water available *ad libitum*. During this time the animals drank and excreted copious amounts of water. He then presented the animals with two liquids, water and a hypertonic 1.8 percent saline solution (which the rats did not drink earlier). The rats avidly consumed the saline solution. This sodium ingestion was useful; at the start of the experiment, isotonic fluid (containing sodium) was drawn into the peritoneal cavity and was subsequently drained out of the body. The rats thus were suffering from a sodium deficiency.

Thus, a treatment that reduces the volume of the extracellular fluid causes a retention of sodium and water by the kidneys and stimulates thirst. When sodium is permanently lost (by removing the fluid collected in the peritoneal cavity), the ingested water cannot be retained; remember, water can be reabsorbed from the distal tubules and collecting ducts only if sodium is first transported out of the tubules and into the surrounding extracellular fluid. If the animal lacks sodium, water cannot be reabsorbed. The volume of the extracellular fluid cannot be maintained, and the animal is chronically thirsty. This thirst can be satisfied only if sodium is ingested; the fact that the animals will drink a concentrated salt solution that is normally rejected suggests that a "sodium hunger" is elicited as well as thirst. In the last section of this chapter I shall discuss the way intake of sodium and other minerals is adjusted to meet the body's requirements.

We have seen that the detectors that initiate internal corrective mechanisms (retention of sodium and water) in response to hypovolemia reside in the left atrium of the heart and in the kidney itself. It would seem plausible that one or both of these detectors might also be involved in extracellular thirst.

In an article on the physiology of thirst, Fitzsimons (1971) reviewed a series of experiments he performed to isolate mechanisms of extracellular thirst. First, he occluded the *vena cava* (the vein that returns blood from the lower part of the body) below the liver. In a short time the rats began to drink. (See **FIGURE 13.7.**) These animals began drinking in response to a fall in venous blood pressure (a result of the obstruction of a large vein). They were not dehydrated, nor were they hypovolemic. This experiment thus provides strong evidence that the baroreceptors and/or receptors in the kidney produce thirst.

In order to locate the detectors for extracellular thirst more precisely, Fitzsimons then restricted the blood supply to the kidneys by partially constricting the renal arteries. This procedure did not lower the venous blood pressure. The animals became thirsty. (See **FIGURE 13.8.**) It would appear, therefore, that the detectors in the kidney, which cause secretion of renin in response to a decreased

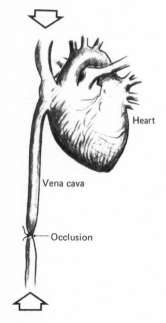

Venous blood pressure falls, rats drink

Heart

Vena cava

Occlusion

From lower part of body

FIGURE 13.7 A schematic representation of the first experiment by Fitzsimons.

renal blood flow, also produce thirst. The rats with restricted kidney blood flow did not drink as much water as the rats with lowered venous blood pressure, suggesting that the baroreceptors might also contribute to osmometric thirst.

To test this hypothesis, Stricker (1973) injected *nephrectomized* rats (those whose kidneys had been removed) with intraperitoneal polyethylene glycol (a colloid that removes fluid from the extracellular compartments, but not from the cells). The reduced volume of the extracellular fluid and the corresponding fall in venous blood pressure could thus stimulate only the baroreceptors, since the kidneys were gone. These rats became thirsty. (See **FIGURE 13.9.**) The experiments thus confirm that the baroreceptors and renal blood flow detectors are independently responsible for drinking produced by depletion of extracellular fluid. The neural mechanism by which this thirst is produced will be discussed later.

Osmometric Thirst

As we saw earlier, thirst can be produced by an injection of hypertonic saline, which draws fluid out of the cells but does not reduce the volume of the extracellular fluid. Therefore, some mechanism must detect either the increased osmotic pressure of the extracellular fluid (as a result of the injection) or the ensuing loss of cellular fluid.

In 1937, Gilman injected dogs with either hypertonic saline or hypertonic urea. The hypertonic saline produced twice as much drinking as did the urea; the results thus suggest that cell shrinkage, and not an increased osmotic pressure, produces thirst.

Let us see why this is so. Sodium is excluded from cells and thus remains in the extracellular fluid. Its presence there produces an osmotic gradient, which causes cellular dehydration—and

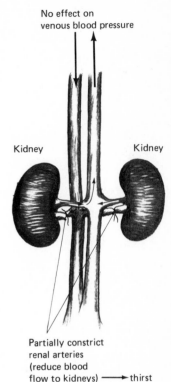

FIGURE 13.8 A schematic representation of the second experiment by Fitzsimons.

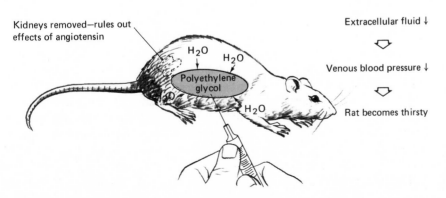

FIGURE 13.9 A schematic representation of the experiment by Stricker (1973).

thirst. Urea, on the other hand, easily crosses the cell membrane. Although the injected urea increases the total osmotic pressure of the body fluid, there is no net movement of water out of the cells. If this analysis is correct, urea should produce no thirst at all. As we shall see, the fact that it produces *some* thirst sheds light on the location of the detectors for thirst produced by cellular dehydration.

Fitzsimons nephrectomized a group of rats (to prevent the kidneys from contributing to fluid regulation) and injected the animals with hypertonic solutions of substances that can enter cells (such as glucose and methyl glucose) and substances that cannot (sodium chloride, sodium sulfate, and sucrose—table sugar). He also injected rats with urea, which, as we shall see, presents a special case.

The results confirm that cellular dehydration produces thirst; the only animals that drank excessively were those receiving substances that could not enter the cells. Glucose, and methyl glucose (which can enter the cells) did not produce thirst. As Gilman had previously found, urea injections produced thirst, but not as much as was produced by the substances excluded from the cells.

Although urea can freely enter the cells of the body, it does not easily cross the blood-brain barrier (Reed and Woodbury, 1962). All other substances Fitzsimons tested can. Therefore, urea present in the rest of the body slowly withdraws fluid from the cells of the brain. This fact suggests that the osmoreceptive cells are within the brain—on the other side of the blood-brain barrier.

Satiety

Anticipatory mechanisms also are involved in regulation of water intake, but these mechanisms are not so important as the ones needed for the regulation of food intake. The time interval between ingestion of water and its absorption into the fluid compartments of the body is much shorter than the 4 hours required to digest an average meal. In the case of water regulation, peripheral and central factors are not so far removed. Oropharyngeal satiety factors do not appear to be very important in water regulation; in 1856, Claude Bernard found that an esophagotamized horse (whose ingested water spilled to the ground) drank to exhaustion. Intubation of water into the stomach, however, led to immediate satiety.

Head factors appear to be more important to a dog than to a horse. Bellows (1939) found that esophagotomized dogs sham-drank approximately twice as much water as they needed, and then stopped. The amount swallowed was proportional to their level of dehydration. Rats, however, depend principally upon gastric and central factors— probably because they drink more slowly (Adolph, Barker, and Hoy,

1954). Dogs, which drink a large volume of water in a short period of time, rely more on head factors in metering their intake. If water is injected directly into a dog's stomach, there is very little immediate effect on drinking, whereas a rat will be immediately satiated.

A hypovolemic animal will drink water, but as the volume of the extracellular fluid increases, the fluid becomes more dilute and thus produces a migration of water into the cells (cellular overhydration). This overhydration is the reverse of the signal for osmometric thirst; will it inhibit drinking produced by hypovolemia?

Stricker (1969) found that overhydration did inhibit drinking in rats that were made hypovolemic by intraperitoneal injections of polyethylene glycol. The rats stopped drinking when their body fluid was diluted by 8 to 10 percent, even though plasma volume was still lower than normal. There seemed to be a trade-off in the excitatory effect produced by hypovolemia and the inhibitory effect produced by cellular overhydration. When the rats were given some sodium chloride (which raised the osmotic pressure in the extracellular fluid and took some of the extra water out of the cells), they again started to drink water.

Since *hyper*volemia produced by increased drinking is not normally a problem (the excess fluid easily enters the interstitial space), we cannot pit hypervolemic satiety against osmotic thirst. Anyway, the ingested water would quickly eliminate the cellular dehydration; if we gave the animals a hypertonic saline solution to drink, which would not permit the cells to become rehydrated, taste factors would then inhibit intake. An osmotically thirsty animal will not accept hypertonic saline.

In the normal animal, with normal kidneys, volumetric and osmometric dehydration generally go hand-in-hand. When the animal is deprived of water, it retains salt and loses water through the lungs and skin, and it loses an irreducible amount of water through the kidneys. The extracellular fluid, as it begins to lose volume and become more concentrated, draws water from the cells. The ensuing cellular dehydration and slight reduction in blood plasma volume both produce thirst, and all fluid compartments are returned to normal by a drink of water.

Anticipation of Future Needs

As we all know, a meal without some beverage is thirst-provoking. In acknowledgment of this fact we almost always drink water (in one form or another) with each meal. So does a rat. Fitzsimons and Le Magnen (1969) showed that rats appear to ingest as much water as they will *subsequently* need to counteract the dehydrating effects of their meal.

All meals produce a certain degree of hypovolemia. Secretion of digestive juices into the digestive tract entails a temporary loss of water (remember, the inside of the gut is actually outside the body). The hypovolemia leads to thirst. A meal rich in protein is particularly dehydrating. The presence of amino acids in the digestive tract produces a considerable rise in the osmotic pressure, thus withdrawing fluid from the extracellular space. If you ate a large steak (even without any added salt) without taking any beverage, you would later become thirsty. (You might prefer this experiment to hitting your thumb.)

Rats ingest an amount of water that is closely related to the osmotic demand placed upon them by their meal (Le Magnen and Tallon, 1966). It appears, however, that they drink the water *before* the body fluid enters the gut (Oatley and Toates, 1969). Fitzsimons and Le Magnen (1969) showed that the matching of water intake to water need appears to be learned. They maintained rats on a carbohydrate diet and noted that the rats ingested almost equal amounts of water and food. The rats were then shifted to a protein diet, and the animals now took 1.47 times as much water as food. At first, however, they drank most of the water *after* the meal, when the osmotic demands were being felt. After a few days the animals began to drink more water with meals. They apparently learned to associate the new diet with subsequent thirst, and they drank to prevent that thirst.

It is interesting to note that when animals were shifted from a protein diet to a carbohydrate diet, they decreased their water intake very slowly. Since the kidneys quickly get rid of any excess water, there is no great pressure on the animal to drink less water; a slight degree of overhydration does not appear to be aversive. The animals probably begin to drink less water because of the effort involved in its ingestion.

There also appears to be a mechanism that produces more immediate anticipation of future water need. Nicolaidis (1968) found that the mouth contains osmoreceptors that convey information to an osmo-sensitive region of the hypothalamus. Possibly, ingestion of hypertonic foods could stimulate drinking by means of this pathway.

BRAIN MECHANISMS IN THIRST

Volumetric Thirst

Hypovolemia is detected by baroreceptors on the venous side of the blood supply, and by a renal mechanism that monitors blood flow through the kidneys. Both of these mechanisms cause the kidney to release renin; the baroreceptors do so via a reflex circuit (which has not been traced) that increases sympathetic activity in the kidneys, and the decreased renal blood flow does so directly. It therefore seems plausible to suggest that renin (or angiotensin, whose synthesis is initiated by renin) acts on some cells in the brain and initiates thirst.

This does indeed appear to be the case. Early studies (e.g., Asscher and Anson, 1963) showed that injections of kidney extracts produced increases in drinking. Later, Fitzsimons and Simons (1969) showed that angiotensin produced drinking in normally hydrated rats. Drinking resulted whether the angiotensin was administered in a single dose or given very slowly for up to 5 hours. Angiotensin produces increased blood pressure (in fact, that is how this chemical got its name; *angeion* means "vessel" and *tensio*, "tension"). Drinking does not appear to be secondary to any vascular changes, since very small amounts of angiotensin, which do not affect blood pressure, nevertheless produce drinking.

Epstein, Fitzsimons, and Rolls (1970) found that intracranial injections of angiotensin produced drinking. Effective sites were found in the septum, preoptic region, and anterior hypothalamus. After receiving the injection through a chronically implanted cannula, the rats would stop what they were doing and begin drinking. A number of control drugs and hormones, some of which produce changes in blood pressure (as angiotensin does), had no effect when injected into the brain regions that respond to angiotensin. Furthermore, Joy and Lowe (1970) found that injections of angiotensin into the blood supply of the medulla produced changes in blood pressure. The neural sites of action for drinking and for increased vascular changes appear to be separate.

Subsequent studies have suggested that angiotensin produces drinking by acting on a very specific brain region. Johnson (1972) found that injections of angiotensin into the ventricles of the brain were very effective in producing drinking. As a matter of fact, the effectiveness of angiotensin injections into various brain regions appeared to correlate very nicely with the likelihood of diffusion (or backflow along the puncture wound produced by the cannula) into a ventricle. Volicer and Loew (1971) found that angiotensin penetrated the blood-brain barrier very slowly, but readily entered the *subfornical organ (SFO)*, a brain structure that is outside of the blood-brain barrier. Simpson and Routtenberg (1975) found that destruction of the subfornical organ markedly decreased drinking produced by intracranial injections of angiotensin.

However, a subsequent set of studies (Buggy, Fisher, Hoffman, Johnson, and Phillips, 1975; Johnson and Buggy, 1976) showed that the subfornical organ does not appear to contain the receptors sensitive to

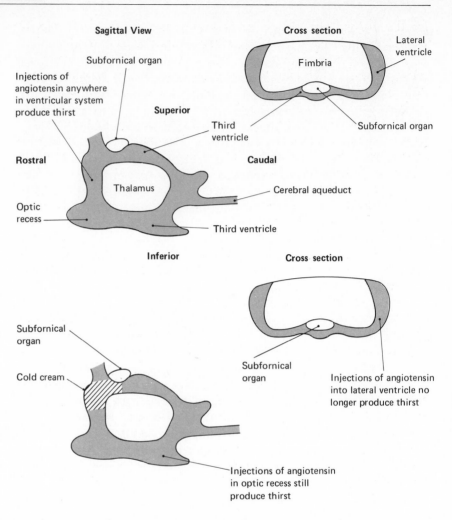

Sagittal View

Cross section

Subfornical organ

Lateral ventricle

Fimbria

Injections of angiotensin anywhere in ventricular system produce thirst

Superior

Third ventricle

Subfornical organ

Rostral

Caudal

Thalamus

Cerebral aqueduct

Optic recess

Third ventricle

Inferior

Cross section

Subfornical organ

Cold cream

Subfornical organ

Injections of angiotensin into lateral ventricle no longer produce thirst

Injections of angiotensin in optic recess still produce thirst

FIGURE 13.10 A schematic representation of the experiment that ruled out the subfornical organ as the receptive organ for angiotensin-produced thirst.

angiotensin. These investigators noted that lesions of the SFO in rats caused tissue swelling that blocked flow of cerebrospinal fluid from the lateral ventricle into the third ventricle. Reasoning that this interruption in flow of CSF could block the access of angiotensin, injected into the lateral ventricle, to other sites "downstream" from the SFO, these investigators injected plugs of cold cream into the third ventricle just rostral to the SFO. Injections of angiotensin into the lateral ventricle now failed to produce drinking. However, injections into the *optic recess* of the third ventricle, on the other side of the block, caused the rats to drink. (See **FIGURE 13.10.**)

Radioactive tracer studies confirmed the fact that lesions of the SFO abolished drinking in response to injections of angiotensin in the lateral ventricle only when the flow of CSF from the lateral ventricle into the third ventricle was blocked by swelling induced by the lesion. In all cases, however, angiotensin was effective when it was placed in the optic recess of the third ventricle.

Where might the receptive tissue be? Lesions were made in a relatively thin layer of tissue around the walls of the optic recess. (Johnson, 1976, notes that there have been several published cases of humans with brain lesions in this region who reported the complete absence of thirst.) After recovery from an initial period of complete adipsia, the rats began drinking, but did not respond to angiotensin injections (either systemically or intraventricularly) or to systemic injections of hypertonic saline solution. They did, however, drink in response to hypovolemia, produced by intraperitoneal injections of polyethylene glycol. It would appear that the periventricular region of the anterior hypothalamus contains cells responsive to angiotensin (and perhaps to cellular dehydration also; this issue will be discussed in the next section). Hypovolemic drinking mediated by the baroreceptors in the walls of the left atrium apparently involves independent neural mechanisms.

To summarize: Hypovolemia results in an increased blood level of angiotensin—directly, by stimulating the kidneys (through decreased renal blood flow) and, indirectly, via a baroreceptor-brain-kidney reflex pathway (not yet identified anatomically). Renin secreted by the kidneys converts blood angiotensinogen to angiotensin, which is detected by cells in the periventricular region of the hypothalamus. Somehow (and this has not been worked out yet) thirst is then stimulated. We also saw, from the fact that hypovolemia stimulates drinking in a nephrectomized animal (which is therefore unable to produce angiotensin), that the baroceptors apparently can stimulate drinking by strictly neural means. The brain mechanisms that mediate hypovolemic drinking, independent of angiotensin, are not known.

Osmometric Thirst

As we have seen, injections of hypertonic solutions produce drinking, so long as the solute administered cannot penetrate cells. The ensuing cellular fluid loss leads to thirst.

Where are the osmoreceptors? In 1947, Verney found that injections of hypertonic saline solution into the blood supply of the diencephalon resulted in water retention, triggered by increased ADH secretion. The results suggested the presence of osmoreceptors, probably in the hypothalamus. Andersson (1953) found that injections of hypertonic saline solution into the rostrolateral hypothalamus produced drinking (but not ADH release), whereas injections into caudal hypothalamic regions stimulated ADH secretion, but not thirst.

Subsequent investigations indicated that the solution Andersson used was very hypertonic and might have directly stimulated neurons involved with drinking or ADH secretion, and not necessarily osmoreceptors. Peck and Novin (1971) and Blass and Epstein (1971) placed lesions in various diencephalic areas in rats and rabbits. Some lesions were ineffective, some caused a reduction in drinking to hypovolemia or cellular dehydration, and still others reduced only the drinking that occurred in response to cellular dehydration. The authors concluded that the lateral preoptic area, which was damaged by lesions that affected only osmotic thirst, appeared to contain the osmoreceptors. In support of this suggestion, the authors found that injections of sodium chloride or sucrose (but not urea, which crosses the cell membrane and fails to produce cellular dehydration) into the lateral preoptic area produced thirst. Furthermore, an injection of water into the same region stopped drinking produced by cellular dehydration, but it did not stop drinking in response to systemic injections of renin.

The more recent studies by Johnson and Buggy (1976) suggest that the periventricular region of the hypothalamus, which appears to contain cells that respond to angiotensin, also contains osmoreceptive neurons. They found that lesions of this area abolish drinking in response to systemic injections of hypertonic saline solution. Research in the next few years will hopefully tell us whether the osmoreceptors responsible for thirst reside in the periventricular region, in the lateral preoptic area, or perhaps in both places.

Experiments by Hatton (1976) provide very strong evidence for the specific location of the osmoreceptors that regulate ADH secretion, in the *nucleus circularis* of the hypothalamus. This nucleus is very small, consisting of approximately 275 cells. None of the standard stereotaxic atlases make mention of it; most people (myself included, before I learned of Hatton's work) tended, if they noticed this structure in a Nissl-stained section, to dismiss it as a staining artefact.

The nucleus circularis appears ringlike in cross section, with a hollow interior. It is actually tubeshaped, its long axis running in a rostral-caudal direction. The neurons in this nucleus lie within a capillary bed and are surrounded by heavily myelinated fibers. These fibers appear to enclose the cells, along with the capillary bed and surrounding interstitial fluid, in a water-tight compartment. (See **FIGURE 13.11.**) According to Hatton, the nucleus lies in the area that, when destroyed, produces deficits in osmometric control of ADH release. The nucleus sends fibers to the supraoptic nucleus (wherein reside the neurons that produce ADH) and also toward the posterior pituitary gland itself.

Electrical stimulation of the nucleus circularis, but not of

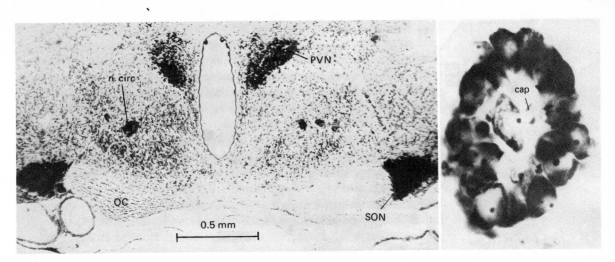

FIGURE 13.11 The location and appearance of nucleus circularis. From Hatton, G. I., *Brain Research Bulletin*, 1976, *1*, 123–131.)

adjacent regions, produced retention of water, which constitutes evidence for ADH secretion. Furthermore, water deprivation led to an increase in the number of nucleoli in the cells of the nucleus. You will recall from chapter 2 that the ribosomes (sites of protein synthesis) are produced by the nucleolus; hence, increases in the number of nucleoli suggest increased protein synthesis, presumably a result of stimulation produced by increased osmotic pressure.

Neural Control of Drinking

As we saw in chapter 12, lesions of the lateral hypothalamus produce temporary aphagia and adipsia, followed by gradual recovery (or rapid recovery, if the animals are first starved to a weight below their new "set point"). When drinking returns, it occurs only during meals. Thirst is no longer produced by injections of hypertonic saline solution (Epstein and Teitelbaum, 1964) or by hypovolemia induced by IP injections of polyethylene glycol (Stricker and Wolf, 1967). Neither of the normal signals, then, produces drinking.

It appears likely that the lateral hypothalamic lesions interrupt a system, directed toward brainstem motor mechanisms, that controls drinking behavior. The neural circuits mediating hypovolemic and osmometric thirst apparently converge at the level of the anterior hypothalamus, since lesions caudal to this area disrupt both kinds of thirst, whereas more anterior lesions disrupt one or the other, depending upon precise location (Peck and Novin, 1971; Blass and Epstein, 1971; Peck, 1973). The fact that lateral hypothalamic lesions do not disrupt drinking necessary for the ingestion of dry food suggests that there are oropharyngeal receptors that can directly activate motor mechanisms of drinking caudal to the hypothalamus.

One other brain region has been shown to play a role in the control of drinking—the septum. Damage to this structure, a part of the limbic system, generally results in polydipsia. The increased drinking appears to be primary, rather than a result of changes in kidney functions (Lubar, Boyce, and Schaefer, 1968). The septum thus appears to play an inhibitory role on water intake. Mogenson (1973) has suggested that this control may be important in mediating the effects of learning, taste, and smell on drinking. It is interesting to note that the septum appears to exert very specific effects; septal lesions enhance water intake only when drinking is stimulated by angiotensin administration or by experimental procedures that cause its release (Blass, Nussbaum, and Hanson, 1974).

CONTROL OF MINERAL AND VITAMIN INTAKE

We saw in the first part of this chapter that an animal suffering from hypovolemic thirst drinks sodium (if it is available) as well as water, in response to its need for this mineral. As we shall see in this section, sodium preference, elicited by sodium need, appears to be independent of learning. However, an animal deprived of calcium must find this mineral through a trial-and-error learning process.

Innate Recognition of Sodium

If an adrenalectomized rat is deprived of sodium, it will develop a strong sodium deficiency because the lack of aldosterone prevents sodium retention by the kidneys. Nachman (1962) found that adrenalectomized rats showed an immediate preference for sodium over other minerals, and he later showed (Nachman, 1963) that sodium-deficient rats also preferred lithium chloride, which has a salty taste. Krieckhaus and Wolf (1968) trained thirsty rats to press a lever for water that contained either sodium or other minerals. A sodium deficiency was then induced in these animals (by giving them a subcutaneous injection of formalin, which damages capillaries and withdraws sodium from the extracellular fluid). The sodium-deficient rats were allowed to press the lever, but no fluid was delivered. Those animals that had previously received a mineral other than sodium when they pressed the lever soon stopped pressing it, now that no fluid was delivered. The rats that had previously obtained sodium, however, continued to press the now-defunct lever for prolonged periods of time. They appeared to be able to associate present sodium need with the prior availability of sodium, even though it was not previously needed.

These studies suggest that sodium recognition is innate. They cannot *prove* this is so, since one would have to demonstrate that the rats had never previously suffered from sodium imbalance that was subsequently relieved by ingestion of sodium (and thus provide the basis for a learned sodium preference in response to sodium need). However, the fact that animals respond so differently to other mineral and vitamin deficiencies suggests that sodium appetite is indeed a special case.

Selection of Other Minerals and Vitamins

It has been known for a long time that it is difficult to kill rats with poison (i.e., poison left out for them in their natural environment). Rats typically exhibit a dietary *neophobia*—fear of a substance with an unfamiliar flavor. More precisely, it should be said that they avoid a novel substance, at first tasting only a small amount of it. A day or two later, assuming nothing bad happens to them, they will eat more of the new diet and add it to their "list" of acceptable foods.

I said they would subsequently eat the new food if "nothing bad happens to them." This is an important qualification. If the rats become ill after eating the new diet, during a period lasting for several hours, they will thereafter permanently avoid the food. (I am assuming, of course, that the animal survives the illness. A dead animal cannot be referred to as "avoiding" anything.) The rats are "bait shy."

We humans are probably also subject to this phenomenon (which is generally called *conditioned aversion*). Probably all of us have one or another aversion to specific foods, and some of these aversions may be a result of fortuitous association of the taste with later illness. Also, we have probably all heard someone (perhaps ourselves) say something like this: "When I was around 13 years old I drank a bottle of cheap sweet wine, and I puked all night. I can't even stand the sight of the stuff now." This possible example of conditioned aversion seems, however, to be contradicted by the countless people who get sick after a bout of drinking, only to do it again. This can probably be explained by the fact that *novel* substances are best associated with ensuing illness. Once a substance has been consumed several times without illness, it is difficult to produce a conditioned aversion to it.

Garcia, Kimmeldorf, and Koelling (1955) showed that rats were indeed capable of associating a novel taste stimulus with sickness that develops several hours later. This caused consternation among some learning theorists; it had been known for many years that a stimulus must precede reinforcement by a very short interval (on the order of seconds) in order for an association to be made. It was suggested that the association could be explained by the presence of postingestional cues around the time of the sickness. For example, the animals might regurgitate when they were sick and thus taste the ingested substance in their vomitus. This explanation does not seem to work, however. Garcia, Green, and McGowan (1969) used a 0.05 percent solution of hydrochloric acid as a taste stimulus, followed one hour later by an injection of lithium chloride (which causes nausea and illness). Hydrochloric acid does not put any novel ions into the stomach (gastric juices contain a high concentration of hydrochloric acid), so nothing is added to the taste of vomitus. (Anyway, rats do not have an effective vomiting mechanism.) Nevertheless, the hydrochloric acid was later avoided only by rats that had been made sick.

Garcia and Koelling (1966) found that taste cues, but not visual or auditory cues, could be associated with illness after a long delay. When visual, auditory, and gustatory stimuli were simultaneously presented prior to illness, only the gustatory stimulus was later avoided. However, a painful electric shock was best associated with visual or auditory stimuli, but only after a short delay interval. Footshock delivered long after the presentation of any of the stimuli had no effect upon the animal's subsequent approach to any of them. Furthermore, Hankins, Garcia, and Rusiniak (1973) found that only the taste, and not the odor, of a novel food was responsible for conditioned aversion.

Paul Rozin has used the phenomenon of conditioned aversion to explain how rats learn to consume selectively diets that provide substances (vitamins or minerals) their bodies require. He fed rats a thiamine-deficient diet (thiamine, also called vitamin B_1, is an essential vitamin). The rats began to eat less food as they began to suffer the ill effects of the vitamin deficiency, and they acted as though the food, formerly quite palatable, had become aversive. They spilled it out of the dish and often ran away from the food, chewing on portions of the cage at the end opposite the food. (Rats given a diet made unpalatable with quinine show much the same behavior.) When the rats were given a new (thiamine-supplemented) food, they ate it avidly, ignoring the old diet.

Why do the rats choose the new food? The best explanation is that the developing illness produces a conditioned aversion to the deficient diet. This aversion overrides their natural neophobia (fear of novelty), and they show a preference for a new diet. Rozin (1968) raised rats on a thiamine-supplemented diet A. He then gave them thiamine-free diet B and allowed a deficiency to develop. When they were later tested with diets A, B, and C (a novel, thiamine-supplemented diet), they preferred A the most, followed by C. B was not eaten at all. The fact that they chose A over C shows that there was still some neophobia (good, old, safe diet A was best), but the rats would take C in preference to the now-aversive B.

Besides the aversion toward a diet associated with a deficiency, rats seem to form a positive association with a diet that makes them feel better. Garcia, Ervin, Yorke, and Koelling (1967) placed rats on a thiamine-deficient diet. After several days the animals were given a drink of saccharine, followed by an injection of thiamine, which produced a quick recovery from their deficiency. These rats subsequently drank more saccharine than did control animals, providing evidence for conditioned preference.

Other investigators have shown that rats respond to mineral deficiencies in a similar way. Rodgers (1967) fed rats a calcium-deficient diet. When given a choice between a novel diet and their old one, they chose the novel one—even if calcium had now been added to the old diet. Rats cannot taste calcium and will choose a new flavor, even if it does not contain calcium.

Nature has evolved an appealing, elegant (and I use the word in its original sense—simple) mechanism for regulation of intake of vital substances. If the regular diet lacks an essential ingredient, an aversion to this diet develops. In the wild, the animal would probably seek other sources of food. If ingestion of a new food is associated with recovery, that food is subsequently preferred. This mechanism appears to operate for calcium intake (Rodgers, 1967) and for specific amino acids (Harper, 1967), as well as for thiamine. I think that it is safe to assume that this mechanism operates for *any* substance we require in our diets.

SUGGESTED READINGS

EPSTEIN, A. N., KISSILEFF, H. R., and STELLAR, E. *The Neuropsychology of Thirst: New Findings and Advances in Concepts.* Washington: V. H. Winston & Sons, 1973. Distributed by Halstead Press, Division of John Wiley & Sons.

FITZSIMONS, J. T. The physiology of thirst: A review of the extraneural aspects of the mechanisms of drinking. In *Progress in Physiological Psychology*, vol. 4, edited by E. Stellar and J. M. Sprague. New York: Academic Press, 1971.

These two volumes cover almost all aspects of thirst and drinking. The chapters are written by the most prominent investigators in the field.

ROZIN, P., and KALAT, J. W. Specific hungers and poison avoidance as adaptive specializations of learning. *Psychological Review*, 1971, 78, 459–486. This article covers the topics of conditioned aversion and dietary selection.

The Nature and
Functions of Sleep

14

Why do we sleep? Why do we spend at least one-third of our lives in a state that provides most of us with only a few, fleeting memories? I shall attempt to answer this question in several ways. In this chapter, I shall describe what is known about the phenomenon of sleep: How much do we sleep? What do we do while asleep? What happens if we do not get enough sleep? What factors affect the duration and quality of sleep? How effective are sleeping medications? Does sleep perform a restorative function? What about sleepwalking and related disorders? When we talk in our sleep, does it mean we are dreaming?

As you shall see, we really cannot say why we sleep. Most investigators believe sleep performs a restorative function, but others consider it to be a response—a state related to periodic availability of food and/or periodic vulnerability to predators. The evidence necessary to prove either of these hypotheses is still incomplete.

In chapter 15, I shall attempt to answer a slightly different question: Given that we do sleep, what brain mechanisms are involved in sleep and in its counterpart, arousal? This question is by no means completely answered, but the issue is much more straightforward and amenable to experimentation than the question of *why* we sleep.

SLEEP: A PHYSIOLOGICAL AND BEHAVIORAL DESCRIPTION

The best research concerning sleep in humans comes from a "sleep laboratory." Usually in a university setting, a sleep lab consists of one or several small, comfortable, homey bedrooms adjacent to an observation room, where the experimenter spends the night (hopefully, awake). The volunteer (or patient, in the cases where observations are made in an attempt to diagnose sleep disorders) is first prepared for electrophysiological measurements. Scalp electrodes are glued on, and electrodes to monitor muscle activity are taped (usually) to the chin. Eye movements are monitored from electrodes taped to the face around the eyes. Other autonomic measures (heart rate, respiration, and skin conductance) are occasionally monitored. Wires from the electrodes are bundled together in a "ponytail," which is then plugged into a junction box at the head of the bed.

As you might imagine, a subject in a sleep experiment often has difficulty in sleeping during the first night. If dreams are monitored then, they typically involve the laboratory situation. Careful investigators always take account of the "first-night phenomenon" and avoid making conclusions based on observations made during this time.

During wakefulness, the electroencephalogram (EEG) of a normal person shows two basic patterns of activity: *alpha* and *beta.* Alpha activity is observed when the person is resting quietly, not particularly aroused or excited and not engaged in strenuous mental activity (such as problem solving). Although alpha waves may be recorded from a person whose eyes are open, they are seen far more often when the eyes are closed. The other type of EEG pattern seen during waking, beta activity, is seen while the person is alert and aroused. Alpha activity will usually be disrupted and be replaced by beta activity when the person is asked to solve a problem (such as the mental addition of two three-digit numbers), or when a sudden loud noise is presented.

Figure 14.1 illustrates these two forms of the waking EEG. Note that beta consists of low-voltage, irregular activity, consisting mostly of high frequencies (13–30 Hz). Alpha activity, on the other hand, is much more regular. A lower frequency (8–12 Hz) of higher voltage predominates. (See **FIGURE 14.1.**)

Stages of Sleep

As a person progresses into sleep, the EEG contains an increasing amount of low-frequency, high-voltage activity. During the transi-

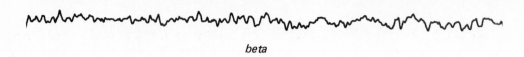

beta

alpha

FIGURE 14.1 Alpha and beta activity from the EEG.

tion from waking to sleep, the EEG record contains mostly irregular, low-voltage waves, but as sleep becomes deeper, more and more slow, high-voltage *delta activity* (1–4 Hz) is seen. Sleep has been divided into stages, according to the type of EEG activity that is present, but since there are no clear-cut boundaries between adjacent stages, the precise definitions of each stage are not of importance to us here. What is important is to note that deeper stages of sleep are accompanied by increasing amounts of delta activity (indicated by the horizontal lines beneath the records). (See **FIGURE 14.2.**)

THE SIGNIFICANCE OF SYNCHRONY.   Since the EEG is produced by the summed postsynaptic activity of neurons in the brain, low frequency, high-voltage activity (such as delta waves) is usually referred to as reflecting neural *synchrony*. There is, presumably, a great deal of similarity in the temporal pattern of activity in a large number of neurons. The activity of the individual neurons is similar to a large number of people chanting the same words (speaking synchronously). Beta activity is, for the same reason, referred to as *desynchrony;* it is more similar to a large number of people broken into many small groups, each carrying on an individual conversation. The analogy helps explain why desynchrony is generally taken to represent activation, whereas synchrony reflects a resting or depressed state. The group of people who are all chanting the same thing is processing very little information; only one message is being produced. The desynchronized group, on the other hand, is processing and transmitting many different messages. The waking state of the brain is more like the desynchronized group of people, with much information processing going on. During delta sleep the neurons of the resting brain (especially the cortex) quietly murmur the same message in unison (following the lead of a group of pacemaker cells, as we shall see in the next chapter).

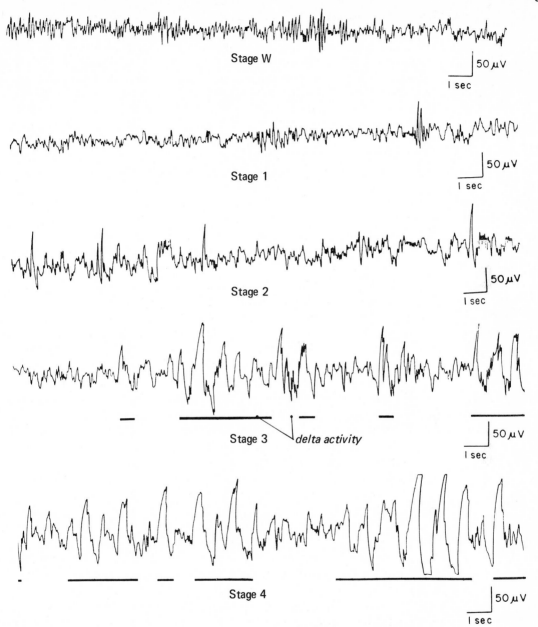

Stage W

50 μV

I sec

Stage 1

50 μV

I sec

Stage 2

50 μV

I sec

Stage 3   *delta activity*

50 μV

I sec

Stage 4

50 μV

I sec

FIGURE 14.2   Stages of sleep. Stage W indicates drowsy
wakefulness immediately preceding the onset of stage 1
of S sleep. (These records were obtained from *A Manual of
Standardized Terminology, Techniques and Scoring
System for Sleep Stages of Human Subjects,* edited by A.
Rechtschaffen and A. Kales. Washington, D.C.: U.S.
Government Printing Office, 1968.)

Description of a Night's Sleep

Let us follow the progress of a volunteer (a male college student) in the sleep lab. Our subject has already slept there, so the sleep patterns we observe will not be unduly influenced by a new, unfamiliar environment. The wires are attached, the lights are turned off, and the door is closed. Our relaxed subject shows mostly alpha activity, which is soon replaced by evidence of stage 1 sleep. Around 10 minutes later he enters stage 2, followed, 15 minutes later, by the occurrence of a few delta waves, signalling entry into stage 3. Gradually, over a 15-minute period, delta waves predominate (stage 4). The subject might very well be snoring loudly now, but if awakened, he might report that he had not been asleep. (This phenomenon is often reported by nurses who awaken loudly snoring patients early in the night—probably to administer a sleeping pill—and find that the patients insist that they were lying there awake all the time.)

We do not gradually slip from waking into sleeping, by the way. The onset of sleep appears to be sudden; it is seen as gradual only in retrospect. Of course, we gradually become sleepier, and gradually become less restless as sleep approaches, but the border between wakefulness and sleep appears to be distinct. Dement (1972) reports a study in which a subject's eyes were taped open (which, Dement assures us, is not uncomfortable). The subject was asked to press a switch every time he saw a bright flash from a strobe light placed 6 inches from his face. The subject pressed repeatedly and then suddenly stopped. The curtain of sleep had suddenly dropped. If the subject were awakened, he would not realize that he had stopped pressing the switch. The cessation of button pressing corresponds with the onset of slow, rolling eye movements (not the rapid eye movements I shall shortly describe) and an EEG record characteristic of stage 1 sleep.

About 90 minutes after the onset of sleep, an abrupt change is suddenly seen in a number of physiological measures. The EEG suddenly becomes desynchronized; if we did not see our subject lying there, asleep, we would assume he was awake. We also note that his eyes are rapidly darting back and forth beneath his closed eyelids. (We can see this in the *electroculogram*, or *EOG*, recorded from electrodes taped to the skin around his eyes, or we can observe the eye movements directly. The cornea produces a bulge in the closed eyelids that can be seen to move about.) We also see that the EMG (a measure of muscular activity) becomes silent; there is a profound loss of muscle tonus. We occasionally see brief twitching movements of the hands and feet, however, and our subject probably has an erection.

This peculiar stage of sleep is quite distinct from the quiet, slow wave sleep we saw earlier. It is usually referred to as *REM sleep* (for the rapid eye movements that characterize it). It has also been called *paradoxical sleep*, because of the presence of a "waking" EEG during sleep. The term "paradoxical" merely reflects surprise at observing an unexpected phenomenon, but the years since its first discovery (reported by Aserinsky and Kleitman in 1953) have blunted the surprise value. In accordance with a suggestion by Hartmann (1973), I shall use the terms *S sleep* and *D sleep* to refer to the two states. S sleep is *s*low-wave, *s*ynchronized, *s*pindling sleep. D sleep, on the other hand, is characterized by *d*esynchrony. Some would call it *d*eep sleep. And, as we shall see, D also refers to *d*reaming.

   If we arouse our volunteer during D sleep and ask him what was going on, he will almost certainly report that he had been dreaming. The dreams of D sleep tend to be narrative in form; there is a storylike progression of events. If we wake him during S sleep and ask, "Were you dreaming?" he will most likely say no. However, if we question him more carefully, he might report the presence of a thought, or an image, or some emotion. I shall return to this issue later.

   During the rest of the night our subject will alternate between periods of S sleep and D sleep, a cycle being approximately 90 minutes long, and containing a 20- to 30-minute bout of D sleep. That means an 8-hour sleep will contain four or five periods of D sleep. Hartmann (1967) has drawn a graph of a typical night's sleep, as shown in Figure 14.3. Note that most stage 4 sleep is accomplished early in the night. D sleep is represented by the heavy horizontal bars. (See **FIGURE 14.3.**)

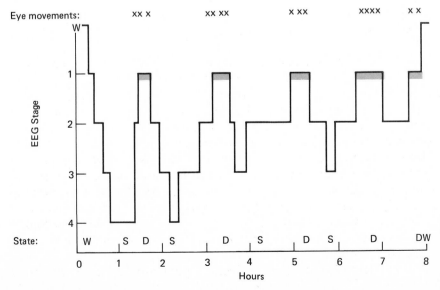

FIGURE 14.3   A typical pattern of the stages of sleep during a single night. (From Hartmann, E., *The Biology of Dreaming,* 1967. Courtesy of Charles C Thomas, Publisher, Springfield, Illinois.)

The regular cyclicity of D sleep suggests that there is some intrinsic brain mechanism that alternately produces the D and S states. Dement and his colleagues (reported by Dement, 1972) tabulated the intervals between successive periods of 1000 cases of D sleep. They found that once a period of D sleep was over for at least 5 minutes (indicating that it was truly over, and not just interrupted temporarily), there was a 95 to 98 percent probability that D sleep would not occur again for at least 30 minutes. By 80 minutes there is almost a 100 percent certainty that another period of D sleep will occur (unless the subject awakens). D sleep, then, cannot randomly occur at any time. There seems to be a refractory period after each occurrence, during which time D sleep cannot again take place.

D Sleep

More attention has been paid to D sleep than to S sleep, partly because it is more interesting. During D sleep we become paralyzed; there is massive inhibition of alpha motor neurons. Tendon reflexes cannot be elicited. At the same time, the brain is very active. Cerebral blood flow and oxygen consumption are accelerated; in fact, a physician long ago reported

> the case of a man who, some time after receiving a severe injury of the head by which a considerable portion of the skull was lost, came under my professional care. Standing by his bedside one evening just after he had gone to sleep, I observed the scalp rise slightly from the chasm in which it was deeply depressed. I was sure he was going to wake, but he did not, and very soon he became restless and agitated while continuing to sleep. Presently he began to talk, and it was evident that he was dreaming. In a few minutes the scalp sank down to its ordinary level when he was asleep, and he became quiet. I called his wife's attention to the circumstance and desired her to observe this condition thereafter when he slept. She subsequently informed me that she could always tell when he was dreaming from the appearance of the scalp. (Hammond, 1883, p. 145, quoted by Freemon, 1972)

EYE MOVEMENTS DURING DREAMS. Eye movements appear to be related to the visual content of the dream. Roffwarg, Dement, Muzio, and Fisher (1962) awakened subjects during D sleep. They carefully elicited a report of the dream, and they determined from the narration what eye movements would have occurred if the dream had been reality. The polygraph record was examined (by a person who did *not* hear the story) and a description of the eye movements was prepared. The investigators found a high degree of concordance between predicted and observed eye movement. A later study by Pivik, Bussel, and Dement (described by Dement, 1972) found that the relationship between EOG and predicted eye movements during D sleep was just as good as the relationship between EOG and actual eye movements during waking. Other investigators have failed to obtain such good agreement, but it is not clear that they questioned their subjects about their dreams so carefully as Dement's group did.

PASSAGE OF TIME DURING DREAMS. It is sometimes said that time is compressed in a dream—that what seems to take hours really occurs in a few seconds. This does not appear to be true, however. Dreams take the same amount of time as they seem to. Dement and Wolpert (1958) sprayed cold water on sleeping subjects during D sleep. They awakened the subjects at various times after the stimulus and questioned them about the dream. When the spray of water was incorporated into the dream, it was found that the perception of time between the stimulus and the subsequent awakening was quite accurate. Time seems to go by at the same rate during dreams as it does during waking. The authors give the following example:

> The S [subject] was sleeping on his stomach. His back was uncovered. An eye movement period started and after it had persisted for 10 minutes, cold water was sprayed on his back. Exactly 30 seconds later he was awakened. The first part of the dream involved a rather complex description of acting in a play. Then, "I was walking behind the leading lady when she suddenly collapsed and water was dripping on her face. I ran over to her and felt water dripping on my back and head. The roof was leaking. I was very puzzled why she fell down and decided some plaster must have fallen on her. I looked up and there was a hole in the roof. I dragged her over to the side of the stage and began pulling the curtains. Just then I woke up." (Dement and Wolpert, 1958, p. 550)

OTHER D SLEEP PHENOMENA. What about the penile erections that occur in male dreamers? Are they related to dreams with sexual content? This does not appear to be the case; erections occur during almost all periods of D sleep, even when the accompanying dreams are devoid of sexual content (Fisher, Gross, and Zuch, 1965). Of course, there are also dreams with frank sexual content that culminate in ejaculation—the so-called *nocturnal emissions,* or "wet dreams." Most investigators believe, by the way, that clitoral engorgement accompanies D sleep in females, but this phenomenon is rather difficult to study.

Many males believe that penile erections are somehow related to a full bladder; they often awaken in the morning with a hard penis and an urge to urinate. The events are correlated, but one does not appear to cause the other. A period of D sleep often occurs shortly before the normal waking time. If a full bladder causes a male to awaken a little early, he is likely to wake from a period of D sleep. He is likely then to believe that the full bladder caused the erection. If sleep is not interrupted prematurely by a full bladder, his dream and the accompanying erection will usually end before he awakens.

I have been describing dreaming as a universal phenomenon, but there are many people who insist that they never dream. They are wrong—everyone dreams. What does happen, however, is that most dreams are subsequently forgotten. Unless a person awakens during or immediately after a dream, memory for the dream is lost. Many people who think they have not had a dream for years are startled by the vivid narrations they are able to supply when roused during D sleep in the laboratory. It is a very interesting fact that such vivid experiences can be so completely erased from consciousness. I am sure that many of you have had the experience of waking during a particularly vivid (and perhaps amusingly bizarre) dream. You decide to tell your friends about it— and all of a sudden, it slips away. You can't even remember the general gist of the dream, which was so vivid and real just a few seconds ago. You have the feeling that if you could remember just one thing about it, everything would come back. I think that an understanding of this phenomenon would tell us a lot about the way in which memories get stored or lost.

What about dreams themselves? Primitive people thought (and many modern people still think) that dreams provide special insights. Prophetic dreams, for example, have altered military campaigns and changed the course of history. However, Freemon (1972) classifies prophetic dreams into three categories: (1) after-the-fact dreams, which can be culled out of a large store of dreams to suit the occasion (if the facts had been otherwise, a different prophetic dream would have been selected); (2) statistical dreams, which are remembered if the predicted event comes true, and conveniently forgotten (or at least not advertised) if it does not; and (3) inner knowledge dreams, which help us to recognize formally something we really know (and are ignoring, perhaps actively).

S Sleep

I have been speaking of dreaming as being synonymous with D sleep. This does indeed appear to be the case, but mental activity also occurs during S sleep. The probability of obtaining a report of a dream during S sleep depends greatly upon one's definition of what constitutes a dream. Freemon (1972) compiled a table (shown in Table 14.1) that shows the great variability in the definitions of dreams used by various

Why Do We Sleep? The Effects of Sleep Deprivation

397

TABLE 14.1   Sleep Mentation and Dreaming

Awakenings from:					
Rem		Nonrem			
Total Number	Dream Recall	Total Number	Dream Recall	Definition of Dreaming	Authors
27	74%	23		"detailed dream description"	Aserinsky and Kleitman (1955)
51	88%	19	0%	self-definition by each subject	Dement (1955)
191	79%	161	7%	"coherent, fairly detailed description"	Dement and Kleitman (1957)
91	69%	99	34%	"a dream recalled in some detail"	Goodenough et al. (1959)
20	60%	30	3%	self-definition by each subject	Jouvet et al. (1960)
67	85%	21	24%	self-definition by each subject	Wolpert (1960)
108	87%	136	74%	"any item of specific content"	Foulkes (1962)
108	82%	136	54%	"visual, auditory, or kinesthetic imagery"	Foulkes (1962)
186	86%	96	23%	"specific content of mental experience"	Rechtschaffen et al. (1963)
108	81%	134	7%	"any sensory imagery with . . . progression of the mental activity"	Kales et al. (1967)
46	74%	150	58%	"a DF rating of at least 2"	Larson and Foulkes (1969)
84	95%	84	8%	"fragmentary reports with little content"	Castaldo and Shevrin (1970)

Source: From Freemon, F. R., *Sleep Research: A Critical Review,* 1972. Courtesy of Charles C Thomas, Publisher, Springfield, Illinois.

authors, along with the accompanying dream frequency during S sleep ("Nonrem") and D sleep ("Rem"). Note that the definitions that stress a narration or progression show the largest difference between S and D sleep   (See **TABLE 14.1.**)

Some of the most terrifying nightmares occur during S sleep, in stages 3 and 4 (Fisher, Byrne, Edwards, and Kahn, 1970). As is typical of mental activity during S sleep, the people do not report a storylike dream as they generally do after D sleep dreaming, but rather a situation, such as being crushed or suffocated. Often, when they awaken, they cannot even remember what frightened them.

WHY DO WE SLEEP?   THE EFFECTS OF SLEEP DEPRIVATION

Sleepiness: An Insistent Drive

We all know how insistent the urge to sleep can be, and how uncomfortable we feel when we have to resist it and stay awake.   If we are engaged in a boring activity, the task is even more difficult. Stossel (1970) found that up to 50 percent of the class found the urge to sleep irresistible during a particularly dull morning class in a medical school, and Pauker (1970) even found cases of neck injury (whiplash) caused when a student's nodding head was suddenly snapped upright. (I hope this does not encourage students to sue their professor for injury.) The loss of muscle tonus during D sleep caused the head to fall forward, only to be snapped back reflexively. The urgent and insistent nature of sleepiness suggests that sleep is a necessity of life. If this is true, then it should be possible to deprive people of sleep and (following the same logic that underlies brain lesion studies) see what capacities are disrupted. We should then be able to infer the role that sleep plays.

We all know that there is a difference between sleepiness and tiredness. We might want to rest after tennis or a vigorous swim, but the feeling is quite different from the sleepiness we feel at the end of a day—a sleepiness that occurs even if we have been relatively inactive. What we must do in order to study the role of sleep, as opposed to the restorative function of rest, is to rest without sleeping. Unfortunately, that is not possible. When Kleitman first began studying sleep in the early 1920's, he hoped to have subjects undress and lie quietly in bed. They would remain awake, however, so that it would be possible to observe the effects of "pure" sleep deprivation. It did not work. People cannot stay awake without engaging in physical activity, no matter how hard they try. So Kleitman had to contend with the fact that his subjects were rest-deprived as well as sleep-deprived.

Kleitman observed that his subjects did not show a steady progression of sleepiness throughout the deprivation period (Kleitman, 1963). They were sleepiest at night, but they recovered considerably during the day. After two sleepless days there did not appear to be any significant increase in sleepiness; there continued to be a cycle of sleepiness, with the worst period occurring at night, but Kleitman noted that after 62–65 hours a person "was as sleepy as he was likely to be."

The amazing thing about these sleep-deprived subjects was how well they could perform, so long as the tasks were short. Prolonged, boring tasks were difficult to do. If the subjects were properly motivated, their performance on short tasks was as good as that of rested subjects.

SLEEP DEPRIVATION AND PERSONALITY DISORDERS. Personality changes are sometimes seen during sleep deprivation, and during the Korean War many American servicemen were induced to sign false

Why Do We Sleep? The Effects of Sleep Deprivation

399

confessions by means of techniques that included sleep deprivation. A famous case that occurred in 1959 lent further support to the belief that sleep deprivation would produce psychotic reactions. Peter Tripp, a New York disc jockey, stayed awake for 200 hours as a publicity stunt to raise money for charity. He made his broadcasts from a glass booth in view of the public, and he was attended at all times, to prevent surreptitious sleep. He developed a severe paranoid psychosis, and believed that he was being poisoned. His suspicion became so marked that he could not even be tested during the later stages of sleep deprivation (Dement, 1972).

However, a subsequent case (reported by Gulevich, Dement, and Johnson, 1966) showed that personality changes did not necessarily occur as a result of sleep deprivation. Randy Gardner, a 17-year-old boy, stayed awake for 264 hours (so that he could find a place in the *Guinness Book of World Records*). He found it difficult to stay awake and had to engage in physical activity. He beat Dr. Dement at 100 straight games on a baseball machine in a penny arcade during the final night of sleeplessness, which suggests that his coordination was unimpaired. (I have no idea how well Dr. Dement plays this game.) After this ordeal, Randy Gardner slept for a little under 15 hours and awoke feeling fine. He slept a normal 8 hours the following night. At no time did Randy exhibit any psychotic symptoms.

The results of this observation suggest that the psychotic symptoms sometimes seen during sleep deprivation result from the stress produced by the deprivation and not from the lack of some basic function carried out by sleep. Presumably the general mental and physical health of the subject (and the conditions under which the sleep deprivation occurs) determines whether the stress will produce psychotic reactions. The servicemen in prisoner-of-war camps in Korea were certainly in an environment different from the one Randy Gardner was in.

SLEEP-DEPRIVATION STUDIES WITH ANIMALS. Sleep-deprivation studies with animals have provided us with no more insight into the role of sleep than have the human studies. The fact that animals cannot be "persuaded" to stay awake makes it even more difficult to separate the effects of sleep deprivation from the effects produced by the method by which the animal is kept awake. We can ask a human volunteer to try to stay awake, and expect some cooperation. He will say, "I'm getting sleepy—help me to stay awake." The animal, however, is interested only in getting to sleep and must be constantly stimulated—and hence, stressed. Webb (1971) summarized the sleep-deprivation literature with the statement that "the effect of sleep deprivation is to make the subject fall asleep."

Selective Deprivation of D Sleep

It may seem strange to say that more is known about the effects of depriving an organism of a particular kind of sleep—D sleep—than of the effects of total sleep deprivation. This is because an organism can be selectively awakened during D sleep but be permitted to obtain S sleep. Control subjects can be awakened the same number of times, at random intervals. Thus, any differences seen as a result of this differential treatment must result from the presence or lack of D sleep.

THE REBOUND PHENOMENON. An early report on the effects of D sleep deprivation (Dement, 1960) noted that as the deprivation progressed, the subject had to be awakened more frequently; the "pressure" to enter D sleep built up. Furthermore, after several days of D-deprivation the subject would show a "rebound" phenomenon when permitted to sleep normally; a much greater percentage of the recovery night was spent in D sleep than would normally occur. These phenomena were subsequently replicated many times. The study also reported anxiety and irritability, and an impaired ability to concentrate. However, later studies (including investigations by Dement and his colleagues) found no such changes, in either humans or animals. Cats have been deprived of D sleep for 70 days, and humans for 16 days, without any major impairment in psychological functions (Dement, 1972).

Some of the phenomena that normally occur only during D sleep will "escape" during D sleep deprivation and occur during S sleep, or even during waking. Penile erections begin to occur during S sleep, for example (Fisher, 1966). The D sleep of animals is characterized by brief, phasic bursts of electrical activity found in the pons, lateral geniculate nucleus, and visual (occipital) cortex (Brooks and Bizzi, 1963). These *PGO waves* are often the first manifestations of D sleep in cats. Whether or not humans also have PGO waves is not known, since their measurement would require the introduction of depth electrodes into the brain—and curiosity is not a good enough reason for such a procedure. Dement, Ferguson, Cohen, and Barchas (1969) found that PGO waves, normally restricted to D sleep, occur during most S sleep and waking after D sleep deprivation. It is quite possible that some of the functions normally accomplished during D sleep are transferred to other times when D sleep deprivation is attempted. Thus, the role played by D sleep may be greater than what we might infer from the missing functions that result from its (only partial) absence.

Why Do We Sleep? The Effects of Sleep Deprivation

401

EMOTIONAL CHANGES.   There do, however, appear to be some subtle impairments after D sleep deprivation.   Performance on simple verbal tasks with no emotional content is not impaired (see Greenberg and Pearlman, 1974, for a review).   However, Greiser, Greenberg, and Harrison (1972) found that D sleep deprivation impaired the recall of emotionally toned words.   Cartwright, Gore, and Weiner (1973) found that subjects who sorted a group of adjectives according to how accurately the words described themselves had a lower recall for these words if the subjects were deprived of D sleep.   Another study examined the effects of D sleep deprivation on the assimilation of anxiety-producing events.   The subjects viewed a film that generally produces anxiety in the observers (a particularly gruesome circumcision rite performed by a primitive tribe).   Normally, less anxiety is shown during the second viewing.   Greenberg, Pillard, and Pearlman (1972) found that subjects permitted to engage in D sleep between the first and second viewings of the film showed more reduction in anxiety than subjects who were deprived of D sleep.   Breger, Hunter, and Lane (1971) found that the dream content of subjects viewing the film was affected by the anxiety-producing material.   Taken together, the studies suggest that D sleep somehow assists the integration of emotional material with memories of other experiences, and allows habituation of the anxiety-producing value of the material.   This is a very fuzzy statement—especially for a textbook of physiological psychology.   Fortunately, I can discuss a similar (but more objective) conclusion based on studies with animals.

LEARNING AND CONSOLIDATION DISORDERS.   A case can be made for two types of learning process, based on the immediacy of the consequences of such learning.   Seligman (1970) speaks of *prepared* and *unprepared* learning.   A rat is *prepared* to learn the whereabouts of food or water; the animal quickly learns to run through a maze for such primary reinforcement (if hungry or thirsty, of course).   An example of *unprepared* learning is given by the fact that most animals show faster learning (for food or water reinforcement) if they have previously been allowed to wander through the maze, in a food-and water-sated condition, and with both of these substances absent. The rat learns something about the layout of the maze in the absence of any obvious drive or reward.   When later made hungry or thirsty and trained to traverse the maze in order to receive the appropriate reinforcement, the rat makes use of what it previously learned.   (The phenomenon is called *latent learning*.)   D sleep deprivation abolished latent learning in this situation; the only rats that profit from wandering through the maze prior to training for primary reinforcement are the ones permitted to get some D sleep (Pearlman, 1971).

Another situation for which the rat is "unprepared" is a two-way avoidance task. The animal is required to avoid a foot shock by running to the opposite side of a two-chambered box each time a stimulus is presented. This is a difficult task for a rat, since it requires the animal to run toward a location where it has just been shocked. Deprivation of D sleep retards the acquisition of such learning (across days), but has little or no effect on one-way avoidance learning (Pearlman and Greenberg, 1973; Joy and Prinz, 1969). A rat is "prepared" for one-way avoidance learning; it need only learn the location of a safe place, which is very quickly accomplished.

As we shall see in chapter 19, memories seem to exist in two forms—a temporary phase (during which the memories can be disrupted by such disturbances as brain seizures) and a long-term, stable phase. Fishbein (1971) found that D sleep deprivation severely retarded the process by which memories were transferred into long-term storage; the memories remained in the fragile state for a considerable period of time. Furthermore, human patients with *Korsakoff's syndrome* (a disease caused by brain damage and characterized by inability to transfer short-term memories into long-term storage) spend less time in D sleep than would be expected (Greenberg, Mayer, Brook, Pearlman, and Hartmann, 1968).

The general results of D sleep deprivation seem to be characterized by difficulty in the assimilation of threatening material and in the learning of incidental or unusual material ("unprepared" learning). The process of fixation of a memory (or *consolidation*, as it is usually called) into long-term storage is also retarded.

Selective Deprivation of S Sleep

Since S sleep normally precedes D sleep, it is not possible selectively to deprive an organism of S sleep alone. What can be done is to deprive an organism of stage 4 sleep. A buzzer (loud enough to lighten sleep, but not loud enough to awaken) can be sounded whenever the EEG record becomes dominated by synchronous delta waves. The procedure seems effective; people deprived of stage 4 sleep show a rebound phenomenon—they engage in more of this type of sleep when permitted to sleep normally (Agnew, Webb, and Williams, 1964). No severe deficits appear to follow deprivation of stage 4 (the deepest stage of S sleep); at the most, some physical lethargy and depression is seen (Agnew, Webb, and Williams, 1967). The results suggest (but *only* suggest) that S sleep might best be described as "sleep as rest"—a physical restoration after the wear-and-tear of a period of waking. D sleep, on the other hand, appears to have more of an intellectual or emotional function.

Why Do We Sleep? The Effects of Sleep Deprivation

403

The Effects of Behavior on Sleep

The results of sleep deprivation experiments have only hinted at the functions of sleep. Another way to approach the problem is to find out what environmental variables might affect sleep. In other words, if we find out that the amount of some stage of sleep depends upon the amount of time we spend at some activity during the preceding day, then perhaps we might get some insight into what it is that particular stage of sleep is doing. Furthermore, we might examine a person's life-style and personality and see whether they correlate with sleep patterns (the problem here is that we do not know whether the sleep patterns are responsible for differences in personality, or vice versa).

Before I present the evidence, let me state the hypothesis: D sleep is important in the cross-indexing of information. Cross-indexing is a metaphorical term, of course. Literally, it refers to a process of recording the relationship of an item to other items (which may or may not themselves be related). Our memories appear to be interrelated, or cross-indexed, in some way. If we recall some memory, other related memories are usually retrieved with it. Memories are seen in the context of other memories. Take a good mystery story as an example. The author slips in dozens of clues throughout the book. Let us assume that you do not figure out who committed the crime, and, just before the culprit is revealed, your memory for the clues is tested. Chances are good that you do not remember too many of them. Suppose you find out who the criminal is and how the clues point to his or her guilt. Now, with a context, you are much more likely to remember the details if you are tested later. When the pieces of information are related to one another, they are much easier to retrieve.

Now let me see if I can explain what I mean by cross-indexing. Greenberg and Pearlman (1974) speak of the importance of D sleep in learning tasks for which the animal is "unprepared." Hartmann (1973) says that D sleep is necessary for reprogramming oneself, for integrating new information that does not relate to present memories or that is at variance with one's prior conceptions. These processes would seem to involve the linking of the new information with the old, and perhaps rearranging some of the relationships about the old memories. For example, imagine the reprogramming that went on in Oedipus' brain when he learned that his wife was his mother! A phenomenal number of memories now had to be viewed in a completely different context. I have no doubt but that his nights were full of dreams, derived from these memories.

Even the fact that D sleep deprivation delays consolidation of memories into long-term storage might be accounted for by the cross-indexing hypothesis. It has been argued (and this point will be considered in chapter 19) that one of the essentials of the consolidation process is a cross-indexing of memories, and this cross-indexing is necessary for later retrieval.

Now for some evidence. Hartmann and his colleagues (summarized in Hartmann, 1973) placed newspaper ads for males over 20 years of age who slept either an unusually short or unusually long time each night. After eliminating people who made up for a short sleeping time at night with naps during the day, and people who complained of insomnia, they were left with men who *needed* either a little or a lot of sleep. They looked at the personality variables of the subjects and tried to see whether they differed according to their sleep requirements. One of their first observations was that the major difference in sleep time was in D sleep; both groups spent nearly the same amount of time in S sleep. This lucky fact means that the personality variables could be related, in particular, to D sleep (which almost everyone—lay person and sleep scientist—finds more interesting than S sleep).

Let me quote Hartmann's conclusions:

> The short sleepers as a group were efficient, energetic, ambitious persons who tended to work hard and to keep busy. They were relatively sure of themselves, socially adept, decisive, and were satisfied with themselves and their lives. They had few complaints either about the study, about their life situations, or about politics and the state of the world. Their social and political views were somewhat conformist, and they wished to appear very normal and "all-American." They were extroverted and definitely were not "worriers"; they seldom left themselves time to sit down and think about problems—in fact, several of them, on being asked what they did in times of stress or worry, made statements such as "I never let my worries go to my head." They seemed relatively free from psychopathology; but insofar as there was pathology, it consisted of a tendency to avoid problems by keeping busy and by denial, which in some cases approached hypomania.
>
> The long sleepers were a less easily definable group than the short sleepers. They worked at a large range of employments; several of them were "eternal students"; and they tended to be nonconformist and critical in their social and political views. The long sleepers were more uncomfortable in many ways than the short sleepers; they complained about the laboratory. Although none of them were seriously ill psychiatrically, most had mild or moderate neurotic problems. Some were overtly anxious, some showed considerable inhibition in aggressive and sexual functioning, and some were mildly depressed. They appeared, in general, not very sure of themselves, their career choices, or their lifestyles; however, several appeared to be artistic and creative persons. A few were aware that they sometimes used sleep as an escape when reality was unpleasant. Most of them valued sleep highly and felt it important to obtain the proper amount of sleep every night. Overall, they were definitely "worriers" who did let their problems "go to their heads" and

Why Do We Sleep? The Effects of Sleep Deprivation

405

spent considerable time worrying over these problems. Likewise the long sleepers worried, or showed concern, about political and social issues far more than the short sleepers, who tended to shrug things off and not get involved. The long sleepers could be seen as constantly "re-programming" themselves as opposed to the relatively "preprogrammed" short sleepers. Thus definite differences were found between the two groups; in a few words, the short sleepers tended to be "nonworriers" or "preprogrammed," while the long sleepers were "worriers" or "repro-grammers." (Hartmann, 1973, pp. 64–65)

Short sleepers, then, appear to brood about things less. If a fact fits in with what they know—fine. Otherwise, it will be ignored. Long sleepers tend continuously to reassess themselves and their concepts, and hence (by Hartmann's reasoning) need a good deal of D sleep to effect these rearrangements.

Hartmann also reported the case of a laborer who entered college, in a special program for bright people with little formal education. Along with the increased intellectual effort and emotional stress went an increased need for sleep. In addition, Hartmann noted that professional people typically report a decreased sleep need upon retirement, which he attributes to a reduction in intellectual activity and a corresponding reduction in the need for D sleep. He also found that manic-depressive patients showed changes in need for D sleep that cycled with their mood. During the manic (hyperactive, compulsively cheerful) phase they required less D sleep than normal people; during the depressed phase (brooding, introspective, hypoactive) they required more. He concluded that, during the manic phase, the patient is "preprogrammed, continuing to do things in his way while pushing away or denying painful realities around him" (Hartmann, 1973, p. 91). During the depressed phase, the patients brood about their problems, their faults, and their guilt, and this requires more D sleep.

These clinical observations are, fortunately, supported by the results of experiments. McGinty (1969) found that a sterile environment decreased D sleep, whereas an enriched environment increased it. Presumably, the animals in the enriched environment had more to remember and integrate. Lucero (1970) found that rats that were trained in a maze spent more time in D sleep, while Leconte, Hennevin, and Bloch (1972) found that the amount of time spent in D sleep was related to the animal's rate of learning of an avoidance task. Lewin and Gombosh (1972) found that humans who are asked to perform peculiar, unexplained tasks require more D sleep the next night.

The functions of sleep are still far from being explained. It does seem likely that D sleep is involved in something like cross-indexing or reprogramming, but until we know what we really mean by these terms—until we learn more about memory consolidation and cognition—we will still have only vague hints about the functions of sleep.

SLEEP PATHOLOGY

Insomnia

Insomnia is a problem that affects at least 20 percent of the population at some time (Raybin and Detre, 1969), but unfortunately, little is known about its causes. William Dement says that one of the things he hopes his students will remember, if they remember nothing else from his course, is that "sleeping pills cause insomnia" (Dement, 1972). This fact, unfortunately, is not appreciated by a very large number of people (or by their physicians, either). According to Freemon (1972), "the promiscuous prescribing of sleep medications is the most common error in medicine." Solomon (1956) classes it as "perhaps the commonest of iatrogenic disorders" (*iatrogenic* means "physician-produced").

I cite these authorities to emphasize the fact that sleeping medications do not induce normal sleep. They suppress D sleep at first, but this effect later habituates—D sleep reemerges (probably because of increased activity of some compensatory mechanism). The D sleep that does reemerge is apparently different from normal D sleep; Carroll, Lewis, and Oswald (1969) found a decrease in the vividness of dreams while under the effects of barbiturates. When sleeping medications are discontinued, a large rebound of D sleep is seen; in fact, the increased D activity leads to sleeplessness and vivid nightmares (Oswald, 1968). The patient then demands more pills in order to get to sleep again.

There are two special forms of insomnia (one that might be called pseudoinsomnia) that present interesting problems. Unfortunately, some people dream that they are awake. They do not dream that they are running around in some Alice-in-Wonderland fantasy, but that they are lying in bed, trying unsuccessfully to fall asleep. In the morning, their memories are of a night of insomnia, and they feel as unrefreshed as if they had really been awake. Others might not dream of being awake, but they nevertheless grossly underestimate the amount of time actually spent asleep. As Hartmann (1973) notes, it is absolutely necessary actually to observe someone's sleep before it is possible to decide whether they get more or less sleep than normal. Fortunately, the knowledge (obtained in the sleep lab) that they are really getting enough sleep is sufficient to make some of these people feel much better.

The second type of special insomnia is rather pathetic. Some people are unable to sleep and breathe at the same time. They fall asleep and cease to breathe (they exhibit what is called *sleep apnea*). The level of carbon dioxide in the blood stimulates chemoreceptors, and the person wakes up, gasping for air. The oxygen level of the blood returns to normal, the person falls asleep, and the whole cycle begins again. Some of these people are aware of a sleep problem and complain of insomnia. Some others, who rapidly forget such awakening, complain of sleeping too much at night. Their total sleep period is prolonged by the large number of awakenings.

Although the issue has not been settled yet, many investigators believe that one of the principal causes for the *sudden infant death syndrome (SIDS)* is sleep apnea; in these cases, however, a high level of carbon dioxide in the blood fails to awaken. Occasionally, infants are found dead in their cribs, without any apparent signs of illness. It is possible that an immature nervous system, depressed by a low-grade infection, is responsible for the cessation of breathing.

Narcolepsy

This disorder is characterized by several symptoms; not all of the symptoms of *narcolepsy* (narke, "numbness"; lepsis, "seizure") need occur in one individual. Although the physiological causes for this disorder have not yet been explained, the symptoms can be described in terms of what we know about the phenomena of sleep. *Sleep attacks,* characterized by a bout of overwhelming sleepiness, can occur at any time. For some reason, they are often precipitated by strong emotion. Even laughter can trigger a sleep attack; some people with this affliction leave the room if a TV show is too amusing. According to Dement (1972), people subject to sleep attacks not infrequently fall asleep during lovemaking.

Another symptom of narcolepsy is *cataplexy* (kata, "down"; plexis, "stroke"). During a cataplectic attack an apparently normal, waking person will suddenly wilt and fall like a sack of flour. The person will lie there, conscious, for a few minutes, and then get up again. (This assumes that the fall itself does not produce an injury leading to unconsciousness.) What apparently happens to these people is that one of the phenomena of D sleep—muscular paralysis—intrudes into wakefulness. You will recall that the EMG taken during D sleep indicates a loss of muscle tonus, as a result of massive inhibition of motor neurons. When this occurs during the day, the victim of a cataplectic attack falls as suddenly as if a switch had been thrown.

D sleep paralysis sometimes intrudes into waking, but at a time that does not present any physical danger—just before normal sleep. This symptom is referred to as *sleep paralysis,* an inability to move just before the onset of sleep. Sometimes the mental component of D sleep intrudes at this time. These *hypnogogic hallucinations* are often alarming or even terrifying—an unpleasant way to fall asleep, I should think. These conclusions are supported by the observations of Rechtschaffen, Wolpert, Dement, Mitchell, and Fisher (1963), who found that narcoleptic patients generally skip the S sleep that normally begins a night's sleep; instead, they go right into D sleep from waking.

Problems Associated with S Sleep

Although you might think that sleep talking should occur during D sleep (the acting out of a dream, for example), most of it occurs during S sleep—during the deepest stage, in fact. (I suppose sleep talking should not be classified as a problem, unless you tend to give away secrets, but since it usually occurs during stage 4 sleep, this seemed to be the best place to mention it.) Bed-wetting (*nocturnal enuresis*) and sleepwalking (*somnambulism*) usually occur during stage 4 sleep, also. So do *night terrors*, a condition (seen most often in children) characterized by anguished screams, trembling, and a rapid pulse (and often no idea at all about what caused the terror). Bed-wetting often can be cured by training methods (having a bell ring when the first few drops of urine are detected in the bedsheet by a special electronic circuit—a few drops usually precede the ensuing flood). Night terrors and somnambulism usually cure themselves as the child gets older. Neither of these phenomena is related to D sleep; a sleepwalking person is *not* acting out a dream. Dement firmly advises that the best treatment for these disorders is no treatment at all. There is no evidence that they are associated with mental disorders or personality variables.

CONCLUSIONS

I have attempted to describe sleep (which is a rather straightforward task) and to summarize the evidence concerning its utility (which is considerably more difficult). I suspect you have come to conclusions similar to my own: yes, sleep seems to perform some function— perhaps to assist in cross-indexing or integration of new material into the existing storehouse of memories—but if sleepiness is such an overwhelming drive, and if it can even take precedence over hunger and sex, then why aren't its functions more obvious?

In the next chapter I shall ignore the mysterious *why* of sleep and concentrate on studies attempting to elucidate the *how* of it.

SUGGESTED READINGS

DEMENT, W. C. *Some Must Watch While Some Must Sleep.* San Francisco: W. H. Freeman, 1974.

FREEMON, F. R. *Sleep Research: A Critical Review.* Springfield, Ill.: Charles C Thomas, 1972.

HARTMANN, E. L. *The Functions of Sleep.* New Haven: Yale University Press, 1973.

WEBB, W. B. *Sleep: The Gentle Tyrant.* Englewood Cliffs, N.J.: Prentice-Hall, 1975.

Sleep is a fascinating subject; these are four of the many excellent books that have been written on this subject. The books by Dement, Hartmann, and Webb are available in paperback.

Neural Mechanisms of the Sleep-Waking Cycle

15

CHEMICAL FACTORS IN SLEEP

I think that you can predict what the earliest theories of sleep suggested—that physical and/or mental activity during the day produced some chemical that caused sleep. During sleep that chemical was destroyed. Or perhaps it went the other way around; some chemical necessary for waking got used up and had to be regenerated during sleep. Perhaps there were several substances, some of which accumulated during waking (and thus served as sleep-producing agents), and some of which (the wakefulness-maintaining agents) were used up.

The obvious way to test this possibility is to transfuse blood from one animal to another. This "experiment" has been accomplished by nature, in the form of Siamese twins with a common circulatory system. Alekseyeva (1958) reported that such twins sleep independently; there does not appear to be a common sleep-inducing factor in the blood that would put both of the twins to sleep.

Nowadays, more attention is being paid to the possibility that some chemicals involved in sleep and waking may accumulate (or be used up) in the brain itself, rather than in general circulation. This hypothesis was tested a long time ago (Piéron, 1913; Legrende and Piéron, 1913). These investigators kept dogs awake for several days. Cerebrospinal fluid was removed from these animals and was injected into the ventricular system of recipient dogs, who subsequently went to sleep for 2 to 6 hours. In 1939, Schnedorf and Ivy replicated the phenomenon, but noted that hyperthermia usually followed injections of CSF (as a result of increased intracerebral pressure), so the notion of a central sleep-producing substance fell into disrepute. More recently, however, Fencl, Koski, and Pappenheimer (1971) have shown that a sleep-promoting factor (with a molecular weight of less than 500) can be concentrated by means of selective filtration from the CSF of sleep-deprived (but not control) goats. This factor (which does not appear to be one of the neurotransmitters thought to be involved in neural sleep mechanisms) increases the duration of sleep and decreases locomotor activity, in recipient subjects. The investigators also discovered a wakefulness-promoting factor (with a molecular weight somewhere between 500 and 10,000) that produces hyperactivity in the recipient that lasts for several days. They found this factor in both control and sleep-deprived goats. Until we find out where the substances are produced and where they exert their effects, we shall not know whether these substances play a role in an animal's sleep-waking cycle. At physiological concentrations these factors might or might not affect the brain of the goat from which the fluid is taken.

Some studies have shown that, under special conditions, the brain might produce some substances that enter the blood (as opposed to the CSF) and can affect the brain activity of another animal. As we shall see later, low-frequency electrical stimulation of the midline nuclei of the thalamus produces cortical synchrony (one of the manifestations of sleep). A number of studies (e.g., Monnier, Koller, and Graber, 1963) have shown that thalamic stimulation of one member of a pair of animals with surgically interconnected circulatory systems will increase the occurrence of cortical synchrony in the other member. The converse effect can also be seen; stimulation of the midbrain reticular formation (which, as we shall see, produces arousal) decreases cortical synchrony in the nonstimulated member. Monnier and Hösli (1964, 1965) were able to concentrate a substance from the cerebral blood of a thalamically stimulated rabbit that would produce this synchronizing effect in a recipient animal. However, Ringle and Herndon (1968) could not find a factor in the blood of sleep-deprived rabbits; thus, the biochemical effects of thalamic stimulation do not mimic sleep. It is possible, of course, that the thalamic stimulation causes the release of a more-than-normal amount of a substance that is really involved in sleep. It is equally possible, however, that the substance has nothing at all to do with sleep, and that it is a consequence of a very abnormal situation—electrical stimulation of the brain.

One other systemic chemical (as opposed to a local one, such as a neurotransmitter) has been found to vary across the sleep-waking cycle, and also to exert effects on sleep; this is the hormone *melatonin*. This substance is produced principally by the pineal gland (Lerner, Case, Takahashi, Lee, and Mori, 1958), an organ situated on the top of the midbrain, between the superior colliculi. Melatonin also appears to be produced in the hypothalamus (Koslow, 1974), and hypothalamic implants of melatonin produce sleep (Marczynski, Yamaguchi, Ling, and Grodzinska, 1964).

Cramer, Rudolph, Consbruch, and Kendel (1974) injected melatonin into human subjects and found that the subjects fell asleep in 55 percent of the time it took to fall asleep after control injections. The subsequent stages of S and D sleep were identical to those normally seen; Figure 15.1 shows that the latency to sleep (dotted lines below the horizontal line denoting the onset of sleep) was the only measure affected by melatonin injections. (See **FIGURE 15.1.**) A battery of personality tests and tests designed to measure the refreshing effects of sleep indicated no significant effects of melatonin. At this point, we have no idea whether melatonin might play a role in sleep. If it does, the role is undoubtedly minor.

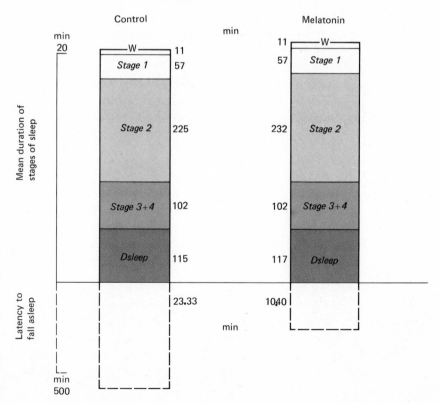

FIGURE 15.1 The effects of melatonin on the latency to fall asleep. Note that the various stages of sleep are unaffected by melatonin. (From Cramer, H., Rudolph, J., Consbruch, U., and Kendel, K., *Advances in Biochemical Psychopharmacology*, 1974, 11, 187–191.)

Many other studies have investigated the role of various chemicals in sleep, but since they are concerned with neurotransmitters and local (rather than systemic) effects, these studies will be covered in a later section.

SLEEP AS AN ACTIVE PROCESS

We can very quickly dispense with the notion that the brain sleeps because it "runs down." There do not appear to be any neurons that get tired (e.g., run out of energy stores for the sodium-potassium pump or deplete the supply of the neurotransmitter) and consequently need a period of sleep in which to rest. Moruzzi (1972) reviewed electrophysiological data that show that neurons in the neocortex, lateral geniculate nucleus, reticular formation, and hypothalamus generally decrease their rate of firing during S sleep, but during D sleep fire as fast as (or faster than) they do during wakefulness. Neurons in motor cortex, for example, fire more often during sleep than during wakefulnss, except when a motor movement is in progress (Evarts, 1965). Other units (such as those of the hippocampus) show a low rate of firing during D sleep. The point to be made is that there is not a *universal* decline in firing rate during sleep.

Effects of Brainstem Transections

Bremer (1937), in an investigation of neural sleep mechanisms, severed the brainstem of a cat between the superior and inferior colliculi. The cat survived for only a few days and showed a permanently synchronized EEG and pupillary constriction. The effects of this *midcollicular transection* (which Bremer called a *cerveau isolé*) are shown in **FIGURE 15.2.**

A transection made at the caudal end of the medulla, just above the spinal cord (the *encéphale isolé* preparation), produced a cat that demonstrated normal sleep and waking cycles. The animal was para-

Cat is comatose

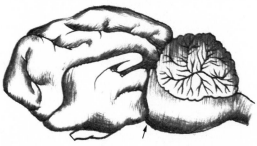

FIGURE 15.2 The cerveau isolé. (From Bremer, F., *Bulletin de l'Academie Royale de Belgique*, 1937, 4, 68–86.)

lyzed, of course, since the brain and spinal cord were disconnected, so waking could not be evaluated in the normal fashion. However, the EEG showed periodic episodes of desynchronized and synchronized activity. During desynchrony, the cat's pupils were dilated, and the eyes followed a moving object. During synchrony, the pupils were constricted, while the eyes showed no reaction to visual stimuli. Therefore, the animal apparently slept and woke in alternate fashion. Figure 15.3 shows the location of the brainstem section and the arousing effects of the cat's having its head handled by the experimenter (in an *encéphale isolé*, the trigeminal nerve, which conveys somatosensory information from the head region, is intact). (See **FIGURE 15.3.**)

Bremer believed that the difference in the arousability of these two preparations could be accounted for by the different amounts of sensory input that could be received by the cerebrum. He believed that the brain was normally inactive, and that it took the tonically arousing effects of sensory stimulation to keep the brain awake. The *encéphale isolé* had all its cranial nerve inputs intact. The midcollicular section, however, isolated the cerebrum from all sensory input except for olfaction and vision (since the other cranial nerves enter the brain caudal to the plane of transection).

This conclusion was clearly shown to be wrong by the experiments of Batini, Moruzzi, Palestini, Rossi, and Zanchetti (1958, 1959a, 1959b), who cut through the midbrain a few millimeters caudal to the midcollicular transection of Bremer. This operation (a *midpontine, pretrigeminal transection*) produced a cat with insomnia; the EEG and ocular signs indicated wakefulness 70 to 90 percent of the time (as opposed to the 30 to 40 percent seen in a normal cat). These animals had exactly the same sensory input as did Bremer's cats with the midcollicular section (the *cerveau isolé*). They showed definite wakefulness, however. Furthermore, if the remaining sensory inputs were removed (Batini et al., 1959b), the animal continued to exhibit signs of wakefulness (after a transient period of EEG synchrony).

Midpontine cats (as these animals are called), like *encéphale isolé* cats, will (during periods of cortical desynchrony) follow an object with their eyes, show pupillary dilation when a visual stimulus

FIGURE 15.3 The encéphale isolé. (From Bremer, F., *Bulletin de l'Academie Royale de Belgique*, 1937, 4, 68–86.)

Asleep

Awake

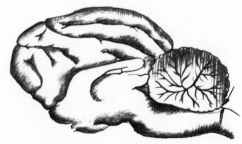

is presented, and show accommodation (adjustment of the lens of the eye) to a near object.   When cortical synchrony is observed, however, visual stimuli have no effect.   The responses also show signs of habituation; a repetitive stimulus, after a while, fails to elicit any ocular responses (perhaps even a midpontine cat can get bored).   Affanni, Marchiafava, and Zernicki (1962) found that these cats could be conditioned; if photic stimulation (which does not produce pupillary dilation) regularly preceded hypothalamic stimulation (which does), the photic stimulation alone eventually elicited the pupillary response.   And Maffei, Moruzzi, and Rizzolatti (1965) showed that the rate of firing of units in the lateral geniculate nucleus was modulated by a flickering light only when cortical desynchrony was seen; during synchrony the units fired randomly.   However, retinal ganglion cells responded to the stimulus at all times, showing that the effect seen in the lateral geniculate nucleus was not produced by some peripheral artifact.   It thus appears to be safe to conclude that midpontine cats demonstrate sleep and waking cycles.   The phenomenon is shown very vividly in **FIGURE 15.4.**

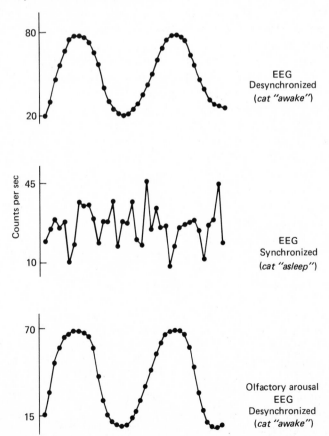

FIGURE 15.4   Single units in the lateral geniculate nucleus fire in response to a flickering stimulus only when a midpontine cat is "awake." (From Maffei, L., Moruzzi, G., and Rizzolatti, G., *Archives Italiennes de Biologie*, 1965, 103, 596–608.)

Three conclusions can be based on these studies:

1. There is a brain region between the midcollicular section of Bremer and the midpontine section of Batini et al. that is important in producing wakefulness. (The rostral section disconnects the cerebrum from this region, whereas the midpontine section does not.)

2. There is a sleep-producing region that lies somewhere between the midpontine section and the rostral part of the medulla—the *encéphale isolé* section of Bremer. (Animals with the midpontine cut show very little sleep, whereas those with the caudal cut show normal sleep-waking cycles.)

3. The brain does not need sensory input in order to show signs of wakefulness. (The midpontine section and the cerveau isolé produce the same effects on sensory input, and de-afferentation of the midpontine animal does not produce permanent sleep.)

These results are summarized in **FIGURE 15.5.**

It would appear, then, that some rostral pontine region is necessary for waking, and some caudal pontine (and/or medullary) region is necessary for sleep. However, some evidence suggests that there is more to the story than that. Some investigators (notably Giuseppe Moruzzi, of Pisa, Italy) believe that there are diencephalic structures that are also involved in sleep and wakefulness, while others (notably Michel Jouvet, of Lyons, France) believe they are not. First we shall examine the evidence concerning (undisputed) midbrain

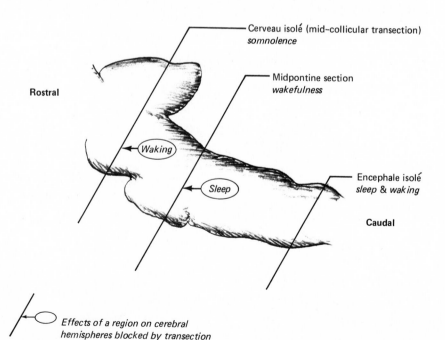

Cerveau isolé (mid–collicular transection)
somnolence

Midpontine section
wakefulness

Rostral

Waking

Sleep

Encephale isolé
sleep & waking

Caudal

FIGURE 15.5   A schematic summary of the results of the three brainstem transections.

Effects of a region on cerebral hemispheres blocked by transection

and hindbrain sleep mechanisms, and then the (disputed) diencephalic mechanisms.

BRAINSTEM MECHANISMS

Magni, Moruzzi, Rossi, and Zanchetti (1959) tied off some cerebral blood vessels so that the arterial blood supply to the medulla and lower pons was separated from the blood supply to the upper pons and cerebrum. (See **FIGURE 15.6.**) Injections of *thiopental* (a general anesthetic) into the blood supply of the rostral pons and cerebrum anesthetized the cat (an unsurprising fact). However, when only the caudal brainstem was anesthetized, the cat woke up (if it had been sleeping). A sleeping (synchronous) EEG was replaced by an aroused (desynchronous) EEG. The conclusion is this: There must be some region in the caudal brainstem whose activity is necessary to put an animal to sleep. When the activity of this region is temporarily suppressed (by thiopental), the sleeping brain awakens.

The brainstem has been implicated in arousal mechanisms for a long time. In 1949, Moruzzi and Magoun found that electrical stimulation of the brainstem reticular formation would produce arousal. The reticular formation, in the core of the brainstem, is known to receive collaterals from ascending sensory pathways. Lindsley, Schreiner, Knowles, and Magoun (1950) produced lesions that dis-

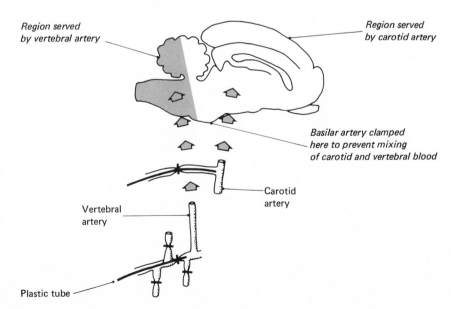

Region served by vertebral artery

Region served by carotid artery

Basilar artery clamped here to prevent mixing of carotid and vertebral blood

Carotid artery

Vertebral artery

Plastic tube

FIGURE 15.6 The procedure of Magni et al., which allowed the injection of an anesthetic into different regions of the brain. (From Magni, F., Moruzzi, G., Rossi, G. N., and Zanchetti, A., *Archives Italiennes de Biologie*, 1959, 97, 33–46.)

rupted the lateral sensory pathways (medial and lateral lemniscus, and trigeminal lemniscus). Tactile stimulation of these subjects produced long-lasting arousal. Since the lateral lesions destroyed the direct sensory pathways (which go to thalamus, and thence to sensory cortex), the arousal was obviously mediated via the reticular formation. Although the animals presumably could not "feel" the stimulation, they nevertheless were aroused by it. If medial lesions were produced (destroying the reticular formation), only a very transient arousal was produced by sensory stimulation. (See **FIGURE 15.7**.) It appears, then, that the reticular formation of the brainstem plays a role in arousal.

Brainstem Arousal Mechanisms

THE DOPAMINERGIC SYSTEM OF SUBSTANTIA NIGRA. There is evidence for two distinct arousal mechanisms situated in the brainstem: a dopaminergic system and a noradrenergic system. According to

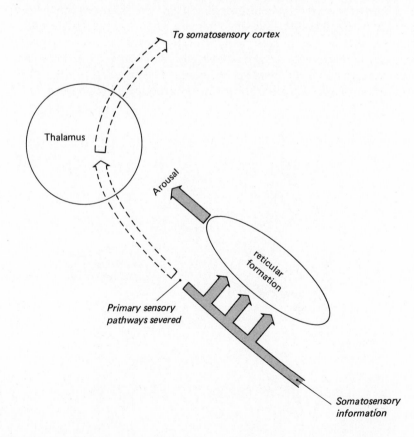

FIGURE 15.7 A schematic representation of the experiment by Lindsley et al. (1950).

Jouvet (1972), there is a system of dopaminergic neurons (whose cell bodies lie in the substantia nigra) that contributes to behavioral arousal. Lesions that destroy the substantia nigra (and also damage the ventral noradrenergic bundle) result in a temporarily or permanently comatose state; the cats remain stuporous and behaviorally unresponsive to sensory stimuli (Jones, 1969; Jones, Bobillier, and Jouvet, 1969). The location of these structures is shown in **FIGURE 15.8.** In the animals that remained permanently comatose, the level of dopamine in the rostral brain was reduced by 90 percent, attesting to the effectiveness of the lesion in disrupting this system. Sensory stimulation produced long-lasting cortical desynchrony without any signs of behavioral arousal. However, lesions of the substantia nigra in rats (as opposed to cats) do not severely affect behavioral arousal; Simpson and Iversen (1971) found that the animals actually increased their activity. The significance of the dopaminergic system in behavioral arousal thus remains doubtful.

Furthermore, when an animal lies in a stuporous state, and yet exhibits electroencephalographic signs of alternating sleep and waking cycles and of desynchrony in response to sensory stimulation, one might question whether an arousal system has really been impaired. After all, Parkinson's disease (which results from damage to the dopaminergic cells of the substantia nigra) is characterized by progressive immobility, along with a tremor at rest. Patients who receive anti-dopaminergic drugs to combat schizophrenia also frequently show signs of hypoactivity and a particular lack of facial expressivity. It would appear to be more reasonable to conclude that the dopaminergic system is involved in the initiation of movements. Its destruction does not, by this reasoning, result in unconsciousness, but rather in

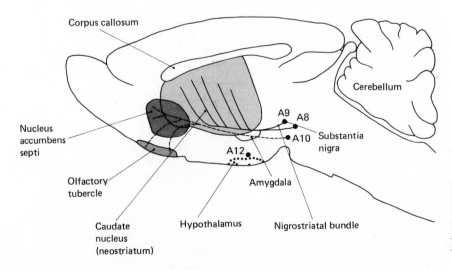

FIGURE 15.8 The pathways followed by dopaminergic neurons in the rat brain. (Redrawn from Livett, B., *British Medical Bulletin*, 1973, 29, 93–99.)

the cessation of movement. The absence of a deficit in rats with lesions of the substantia nigra suggests that the motor system in these two species (rats and cats) might be organized differently.

THE NORADRENERGIC SYSTEM OF LOCUS COERULEUS.   There also appears to be a noradrenergic system involved in sleep. This system arises mainly from the rostral portion of *locus coeruleus*, a structure in the pons. (See **FIGURE 15.9.**) Amphetamine, a potent stimulant, facilitates the release of dopamine and norepinephrine and retards the re-uptake of these neurotransmitters by the terminals. Thus, this drug acts as a very effective stimulator of catecholaminergic neurons. Amphetamine injections produce several hours of arousal and sleeplessness. The effects can be blocked by *α-methyl-para-tyrosine* (AMPT), which blocks biosynthesis of norepinephrine and dopamine.

The activating effects of amphetamine appear to be produced in the pontine-midbrain reticular formation; injections of amphetamine have no effect on activity levels after lesions are made in this region (Fujimori and Himwich, 1969). Furthermore, injections of amphetamine into the vertebral artery have no effect if the basilar artery is tied off at the midpontine level (restricting the drug to the caudal pons and medulla), according to van Meter and Ayala (1961). Thus, we can rule out caudal brainstem mechanisms in amphetamine-produced arousal.

If a lesion is made in the dorsal noradrenergic bundle (interrupting the axons from the neurons of the rostral locus coeruleus), the animals show hypersomnia; D sleep and S sleep increase dramatically (Jones, Bobillier, and Jouvet, 1969). Thus, there is good evidence

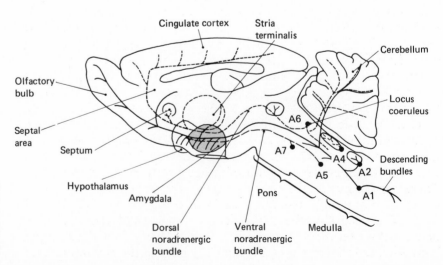

FIGURE 15.9   The pathways followed by noradrenergic neurons in the rat brain. (Redrawn from Livett, B., *British Medical Bulletin*, 1973, *29*, 93–99.)

that the dorsal noradrenergic bundle is involved in arousal (or in the suppression of sleep).

Stimulation of this region produces arousal; indeed, when Moruzzi and Magoun (1949) stimulated the reticular formation, their electrodes were very near the dorsal noradrenergic bundle. The effects of electrical stimulation are not very localized, however, so it is impossible to say with any certainty that this system mediates the arousing effects produced by stimulation of the reticular formation.

Brainstem Sleep Mechanisms

As we saw earlier (from the insomnia produced by the midpontine section and from the antisleep effects of caudal brainstem anesthesia), there appears to be a brainstem mechanism (located behind the middle of the pons) that is important for the occurrence of sleep. That structure appears to be the *raphe* (say "ruh-FAY"), a complex of nuclei running through the core of the brainstem, from the medulla to the back of the midbrain. There is also evidence suggesting a deactivating role for the nucleus of the *solitary tract,* a structure located in the medulla, which receives taste information and visceral sensation. Finally, the caudal two-thirds of the locus coeruleus and cells of the *FTG* (another region of the pons) appear specifically to be involved in D sleep.

The Raphe. Figure 15.10 shows the location of the raphe in a midsagittal section through the brainstem; you can see how the midpontine section separates most of the raphe from the cerebrum. (See **FIGURE 15.10.**) The transverse section in the same figure shows how this structure got its name—raphe means crease, or seam. (See **FIGURE 15.10.**) Jouvet and Renault (1966) produced large lesions that destroyed 80 to 90 percent of the raphe and observed complete insomnia for 3 to 4 days. S sleep (but not D sleep) gradually returned, but never exceeded approximately 2.5 hours per day. Smaller lesions resulted in more recovery, but D sleep did not reappear until S sleep totalled approximately 3.5 hours per day. Attempts have been made to produce sleep by electrically stimulating the raphe, but results have been mixed; some investigators (e.g., Gumulka, Samanin, Valzelli, and Consolo, 1971) have met with success, while others (e.g., Polc and Monnier, 1966) produced *arousal* with raphe stimulation. These conflicting results probably say more about the vagaries of electrical stimulation than about the functions of the raphe.

The nuclei of the raphe are rich in cells that contain the neurotransmitter 5-HT (serotonin). Jouvet (1968) found that raphe lesions depressed cerebral levels of 5-HT, and that the amount of time

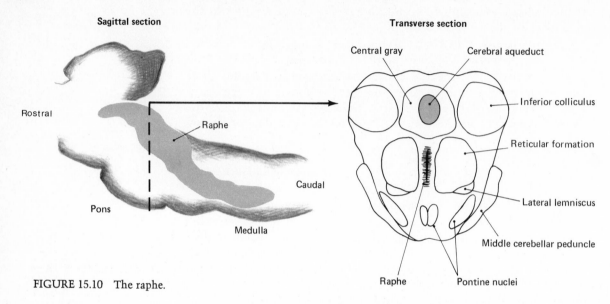

Sagittal section

Transverse section

Rostral

Raphe

Pons

Medulla

Caudal

Central gray

Cerebral aqueduct

Inferior colliculus

Reticular formation

Lateral lemniscus

Middle cerebellar peduncle

Raphe

Pontine nuclei

FIGURE 15.10   The raphe.

the animals spent sleeping correlated with the amount of 5-HT present in the brain (decreases in 5-HT being associated with decreases in sleep). Furthermore, administration of a single dose of *para-chloro-phenylalanine* (PCPA), which suppresses biosynthesis of 5-HT, also suppressed sleep. Figure 15.12 shows the effects of PCPA on the brain levels of 5-HT and on sleep; note that the percentage of sleep (top curve) and the percentage of 5-HT (bottom curve) both drop at approximately 16 hours after the injection and show a parallel recovery course. (See **FIGURE 15.11.**)

Brain levels of 5-HT can be restored after treatment with PCPA by injecting 5-HTP, the immediate precursor of 5-HT. Figure 15.12 shows the biosynthetic pathway for 5-HT and shows how PCPA blocks, but 5-HTP restores, production of 5-HT. (See **FIGURE 15.12.**) It would be much more straightforward, of course, to inject 5-HT itself, but this substance does not cross the blood-brain barrier, whereas 5-HTP will. Insomnia produced by an injection of PCPA can be quickly reversed (sleep is reinstated) by an injection of 5-HTP (Pujol, Buguet, Froment, Jones, and Jouvet, 1971).

Unfortunately, the story becomes complicated when PCPA is administered chronically. When a cat is given daily injections of PCPA, the insomnia eventually disappears; both D sleep and S sleep return to approximately 70 percent of their normal levels (Dement, Mitler, and Henriksen, 1972). This occurs despite a chronically depressed (by 90 percent) level of 5-HT. (See **FIGURE 15.13.**) Some investigators have suggested that there is some small pool of 5-HT that somehow escapes the effects of PCPA, or that homeostatic mechan-

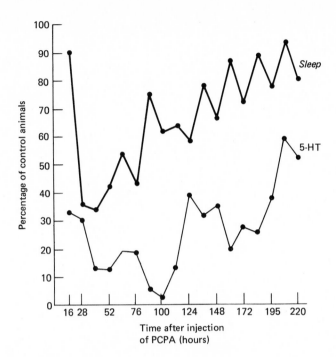

FIGURE 15.11 Effects of a single injection of PCPA on sleep and the amount of 5-HT in the brain. (From Mouret, J. R., Bobillier, P., and Jouvet, M., *European Journal of Pharmacology*, 1968, 5, 17–22.)

isms cause the production of sleep by other means, or that the cerebral neurons that are stimulated by the 5-HT-containing terminals become more sensitive to the transmitter. These explanations are not very convincing; as King (1974) notes, acceptance of these explanations means that one must assume that sleep disappears because "brain 5-HT is depleted, but . . . returns because brain 5-HT is *not* depleted."

We cannot discount the role of 5-HT in sleep, however. Although sleep returns to a cat that receives injections of PCPA every day, the phasic effects of D sleep (PGO waves, muscular twitches, rapid eye movements) "escape" and begin to intrude during S sleep

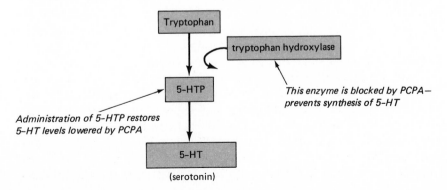

FIGURE 15.12 Biosynthesis of 5-HT and the effects of PCPA.

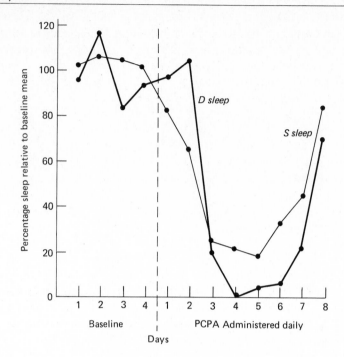

FIGURE 15.13 Effects of daily administration of PCPA on sleep. (From Dement, W., Mitler, M., and Henriksen, S., *Revue Canadienne de Biologie*, 1972, 31, 239–246.)

and even during waking (Henriksen, Dement, and Barchas, 1974). Even when sleep is suppressed, the cats show this phasic activity. They have sudden attacks of "hallucinatory episodes"; the animals jump and exhibit emotional behavior, such as snarling and hissing. We cannot determine whether the cat is really having a hallucination—all we can say is that if the cat were to have one, the animal would probably act the way it is observed to. Dement and his colleagues believe that these episodes are very disturbing to the cat, and that they are what keeps the 5-HT depleted animal awake. After a few days the animal becomes habituated to these attacks and manages to sleep.

The best evidence at this time suggests that 5-HT neurons (probably in the rostral raphe) are involved in restricting PGO spikes (and the other phasic phenomena) to D sleep. But the raphe obviously is involved in a general sleep mechanism, since its destruction produces long-lasting insomnia. The lesions must destroy many kinds of neurons (besides those which produce 5-HT) and it will take much more study to determine the means by which the intact raphe produces sleep. I shall return to the role that the rostral raphe appears to play in the suppression of untimely PGO spikes when I discuss mechanisms of D sleep in a later section.

THE NUCLEUS OF THE SOLITARY TRACT. There is evidence for another brainstem sleep mechanism—or, at least, a synchronizing region.

This area does not produce insomnia when it is removed, but it appears to have a sleep-promoting effect when it is active (perhaps it inhibits arousal mechanisms rather than actually produce sleep).

Berlucchi, Maffei, Moruzzi, and Strata (1964) found that cooling of the medulla (which produces a temporary lesion) at the floor of the fourth ventricle produced behavioral and EEG arousal. (The cat's spinal cord was severed just below the medulla to prevent peripheral effects controlled by the medulla from indirectly producing arousal.) Figure 15.14 shows the appearance of one of these cats during sleep and during arousal produced by cooling of the medulla. (See **FIGURE 15.14.**)

Magnes, Moruzzi, and Pompeiano (1961) used low-frequency current electrically to stimulate the region of the nucleus of the solitary tract (which is located within the medulla, and which was cooled in the study by Berlucchi et al.). These investigators observed a synchronizing effect of the stimulation on the EEG. The synchrony often outlasted the stimulation. Figure 15.15 shows the effects of such stimulation on the EEG. The tick marks on the lower line represent the stimulation; note that the cortical synchrony outlasts the stimulation. (See **FIGURE 15.15, TOP.**) The lower record shows the effects of the same stimulation immediately after an arousing noise was produced; note that the electrical stimulation produced no effect in this case. (See **FIGURE 15.15, BOTTOM.**)

Bonvallet and Allen (1963) placed small transverse sections rostral to this region and found that the phasic arousal effects of electrical stimulation of the reticular formation were enhanced and prolonged. These results suggest that the region of the nucleus of the solitary tract normally exerts an inhibitory effect upon the reticular activating system.

This portion of the medulla receives sensory information from the tongue and from various internal organs. Stimulation of afferent fibers of the vagus nerve (which sends fibers to this region) produces EEG synchrony (Bonvallet and Sigg, 1958). Even slow stimulation of the skin (Roitbak, 1960) produces slow-wave activity and drowsiness. Pompeiano and Swett (1962) stimulated cutaneous nerves in unanesthetized, freely moving cats and found that repetitive, low-frequency (3–8 pulses per second) stimulation produced EEG synchrony, when the cat was in a relatively quiet state. Pompeiano and Swett (1963) subsequently found that medullary neurons responded to the cutaneous nerve stimulation that produced synchrony. However, high-intensity nerve stimulation, which produces arousal, activated neurons in the pontine and midbrain reticular formation. It would seem to be very likely that the calming effects of gentle rocking (which usually soothes a baby) are mediated by the mechanism located in the vicinity of the nucleus of the solitary tract. Perhaps we can also thus account for the fact that a large meal makes us sleepy; we

Before medullary cooling (cat is asleep)

During medullary cooling (cat is aroused)

FIGURE 15.14   Effects of medullary cooling on the arousal level of the encéphale isolé cat. (Drawings based on photographs from Berlucchi, G., Maffei, L., Moruzzi, G., and Strata, P., *Archives Italiennes de Biologie,* 1964, 102, 372–392.)

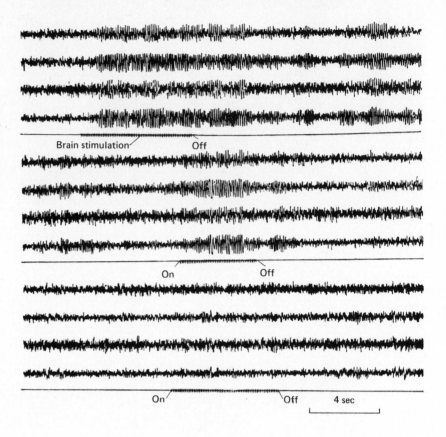

Brain stimulation — Off

On — Off

On — Off — 4 sec

FIGURE 15.15 The effects of stimulation of the region of the nucleus of the solitary tract. (From Magnes, J., Moruzzi, G., and Pompeiano, O., *Archives Italiennes de Biologie*, 1961, 99, 33–67.)

receive increased activity from afferents of the digestive tract, which stimulates the nucleus of the solitary tract.

Koella (1974) reported that evoked potentials could be recorded in the nucleus of the solitary tract after the application of brief pulses of stimulation in the midbrain reticular formation, and that the information was subsequently relayed back to the reticular formation. This evidence (along with that previously presented) suggests that the area of the nucleus of the solitary tract (an unwieldy phrase, I must admit) is capable of detecting the activity of the reticular activating system and of modulating reticular activity. The nature of this modulation depends on other factors (such as the nature of the sensory input to this region).

Modulating Effects of the Area Postrema. One very peculiar and unexplained factor that influences the region of this medullary nucleus arises in the *area postrema*. Koella found that the modulating effect of the area of the nucleus of the solitary tract upon the reticular activating system was strongly influenced by the area postrema. Depression of the area postrema (with a local anesthetic) reduced the influence of the solitary region on the reticular formation. Another substance (I'll identify it in a moment) produced the opposite effect. When applied to the area postrema, this substance enhanced the modulating effects of the solitary region upon the reticular formation. This substance, therefore, indirectly caused a depression of the activating system. This complicated mechanism is outlined in **FIGURE 15.16.**)

The area postrema lies on the blood side of the blood-brain barrier. (You will recall from chapter 2 that this structure is capable of detecting the presence of a toxin in the blood and of triggering the vomiting reflex.) So this area can also detect sleep-promoting compounds that cannot cross the blood-brain barrier. What was the substance Koella placed on the area postrema? It was 5-HT. This does *not* mean that the serotonergic raphe neurons exert an effect on the area postrema through the circulatory system. Just as 5-HT cannot enter the brain through the blood-brain barrier, this substance cannot leave it. Then what is the significance of this mechanism? We do not know. Serotonin is produced in the pineal gland and in the gastrointestinal system in quantities much greater than are found in the brain. But there is, at present, no logical way to explain why systemic 5-HT, acting on the area postrema, exerts an antiarousal effect. Perhaps the effect is incidental, and the area postrema is actually sensitive to melatonin, produced by the pineal body, which also produces a hypnotic effect. These substances are both *indolamines,* and their molecular structures are quite similar, as indicated in **FIGURE 15.17.**

To summarize: The most important sleep-producing region of the brainstem is the raphe, whose destruction leads to insomnia. The raphe contains many serotonergic neurons, and these neurons

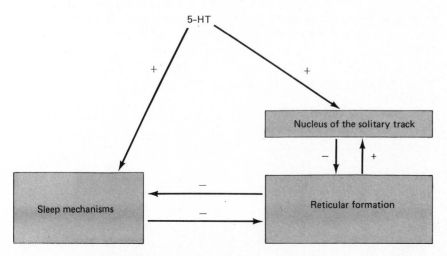

FIGURE 15.16 The hypothesized relationship between the nucleus of the solitary tract and the reticular formation. (From Koella, W. P., *Advances in Biochemical Psychopharmacology*, 1974, *11*, 181–186.)

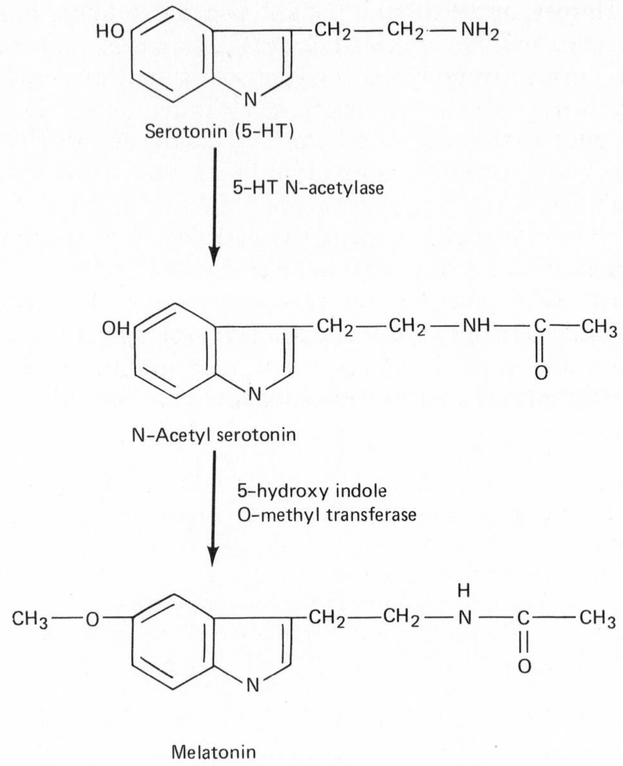

FIGURE 15.17 The chemical
structures of 5-HT and
melatonin.

may be related to sleep, but since chronic interference with 5-HT synthesis does not permanently disrupt sleep, other kinds of raphe neurons must also be involved. It appears that the serotonergic neurons
(especially of the anterior raphe) are involved in the suppression of
PGO spikes during inappropriate times, releasing this inhibition during D sleep. There also appears to be a medullary system that modulates the activating effects of the reticular formation. This system
(located in the vicinity of the nucleus of the solitary tract) is affected
by somatosensory and visceral input and by the area postrema, which
is, in turn, affected by blood-borne indolamine(s).

Brainstem Mechanisms in D Sleep

Desynchronized sleep deserves its own section, especially since so
much is known about the brainstem mechanisms that control it. As

we saw in the last section, serotonergic neurons in the rostral portion of the raphe normally suppress PGO waves, the electrophysiological indication of the event that triggers phasic components of D sleep. McGinty, Harper, and Fairbanks (1974) found that some neurons in the dorsal raphe fire at a maximal rate during waking and drastically decrease their rate during D sleep. Some of the neurons ceased firing specifically during PGO waves, whereas others remained silent during the entire bout of D sleep. Presumably, these neurons inhibit D sleep mechanisms; their silence during D sleep indicates a cessation of this inhibition.

In 1962, Jouvet reported that large lesions of the pontine reticular formation (*nucleus reticularis pontis oralis* and *nucleus reticularis pontis caudalis,* usually referred to as *rpo* and *rpc)* abolished both behavioral and electrophysiological signs of D sleep. Smaller lesions caudal to this region abolished the profound muscular inhibition that normally accompanies D sleep; as a matter of fact, the cats "acted out their dreams."

> ... to a naive observer, the cat, which is standing, looks awake since it may attack unknown enemies, play with an absent mouse, or display flight behavior. There are orienting movements of the head or eyes toward imaginary stimuli, although the animal does not respond to visual or auditory stimuli. These extraordinary episodes ... are a good argument that "dreaming" occurs during [D sleep] in the cat. . . ." (Jouvet, 1972, pp. 236–237)

Jouvet later concluded (1972) that his large lesions destroyed a number of structures, and that the locus coeruleus appeared to be the structure responsible for the occurrence of D sleep. He noted that many pharmacological manipulations that affect noradrenergic systems (the locus coeruleus is rich in noradrenergic cells) also affect D sleep. However, as Jouvet himself noted, injections of AMPT, which suppress biosynthesis of noradrenalin, do not abolish D sleep in cats (King and Jewett, 1971) or rats (Marantz and Rechtschaffen, 1967).

GIGANTOCELLULAR TEGMENTAL FIELD. It appears clear now that the locus coeruleus does *not* contain the executive mechanism that initiates D sleep; this distinction belongs to cells of the nucleus of the *gigantocellular tegmental field* (henceforth referred to as *FTG),* the currently accepted name for the area of the pons that encompasses both rpc and rpo (Berman, 1968). One of these cells is shown in a sagittal section through a rat brain; the cell body (which has many dendrites with prominent spines) is located near the letter R (the location of FTG). Note how the axon divides and sends axonic processes throughout the telencephalon, diencephalon, midbrain, and hindbrain. (See **FIGURE 15.18.**) As Scheibel and Scheibel (1961) note, 300 FTG cells (10 percent of the population of this

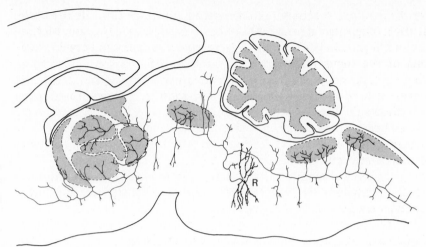

FIGURE 15.18   The extensive arborizations of an FTG neuron. (From Brazier, M. A. B., *The Electrical Activity of the Nervous System*, ed. 4. London: Pitman Medical Publishing Co., 1976.)

region) can potentially affect 9 million cells of the brainstem reticular formation (90 percent of the population of this region).   If there were ever a system whose anatomy suggested some sort of a controlling role in sleep-waking mechanisms, this is it.

We do not have to rely just on the anatomy, however.   Stimulation of this region by means of *carbachol* (a drug that provides long-lasting stimulation of cholinergic synapses) produces muscular flaccidity, cortical desynchrony, and rapid eye movements (McKenna, Mc-Carley, Amatruda, Black, and Hobson, 1974).   Furthermore, Sitaram, Wyatt, Sawson, and Gillin (1976) administered intravenous injections of *physostigmine* (a drug that inhibits AChE, and therefore increases postsynaptic activity mediated by acetylcholine) to human subjects during sleep.   If the subjects were in S sleep, the injections induced D sleep.   If the subjects were in D sleep, the injections awoke them. The authors conclude that cholinergic mechanisms might play a role in D sleep and in arousal.

Electrical recordings appear to provide the most persuasive support for the participation of pontine neurons in D sleep.   A number of studies from Hobson's laboratory at Harvard (e.g., McCarley and Hobson, 1975) have shown that there are two populations of neurons in the pontine tegmentum that fire *immediately before and during* D sleep.   These neurons provide the earliest electrophysiological signs of D sleep and appear to be the cells that initiate this state. Two populations of cells were found: *phasic cells,* which are probably responsible for PGO waves, rapid eye movements, and muscular twitches, and *tonic cells,* which are probably responsible for cortical desynchrony and muscular immobility.   The phasic cells tend to cluster in FTG itself, whereas the tonic cells are mainly found nearby, in the *central tegmental field (FTC).*

THE CYCLICITY OF D SLEEP.   The mechanism that controls the cyclicity of D sleep also appears to have been discovered. Hobson, McCarley, and Wyzinski (1975) found a reciprocal arrangement between neurons of the locus coeruleus and those of FTG. They found that whereas cells in FTG fired most rapidly during D sleep, cells in locus coeruleus fired least often then. Furthermore, the firing rate of these cells showed a reciprocal relationship during the transition between S and D sleep. Figure 15.19 shows the average firing rate (expressed as a percentage of the total number of action potentials) of locus coeruleus cells and FTG cells before and after the onset of sleep. Note how precisely the cells mirror each other; when one curve is climbing rapidly (signifying a high rate of firing), the other is climbing slowly (signifying a low rate of firing). (See **FIGURE 15.19.**)

McKenna et al. (1974) presented a model, shown in Figure 15.20, which suggests how an interaction between the locus coeruleus and FTG produces periods of D sleep. (See **FIGURE 15.20.**) McCarley and Hobson (1975) derived a mathematical model that describes what is shown in Figure 15.20; the predictions from the mathematical model

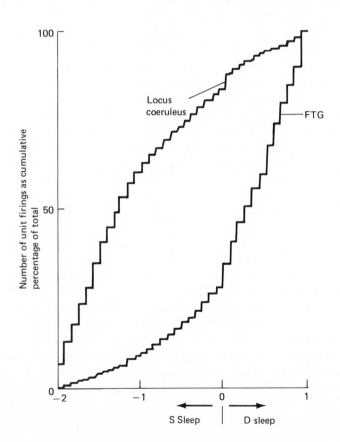

FIGURE 15.19   Reciprocity of firing rate of FTG neurons and neurons of locus coeruleus during S and D sleep. (From Hobson, J. A., McCarley, R. W., and Wyzinski, P. W., *Science*, 4 July 1975, *189*, 55–58. Copyright 1975 by the American Association for the Advancement of Science.)

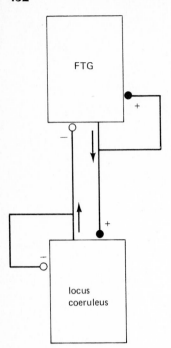

FIGURE 15.20 A neural model that accounts for the reciprocal relationship between FTG neurons of locus coeruleus. (Adapted from McKenna, T., McCarley, R. W., Amatruda, T., Black, D., and Hobson, J. A. In *Sleep Research*, Vol. 3. Los Angeles: Brain Information Service/Brain Research Institute, UCLA, 1974.)

very closely describe the cyclical behavior of an FTG neuron, recorded for over 10 hours. I shall not discuss the mathematical model here; I only want to make the point that the model presented in Figure 15.20 will actually work cyclically, with locus coeruleus and FTG alternately being dominant. We need not look for "pacemaker" cells with some intrinsic rhythm.

To summarize: The anterior dorsal raphe suppresses the D sleep mechanism during waking. When sleep occurs, this inhibition is removed, and cells of the FTG and locus coeruleus alternately become active. When the FTG cells are active, D sleep results. The phasic phenomena of D sleep are produced by cells in FTG proper, whereas the tonic phenomena are produced by cells located nearby (in FTC, or the nucleus of the central tegmental field), although there is overlap in these two populations. Both locus coeruleus and FTG are excited by acetylcholine and inhibited by norepinephrine.

FOREBRAIN MECHANISMS

Forebrain Waking Mechanisms

EVENTUAL RECOVERY OF THE CERVEAU ISOLÉ. There is evidence that the isolated cerebrum is capable of periodic wakefulness. Genovesi, Moruzzi, Palestini, Rossi, and Zanchetti (1956) found that multistage lesions (i.e., a little bit at a time) that eventually transected the brainstem between the superior and inferior colliculi did not produce totally comatose animals; the animals showed ocular and electroencephalographic signs of periodic arousal.

Batsel (1960) produced single-stage brainstem transections in dogs, which he was able to keep alive for up to 73 days by very careful nursing. As time passed, the animals showed increasing amounts of cortical desynchrony. The level of transection was too far rostral to allow observation of ocular behavior, so only the EEG could be used to determine whether the animal was asleep or awake. When a more caudal transection was made (Batsel, 1964), the EEG again showed a gradual recovery of desynchronized activity. This time some ocular signs of arousal could be seen. However, as Jouvet (1972) has noted, the more caudal transection might leave some of the noradrenergic brainstem arousal mechanism still attached to the cerebrum.

These results suggest that there is a forebrain waking mechanism that is able to produce arousal independently of the brainstem. Jouvet (1972) has suggested alternative explanations: (a) norepinephrine or dopamine, produced in the brainstem, might be conveyed by the blood supply to the forebrain, where it might stimulate postsynaptic neurons; (b) there might be some sprouting of catecholaminergic neurons of the brainstem that reestablish some connections with the forebrain; or (c) there might be some degenerating neurons in the forebrain that show abnormal discharge patterns that produce cortical desynchrony actually unrelated to arousal. These alternatives have some degree of plausibility, but there is no direct evidence at the present to support any of them. Until such time, it would appear to be safest to conclude that an animal can eventually awaken after a transection that isolates the forebrain from the brainstem waking mechanism; hence, there appear to be waking mechanisms in the forebrain itself.

POSTERIOR HYPOTHALAMUS. Where might these mechanisms be? In 1936, Ingram, Barris, and Ranson reported that lesions in the vicinity of the posterior hypothalamus resulted in a state of somnolence, with hypoactivity. The animals could be aroused by sensory stimulation, but the arousal was minor and short-lived. The animals' "instinctive" behavior appeared deficient; the cats would show only mild interest, but no emotion, when put in front of a group of barking dogs. The cats ignored a rat—even when the rodent was placed on the cats' backs. Nauta (1946) reported that posterior hypothalamic lesions produced a state of lethargy; the animals could be aroused by pinching the tail, but soon afterward "they would yawn and stretch and settle down in a comfortable position to go to sleep again" (Nauta, 1946, p. 292). These results were further corroborated by Naquet, Denavit, and Albe-Fessard (1966), who found that lesions in the vicinity of the posterior hypothalamus of the cat produced almost total somnolence for 8 to 10 days. The cats could be aroused briefly by sensory stimulation. D sleep was not disrupted.

The issue is not at all clear, however. To produce hypersomnia effectively, the lesions must include both the medial and lateral portions of the posterior hypothalamus (Swett and Hobson, 1968). Ascending catecholaminergic fibers and descending fibers of the extrapyramidal motor system are also destroyed by these lesions. And one often sees "somnolent" behavior even when the EEG is desynchronized. Electrical stimulation of this area results in such well-integrated and organized behaviors as attack and flight (I shall discuss this more in chapter 16). These effects contrast with the more "pure" arousal seen after stimulation of the reticular formation. With the evidence we have so far, it would be safest to conclude that the principal effect of posterior hypothalamic lesions is to disrupt a system that activates mechanisms controlling complex motor behavior (especially emotional behavior). The lack of emotional reactivity and hypoactivity cannot really be called sleep. These lesions sometimes also enhance true sleep, but we cannot rule out the possibility that they do so by interrupting fibers that convey activating influences from brainstem structures.

Forebrain Sleep Mechanisms

BASAL FOREBRAIN REGION. Destruction of the preoptic–basal forebrain region produces insomnia. Nauta (1946) produced these lesions in rats and observed total insomnia. The animals subsequently fell into a coma and died; the average survival time was only 3 days. McGinty and Sterman (1968) found that cats reacted differently; the animals did not show any insomnia until several days after the lesion. Figure 15.21 illustrates this effect. (See **FIGURE 15.21.**)

The effects of basal forebrain stimulation are consistent with the lesion experiments. Sterman and Clemente (1962a, 1962b) found that electrical stimulation of this region in an unanesthetized, freely moving cat produced cortical synchrony. The average latency between stimulation and EEG synchrony was 30 seconds; often, the effect was immediate. Drowsiness and behavioral sleep often followed. (See **FIGURE 15.22.**)

As we shall see, it is difficult to prove that electrical stimulation has put an animal to sleep. There are several pieces of evidence, however, that suggest that the stimulation actually produces sleep. Clemente, Sterman, and Wyrwicka (1963) presented a tone for a total of 30 seconds. During the last 20 seconds they also electrically stimulated a basal forebrain region that produced cortical synchrony. After several pairings of tone and stimulation, the tone presented by itself became capable of producing EEG synchrony and behavior asso-

FIGURE 15.21 Effects of lesions of the preoptic area on sleep. (From McGinty, D. J., and Sterman, M. B., *Science,* 1968, *160,* 1253–1255. Copyright 1968 by the American Association for the Advancement of Science.)

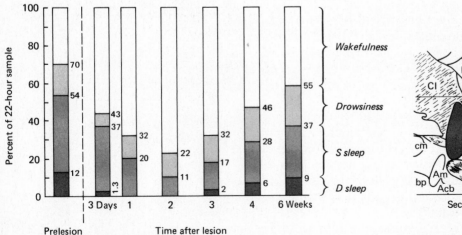
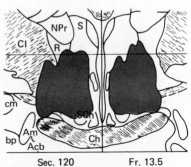

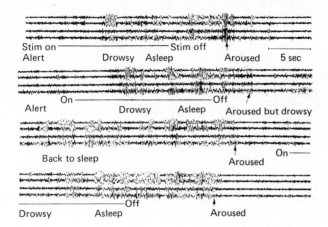

Stim on ———————— Stim off
Alert   Drowsy Asleep   Aroused   5 sec

On ——————————— Off
Alert   Drowsy   Asleep   Aroused but drowsy

                                        On ———
Back to sleep   Aroused

——————————Off
Drowsy   Asleep   Aroused

FIGURE 15.22 Sleep produced by prolonged electrical stimulation of the basal forebrain region. (From Sterman, M. B., and Clemente, C. D., *Experimental Neurology*, 1962b, *6*, 103–117.)

ciated with the preparation for sleep (the cat would lie down, drop its head, and close its eyes). (See **FIGURE 15.23.**)

Roberts and Robinson (1969) warmed the preoptic region (which results in stimulation of thermoreceptors in this area) and observed drowsiness and EEG synchrony. Thus, a more "natural" stimulation mimics the effects of electrical stimulation. Perhaps the excessive sleep that accompanies a fever is produced by this mechanism. Peripheral thermoreceptors also relay information to the preoptic area, and perhaps preoptic stimulation accounts for the drowsiness and lassitude we feel on a hot day. Pavlov (1923) even noted that when thermal stimulation of the skin was used as a conditioned stimulus, the dogs being trained often fell asleep.

Bremer (1970) provided further support for the synchronizing effects of preoptic stimulation. He obtained electrophysiological evidence for an inhibitory influence of the preoptic region on activating effects of the reticular formation. When the preoptic stimulation was presented simultaneously with sensory stimulation or electrical stimulation of the reticular formation, the arousing effects of the latter two procedures were diminished. The evidence implicating the preoptic region as a part of a sleep mechanism is, therefore, quite strong.

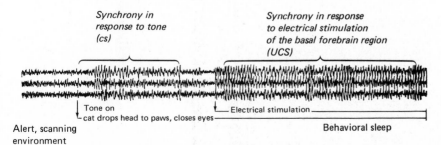

Synchrony in response to tone (cs)

Synchrony in response to electrical stimulation of the basal forebrain region (UCS)

Tone on
cat drops head to paws, closes eyes —— Electrical stimulation ——

Alert, scanning environment

Behavioral sleep

FIGURE 15.23 Conditioning of the effects of stimulation of the basal forebrain region to a neutral stimulus. (From Clemente, C. D., Sterman, M. B., and Wyrwicka, W., *Experimental Neurology*, 1963, *7*, 404–417.)

MIDLINE THALAMUS.   Another forebrain region has been implicated in the production of sleep.   Morison and Dempsey (1942) found that repetitive stimulation of the midline thalamus produces a "recruiting response"; successive pulses evoke larger and larger cortical evoked potentials.   These potentials can be abolished by stimulation of the reticular formation (Moruzzi and Magoun, 1949).   Furthermore, cortical spindles seen during stage 2 of S sleep are abolished by thalamic lesions (Naquet, Denavit, and Albe-Fessard, 1966).   However, except for the loss of sleep spindles, there is no alteration in the occurrence and distribution of S or D sleep (Angeleri, Marchesi, and Quattrini, 1969).   Although the midline thalamus exerts powerful control on the electrical activity of the cortex, the label "sleep center" would not appear to apply to this region, since lesions do not produce even partial insomnia.

There have been suggestions that low-frequency stimulation of the midline thalamus can produce sleep, but this issue is very controversial.   Hess (1944) observed sleep in cats after such stimulation; high-frequency stimulation, on the other hand, would awaken a sleeping cat.   These results were confirmed by Akert, Koella, and Hess (1952) and by Parmeggiani (1968). However, we must note that a cat normally sleeps 60 to 70 percent of the time, and low-frequency thalamic stimulation will never put an active, aroused cat to sleep. The electrical stimulation is effective only if the cat is already quiet and drowsy in appearance—but then who can say that the stimulation is what produced sleep?   Perhaps the cat would have fallen asleep anyway.

Hunsperger (1972) placed cats in a chamber once a day and noted the latency to fall asleep.   The cats received thalamic stimulation (which produced cortical synchronization) but he observed that the stimulation had no effect on the time it took the cats to fall asleep. Sterman (1972) suggested that the animals had become conditioned to the testing chamber and always fell asleep quickly because of the pairing between the stimulation and the environmental cues provided by the chamber.   However, Hunsperger removed the rug from the chamber after the cats had become accustomed to it, and this disturbed the cats, which then took longer to fall asleep.   Thalamic stimulation did not reduce this disturbing effect.

The effects of midline thalamic stimulation on sleep are in sharp contrast with the effects of basal forebrain stimulation (where either high or low frequencies produce cortical synchrony and sleep). Furthermore, thalamic lesions do not affect sleep, whereas basal forebrain lesions produce insomnia.   These facts make it difficult to conclude that the midline thalamus plays a major role in sleep mechanisms.

CONCLUSIONS

As we have seen, there is very good evidence for brainstem sleep and waking mechanisms, and for a forebrain sleep mechanism. The evidence for a forebrain waking mechanism (in the posterior hypothalamus) is not quite so compelling. This, of course, leaves open the issue of what causes the periodic arousal of the chronic *cerveau isolé*. What we definitely lack, at the present time, is a unifying concept that can bring all the evidence together. Hobson's experiments apparently explain the cyclic nature of D sleep, but what mechanism controls the alternation between sleep and waking? The raphe is apparently necessary for sleep, but what factors control the raphe? The past few years have provided us with much information about neural mechanisms of the sleep-waking cycle, but the basic process still remains a mystery.

SUGGESTED READINGS

DEMENT, W. C. *Some Must Watch While Some Must Sleep.* San Francisco: W. H. Freeman, 1974.

FREEMON, F. R. *Sleep Research: A Critical Review.* Springfield, Ill.: Charles C Thomas, 1972.

HARTMANN, E. L. *The Functions of Sleep.* New Haven: Yale University Press, 1973.

WEBB, W. B. *Sleep: The Gentle Tyrant.* Englewood Cliffs, N.J.: Prentice-Hall, 1975.

Ergebnisse der Physiologie, 1972, Vol. 64.

In addition to the suggested readings I listed for chapter 14, I have included volume 64 of *Ergebnisse der Physiologie.* This volume contains two lengthy review articles, one by Giussepe Moruzzi and the other by Michel Jouvet. (The articles are in English.) For more recent information, write to the Brain Information Service/Brain Research Institute, UCLA, Los Angeles, California, for the latest list of sleep-related volumes they publish each year. Besides publishing original articles, BIS/BRI provides an excellent abstracting service.

Emotion, Aggression, and Species-Typical Behavior

16

Emotions constitute a very important part of our lives. Basic motives, such as those produced by lack of food or suitable shelter from the cold, are not important issues for most people in industrially developed countries. We tend to evaluate our lives by our jobs, our incomes, our friends, and our material possessions. But ultimately, we ask ourselves whether we are happy or satisfied with our lives. We all acknowledge a relationship between wealth and happiness, but most of us would agree that a rich, lonely, unhappy person is worse off than a materially poor but happy and contented member of a "less civilized" society.

I do not intend to present here a brief for the life of the "innocent savage." I merely wish to make the point that a surfeit of the goal objects sought by people to satisfy their biological drives—for example, plenty of food, warm clothing, and shelter—does not guarantee "happiness." Although countless writings and lectures have been devoted to telling us how to be "happy," we still cannot specify the conditions that lead to this state. And we do not know how to eliminate hate, jealousy, and other negative emotions that exist even in people who are able to satisfy their material needs.

We know that lack of food causes hunger; consequently, we have an idea of how to investigate its physiological basis. As we saw in chapter 12, much progress has been made. In fact, the relationship between food deprivation and hunger is so clear that we do not refer to hunger as an emotion. We cannot analyze the causes for other feelings so easily, however. What makes someone happy might bore someone else. A situation that terrifies one person might merely amuse another. We have no knowledge of the physiological basis that determines why a person reacts in a given way to emotion-producing stimuli.

Where we *have* made some progress is in the investigation of the physiological mechanisms controlling behaviors that accompany various emotions. For example, we know something about the physiological basis of aggressive behavior, although we do not know why a given situation makes a person angry. Similarly, we know quite a bit about neural and hormonal mechanisms of sexual behavior, but not of love.

In this chapter I shall discuss what is known about the physiological bases of aggressive and defensive behavior, and of parental behavior. (Sexual behavior has already been covered in chapter 11.) The stress is on behavior, not on the emotions that presumably accompany the behavior. There has been some study of the effects of physiological manipulations (brain damage, alteration of hormone levels, administration of drugs) on emotions expressed by humans, but most of the objective work has been performed with animals, and this work is necessarily restricted to observable behavior. Even the human studies, as we shall see, emphasize emotional behavior, since there are no methods by which we can directly measure feelings of emotion.

This chapter will also contain a discussion of attempts to control undesirable human behavior—specifically, violent aggressive behavior—by surgical and chemical means. As we shall see, serious questions have been raised about the effectiveness of these procedures and about the moral and ethical issues involved in producing irreversible brain damage.

FEELINGS OF EMOTION

The James-Lange Theory

An early theory attempted to explain feelings of emotion as feedback from peripheral effects of the autonomic nervous system, and from skeletal muscles. This theory, formulated by William James and Carl Lange in the late nineteenth century (see Cannon, 1927), argued that environmental stimuli produced reflex autonomic and somatic effects, and that afferent feedback from these effects constituted the expression of emotion. This theory is no longer taken seriously, but it has yet to be disproved. In fact, it is unlikely that it can be. Sherrington (1900) operated on dogs, cutting the spinal cord below the brain and severing the vagus nerves. The animals continued to exhibit growling and biting response to painful stimulation of the head. Similarly, Cannon (1927) removed the sympathetic chains and found that cats continued to express emotional behavior. However, one cannot say that the cats and dogs continued to "feel" their emotions. To test the theory one would have to sever the spinal cord and various cranial nerves of a human and see whether the person would still report feelings of emotions.

This issue would seem to be rather sterile. An intact animal does, in fact, experience sensations from the muscles and from the autonomic nervous system, and this feedback certainly is an important factor in feelings of emotion. Sweet (1966) reports the case of a person whose sympathetic nervous system was severed on one side of the body (for therapeutic reasons). He subsequently found that the shivering sensation he previously felt while listening to music now occurred only on the unoperated side. Clearly, his autonomic reaction constituted part of the enjoyable experience of listening to music that he found emotionally moving.

Interactions between Physiological and Cognitive Factors in Emotion

Schachter (1967) administered injections of epinephrine (which activates the sympathetic nervous system) or a saline solution (as a control) to various groups of human subjects. Some were told that the drug would make their hands tremble, their face get warm, and their heart pound (that is, they were advised about the normal effects of epinephrine injections). Others were told that the drug would have no side effects (although, of course, the side effects would actually occur). The subjects were placed in one of two situations. In the first, a stooge (who had supposedly received the same drug) simulated euphoria, running around, talking continuously, flying paper airplanes, and engaging in other "manic" behaviors. In the second situation, the subjects were given an anger-producing task. They had to fill out a long, personal, insulting questionnaire. The stooge, ostensibly taking the test with the subjects, showed increasing signs of anger, finally tearing up the form and stamping out of the room. After the treatment the subjects were given tests to measure anger or euphoria.

The uninformed subjects (those who were told that the drug would produce no side effects) interpreted their (unexpected) autonomic reactions as manifestations of euphoria or anger, depending on the situation. They consequently *felt* more euphoric or angry. It was as if they said to themselves "my heart is pounding, so I must be angry (or euphoric), too." The informed subjects perceived their autonomic reactions as side effects of the drug, and they did not feel any more euphoric or angry than did the subjects who received control injections of saline. These observations clearly show that our bodily reactions comprise a part of our emotional experience but that, depending on cognitive factors, the same reactions can be part of very different emotions. In different environmental situations the same physical symptoms were interpreted in completely different ways. Thus, feelings of emotions would appear to entail more than a set of peripheral physiological reactions.

AGGRESSION AND FLIGHT

Aggression is difficult to define precisely. Some instances—a fight between two dogs, for example—are clear. Others are not. People can certainly express aggression verbally. A person's silence could even be interpreted as aggression, if that person knows that the silence will frustrate and infuriate the other person. So we need not restrict a definition of aggression to the production (or threat) of bodily harm. Nor should all behaviors that intentionally result in harm to another be interpreted as aggressive. Certainly a surgeon is not expressing aggression by cutting the patient's abdomen open. Nor is an employee in a slaughterhouse, by killing dozens of animals each day.

Types of Aggression

Moyer (1968) has identified seven kinds of aggression, classified partly by the object of the attack, partly by the situation that elicits the attack, and partly by the way in which the animal carries out the attack.

1. *Predatory attack* is different from all the others, and a good case could be made for its not really being a form of aggression. When a lion attacks a zebra, or a fox attacks a rabbit, the predator does not appear to be "angry" at its prey.
2. *Inter-male aggression* is usually restricted to fights between strangers. A male mouse raised in isolation will attack other males, but it will not fight with other males if it is raised with them.
3. *Fear-induced aggression* can be seen in a cornered animal; even a rat will turn and fight, as the saying goes.
4. *Irritable aggression* can be elicited by frustration or (more frequently, at least in experimental settings) by pain. If a pair of

normally docile animals are given a painful foot shock, they will often attack each other viciously. (We are all familiar with the warning not to approach a wounded animal too closely.) This category also includes attack upon an inanimate object (a frustrated tennis player breaking his racket, for example).

5. *Territorial defense* is usually an inter-male phenomenon. It is often accompanied by an elaborate set of behaviors (such as scent marking or vocalizing) that define the boundaries of the animal's territory. In form, it would probably be hard to distinguish from inter-male aggression.

6. *Maternal aggression* is displayed by a lactating mammal when disturbed near her nesting site, or near her young.

7. *Instrumental aggression* is that attack that can be trained by conditioning procedures. For example, a dog can be trained to be vicious by rewarding it for attacking, and punishing it for being affectionate toward, a (well-padded) human.

As we shall see, very little is known about the physiological bases of some of these types of aggression; predatory attack, inter-male aggression, and irritable aggression have been the subjects of most of the investigations. And sometimes the type of aggression seen in a study is not specifiable. For example, if electrical stimulation of some brain region makes a cat hiss and snarl (at no particular object), we would conclude that we were stimulating neural circuits involved in aggression, but not necessarily any particular type.

Attack Elicited by Electrical Brain Stimulation

AFFECTIVE ATTACK AND QUIET-BITING ATTACK. It is possible to electrically stimulate various parts of the brain and elicit at least three types of aggressive behavior: irritable aggression, predatory attack, and fear-induced aggression. Although electrical stimulation occasionally produces only elements of attack, or a half-hearted display of aggression, full-blown attack, when it occurs, appears identical to that which is elicited naturally. Flynn and his colleagues (Flynn, Vanegas, Foote, and Edwards, 1970) have reviewed a series of investigations on the neural bases of rat killing by cats. They find two general types of attack that can be elicited by brain stimulation: *affective attack* and *quiet-biting attack,* which probably correspond to Moyer's irritable aggression and predatory attack, respectively. It may seem surprising that a cat should need any special treatment to induce it to attack a rat, but most laboratory cats do *not* spontaneously attack rats.

Affective attack is by far the more dramatic. The animal adopts a "Halloween-cat" posture, with arched back, erect fur on the back and neck, dilated pupils, and bared teeth. A nearby rat will be viciously attacked with the claws, sometimes to the accompaniment of screams. If the stimulation continues, the cat will often begin biting the rat. We do not know how the cat feels, of course, but it acts as if it were brimming over with rage.

Quiet-biting attack is quite different. This type of attack does not appear to be accompanied by strong emotion. The cat begins searching, and it suddenly pounces on the rat, directing powerful bites to the head and neck region. The cat does not growl or scream, and it stops attacking once the rat ceases to move. This type of attack appears more cold-blooded and ruthless than affective attack (it is more efficient, too, in terms of the probability of the rat being killed). Almost certainly, this behavior is identical with the attack normally seen when a cat is hunting.

QUIET-BITING ATTACK AND HUNGER. Quiet-biting attack is related to feeding behavior, but these behaviors are clearly mediated by different neural circuitry. Food deprivation will increase the probability of spontaneous mouse killing in rats (Paul, Miley, and Baenninger, 1971), but some rats never become killers and will starve to death in the presence of live mice—even if they have learned to eat dead ones (Karli, 1956).

Hutchinson and Renfrew (1966) found that all brain-stimulating electrodes that elicited eating in cats would produce quiet-biting attacks on rats if the intensity of the stimulating current were increased. The animals did *not*, however, eat the rats they killed. Roberts and Kiess (1964) implanted electrodes in the brain of cats and obtained quiet-biting attacks on rats when electrical stimulation was delivered through the electrodes. The cats learned to traverse a maze in order to obtain a rat to attack, but they would do so only while the brain stimulation was turned on. When it was off, they would not seek out the rat. When stimulation was turned on, a hungry cat would even leave a dish of food to run through the maze and attack the rat, which it would *not* subsequently eat. Therefore, quiet-biting attack is not synonymous with hunger.

THE DISTINCTION BETWEEN QUIET-BITING ATTACK AND AFFECTIVE ATTACK. Panksepp (1971b) found that both quiet-biting attack and affective attack could be obtained from rats by electrical brain stimulation. Most rats would quickly learn to turn off the stimulation that produced affective attack (suggesting that this stimulation was aversive), but they would press a lever that turned *on* stimulation that elicited quiet-biting attack. Furthermore, administration of amphetamine accentuated affective attack but diminished quiet-biting attack (Panksepp, 1971a). These physiological data only reinforce the behavioral differences between these two forms of electrically elicited attack.

A POSSIBLE DISTINCTION BETWEEN AFFECTIVE ATTACK AND FEAR-INDUCED AGGRESSION. There appear to be differences in the physiological mechanisms underlying affective attack and fear-induced aggression. It is possible to elicit flight reactions characteristic of fear-induced aggression by means of brain stimulation, and the subjects (cats) readily learn a task (pressing a paddle) to turn off the stimulation (Nakao, 1958). It is much more difficult to train a cat to turn off stimulation that produced attack. Furthermore, MacLean and Delgado (1953) were able to obtain a display of rage (presumably affective attack) without any evidence of a tendency toward escape.

Flynn and his colleagues (1970) report a study in which cats could be induced to attack a rat or to flee from the chamber, in response to electrical stimulation of the brain. In some cats, the behaviors occurred in response to stimulation through different electrodes. In other cats, both behaviors could be elicited through the same electrode—attack if a rat were present, and escape if one were not. (Presumably, the electrode was located so that circuits involved in escape and attack were simultaneously stimulated.) The investigators destroyed the medial thalamus; Mitchell and Kaelber (1967) had reported earlier that these lesions reduce the intensity of painful stimuli, and will eliminate escape from painful electrical stimulation of a tooth or paw. After these thalamic lesions were made, the cats could no longer be induced to escape by means of electrical brain stimulation. Attack behavior, however, was undamaged. Unfortunately, the investigators did not distinguish between affective attack and quiet-biting attack in this study; they noted only that the data on affective attack were limited. There is no reason to assume that quiet-biting attack is elicited through painful stimulation, since it is clearly different in its form. If affective attack could indeed be elicited after these lesions, which eliminate escape previously elicited by brain stimulation, there would be good evidence for a real distinction between these two behaviors. At the present, however, we cannot determine whether fear-induced aggression and affective attack are produced by different physiological mechanisms.

SIMILARITIES BETWEEN AFFECTIVE ATTACK AND IRRITABLE AGGRESSION. There are similarities between affective attack and the aggressive behaviors that often accompany the delivery of aversive stimuli. It is quite possible that affective attack does not result from direct stimulation of "attack circuits," but rather results from aversive effects of the brain stimulation (not necessarily identical with pain) that cause the animal to lash out at living objects in its vicinity. For example, a monkey, when given a painful shock, will learn a task that results in the delivery of a tennis ball it can bite (Azrin, Hutchinson, and McLaughlin, 1965), and a pigeon subjected to the frustration of an extinction schedule will peck at a key in order to gain access to another pigeon that it can attack (Azrin, 1964). Electrical stimulation of the brain could be eliciting aversive feelings similar to the ones that are apparently produced in these experiments, and could then indirectly produce affective attack. Thus, a map of brain regions where electrical stimulations produce affective attack does not necessarily identify the neural circuits that mediate this behavior.

Evidence for similarity between affective attack elicited by brain stimulation and irritable attack elicited by foot shock is the fact that both forms of attack are accentuated by amphetamine and are diminished by *chlordiazepoxide* (a tranquilizer), according to Horovitz, Piala, High, Burke, and Leaf (1966) and Panksepp (1971a).

Neural Pathways Mediating Electrically Elicited Attack

HYPOTHALAMUS AND MIDBRAIN. Attack can most readily be elicited from hypothalamic stimulation; in general, affective attack is produced by medial hypothalamic stimulation, whereas quiet-biting attack occurs after stimulation of the lateral hypothalamus. This appears to be true for cats (Flynn et al., 1970), opossums (Roberts, Steinberg, and Means, 1967), monkeys (Delgado, 1969), and rats (Panksepp, 1971b). Furthermore, electrodes in the dorsal portion of the hypothalamus often produce flight when current is passed through them; the animal breathes rapidly, its pupils dilate, it might urinate or defecate, and it exhibits frantic attempts to escape the chamber in which it is confined (Clemente and Chase, 1973). If restrained, the animal will frequently attack in an attempt to flee. (This fear-induced aggression is thus not directly elicited by the brain stimulation, but resembles the natural attack of a cornered animal.)

The effects of hypothalamic stimulation appear to be mediated caudally, through the midbrain. Both affective attack and quiet-biting attack can be elicited by stimulation in various midbrain locations (Flynn et al., 1970; Clemente and Chase, 1973), especially in the *central gray* of the tegmentum, shown in **FIGURE 16.1.** This region of the midbrain (which contains a number of specific nuclei) receives fibers (via the *dorsal longitudinal fasciculus*) from preoptic and hypothalamic regions. It is extensively connected with midbrain sensory and motor systems. When lesions are placed in the central gray, affective attack, previously produced by hypothalamic stimulation, can no longer be elicited. Nor will such a cat show an emotional reaction to the presence of a dog.

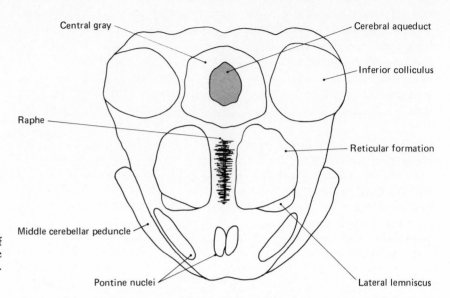

FIGURE 16.1 Location of the central gray of the midbrain.

The fact that attack can be elicited by hypothalamic stimulation, and that this attack can be blocked by midbrain lesions, suggests that either (a) the neural circuitry that organizes the complex motor patterns of attack is located in the hypothalamus and exerts its effects by means of axons passing caudally through the midbrain, or (b) these patterns are organized in the midbrain and/or more caudal regions, and the hypothalamic stimulation serves merely to turn on these circuits by means of descending fiber systems. (It is also possible, of course, that some organization is accomplished in the hypothalamus and some in the midbrain.)

AGGRESSIVE BEHAVIOR NOT MEDIATED BY THE HYPOTHALAMUS. In order to ascertain whether the hypothalamus is uniquely involved in organizing aggressive behavior, Ellison and Flynn (1968) produced a hypothalamic "island" with a specially designed surgical instrument. The device contained two small knives that could be rotated around the hypothalamus, thus severing all connections between the hypothalamus and the rest of the brain. (This complicated technique is used because large hypothalamic lesions will kill the animal because of severe disruption of the endocrine system. The hypothalamic "island" technique leaves the pituitary gland attached to the isolated hypothalamus.)

Even after hypothalamic isolation, midbrain stimulation could still effectively elicit both affective and quiet-biting attack, although higher levels of electrical current had to be used than were necessary before the isolation. The cats also reacted aggressively to a tail pinch, and natural mouse-killers continued to attack mice. The behavior was not quite so intense as before the surgery, but it is safe to conclude from these results that the hypothalamus is not necessary for the organization of motor control of aggressive behavior. The fact that the cats were inactive when not stimulated (naturally or electrically) suggests that the hypothalamus plays a role in the initiation or facilitation of behaviors that are organized and integrated elsewhere.

SINGLE UNITS AND DEFENSIVE BEHAVIOR. There is some electrophysiological evidence for the participation of neurons of the midbrain in emotional behavior. Adams (1968) placed a cat in each of two compartments of a divided box with a removable partition. A stimulating electrode was located in the hypothalamus of one cat (the attacker); single-unit recording electrodes were placed in the hypothalamus and midbrain of the other cat (the attackee). It was possible, then, to stimulate the attacker and record the activity of neurons in the attackee as this cat defended itself. A wide variety of "control" stimuli were also applied to the attackee, such as pinching its tail, dropping it, flashing lights, making noises, etc., to try to identify those cells that might respond to some nonspecific elements of the attack or of motor activity not related to the cat's own defensive behavior. Of the ninety-five cells recorded, ten responded much more during affective defense than during the control procedures. (Four of these altered their activity *only* during affective defense.) Eight of these ten cells (including the four that responded only during defensive behavior) were found in the midbrain. The results are not conclusive, but they are consistent with the fact that midbrain stimulation may elicit attack, whereas midbrain lesions disrupt attack and defensive behavior—even that which was formerly elicited by hypothalamic stimulation.

ORGANIZATION OF AGGRESSIVE BEHAVIOR CAUDAL TO THE MIDBRAIN. Some elements of aggressive and defensive behavior appear to be organized at levels even lower than the midbrain. Early work (Woodworth and Sherrington, 1904) showed that animals with brainstem transections at the level of the pons would still bite, scratch, vocalize, and show facial gestures of rage when noxious stimuli were applied to the body. The behavior was very poorly coordinated; it appeared quite fragmented in form. Since the lower brainstem was the only part of the brain attached to the muscles being used for the aggressive display, this part of the brain must play at least a partial role in the organization of these behaviors.

INTERACTION BETWEEN BRAIN STIMULATION AND SENSORY AND MOTOR MECHANISMS. Flynn and his colleagues have investigated interactions between electrical stimulation of the brain and the sensory and motor systems that mediate attack. They report that stimulation of various locations in the midbrain leads to attack with the forepaw contralateral to the stimulating electrode. The cats never used the ipsilateral forepaw. This result strongly argues against the possibility that the stimulation merely produced some emotional effects (making the cat "angry" at the rat), which then triggered the normal attack sequence. Instead, the motor systems involved in the attack were directly facilitated; otherwise, the cat would always have used its preferred paw (cats and other animals usually show some degree of "handedness," just as humans do). Even when the pyramidal tract was cut on one side, resulting in the cat's reluctance to use the contralateral limb, electrical stimulation of the midbrain would elicit attack with the normally disused paw. The results are what would be expected if there were a natural tendency for the sight of a rat to elicit an attack with a paw. This tendency is represented in the form of increased synaptic potentials on the neurons appropriate for the motor movements made in the cat's strike at the rat. The attack does not normally occur (except in a cat that spontaneously kills rats) because of overriding neural inhibition. The electrical stimulation excites all cells, but not all cells will actually respond—only those already facilitated by the increased synaptic activity that accompanies the sight of the rat. (It is possible that the electrical stimulation instead disrupts inhibitory cells, thus releasing the effector cells from the neural inhibition that normally prevents the attack. The result would be the same.)

Flynn and his colleagues also report electrophysiological evidence in support of this motor facilitation. Stimulation of the central gray produces action potentials in the nerves serving the biceps and triceps muscles, which are involved in the attack on the rat. Furthermore, if motor cortex and central gray are stimulated together, a larger response is seen than the one accompanying cortical stimulation alone.

A clear picture of the facilitatory effects of brain stimulation was shown by MacDonnell and Flynn (1966). They noted that a cat normally turns its head away when a stick is touched to the side of its cheek. If a cat is stimulated through an electrode in the hypothalamus that normally elicits a quiet-biting attack, the animal will instead turn toward the stick so that the object meets its lips; when this contact occurs, the cat's mouth opens. At low levels of stimulation a rather small region of the cat's face will produce this set of responses when touched, but as the intensity increases, the sequence can be elicited by touching the cat farther and farther from the front of its mouth. This effect is shown in **FIGURE 16.2.**

The experiments cited so far show that electrical stimulation of the hypothalamus or midbrain will facilitate sensory and motor mechanisms involved in attack and defensive behavior. Furthermore, hypothalamic stimulation appears also to facilitate some sort of drive mechanism; the animal will learn a maze to find a rat it can then attack. There appears to be no one brain location where these behaviors are organized, but the midbrain (especially the central gray) appears to be the most important region for this organization. If the brainstem is transected beneath the midbrain, fragments of emotional behavior can be seen, but they are not coordinated. It is impossible to say at this time what role is played by the hypothalamus in the organization of the response patterns.

Modulation of Emotional Behavior by the Limbic System

Various portions of the limbic system appear to be involved in the modulation of emotional behavior. Concerning aggressive and defensive behavior, the most important regions appear to be the septum and the amygdala. The septum appears to be involved in suppression of these behaviors; the amygdala appears to be involved in both suppression and facilitation, but it appears, on the balance, principally to play a facilitatory role.

Most extensive region from which head-orienting response could be elicited during brain stimulation

THE AMYGDALA. The amygdala is located in the rostromedial temporal lobe in humans, and in analogous locations in other mammals. There are several nuclei in the amygdaloid complex, but they are divided into two principal groups: the *corticomedial group* (phylogenetically older) and the *basolateral group* (evolved more recently). The separation between the nuclear groups is not complete, but the *stria terminalis* conveys efferent information principally from the corticomedial group to the hypothalamus and other forebrain structures, while the outflow from the basolateral group is chiefly carried by the *ventral amygdalofugal pathway*. The ventral pathway reaches the hypothalamus and preoptic region and also sends fibers to the midbrain tegmentum and central gray. The amygdalar connections are shown schematically in **FIGURE 16.3**. The amygdala receives fibers from the olfactory system, from surrounding cortex, and from the thalamus and hypothalamus. Electrical recordings have shown that the amygdala is responsive to a variety of sensory stimuli. The anatomical evidence thus provides a basis for a role for the amygdala in the modulation of hypothalamic-midbrain mechanisms in aggressive and defensive behavior.

Region from which Jaw-opening response could be elicited during brain stimulation

FIGURE 16.2 Tactile stimuli applied to these regions of the cat's face caused head turning or mouth opening during electrical stimulation of the hypothalamus. (From MacDonnell, M. F., and Flynn, J. P., *Science*, 1966, 152, 1406–1408. Copyright 1966 by the American Association for the Advancement of Science.)

Effects of Electrical Stimulation of the Amygdala. Electrical stimulation of the amygdala has been found to produce either affective

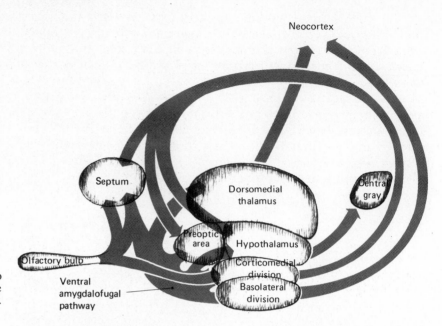

FIGURE 16.3 The two
efferent fiber systems of the
amygdala.

attack (usually characterized as "defensive reactions" by the authors
of these studies) or escape behavior (usually called "fear reactions").
Predatory attack does not appear to occur as a result of amygdaloid
stimulation, but the amygdala nevertheless appears to exert some influence on this behavior. Egger and Flynn (1963) found that stimulation of different portions of the lateral nucleus (a part of the basolateral complex) either facilitated or inhibited quiet-biting attack
elicited by hypothalamic stimulation. Furthermore, quiet-biting
attack was shown to be facilitated by lesions of the amygdalar area
in which stimulation produced an inhibitory effect (Egger and Flynn,
1967).

A wide variety of locations within the basolateral amygdala
will produce alerting and increased attentiveness when stimulated
(Ursin and Kaada, 1960). At higher current intensities about half of
the electrode locations that produce alerting will elicit an affective
reaction: fear or attack. The regions that elicit these behaviors do
not correspond precisely to anatomical subdivisions, but the basolateral electrodes that produce attack tend to be located caudally and
laterally to those that produce escape. Lesions in either of these regions
tend to suppress (but do not eliminate) the corresponding emotional
behaviors. The amygdalar neurons involved in these behaviors
appear to respond to acetylcholine; Hernandez-Peon, O'Flaherty, and
Mazzuchelli-O'Flaherty (1967) elicited both affective rage and flight
(but not predatory attack) by applying this neurotransmitter to the
amygdala.

Neural Pathways Mediating the Effects of Amygdala Stimulation. The amygdala appears to exert most of its effects on emotional behavior via the hypothalamus; hypothalamic lesions abolish the effects of amygdaloid stimulation, and the behaviors elicited by stimulation of the amygdala tend to begin gradually and continue for a while after the stimulus is turned off, whereas the behaviors associated with hypothalamic stimulation generally start and stop more abruptly (Clemente and Chase, 1973). Hilton and Zbrozyna (1963) found that affective attack could be elicited by amygdalar stimulation even after the stria terminalis was cut, and they suggested that the relevant connections between the amygdala and hypothalamus were made by means of the ventral amygdalofugal pathway.

THE SEPTUM. Although discrete regions of the amygdala exert either excitatory or inhibitory effects on emotional behavior, large lesions of the amygdala tend to suppress attack and flight. The septum, on the other hand, has been assigned a role as a mediator of inhibitory influence on the same behaviors, but as we shall see, this statement must be qualified. Brady and Nauta (1953) found that septal lesions produce a profound lowering of a rat's "rage threshold." These animals will show signs of extreme emotional arousal if someone aproaches their cage, and they will usually scream and jump wildly around the cage if poked at with some object or even if disturbed with a puff of air. If someone is so foolhardy as to put a hand into the cage, the rat will launch a vicious, bloody attack upon it. (One of my most memorable experiences as an undergraduate was to watch an escaped "septal" rat chase two laboratory instructors around the animal room.) This increased emotionality subsides within a couple of weeks, however, and the speed with which the syndrome disappears seems to be a function of environmental variables such as handling (Gotsick and Marshall, 1972). Other rodents, such as mice (Slotnick, McMullen, and Fleischer, 1974), show increases in flight behavior rather than increases in what appears to be affective rage. A "septal" mouse, for example, will jump wildly around in its cage if it is disturbed, and it is extremely difficult to catch if (perhaps I should say when, because these animals are faster than most experimenters) it escapes, in contrast with the more placid unoperated laboratory mouse. The animals will not attack a human, although they will attempt to bite if they are held. Also in contrast with rats, these animals remain hyperemotional indefinitely; in fact, they get better at escaping if they are handled repeatedly. If a battle is staged between a normal and a "septal" mouse, the brain-damaged animal will invariably lose (Slotnick and McMullen, 1972), so these animals cannot be called "aggressive."

The hyperemotionality (increased aggressiveness or fearfulness) seen in rodents is not seen in most other animals; some investigators report slightly increased rage in cats with septal lesions (Moore, 1964), whereas others find that some of these cats act more affectionate (Glendenning, 1972). Monkeys apparently show no change in emotionality after septal lesions (Buddington, 1967). The effects of these lesions appear to depend upon the species used; therefore, no general statement can be made about the role of the septum in emotional behavior.

Hormonal Influences on Aggression

TESTOSTERONE. In most species the male is more aggressive than the female. Furthermore, castration generally reduces this aggressiveness. We saw in chapter 11 that early androgenization modifies the developing brain, making neural circuits that underlie male sexual behavior more responsive to testosterone. Similarly, early androgenization appears to stimulate the development of testosterone-sensitive neural circuits underlying aggressive behavior. Conner and Levine (1969) found that neonatal castration reduced irritable (pain-elicited) aggression when the rats were tested as adults, as compared with rats that were castrated after puberty. The late-castrated rats could be made as aggressive as normal animals if they were given injections of testosterone, but this replacement therapy did not increase the aggressiveness of the early-castrated rats. Edwards (1968) found that the androgen-sensitive neural circuits underlying aggression could also be "masculinized" in females; administration of testosterone to newborn female mice resulted in animals that reacted like males (i.e., with increased aggression) when given injections of testosterone during adulthood. Female mice given control injections immediately after birth did *not* respond this way when they were given testosterone as adults.

Inter-male (isolation-induced) aggression appears to be very similar to the irritable aggression (elicited by pain) just described. This form of aggression does not appear until puberty (Fredericson, 1950) and does not occur after castration unless testosterone is administered (Beeman, 1947). Administration of *thyroxine* (one of the hormones of the thyroid gland, which has a stimulating effect on metabolism) decreases the amount of isolation time necessary to induce inter-male aggression, whereas animals given *thiouracil* (a drug that blocks the biosynthesis of thyroxine) must be isolated for longer times (Sigg, Day, and Colombo, 1966).

ADRENOCORTICOTROPHIC HORMONE. Other endocrine systems appear to be involved in inter-male aggression. Adrenalectomy decreases aggressiveness in male mice even after prolonged periods of isolation (Harding and Leshner, 1972). Administration of *corticosterone* (one of the principal hormones of the adrenal cortex) to the adrenalectomized mice will restore the aggressiveness (Walker and Leshner, 1972). One cannot conclude that the decreased corticosterone levels are responsible for the decreased aggression seen in the adrenalectomized mouse, since at least two other hormonal changes accompany a fall in corticosterone. (1) A fall in adrenal *glucocorticoids* (corticosterone is one of them) leads to a compensatory increase in *ACTH (adrenocorticotrophic hormone)*, the pituitary hormone that stimulates the adrenal gland to produce more corticosteroids. Normally the adrenal gland responds, and the subsequent rise in glucocorticoid level in the blood causes a fall in the pituitary output of ACTH. Adrenalectomy prevents the production of glucocorticoids, and the level of ACTH remains high. (2) It appears that high levels of ACTH suppress production of testosterone (Bullock and New, 1971); since testosterone is involved in inter-male aggression, a fall in this hormone could be responsible for the inhibitory effects of adrenalectomy on aggressiveness. These hormonal interactions are schematized in **FIGURE 16.4.**

Leshner, Walker, Johnson, Kelling, Kreisler, and Svare (1973) performed a series of experiments to determine the hormone(s) responsible for the decreased inter-male aggressiveness seen after adren-

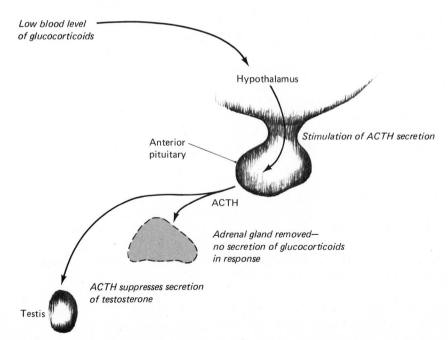

Low blood level
of glucocorticoids

Hypothalamus

Anterior
pituitary

Stimulation of ACTH secretion

ACTH

Adrenal gland removed—
no secretion of glucocorticoids
in response

ACTH suppresses secretion
of testosterone

Testis

FIGURE 16.4 A schematic representation of the effects of adrenalectomy on production of ACTH and testosterone.

alectomy. They found that administration of testosterone failed to restore inter-male aggression after adrenalectomy; therefore, a decreased androgen level did not appear to account for the fall in aggressiveness. They also adrenalectomized and castrated a group of mice and gave these animals controlled amounts of corticosterone and testosterone as replacement therapy. When these animals were also given ACTH, their aggressiveness declined. Since the increase in ACTH did not alter the blood levels of either testosterone or corticosterone (since these hormones were administered daily by injection), we must conclude that ACTH itself has an antiaggressiveness effect. Finally, they showed that replacement injections of a synthetic glucocorticoid restored aggressiveness in adrenalectomized mice, apparently because the hormone, by feeding back on the hypothalamus-pituitary system, inhibited further secretion of ACTH. However, when mice were adrenalectomized *and* castrated, the glucocorticoid did *not* restore aggressiveness. Without testosterone, the mice did not fight.

The study by Leshner and his colleagues allows us to conclude that (1) inter-male aggression is suppressed by ACTH, (2) this suppression is independent of the inhibitory effects of ACTH on testosterone secretion, and (3) testosterone is necessary for inter-male aggression—aggression is not seen without this hormone, no matter what the levels of ACTH and glucocorticoids are.

PSYCHOSURGERY AND THE SUPPRESSION OF HUMAN VIOLENCE

No reasonable person would deny that there is too much violence in the world. Wars and individual acts of aggression produce a great deal of human misery. It is questionable, however, whether the neuroscientist can contribute very much, at least at the present time, to solving this problem. First of all, even the environmental variables that produce violence have not been identified by social scientists. Although studies of mice and rats have found that overcrowding causes increased aggression and even cannibalism, it is not at all clear that crowding produces violence in humans. In fact, careful studies that control for socioeconomic level and ethnic origin have failed to find any effects on violence and crime that can be attributed solely to increased population density (Lawrence, 1974). A crowded, squalid slum with poorly maintained buildings and a high level of unemployment will surely tend to produce frustration and violence in many of its inhabitants, but luxury high-rise apartment buildings, with even higher population densities, will probably be very peaceful. Whatever the causes of violence are, we are certainly a long way from isolating the variables and identifying their physiological bases.

Even more people are killed by wars than by individual acts of violence, but the factors that cause wars are probably very different from those that are responsible for the attack of one organism upon another. Fear-induced aggression is certainly prominent in battle, but even a complete understanding of this phenomenon will not explain why politicians and rulers send the soldiers off to engage in these battles.

Aside from wars (which probably are not started primarily by aggressive emotions) and crimes of violence endemic to many slums, there are individual acts of irrational violence that might very well have a basis in some kind of pathology. For example, Charles Whitman, who killed fourteen people (and then himself, in addition) from a tower at the University of Texas, was found to have a malignant tumor in the vicinity of the amygdala. The obvious inference is that the tumor caused the violence by stimulating neural circuits involved in aggressive behavior, and that prompt diagnosis and surgery could have prevented the tragic results of this violence. It is to issues like these that the following discussion is addressed.

Control of Violence by Brain Surgery

Most brain surgery is performed for reasons that are not at all controversial—removal of brain tumors, repair of *aneurysms* of blood vessels (balloon-shaped widenings due to local weakness), removal of scar tissue triggering epileptic attacks, reduction of intractable pain by destruction of brain circuits conveying this sensation, and alleviation of motor disturbances by localized brain lesions (for example, Parkinson's disease is sometimes treated by destroying parts of the globus pallidus to restore the normal balance of excitation and inhibition in the extrapyramidal motor system). Psychosurgery—intentional damage to brain tissue in an attempt to alter behavior, but in the absence of any observable neuropathology—has, however, been criticized a great deal in recent years.

Elliot Valenstein has written an excellent review and critique of attempts to correct human behavior problems by means of brain stimulation and ablation procedures (Valenstein, 1973). His conclusions are rather pessimistic; a good relationship between malfunctioning limbic system mechanisms and violent behavior has not been established, and most of the clinical reports that purport to show improvement after psychosurgical correction of this behavior do not contain adequate, impartial descriptions of preoperative and postoperative behavior.

One of the first neurosurgeons to attempt to control violent behavior by means of ablation of portions of the limbic system was Dr. Hirataro Narabayashi, of Japan. At first he performed amygdalectomies on people who showed signs of temporal lobe epilepsy along with hyperexcitability and aggressive tendencies. Later he began to try to treat people with behavior disorders, but without accompanying signs of neuropathology (such as epilepsy or severe EEG abnormalities). His earlier technique was to position the tip of a hypodermic needle in the amygdala by means of a stereotaxic apparatus. An oil-wax mixture (which causes localized brain destruction) was then injected into the brain. Currently, however, he uses a radio-frequency lesion maker.

The following quotation is a case history cited by Dr. Narabayashi and his colleagues.

> This 7-year-old boy had been diagnosed as having symptomatic epilepsy with right spastic hemiplegia and imbecility. The child maintained a severe behavior disturbance with . . . explosiveness and uncontrollable hyperactivity. The EEG revealed a general dysrhythmia with spike discharges bilaterally. . . .
>
> When he reached the age of 5, he began to have convulsions once or twice a week, such attacks lasting approximately one hour. . . .
>
> [Following surgery] the change in behavior was so complete, the patient had become so obedient and cooperative, that it was almost impossible to imagine that it was the same child who had been so wild and uncontrollable preoperatively. The electroencephalogram no longer revealed spike discharges on either side. (Narabayashi, Nagao, Saito, Yoshida, and Nagahata, 1963, pp. 6–7)

Narabayashi reported that a "marked and relatively satisfactory improvement consisting in calming and taming effects" was seen in twenty-seven out of forty cases reported on in a conference on psychosurgery (Narabayashi, 1972). Since his patients were classified as idiots or imbeciles to begin with, it is difficult to assess effects of the lesions on intellectual capacities.

PROBLEMS WITH EVALUATION. In general, attempts to evaluate the effects of psychosurgical procedures on intellectual capacities and on behaviors other than aggressiveness have not been very serious or concerted. For example, Balasubramaniam, Kanaka, and Ramamurthi (1970) use the following rating form in assessing the effects of surgery on the hyperactive or violent behavior of their patients:

Grade	Criteria
A	There is no need of any drug. Patient is able to mingle with others.
B	Very much docile and given to occasional outburst only.
C	Manageable when given drugs though not leading a useful life.
D	Transient improvement.
E	No change.
F	Died.

Note that there is no category for patients whose condition was made worse by the surgical procedure, and that the manageability of the patient is the most prominent characteristic that is rated. For example, the following case would be rated as "Grade A" by the classification system.

> Case 34 was admitted and kept in Mental Hospital. . . . He was a young man of 25 years . . . admitted into the Mental Hospital because he was always violent. He was constantly aggressive and was destructive. He could not be kept in the general wards and had to be nursed in an isolated cell. It was difficult to establish any sort of communication with him. Bilateral stereotaxic amygdalectomy was performed. Following the operation he was very quiet and could be safely left in the general wards. He started answering questions in slow syllables. (Balasubramaniam et al., 1969, p. 381)

This person can hardly be classified as cured, although he is certainly easier to manage (and I do not want to suggest that control of violent patients is a trivial matter). Dr. Balasubramaniam not only performs amygdalectomies, but also destroys the posterior hypothalamus and even the central gray of the midbrain if the patient is not sufficiently calmed down by destruction of the amygdala. Many of his patients are children; some of them were operated on when they were under the age of 5. He does not provide documentation to show that drug therapy was tried and found to be inadequate. This is a crucial issue, since tranquilizers, anticonvulsants, and amphetamines have been found to reduce various forms of violence and hyperactivity, especially in children. Certainly it is better to try to find a drug treatment that will control a child's behavior than to produce irreversible damage to the brain.

ALTERNATIVES TO PSYCHOSURGERY. An example of the beneficial effects that can often be achieved with drugs is given in the following case, in which an anticonvulsant drug was used to treat a child who exhibited violent behavior, apparently associated with a seizure-producing focus in the temporal lobe.

> A good example is Jimmy, whom we saw at age 9 because of serious rage reactions and aggressiveness leading to threatened expulsion from school. He was one of nine children, and the only one who had any behavior problem. In fact, the other children were considered outstanding in the community and at school. Jimmy had an identical twin, Johnny, who was considered a "model child." Jimmy's EEG showed left temporal spikes; Johnny's was negative. On methsuximide, Jimmy became an entirely different boy, a "model child" like his twin. When medication was omitted for a short time, he reverted to his old self by the third day. . . . (Gross, 1971, p. 89)

Not many cases are so clear-cut as this; we have evidence that the home environment of the nine children was such that they did not all become violent. In fact, the contrary was seen. The violent boy even had a normal identical twin, so we cannot blame any genetic factors. Furthermore, his EEG was abnormal, indicating that there very probably had been some degree of brain damage. I think that everyone would agree that this child is much better off with the drug treatment, and that this means of therapy should be explored thoroughly before resorting to psychosurgery.

THE "DYSCONTROL SYNDROME." Doctors Vernon Mark and Frank Ervin are among the most prominent supporters of the use of psychosurgery to treat violent and aggressive behavior. They believe that a substantial number of people suffering from the "dyscontrol syndrome" have localized brain abnormalities that trigger neural circuits responsible for aggressive behavior (Mark and Ervin, 1970). They appear to be careful and conservative in their choice of candidates for surgery, but even their results do not appear to be uniformly good. Mark, Sweet, and Ervin (1972) report on patients exhibiting violent or fearful behavior who were treated by lesions of the amygdala. Most of the patients showed some improvement, but side effects (hyperphagia, impotence) were also seen in some cases. Some people were not helped, or showed only a temporary reduction of violent behavior. The most successfully treated case was that of a woman who fell and injured her head. She subsequently had seizures and assaulted people violently. Amygdalectomy reduced the number of seizures and eliminated her attacks of rage. In this case, however, there was clear evidence of brain injury.

Even some clear cases of brain pathology might not necessarily be related to accompanying violent behavior. Charles Whitman did indeed have a rapidly growing temporal lobe tumor, but his diary shows that he had been carefully planning the shooting episode. His diary also shows evidence of severely disordered thought processes. Valenstein points out that we cannot ever determine what triggered Whitman's behavior, but it certainly does not appear that he was "in the throes of a sudden, episodic attack of violence." The history of careful planning stands in contrast with the spasms of rage we might expect to see if the developing brain tumor were stimulating neural circuits underlying aggressive behavior.

PROBLEMS WITH INTERPRETATION OF ANIMAL STUDIES. Valenstein points out that neurosurgeons generally base their psychosurgical procedures on data from experiments performed with animals. He also points out, however, that they tend to have "tunnel vision" when they look at the data. They tend to see only the potentially beneficial aspects of the operation and to ignore its harmful aspects. For example, some neurosurgeons produced lesions in the region of the anterior *cingulate gyrus* (a portion of limbic cortex) based on studies with monkeys that reported taming effects from these lesions. However, Ward (1948) notes that "tameness" is a poor word to use in describing the postoperative behavior of the monkeys.

> . . . the most marked change was in social behavior. The monkey's mimetic activity decreased and it lost its preoperative shyness and fear of man. It would approach me and curiously examine my finger instead of cowering in the far corner of the cage. It was more inquisitive than the normal monkey of the same age. In a large cage with other monkeys of the same size it showed no grooming or acts of affection toward its companions. In fact, it behaved as though they were inanimate. It would walk over them, walk on them if they happened to be in the way, and would even sit on them. It would openly take food from its companions and appeared surprised when they retaliated. . . . (p. 15)

Another example of the selective use of animal data is provided by the use of ventromedial hypothalamic (VMH) lesions by Roeder, Orthner, and Müller (1972). These surgeons saw a film of cats and monkeys that became hypersexual after lesions of the amygdala. Subsequent VMH lesions reversed the hypersexuality. As we saw in chapters 11 and 12, the region of the VMH is implicated in endocrine control and in food regulation. It certainly cannot be characterized as a region responsible for pedophilic homosexuality, the condition Roeder and his colleagues wished to treat. They describe the operation as restoring a balance between "male and female sex-behavior centers." First of all, it has certainly not been established that pedophilic homosexuality (the desire of a man to engage in sexual activity with young boys) is a result of overactive neural circuits mediating female sexual behavior. Secondly, there is no evidence that there is a distinct "female sex-behavior center" in the VMH. Finally, even the results of the surgery refute the notion that a balance has been achieved; as Valenstein notes, "The major effect of the surgery seems to be a general reduction of sexual drive to the point where it is possible for the patient to control his deviant behavior." If a lowering of sexual drive is the result of the operation, it would appear that it would be preferable to administer antiandrogenic drugs instead.

The rationale for amygdalectomy in humans is, of course, that it suppresses violent behavior. However, Kling, Lancaster, and Benitone (1970) reported that amygdalectomized monkeys do appear less aggressive and more friendly toward humans, but that these animals did not get along very well with their peers in the wild. They acted confused and exhibited *more,* rather than less, fear. They sometimes responded to dominance gestures from higher-ranked monkeys in an inappropriate way and consequently got thrashed. In general, they appeared to have trouble interpreting the signs by which monkeys communicate with each other, and they eventually became outcasts. The amygdalectomized monkeys all subsequently died. Although humans with amygdala lesions do not show these severe defects, it would be absurd to attend solely to the interaction of the brain-damaged monkeys with humans in the laboratory, ignoring their fate in the wild, and thus conclude that "amygdalectomy has a taming affect on monkeys."

Further evidence obtained from monkeys suggests that the "taming" seen might be a result of impaired visual recognition. (You will recall from chapter 9 that the temporal lobe is involved in visual recognition.) Downer (1962) cut the corpus callosum and other forebrain commissural fibers, including the optic chiasm. Thus, visual information received by one eye was relayed solely to the ipsilateral hemisphere. A unilateral amygdalectomy was also performed. The rather wild monkey continued to react emotionally when visual stimuli were presented to the intact side of the brain. The same stimuli were treated with aplomb when they were presented to the amygdalectomized side; the monkey appeared quite tame. However, the animal reacted aggressively to tactile stimuli, suggesting that the *mechanism* for violence was not impaired, but rather the means by which visual stimuli can trigger this mechanism.

It should be noted that amygdaloid stimulation in humans does *not* appear to result in aggressive behavior unless the patient normally shows episodes of violent behavior (Kim and Umbach, 1972). These results suggest that the stimulation, instead of directly triggering aggressive circuits, might be producing some aversive effects, which, in turn, trigger aggression in a person who has a low threshold for violent behavior. Alternatively, there could be pathology at some other brain region, and the amygdaloid stimulation might summate with the effects of this pathology (just as subthreshold brain stimulation in the hypothalamus and amygdala can summate).

In conclusion, it would appear that although psychosurgery might indeed ameliorate some instances of violent behavior, preoperative and postoperative observations are generally inadequate to provide conclusive evidence. It would appear that surgery is most effective when there are definite signs of some form of neuropathology, above and beyond the behavioral manifestations of violence. Animal research has not yet provided us with a clear enough picture of the neural mechanisms underlying aggressive behavior to justify any particular types of brain ablation. It would be a wonderful thing if we could indeed locate and isolate neural circuits that mediate violence, and nothing else, and then destroy these circuits in people who wish to be free of uncontrollable fits of rage (and there is no doubt about the existence of such people, who would gladly be rid of these irresistible bouts of violence). However, until such a happy occurrence comes about (and I doubt that it will), we should be very cautious in our use of neurosurgical procedures and concentrate on controlling these forms of violence by means of chemical treatments.

MATERNAL BEHAVIOR

We can now turn our attention to a much more pleasant topic. Maternal behavior is the antithesis of aggressive behavior. It involves nurturance and protection rather than attack and injury (although the mother may very well direct some violent behavior toward animals that appear to endanger her brood). This section will examine the role of hormones in the initiation and maintenance of maternal behavior, and the role of the underlying neural circuits that are responsible for their expression. The research is principally restricted to rodents; very little is known about the neural and endocrine bases of maternal behavior in primates. Harlow has shown the importance of experience (especially of interaction between a young monkey and its peers) in the later development of proper sexual and maternal behavior (Harlow, 1973). Maternal behavior, especially, is much more complex in primates than the relatively stereotyped behavior sequences seen in rodents, and the underlying neural and hormonal substrates will undoubtedly be found to be different in these species.

In concentrating on maternal behavior I do not deny the existence of paternal behavior, but male parental behavior is seen most prominently in higher primates like humans, where the least is known neurologically. Male rodents do not show parental behavior except under special circumstances. There are, of course, other animals (e.g., some species of mouth-breeding fish) in which the male takes care of the young, and in many species of birds the task of caring for the offspring is shared equally. Neural mechanisms of parental behavior have not received much study in these species, however.

Maternal Behavior in Rodents

The final test of the "superiority" of a given animal's genes is the number of offspring that survive to a reproductive age. Just as reproductively competent animals are selected for, so are animals that will care adequately for their young (if their young in fact require any care). Rat and mouse pups certainly do require care, and they cannot survive without a mother who will attend to their needs.

At birth, rats and mice resemble fetuses. The infants are blind (their eyes are still shut) and they can only helplessly wriggle. They are *poikilothermic*; their brain is not yet developed enough to regulate body temperature. They even lack the ability to spontaneously release their own urine and feces; they must be helped to do so by their mother. As we shall see shortly, this phenomenon does not appear to be merely one of the consequences of bearing young that are quite immature; it serves a useful function.

Why, in fact, are rodent young so immature at birth? They do not even look like mice or rats at all. We might speculate as follows: There will obviously be genetic selection for an organism that produces a large number of young. This means large litters, spaced closely together. A mouse can carry a litter of twelve (or even more) pups. A pregnant mouse looks like she swallowed a golf ball; one cannot imagine the mouse carrying any more weight than she does. Therefore, if mice (or rats) gave birth to young that were larger and more mature, they would have to carry a smaller number of them. Also, the sooner the uterus is cleared out, the sooner the mouse can start cooking up another batch. As a matter of fact, some mice have a rather clever trick; they can get pregnant on top of a current pregnancy. This phenomenon, called *superfetation*, is supposedly rare, but I have observed it commonly in a breeding colony I ran in my laboratory when I left a male with the females for around 15 days. One litter of pups would be born, and just around the time the first litter was weaned (around 15 days of age), a second litter was born.

During gestation, female rats and mice build a nest. The form this structure takes depends, naturally, on the material available for its construction. In the laboratory the animals are usually given

FIGURE 16.5   A mouse's brood nest. Alongside it is a length of the rope from which it was constructed.

strips of paper or lengths of rope or twine. A good *brood nest,* as they are called, is shown in Figure 16.5. This nest is made of a piece of hemp rope, shown below. The mouse laboriously shredded the rope and then wove an enclosed nest, with a small hole for access to the interior. (See **FIGURE 16.5.**)

At the time of parturition the female begins to groom and lick the area around the vagina. As a pup begins to emerge, she assists the uterine contractions by pulling the pup out with her teeth. She then eats the placenta and umbilical cord, and cleans off the fetal membranes—a quite delicate operation. (A newborn pup looks like it is sealed in very thin Saran Wrap.) After all the pups are born and cleaned up, the mother will probably nurse them. Milk is usually present very near the time of birth.

Periodically, the mother will lick the anogenital region of the pups which stimulates reflexive urination and defecation. Friedman and Bruno (1976) have shown the utility of this mechanism. They noted that a lactating female rat produces approximately 48 gm of milk (containing approximately 35 ml of water) on the tenth day of lactation. They injected some of the pups with radioactive tritiated water and later found radioactivity in the mother and in the litter-mates. Friedman and Bruno calculated that a lactating rat normally consumes 21 ml of water in the urine of her young, thus recycling approximately two-thirds of the water she gives to the pups in the form of milk. The water, traded back and forth between mother and young, serves essentially as a vehicle for the nutrients contained in milk. Since the milk production of a lactating rat each day is approximately 14 percent of her body weight (for a human weighing 120 pounds that would be around 2 gallons), the recycling is extremely useful, especially where the availability of water might be a problem.

Besides cleaning, nursing, and purging her offspring, a female rodent will retrieve pups if they leave or are removed from the nest. The mother will even construct another nest in a new location and move her litter there, should the conditions at the old site become unfavorable (e.g., when an inconsiderate experimenter puts a heat lamp over it). The way in which a female rodent picks up her pup is quite consistent; she gingerly grasps the animal by the back, managing not to injure it with her very sharp teeth (I can personally attest to the ease with which these teeth can penetrate skin) and carries the pup with a characteristic prancing walk, her head held high. (See **FIGURE 16.6.**) The pup is brought back to the nest and is left there. The female then leaves the nest again to search for another pup. She will continue to retrieve pups until she finds no more; she does not count her pups and stop retrieving when they are all back. A mouse or rat

FIGURE 16.6 A female mouse carrying one of her pups.

does not appear to discriminate between her own young and that of another female, but will accept all the pups she is offered. I once observed two lactating female mice with nests in corners of the same cage, diagonally opposite each other. I disturbed their nests, which triggered a long bout of retrieving, during which each mother stole youngsters from the other's nest. The mothers kept up their exchange for a long time, passing each other in the middle of the cage.

Maternal behavior begins to wane as the pups become more active and begin to look more like adult mice. At around 16 to 18 days of age they are able to get about easily by themselves, and they begin to obtain their own food. The mother ceases to retrieve them when they leave the nest (although they still return to the nest to nurse), and she will eventually run away from them if they attempt to nurse.

Stimuli that Elicit and Maintain Maternal Behavior

Most virgin female rats will begin to retrieve and care for young pups after having infants placed with them for several days, a process called *sensitization* or *concaveation* (Wiesner and Sheard, 1933). The same phenomenon can be observed in mice, but a higher percentage of these animals are spontaneously "maternal" anyway. Olfaction and audition appear to be the primary senses involved in sensitization, but they act in different ways. Noirot (1970) exposed virgin female mice to the sound of the distress calls of an isolated pup; these mice engaged in more nest-building behavior than did controls. On the other hand, exposure to the odor, but not the sound, of pups (the presence of a nest that previously held a litter of mice) enhanced subsequent handling and licking of pups, but not nest-building.

Mouse, rat, and hamster pups emit at least two different kinds of ultrasonic calls (see Noirot, 1972). These sounds cannot be heard by humans, but have to be translated into lower frequencies by a special device (a "bat detector") in order to be perceived by the experimenter. The mother can, of course, hear these calls. When a pup gets cold (as it would if removed from the nest), it emits a characteristic call that brings the mother (or any other sensitized female) out of her nest. The sound is so effective that female mice have been observed to chew the cover off of a loudspeaker that is transmitting a recording of this call. Once out of the nest, the female uses olfactory cues as well as auditory ones to find the pups, since she can even find a buried, anesthetized baby mouse that is unable to make any noise. The second call is made in response to rough handling. When a mother hears this sound, she stops what she is doing. Typically, it is she who is administering the rough handling, and the distress call makes her stop. This mechanism undoubtedly plays an important role in the training of mother mice in the proper handling of pups.

Olfaction and the olfactory bulbs play an important role in controlling maternal behavior, but the means by which this occurs is uncertain. Removal of the olfactory bulbs causes pup killing and eating in female rats (Fleming and Rosenblatt, 1974a) and mice (Gandelman, Zarrow, Denenberg, and Myers, 1971). However, elimination of olfactory sensitivity by application of zinc sulfate to the olfactory mucosa was found to facilitate sensitization of virgin female mice by pups (Fleming and Rosenblatt, 1974b). These rats showed less of the ambivalence normally shown by naive rats toward pups; instead of approaching them gingerly, sniffing them, and then sudenly jumping back, the animals approached them more boldly. Apparently some aspect of the odor of the pups had an inhibitory effect. The fact that removal of the olfactory bulbs induces killing and cannibalism attests to the fact that this structure does more than simply transmit olfactory information to the brain.

Hormonal Control of Maternal Behavior

Nest building behavior appears to be primarily dependent on progesterone, the principal hormone of pregnancy. Lisk (1962) found that nonpregnant female mice built brood nests after a pellet of progesterone was implanted under the skin. The pellet slowly dissolved, maintaining a continuously high level of progesterone. The enhanced nest building was suppressed by the administration of estrogen. After parturition, the mothers continued to maintain their nests, and they constructed new nests if necessary. Their blood level of progesterone was very low then, but Voci and Carlson (1973) found that hypothalamic implants of prolactin (the principal hormone of the lactation period) as well as progesterone facilitated nest building in mice. Presumably, nest building can be facilitated by either hormone: progesterone during pregnancy and prolactin after parturition.

A pregnant female rat might retrieve and take care of a young pup if one is offered to her (she cannot provide milk, of course); the probability that she will do so increases as the gestational period proceeds (Rosenblatt, 1969). She will not attend to the pups immediately, but only after they have been around for a while. Figure 16.7 shows the percentage of females that began to retrieve pups as a function of days of pregnancy. (A fresh batch of pups was presented each day.) Note that the females given pups on day 17 of the gestational period (which takes 21 to 23 days) show an interest in them sooner than do females that receive the pups on day 11. (See **FIGURE 16.7.**)

At the time of parturition, the mother is immediately ready to

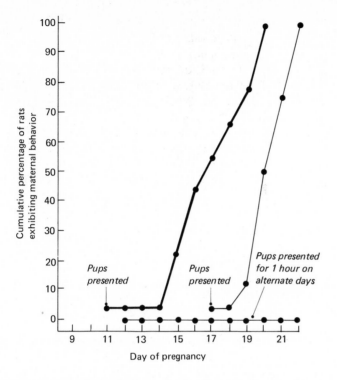

FIGURE 16.7 Cumulative percentage of pregnant female rats exhibiting maternal behavior as a function of days of exposure to pups. (From Rosenblatt, J. S., *American Journal of Orthopsychiatry*, 1969, 39, 36–56. Copyright © 1969 by the American Orthopsychiatric Association, Inc.)

care for her pups. She will do so even if her pups are taken by caesarian section and presented to her later (Moltz, Robbins, and Parks, 1966); the experience of parturition is not necessary for the initiation of maternal behavior.

It would appear likely that some hormone is responsible for the initiation of maternal behavior, and the assumption is commonly made that this hormone is prolactin, which is present in high levels around the time of birth. Riddle, Lahr, and Bates (1942) found that injections of prolactin induced maternal behavior in virgin female rats, but later investigators criticized their experimental procedure and found that prolactin alone did *not* initiate maternal behavior (Lott and Fuchs, 1962; Beach and Wilson, 1963). In a series of hormonal administrations that attempted to simulate the estrogen-progesterone-prolactin sequence of pregnancy and parturition, Moltz, Lubin, Leon, and Numan (1970) were able to facilitate maternal behavior in virgin female rats. Almost all rats will eventually exhibit maternal behavior, but they require around 7 days of sensitization, as we saw earlier. Moltz and his colleagues were able to shorten this sensitization time to between 1 and 2 days. Rats that received only estrogen and progesterone in the sequence also showed facilitated maternal behavior, but this sequence itself has been shown to stimulate prolactin secretion (Amenomori, Chen, and Meites, 1970).

The entire story of the role of the endocrine system in the initiation of maternal behavior has not yet been told, however. Terkel and Rosenblatt (1968) found that blood plasma taken from a lactating rat induced maternal behavior (within an average of 2 days) when injected into a virgin female. Only one injection was necessary, as opposed to the long series of injections used by Moltz and his colleagues. And a special technique that allows the continuous exchange of blood between a virgin female and one giving birth induced maternal behavior in about half a day (Terkel, 1970; 1972). No studies using pure hormones have been able to accomplish such rapid sensitization, so it remains distinctly possible that some unidentified humoral factors (besides the known female hormones) are responsible for the induction of maternal behavior.

Neural Control of Maternal Behavior

The most critical brain region responsible for maternal behavior appears to be the medial preoptic area. Numan (1974) found that medial preoptic lesions, or knife cuts that isolated this region from the medial forebrain bundle, disrupted both nest building and pup care. The mothers simply ignored their offspring. Female sexual behavior was unaffected by these lesions, however. Numan noted that similar lesions have been shown to disrupt male sexual behavior (Hitt, Hendricks, Ginsberg, and Lewis, 1970; Paxinos and Bindra, 1973). More caudal hypothalamic damage was shown to disrupt female sexual behavior (Kalra and Sawyer, 1970) but not maternal behavior or male sexual behavior (Yokoyama, Halasz, and Sawyer, 1967; Paxinos and Bindra, 1972).

Numan did not observe any deficits in maternal behavior or nest building after lesions of the stria terminalis (one of the two fiber systems that interconnect amygdala and hypothalamus). Data from my laboratory are contradictory, however. Leanna Standish, Richard Valcourt, and I found that lesions of the stria terminalis eliminated nest building in both pregnant and lactating mice. Maternal behavior is apparently normal, but we do not yet have enough data to be sure. Even when the mice were put into a refrigerator (a procedure that normally stimulates them to build a nest to conserve body heat), the brain-damaged mice failed to build nests. (I should note that the refrigerated mice did not seem to suffer any ill effects from their ordeal.) Since Numan noted that half of the lesions produced in his experiments missed the stria terminalis on one side of the brain, it is possible that he did not totally interrupt the fibers of this system.

Various lesions of the limbic system will disrupt the sequence, but not the elements, of maternal behavior. Slotnick (1967) found that lesions of the cingulate cortex in rats resulted in a scrambling of the normal sequence of pup retrieval. The mother would pick up a pup, enter the nest, walk out again still carrying the pup, drop it, try to nurse one pup outside the nest, remove pups from the nest, and, in general, act extremely confused. The component behavioral acts that make up pup care (e.g., picking up the pup and licking its anogenital region) were still present, but the behaviors appeared to occur at random. Garth Thomas and I (Carlson and Thomas, 1968) observed an even more severe deficit (including a total lack of nest building) after lesions of the septum (a structure in the limbic system) of mice. Cingulate lesions, in comparison, produced only a slight deficit. The animals with septal lesions did not improve in their performance, as do both rats and mice (Slotnick and Nigrosh, 1975) with cingulate lesions. Miriam Portnoy and I found that even experienced mothers showed this confused behavior after they were given septal lesions.

It is interesting to note that septal lesions do not seem to impair the ability of a mouse to carry things from one place to another in the cage. Julie Virta and I found that mice with septal lesions could be trained to pick up plastic tokens from anywhere in the cage and carry them over to a small dish. When the tokens were deposited into the dish, a food pellet was dropped into another container. However, these same females were unable to get their pups back into the nesting box where they normally stayed; once they picked up a pup they did not seem to know what to do with it.

The most plausible explanation for this behavior (at least for me) is the following: The hippocampus has been shown to be important in finding one's way around; lesions of this structure severely impair maze-learning ability (Douglas, 1967) and, indeed, maternal behavior (Kimble, Rogers, and Hendrickson, 1967). Septal lesions disrupt connections between hypothalamus and hippocampus, but not between cortex and hippocampus. (See **FIGURE 16.8.**) Septal lesions produce only slight disruption in the ability to learn a maze (Thomas, Hostetter, and Barker, 1968), presumably because the corticohippocampal connections are not damaged by septal lesions. Perhaps these corticohippocampal connections also function in token retrieving. It is possible that mice and rats cannot perform the behavioral sequence of pup retrieval because the hypothalamic and preoptic circuits that mediate maternal behavior can no longer communicate with the hippocampus, which is so important to spatial orientation.

Jeff Blaustein and I found that another species-typical behavior that requires spatial integration (hoarding of food) was disrupted by septal lesions, whereas cockroach killing was not. This predatory behavior consists of an extremely excited chase and a stereotyped bite at the head, very similar to rat killing by cats. The mice did not have to integrate their behavior spatially; they only had to follow the cockroach (an enormous variety of *Blattis americanis*) as it ran around the cage. These studies suggest that septal lesions do not

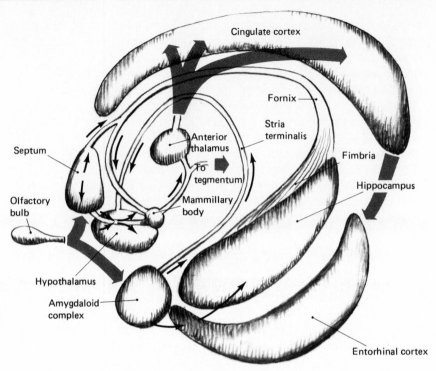

Cingulate cortex

Fornix

Stria terminalis

Anterior thalamus

Fimbria

Septum

To tegmentum

Hippocampus

Olfactory bulb

Mammillary body

Hypothalamus

Amygdaloid complex

Entorhinal cortex

FIGURE 16.8 A schematic and simplified representation of the limbic system. Note that septal lesions disconnect the hippocampus and hypothalamus, but spare the connections between hippocampus and cortex.

impair the sequences, but disrupt the connections between neural circuits that initiate species-typical behaviors (such as pup retrieving and the circuits necessary for spatially guided behaviors).

It must be concluded that the analysis of the hormonal and neural mechanisms involved in maternal behavior is still in its infancy (is that a pun?) and that much more work must be done before a clearer picture of its physiological control will emerge.

SUGGESTED READINGS

CLEMENTE, C. D., and CHASE, M. H. Neurological substrates of aggressive behavior. *Annual Review of Physiology*, 1973, 35, 329–356.

FLYNN, J., VANEGAS, H., FOOTE, W., and EDWARDS, S. Neural mechanisms involved in a cat's attack on a rat. In *The Neural Control of Behavior*, edited by R. F. Whalen, R. F. Thompson M. Verzeano, and N. M. Weinberger. New York: Academic Press, 1970.

MOYER, K. E. *The Physiology of Hostility*. Chicago: Markham, 1971.

These references review most of the research concerning the physiology of aggression.

SLOTNICK, B. M. Neural and hormonal basis of maternal behavior in the rat. In *Hormonal Correlates of Behavior, Vol. 2*, edited by B. E. Eleftheriou and R. L. Sprott. New York: Plenum Press, 1975. This chapter is an up-to-date review of the literature on the physiology of maternal behavior in rats.

VALENSTEIN, E. S. *Brain Control*. New York: Wiley, 1973. This book is a must for people interested in the topic of psychosurgery and electrical stimulation of the human brain.

Reward and
Punishment

17

The phenomenon of reinforcement is very important in the lives of higher organisms. If a given behavior is followed by a certain class of stimuli (positive reinforcers), there will be an increase in the likelihood of the subsequent occurrence of that behavior. If the behavior is followed by another class of stimuli (punishers or aversive stimuli), it is less likely to occur again. The animal can thus be *rewarded* or *punished* for a given behavior.

Most classes of positively reinforcing (rewarding) stimuli are closely related to homeostatic needs, such as food, water, and body temperature. Others are related to nonhomeostatic drives, such as sex. The effectiveness of many reinforcing stimuli depends on the presence of a particular drive (e.g., water can be used as a reward only if the animal is already thirsty); therefore, many investigators have assumed that rewarding stimuli exert their effect by reducing the level of drive. Drive, then, is seen by some people to be an aversive state, and its reduction is thus seen to be rewarding.

The fact that some kinds of drive are not based on homeostatic need makes it very difficult to test the hypothesis that drive reduction is a necessary aspect of reinforcing stimuli. Sex drive is a clear-cut example of a drive, and it is one that is of obvious biological utility. But what can we conclude about the fact that the behavior of an animal can be rewarded by giving it the opportunity to explore another chamber, or even to look out a window? We can, of course, postulate an "exploratory drive." However, if we name a new drive every time a new class of reinforcing stimuli is discovered, we are not proving that drive (and its reduction) is a necessary component of reward. What we have done is to construct a circular argument: A must be present for B to occur, so whenever we observe B, we know that A must have been present. In order to prove that A is a necessary condition for the occurrence of B, we must be able to detect the presence of A by some independent means. We can (theoretically at least) detect the presence of physiological conditions that underlie homeostatic drives such as thirst; we can measure the volume and osmotic pressure of the blood plasma, for example. But the presence of an "exploratory drive" can be detected only by the fact that an animal will alter its behavior for the opportunity to explore. Unless we can measure some physiological manifestation of "exploratory drive" and determine that the animal will work for the opportunity to explore when the drive is present, but not when it is absent, we cannot evaluate the role of drive reduction in rewards not related to homeostasis.

A discovery made in 1953 by James Olds and Peter Milner produced a revolutionary change in the approach to the problem of reinforcement. They found that electrical stimulation of the brain could be reinforcing. Furthermore, it was soon discovered that the rewarding brain stimulation was found in regions of the brain associated with *increases*, rather than decreases, in drives.

The first part of this chapter will be concerned with the phenomenon of reinforcing brain stimulation, and a discussion of what this phenomenon tells us about drive and reward. I shall also consider the implications of such brain stimulation for human society, and I shall evaluate a theory that implicates neural reward mechanisms in schizophrenia. In the second part of the chapter I shall deal with aversive stimulation: pain and brain mechanisms of punishment.

REWARDING BRAIN STIMULATION

Its Discovery

The discovery of the rewarding properties of brain stimulation was made by accident. Dr. James Olds was investigating whether electrical stimulation of the reticular formation might increase arousal and thus facilitate the learning process. He was assisted in this project by Peter Milner (who was a graduate student at the time).

Olds had heard a paper, presented by Neal Miller, that described the aversive effects of electrical stimulation of the brain. Therefore, he decided to make sure that stimulation of the reticular formation was not aversive—if it would be, the effects of this stimulation on the speed of learning would be difficult to assess. Fortunately for the investigators, one of the electrodes missed its target; the tip wound up some millimeters away, probably in the hypothalamus (the brain of this animal was lost).

Here is Olds's description of what happened when he tested this animal to see if the brain stimulation was aversive:

> I applied a brief train of 60-cycle sine-wave electrical current whenever the animal entered one corner of the enclosure. The animal did not stay away from that corner, but rather came back quickly after a brief sortie which followed the first stimulation and came back even more quickly after a briefer sortie which followed the second stimulation. By the time the third electrical stimulus had been applied the animal seemed indubitably to be "coming back for more." (Olds, 1973, p. 81)

Olds and Milner then implanted electrodes in the brain of a group of rats and allowed the animals to administer their own brain stimulation by pressing a lever-operated switch in an operant chamber. (See **FIGURE 17.1.**) The animals readily pressed the lever; in the initial study (Olds and Milner, 1954) they reported response rates of over 700 per hour. In subsequent studies, rates of many thousands of responses per hour have been obtained.

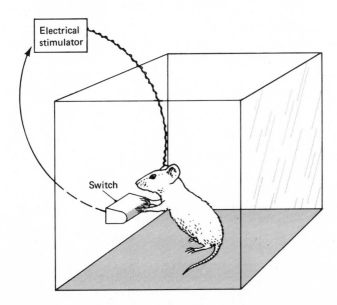

Electrical stimulator

Switch

FIGURE 17.1 A rat in a self-stimulation apparatus.

The Potency of Rewarding Brain Stimulation

The reinforcing effect of brain stimulation is very potent; a hungry rat will often ignore food when it is able to press a lever for shocks to the brain. Routtenberg and Lindy (1965) trained rats to press two levers—one delivered rewarding electrical brain stimulation (ESB), whereas presses on the other one produced food pellets. The animals were allowed to press the levers for only one hour each day, and some of them spent so much time at the bar that administered ESB that they starved to death. When food and ESB are continuously available, however, rats will alternately eat, press the lever for ESB, and sleep; they will not remain at the lever to the exclusion of other activities (Valenstein and Beer, 1964). ESB is a powerful reinforcer, but subjects will not starve in preference to leaving the lever, except under very special circumstances (i.e., when the opportunity to obtain food is sharply restricted).

Anatomy of the "Reward System"

Electrical stimulation delivered to a wide variety of locations will reinforce lever pressing (or other behaviors). Self-stimulation can be elicited most reliably from electrodes placed in the medial forebrain bundle (MFB) and the septum, although various other positive locations have been reported: amygdala, hippocampus, basal ganglia, thalamus, reticular formation, limbic cortex, and neocortex (Wetzel, 1968; Gallistel, 1973). Most investigators agree that the most important system is the MFB, and this region has received the most attention.

The medial forebrain bundle consists of a diffuse system of fibers near the base of the brain, running from the anterior telecephalon to the ventral tegmentum. It carries both ascending and descending fibers, and it communicates with the hippocampus (via relays in the septum), with various hypothalamic nuclei, and with tegmental sensory and motor systems.

The neural pathways followed by the reinforcing stimuli have not been clearly charted. Lesions in a wide variety of structures—amygdala, fornix, dorsal thalamus, septum, central gray—do *not* disrupt self-stimulation (Asdourian, Stutz, and Rocklin, 1966; Valenstein, 1966). Even lesions of the MFB anterior to or posterior to the electrode site do not disrupt self-stimulation, according to Lorens (1966) and Valenstein (1966). However, Olds and Olds (1969) found that lesions in the MFB caudal to the electrode tip *did* disrupt self-stimulation. The disruption was not due to debilitation; the animals still pressed the lever for stimulation delivered to electrodes *caudal* to the lesion. It would appear, then, that the reinforcing effect is exerted upon more caudal structures, where the motor mechanisms producing the responses are located, perhaps.

The "Naturalness" of Rewarding Brain Stimulation

ESB appears to produce effects that are different from what one would expect if the stimulation were producing pure "reward." These phenomena are all, in one way or another, related to the interval between one reinforcement and the next.

OVERNIGHT DECREMENTS AND PRIMING. As we have seen, ESB is very reinforcing; behaviors rewarded by ESB will persist at a very high rate for many hours, until the animal becomes exhausted. The only natural reward that comes close to sustaining long bouts of responding is a mixture of saccharin and dilute glucose (Valenstein, Cox, and Kakolewski, 1967). Despite the fact that ESB seems to be so reinforcing, an animal that responded at very high rates on one day is often observed to ignore the lever the next day when put into the testing chamber. If the animal is then given one or two "free" shots of ESB, it will run to the lever and begin responding again. These phenomena, *overnight decrements* and the *priming* effect of a few rewarding stimulations delivered by the experimenter, have been observed in a large number of studies (e.g., Olds and Milner, 1954; Wetzel, 1963). It should be noted, however, that not all rats show these phenomena. Kent and Grossman (1969) observed that the performance of some of their rats did not decline overnight, and hence these animals did not require any "priming."

RAPID EXTINCTION. Just as most animals show overnight decrements, their responding will also extinguish very quickly when reinforcement is withheld. If a rat is trained to depress a lever for a natural reward such as food or water, it will eventually stop responding when the lever is disconnected (so that reinforcements are no longer delivered). When the same is done for an animal pressing the lever for ESB, the extinction is much more rapid (Seward, Uyeda, and Olds, 1959). In fact, Howarth and Deutsch (1962) found that extinction seemed to be more a function of time since the last reinforcement than the number of nonreinforced responses made. These investigators withdrew the lever from the apparatus (so that the rats could not respond) for a short period of time (2.5 to 10 seconds) and then replaced it, counting the number of responses the rats made before they stopped. They found that rats made fewer responses the longer the lever was kept outside the apparatus. It did not appear to matter whether or not the animals were permitted to respond; probability of making a response declined as a function of time since the last reinforcement. (See **FIGURE 17.2.**) This phenomenon does *not* occur when a rat is given a natural reinforcer; Quartermain and Webster (1968) found such a time-dependent decline when rats were reinforced with ESB, but not when they were made thirsty and reinforced with water.

THE IMMEDIACY OF ESB: AN EXPLANATION FOR RAPID EXTINCTION? Gibson, Reid, Sakai, and Porter (1965) noted that there is a basic difference in the way that ESB and natural reinforcers are delivered in an operant situation, and perhaps these differences might account for the fact that responding for rewarding brain stimulation is so rapid. ESB is administered as soon as the lever is pressed, whereas the lever press for food reward is only the first in a sequence of responses, including approach to the foodcup and the act of consuming the food. Perhaps it is the "immediacy" of the presentation of ESB that makes behaviors learned for this type of reward so subject to extinction.

Experimental Evidence. This explanation does not appear to be true. Panksepp and Trowill (1967a) designed an experiment that closely simulated the time factor of ESB delivery. They attached chronic *fistulas* to a group of rats. These devices permitted injection of liquid directly into the mouth. Panksepp and Trowill trained rats to press a lever for chocolate milk—a highly preferred food, for rats. Some rats received chocolate milk immediately after a lever press (group *oral-immediate*) whereas others received it only after a 3.3-second delay (group *oral-delay*). Members of group *oral-immediate* showed very rapid acquisition (in 1 to 3.5 minutes), whereas rats that received the milk after a delay (group *oral-delay*) took 18 to 35 minutes to learn the task. When the lever was disconnected, however, these

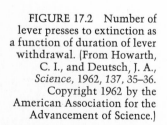

FIGURE 17.2 Number of lever presses to extinction as a function of duration of lever withdrawal. (From Howarth, C. I., and Deutsch, J. A., *Science*, 1962, 137, 35–36. Copyright 1962 by the American Association for the Advancement of Science.)

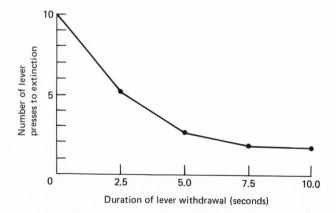

two groups showed nearly identical rates of extinction, as is shown in **FIGURE 17.3.**

The rats in Panksepp and Trowill's study did not show the rapid extinction seen in animals that respond for ESB, despite the fact that the intraoral injection closely simulated the way in which brain stimulation is delivered. However, in a second study, using a different procedure, Panksepp and Trowill (1967b) *did* succeed in obtaining rapid extinction of responding for intraoral reward. They noted that animals responding for ESB are generally trained in the absence of any obvious drive state, whereas subjects that are given food reward are first made hungry. Perhaps the drive (hunger) retards the process of extinction when the response was originally rewarded by the delivery of food. They suggested that it would be more appropriate to compare rats responding for ESB with *nonhungry* rats responding for food.

Rats, like humans, have a "sweet tooth." Even if they have just finished a meal, they manage to find some room for a highly preferred food like chocolate milk, and they will, in fact, press a lever for intraoral delivery of this substance. Panksepp and Trowill compared the rates of extinction of hungry rats and sated rats pressing a lever for injections of chocolate milk into the mouth. When the lever was turned off, the hungry rats pressed the lever almost three times more than the sated rats did. Furthermore, extinction of the response of sated rats occurred even when the animals were prevented from responding for a period of time; they showed the same decline that was seen by Howarth and Deutsch (Figure 17.2). The animals whose responses had been extinguished could even be "primed" to begin responding again. The behavior shown by sated animals receiving a very palatable food is thus similar to that of an animal receiving reinforcing brain stimulation. Trowill, Panksepp, and Gandelman (1969) suggested that this similarity might be due to the *incentive* effects of both kinds of reward. Incentive is defined as some sort of "anticipation" of reinforcement: an effect that "seems to depend primarily on the animal's recent history of reinforcement . . ." (Bolles, 1967). It is an energizing system, the level of which can be raised or lowered quickly, depending on the animal's expectancy of reward.

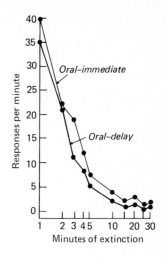

FIGURE 17.3   Rate of extinction of lever pressing of rats that received oral reinforcement immediately or after a delay. (Redrawn from Panksepp, J., and Trowill, J. A., *Psychonomic Science*, 1967, *9*, 405–406.)

Two-Factor Theory

A prominent theoretical account of the way in which ESB affects behavior has been presented by Deutsch and Howarth (1963) and by Gallistel (1973). This theory suggests that ESB has two effects: (1) A *rewarding effect* raises the probability of recurrence of the response that immediately preceded it (just as delivery of a natural reinforcer would do). The rewarding effect is important for learning to make the response, therefore. (2) A *drive-inducing effect* produces a temporary mobilizing effect, which is necessary for *performance* of the response. Just as food deprivation will cause an animal to perform a previously learned task in order to obtain food, the drive-inducing effect of ESB is assumed to energize the animal to perform a response to obtain rewarding brain stimulation. In other words, the immediate, primary effect of ESB is rewarding. The aftereffect of ESB is to make the animal want more.

There is considerable merit in the two-factor theory. It very nicely explains the priming effect (drive is raised by administering ESB) and the fact that extinction takes place rapidly and even occurs if the animal is not allowed access to the bar (the drive decays with time). Other evidence supports this theory.

INVESTIGATION OF THE DRIVE-INDUCING EFFECTS OF ESB. Gallistel (1969) investigated the decay of the hypothesized drive-inducing effects of ESB. He reinforced the animals with "trains" of brief pulses of current to the brain. The rats were taught to traverse a runway for ESB delivered when the animal reached the far end. The rats were given a variable number (one to twenty) of "priming" pulse trains of ESB (sixty-four pulses in each train) just before they were placed in the starting box, and they were then given a fixed number of pulses (sixteen) as a reward when they reached the goalbox at the end. The procedure is outlined in **FIGURE 17.4.**

Gallistel found that the speed of running depended on two factors: the number of priming shocks the subject received and the amount of time since the priming shocks were administered. Figure

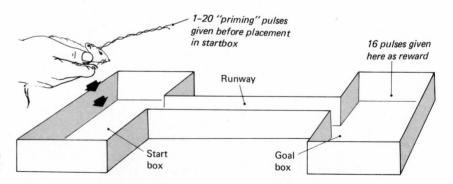

1–20 "priming" pulses given before placement in startbox

16 pulses given here as reward

Runway

Start box

Goal box

FIGURE 17.4 The procedure used by Gallistel (1969).

17.5 shows data obtained from one rat; note how one priming pulse train facilitated running only slightly (the effect lasted less than 30 seconds), whereas twenty priming pulse trains produced a much more striking increase in running speed. (See **FIGURE 17.5.**)

Another experiment (Gallistel, Stellar, and Bubis, 1974) clearly separated the rewarding and drive-inducing effects of ESB. The rats were given priming ESB and were then allowed to traverse a runway, where they could receive ESB for pressing a lever. The priming and rewarding stimulations were varied. Figure 17.6 shows the effects of manipulating the magnitude of priming ESB or rewarding ESB on running speed. Note that increases or decreases in priming ESB (thick lines) had an *immediate* effect on running speed, as would be predicted if the brain stimulation caused an increase in drive. (See **FIGURE 17.6.**) Increases or decreases in rewarding ESB (thin lines) delivered at the end of the runway had a *gradual* effect on performance—it was as if the animals had to learn to run faster for the reward. (See **FIGURE 17.6.**)

The data appear to show quite conclusively that ESB can have an aftereffect that influences subsequent behavior. Not all in-

FIGURE 17.5 Data from the procedure shown in Figure 17.4: Running time as a function of delay after varying amounts of priming stimulation. (From Gallistel, C. R., *Journal of Comparative and Physiological Psychology,* 1969, 69, 713–721.)

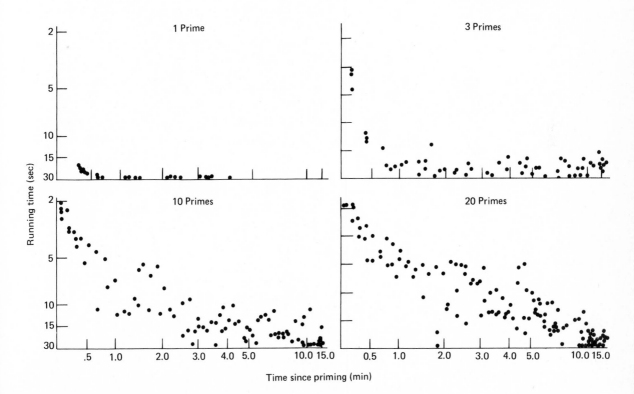

Time since priming (min)

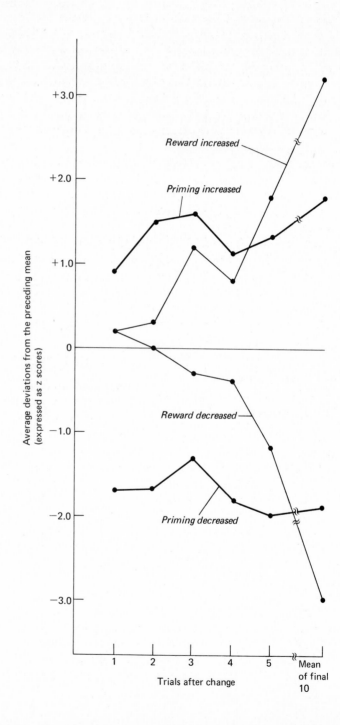

FIGURE 17.6   The immediate
effects of change in magnitude
of priming stimulation as
contrasted with the gradual
effects of change in magnitude
of reinforcing stimulation.
(From Gallistel, C. R., Stellar,
J. R., and Bubis, E., *Journal of
Comparative and
Physiological Psychology,*
1974, 87, 848–859.)

vestigators, as we shall see, would agree with Deutsch and Gallistel that the aftereffects, when they occur, should be called drive.

INTERACTIONS BETWEEN ESB AND HOMEOSTATIC DRIVES.   There appears to be a relationship between ESB and natural drives.   For example, brain stimulation that elicits such behaviors as eating and drinking will usually be found to be reinforcing, if the animal is permitted to press a lever for its delivery.   Why should an animal press a lever in order to make itself hungry or thirsty?   This fact is certainly not consistent with theories that state that the reduction in drive is what constitutes reward.   It should be aversive to become more hungry or more thirsty.

Rates of responding for ESB (when the shock is delivered to the region of the MFB that is also involved with feeding behavior) have been found to co-vary with alterations in hunger, no matter how these alterations are produced.   Increases in both hunger and response rate were produced by food deprivation and injections of insulin.   Decreases were produced by normal feeding, gastric feeding, and glucagon injections (Balagura and Hoebel, 1967; Mount and Hoebel, 1967; Hoebel, 1968).   Furthermore, Deutsch and DiCara (1967) found that it took longer to extinguish behavior previously reinforced by ESB when the animals were deprived of food prior to starting the extinction procedure.   ESB thus appears to be even more reinforcing when the animal's drive state is increased.

How can we explain these results?   Deutsch and Gallistel would suggest that the natural drive is added to the aftereffects of ESB, thus providing the animal with more motivation to work for the stimulation.   We saw earlier that increases or decreases in priming pulses of ESB had an immediate effect on running speed in the runway–lever press experiment of Gallistel, Stellar, and Bubis.   Alterations in the amount of rewarding ESB delivered after lever presses at the end of the runway had gradual effects on running speed.   Thus, the researchers concluded that the effect of the priming stimulation appeared to be a drivelike phenomenon.   In a later study, Stellar and Gallistel (1975) found that when a hungry rat was trained to traverse the runway and press the lever for ESB, the running speed could be facilitated by "priming" the animal with food pellets just before placing it in the start box.   Thus, a shot of ESB acted like a piece of food; both facilitated performance.

Gallistel has presented a diagram that summarizes this hypothesis.   Drive is normally produced by a variety of means (homeostatic imbalance, the appropriate hormones, presence of a receptive sex partner).   The "energy" of this drive can be channeled into a number of different activities; for example, a hungry rat will press a lever, or run through a maze, or do whatever is necessary to obtain food. The particular behavior that occurs depends upon the animal's past history. Whichever behaviors have been rewarded in the past by the presence of food will tend to occur again. Reward thus has a selecting function; drive, when present, will be channeled into the appropriate behavior. ESB is assumed to artificially stimulate both mechanisms, the reward system and the drive system; the drive enhancement supposedly lasts for a period of time. (See **FIGURE 17.7.**)

Alternatives to the Two-Factor Theory

POSITIVE FEEDBACK THEORIES.   Regulatory mechanisms are characterized by negative feedback loops: an imbalance elicits a correctional mechanism, which restores the balance and thus shuts itself off. Such a system is schematized in **FIGURE 17.8.** As we saw in chapter 12, there also appear to be positive feedback mechanisms; the effect of the sight, odor, and taste of food, and of the act of ingestion itself, is to *increase* hunger, not to decrease it. A particularly dramatic ex-

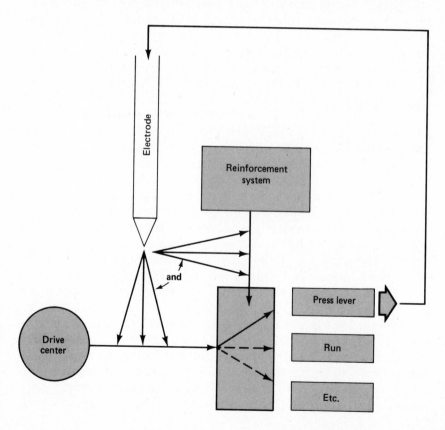

FIGURE 17.7   A schematic representation of Gallistel's two-factor theory of reinforcing brain stimulation. (From Gallistel, C. R. In Deutsch, J. A. (ed.), *The Physiological Basis of Memory.* Copyright 1973 by Academic Press, New York.)

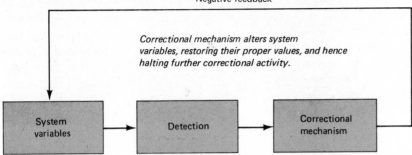

Negative feedback

Correctional mechanism alters system
variables, restoring their proper values, and hence
halting further correctional activity.

System variables → Detection → Correctional mechanism

FIGURE 17.8   A negative feedback loop.

ample of this positive feedback would be the "feeding frenzy" sometimes seen in groups of sharks or other fish. Ultimately, of course,
the satiety signals arising as a result of the ingestion of food suppress
further eating; the positive feedback loop is overwhelmed by a more
powerful negative feedback loop. As I noted in chapter 12, a clearer
example of positive feedback is provided by sexual behavior. One
can only conclude that increases in sexual arousal are positively
reinforcing—otherwise, why would people engage in foreplay? Similarly, most people enjoy momentary frights, or "thrills," such as roller
coasters or horror films. Children generally like to be thrown into
the air, or to be startled by a loud "Boo!" They may run away, but
usually the children will come back to say "Do it again!" So, perhaps,
at least some increases in drive are positively reinforcing.

If there is a brain mechanism responsible for the fact that increases in drive are reinforcing, then perhaps electrical stimulation
of the brain, by artificially exciting this system, could produce an
effect that is both rewarding and activating. Instead of hypothesizing
two different effects, perhaps there is only one.

Experimental Evidence.   There is evidence in support of this
positive feedback hypothesis. Nearly all electrode locations whose
stimulation elicits a particular "motivated behavior" (i.e., one that
appears to be related to a particular drive) will also sustain self-stimulation. Furthermore, stimuli that would be presumed to increase the
drive should also serve to increase the rate of self-stimulation.

Mendelson (1967) tested rats that would press a lever for brain
stimulation that would also elicit drinking. He adjusted the current
level to a point just sufficient to elicit drinking. At this intensity,
ESB was too low to elicit self-stimulation in some of his subjects.
When the same subjects were presented with water, they rapidly began to press the bar; the availability of water made the brain stimulation reinforcing. Figure 17.9 illustrates the performance of one of
Mendelson's subjects—the upper curve represents the number of lever

presses made for ESB with water available, while the lower curve represents performance for ESB alone.   (See **FIGURE 17.9.**)

In a similar study, Coons and Cruce (1968) found that the availability of food would also increase the reinforcing effects of brain stimulation that would elicit eating.   The effect does not even appear to be restricted to homeostatic drives; De Sisto and Zweig (1974) tested bar pressing of rats that would either (a) eat food or (b) kill a frog when brain stimulation was administered.   The "eaters" pressed the lever for a longer time when food (but not a frog) was present, whereas the "killers" pressed the lever for a longer time when a frog (but not food) was present.   (See **FIGURE 17.10.**)

Positive Feedback and Natural Rewards.   Positive feedback can be demonstrated in experiments using natural reinforcers, but it is often obscured by satiety mechanisms (negative feedback).   Since ESB does not alter system variables, (e.g., it does not cause the stomach and duodenum to fill up with food), satiety mechanisms are not engaged, and the behavior is maintained by means of positive feedback.

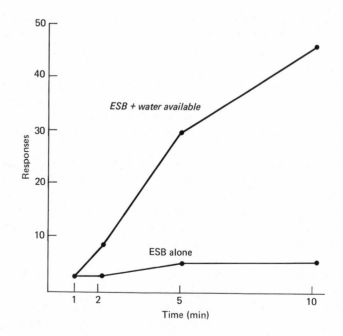

FIGURE 17.9   The effects of the presence of water on lever pressing for electrical stimulation delivered through electrodes that elicit drinking and have a reinforcing effect. (Redrawn from Mendelson, J., *Science, 1967, 157,* 1077–1079. Copyright 1967 by the American Association for the Advancement of Science.)

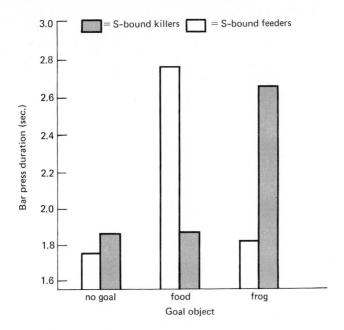

FIGURE 17.10 Effects of the presence of food or frogs on lever pressing of rats that eat or kill frogs in response to electrical stimulation of the brain. (From DeSisto, M. J., and Zweig, M., *Physiological Psychology*, 1974, 2, 67–70.

We saw in chapter 12 that an animal will press a lever longer when responses result in the intraoral, rather than intragastric, administration of food. The animal can taste and swallow the food delivered to the mouth, and this stimulation is apparently reinforcing (i.e., it provides positive feedback to the feeding mechanism). This positive feedback then competes with the negative feedback that results from ingestion; the animal will tolerate more intense satiety signals from the viscera before it ceases eating because of the positive effect of the taste of the food.

Furthermore, Hunsiker and Reid (1974) found that thirsty rats would run faster for water reinforcement when the individual trials were separated by 7 seconds than when they were separated by 95 seconds. Presumably, positive feedback from each trial lasted long enough to facilitate performance on the next trial. That is, one reinforcement "primed" the performance for the next trial, just as ESB can do.

These results are consistent with the hypothesis that drive might involve a positive feedback mechanism that can be excited by the administration of reinforcing brain stimulation. Presumably the same reward system that is excited by the act of eating (or drinking, or frog killing), and that serves to reinforce and maintain this behavior, is also excited by ESB.

CONFLICT THEORIES

Mixed Effects of ESB. It is an interesting fact that the same animal that will respond for a burst of ESB will also respond to *turn off* the same stimulation. Roberts (1958a) found that cats would escape from hypothalamic stimulation but, curiously, did not learn to *avoid* it. They waited until it came, and then they responded. Later, Roberts (1958b) found that the animals would, in fact, work to turn on the same stimulation they would subsequently escape from. Similarly, Bower and Miller (1958) were able to train rats to press one lever to turn ESB on, and to press another to turn it off. Valenstein and Valenstein (1964) found that a wide variety of placements gave these ambivalent effects. It does not appear, then, that the electrode has to be positioned between rewarding and punishing circuits. Rather, prolonged ESB appears to be aversive.

Some investigators (e.g., Kent and Grossman, 1969) have suggested that the drive-inducing effect hypothesized by Deutsch and Gallistel might merely be a consequence of the mixed rewarding and punishing effects of ESB. They noted that some of their rats required priming shots of ESB after they had been away from the lever for a while; others did not. (As I noted before, a considerable amount of evidence indicates that not all rats show the overnight decrement or deleterious effect of long intertrial interval on responding for ESB.) Kent and Grossman suggested that ESB was purely rewarding for the rats that did not need priming, but that it was both rewarding and punishing for rats that required priming.

To test this hypothesis, the investigators attached a pair of shock electrodes to the tails of the "nonprimers." The animals were then given painful tail shocks along with ESB when they pressed the levers. The rats continued to respond, but they now acted like primers. They avoided the lever after they had been away from it for a while, but would return and commence pressing when a "free" shot of ESB plus tail shock was administered. It is interesting to note that a tail shock alone, or even a loud noise, would send the rats back to the lever.

Drug Addiction as a Model for ESB. A particular hypothesis suggests that brain stimulation per se is not reinforcing, but that it temporarily blocks the aversive aftereffects of the *previous* brain stimulation. Ball and Adams (1965) found that rats will learn to go to a place where brain stimulation will *not* be delivered if the stimulations are administered 30 minutes apart, but will go to a place where it *will* be delivered if the stimulation occurs every 20 seconds. Perhaps a single stimulation produces aversive aftereffects lasting more than 20 seconds but less than 30 minutes. The rat would thus be "driven" to receive brain stimulation because only a shot of ESB will remove this unpleasant consequence of the previous administration. Ball (1967) has suggested that ESB produces a profound suppression of sensory input, and that the sudden release of this inhibition produces an unpleasant "rebound." This explanation resembles the model of drug addiction. Morphine, for example, suppresses gastric and intestinal motility, and one of the painful effects of drug withdrawal is the sudden hypermotility—"cramps"—that occurs when the suppression is removed.

Ball's hypothesis can explain why Kent and Grossman's "primers" would not approach the bar after a delay period, and it even accounts for the fact that a tail shock or a loud noise will bring the rats receiving ESB plus tail shock back to the bar—they go there because ESB gets rid of the "unpleasant feelings." However, Ball's hypothesis does not explain why some of Kent and Grossman's rats did not hesitate to approach the bar, even after long intervals; nor does the two-factor theory of Deutsch and Gallistel, for that matter.

Conclusions

It is obvious that ESB produces a variety of effects that are difficult to reconcile, and it seems likely that placement of the electrode is a very crucial matter. There are probably many ways to reinforce behavior, and any single, unitary explanation is undoubtedly doomed to failure. A study by Olds and his colleagues (Olds, Allan, and Briese, 1971) provides evidence that suggests why such a variety of hypotheses have been put forward to explain the effects of ESB. These investigators placed extremely small electrodes (62.5 μm, or approximately 0.002 inches in diameter) in various locations. They hoped that use of such small electrodes would make it likely that stimulation would not affect a wide variety of neural systems. They observed the effect of stimulation on eating and drinking, and they noted whether the stimulations were reinforcing—that is, whether the rats would press a lever for ESB.

Olds and his colleagues found several regions where stimulation had distinctly different effects: (1) eating, but not drinking or self-stimulation; (2) drinking, but not eating or self-stimulation; (3) self-stimulation alone; (4) eating, drinking, and self-stimulation (all from the same electrode); and (5) *suppression* of eating and drinking.

These results suggest that hunger and thirst mechanisms are separable from reward mechanisms; it is possible to elicit eating and drinking with brain stimulation that is not in itself reinforcing. Some people have suggested that ESB is rewarding because it induces a drive that falls again as soon as the current is turned off. The reduction in drive is presumably reinforcing. However, Olds and his colleagues found locations where nonreinforcing electrical stimulation resulted in the execution of behaviors (pressing the appropriate lever) previously reinforced with food or water. Thus, it would appear that the stimulation did indeed elicit drive, and not just the motor patterns of eating or drinking. The fact that this stimulation was not reinforcing argues against the drive-reduction hypothesis as an explanation for the rewarding effects of ESB.

Olds and his colleagues also found brain locations where reinforcement was associated with induction of eating and drinking, but they did not find any places where reinforcement was associated with the *inhibition* of ingestive behaviors. In fact, other studies have shown that stimulation that inhibits feeding and drinking is also aversive. (We have to be careful in determining which phenomenon is cause and which is effect; aversive effects of the stimulation might interfere with ingestive behaviors in a nonregulatory sense, as foot shock would.) Nevertheless, we can still conclude that there is no evidence that drive-reducing stimulation is also reinforcing.

The fact that stimulation delivered through some electrodes produced a rewarding effect without making the rat hungry or thirsty does not prove that reward can be obtained independently of drive. The animals were not given an opportunity to kill mice or frogs, to copulate, or to perform any one of a variety of behaviors that might have resulted from this stimulation. Drive could have been raised, but without the presence of the appropriate goal object, the behaviors associated with this drive could not be seen. Olds and his colleagues demonstrated drive without reward, but we cannot conclude that they demonstrated reward without drive.

Since reward was sometimes associated with drive induction, but never with drive reduction, the results (of this study and others) would appear to favor a positive feedback mechanism as an explanation for the rewarding effects of ESB. Reinforcement, then, might be seen as being the attainment and consumption of the goal object in the presence of the appropriate drive. Drive in itself is *not* aversive (at least at moderate levels); it is one of the necessary components of reinforcement. Animals do not work in order to reduce their drive—they work to obtain the rewarding effect that occurs when they obtain the goal object in the presence of drive. How else can we explain the fact that wealthy Romans used to consume *nux vomicae* (seeds from a certain tree) after a big meal so that they would vomit and could start all over again? Which aspect of a Thanksgiving meal is most pleasant—eating the food or having a distended stomach afterward? In fact, drive reduction would appear to be aversive, resulting from mechanisms of negative feedback that prevent further ingestive behavior.

Study of the phenomenon of rewarding brain stimulation has provided some hints, but we still do not know what reinforcement is, and we will certainly continue to be plagued by contradictory results and by alternative explanations for a given piece of data. The intermingling of different neural systems of rewards, drive, and punishment makes the study of this phenomenon a formidable task.

IMPLICATIONS OF ESB FOR THE CONTROL OF HUMAN BEHAVIOR

The fact that ESB can be so reinforcing—that it is possible to arrange conditions so that a self-stimulating rat will ignore food (Routtenberg and Lindy, 1965) or even neglect its newborn pups (Sonderegger, 1970)—has raised fears that ESB could possibly become, in the hands of a tyrant, a means by which human behavior could be absolutely controlled. Fortunately, there are two sets of arguments against this fear.

Practical Arguments against the Use of ESB

The first argument is practical. If the population can be controlled well enough so that people will submit to surgical implantation of stimulating electrodes, the tyrant's objective has already been achieved. There is no need for inserting these wires. Furthermore, even if electrodes were somehow placed in the brains of unwilling subjects, who would control the buttons? It is conceivable that a factory worker could automatically be administered a shot of ESB whenever a part was assembled, but there would have to be some process that detected that the part was assembled correctly. If the part were simple and could be easily evaluated by machinery, then it is probably the case that a human was not needed to construct the part—it could have been constructed more cheaply by a machine. If the work is more complicated, then it could probably be evaluated only by an inspector, and this means that one would need people present to administer the ESB at the appropriate times. But why bother with all this rigamarole? Hitler had no trouble getting a considerable amount of work out of slave laborers, without recourse to ESB. Fear and pain can be used very effectively to get people to work.

A more fundamental fear might be that our thoughts and attitudes could be controlled by use of ESB. Again, it is difficult to imagine how this could be accomplished. One can only reinforce observable responses, and thoughts are the most private phenomena there are. To effectively control a person's political or social behavior, that person would have to be followed around and given ESB whenever a "correct" behavior occurred. This means that half the population would have to monitor the behavior of the other half. Remember, behaviors reinforced by ESB are subject to rapid extinction; it would not be sufficient merely to monitor and reinforce behaviors periodically. The techniques of social control that are available now seem much more effective than ESB could ever be. If, in a totalitarian society, a person's livelihood, physical amenities, and possibility of advancement depend upon making the "correct" social and political responses, that person's behavior is very likely to come into line.

Rewarding Effects of ESB in Humans

The second argument against the possible use of ESB as an agent for control has been raised by Valenstein (1973). He notes, in a review of the effects of psychosurgery and brain stimulation in humans, that studies have not yet shown ESB to be all that effective in humans. There are problems with this conclusion, since most of the people who have received brain-stimulating electrodes have received them because of some pathology, so the effects of ESB in normal people might be different. Furthermore, the brain of humans has not been mapped the way the rat brain has; perhaps the really effective sites have yet to be discovered. With these reservations in mind, the data argue that whereas ESB can elicit reactions of pleasure and can sustain self-stimulation (button pushing), people can "take it or leave it." For example, Sem-Jacobsen (1968) noted: "In man, curiosity is probably the most dominant causative factor in initiating self-stimulation. If a patient feels 'something,' he might wonder 'Precisely what is the nature of this sensation? What am I feeling? Let me try it once more. Once more! Is it tickling? Is it real pleasure?'" Heath (1964) noted that one of his patients repeatedly pressed the switch because each shot of ESB evoked a vague memory—he kept responding in order to bring the memory more clearly in focus. Another reported: "I have a glowing feeling. I feel good."

Thus, there is not yet any evidence that ESB produces an overwhelming reinforcing effect that could be used to control human behavior to any significant degree. It is interesting that no particular fears have been raised over a manipulation that can, demonstrably, produce a very powerful reinforcing effect—injection of drugs such as heroin. Certainly heroin is a much-feared and much-legislated-against substance. But one does not read articles about the dangers of a dictator first making us become addicted to heroin and then attaching infusion devices to us that could administer small shots of heroin when we perform the "correct" behavior. And yet this is much more practical than ESB ever could be. A shot of heroin is extremely reinforcing, especially if some time has elapsed since the last shot. A person could be induced to work very hard toward some goal in the hopes of getting his injection of heroin, whereas no such overwhelming drive accompanies the absence of ESB. (In fact, to the extent that a "drive" for ESB occurs, it decays quickly after the previous stimulation, as Deutsch and Gallistel have shown.) Perhaps the reason for the fear of ESB (and Valenstein quotes a number of popular articles that express this fear) and the lack of fear of drug addiction as a means of social control can be attributed to relative ignorance about the surgical and technical procedures necessary for the administration of ESB, and a general feeling that electrical stimulation could be used to "control the brain."

THE "REWARD SYSTEM" AND SCHIZOPHRENIA

Stein and Wise (1971) note that many investigators have characterized the cardinal symptom of schizophrenia as a relative lack of *affect* (pronounce it A-fekt, rather than a-FEKT)—a decrease in the expression of emotion. Bleuler (1950) says that "the fundamental symptoms consist of disturbances of association and affectivity," and thoughts "are not related and directed by any unifying concept of purpose or goal." Rado (1964) characterizes lack of affect as resulting from deficiencies in "pleasure resources." These considerations led Stein and Wise to hypothesize that damage to neural reward mechanisms might produce this lack of affect or directedness; the mechanism by which appropriate behaviors can be selected does not function normally in schizophrenia. Therefore, abnormal and inappropriate behaviors begin to intrude.

Stein and Wise present the following evidence for their theory:

1. An inborn "error of metabolism" can selectively destroy noradrenergic terminals.
2. The neural reward mechanism appears to consist of noradrenergic neurons (i.e., those which utilize norepinephrine as a transmitter substance).
3. The enzyme that converts dopamine to norepinephrine is found in lower quantities in the brain of schizophrenic patients, thus suggesting that these brains contain fewer noradrenergic terminals (where the enzyme would be expected to occur).

Schizophrenia and 6-Hydroxydopamine

Stein and Wise note that *6-hydroxydopamine,* a chemical commonly used experimentally to destroy catecholaminergic nerve terminals (i.e., those which use norepinephrine or dopamine as a transmitter substance), can be found to occur naturally in the brain (Senoh, Creveling, Udenfriend, and Witkop, 1959). 6-Hydroxydopamine (6-HD) apparently damages catecholaminergic neurons because it is selectively taken up by the axons and (especially) terminal buttons of the cells. The entry of 6-HD appears to be produced by the same process (the re-uptake mechanism) that removes recently liberated neurotransmitters from the synaptic cleft and thus prevents the postsynaptic potential from lasting too long. (See chapters 4 and 5.) Once 6-HD enters the catecholaminergic nerve terminals, it destroys them, probably because a high concentration of poisonous peroxide is formed. If a genetic error of metabolism resulted in production of high levels of 6-HD, then catecholaminergic terminals might selectively be destroyed, with schizophrenia as the result.

The way in which relatively high levels of 6-HD might be produced in the brains of schizophrenics is not very clear. Stein and Wise suggest that deficits in *dopamine-β-hydroxylase* result in excessive amounts of domapine accumulating in noradrenergic nerve terminals. The enzyme dopamine-β-hydroxylase is necessary for the production of norepinephrine from its precursor, dopamine. (See **FIGURE 17.11.**) If insufficient amounts of this enzyme produce incomplete conversion of dopamine into norepinephrine within the synaptic vesicles, perhaps some dopamine is released into the synaptic cleft of noradrenergic synapses. The dopamine then gets converted, in the synaptic cleft, into 6-hydroxydopamine. The 6-HD then is taken up by the terminals and poisons them. (See **FIGURE 17.12.**)

There is one puzzling fact, however. Some terminals are dopaminergic and consequently release *only* dopamine. Why doesn't the dopamine released from these terminals get converted to 6-hydroxydopamine and thus poison dopaminergic neurons as well? 6-HD does not appear to have a specific affinity for noradrenergic terminals; it kills dopaminergic ones as well. However, since the hypothesized mechanism by which 6-HD might be produced in the brain is admittedly speculative, we cannot rule out Stein and Wise's theory on this basis. Perhaps 6-HD is produced in some other way. Let us therefore turn to evidence concerning the role of norepinephrine in mechanisms of reward.

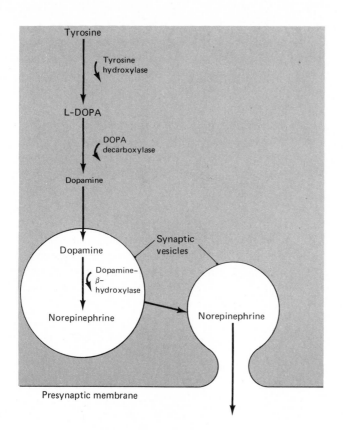

FIGURE 17.11 Normal production of norepinephrine from dopamine within the synaptic vesicles.

The Role of Norepinephrine in Rewarding Brain Stimulation

The participation of noradrenergic neurons in neural systems of re-ward was suggested by the fact that the most effective electrode placements appear to be within the medial forebrain bundle, which contains many noradrenergic fibers. It was found, moreover, that delivery of rewarding brain stimulation produced an increase in norepinephrine in the brain. Nonrewarding stimulation, however, did not (Stein and Wise, 1969). Further studies found that drugs that facilitate the release of norepinephrine from the nerve terminals (e.g., amphetamine) also facilitate responding for ESB. In contrast, drugs such as *α-methyl-para-tyrosine* (AMPT), which prevent the syn-thesis of norepinephrine (but also dopamine), decrease the rate of self-stimulation. So do those drugs (e.g., *chlorpromazine*) that block noradrenergic (and also dopaminergic) receptor sites. Moreover, drugs that inhibit dopamine-β-hydroxylase and thus decrease brain

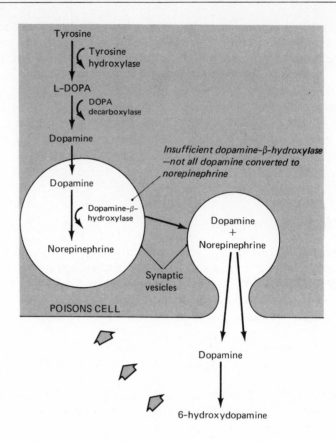

FIGURE 17.12   The Stein and Wise hypothesis: An insufficiency in the amount of dopamine-β-hydroxylase might result in incomplete conversion of dopamine to norepinephrine. The noradrenergic synapse might then liberate some dopamine, which might be converted to 6-hydroxydopamine, which would subsequently kill the nerve terminal.

levels of norepinephrine (but not dopamine) suppress responding for ESB (Stein, Belluzzi, Ritter, and Wise, 1974).

There are two problems with the preceding argument. (1) If schizophrenia resulted from a *deficiency* in norepinephrine, the neurotransmitter in the reward system, then one would expect that chlorpromazine, which blocks postsynaptic receptor sites for norepinephrine (and dopamine) and suppresses self-stimulation, should produce schizophrenic symptoms (or at least aggravate them).   In fact, chlorpromazine is a very effective *antipsychotic* drug, used extensively to alleviate the symptoms of schizophrenia.   (2) Amphetamines (which facilitate the release of norepinephrine and dopamine) facilitate self-stimulation and also produce psychotic symptoms. Stein and his colleagues note, in defense of their theory, that high doses of amphetamine, which induce psychotic symptoms, also suppress, rather than facilitate, self-stimulation.   To counter this argument, we can note that large doses of amphetamine also produce obvious motor effects (stereotyped repetition of behaviors such as sniffing, pacing back and forth, grooming, and rearing up on the hindlegs).   Therefore, it could very well be that these "side effects" interfere with lever pressing. We cannot conclude, as Stein and his colleagues maintain, that large doses of amphetamine decrease the rewarding effect of ESB. We can only say that the animals' response rates go down.

It should also be noted that dopaminergic neurons, as well as noradrenergic neurons, appear to be involved in a system of reward. Fuxe, Nyström, Tovi, Smith, and Ögren (1974) noted that rats will press a lever at very high rates (6000 responses per hour) for stimulation delivered through electrodes in ascending dopamine fiber bundles in the lateral hypothalamus. Administration of AMPT (which blocks the synthesis of norepinephrine and dopamine) suppressed this responding, while the administration of an inhibitor of dopamine-β-hydroxylase (which thus suppressed only norepinephrine synthesis) actually *increased* the rate of self-stimulation. (See **FIGURE 17.13**.) Moreover, an agent that specifically blocks the postsynaptic receptor sites for dopamine (*pimozide*) blocked self-stimulation behavior. These studies from Fuxe's laboratory provide excellent evidence that there is a dopaminergic reward system, apparently independent of the noradrenergic system of reward.

Biochemical Assays of the Brain of Schizophrenics

Wise and Stein (1973) and Wise, Baden, and Stein (1974) analyzed the brain of deceased schizophrenic patients and noted that there appeared to be a lower level of dopamine-β-hydroxylase activity in the brain of these patients, as compared with normal control subjects. Since this enzyme is necessary for the synthesis of norepinephrine

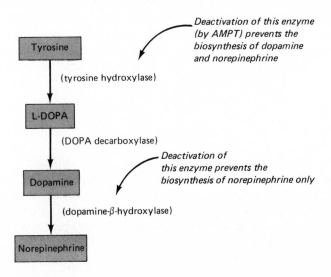

FIGURE 17.13 A schematic description of the experiment by Fuxe et al. (1974).

from dopamine, the supposition is that the brain of the schizophrenic patient contains fewer noradrenergic nerve terminals. Whether the enzyme insufficiency caused the terminals to die by allowing 6-HD to accumulate or whether noradrenergic terminals were killed by some other means cannot be determined from the data. Either way, the results are consistent with the hypothesis that schizophrenia results from damage to noradrenergic neurons.

There are problems with the study, however, that plague any attempt to compare schizophrenic patients with normal subjects. The schizophrenics had spent a mean of 34.4 years in a mental institution; the normal subjects had died suddenly from heart attacks or automobile accidents. The schizophrenics had been receiving antipsychotic drugs that are known to affect catecholaminergic cells; the normal subjects had not. Wise and his colleagues did note that rats that received an antipsychotic drug for 5 or 12 weeks prior to being killed did not show decreases in dopamine-β-hydroxylase activity—in fact, a 16 percent *increase* was shown. However, there is evidence that the rat enzyme differs from the human enzyme (Goldstein, 1974). Furthermore, the effects of years of drug treatment in human schizophrenia might not be mimicked by a 5-to-12-week drug treatment in rats.

Olson (1974) made more direct measurements of catecholamine-containing neurons (and also neurons that contain 5-HT, another transmitter substance). He found no difference in the number or appearance of these terminals in the brains of deceased schizophrenic and normal people. Thus, no evidence was found for destruction of nerve terminals by 6-HD, as suggested by Stein and Wise.

It must be concluded that the data do not clearly indicate whether a reduction in dopamine-β-hydroxylase activity (and, therefore, a decrease in norepinephrine) is related to schizophrenia. Therefore, let us turn to another line of evidence, which suggests that schizophrenia results from excessive activity of dopaminergic terminals rather than from insufficient activity of noradrenergic ones.

Dopamine and Schizophrenia

THE ANTIPSYCHOTIC DRUGS. There is excellent evidence that implicates dopaminergic neurons in schizophrenia. The effectiveness of antipsychotic drugs appears to be related to their ability to block the postsynaptic receptors for dopamine. Furthermore, drugs that facilitate the release of dopamine (or retard its re-uptake, thus prolonging the effectiveness of the neurotransmitter) can induce psychotic behavior. For example, Angrist, Sathananthan, Wilk, and Gershon

(1974) injected volunteers with *d*-amphetamine and *l*-amphetamine. Both forms of amphetamine stimulate dopaminergic and noradrenergic synapses; however, *d*-amphetamine is ten times more effective than *l*-amphetamine in stimulating noradrenergic synapses, whereas these drugs are about equally effective in stimulating dopaminergic synapses. If psychotic symptoms were related to norepinephrine, one would expect that a given dose of *d*-amphetamine would be just as effective as ten times as much *l*-amphetamine. However, the two drugs are approximately equal in their ability to produce psychotic symptoms, suggesting that the dopaminergic stimulation is what produces the psychosis. Furthermore, drugs that selectively block dopaminergic synapses reduce the psychotic symptoms that accompany the administration of amphetamine.

Davis (1974) provided a particularly dramatic illustration of the way that symptoms of schizophrenia can be exacerbated by dopaminergic stimulation. He and his colleagues injected small doses of *methylphenidate* (a drug that causes dopamine to be released by the terminals and that also inhibits re-uptake) into the veins of schizophrenic patients who were in a fairly quiet state. Within a minute after the injection, each patient was transformed "from a mild schizophrenic into a wild and very florid schizophrenic." One of the patients began to make a clacking noise. He then took a pad of paper which he pounded repeatedly, and ultimately shredded, with the pencil. He had been "sending and receiving messages from the ancient Egyptians." Other catatonic patients became more catatonic, displaying a *waxy flexibility* characteristic of this disorder. If such a patient is "molded" into some posture, the posture will be retained for a long period of time. Thus, it cannot be said that the drug merely made the patients more active—whatever their symptoms were, they became worse.

THE DOPAMINERGIC PATHWAYS OF THE LIMBIC SYSTEM. There is evidence that a particular dopaminergic circuit is involved in schizophrenia. Many antipsychotic drugs produce extrapyramidal side effects, that is, symptoms resembling Parkinson's disease. This disorder results from degeneration of the dopaminergic fibers of the nigrostriatal bundle (which travels from the substantia nigra to the caudate nucleus, or neostriatum). Andén and Stock (1973) found that a particular antipsychotic drug (*clozapine*) had a minor effect on the postsynaptic dopaminergic receptor sites in the caudate nucleus, but had a strong inhibitory effect on dopaminergic receptors in the limbic system. Clozapine, furthermore, is known to produce minimal extrapyramidal side effects. Thus, the evidence suggests that schizophrenia is associated with hyperactivity of the dopaminergic neurons of the limbic system.

Role of Dopaminergic Neurons in Behavior. What function, normally performed by these neurons, produces schizophrenia when the system is hyperactive? The deficit that occurs when the dopaminergic circuits are damaged is usually characterized as *sensory neglect*. Ungerstedt and Ljungberg (1974) found that animals with a unilateral lesion in the dopaminergic pathways did not orient toward sensory stimuli on the side of the body contralateral to the lesion. Reactions to ipsilaterally presented stimuli were normal. The investigators noted that there was a recovery period during which reactions to the contralateral stimuli returned. However, they did not all return at once; reactions to each sense modality had a different time course of recovery. Thus, the lesions would appear to impair sensory functions rather than motor functions.

If we assumed that the hyperactivity of the dopaminergic system would produce results contrary to what occurs after lesions, then we would conclude that the symptoms of schizophrenia might result from some sort of overstimulation—a failure, perhaps, to be able to sort out important and trivial stimuli (and, perhaps, important and trivial thoughts). Schizophrenics might, because of hyperactivity of the dopaminergic system, be struck by an overwhelming barrage of sensory information that is so confusing that many patients eventually retreat from it.

Conclusions

I must note that the causes of schizophrenia are by no means settled. The dopamine hypothesis certainly appears to be the most promising breakthrough that we have had so far, but we are a long way from reaching final conclusions. Those of you who are interested in a further discussion of this topic should obtain an excellent and very readable book by Snyder (1974).

We have come a long way from a discussion of the rewarding effects of ESB to a dopaminergic hypothesis of schizophrenia. I hope it has been profitable, nevertheless. Stein and Wise's theory has received a considerable amount of interest, and it is impossible to evaluate a theory without presenting an alternative. I should note that people are still mystified as to why electrical stimulation of dopaminergic fibers is reinforcing (at least in rats). Perhaps it is reinforcing for the same reason that self-administered intravenous injections of amphetamines are reinforcing; the overwhelming "rush" of sensory stimulation is pleasurable. (Note again that reinforcement appears to be associated with *increased* afferent activity.) And perhaps schizophrenia and amphetamine psychoses result from the same chronic hyperstimulation of this system, which is so pleasurable in briefer doses.

PAIN

Pain is a curious phenomenon. It is more than a mere sensation; it can be defined only by some sort of withdrawal reaction or, in humans, by verbal report. Pain can be modified by opiates, by hypnosis, by emotions (such as the joy of childbirth or the relief of escaping alive from a dangerous situation), and even, perhaps, by other forms of stimulation such as acupuncture.

The importance of emotional and other "psychological" factors in the perception of pain (documented very well by Sternbach, 1968) suggests that there must be neural mechanisms that modify either the transmission of pain or the translation of central pain messages into negative affect. As we shall see, there is excellent evidence for both types of interactions.

We might reasonably ask why we experience pain. A person suffering from the terminal stages of cancer presents a particularly distressing case. Pain, for this person, serves no useful purpose. Damage has already occurred, and no action can be taken on the part of the patient to avoid further damage. The pain only turns the patient's last days into misery.

In most cases, however, pain serves a more constructive role. The best examples of the importance of pain come from cases of people who have congenital insensitivity to pain. These people suffer an abnormally large number of injuries, such as cuts and burns. One woman eventually died because she did not make the normal shifts in posture that we normally do when our joints start to ache. As a consequence, she suffered damage to the spine that ultimately resulted in death. Other people have died from ruptured appendixes and ensuing peritonitis (infection within the abdomen) that they did not feel (Sternbach, 1968). I am sure that a person who is passing a kidney stone would not find much comfort in the fact that pain does more good than ill, but it is, nevertheless, vital to our existence.

Neural Pathways for Pain

As we saw in chapter 8, there is general agreement that the free nerve endings generate the messages that are ultimately interpreted as pain. These sensory endings are found in the skin, in the sheath surrounding muscles, in the internal organs, and in the membrane surrounding bones. They are also located in the cornea of the eye, and (as many of you know only too well) in the pulp of the teeth. As we saw in chapter 8, just about any kind of manipulation that causes tissue damage will cause pain, and thus most investigators believe that pain receptors are chemically stimulated by substances liberated by the damaged tissue.

Pain messages arise from two types of peripheral pain fibers, the *C fibers* (thin, unmyelinated, slow-conducting) and the *A-delta fibers* (thicker, faster-conducting, myelinated). Pain fibers (from the regions below the head) enter the dorsal roots of the spinal cord and synapse in the dorsal horn. The second-order neurons located there send axons to the other side of the spinal cord and ascend via the contralateral *spinothalamic tract*. As this tract ascends, it sends collaterals into the reticular formation. A secondary route to the thalamus thus consists of a polysynaptic pathway: the *spinoreticulothalamic tract*. The thalamus appears to be the "end station" for pain, in that projections to the cortex do not seem necessary for its perception. The pathways are shown in Figure 17.14; note that there is a considerable amount of divergent branching (up and down the spinal cord) by the primary sensory neurons. (See **FIGURE 17.14.**)

Pain fibers originating in the trigeminal nerves (i.e., those which serve the face and head) follow a similar set of pathways. There are multisynaptic projections through the reticular formation (the *trigeminoreticulothalamic tract*) and a straight-through pathway that lies alongside the spinothalamic tract (the *anterior trigemino-thalamic tract*). (See **FIGURE 17.14.**)

Gate-Control Theory

A very influential theory, developed by Melzack and Wall (1965), attempts to account for some of the ways in which pain differs from the other senses. The most significant differences are the ways in which emotions or other cutaneous stimuli can alter the perception of pain. The authors suggest that a level of control is exerted, in the case of spinal nerves, in the *substantia gelatinosa* of the dorsal horn. They hypothesize that the second-order neurons, which ascend to the brain, receive input from two populations of fibers: the *S fibers* (small diameter) and the *L fibers* (large diameter). The S fibers correspond to the "classical" C pain fibers, while the L fibers correspond to the *A-alpha* fibers that mediate other somatosenses. There are also interneurons in the substantia gelatinosa that are inhibited by collaterals from the S fibers and excited by collaterals from the L fibers. The brain also is assumed to exert control on this system, but the nature of this control is not specified. When the interneurons are active, they provide presynaptic inhibition on the terminals of both the L and S fibers, thus blocking the transmission of pain messages to the brain. Study Figure 17.15; note how the interneurons serve as "gate cells." If the interneurons are active, pain messages do not get through. The interneurons are activated by L fibers and inhibited

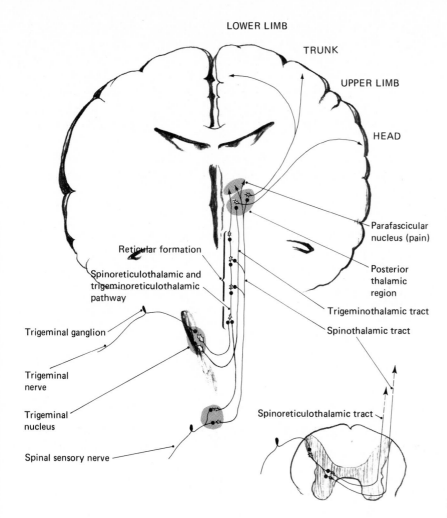

LOWER LIMB

TRUNK

UPPER LIMB

HEAD

Parafascicular
nucleus (pain)

Posterior
thalamic
region

Reticular formation

Spinoreticulothalamic and
trigeminoreticulothalamic
pathway

Trigeminothalamic tract

Spinothalamic tract

Trigeminal ganglion

Trigeminal
nerve

Trigeminal
nucleus

Spinoreticulothalamic tract

Spinal sensory nerve

FIGURE 17.14   The pathways
of nerve fibers mediating pain.

by S fibers; thus, the relative activity of these fibers "opens or closes the gate." (See **FIGURE 17.15.**)

NEUROPHYSIOLOGICAL EVIDENCE.   Melzack and Wall's theory predicts that somatosensory stimulation should produce presynaptic inhibition on the small and large diameter fibers that synapse upon the neurons that transmit pain information to the brain.   To test this, Whitehorn and Burgess (1973) stimulated two kinds of large afferent fibers (A-alpha and A-delta) and looked for evidence of presynaptic inhibition on the small C fibers.   They found none. They did see evidence of presynaptic inhibition on C fibers, but only

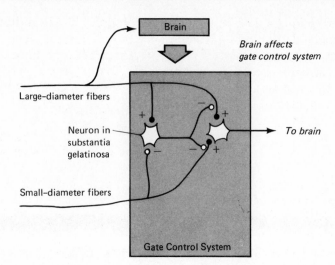

FIGURE 17.15 The gate-
control theory of pain.
(Adapted from Melzack, R., and
Wall, P. D., *Science*, 1965, *150*,
971–979.)

when the C fibers themselves were stimulated (by noxious stimuli applied to the skin). Similarly, gentle mechanical stimulation produced evidence of presynaptic inhibition, but only in the large-diameter fibers that mediate this information. The mechanism suggested by Melzack and Wall (Figure 17.15) thus did not receive empirical support.

CLINICAL RELEVANCE OF THE GATE-CONTROL THEORY. Why bother to discuss the gate-control theory if it does not appear to be correct? There are two reasons. First, there does appear to be some kind of gate that, as we shall see, can be closed by central mechanisms. Second, clinical use has been made of the theory; even if the proposed mechanism is wrong, some of its predictions have been found to be correct.

The most useful prediction from this theory has been that stimulation of the large-diameter fibers should close the gate and thus diminish the perception of pain. In fact, Wall and Sweet (1967) reported that direct electrical stimulation of sensory nerves or roots (which by itself produces a buzzing or tingling sensation) provided pain relief that lasted for up to half an hour. They note that they avoided suggesting that the treatment would alleviate pain, and they even told one patient that his pain would remain; nevertheless, the stimulation did produce *analgesia* (lowering of the perception of pain). It has been suggested that acupuncture might produce analgesia in this way (assuming that acupuncture actually works).

Although others have used peripheral stimulation to alleviate clinical pain, Nathan and Rudge (1974) failed to obtain analgesia from nerve stimulation in normal subjects in whom pain was induced by heat, pinprick, and occlusion of circulation. These authors therefore concluded that the prediction of the gate-control theory was incorrect. It is not at all clear why different results should be obtained from normal and pathologically produced pain. It is clear that more research must be done before we understand how the transmission of pain is gated in the spinal cord.

Perception and Tolerance of Pain

There are manipulations that diminish the perception of pain. For example, Beecher (1959) noted that wounded American soldiers back from the battle at Anzio reported that they felt no pain from their wounds—they did not even want medication. It would appear that their perception of pain was diminished by the relief felt from surviving such an ordeal. There are other instances where people still report the perception of pain but are not bothered by it. Some tranquilizers have this effect.

There is clear-cut physiological evidence for such a distinction between the perception and tolerance of pain. Mark, Ervin, and Yakovlev (1962) made stereotaxically placed lesions in the thalamus in an attempt to relieve the pain of patients suffering from the advanced stages of cancer. Damage to the sensory relay nuclei (VPM and VPL) produced a loss of cutaneous senses: touch, temperature, and cutaneous pain (the ability to detect pinpricks). However, patients obtained no relief from deep, chronic pain. Lesions in the parafascicular nucleus and in the intralaminar nucleus were successful; pain, but not cutaneous sensitivity, was gone. Finally, destruction of the dorsomedial and anterior thalamic nuclei left cutaneous sensitivity and the perception of pain intact. However, the patients did not pay much attention to the pain. The lesions appeared to reduce or remove its emotional component. It is noteworthy that these nuclei are intimately involved with the limbic system, and that the dorsomedial nuclei project to prefrontal cortex. Removal of this region (*prefrontal lobotomy* or *prefrontal leucotomy*) also reduces the emotional aspects of pain perception.

It seems clear that pain perception and pain tolerance are separate phenomena. It would appear that the intralaminar and parafascicular nuclei are the thalamic nuclei necessary for the perception of pain, and that the limbic system and prefrontal cortex mediate its emotional component.

PHYSIOLOGICAL EVIDENCE. Mark and his colleagues also noted a very interesting fact: electrical stimulation of the thalamus never resulted in reports of pain. Neither did the patients report any specific sense, such as temperature or touch. Instead, they reported tingling sensations like "pins and needles." This fact suggests that the *pattern*, temporal and/or spatial, of incoming activity is of paramount importance in somatic sensation. It is not enough to produce excitation of thalamic neurons—they must be stimulated in a particular way that has not been duplicated by electrical stimulation.

Finally, this study confirms the long-standing supposition that there are two types of pain: a rapidly felt "sharp" pain and a more gradual, but more aversive, "dull" pain. Stub your toe and you will see what I mean. The first flash of pain subsides fairly quickly, to be replaced by another that is longer-lived and more poorly localized. The fact that lesions of VPM and VPL abolished pain felt from pinpricks, but not deep-seated pain, suggests that the "bright pain" but not the "dull pain" component is mediated by these nuclei.

Treatments that Relieve Pain

The group of drugs that most effectively relieve pain are, of course, the opiates. These drugs apparently diminish the perception of pain; they do not just raise the tolerance for it. As we shall see, excellent evidence suggests that opiates act by *stimulating* neural systems in the brain that affect pain transmission in the spinal cord (and also, presumably, in the trigeminal pathway). The mechanism is consistent with the gate-control theory, in that central mechanisms can control the transmission of pain, although the "gate" probably does not work in the way that Melzack and Wall have suggested. Fewer details are known about manipulations that modify tolerance of pain, such as administration of certain tranquilizers.

Analgesia Produced by Brain Stimulation. It has been known for some years that electrical stimulation of the brain can attenuate pain. It seems likely that stimulation at some loci produces true analgesia (elimination of pain perception) and increased pain tolerance at others. Furthermore, there is very good evidence that stimulation-produced analgesia works by means of the same mechanisms that mediate analgesia produced by morphine. Mayer and Liebeskind (1974) reported that electrical stimulation of the central gray of rats resulted in analgesia equivalent to that produced by at least 10 milligrams of morphine per kilogram of body weight (a large dose). The rats did not react to pain of any kind; the authors pinched the tails and paws, applied electric shock to the feet, and applied heat to the tail. Stimulation of the septum, dorsomedial thalamus, and ventral tegmentum produced a less striking analgesia. Stimulation of the lateral hypothalamus or ventrobasal thalamus (the somatosensory area) had no effect.

The investigators found no causal relationship between rewarding and analgesia-producing brain stimulation. Rats failed to press a lever for analgesic stimulation at some locations, and some rewarding stimulation was found not to produce analgesia. Furthermore, they noted that analgesia and self-stimulation elicited by stimulation of the central gray are differently affected by pharmacological means; depletion of serotonin diminishes analgesia without affecting self-stimulation, whereas depletion of norepinephrine facilitates analgesia but diminishes self-stimulation (Margules, 1969; Akil, 1972; Akil and Mayer, 1972).

It should be noted that other investigators (e.g., Balagura and Ralph, 1973; Yunger, Harvey, and Lorens, 1973) have obtained analgesia from stimulation of other brain regions, including the medial forebrain bundle and midbrain reticular formation. These investigators agree, however, that the rewarding effects of brain stimulation can be dissociated from the analgesic effects. In humans, septal stimulation has been found to produce analgesia. Heath and Mickle (1960) noted that their patients reported a true loss of pain, and not just increased tolerance for it. It is not yet known whether stimulation of these more rostral brain regions produces the same kind of analgesia produced by morphine or stimulation of the central gray; perhaps there are "gates" in the brain itself that can be closed by electrical stimulation.

What might be the biological significance of the phenomenon of analgesia produced by electrical brain stimulation? Liebeskind, Giesler, and Urca (1976) note that stimulation of the central gray of the midbrain produces aggressive and defensive behaviors, as well as analgesia. It therefore seems plausible to suggest that the analgesic mechanism is related to the suppression of pain when such behaviors are being performed. It is a common observation that great fear or rage diminishes perception of pain; during battle, some wounds may go unnoticed until afterwards. Even engaging in sexual behavior may lower the perception of pain. Komisaruk (1974) observed electrophysiological and behavioral evidence of decreased responsiveness of a female rat to noxious stimulation when the animal's genitals were mechanically stimulated.

THE ROLE OF MORPHINE IN PAIN PERCEPTION. Mayer and Liebeskind note that microinjections of morphine produce analgesia when delivered to the periventricular gray of the hypothalamus and the central gray of the midbrain and pons (Tsou and Jang, 1964; Foster, Jenden, and Lomax, 1967; Herz, Alberts, Metyš, Schubert, and Teschemacher, 1970). Morphine does *not* appear to block transmission of pain impulses at this level; the effects appear to be exerted more caudally. Depletion of serotonin with PCPA or lesions of the raphe nuclei block the ability of morphine to diminish pain (Lee and Fennessy, 1970;

Samanin and Bernasconi, 1972). Thus, it would appear that the analgesic effects of morphine depend on an intact system of serotonergic neurons. Furthermore, the effect seems to be produced by fibers that travel caudally from the brain. Dewey, Snyder, Harris, and Howes (1969) found that morphine no longer abolished the tail-flick response to painful stimulation when the spinal cord was transected below the brain. The most likely explanation is that morphine causes the stimulation of brain mechanisms that inhibit pain transmission in the cord (it closes the gate?).

Morphine and analgesic brain stimulation appear to have similar effects. As I already noted, analgesia produced by brain stimulation, like that produced by morphine, is blocked by depletion of serotonin with PCPA (Akil and Mayer, 1972). Even more significantly, *naloxone*, a drug that blocks the analgesic effects of morphine (by blocking *opiate receptors*, to be described later) partially blocks analgesia produced by electrical stimulation (Akil, Mayer, and Liebeskind, 1976). Furthermore, simultaneous administration of low levels of brain stimulation and low doses of morphine (neither of which by itself will inhibit pain) will summate and produce analgesia. Finally, Liebeskind, Guilbaud, Besson, and Oliveras (1973) recorded the activity of interneurons in the dorsal horn of the spinal cord and found that the responsiveness of these neurons to noxious stimuli was blocked by analgesic brain stimulation.

There remains the possibility that morphine exerts an inhibitory effect on central pain transmission as well as this clear-cut effect on spinal transmission. This does not appear to be the case, however. Rosenfeld and Kowatch (1975) produced pain in two ways: peripherally (by means of foot shock) and centrally (by electrically stimulating three different points along the central pathways in the brainstem that mediate pain). They found that morphine blocked the aversive effect of peripherally induced pain, but did not affect pain produced by central stimulation. Therefore, it would appear that the pain-reducing effects of morphine are mediated solely by blocking transmission of pain impulses at the level of the first synapse in the spinal cord and, perhaps, in the trigeminal nucleus as well.

OPIATE RECEPTORS. Opiates such as morphine appear to exert their effects by interacting with specific postsynaptic receptors. Pert, Snowman, and Snyder (1974) homogenized the brains of rats and extracted synaptosomes by means of differential centrifugation (described in chapter 4). They further separated the terminal buttons from the postsynaptic membrane to which the terminal buttons were attached, and they found that the membrane would selectively take up radioactive naloxone and dihydromorphine. Thus, it would appear that there are postsynaptic receptors that "recognize" the opiates. The authors note that the regional distribution of opiate receptors in the anterior amygdala, central gray, hypothalamus, and head of the caudate nucleus (Kuhar, Pert, and Snyder, 1973) corresponds to no single transmitter substance.

ENDOGENOUS OPIATES. The puzzle as to why the brain contains opiate receptors has been solved—the brain produces its own opiates. Terenius and Wahlström (1975) reported the existence of a substance in human cerebrospinal fluid that had a specific affinity for opiate receptors extracted from rat brain. They called this chemical "morphinelike factor." They found that more of this substance was found in the CSF of patients with *trigeminal neuralgia,* a disease that produces severe facial pain; perhaps the brain produces its own opiates as a result of prolonged painful stimulation.

Hughes, Smith, Kosterlitz, Fothergill, Morgan, and Morris (1975) found that there were actually two morphinelike factors and identified them as two very small peptide chains, each containing five amino acids. They synthesized these substances and found that the artificial *enkephalin* (the authors' name for the substance) acted as a potent opiate. Enkephalin was found to be three times as potent as morphine in binding with opiate receptors in the guinea pig brain.

It appears likely that one of the reasons that electrical brain stimulation produces analgesia is that the stimulation causes the release of enkephalin by the brain. The enkephalin then stimulates the opiate receptors and produces analgesia. As we saw earlier, the analgesic effects of brain stimulation are partially blocked by naloxone (Akil, Mayer, and Liebeskind, 1976). The fact that total blocking was not seen suggests that the stimulation produces analgesia by means of more than one mechanism.

These results are very exciting and will undoubtedly have significant implications in the management of pain. Will enkephalin have fewer side effects than morphine? Will it be as addictive as the opiates? I am certain that investigators in many laboratories are working on answers to these and related questions.

CONCLUSIONS

Electrical stimulation of the brain produces a variety of effects: induction of drive (which is usually also rewarding), production of pain, and the diminution of pain. Although no really conclusive statements can be made, the effects of rewarding brain stimulation can be said to support the notion that drive induction (or some kind of positive feedback mechanism) is positively reinforcing, and that aversive effects result from stimuli (such as a full stomach and duo-denum) that suppress appetitive behaviors. It seems likely, however, that ESB can support self-stimulation behavior by a variety of means; we saw that humans will press a button for intracranial stimulation just out of curiosity. We also saw that there are many things to fear more than the possibility that our behavior will be controlled by reinforcing brain stimulation, and we saw that, whatever role reward circuits play in our behavior, schizophrenia does not appear to result from their damage. Finally, we saw that, whereas pain can be diminished by brain stimulation that is also reinforcing, the two mechanisms appear to be independent.

SUGGESTED READINGS

GALLISTEL, C. R. Self-stimulation: The neurophysi-ology of reward and motivation. In *The Physiological Basis of Memory*, edited by J. A. Deutsch. New York: Academic Press, 1973. Gallistel summarizes the dom-inant theories concerning the nature of rewarding brain stimulation, covering a number of approaches besides his own.

VALENSTEIN, E. S. *Brain Control*. New York: John Wiley & Sons, 1973. Valenstein's book should con-vince you, if I have not done so, that we need not fear the use of rewarding brain stimulation as a means of social control.

SNYDER, S. *Madness and the Brain*. New York: Mc-Graw-Hill, 1974.

Journal of Psychiatric Research, Vol. 11, 1974.

Snyder's book (available in paperback) provides a simple but noncondescending description of the bi-

ology of schizophrenia. The entire issue of the *Journal of Psychiatric Research* is devoted to this topic. The articles in it are considerably more detailed than is Snyder's book.

LIEBESKIND, J. C., GIESLER, G. J., and URCA, G. Evidence pertaining to an endogenous mechanism of pain inhi-bition in the central nervous system. In *Sensory Func-tions of the Skin in Primates, with Special Reference to Man*, edited by Y. Zotterman. Oxford: Pergamon Press, 1976.

STERNBACH, R. A. *Pain: A Psychophysiological Analy-sis*. New York: Academic Press, 1968.

Sternbach's book provides a good overview of the topic of pain, whereas the chapter by Liebeskind et al. will bring you up to date on the issue of the neural mechanisms of analgesia.

Memories: Where Are They?

18

The mechanisms by which we learn and remember information represent the most complicated capacity of our nervous system. The memory process cannot function without properly working sensory, attentional, arousal, and motivational mechanisms. We must perceive the stimuli bearing the information in order that this information be remembered, and unless it has some motivational significance, we will probably not pay attention to it. Furthermore, even if we form a memory for the occurrence of an event, this representation is useless unless it can, at a later time, be withdrawn from storage. And if we wish to infer the presence of a memory in an organism other than ourselves, there must be some observable behavior that is produced by this act of remembering. Memory, therefore, involves sensation, perception, attention, motivation, reinforcement, and motor behavior, as well as purely *mnemonic* processes (those which pertain to memory, or *mnēmē*, in Greek). Thus, to the extent that we do not understand the physiological bases for those processes that are necessary for memory formation and retrieval, we do not understand memory itself. I think the preceding chapters will have convinced you that we have a long way to go before we understand these processes. Nevertheless, some very positive things can be said about the physiological bases of memory.

An Overview of the Memory Process

We perceive and remember events, and the memory of these events is capable of changing our later behavior. For example, we observe an event and later tell someone about it. Or we flinch when we see a child blowing up a balloon to the bursting point, having had them explode in our own face in the past. From what I have already discussed about the nervous system, I can safely offer some conclusions about the physical nature of the memory process.

First, the event must be represented by activity of afferent neurons (the process of *sensory coding*). This activity must be specific for the event that produces it, and for no other event. If we can tell the difference between two stimuli, then their neural representations must be different.

Second, the neural activity that encodes the sensory experience of the event must somehow alter characteristics of other (nonsensory) neurons in a manner that represents the event (the process of *storage*). We know that the presentation of a visual stimulus, for example, does not destroy our memories for all the visual stimuli we saw earlier. This means that the peripheral parts of the visual system serve as an input to other parts of the brain, but activity in the periphery does not constitute the memory itself (or the memories would be erased by subsequent visual input). The neurons that contain the memory must be more centrally located. Without physiological evidence, however, we cannot say how "central" the memory representation must be. It is possible that the process of feature extraction in sensory systems depends on neural alterations produced by exposure to stimuli —see Spinelli's work, cited in chapter 9. These alterations, if they occur, *would* change the way subsequent stimuli are perceived. Perhaps, for example, our sensory systems can identify vertical lines only because we were exposed to vertical lines at a very early age. If they occur, these alterations will have something to tell us about the memory process, but for the present, I am not including them in my definition of "memory."

Third, the stored memory must be subject to *retrieval*. That is, there must be at least one stimulus that will now produce a behavioral event different from what would have occurred if the memory had not been stored. If you have never seen a balloon burst, you will have no reason to flinch when you see one blown up. The fact that retrieval can occur means that the stored memory is not walled off like a little cyst; the cells that represent the memory must be capable of receiving the coded sensory input that initiates retrieval.

As we shall see, the process is very much more complicated, but even this description will serve as a basis for a discussion of some physiological evidence.

THE SEARCH FOR THE LOCATION OF STORED MEMORIES

This chapter will be addressed to the following question: Where are memories stored? All investigators would agree that there is not a single brain region that serves as a "filing cabinet" for the storage of all memories. In fact, some neuroscientists believe that memories are stored diffusely, throughout all regions of cortex (and, very possibly, subcortical regions as well). Even a single memory is believed to be stored by means of subtle alterations in a vast number of neurons scattered throughout cortex; thus, a given neuron participates, in some small way, in the storage of a large number of memories.

Data collected from sub-primate mammals appears to support this conceptualization. However, I believe that studies with primates and with brain-damaged humans argue for a different conclusion: Memories are stored principally in particular regions of the brain, namely, association cortex related to the sensory modality in which the new information was received. Complex memories that require interaction of various sensory modalities are mediated by fiber bundles running beneath cortex that specifically interconnect these association areas, and that connect these regions with motor mechanisms.

Support for both of these conceptualizations can be found among eminent and capable neuroscientists. We do not yet have enough evidence to rule out either of these schemes. It is even possible that memories are organized differently in the brain of a rat and in the brain of a human or chimpanzee. On a cellular level, I have no doubt but that rat neurons and human neurons undergo the same kinds of alterations when they participate in memory storage (the issue that will be discussed in chapter 20). But on a more complex level of organization, the differences between rat brain (or even cat brain) and the brain of higher primates are substantial. Humans have distinct areas of association cortex interconnected by specific fiber bundles. The distinction between sensory, motor, and association cortex is less definite in lower mammals, and the specific fiber bundles are not found (Geschwind, 1965). If there is a difference between lower mammals and higher primates in the higher-level organization of memory in the brain, I think it is appropriate to devote more attention to the human brain.

Rationale for Use of the Lesion Method

How can we find the location of a given memory? On principle, it would appear to be simple. Train an animal and remove a part of its brain. Test the animal later to see if it has retained what it learned. If it remembers the task, the memory must not have been exclusively stored in that brain region. If it does not perform, then the memory must have been located there.

It does not take too much reflection to see the problems with this procedure. Removal of an animal's eyes would, of course, abolish a learned response to a flash of light, but no one would conclude that the memory for this task is stored in the eyes. The same would hold for the optic nerves, optic tracts, and lateral geniculate nucleus. But what about visual cortex? Does this brain region participate in the storage of memory as well as in purely visual functions?

The Visual System and Retention of Memory in Rats

In a series of experiments with rats, Lashley (1950) found that the only brain lesions that abolished performance of a simple brightness discrimination learned preoperatively was total destruction of visual cortex. The rats could relearn the task, however, in approximately the same number of trials. If they were then subjected to an operation that destroyed the optic tectum (superior colliculus and surrounding tissue), performance was gone again, and this time the task could not be relearned (no surprise, since the rats were now blind). But animals that relearned the task after removal of visual cortex continued to perform even if other cortical regions were destroyed; the memory for the task relearned by means of input to the optic tectum did not appear to be stored in any portion of cortex. Other groups of rats that received the tectal lesions (but not lesions of the visual cortex) continued to perform normally. Apparently the tectum does not play an important role in retention of simple visual memories when visual cortex is intact. (See **FIGURE 18.1.**)

What can we conclude from these studies? First of all, I must emphasize that the rats were required only to respond to the presence or absence of light; after removal of visual cortex a rat cannot learn (or relearn) a task that requires recognition of visual patterns; the patterns apparently just cannot be perceived. But for a simple problem, all that appears to be necessary is the presence of a brain region capable of mediating the sensory functions necessary for the perception of the necessary stimuli. No other cortical region appears to be necessary. It goes without saying that there must be some way for information from the sensory region to be transmitted to motor mechanisms that mediate the response. In the case of the rats that relearned the task after lesions of visual cortex, retrieval of the memory probably involved the transmission of information from optic tectum to subcortical motor mechanisms (e.g., basal ganglia, reticular formation).

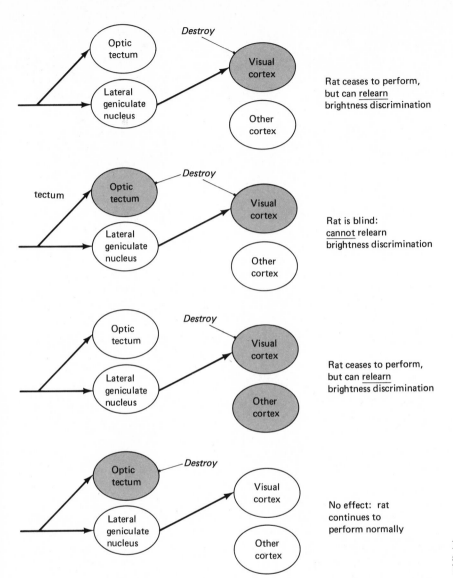

Rat ceases to perform, but can <u>relearn</u> brightness discrimination

Rat is blind: <u>cannot</u> relearn brightness discrimination

Rat ceases to perform, but can <u>relearn</u> brightness discrimination

No effect: rat continues to perform normally

FIGURE 18.1 A schematic summary of the experiments by Lashley.

Learning in the Absence of Cortex

Even animals subjected to total cortical removal are still capable of learning certain problems. Girden, Mettler, Finch, and Culler (1936) demonstrated that a decorticate dog could learn a classically conditioned leg withdrawal about as rapidly as a normal dog. The top graph of Figure 18.2 shows the acquisition of a leg withdrawal in anticipation of an electrical shock that was preceded by a signal (auditory, thermal, or tactile). (See **FIGURE 18.2.**) The lower graph shows that the animal was even capable of learning to respond to a bell (followed by shock) but could withhold its response when a tone was presented. (The tone was *not* followed by a shock.) Thus, it cannot be argued that the dog just became sensitized to respond to all kinds of stimuli over the course of the experiment. The experiment, then, clearly demonstrates associative learning by a dog lacking cerebral cortex. (See **FIGURE 18.2.**)

Conclusions from the Preceding Studies

The conclusion I should like to draw from these studies is that the capacity for memory does not appear to be restricted to any one region of the brain. The only way to destroy simple (and I must emphasize the word *simple*) visual memory is to produce lesions that destroy the animal's visual capacity. The same is true for other sensory modalities. All the animal needs in order to learn and perform a simple sensory discrimination is sufficient cortical tissue to analyze the incoming sensory information. No other cortical tissue appears to be needed. (Of course, there must be connections with motor mechanisms that can produce the response.)

Equipotentiality

FIGURE 18.2 Classical conditioning of a dog whose cortex was removed. (From Girden, E., Mettler, F. A., Finch, G., and Culler, E., *Journal of Comparative Psychology*, 1936, 21, 367–385.)

This raises some interesting questions. As Lashley (1950) has shown, visual cortex is the only portion of cortex uniquely necessary for the

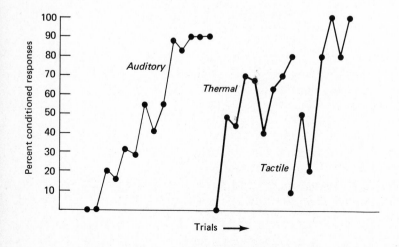
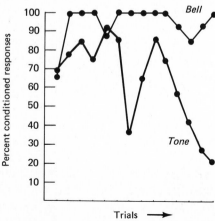

learning and retention of a discrimination task involving recognition of a visual pattern. This task cannot be relearned subcortically; apparently the optic tectum cannot mediate pattern vision although it can detect changes in brightness. The fascinating thing is that an animal trained preoperatively on a pattern discrimination can continue to perform the task after removal of all but a very small portion of primary visual cortex. This is true for rats (Lashley, 1939) or monkeys (Harlow, 1939; Settlage, 1939). The animals were apparently left with a small spot of visual function, and had to learn to orient themselves so that they could observe the discriminative stimulus with this little spot. Harlow and Settlage found that monkeys would perform the task postoperatively only if they were given some recovery time in a lighted cage; when they were kept in a dark cage, where they could not practice looking at things with their small spots of residual vision, they did not show retention of the task.

Lashley concluded that these results mean that neurons in all regions of visual cortex must participate in the formation of visual memories; otherwise, how could retention be demonstrated with survival of a small number of neurons located anywhere in visual cortex? He named this phenomenon the *principle of equipotentiality*: All neurons within a brain region that mediate a particular sensory modality are equally capable of participating in the storage of a sensory event received by that modality.

Lashley calculated that, for every afferent fiber to a rat's visual cortex, there are approximately nineteen cortical neurons. This obviously means that there is no great reservoir of cells there that is not needed for purely visual functions and may be used to store memories. It also suggests that a given neuron must participate in more than one memory. The minimum number of visual cortical cells it takes to specify memory for a given pattern must surely be fairly large. When we consider the huge number of visual memories that can be retained by an animal, it becomes obvious that a given neuron in any part of visual cortex must be a part of the representation of a large number of different memories. There simply are not enough cells in visual cortex to permit neurons to be reserved for the exclusive use of individual memories. And when we consider that the preservation of any small part of visual cortex leaves the memory intact, the point is made even more forcefully.

Visual Memory in Primates

ANATOMY OF THE VISUAL SYSTEM. Experiments performed since Lashley's time have complicated this story somewhat. In monkeys, primary visual cortex contains only the first stage of cortical analysis of visual information. There is a second band of cortex around *striate cortex* (primary visual cortex) called the *circumstriate belt*. The most crucial region of the circumstriate belt has been called the *foveal prestriate* area; this area receives and processes information from the central (foveal) portion of the visual field, where a monkey's acuity is greatest. Indeed, when we "look at" an object, what we are doing is moving our eyes (and perhaps also our head) so that the image of the object falls within the foveal field of vision. Finally, there is a third cortical area important to the processing of visual information: *inferotemporal cortex*. These three regions are shown in **FIGURE 18.3.**

Visual information proceeds from striate cortex to the ipsilateral circumstriate belt by means of corticocortical connections. Circumstriate cortex is then connected to both ipsilateral and contralateral inferotemporal cortex; the contralateral connections are made by means of fibers of the corpus callosum. Furthermore, striate cortex and superior colliculus both project to the *pulvinar* (a thalamic nucleus), which in turn projects to and receives fibers from both circumstriate and inferotemporal cortex. (See **FIGURE 18.4.**)

ROLE OF INFEROTEMPORAL CORTEX IN VISUAL PROCESSING. You will recall from chapter 9 that monkeys with lesions of temporal cortex show "psychic blindness"; they can get around very nicely without bumping into things, but they appear to have trouble recognizing what

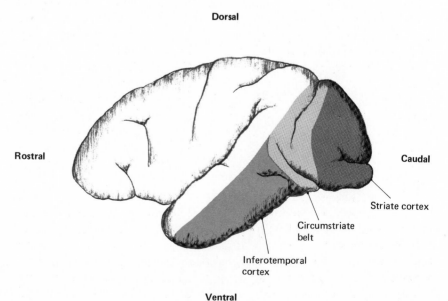

Dorsal

Rostral

Caudal

Striate cortex

Circumstriate belt

Inferotemporal cortex

Ventral

FIGURE 18.3 Primary visual cortex (striate cortex), inferotemporal cortex, and the circumstriate belt. (Redrawn from Gross, C. G. In Jung, R., editor, *Handbook of Physiology.* Vol. 7/3B. Berlin: Springer-Verlag, 1973.)

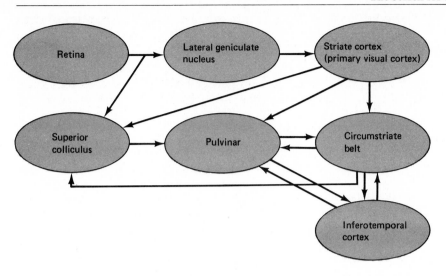

FIGURE 18.4 A schematic and simplified representation of the interconnections of various regions of the visual system.

these objects are. They will pick up items from a tray containing small edible and inedible objects, eating the pieces of food and dropping the pieces of hardware. They show no fear of objects that monkeys normally avoid; Klüver and Bucy (1939) reported that these monkeys will even try to investigate the tongue of a living snake. Mishkin (1966) made brain lesions in a series of three stages and tested the monkeys' ability to perform a visual discrimination after each lesion. First he removed striate cortex on one side: no deficit. Then he removed the contralateral inferotemporal cortex: no deficit. Finally, he cut the corpus callosum. The last operation isolated the remaining inferotemporal cortex from the remaining striate cortex, and the animals now suffered from a deficit in visual pattern discrimination. Striate cortex alone could not mediate memory for this task. Neither could inferotemporal cortex that was deprived of its visual input. (See **FIGURE 18.5.**) Lesions of the pulvinar (the only subcortical area that projects to inferotemporal cortex) do not, however, produce such deficits (Chow, 1961). Thus, we must conclude that the transcortical connections from striate cortex to circumstriate cortex to inferotemporal cortex are the ones that convey the essential visual information.

Inferotemporal cortex appears to participate in a very high level of analysis of visual information; it is here, perhaps, that meaning is assigned to visual stimuli. Gross (1973) summarized the results of a series of studies performed in his laboratory. He reported that it was very difficult to characterize features of the stimuli that most effectively altered the firing rate of single units located there. For example, one unit responded most vigorously to the sight of a bottle brush, another to the shadow of a pair of hemostatic forceps (which

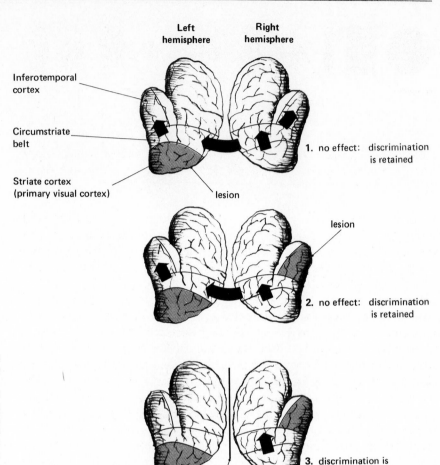

Left hemisphere

Right hemisphere

Inferotemporal cortex

Circumstriate belt

Striate cortex (primary visual cortex)

lesion

1. no effect: discrimination is retained

lesion

2. no effect: discrimination is retained

3. discrimination is not retained

Corpus callosum is cut

FIGURE 18.5   A schematic representation of the procedure used by Mishkin et al. (1966). Not all of the control groups used in this experiment are represented here. (Adapted from Mishkin, M., Visual mechanisms beyond the striate cortex. In *Frontiers in Physiological Psychology,* edited by R. W. Russell. New York: Academic Press, 1966.)

are shaped somewhat like scissors), and another to a monkey hand. The shapes shown in Figure 18.6 are ordered according to the magnitude of the response they produced in this last neuron.   (See **FIGURE 18.6.**)   Gross does not say that this neuron detects monkey hands, because this claim could be made only after showing that no other stimulus produced a better response. But it is the case, nevertheless, that neurons in inferotemporal cortex are most idiosyncratic in the features they respond to. Many of them, as Gross reports, respond better to a particular three-dimensional stimulus than to any silhouette made from it, suggesting a high level of analysis of the visual information.   It would be interesting to know whether small lesions of inferotemporal cortex (they would have to be made bilaterally, or in one hemisphere of a split-brain monkey) would result in losses in

Ineffective   Most effective

Relative effectiveness of various stimuli
in changing activity of unit

FIGURE 18.6 A rank-ordering of the effectiveness of various stimuli in producing a response in a single neuron located in inferotemporal cortex. (From Gross, C. P., Rocha-Miranda, C. E., and Bender, D. B., *Journal of Neurophysiology*, 1972, 35, 96–111.)

ability to recognize particular classes of stimuli in the way that lesions of striate cortex produce blindness in particular parts of the visual field.

INFEROTEMPORAL CORTEX AND VISUAL MEMORY. If the tempting inference from these results is correct, that there are cells in inferotemporal cortex that respond to very specific visual stimuli, then we must alter our view of the role of primary visual cortex in memory. In primates, at least, the finding that memory for a visual pattern discrimination remains after lesions destroying all but a small part of striate cortex does not prove that the surviving cells had necessarily participated in storage of the memory for that pattern. To put it another way, if memory involves alterations in the properties of neurons (an inescapable conclusion, I think), then we need not assume that any changes are taking place in neurons of visual cortex. The changes that represent the association between a complex visual stimulus and some other stimulus (or some response performed by the animal) could be made "downstream" from the neurons in inferotemporal cortex that respond to that pattern. Neurons in inferotemporal cortex could serve as the starting point for memory circuits involved in an association between the stimulus they represent and circuits mediating a response or the representation of some other stimulus. This suggestion leaves unanswered the question of why a particular inferotemporal neuron responds to a particular visual stimulus; does inferotemporal cortex contain a huge number of "wired-in" complex feature detectors, or do units there "learn" to recognize visual stimuli? (I think the neurons "learn" the patterns.)

Figure 18.7 contains a diagram that might help summarize the conclusions that can be made from the evidence presented so far. Simple visual habits can be disrupted only by lesions that destroy the animal's ability to process that information; a brightness discrimination, for example, does not require any visual cortex at all. A preoperatively learned brightness discrimination is not retained after striate lesions, but can be relearned by means of subcortical mechanisms. This fact suggests that intact sensory cortex somehow inhibits the formation of memories by subcortical processes. (See **FIGURE 18.7.**) As the stimuli become more complex, more levels of analysis

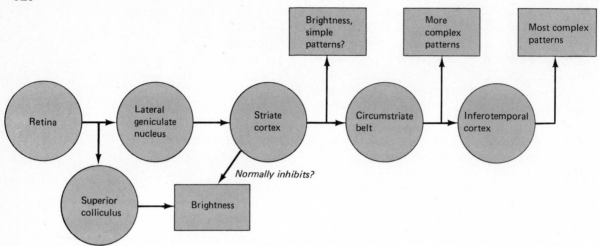

FIGURE 18.7 A schematic representation of the way in which information might be analyzed in the visual system, and the relationship of this analysis to the formation of memory.

are needed for the central nervous system to encode the sensory information and thus provide the input necessary for the formation of an association.

Association Cortex and Memory

Lesions in other regions of association cortex appear to produce similar modality-specific deficits in discrimination learnng. For example, Brown, Rosvold, and Mishkin (1963) observed impairments in olfactory discriminations after lesions of the temporal pole; Weiskrantz and Mishkin (1958) found that superior temporal lesions (auditory association cortex) disrupted complex auditory discriminations; and Wilson (1957) produced lesions in posterior parietal cortex (somatosensory association cortex) and observed deficits in tactual discriminations. In all of these experiments, the impairments were modality-specific; only discriminations made by means of the sense modalities mentioned were disrupted.

PROBLEMS OF INTERPRETATION. The data presented so far suggest that when an animal is required to make a simple response to a simple stimulus, the only cortical lesions that will disrupt performance are those which obviously disrupt perceptual processing of the stimulus. Experiments showing that damage to nonsensory areas impairs performance on a simple task invariably involve tasks that are, upon subsequent analysis, not so simple after all. For example, Lashley (1950) reports data of Klüver that show an apparent loss of memory based on simple stimuli after he made large cortical lesions in a variety of locations. Monkeys were preoperatively trained on a number of discrimination tasks requiring different sense modalities. After the lesions were made, the animals' performance fell to chance levels; they selected the stimuli at random. Klüver then retrained the monkeys on one of the problems—the selection of weights. Once this task was relearned, the animals were tested again with the other stimuli. This time, the monkeys selected the appropriate objects. Klüver concluded that the lesions had damaged the animals' *behavioral set* to compare the stimuli, but had not affected memories relating to the stimuli themselves.

Behavioral set is a tendency to perceive or respond to a stimulus in a particular way. The set can be explicitly established, by presenting instructions or rules. For example, if I say, "Add these numbers together and say the answer: two and three," you will respond, "Five." Any subsequent pair of numbers will be added together. If I say, "Multiply these numbers and say the answer," your response— to the same stimuli presented earlier—will be different. Your behavioral set, established by means of instruction, will cause you to perceive and respond to my utterances in a certain way. Behavioral set can also be established implicitly, by context. Figure 18.8 illustrates this principle. Recite the symbols to yourself. (See **FIGURE 18.8**). One of the symbols in this figure appears in identical form in both the top and the bottom lines, but you probably perceived it in two different ways, depending on the behavioral set established by means of context; the upper line contains numbers, and the lower one, letters. (See **FIGURE 18.8**.)

Behavioral set, in the task Klüver used, can be translated roughly as the "rules of the game." The monkeys had to compare the stimuli and respond to the one that was previously reinforced. The brain lesions probably disrupted this behavioral set in some way, so that the monkeys did not attend to and respond to the stimuli in the proper manner. Retraining on the weight discrimination reestablished their set to compare stimuli, but it obviously did not convey any information about which of the other stimuli should be selected. Then, having mastered the rules of the game, the monkeys could apply these rules to the stimuli they had learned earlier.

This experiment is a good example of the difficulty we have in deciding whether a memory for a simple stimulus is lost. An experiment that uses brain lesions to assess the location of memories can really be conclusive only if the animal can still perform the task—we know then that the memory was not lost. If the animal cannot perform, we must prove that the deficit cannot be attributed to any other function, such as behavioral set.

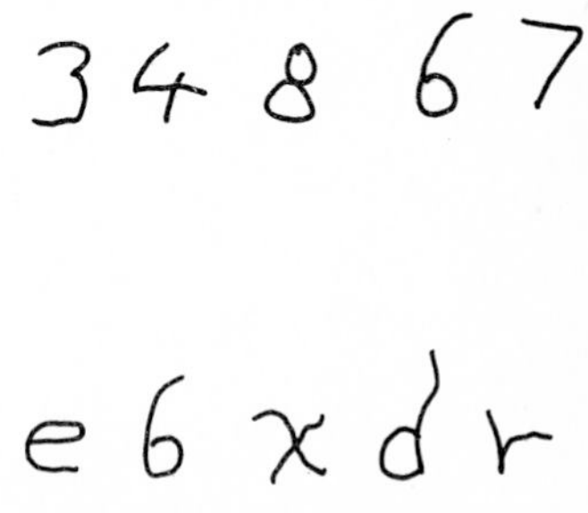

FIGURE 18.8   Read these symbols aloud.

Complex Tasks and the Diffuse Representation of Memory

So far I have restricted my discussion to instances of learning a simple discrimination task. But what about a more complex task? Lashley (1950) concluded that a rat's performance on a complex task such as a maze problem depended more on the *amount* of cortex that remained than upon the particular *location* of the surviving tissue. (He referred to this as the principle of *mass action*.) Decrements in retention were seen to be proportional to the amount of cortex that was damaged. Results such as these led to speculations that memories might be very diffusely represented in the brain, each association being represented by a large number of neurons scattered throughout cortex.

Analogies have been developed that emphasize spatial and temporal dimensions on the surface of the brain in preference to specific neural connections. For example, memory could be likened to the ripples on a pond produced when a stone is thrown in; the spatial and temporal patterns of waves specify the location where the object entered the pond, the time it entered, and something about its size and/or the force with which it entered. A large pond will, of course, encode this information more precisely, and if it were not for the problem of the waves eventually dying down, we could (if we knew how) read the history of the pond's disturbances. More complicated analogies have been used; the cortical representation of information has been likened to a *holographic* process (Pribram, 1971). A hologram is a kind of photograph produced by the interference patterns made by bouncing coherent light from a laser off of a three-dimensional object and onto a sheet of film. The result is a photographic transparency that looks, in ordinary light, like a set of meaningless abstractions. However, when illuminated by a laser, it produces an image of the object that appears to float in space. It is even possible to move one's head and "look behind" the image. If pieces of the hologram are cut out, corresponding pieces of the image are not lost; instead, the image begins to get fuzzy. (You have to move your eye closer to the remaining piece of the hologram, but you still see the entire image.) Each part of the hologram participates in representation of the whole, but no one part is essential.

The sharpness of a holographic image, then, depends on the amount of the hologram left intact, and since performance on a complex task is proportional to the amount of cortex left intact, perhaps cortical representations of memory are similar to holographic representations of a visual image. That is, perhaps all parts of cortex participate in the storage of all memories.

EVIDENCE IN FAVOR OF DIFFUSE REPRESENTATION OF MEMORY.   Let us examine some of the data that pertain to this issue.   I have already noted that Lashley reported that the amount, not the location, of cortical damage was the best predictor of an animal's performance on a complex task, such as a maze problem.   The simplest explanation for the fact that a complex task can be disrupted by lesions placed in any of a wide variety of cortical locations is that a complex task is learned by means of several sensory modalities, and that damage to a given region of cortex impairs a particular sensory function.   For example, visual, tactile, kinesthetic, olfactory, and probably even auditory cues may be utilized in the acquisition of a maze task by a rat.   The fact that sufficient cortical damage just about anywhere will impair acquisition or retention of this task might be attributed to deficits in one or more of the several sensory modalities.   The animal is left with less sensory information than it had before the operation. There is evidence against this explanation, however.

Lashley (1943) found that even unexpected regions of cortex participated in retention of a complex habit.   He blinded rats by removing their eyes and then had them learn a maze problem.   He then destroyed visual cortex and found that its removal produced very severe deficits in the animals' subsequent performance on this task. If the rats were blind, what use were they making of visual cortex? Perhaps they formed a "visual image" of the maze based on prior associations (before blinding) of visual stimuli with tactile and kinesthetic feedback received from moving about the environment.   When they traversed the maze, these associations might have triggered activity in visual cortex.   However, Tsang (1934) observed similar deleterious effects of lesions of striate cortex even in adult animals that had been blinded at birth.   Apparently, the animals do not need practice in making associations between visual and kinesthetic input in order for visual cortex to play a role in nonvisual learning.

Nonsensory participation in complex habits is not restricted to visual cortex.   Rats that were made blind, whose whiskers (*vibrissae*) were cut off, and that had the dorsal half of the spinal cords severed at the cervical level (cutting the dorsal columns and thus producing anesthesia for both touch and kinesthetic feedback provided by movement) suffered less of a deficit on a complex latchbox-opening task than did animals deprived of any single sensory area of cortex (Lashley, 1935).

In general, whenever a task requires an animal to respond to stimuli of more than one sense modality, performance will be disrupted by a sufficiently large lesion placed almost anywhere within cortex.   And, in general, more difficult tasks (i.e., those which take longer for a normal animal to learn) can be disrupted by a relatively small lesion, which would not affect performance on an easier task. This suggests, again, that a complex memory is represented by neurons in a wide area of cortex.

In a general sense, this conclusion is undoubtedly true. Memories *are* contained in wide regions of cortex, and when an animal makes a particular association, this event undoubtedly produces alterations all over the cortex (and in subcortical regions also). The issue is whether (a) a memory is diffusely stored, all parts of the memory for a complex task being represented in all parts of cortex, or whether (b) individual elements are each stored in relatively discrete neural circuits. In other words, the question is whether visual components of a complex task are stored in visual cortex (primary and/or association areas), auditory components in auditory cortex, and so on, or whether all components are diffusely represented in all portions of cortex.

PROBABILISM VERSUS DETERMINISM IN THE REPRESENTATION OF MEMORY.   One of the foremost proponents of the hypothesis that memories are represented almost everywhere is E. Roy John.   In his book on brain mechanisms of memory he states:

> . . . it seems unlikely that any one structure, or set of neurons therein, is uniquely responsible for the storage of memory about a specific experience.   The evidence argues against the proposition that memory is stored as a requirement that a specific set of cells must discharge when a familiar event occurs, or that remembering that event demands the deterministic discharge of a specific set of cells.   It does not seem likely that the discharge of a given set of cells is either a necessary or sufficient condition for the activation of a particular memory.   (John, 1967, p. 418)

John is clearly not saying that the individual elements of a specific task are each stored in fairly discrete neural circuits; he is saying that representation of *each* of the elements is widely distributed in the brain.   He refers to the representation of memories as being "probabilistic."   Since neurons are actively firing at almost all times, the occurrence of a single action potential in one neuron is meaningless.   Only when we examine a neuron's rate or pattern of discharge, across time, can we detect any information.   And since there are so many neurons in the brain (and since we lose several hundred neurons a day as a result of natural causes), it seems unlikely that any information is stored or transmitted solely by a single neuron.   Information must be represented redundantly, in the firing patterns of a large number of neurons.   This seems eminently reasonable; we know that a large number of sensory neurons must respond (in most cases) for us to perceive a stimulus, and many motor neurons must fire to make a response. It seems likely that, between stimulus and response, neural representation of memory for an event also requires the participation of a large number of neurons. There are cases where we can discriminate very minute stimulus changes; for example, we can apparently detect the firing of a single afferent axon mediating tactile information, and we can learn to control the firing of a single muscle fiber without also firing its neighbors (at least the particular neighbors whose activity is being recorded). It is unlikely, however, that the representation of either of these events is mediated by a chain of individual neurons. Considering the input of a single afferent neuron, there is a tremendous amount of divergence on the way up to somatosensory cortex, and undoubtedly a large number of cortical neurons respond to a sensory event, the input. And control of a single motor unit must require a complex pattern of afferent discharge on lower motor neurons, inhibiting the ones to be kept silent as well as exciting the one to be fired.

When John refers to neural coding as being *probabilistic* rather than *deterministic*, he is essentially describing the problem of signal versus noise. For example, it is not very likely that you will detect the bending of a single hair on one part of your forearm if simultaneously someone is rubbing another part. There is just too much afferent activity arising at that time for such a small stimulus to be detected. And you might be able to hear a whisper across a quiet room, but you will not be able to do so if an airplane goes overhead just then. The probability of detecting the information depends on two things: the size of the signal (number of neurons conveying the information and magnitude of the change in their firing patterns from baseline patterns) and the amount of noise (degree to which the neurons are also subjected to other inputs).

Representation of a stimulus, then, can be thought of as probabilistic. The likelihood of detection increases as more neurons participate in the representation. It seems likely that the representation of the *memory* for an event can similarly be referred to as probabilistic. The more neurons undergoing some sort of alterations that encode that event, the more likely it is that the event will be available for retrieval at a later time. Most people, I think, would agree with that statement. Even investigators who believe that a single association can be represented by a very specific and discrete assembly of neurons will agree that memories are more likely to withstand the ravages of time and interference if a large number of cells participate in the storage of the information—perhaps in a redundant, parallel manner. In other words, even if a particular memory is encoded by changes occurring in a distinct subset of neurons, the greater that number is, the more stable the memory will be.

The fact that performance on a complex task is disrupted by

sufficiently large lesions anywhere in cortex is taken, by John, as evidence for the diffuseness of the representation of memory. On the other hand, the evidence could equally well support the hypothesis that individual associations are stored in relatively discrete locations, since a complex task requires a very large number of associations; a large lesion would disrupt more of these individual associations than a small one.

The issue of diffuse versus specific representation of memories can best be resolved by examining data from humans and from other higher primates. As we shall see, there is good evidence that simple associations are mediated within specific regions of association cortex. More complex associations that involve information from more than one sensory modality are mediated by means of specific bundles of axons that interconnect these regions of cortex. Data from animals such as rats are not as useful in resolving this issue, since the distinction between primary sensory cortex and association areas is not so clear-cut as it is in primates. Cortex itself, in rats, is less specialized and functions are more diffusely represented; therefore, finding diffuse representation of memory in rats does not imply that the same holds true for primates.

CROSS-MODAL TRANSFER OF INFORMATION AND THE LOCATION OF STORED MEMORY

A very important phenomenon that must be explained by any physiological theory of memory is that, in humans, an association can be retrieved by stimuli other than the ones that originally led to its formation, and the memory can produce responses other than the ones originally made when the task was learned. To be more specific: an auditory stimulus may, for example, be used to initiate the retrieval of a memory that was originally learned visually. And once a person is taught to draw a geometric figure, that same figure could be drawn with the other hand, with the foot, with a pencil held between the teeth, or even by proxy, with verbal instructions given to another person: "Draw a short vertical line, now a long one slanting down to the right," etc. These facts are so obvious to us that they seem trivial. We tend to think of our memories as being all of one piece. The fact that we can describe a visual memory verbally comes as no surprise to us. We can even modify the mental image on the basis of nonvisual information. Suppose a person is describing an image of a memory formed visually. He says, "I remember the first time we met. You were wearing a blue dress when you walked into the room." "No, I was wearing a yellow dress." "Oh, were you? A yellow dress, huh?" And suddenly a part of the mental image changes. In subsequent retrievals of that memory, she will probably be wearing a yellow dress.

These phenomena show how interrelated and interconnected our memories are, and how available they are to all kinds of response systems. The intimate interconnections among memories might be accomplished in one of two ways: (1) Individual memories are stored in rather specific locations. Associations among them are mediated by neurons that interconnect these regions. (2) Individual memories are represented in a very diffuse manner by means of small changes in a very large number of neurons, resulting in changes in the properties of the brain as a whole. Associations among memories would not be attributed to any one set of connections, but would be as diffuse as the memories themselves. As we shall see, the evidence favors the first alternative.

Cross-Modal Transfer of Information in Animals

Studies with animals have shown that performance on a simple, single-modality task is most likely to be impaired by lesions that damage the appropriate sensory cortex or the sensory association area. These results indicate a loss of memories and the ability to form new ones, but they could just as well indicate that the stimuli needed to elicit retrieval of the memory can no longer be perceived. The memory is still there, perhaps, but can no longer be accessed by the appropriate stimulus because of a sensory or perceptual deficit.

The obvious way to discriminate among these alternatives is to do the following: Train an animal with a particular sense modality and then destroy the appropriate area of association cortex. Afterwards, test for the memory, using a *different* sense modality, and see whether the animal remembers the original association. There is just one problem. Very few studies have successfully shown that even a *normal* animal (other than one of the higher primates) can gain access to information learned through one sense modality by the use of another one. For example, a particular cross-modality transfer task that is quite easy for humans does not appear to be possible for monkeys. (Monkeys have less complex brains than do apes, such as chimps or gorillas.) Ettlinger (1960) trained monkeys to visually discriminate between a circle and a cross. The animals were then trained to discriminate between a circle and a cross they could touch but not see. Their prior visual experience with the stimuli did not help them with the tactual discrimination; the visual memories were not available to the somatosensory system. In humans, of course, there would be no problem. I am sure that if any of you were shown (but not allowed to touch) a gold cube and a lead sphere and then were blindfolded and were allowed to choose and keep one of the objects, you would choose the cube. Your visual memory is easily available for retrieval by means of tactual input. It probably comes as a surprise to learn that the same is not true for a monkey.

Ettlinger's results contrast with the performance of apes such as chimpanzees (Davenport, Rogers, and Russell, 1975) or of human children (Blank, Altman, and Bridger, 1968), who are quite adept at cross-modal retrieval of memory. This ability appears to be a relatively specialized capacity that is characteristic only of highly developed brains. If the stimuli are made especially important to the subjects, cross-modal transfer can be demonstrated in monkeys (which have less complex brains than do the higher apes). Cowey and Weiskrantz (1975) presented pairs of cookies to monkeys kept in absolute darkness; the shapes of the cookies are shown in **FIGURE 18.9.** One member of each pair (the positive stimulus) was molded of commercial monkey food. The other member (the negative stimulus) was made of equal parts of monkey food and sand, with added quinine for bitterness. (It should be obvious why this stimulus was referred to as negative.) The monkeys readily ate the positive stimulus and, not unexpectedly, left the negative stimulus alone after a few nibbles. When permitted to select the shapes visually (but not by touch), the monkeys showed a distinct preference for the positive ones, which they had not previously seen.

This study and a subsequent experiment by the same authors (Weiskrantz and Cowey, 1975) appear to be the only ones that unequivocally demonstrate cross-modal transfer of a discrimination task learned on the basis of form. Other studies have demonstrated auditory to visual or visual to auditory transfer of frequency discrimination (i.e., response to one frequency of click or flash, but not to another frequency) in rats (Over and Mackintosh, 1969) and rabbits (Yehle and Ward, 1969). The fact that frequency of an intermit-

Pairs of stimuli

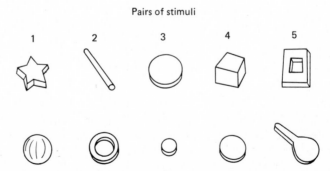

FIGURE 18.9 Pairs of stimulus cookies used by Cowey and Weiskrantz (1975). Redrawn from Cowey, A., and Weiskrantz, L., *Neuropsychologia*, 1975, *13*, 117–120.)

tent stimulus can be transferred cross-modally even in rodents suggests the possibility that some rhythmic response serves to mediate the transfer. Perhaps a set of neurons (of the motor system, perhaps) responds differently to different frequencies of sensory input, and feedback from these neurons serves as one of the cues by which the animal learns to respond to the positive, but not the negative, stimulus. The response-produced stimuli could then account for the transfer from one sense modality to another. This suggestion is advanced because it would seem strange, otherwise, that monkeys, which have excellent vision and tactile sensitivity along with a highly developed brain, nevertheless show cross-modal transfer only under special conditions.

IMPLICATIONS FOR SPECIFIC VERSUS DIFFUSE REPRESENTATION OF MEMORY. Why is cross-modal transfer of *form* information (as opposed to frequency) apparently restricted to higher primates? One could say that such a facility shown by humans can be explained by the fact that we are much more capable of mediating cross-modal associations via language. But, as Geschwind (1965) points out, this explanation is probably backwards. That is, humans are capable of learning and using language *because* we are so facile at making cross-modal associations. Without the ability quickly and easily to form an association between the sight of an object and the sound of the word representing it, we would not be capable of a language.

The failure, prior to the studies by Cowey and Weiskrantz, to obtain results showing good cross-modal transfer of memories for form in animals other than apes means that perhaps we need not take the diffuseness theory of memory quite so seriously. At the very least, if memories pertaining to all sensory modalities are distributed throughout the brain, they nevertheless do not interact across sensory modalities, except in the most highly developed brain. They do, however, interact *within* a sense modality. If an animal is taught to respond to a tone of a high frequency but not to one of a low frequency, the probability that it will respond to a tone of an intermediate frequency depends on the similarity between the test tone and the one that was originally reinforced. In other words, the animals show *stimulus generalization*. The same is true for other dimensions within any given sense modality: the more similar the test stimulus is to the training stimulus, the more likely it is that the response will be emitted, even though the test stimulus itself was never associated with reinforcement. If all memories are diffusely represented throughout the brains of lower mammals, it is interesting that memories can interact intramodally but somehow are kept separate from memories of other sense modalities.

Disconnection Syndromes in Humans

Why is there such a difference in the ease with which cross-modal transfer occurs in humans and in other animals? Geschwind (1965) has suggested that the answer can be found in the fact that, in the human brain, various sensory association areas and the motor association area rostral to the precentral gyrus are extensively interconnected by specific fiber systems. These interconnections are not seen to nearly the same extent in lower animals, and they are not very prominent even in subhuman primates. Brains of apes (e.g., chimps and gorillas) contain many more of these fibers than do brains of monkeys. The significance of these axonal interconnections is shown by the fact that their destruction produces a very definite impairment in cross-modal transfer in humans. If, for example, you had a lesion that destroyed fibers connecting visual association cortex with somatosensory association cortex, you would *not* deliberately pick up the gold cube, as opposed to the lead sphere, when you chose the objects blindfolded. Tactual input would not have access to visually stored information. If, however, your connections between auditory association cortex and somatosensory association cortex were still intact, you would be able to choose the correct object if you had been previously told, "The cube is made of gold, but the sphere is lead." Tactual input would still have access to auditory memories. Let us examine the evidence that permits me to make statements like these.

WERNICKE'S APHASIA. Some very specific, and rather bizarre, deficits may be seen after brain lesions in humans. For example, human auditory cortex is located in the posterior part of the *superior temporal gyrus* of the left hemisphere. (It is located in the right hemisphere in a few people, but it is *not* generally associatd with handedness, as most people assume. Even left-handed people are more likely to have a verbally dominant left hemisphere, as was demonstrated by Milner, Branch, and Rasmussen, 1966.) This auditory association area is usually referred to as *Wernicke's area*, after its discoverer. (See **FIGURE 18.10**.) Subtotal damage to this region (which might occur as a result of occlusion of a small artery by a blood clot) results in difficulty in discriminating between closely related sounds, such as *b* and *p* or *d* and *t* (Luria, 1970). These results are not difficult to interpret; it would be expected that a considerable degree of analysis is necessary to distinguish between such similar sounds. However, damage to Wernicke's area produces another effect, which is not quite so obvious. The patient will also have difficulty in writing; words will tend to be misspelled. The errors will not be random, however. Letters representing similar sounds will tend to be interchanged. For

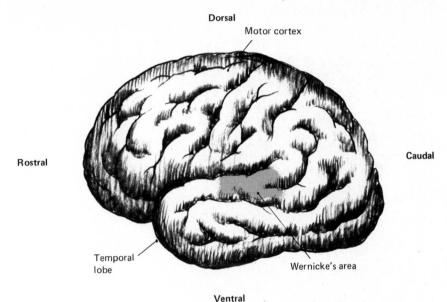

Dorsal

Motor cortex

Rostral

Caudal

Temporal
lobe

Wernicke's area

Ventral

FIGURE 18.10 The location
of Wernicke's area in the left
hemisphere of the brain.

example, the patient might write *tip* instead of *dip*. The letters *o* and *c*, which are certainly more similar in shape than *d* and *t*, are less likely to be interchanged, since they produce different sounds. Why should spelling errors made by people with damage to auditory association cortex be related to sounds made by the letters that are written?

The easiest way to explain the deficit is to assume (a) that words are learned acoustically, by association between the auditory representation of the word and the corresponding visual, tactual, etc., representation of the object being denoted (in the case of object nouns, at least) and (b) that writing, which comes later, apparently depends upon associations between writing movements made by the hand and acoustically learned representations of the words. If you observe children learning to write, you will notice that they spell out the sounds each letter makes as they write a word. Even when an adult spells a long, relatively unfamiliar word, the sounds of the letters are pronounced, or at least imagined in an acoustic manner. You will probably find it impossible to write the word *antidisestablish-mentarianism* without conjuring up an "auditory image" of the sounds made by the letters. Sing "When the Saints Go Marching In" as you write the word—you will probably find that you have to write the successive letters during pauses between the words of the song. If you try to draw a picture, however, singing a song will probably produce no interference at all. (Try it—talking and singing do not interfere with complex hand and finger movements, since drawing is not impeded by unrelated verbalization. Writing, however, certainly is.) Access to auditory representation of the words being sung or spoken and access to visual memory of an object being drawn can be accomplished much more independently than can simultaneous access to two different auditory memories.

I do not want to suggest that I have proved anything with this example. One could argue that it takes more information-processing ability to spell *antidisestablishmentarianism* than to draw a picture, and less information-processing capacity is left over for singing a song while writing than while drawing a picture. I merely want to show you that it is at least plausible to refer to separate access to visually stored and acoustically stored memories, and to give you a specific instance that is easy to think about and remember.

If our ability to write depends upon a transfer of information between acoustically acquired representations of sounds and motor movements that represent those sounds, then damage to auditory association cortex should not impair written symbols that represent visually acquired memories. This does indeed seem to be true. Damage to Wernicke's area in the left hemisphere does not impair a person's ability to draw pictures that represent visual memories. Even more impressively, Chinese patients with these lesions suffer the same impairment in auditory recognition, mistaking words that sound similar; nevertheless, they are able to write very accurately, unlike Westerners (Luria, 1970). Chinese is written in the form of ideographs, which are not related to the sounds of the words they represent. When Chinese people write a word, they do not need to gain access to its acoustic representation in memory in order to spell it; a character representing an object noun can be based upon associations between a visual representation of that word and the movements necessary to produce it. Similarly, the writing ability of deaf people is not affected by lesions in Wernicke's area, nor is the representation of words by means of *kanji* symbols (ideographs) in Japanese. The lesions do, however, interfere with the writing of Japanese *kana* symbols, which are phonetic, representing the sounds the words make (Sasanuma, 1975). Lesions of auditory association cortex, then, impair the execution of hand movements based on acoustically learned memories, but not visually learned ones. Deaf patients can write, Oriental patients can write ideographs, and all of the patients can draw pictures.

CONDUCTION APHASIA. Norman Geschwind (1965; 1972; 1975) has described a number of specific disorders in humans that can best be explained in terms of interrupted connections between various cortical association areas. For example, a syndrome known as *conduction aphasia* appears to result from damage to fibers of the *arcuate fasciculus*. This fiber bundle interconnects auditory association cortex with a region of motor association cortex that, in turn, relays information to *Broca's speech area.* Broca's speech area is concerned with speech production; lesions here damage the ability of a patient to articulate words, but not necessarily to write them. Patients with *Broca's aphasia* have a great deal of difficulty in speaking; words are laboriously and slowly produced. A deficit in comprehension or intellectual ability is not seen when the lesions are limited to this area. (See **FIGURE 18.11.**) Patients with conduction aphasia (disconnections between Wernicke's area and Broca's area caused by lesions that damage the arcuate fasciculus) generally exhibit very good spontaneous speech; they can express their thoughts in words. They can usually carry out verbal commands by means of movements, so they obviously comprehend the meaning of words they hear. However, they are very poor at *repeating* words. Geschwind cites the example of a patient who was asked to repeat the word *president.* He replied, "I know who that is—Kennedy." (The patient was tested in the early 1960's.) So information can get from Wernicke's area to Broca's area, but only in an indirect fashion. Presumably the word *president* evoked an association between the word and some sort of representation (visual, perhaps) of John Kennedy. Connections between visual association cortex and Broca's area conveyed this information, and the patient verbalized the image.

A surprising fact is that patients who suffer from conduction aphasia are usually able to identify numbers. They can read them,

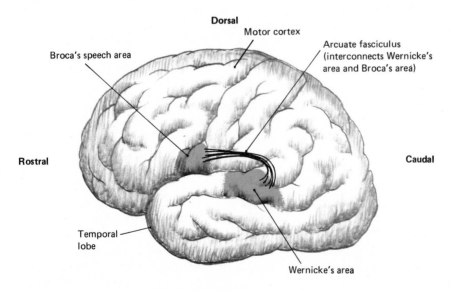

FIGURE 18.11 The location of Broca's speech area in the left hemisphere of the brain.

and can repeat them back. In fact, they show obvious signs of relaxation when they are asked to repeat numbers, as opposed to nonnumerical words. In these patients, auditory association cortex is disconnected from Broca's area but remains connected to visual association and somatosensory association cortex, so the route from temporal lobe to speech center must be mediated indirectly, by arousing associations elsewhere. Geschwind points out that numbers are usually associated with specific visual and somatosensory representations. We teach a child to count on his or her fingers, and to associate numbers with images—the number "two" with a visual image of two objects, for example. Thus, there are previously learned mediators that represent numerical information. There are, of course, mediators for nonnumerical information, but they are generally more ambiguous. The image evoked by the word *chair* might be verbally described by a patient suffering from conduction aphasia as "sit," or "furniture."

The likelihood that this explanation is correct is enhanced by close examination of the errors patients make when asked to repeat numbers. "Fifty-five percent" becomes "fifty-five progum," and "eleven plus eight" becomes "eleven, eight . . . nineteen." "Three-*quarters*" becomes "three, four," even though the patient could say "penny, nickel, dime, *quarter*." Presumably, there are good visual associations available to mediate the transmission of the representation of the coins. A patient could read "28" or "twenty-eight" equally well, but could not, for instance, read "train." He said "travel" instead. Presumably, an image went from visual association cortex to auditory cortex, where the "meaning" of the image was evoked. The "meaning" was communicated back to visual cortex, and then Broca's area translated the concept into words: "travel" for "train." The numerical information survived the successive transformations much better. In more severe cases, patients lose the ability to say "sixty-eight" but will say "six, eight" instead.

ISOLATION OF AUDITORY AND SPEECH MECHANISMS. Geschwind concludes that auditory associations can no longer be put into speech, but can evoke visual and/or somatosensory associations, when the arcuate fasciculus is cut. Comprehension is good, but speech cannot be repeated. The clincher for this argument comes from the case of a woman who suffered a brain lesion that did not damage Wernicke's area, or Broca's area, or their interconnections via the arcuate fasciculus, but did isolate both of these areas from visual and somatosensory cortex (Geschwind, Quadfasel, and Segarra, 1968). (See **FIGURE 18.12**.) The lesion, produced by methane poisoning, is almost the reverse of the lesion produced in the case of conduction aphasia. Instead of damaging the connections between Wernicke's

Dorsal

Rostral

Caudal

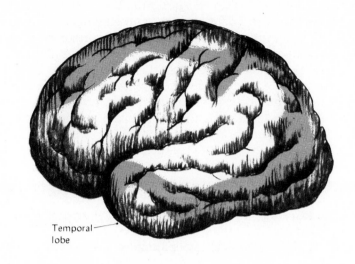

Temporal
lobe

Ventral

FIGURE 18.12   Brain damage
produced by methane poison-
ing in the patient reported by
Geschwind et al. (1968).
(Redrawn from Geschwind, N.,
Quadfasel, F. A., and Segarra,
J. M., *Neuropsychologia*, 1968,
13, 229–235.)

area and Broca's area, leaving everything else intact, the lesion destroyed the other connections, leaving the Wernicke-Broca circuit
intact.

The symptoms were also the reverse of conduction aphasia;
what this woman could do, the conduction asphasic could not, and
vice-versa. She could repeat everything that was said to her, but
she never, during the nine years she survived after the lesion occurred,
spoke spontaneously. Nor did she give any sign of understanding
what was said to her. If the first part of a poem were recited she would
continue with the last part. She could sing and was even capable
of learning new songs.

This patient was helpless and had to receive complete nursing
care. Was she conscious? I cannot answer that question, but you
might think about what consciousness means. She certainly did not
picture flowers when she repeated "roses are red, violets are blue,"
but she obviously knew the rest of the verse, because she went on to
say it by herself. Her visual association area was intact, and her eyes
moved in response to moving stimuli; does this mean she "knew"
what was going on, even though she could not make cross-modal associations, or, indeed, any kind of voluntary movement? If she saw
a picture of a person with an extra eye in the middle of the forehead,
would she recognize this as incongruous, even though she could not
tell us about it? It is difficult to imagine our consciousness as being
separated into visual awareness and auditory awareness and somatosensory awareness, but consider people whose hemispheres have been

disconnected by means of cutting the corpus callosum (chapter 1). These people clearly have heads occupied by two "selves," with two different personalities. They can even learn to communicate with each other by means of gross body movements that they can both initiate and feel, such as head-shaking.

CONCLUSIONS FROM DISCONNECTION SYNDROMES IN HUMANS. The disconnection syndromes, as Geschwind calls them, seem to provide the most clear-cut data that pertain to the issue of whether memories are localized or diffusely represented. The data appear to indicate that, in humans, access to modality-specific memories is lost when the association cortex for that sense modality is destroyed. Furthermore, sensory-sensory associations are specifically destroyed when the interconnections between the relevant association areas are damaged. It is difficult to escape the conclusion that memories are located in distinct regions of the brain, and that cross-modal associations are mediated by interconnecting fiber bundles. A particularly telling piece of evidence is the fact that when people with conduction aphasia give a verbal response to a spoken stimulus the detour around the damaged connection is by means of prior associations. The information from auditory association cortex arrives at Broca's area not by means of diffuse connections through cortex that convey the information in a representative manner, but by arousing specific visual or somatosensory associations that are then described verbally.

What the data do *not* tell us is whether memories for specific stimuli are represented by specific sets of neurons within the appropriate association cortex, or whether they are coded in a more diffuse manner, by subtle alterations in neurons located all over this region. We will have to know a lot more about the memory process before we can determine which of these alternatives is correct.

Disconnection Syndromes in Animals

As we have seen, the only animals that can readily demonstrate cross-modal transfer of complex associations are the higher apes. These are the only animals that also possess distinct fiber bundles interconnecting various association areas of cortex. (The corpus callosum is the only exception, and all mammals quite readily transfer information from one hemisphere to the other.) Apes are very valuable animals, and so far no one has tried to see whether "disconnection syndromes" can be produced by making brain lesions in these animals.

However, two studies have shown that disconnection syndromes can be produced in monkeys by destruction of a region of frontal cortex that receives input from long association fibers. *Peri-*

arcuate cortex (cortex in the vicinity of the *arcuate sulcus*—not to be confused with the *arcuate fasciculus* that interconnects Wernicke's area and Broca's area) receives fibers from visual, auditory, and somatosensory cortex (Pandya and Kuypers, 1969). (See **FIGURE 18.13.**) Monkeys can be taught to respond to the simultaneous presence of an auditory and a visual stimulus, but to withhold the response to either of the stimuli presented alone. This task requires a certain amount of cross-modal communication, if not cross-modal transfer of memory. Van Hoesen, Vogt, Pandya, and McKenna (1974) made lesions in this area and found that preoperatively trained monkeys could no longer respond to the conjoint presence of the stimuli. They could learn to respond selectively to a visual stimulus or to an auditory stimulus, or even to one of two auditory stimuli. They could not, however, respond to the simultaneous presence of the auditory and visual stimuli. Visual-motor and auditory-motor associations could be made, but not associations based on the integration of auditory and visual information.

As we saw earlier, Cowey and Weiskrantz (1975) were able to demonstrate cross-modality matching of stimuli in rhesus monkeys when the monkeys were presented with palatable and unpalatable cookies of different geometric shapes. Petrides and Iverson (1976) presented these cookies, in the dark, to monkeys with lesions of periarcuate cortex and to normal control monkeys and monkeys that had lesions in other brain regions. The monkeys with periarcuate lesions

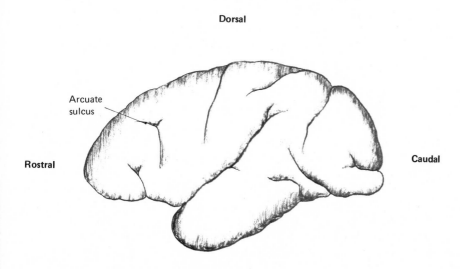

Dorsal

Arcuate
sulcus

Rostral

Caudal

Ventral

FIGURE 18.13 Location of the arcuate sulcus in the brain of the rhesus monkey.

failed to show cross-modality transfer of learning, in contrast with the control subjects.

The data on the neural basis of cross-modality transfer of information in nonhuman primates is still limited, but the evidence reported so far is consistent with the human disconnection syndromes; interactions among memories obtained by means of different sense modalities are made by means of specific long-fiber connections of the cortex. Cross-modal transfer (at least in primates) is not accomplished by means of diffuse, polysynaptic pathways through cortex.

Polysensory Neurons and Representation of Memory

In contrast to the data obtained from brain lesions, there is a considerable amount of electrophysiological data, summarized by John (1972), that, he believes, indicates that information is represented in a diffuse manner throughout the brain. For example, many neurons, especially in motor cortex, will alter their response rate to stimuli of more than one sensory modality. O'Brien and Fox (1969) found that approximately 80 percent of motor cortex neurons in the cat are *polysensory*, responding to more than one sense modality. I do not believe that evidence such as this argues for diffuse representation of memory in the brain. It is certainly true that animals are capable of making sensory-motor associations with all sense modalities. Thus, it is not surprising that neurons in motor cortex will respond to a wide variety of stimuli; after all, the animal can learn to make a given response to a number of different stimuli. When we consider that motor neurons are not restricted to the precentral gyrus, but are found in a variety of cortical regions, it is not surprising to find that polysensory neurons are relatively common. It is noteworthy that these neurons are found most often in motor cortex, but they are more rarely found in primary sensory cortex. This evidence shows that a motor neuron can be influenced by more than one sense modality, but it does not prove that access to information stored by means of one modality can be gained by means of input to another modality.

CONCLUSIONS

The data seem to support connectionistic, rather than diffuse or holistic, theories of memory. Associations appear to be closely tied to the cortical regions that receive and analyze sensory information. In animals capable of making them, sensory-sensory associations appear to depend upon intact connections between the relevant association cortex, and performance depends upon access of these regions to the brain's motor mechanisms.

SUGGESTED READINGS

BEACH, F. A., HEBB, D. O., MORGAN, C. T., and NISSEN, H. W., editors. *The Neuropsychology of Lashley*. New York: McGraw-Hill, 1960.

GESCHWIND, N. Disconnexion syndromes in animals and man. *Brain*, 1965, 88, 237–294; 585–644.

JOHN, E. R. *Mechanisms of Memory*. New York: Academic Press, 1967.

The volume edited by Beach et al. contains a selection of papers by Karl Lashley that should be read by every serious student of the physiology of memory. I especially recommend *In Search of the Engram* and *The Problem of Serial Order in Behavior*. John's case for the diffuse representation of memory is ably stated in his book. Geschwind's articles discuss the anatomy of association cortex in humans and other animals and describe the disconnection syndromes.

Physiology of the Memory Process

19

I am sure that you are all aware of the fact that not everything you perceive can later be remembered. You are also aware of the fact that it takes some effort to learn and remember information—especially if it is not intrinsically interesting. For example, it takes a certain amount of time and rehearsal in order to learn a telephone number.

THE TWO STAGES OF MEMORY

Most learning theorists believe that there are two stages of memory: a short-term and a long-term storage (Wickelgren, 1973). *Short-term memory (STM)* is seen to mediate information that has just been received; we use STM to retain an image of something we just saw, or a sentence we just heard, or something we just touched. The information is quickly replaced by representations of new stimuli, unless some active process intervenes—unless we stop attending to new information, and rehearse the information currently in STM.

For example, suppose that you look up a number in the telephone directory. You repeat the number to yourself and dial it. The number does not ring, so you dial it again; obviously, you still have the number in short-term memory. This time you hear the number ringing and you relax a little, because you do not need to keep remembering the number. Then, you hear a voice saying, "The number you have reached is not in service. What number did you dial?" And you don't remember. Once you relaxed and stopped rehearsing, the number left your short-term memory.

We can, of course, memorize telephone numbers so that they will remain in memory without having to be constantly rehearsed. The process of rehearsal, carried out for a long enough period of time, seems to produce a stable, long-term memory for the information. We can do our rehearsing all in one bout, or we can learn a telephone number by looking it up on repeated occasions. The more time a given piece of information spends in short-term memory, the more likely it becomes that it can be retrieved later from a long-term memory. The transition from short-term memory into long-term memory has the appearance of a gradual process.

Effects of Head Injury in Humans

A severe enough blow to a person's head produces disturbances in memory. These disturbances are most likely to occur when there is diffuse, rather than localized, head injury, such as that produced by a blow to the head with a blunt object (Russell and Nathan, 1949). The following example (which I have adapted from a talk delivered by Hans-Lucas Teuber to a meeting of the New England Psychological Society) shows how temporary disruption of normal brain functions produces effects that can best be understood in terms of a two-proces model of memory.

Bill and John are walking down the street, engaged in conversation. They pass the drugstore, the hardware store, and the dress shop on the corner, and start to cross the street. Suddenly John looks up and shouts, "Look out!" jumping back to the curb as he does so. Bill reacts too late and is struck by an oncoming car. He is thrown several feet, and his head strikes the pavement.

When he awakens in the hospital, Bill has enough presence of mind to avoid the obvious "where am I" question. Instead, he says to a nurse entering the room, "What happened to me? My head hurts."

"You were hit by a car."

"I was? Am I badly hurt?"

"No, we don't think so. Some X-rays have been taken to be sure."

"Will you see that my wife is called? I don't want her to worry. We were supposed to meet for lunch." And he gives the nurse the telephone number she should call. The nurse leaves the room to place the call.

Several minutes later she returns. Before she can say anything, Bill says, "What happened to me?"

"Why, you were hit by a car."

"Will you call my wife for me? I was supposed to meet her for lunch, and I don't want her to worry."

Obviously, Bill has a memory problem.

There are still other symptoms. Some days later, after recovering from his injury, Bill discusses his accident with John. He says, "For the life of me, I can't remember what happened. The last thing I can recall was passing the hardware store."

"But don't you remember watching that deliveryman rolling the rack of clothes into the dress shop? You were looking at them and said you'd have to remember to mention them to your wife. As a matter of fact, I think that's why you didn't notice the car—you were looking back at the dress shop."

"I don't remember that at all."

So Bill has more than one memory problem. Let us review the evidence. (1) He has forgotten events immediately before the time of his head injury, but he remembers more remote events. He has *retrograde amnesia*. He remembers passing the drugstore and the hardware store, but he doesn't remember anything after that. Conveniently, we have a witness who can attest to the fact that there were events that Bill would have been expected to remember later. (2) For a time after regaining consciousness, Bill was able to converse and could remember past events (his telephone number, the fact that he was supposed to meet his wife). However, he did not later remember things that occurred during this period; he repeated his conversations with the nurse. He had *anterograde*, or *posttraumatic*, *amnesia*. (See **FIGURE 19.1**.)

IMPLICATIONS FOR THE MEMORY PROCESS. The best way to explain these symptoms is to hypothesize that (1) immediate memory is re-

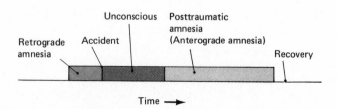

FIGURE 19.1 A schematic representation of retrograde and posttraumatic amnesia.

tained in short-term memory, which is in a different form from long-term memory; (2) STM can be converted into LTM, and the process takes time; and (3) events stored in STM can be disrupted by diffuse brain damage, but events stored in LTM are much more durable. The reasoning for these statements is as follows: While walking down the street, Bill had experiences that entered STM. Some elements of these temporarily retained memories were stored in LTM, but the transition takes time. The head injury interrupted this transition (from STM to LTM) in one of two ways: either (a) events represented in STM were lost (i.e, the "slate was cleared") or (b) STM decayed normally, but the brain mechanism that transfers the memories into LTM was temporarily disrupted by the trauma. Let us refer to the transition from STM to LTM as the process of *consolidation*. Some evidence that provides a bit of support for alternative (b) comes from the fact that Bill forgot his first conversation with the nurse. Clearly his STM was working, or he could not carry on a conversation. In order to respond to something said by someone else, it is necessary to retain information about what was said long enough to phrase an answer. If we hypothesize that some brain mechanism must function normally in order for consolidation to occur, and that this mechanism is disrupted by the injury for a period of time, we can account for the forgetting of the conversation with the nurse. The STM gradually decays, but no transfer to LTM occurs.

I must emphasize that the evidence concerning the consolidation process is not conclusive. During the stage of posttraumatic amnesia, patients are usually confused to varying degrees, and one could just as well attribute the lack of consolidation to a more rapid decay of memories in STM; perhaps they do not stay around long enough for consolidation to take place. Whether consolidation requires operation of a special mechanism, or whether it occurs automatically when memories remain long enough in short-term storage, we can still conclude that STM and LTM are separate processes.

Experimental Amnesia

The evidence obtained from the effects of head injury in humans tells us something about the memory process, but further study with animals obviously requires a better method for producing amnesia. One *could*, I suppose, train some rats and then hit them on the head, but fortunately there are better techniques available.

ELECTROCONVULSIVE SHOCK: HISTORY. For many years, attempts have been made to treat schizophrenia and other mental disorders with various sorts of shock treatments, such as dunking the patient in cold water, exposing him to snakes, producing a fever—doing something to shake the patient up and initiate some change, hopefully for the better (Valenstein, 1973). Particularly popular types of shock treatment were the induction of comas by injections of insulin or of seizures by injections of *metrazol* (the active ingredient in camphor). The rationale for the therapeutic application derived partly from the fact that schizophrenia and epilepsy appeared to occur infrequently in the same person, and from the observation that a seizure appeared to produce a remission in the psychotic symptoms (von Meduna, 1938).

The production of electrically elicited seizures was first performed by Ugo Cerletti, an Italian psychiatrist (Cerletti and Bini, 1938). He noted that pigs in the local slaughterhouse were first made unconscious by electric shock across the temples and were then killed with a knife. He tried the same treatment (the electric shock, that is, not the stabbing) on experimental dogs and observed that seizures could be produced by application of current to the head for a few tenths of a second. The dogs did not appear to suffer any long-term ill effects.

Cerletti then went on to try the procedure on a schizophrenic patient, who apparently experienced hallucinations, and whose speech was full of meaningless babbling. He applied a low-current shock to the head, which was insufficient to produce unconsciousness. When the patient heard Cerletti say that he would try it again tomorrow with higher current, the patient said, "Not another one! It's deadly!" Encouraged by this sudden display of rational speech, Cerleti immediately tried a more intense shock. Here are his observations:

> We observed the same instantaneous, brief, generalized spasm, and soon after, the onset of the classic epileptic convulsion. We were all breathless during the tonic phase of the attack, and really overwhelmed during the apnea as we watched the cadaverous cyanosis of the patient's face; the apnea of the spontaneous epileptic convulsion is always impressive, but at that moment it seemed to all of us painfully endless. Finally, with the first stertorous breathing and the first clonic spasm, the blood flowed better not only in the patient's vessels but also in our own. Thereupon we observed with the most intensely gratifying sensation the characteristic gradual awakening of the patient "by steps." He rose to sitting position and looked at us, calm and smiling, as though to inquire what we wanted of him. We asked: "What happened to you?" He answered: "I don't know. Maybe I was asleep." Thus occurred the first electrically produced convulsion in man, which I at once named "electroshock." (Cerletti, 1956)

Electroconvulsive shock, or *ECS,* soon caught on and largely supplanted the use of insulin or metrazol. Some patients suffered broken limbs or backs as a result of the convulsions, but physicians soon learned to use paralytic agents such as *succinylcholine* in order to prevent these injuries. The interesting thing about ECS is that it was soon discovered that patients forgot events that occurred shortly before production of the seizure. That is, they showed a retrograde amnesia. Apparently, the ECS did something to disrupt the consolidation process.

A number of studies have documented the amnesic effect of ECS and have demonstrated a *temporal gradient* of retrograde amnesia. The shorter the learning–ECS interval, the greater the likelihood that the material will be forgotten. ECS also produces posttraumatic amnesia; patients later do not remember events that occurred during a period of time after the seizure (Cronholm, 1969). The effects of ECS, then, are quite similar to those of blunt head injury. I should note that the use of ECS is usually restricted to cases of severe depression that do not respond to drug therapy. Most clinicians agree that ECS has very little therapeutic value for other disorders. Morover, repeated ECS treatments cause a general deterioration in the ability to recall *all* memories, recent or old (Squire, 1974). For these reasons, ECS should be used very cautiously, and only as a last resort.

Electroconvulsive Shock: Use in Research on the Memory Process

As you might expect, ECS has been used by many investigators to study the consolidation process in animals. For example, Duncan (1949) trained rats to run from a dark to a lighted compartment in order to avoid receiving a shock from the floor, which was composed of a series of parallel metal rods. The rats were trained for 18 days, receiving one trial each day. Each training trial was followed by an ECS treatment at varying intervals (20 seconds to 14 hours). Animals that received the shock shortly after the training showed the least evidence of learning, whereas the subjects that received the ECS an hour or more after training performed as well as control animals that received no shock at all. (See **FIGURE 19.2**.)

PROBLEMS OF INTERPRETATION: PUNISHMENT VERSUS AMNESIA. There is a problem with this procedure, as was pointed out by Coons and Miller (1960). Clinical observations with humans showed that patients exhibited signs of fear when they approached the room where the ECS had been previously given to them, even though they could not describe any details of what went on there. Perhaps the performance of the rats in Duncan's experiment could be explained in terms of punishment of the avoidance response by ECS treatment. Perhaps ECS was such an unpleasant experience that it served to punish responses that occurred in the period prior to its administration.

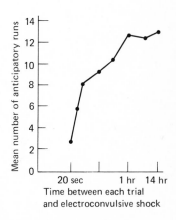

FIGURE 19.2 Effects of ECS on maze learning. (From Duncan, C. P., *Journal of Comparative and Physiological Psychology*, 1949, 42, 32–44.)

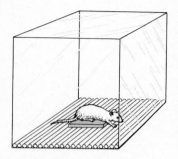

FIGURE 19.3 The step-down apparatus for testing retention of passive avoidance.

Experimental Evidence. This hypothesis was tested by Chorover and Schiller (1965). These investigators used a special task that could be learned in a single trial. The apparatus consisted of a chamber with a grid floor, in the middle of which was a small wooden platform. (See **FIGURE 19.3.**) The rat was placed on the platform and was given a brief foot shock shortly after it stepped off the platform onto the floor (rats do not have to be trained to step off the platform —they do so normally). The animal was removed from the chamber after receiving the foot shock, and was put back into its home cage. The next day the rat was again placed on the platform. This time the animal stayed put for a relatively long time; it showed evidence of remembering the fact that it previously received a painful shock. Animals that were *not* previously shocked stepped off the platform almost immediately.

This procedure is an excellent one for determining whether ECS has an amnesic or an aversive effect. Suppose ECS had an aversive, but not amnesic, effect. It would be like receiving a "super foot shock." If a rat received a foot shock for stepping down, and then received an ECS treatment, the animal would have even more reason to stay on the platform the next day. However, if the ECS disrupted the consolidation process, the rat would forget receiving the foot shock if the ECS were given soon afterwards.

Figure 19.4 shows the data from the experiment by Chorover and Schiller. Animals that received ECS within a few seconds of getting shocked through the feet stepped off the platform quickly the next day; they did not appear to remember the shock. (The ECS was delivered through metal snaps that had been fastened to the rats' ears before the start of the experiment.) As the foot shock–ECS interval lengthened, more and more subjects remained on the platform when tested the next day. (See **FIGURE 19.4.**) Results from another group of rats (the data are not shown) indicated that an aversive effect, as well as an amnesic effect, could be produced by ECS. I shall say more about this later.

AN ALTERNATIVE EXPLANATION: THE CATALOGING PROCESS. Although thousands of rats and mice have received ECS treatment, not all investigators agree that the observed impairment in subsequent performance is a result of disrupted consolidation. Some investigators (e.g., Miller and Springer, 1973) believe that short-term memories are consolidated in a fraction of a second and that some sort of cataloging function is performed subsequent to this consolidation. The cataloging process, and not long-term memory storage, is disrupted by ECS. They do not explicitly define what is meant by cataloging, but they present, instead, an analogy. Consolidation is similar to the placement of a new book on the shelf of a library. It is there, but unless

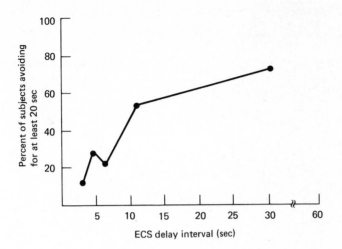

FIGURE 19.4 Data obtained from an experiment using an apparatus similar to that pictured in Figure 19.3. (From Chorover, S. L., and Schiller, P. H., *Journal of Comparative and Physiological Psychology*, 1965, *59*, 73–78.)

you know of its existence and how to find it, it will not be available. The cataloging process of memory presumably makes the consolidated memory somehow *locatable.*

The most important evidence in support of this hypothesis is that, under some conditions, a memory apparently lost by ECS treatment can be shown to be available, after all. For example, a "reminder shock," given to rats in an apparatus different from the one in which they received the original training, sometimes "reinstates" the memory whose consolidation was previously thought to have been disrupted (Lewis, Misanin, and Miller, 1968). James McGaugh and his colleagues dispute this interpretation. Animals in their experiments (reviewed by McGaugh and Herz, 1972) generally do not show recovery of memories disrupted by ECS. They attribute most of the differences to the intensity of the ECS treatment. McGaugh and his colleagues generally use mice and administer ECS by means of saline-soaked cotton electrodes applied to the eyes. Investigators who observe recovery more often use rats, and they apply the ECS through the ears. McGaugh suggests that this method of ECS administration (through the eyes) applies more electrical current to the brain and produces a more thorough interference with the memory process, thus resulting in a more profound amnesia. As he notes, if consolidation of a memory were only partially disrupted, then there might be conditions under which it could later be retrieved.

I will not review the numerous studies that address this issue. Instead, I would like to suggest the following: (1) ECS does disrupt the consolidation process and does indeed produce a true amnesia. The disruption is not an all-or-none phenomenon; it depends upon such variables as the complexity of the task to be learned and the intensity of the ECS. If consolidation is not completely blocked, an apparent reversal of the amnesia can be seen under conditions that favor retrieval. (2) There is also a cataloging mechanism, such as the one described by Miller and Springer, which can also be disrupted by the administration of ECS. I shall describe another experiment that bears on the first conclusion; this study shows how "recovery" for a memory can occur, even though its consolidation was disrupted. Then I shall describe some evidence for the existence of a cataloging mechanism.

Recovery from Amnesia: Resistance of Some Memories to ECS. Schneider, Tyler, and Jinich (1974) shocked rats for entering a large dark compartment from the small, lighted one into which they had been placed. (Rats normally leave a lighted area in preference for a dark one, just as they normally step off a low platform.) The subjects were given an ECS one second after receiving the foot shock, and were tested for retention on the next 6 days. On the second day of testing they showed no evidence of remembering the shock; they readily entered the compartment where they had been punished. However, by day 4, they started showing evidence of memory for the shock—they began to show more and more hesitation before stepping through the doorway, even though they did *not* receive any shocks after day 1. Figure 19.5 compares the behavior of these subjects with controls that received foot shock but no ECS; control subjects avoided the dark compartment the day after receiving the foot shock. Remembering is indicated by *high* scores. (See **FIGURE 19.5.**)

One could hypothesize that the ECS did not produce retrograde amnesia, but, instead, just disrupted the retrieval mechanism for several days. The rats, by this explanation, had long-term mem-

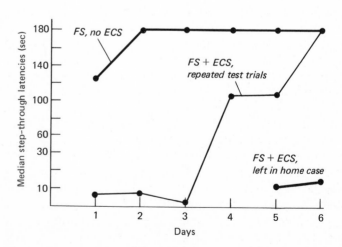

FIGURE 19.5 Effects of retesting on retention of a step-through response. (From Schneider, A. M., Tyler, J., and Jinich, D., *Science*, 1974, *184*, 87–88. Copyright 1974 by the American Association for the Advancement of Science.)

ories for the shock, but they could not retrieve them until they recovered from prolonged effects of the ECS treatment. However, another group of rats received the foot shock–ECS treatment on day 1, but were left in their cages during days 2–5. When they were tested on day 6, they showed no evidence of remembering the shock; they readily went into the large compartment. Time alone does not reinstate the animals' memories. The performance of these animals is represented by the two data points at the lower right of **FIGURE 19.5.**

Rats in this study did not recover their memory for the shock with the passage of time—they had to receive practice in entering the large compartment. But since no punishment was administered on these days, why did the rats start showing signs of avoiding the large chamber?

Schneider and his colleagues suggested that originally two types of learning occurred; the response of entering the compartment was punished (instrumental conditioning), and autonomic responses to the foot shock were associated with the stimuli present in the compartment where the rats received the shock (classical conditioning). ECS treatment abolished consolidation of the instrumental conditioning (the punishment of the response of going through the doorway) but did not affect the association between the environmental stimuli and the aversive effects of the shock. In support of this hypothesis, Schneider et al. note that decorticate rats are capable of being classically conditioned but cannot learn an instrumental response (DiCara, Braun, and Pappas, 1970). So perhaps the ECS differentially affects cortical and subcortical processes, disrupting consolidation of some kinds of memories but not others.

If the classically conditioned association between the stimuli in the large compartment and unpleasant autonomic responses were still intact, then these autonomic responses would occur as soon as the rats passed through the door and entered the large compartment. These aversive effects would become associated with entry into the compartment, and they would, in time, lead to the animals' avoidance of the compartment. (I am sure each of you has experienced a queasy feeling in some situation that you know is due to a prior association, even before you remember the precise nature of that association. Presumably, the rats get this same "queasy feeling" and consequently learn to stay away from the compartment in order to avoid the feeling. This "queasy feeling" might be similar to the fear ECS patients report about the treatment even though they can recall none of the details.) Schneider and his colleagues extinguished this "queasy feeling" by leaving some rats in the chamber for 8 minutes on day 2. These subjects did *not* subsequently avoid entering the chamber on the next 5 days; the "queasy feeling" was gone, and the animals continued to enter the compartment. (If you are made uncomfortable by my use of such an imprecise term as "queasy feeling," please substitute "aversive effects of autonomic responses classically conditioned to the environmental stimuli by the presentation of foot shock.") It is very possible that other studies showing recovery from amnesia do so by means of similar mechanisms.

EVIDENCE FOR EFFECTS OF ECS ON CATALOGING. There are other effects of ECS, however, that do not result from disrupted consolidation, but instead appear to involve a cataloging process. Robbins and Meyer (1970) trained several groups of rats in a series of three different discrimination tasks. The tasks could be appetitively or aversively motivated; the animals could be taught to choose the proper stimulus in order to get a food pellet or to avoid mild foot shock. The animals learned each of the three discriminations, but for different reinforcers. For example, some rats first learned a shock-motivated task (S_1), then a second, food-motivated, task (F_2), and then a third, shock-motivated task (S_3). The sequence for these rats would be $S_1F_2S_3$. There were six groups of animals learning the tasks under different orders of motivational conditions.

After learning the third task, the rats received an ECS treatment. They were then retrained on problems 1 and 2. The surprising fact is that an impairment was seen in the animals' performance on the tasks learned earlier. One would not expect the ECS to affect performance on a task learned several days ago. Furthermore, the impairment was selective; if task 3 (the one followed by ECS treatment) had been food-motivated, performance on the previous food-motivated task (but *not* the shock-motivated task) was impaired. Similarly, if task 3 had been shock-motivated, performance on the previous shock-motivated task was impaired. (See **FIGURE 19.6**.)

ECS treatment was found by Robbins and Meyer to affect not just the most recent memories, but also memories for previously learned habits that were acquired under similar motivatonal conditions. The investigators suggested that what was disrupted was not the long-term memories themselves, but their accessibility. Perhaps some sort of cataloging mechanism was active at the time, and its disruption somehow altered the "entries" relating to tasks learned under a particular motivational condition. To continue with the library analogy suggested by Miller and Springer: Perhaps the entries for books of a particular category were being altered because a new book had been added to the collection. If we disrupt the person doing the cataloging, we lose the entry not only to the new book, but also to the other books in that category. I shall elaborate upon this explanation later and provide some more data.

Training	Test	Retention?
(S₁) F₂(S₃)+ ECS	(S₁)	NO
	F₂	YES
S₁ S₂ (F₃)+ ECS	S₁	YES
	S₂	YES
F₁(S₂)(S₃)+ ECS	F₁	YES
	(S₂)	NO
(F₁)S₂ (F₃)+ ECS	(F₁)	NO
	S₂	YES
F₁ F₂ (S₃)+ ECS	F₁	YES
	F₂	YES
S₁ (F₂)(F₃)+ ECS	S₁	YES
	(F₂)	NO

FIGURE 19.6 A summary of the data from the experiment by Robbins and Meyer (1970).

The Physical Characteristics of Short-Term Memory

The hypothesis that best accounts for the data we have examined so far is the following: A stimulus is represented in short-term memory by some process that requires continuous neural activity. This activity, if it persists long enough, causes long-term physical changes in neurons (perhaps the ones that are representing the STM, or perhaps other neurons that receive inputs from them). The long-term changes alter the "circuitry" of the brain and hence change the way it responds to a subsequent presentation of that stimulus.

Short-term memories appear to be disrupted by blunt head injury or ECS. This fact suggests that STM involves coherent neural activity that can be disrupted by treatments that temporarily suppress neural activity or that induce incoherent, meaningless firing of neurons (for example, ECS). Head injury and ECS are not the only treatments that disrupt STM; anesthesia, cooling of the brain, anoxia, and treatment with various drugs will also do so (Jarvik, 1972). Long-term memories, however, are not susceptible to damage from these treatments. (There are exceptions, as shown by the data of Robbins and Meyer, but this issue will be dealt with later.)

REVERBERATION AS THE PHYSICAL BASIS OF SHORT-TERM MEMORY. What kind of neural activity can represent short-term memories? The mechanism that has most often been proposed is *reverberation*. If activity is initiated in a complex, interconnected network of neurons, it is very likely that loops of interconnected neurons will recurrently circulate bursts of excitation. Figure 19.7 presents that concept more concretely. *Theoretically*, the initiation of an action potential in neuron A could cause incessant firing of the circuit; A excites B, which fires and then excites C . . . and so on, back to A, where the process begins again. (See **FIGURE 19.7.**)

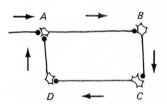

FIGURE 19.7 A schematic representation of a reverberatory circuit.

Of course, we know that a circuit of four neurons would not continue to fire in this manner. It takes more than one EPSP from a single terminal button to trigger an action potential in a neuron. But consider Figure 19.8, which is merely a more redundant version of the simpler circuit. Neural activity might continue in this circuit for a much longer tme. (See **FIGURE 19.8.**)

Evidence for the Existence of Reverberation. First of all, is there any evidence that reverberation does, in fact, take place? Burns (1958) studied the properties of the *isolated cortical slab* and obtained data that argue very strongly for the existence of reverberatory activity. An isolated cortical slab is produced by undercutting a section of

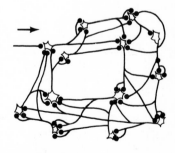

FIGURE 19.8 A representation of a reverberatory circuit, slightly more realistic than that shown in Figure 19.7.

cortex so that it is not connected neurally to any other region of the brain. Care is taken to preserve the blood supply that runs along the top of the cortex. (See **FIGURE 19.9**.) The tissue can be recorded from after it has recovered from the immediate effects of surgery. Neurons in these slabs are normally silent, but if the tissue is stimulated with a train of electrical pulses, bursts of activity can be recorded. If the stimulus is intense enough, firing will continue for up to 30 minutes.

This prolonged neural activity suggests that reverberation can indeed occur in networks of neural tissue. Burns noted that if the activity is a result of recirculation of excitation in loops of neurons, then one should be able to halt this activity by stimulating the neurons to discharge all at the same time. That way, the cells would simultaneously be in the refractory period, during which an action potential cannot be elicited. The neurons would all quickly recover, but none of them would be firing. (Picture what would happen if all four neurons in Figure 19.7 fired simultaneously. Reverberation could not continue.) (See **FIGURE 19.7**.) Burns' prediction was borne out; a single shock of sufficient intensity, delivered to the center of the slab, halted the neural activity of the slab.

It would appear from the experiment by Burns that reverberation *can* occur in the brain, even in small isolated regions. But can a reverberatory circuit represent information? First, we should make sure that information, coded by the sensory system, can (potentially, at least) produce reverberatory activity unique to the perceived stimulus. In other words, can the hypothesized mechanism represent, in different and distinct ways, the great variety of stimuli that an organism can perceive? Secondly, is there any experimental evidence that recurrent activity in fact bears any relationship to perceived stimuli?

The particular set of reverberatory circuits that represent a stimulus depends on the particular neurons that receive the coded

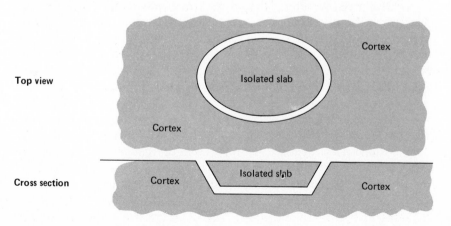

FIGURE 19.9 An isolated cortical slab.

sensory information. If an auditory stimulus is presented, then the reverberatory loops will begin with cells that receive auditory input. And if the stimulus is a high tone, only those cells that respond to high frequencies will provide excitation that initiates reverberatory activity. The particular reverberatory circuits that represent the short-term memory thus will depend on the feature-detecting mechanisms that respond to the stimulus being perceived. Complex visual stimuli, for example, would trigger the response of feature-detecting cells within inferotemporal cortex (or its analog in the human brain), and reverberatory activity would be initiated by these neurons.

Evidence for Reverberation as a Mechanism of Encoding Information. Is there evidence of any reverberatory activity occurring in response to sensory stimulation? There are some suggestive data, such as that obtained by Verzeano and his colleagues (Verzeano and Negishi, 1960; Verzeano, Laufer, Spear, and McDonald, 1970). These investigators believe that short-term memories are represented by circulating activity between cortex and thalamus. They have recorded unit activity from closely spaced electrodes (30–200 μm apart) arranged in a row, in order to determine the firing patterns of neurons in relation to their neighbors. There appeared to be consistent patterns of discharge; it was possible to follow recurrent waves of excitation from one location to the next, suggesting some sort of recirculating activity. Moreover, the observed patterns appeared to vary as a function of the stimulus that was being presented. There is, then, some evidence that reverberatory activity can indeed take place in the brain, and, furthermore, that this activity is related to the stimuli being perceived by the animal. The evidence is, of course, not conclusive; we are a very long way from specifying the way in which reverberatory activity encodes short-term memory.

Evidence for Physical Change Produced by Neural Stimulation. Finally, is there any evidence that neural activity can produce any long-term changes in the properties of neurons? In other words, is a link between STM (reverberatory activity) and LTM (some stable change in neurons) at least plausible? The answer appears to be yes; a number of experiments have demonstrated alterations in the properties of neural tissue after prolonged neural activity. I shall review some of these studies, but shall not discuss the *nature* of these changes; that topic will be covered in the next chapter.

There is an interesting phenomenon known as a *secondary epileptogenic lesion.* If a primary epileptogenic lesion is established on one side of the brain, a secondary focus can soon be detected in the homotopic region of the contralateral hemisphere. That is, excitation is transmitted from the primary lesion by means of the corpus callosum and, apparently, by means of subcortical connections, to the opposite side of the brain.

Experimentally, primary epileptogenic lesions can be produced by drilling a small hole in the animal's skull and applying *ethyl chloride* to the exposed brain. This chemical (often applied to the skin as a local anesthetic) evaporates rapidly and freezes a small part of the cortex. This treatment produces localized brain damage and leaves an irritative lesion, which produces hyperexcitation of the surrounding region. This local excitation is transmitted to the contralateral hemisphere. At first, the secondary focus passively responds to the primary lesion; if the primary lesion is removed, the electrical activity of the secondary focus will return to normal. However, if the primary lesion is removed several months after its establishment, the secondary focus in the contralateral hemisphere will remain abnormally hyperactive; a *mirror focus* has been established. If a mirror focus is separated from the rest of the brain by isolating it on a cortical slab, the focus remains hyperirritable; it will respond to stimulation that will not trigger activity in a similar isolated slab that does not contain a mirror focus (Morrell, 1969). (See **FIGURE 19.10.**)

Long-term changes in properties of the brain can be produced in other ways. Goddard (1967) reported a phenomenon that he called *kindling*. Electrodes were implanted in various brain regions of rats.

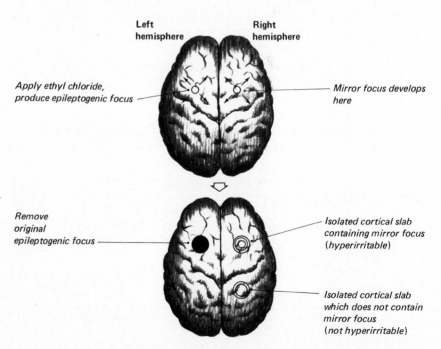

Left hemisphere   Right hemisphere

Apply ethyl chloride, produce epileptogenic focus

Mirror focus develops here

Remove original epileptogenic focus

Isolated cortical slab containing mirror focus (*hyperirritable*)

Isolated cortical slab which does not contain mirror focus (*not hyperirritable*)

FIGURE 19.10 A schematic representation of the way in which Morrell isolated a mirror focus on a cortical slab.

A very weak stimulus was presented once a day. At first, no behavioral disruption was observed, but after a number of days the stimulation began to trigger convulsions. The same total amount of stimulation applied in a short period of time did not produce these effects. Furthermore, the effect seemed to be permanent; once kindling occurred, convulsions could be triggered by the stimulation even if the animal had been left alone for three months.

Figure 19.11 illustrates a "learning curve" for the kindling effect. Goddard and Morrell (cited by Morrell, 1969) delivered a weak, brief stimulus (200 μamp, 62.5 pulses/sec for 5 sec) each day through electrodes in the amygdala. They measured the duration of the electrical *after discharge* (hyperactivity recorded after the stimulus was turned off) each day. As you can see in their graph, the after discharge, nonexistent at first, became more and more prolonged. (See **FIGURE 19.11.**)

It does appear, then, that neural activity can produce a long-term change in the properties of neural tissue, so there is some physiological basis for hypothesizing that permanent alterations in neurons (LTM) can be produced by reverberatory activity (STM).

The Anatomy of Short-Term Memory

The reverberatory hypothesis is consistent with several phenomena of short-term memory. First, the capacity of STM is quite limited. A person can retain about seven to nine items of information in short-

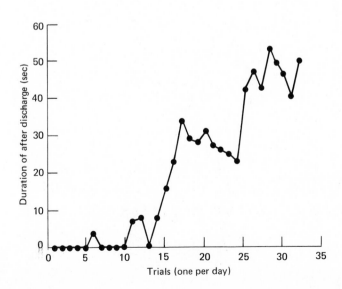

FIGURE 19.11 Effects of repeated amygdaloid stimulation on duration of after discharge. (From Morrell, F. In Jasper, H. H., Ward, A. A., and Pope, A., *Basic Mechanisms of the Epilepsies*. Copyright 1969 by Little, Brown and Company, Boston.)

term storage. It would be expected that the redundancy needed to sustain recirculating activity would be such that only a limited amount of information could be represented at a single time. Second, the decay that occurs when rehearsal is prevented could be explained as a gradual fading in neural activity as random events ("noise") begin to disrupt coherent firing. Third, new information, if attended to, interferes with older information in STM; continued activity of sensory neurons presumably establishes new reverberatory circuits that disrupt ongoing activity.

VISUAL AND AUDITORY SHORT-TERM MEMORY IN HUMANS. There appears to be a certain amount of cross-modal independence in short-term memory. There may, in fact, be separate short-term storage for each sense modality. If a person is presented with a particular stimulus, the information is quickly forgotten (dropped from STM) if the subject is required to attend to other stimuli of the same sense modality. However, the information is much more likely to be retained if distracting stimuli are presented by means of a different modality (Shiffrin, 1973).

There is physiological evidence that each sense modality may have an anatomically distinct area in which its short-term memories are stored. This appears to be true, at least, for auditory and visual stimuli. Warrington and Shallice (1972) report on a patient (K. F.) who had a lesion of the left parietal area. K. F. could repeat a single letter or a series of two letters if they were presented acoustically, but he had a considerable amount of trouble repeating a series of three letters. When he was presented with one-, two-, or three-letter sequences visually, he had no trouble repeating them. Warrington and Shallice presented K. F. with a stimulus and then made him perform a distraction task (reading numbers aloud) for 5, 10, 30, or 60 seconds. As soon as the distraction interval was over, the patient was asked to repeat the original stimulus. By plotting the percentage of correct responses given after various delay intervals, the authors could obtain an estimate of the rapidity of the decay of STM. The distraction task was used to prevent rehearsal, which can prolong STM indefinitely.

The results are shown in Figure 19.12. K. F. had no trouble remembering a single letter presented acoustically or visually. However, short-term memory for two- and three-letter sequences showed signs of decay, the rate of forgetting being much more pronounced for acoustically presented material. (See **FIGURE 19.12.**)

Warrington and Shallice also found that K. F. did not show the kinds of acoustic confusion that a normal person would exhibit when attempting to recall visually presented material. For instance, the letters B and D, and Q and U are very similar acoustically, whereas E and F, and O and Q are similar visually, but not acoustically. When

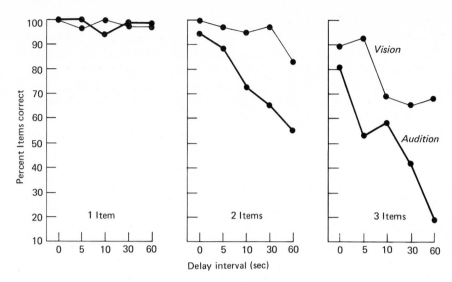

FIGURE 19.12 Short-term retention of one-, two-, and three-letter sequences presented acoustically and visually to patient K. F. (From Warrington, E. K., and Shallice, T., *Quarterly Journal of Experimental Psychology,* 1972, *24,* 30–40.)

trying to recall letters presented earlier, normal people tend to make acoustic errors; that is, their incorrect responses are likely to be letters that sound like the correct responses. K. F., on the other hand, made acoustic errors when the letters were presented acoustically, but he did not tend to do so when the letters were presented visually.

These results suggest that normal people have more than one short-term store available to them. Visually presented verbal material can be stored as an "image" in visual STM and also a "sound" in auditory STM. Because of this acoustic coding, when errors are made in retrieval, they tend to show acoustic confusions. K. F., on the other hand, showed a severely impaired ability to remember more than one or two letters when they were spoken to him, but he could recall visually presented material well. Furthermore, he did not encode visual information acoustically, as evidenced by the lack of acoustic confusions when the material was visually presented.

There are two interpretations of K. F.'s impairment, both of which support the existence of separate locations for visual and auditory short-term memories. The one favored by Warrington and her colleagues is that his auditory STM is largely gone, but visual STM is intact. The other possibility is that K. F. suffers from a form of conduction aphasia that leaves auditory STM relatively intact but does not permit much information to be transmitted, via the arcuate fasciculus, from Wernicke's (auditory association) area to Broca's speech area. There are data supporting the disconnection hypothesis. Shallice and Warrington (1975) note that K. F. was able to read concrete nouns very well, but he was unable to read abstract ones. This reading impairment contrasted with his ability to *use* abstract words in his own speech. He presumably described the visual and/or somatosensory images produced by the sight of the words; when these images were lacking, he failed to read the word. (Try to picture the meaning of the word *apparently*, for example.)

It is possible, then, that the increased rate of decay of auditory STM shown in Figure 19.12 results from the fact that the sounds of the letters had to be translated into images, and the images then had to be described. When K. F. heard the letter *T*, for example, he had to picture the letter and then verbalize this image. That would be a fairly easy task. However, a series of letters presented acoustically would be much more difficult to visualize. Even normal people sometimes find it difficult to recognize a word when someone spells it out; "picturing the letter" is a difficult task for most people. K. F., then, could have had a normally functioning auditory STM, but with the connections between auditory association cortex and Broca's area interrupted, transfer out of auditory STM into his mechanism controlling speech was by means of a very inefficient route. Note, however, that *both* hypotheses suggest different locations for visual and auditory short-term memory storage.

VISUAL SHORT-TERM MEMORY IN ANIMALS. Further evidence for anatomical specificity in short-term memory storage was provided by Kovner and Stamm (1972). These investigators trained monkeys to perform a *delayed matching-to-sample* task. The animals were shown a visual pattern (the sample), which was then turned off for several seconds. At the end of the delay interval, they were shown two different patterns, one of which was the one just shown to them. If they responded to the appropriate pattern (i.e., if they chose the pattern that matched the sample), they were rewarded with a piece of food. Electrical stimulation applied (through chronically implanted electrodes) to inferotemporal cortex just before or during the time the animal was shown the matching stimuli resulted in severe decrements in performance. However, stimulation in foveal prestriate cortex (which projects to inferotemporal cortex) had no effect. Nor did stimulation of prefrontal association cortex. The deficit produced by the interfering stimulation would not appear to be perceptual, since stimulation of inferotemporal cortex did not impair performance on a *simultaneous* matching-to-sample task. In this task, all three stimuli were present at the same time; the monkeys had to select which of the two stimuli matched the upper stimulus. It is only when the animals had to compare visual stimuli with their short-term memory for a previously presented stimulus that the electrical stimulation had a deleterious effect.

It would appear that inferotemporal cortex is important for visual short-term memory in monkeys. Since only visual stimuli were used in this study, we cannot conclude that only visual STM is disrupted by inferotemporal stimulation, but this fact does seem likely, since inferotemporal lesions impair visual, but not olfactory, auditory, tactile, or gustatory, discriminations (Gross, 1973).

CONCLUSIONS. There is good evidence that short-term memory is stored in a form different from that of long-term memory; events such as ECS, anoxia, anesthesia, and hypothermia disrupt short-term memories, but leave long-term memories largely intact. It would appear, then, that STM is represented by some form of neural activity, while LTM is encoded in stable physical alterations in the property of neurons. There is anatomical and electrophysiological evidence for reverberation, and there is evidence that neural activity by itself can result in long-term changes in the properties of neurons. Finally, evidence suggests that short-term storage is accomplished independently for the various sense modalities, although this is complicated by the fact that humans, at least, are capable of a high degree of cross-modality coding. It appears most likely that short-term memories, like long-term ones, are represented in the appropriate association areas of cortex.

THE LIMBIC SYSTEM AND THE CONSOLIDATION PROCESS

Korsakoff's Syndrome

A very dramatic memory deficit occurs when a person sustains bilateral damage to portions of the limbic system. Korsakoff, a Russian physician, first described the syndrome in 1889, and the disorder was given his name. The most profound symptom of Korsakoff's syndrome is a severe anterograde amnesia; the patients are unable to form new memories, although old ones still remain. They act like our head-injured patient did after waking in the hospital; they can converse normally and can remember past events, but they cannot later recall events that occur after the brain damage. Unlike the head-injured patient, people with Korsakoff's syndrome suffer this impairment *permanently.*

Korsakoff's syndrome occurs most often in chronic alcoholics. It is thought (Adams, 1969) to result from a thiamine deficiency caused by the alcoholism. Alcoholics, receiving a substantial number of calories from the alcohol they ingest, usually eat a very poor diet, so their vitamin intake is consequently low. Furthermore, alcohol appears to interfere with intestinal absorption of thiamine (vitamin B_1), and the ensuing deficiency produces brain damage. There is some controversy about the critical brain regions whose destruction leads to Korsakoff's syndrome. Brion (1969) suggests that bilateral change anywhere along *Papez's circuit* of the limbic system will produce this disorder. Cell bodies in the *mammillary bodies* send fibers via the *mammillothalamic tract* to the *anterior thalamic nuclei*, where they synapse on another set of neurons. These neurons project to the limbic cortex of the *cingulate gyrus*. Neurons there project, via polysynaptic cortical pathways, to the hippocampus. Fibers arising in the hippocampus project via the *fornix* to the mammillary bodies, thus completing Papez's circuit. (See **FIGURE 19.13.**)

Korsakoff's syndrome in alcoholics, according to Brion, usually results from bilateral damage to the mammillary bodies, as well as damage in various regions of the thalamus. Brion attributes more importance to the mammillary lesions, since he notes that all of his alcoholic patients with this disorder sustained damage there. He also reports that the disorder may be produced by tumors that destroy the fornix or anterior thalamic nuclei. Occasionally, blood clots produce Korsakoff's syndrome by damaging the hippocampus or the cingulate gyrus. In two cases the damage to Papez's circuit was bilateral but nonsymmetrical; in one of them hippocampal fibers were damaged

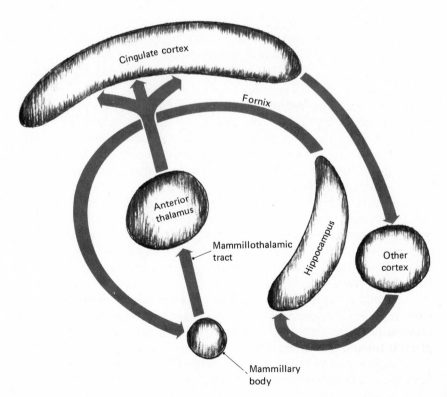

FIGURE 19.13 A schematic diagram of Papez's circuit.

on the left side and the cingulate gyrus on the right, for example. It appears, therefore, that the damage to Papez's circuit must be bilateral, but the interruptions need not be symmetrically placed, just as telephone service could be interrupted by severing the cable halfway through in two different places. (This analogy is, of course, an oversimplification, since the various structures that compose Papez's circuit are more than simple relay stations.)

Damage to other brain regions may also produce Korsakoff's syndrome, but the evidence is still unclear. Adams (1969) believes that damage to the dorsomedial thalamus (which is interconnected with many parts of the limbic system) may be the critical cause for the memory impairment produced by thiamine deficiency. As he notes, however, cases of Korsakoff's syndrome that have been autopsied did not receive careful psychological testing, and those people who have been thoroughly tested are still alive. Therefore, it will take a number of years to determine which structures are most crucial. The patients who have been carefully tested will some day die, and hopefully the brains can then be studied. One of the problems associated with the testing of brain-damaged humans is that the subject may very well outlive the experimenter!

Temporal Lobectomy in Humans

Scoville, in 1954, reported that bilateral removal of the medial temporal lobe produced a memory impairment that was apparently identical to that seen in Korsakoff's syndrome. Thirty operations had been performed on psychotic patients in an attempt to alleviate their mental disorder, but it was not until this operation was performed on patient H. M. that the anterograde amnesia was discovered.

Patient H. M. had very severe epilepsy before his operation. Even though he received medication at what is described as near-toxic levels, he suffered major convulsions approximately once a week and had dozens of minor attacks each day. After bilateral removal of the medial temporal lobes, he showed a considerable amount of recovery. He receives moderate doses of dilantin and has only one or two minor seizures each day. Major convulsions are seen very rarely—one every two or three years. In terms of treatment of his epilepsy, the surgery was very successful.

However, it quickly became apparent after surgery that the patient suffered a severe memory impairment. The deficit had not previously been seen in the psychotic patients because of the severity of their mental disorders. H. M., however, was quite normal, except for his epilepsy, and the memory impairment was only too easily detected. Subsequently, Scoville and Milner (1957) tested eight of the psychotic patients who were able to cooperate with them. They found that some of these patients also had anterograde amnesia; the deficit appeared to occur when the hippocampus was removed, but not when the amygdala, uncus, and overlying temporal cortex were removed, sparing the hippocampus.

These results were compatible with findings in the case of P. B., reported by Penfield and Milner (1958). The left temporal lobe of this patient was removed, in two stages, on separate occasions. No memory disorder was seen after the first operation. The amygdala, uncus, and hippocampus were removed during the second operation and a severe anterograde amnesia resulted. Unilateral temporal damage does not normally result in memory impairment, so this effect was unexpected. Patient P. B. died 12 years later (of unrelated natural causes) and his brain was examined. The right hippocampus was found to have been damaged, probably as a result of a cerebrovascular accident that occurred many years previously. The left temporal lobectomy removed the only functioning hippocampus. No other brain abnormalities were seen; therefore, it seems safe to conclude that the hippocampal removal produced the amnesia.

THE CASE OF H. M.: HIS MEMORY DEFICITS. Now let us examine H. M.'s case in more detail (Milner, Corkin, and Teuber, 1968; Milner, 1970). His intellectual ability and his short-term memory appear to be normal. He can carry on a conversation, rephrase sentences, and perform mental arithmetic. His immediate memory for a series of numbers (*digit span*) is low-normal; he can repeat seven numbers forward and five numbers backward. He has a partial retrograde amnesia for events of the 2 years preceding the operation, but he can retrieve older memories very well. He showed no personality change after the operation, and he appears to be a polite and well-mannered person.

Since the operation, however, H. M. has, with rare exceptions, been unable to learn anything new. He cannot identify people he met since the operation (performed in 1953, when he was 27 years old) nor can he find his way back home if he leaves his house (his family moved to a new house after his operation and he has been unable to learn how to get around the new neighborhood). He is aware of his disorder and often says something like this:

> Right now, I'm wondering. Have I done or said anything amiss? You see, at this moment everything looks clear to me, but what happened just before? That's what worries me. It's like waking from a dream; I just don't remember. (Milner, 1970, p. 37)

H. M. is capable of remembering a piece of information if he is not distracted; constant rehearsal can keep an item in his short-term memory for a very long time. He does not show any long-term effects of this continuous rehearsal, however. If he is distracted for a moment, he will completely forget the item he had been rehearsing so long. He works very well at repetitive tasks; since he so quickly forgets what previously happened, he does not become bored easily. He can endlessly reread the same magazine or laugh at the same jokes, finding them fresh and new each time. H. M. also shows a few symptoms that do not appear to be related to his memory impairment. He has no interest in sexual behavior; he does not express feelings of hunger, although he will eat normally when food is in front of him; and he shows no reaction to pain. As a matter of fact, an attempt was made to ascertain whether H. M. could be classically conditioned to give an autonomic response to a stimulus paired with a painful shock. The attempt was abandoned when it was found that H. M. did not react to shock levels that normal people would find quite painful. He could feel the shock, but it did not appear to bother him. (Recall, from chapter 17, that damage to the dorsomedial thalamus—which is intimately connected with the limbic system—similarly disrupts reactivity to painful stimuli.)

THE CASE OF H. M.: EVIDENCE OF CONSOLIDATION. There *are* a few tasks on whch H. M. shows some evidence of learning. Milner (1965) presented him with a *mirror-drawing* task. This procedure requires the subject to trace the outline of a figure (in this case, a star) with a pencil, being able to see the procedure in a mirror, but not directly. (See **FIGURE 19.14.**) The task may appear to be simple, but it is actually rather difficult. Left and right are maintained normally in the mirror, but movements toward or away from the body are reversed. That makes it somewhat complicated to follow a diagonal line. I have observed college students trying this task; when it was explained to them they began, confident that they would be able to quickly trace around the star. Instead, they found themselves repeatedly leaving the confines of the double lines. Some of the students got so rattled that they broke the points of their pencils while trying to figure out which way to move next. With practice, however, people can eventually become quite proficient at this task.

The interesting thing is that H. M., also, has become better at mirror-drawing. Figure 19.15 illustrates his improvement; his errors were reduced considerably during the first session, and his improvement was retained on subsequent days of testing. (See **FIGURE 19.15.**) H. M. did not remember having performed the task previously, however. He reported no sense of familiarity with it.

Another task on which H. M. has shown long-term improvement is the recognition of incomplete pictures. Figure 19.16 shows two sample items from this test; note how the drawings are succes-

FIGURE 19.14 The mirror-drawing task.

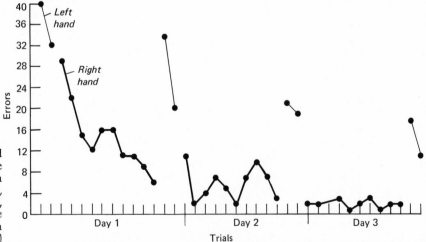

FIGURE 19.15 Data obtained from patient H. M. on the mirror-drawing task. (From Milner, B. In Milner, P. M., and Glickman, S., editors, *Cognitive Processes in the Brain*. Princeton: Van Nostrand, 1965.)

sively more complete. (See **FIGURE 19.16.**) The subjects are first shown the least-complete version (set I) of each of twenty different drawings. They are asked to identify as many items as possible. They are then shown more complete versions until each of the items is identified. One hour later the subjects are tested again for retention, starting with set I.

H. M. was given this test and, when retested an hour later, showed considerable improvement (Milner, 1970). When he was retested 4 months later, he still showed this improvement. His performance was not so good as that of normal control subjects, but unmistakable evidence of long-term retention was obtained. (See **FIGURE 19.17.**)

MILNER'S CONCLUSIONS. Milner, who has studied H. M. and other cases like his, concludes that the hippocampus plays a vital role in the consolidation process. It seems obvious, she notes, that neither short-term nor long-term memories are stored there. H. M. has a normal STM, as is shown by his digit span and by the fact that he can carry on a normal conversation. His long-term memories are not lost, since memories for events that occurred prior to the operation can be retrieved. Because these memories can be retrieved, we also know that the retrieval mechanism is still functioning. The hippocampus, Milner says, must exert some function that permits the transition of STM to LTM to occur; apparently, the transition itself occurs somewhere else. Furthermore, evidence from patients with Korsakoff's syndrome would argue that consolidation is not a function of the hippocampus alone, but requires the coordinated activity of all of Papez's circuit.

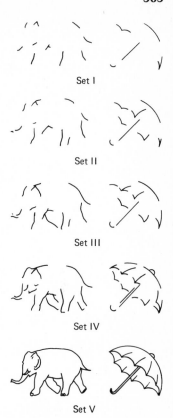

Set I

Set II

Set III

Set IV

Set V

FIGURE 19.16 Examples of broken drawings. (Reprinted by permission of author and publisher from Gollin, Eugene S. Developmental studies of visual recognition of incomplete objects. *Perceptual and Motor Skills*, 1960, 11, 289–298.)

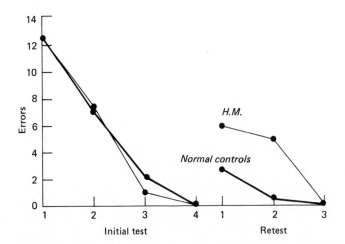

FIGURE 19.17 Learning and long-term retention demonstrated by patient H. M. on the broken-drawing task. (From Milner, B. In Pribram, K. H., and Broadbent, D. E., editors, *Biology of Memory*. Copyright 1970 by Academic Press, New York.)

Temporal Lobectomy in Animals

As you might have predicted, investigators have studied the effects of these lesions in animal subjects. A good example is the experiment of Orbach, Milner, and Rasmussen (1960), who performed bilateral temporal lobectomies in monkeys. The operations were similar to those producing memory impairments in humans. The monkeys did not, however, suffer a similar anterograde amnesia. They were capable of learning visual object discriminations, even when they were distracted between trials. They could also perform a delayed-response task, which required them to remember where the experimenter had placed a piece of food that was subsequently hidden from view.

Many thousands of monkeys, cats, and rats have been tested on a variety of tasks after receiving bilateral hippocampal lesions in an attempt to find out what role this structure plays (see Isaacson, 1974, for a general review). A number of deficits accompany these lesions, but there does not appear to be an overwhelming amnesia such as is seen in humans. Animals can learn many different kinds of tasks and show long-term retention later. They have little or no difficulty with brightness discriminations, for example. When the task involves spatial elements, more severe deficits are seen. Hippocampal lesions severely impair the learning or retention of a maze, for example. Conditional discriminations (if the alley is dark, turn right; if it is light, turn left) are also difficult for animals with these lesions. Nevertheless, the expectation that temporal lobe lesions would produce a permanent and global anterograde amnesia in animals was clearly not fulfilled.

A New Function for the Hippocampus in Humans? How can this discrepancy be explained? I think the suggestion that the human hippocampus and the animal hippocampus perform unrelated functions should be seriously considered only as a last resort. It is certainly true that our brains can do more than those of other animals, and thus the hippocampus could be called upon to do things in humans that it does not do in other species. However, other animals can consolidate memories. Why should this function have been transferred over to the hippocampus so abruptly, so that hippocampal removals produce amnesia in humans but not in monkeys?

It has been suggested that such a change in the function of the hippocampus is not unprecedented, since this structure used to be (earlier in evolutionary history) a part of the olfactory system, but no longer serves this function in mammals. However, Milner, Corkin, and Teuber (1968) report that H. M. appears to have difficulty in identifying odors, although they did not perform any careful test of this function. Jones, Moskowitz, and Butters (1975) tested odor discrimination in patients with Korsakoff's syndrome and found a severe deficit. Of course, the location of the critical brain lesion is not known in these patients, and there may well be damage outside the limbic system. Nevertheless, it would appear likely that the hippocampus and other limbic system structures retained some of their old functions when new ones were acquired, since damage results in deficits in at least one of these old functions, olfaction.

Language: A Possible Explanation for Discrepant Results?

The most obvious functional difference between humans and other animals is our use of language and our facility at cross-modality information transfer (which, as Geschwind notes, is probably the function that makes language possible). Could it be that the hippocampus plays a role in verbal memories, which humans alone are capable of forming, but is not involved to the same extent in nonverbal memories?

TEMPORAL LOBECTOMY AND NONVERBAL MEMORY IN HUMANS.   One of the first experiments addressed to this question appeared to say no —humans with temporal lobectomies appear to have problems with nonverbal material as well as with verbal material. Prisko (1963) presented H. M. with a series of nonverbal stimuli (other patients were tested as well, but they did not show as severe a deficit as H. M. did). A single stimulus (a particular frequency of a flashing light or click, a particular pattern, or a shade of pink) was presented, and after a delay interval another stimulus was presented. The patient was required to say whether or not the second stimulus was the same as the first. H. M. showed a very severe deficit; at a delay interval of 60 seconds, he was correct on only 60 percent of the trials. That is a poor performance, when we realize that a score of 50 percent could be achieved by guessing. Normal subjects were correct 92 percent of the time at a 60-second delay. It appears that H. M.'s deficit is not limited to verbal material. (See **FIGURE 19.18.**)

But there is a problem with this interpretation. The test is not really one of consolidation, since only a 60-second interval was used. Instead, the task would appear to be measuring the subject's ability to maintain a nonverbal stimulus in short-term memory. We know that H. M. can easily retain *verbal* material in this fashion. If he is not distracted, he can easily rehearse a number for 15 minutes. Why can't he retain nonverbal information in STM, as well?

A FAILURE OF VERBAL ENCODING.   Sidman, Stoddard, and Mohr (1968) tested H. M. on a delayed matching-to-sample problem with verbal

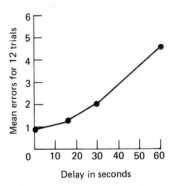

FIGURE 19.18   Short-term retention of nonverbal stimuli by patient H. M. (Data of Prisko reported by Milner, B. In Pribram, K. H., and Broadbent, D. E., editors, *Biology of Memory.* Copyright 1970 by Academic Press, New York.)

and nonverbal material. A stimulus (the sample) would appear on a square of frosted Plexiglas in the middle of an array of nine squares. H. M. would press the square, and the stimulus would disappear. After a delay interval, a number of stimuli would appear in the surrounding squares. One of these stimuli would be the same as the sample stimulus, and depression of the proper square would cause a penny to be delivered into a dish. The apparatus is illustrated in Figure 19.19. Also shown are the two types of items used: verbal stimuli (nonsense words composed of three consonants) and nonverbal stimuli (ellipses of various shapes). (See **FIGURE 19.19.**)

H. M.'s performance on the matching-to-sample problem for the nonverbal stimuli (ellipses) is shown in Figure 19.20, along with data from two normal preadolescent children (shown below), for comparison. The numbers on the horizontal axis to the right and left of the 0 (correct choice) refer to responses made to ellipses "fatter" or "thinner" than the sample. Note that H. M. could do fairly well when there was no delay, but his performance quickly deteriorated as a delay was introduced. On the other hand, the children had no trouble remembering the sample stimulus. (See **FIGURE 19.20.**)

When H. M. was presented with a three-letter nonsense word, he had no trouble at all selecting the matching stimulus, even after a 40-second delay. Why should there be such a difference in his abil-

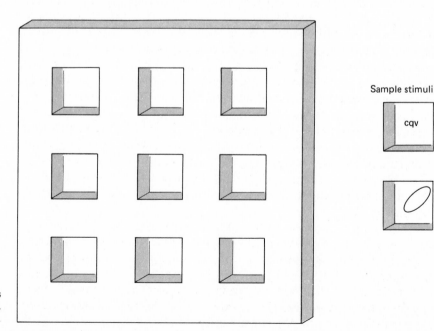

Sample stimuli

cqv

FIGURE 19.19 The apparatus used by Sidman, Stoddard, and Mohr (1968).

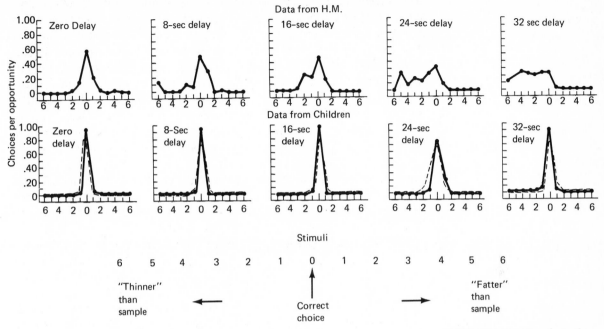

FIGURE 19.20 Data from the ellipse matching-to-sample test. (From Sidman, M., Stoddard, L. T., and Mohr, J. P., *Neuropsychologia*, 1968, 6, 245–254.)

ity to retain verbal as opposed to nonverbal material in STM? As Sidman and his colleagues note, H. M. can easily rehearse verbal information. In fact, he can be observed to form the letters of the stimulus with his lips. If the sample is *cqv*, for example, he repeatedly says "c-q-v" to himself, and thus retains the information. There is no such verbal code presented by an ellipse of a particular shape. However, normal subjects manage to invent a code of their own. Sidman and his colleagues reported that normal subjects soon learn to identify the shapes and remember them as "the largest one, the next-to-largest, the smallest," etc., or give them numbers from 1 to 8. Then, they have a verbal code that can easily be retained. H. M., on the other hand, does *not* construct these verbal codes. He does not write notes to himself or even ask others to help him get around. His deficit in this short-term task is in the ability (or motivation) to construct an easily retained verbal code. He must retain an image of the ellipse, which is difficult to do.

It may not seem immediately obvious that we rely on verbal codes so extensively. We are much poorer than we think at retaining a purely nonverbal image in STM. This fact was clearly shown in an experiment by Warrington and Taylor (1973). Normal subjects and patients with Korsakoff's syndrome were shown photographs of one, two, three, or four different faces. They were then *immediately* shown another set of faces, consisting of two test stimuli (one of which

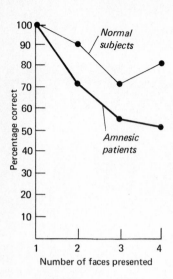

FIGURE 19.21 Ability of subjects to recognize faces they have just seen. (From Warrington, E. K., and Taylor, A. M., *Quarterly Journal of Experimental Psychology,* 1973, 25, 316–322.)

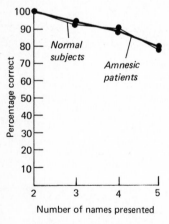

FIGURE 19.22 Ability of subjects to recognize surnames they have just seen. (From Warrington, E. K., and Taylor, A. M., *Quarterly Journal of Experimental Psychology,* 1973, 25, 316–322.)

was correct) for each sample stimulus. They were required to choose the faces they had just seen. As shown in Figure 19.21, only *one* face could be reliably remembered. When only two faces were presented, even normal people made errors on 10 percent of the trials. This contrasts sharply with memory span for numbers, where seven digits can be retained easily. Patients with Korsakoff's syndrome were found to be even worse than normal controls at recognizing the faces. (See **FIGURE 19.21.**)

Figure 19.22 shows the data from a similar test, using surnames instead of faces. Performance was much better in this case; it was easier to retain a verbal stimulus than a nonverbal one. Furthermore, the amnesic patients performed as well as normal subjects. These results emphasize the importance of verbal coding, even for normal people. (See **FIGURE 19.22.**)

The results presented so far suggest that amnesic patients can retain verbal material in short-term memory quite normally, but that they fail, when compared with normal subjects, to retain nonverbal material (such as the ellipses) that can be verbally encoded. They do not apply a coding scheme. When nonverbal material that cannot be so easily encoded (human faces) is presented, then normal subjects and amnesics *both* have trouble retaining more than one item in STM. The reason the normal subjects do better is probably that a limited amount of verbal coding is possible (e.g., "high forehead, curly hair," etc.). These codes are not absolutely reliable, of course, since some of the test stimuli may also have these characteristics; therefore, even normal subjects have to rely mainly on nonverbal STM.

Consolidation without Verbal Awareness. What about the problem of consolidation? Few studies have tested amnesic humans for nonverbal *consolidation.* Most experiments have tested retention after one-minute delay intervals; thus, they might very well be testing the efficiency with which the subject encodes material in STM. Some exceptions, already noted, have been the mirror-drawing and the incomplete pictures task, and amnesic patients do well on these tasks. Very few studies have tested amnesic patients in the same nonverbal way one would use to train animals. Sidman, Stoddard, and Mohr (1968) did so, and they found that H. M. was able to learn a nonverbal discrimination task very well. He was trained to press the square that contained the image of a circle (using the apparatus pictured in Figure 19.19) no matter where the circle appeared. No verbal instructions were offered, except those necessary to seat the patient and get him started on the task. A penny was dispensed each time a correct response was made. H. M. quickly learned to press the circle, and he would select this stimulus from a display containing one circle and seven ellipses of various shapes. He was then interrupted and asked to count his pennies (distraction task). Then he was asked how he earned them.

> H. M: Well, let's see. Something would flash up there and the idea was to pick out one of those squares and to point it toward dark. To tip it—to hit it with my finger tip and to match up. Each time the two matched a penny would drop in.
>
> E: Each time the two matched?
>
> H. M: The two matched.
>
> E: Uh-huh. What was on them?
>
> H. M: X.
>
> E: X was on them?
>
> H. M: Yeah.

A few minutes later:

> E: Can you tell me once more what you did to earn all those pennies?
>
> H. M: Well, one of those would flash up and actually I made a decision to point or to hit one of them with my finger tip . . .
>
> E: What were you pointing to—what were you pressing over there?
>
> H. M: Well, one of these would light up and get one of them matched and every time one would match, of course, a penny would drop in.
>
> E: What did the one that matched look like?
>
> H. M: Cross.
>
> E: A cross. Uh-huh. A plus sign?
>
> H. M: Uh-huh.
>
> E: Or a multiplication sign?
>
> H. M: Well, you'd say, uh, it wouldn't be multiplication—addition. (Sidman, Stoddard, and Mohr, 1968)

Judging by what H. M. said, he had already forgotten the task. However, when another series of stimuli was presented, he continued to select the circle. After several trials he was again asked what he had been doing.

> H. M: Get the circles that were round. . . . Some were oval-shaped and definitely the roundest one.

After this accurate description he counted his pennies, and two minutes later he was asked again to tell what he had done to earn the pennies:

> H. M: Well, I pressed matching up to that would be exactly alike of, uh, well, crosses. . . . There would be several of them on there, but two of them would be exactly alike. . . . Pointing to one of them would naturally mean that there was another one just like it.

He was tested once more, and again he selected the circle. H. M. showed amnesia for the task when tested verbally, but he showed perfect retention when tested nonverbally.

STIMULUS-SPECIFICITY AND THE RETRIEVAL OF MEMORIES. What can we say about the nature of anterograde amnesia in humans? When the patient is trained with nonverbal stimuli and is then tested with the identical stimuli, he shows evidence of very good retention. In this way his performance resembles that of animals with similar brain lesions. It is possible that even verbal material can be retained this way. Warrington and Weiskrantz (1968) found that amnesic patients showed evidence of long-term retention of fragmented words, as well as fragmented pictures. (See **FIGURE 19.23**.) Perhaps the important thing is that the test stimulus be the same as the training stimulus. Perhaps memories are normally consolidated in amnesic patients, but no coding or cross-indexing takes place that allows the memories to be retrieved by stimuli different from the ones originally learned. When H. M. sees the circle, the stimulus serves to elicit the appropriate response. But when he is asked to describe what he did, the verbal input (the question) cannot initiate retrieval of the stored information. If we just asked him to study a picture of a circle, we would find that, after distraction, he would not be able to remember what he was looking at. But he obviously *can* form a long-term association between the presence of a circle and the performance of a response.

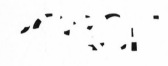

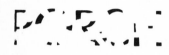

PORCH

FIGURE 19.23 Fragmented words, similar to Gollin's fragmented drawings. (From Warrington, E., and Warrington, L., *Nature*, 1968, 217, 972–974.)

El-Wakil (1975) found that amnesic patients do not even have to be taught a particular response in order to consolidate information. He prepared twenty-nine pairs of color slides: two different trees, two different automobiles, two different houses, etc. The patients were shown one member of each pair for 15 seconds. Twenty-four hours later they were shown each pair of slides, side by side, and were asked to point to the one they remembered. Some patients said that they hadn't seen the slides before, but nevertheless all of them pointed to the correct member of each pair. They were tested again 18 days later and this time none of them remembered seeing the slides; nevertheless, they again showed almost perfect retention.

We can reach at least two conclusions from the foregoing results about the nature of the deficit seen in amnesic patients: (1) they are very poor at using semantic codes to simplify the storage process, and (2) when consolidation can be demonstrated, the stimulus that elicits the retrieval must be the same one that was originally learned. Verbal stimuli cannot be used as cues to retrieve material learned non-verbally, for example. Normal humans are phenomenally efficient at learning verbal material, probably because we can so easily encode information in terms of its meaning. If we heard someone utter a

2-minute speech, we would be able to repeat most of it back, paraphrasing the ideas even if we could not reproduce the exact wording. But suppose we were subjected to 2 minutes of a language we could not understand? The chances are very slim that we could reproduce even a few of the sounds we heard. Perhaps a person like H. M. cannot make use of language in encoding information for storage. We have seen enough evidence from the disconnection syndromes to realize that brain lesions can cause the separation of functions that would appear to be parts of a single entity. The fact that certain brain lesions can cause a patient to be able to write but not be able to read his or her own writing is certainly contrary to one's own introspection. So perhaps it is not too implausible to suggest that a brain-damaged patient can recognize and make use of the meanings of words in short-term memory but cannot use the same meanings in the consolidation process. Perhaps a brain-damaged patient can read and understand a printed word, but can store the visual image of it only as a meaningless pattern, the way an English-speaking person might memorize a Chinese character. We would not then expect the patient to be able to retrieve the information on the basis of its meaning, since it was never encoded for storage that way. Given sufficient exposure, however, the patient would be able to recognize it if tested appropriately. The fact that memory for fragmented letters can be demonstrated suggests that this is indeed the case.

Conclusions

The discrepancy between the effects of hippocampal lesions in animals and those in humans, then, might be explained by the fact that humans possess coding skills that are not available to other animals. In humans, the limbic system might be involved in the consolidation of semantically encoded information, but not simple associations. One might even predict that chimpanzees like Washoe, who have been taught to converse in sign language with humans (Gardner and Gardner, 1969), would show memory problems for verbal material similar to those seen in humans whose temporal lobes were removed. I am quite confident, however, that the trainers of such animals (who come to view their subjects almost in the way that parents view their children) would not be likely to test this hypothesis.

It is very possible that the function performed by the hippocampus (and the rest of Papez's circuit) is related to the phenomenon observed by Robbins and Meyer (1970). As we saw earlier, these investigators found that ECS treatment administered shortly after training disrupted subsequent performance on tasks learned earlier under the same motivational condition. Meyer (1972) has suggested that when new information is learned, it is integrated with similar material that was learned earlier. This integration requires establishment of associations between new memories and old, and if ECS is applied during this period, new *and* old memories are disrupted. Perhaps the wild, unnatural firing of neurons during the seizure causes alterations in the neurons that encode the information (new and old) that is being cross-indexed. Somehow the process of cross-indexing causes the memories to become vulnerable to the effects of ECS.

You will recall from chapter 14 that a possible function of D sleep is the cross-indexing of memories. Several pieces of information support this hypothesis and suggest that Papez's circuit is involved in this activity. (1) As we saw in chapter 14, D sleep increases for animals being trained in a new task. (2) Patients with Korsakoff's syndrome show less D sleep than control subjects (Greenberg, Mayer, Brook, Pearlman, and Hartmann, 1968). (3) If an animal is trained on a task and is then deprived of D sleep, the memory for the newly learned task will remain vulnerable to the damaging effects of ECS (Fishbein, McGaugh, and Swarz, 1971; Linden, Bern, and Fishbein, 1975). Normally, ECS will not have an amnesic effect if it is administered the day after training. If the animals are not permitted to engage in D sleep (thus delaying the cross-indexing process), ECS given the next day will impair subsequent performance on that task. (4) Hippocampal removal decreases the susceptibility of newly formed memories to ECS (Hostetter, 1968). Perhaps cross-indexing does not take place when the hippocampus is removed, so that fewer associations remain in a vulnerable condition.

The evidence for a cross-indexing mechanism is much weaker than the evidence for a mechanism that encodes new information for long-term storage. The two processes are quite similar, and they might even be different facets of the same mechanism. Encoding must depend on prior associations; we can encode a verbal message in terms of meaning only because we previously learned what the words mean. Furthermore, a newly learned item of information can produce changes in associations made earlier. In reading a mystery novel, the clues, which we were informed of earlier, suddenly take on a new significance when we find out who the murderer is. The separate pieces of evidence are now linked together in a way that makes sense; surely there are physical changes in our brains that correspond to these interconnections. This process might make use of the same mechanism that permits us to encode new information in terms of its meaning (i.e., its relationshp to previously learned material) and thus store it more efficiently. In so doing, the new material becomes cross-indexed with older, related, memories.

The nature of the consolidation deficit in human patients has certainly not yet been explained. The semantic encoding hypothesis is not very well formulated and probably cannot completely account for the deficit. All we can really say is that the syndrome is considerably more complex than a failure to transfer memories from STM into LTM. There is probably some continuity in the role of Papez's circuit in humans and other animals, but we still have not identified it. To do so, we will probably have to know much more about language and the process of the symbolic encoding of meaning.

SUGGESTED READINGS

LEWIS, D. J. A cognitive approach to experimental amnesia. *American Journal of Psychology*, 1976, *89*, 51–80.

McGAUGH, J. L. AND HERZ, M. J. *Memory Consolidation.* San Francisco: Albion, 1972.

These references present the conflicting views concerning the nature of the consolidation process and the reasons for experimentally produced amnesia.

PRIBRAM, K. H., AND BROADBENT, D. E., editors. *Biology of Memory.* New York: Academic Press, 1970. This book contains individual chapters concerning cognitive and physical aspects of the two phases of memory. Brenda Milner's chapter describes the case of patient H. M. in detail.

Physical Bases
of Memory

20

In the previous two chapters I presented some of the evidence suggesting that memory consists of two stages, short-term memory (STM) and long-term memory (LTM), and that the means by which information is stored in these two states is different. Short-term memories are apparently encoded by some form of neural activity, such as reverberation, whereas long-term memories are retained by means of relatively permanent physical changes. In this chapter I shall describe the approaches that have been used to ascertain the nature of these physical changes. I must emphasize the word *approaches;* no methods yet discovered allow us unequivocally to identify changes in neural structure or biochemistry as being those that encode specific information. However, many interesting and suggestive results have been obtained, as you shall see.

There are several different approaches to the problem of locating physical changes that relate to learning.

1. One can train animals, and then look for alterations in the biochemistry or morphology of neurons. There are two basic problems with this approach, which will be discussed in more detail later. First, it is difficult to detect subtle biochemical changes; new developments in analytical techniques continue to point out problems with earlier experiments. Second, it is extremely difficult (if it is possible at all)

to isolate changes that are a result of *learning* and not of the other physiological states that accompany it: attention, arousal, and sensory stimulation, for example.

2. One can inhibit biochemical systems that are necessary links in the chain of events ultimately producing a certain physical change. If a failure in learning is observed, then perhaps the physical changes that were blocked are those which mediate the memory storage. Unfortunately, the biochemical inhibitors that are presently available are not very specific in their effects; they block a wide range of physical changes and do not permit us to conclude much about the kind of change that takes place.

3. One can facilitate certain biochemical systems and thereby accomplish effects opposite to the ones proposed in (2); the acquisition of a memory should thus take place more rapidly. Unfortunately, it is not at all easy to speed up biosynthetic processes in a living organism, and attempts such as these have not met with success.

4. Finally, perhaps one can extract chemicals from the brains of animals that have learned a task and then give a group of recipient subjects the benefit of the trained animals' experience by injecting them with these chemicals. The nature of the chemical would tell us something about the nature of memory. As we shall see, some positive results have been obtained, but we cannot yet conclude that *learning* has been transferred.

PHYSICAL CHANGES IN CELLS

We cannot evaluate any of these approaches without first being acquainted with the way in which cells may undertake physical changes. There are a great variety of ways in which short-lived changes may occur in neural systems: transmitter substances (or the enzymes that destroy them) may be used up, or ionic changes may occur when the rate of neural firing is high enough to "get ahead" of the sodium-potassium pump, to give two examples. However, these changes cannot account for *long-term* alterations that are capable of storing memories for many years. It is much more likely that some structural changes take place—changes in the size of synapses, growth of new synaptic terminals, or permanent changes in the amount of transmitter substance or destructive enzymes, for example. One type of substance is particularly important in the production of these alterations and in their continued maintenance—proteins.

The Structure and Function of Proteins

Types of Proteins

Structural Proteins. Proteins serve as structural elements of the body. The organic matrix of bones is made of the protein *collagen;* upon this matrix are deposited the inorganic salts that give the bones their strength. Hemoglobin, the molecule that provides the oxygen-carrying capacity of the blood, is a protein; so are the pituitary hormones. Proteins are vital constituents of the membrane that bounds the cell and forms many of its organelles. The motive force of the body, provided by actin and myosin filaments of muscles, or by the filaments of cilia, is provided by proteins. Proteins even provide the mechanism by which packages of transmitter molecules (the synaptic vesicles) are extruded, and proteins apparently constitute the sodium-potassium pump. If learning involves physical changes within the nervous system, it is difficult to imagine how proteins could *not* be involved.

Enzymes. But the second role played by proteins makes them even more ubiquitous in cellular mechanisms. The cell is a biochemical factory that assembles or disassembles various chemical compounds according to the requirements of the moment. The control of these synthetic or destructive processes is accomplished by complex systems of feedback between cytoplasmic constituents and the genetic material within the nucleus of the cell. The tools used by these systems to produce these changes are the enzymes, a special class of proteins.

Let us consider the nature of the cytoplasm, where these biochemical processes take place. The raw materials necessary to construct a vast variety of substances are present. The environment is close to neutral in its acid-base balance. Temperature rarely exceeds 37° C. Under these conditions a chemist would be hard put artificially to synthesize or destroy organic compounds. These processes require changes in the acid-base balance or high temperatures—changes that would kill a cell. Here is where enzymes are important. Enzymes combine with their *substrate* (the substance they act upon) in such a way that other substances can be attached (they facilitate synthetic processes) or they break the substrate molecules apart in some particular way (they facilitate destructive processes).

Amino Acids: The Elements of Proteins. Proteins are constructed of long chains of *amino acids.* A few representative amino acids (most proteins are constructed from a group of twenty amino acids) are

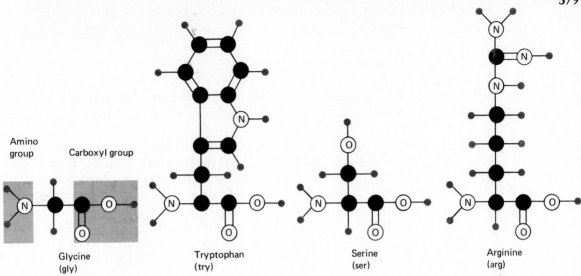

Amino group

Carboxyl group

Glycine
(gly)

Tryptophan
(try)

Serine
(ser)

Arginine
(arg)

FIGURE 20.1 Structures of some amino acids.

shown in Figure 20.1. Note that each amino acid contains a *carboxyl group* (COOH), shown on the right, and an *amino group* (NH₂), shown on the left. (Small gray dots represent hydrogen atoms; large black dots represent carbon atoms.) (See **FIGURE 20.1.**)

The carboxyl group of one amino acid can couple with the amino group of another. This junction, the *peptide bond,* is the link that connects a string of amino acids together to make proteins. (A molecule that consists of a few amino acids is referred to as a *poly-peptide;* a protein consists of a larger number—somewhere over fifty.) Figure 20.2 shows how two amino acids (serine and glycine) can be linked together with a peptide bond. (See **FIGURE 20.2.**)

FIGURE 20.2 A peptide bond between two amino acids.

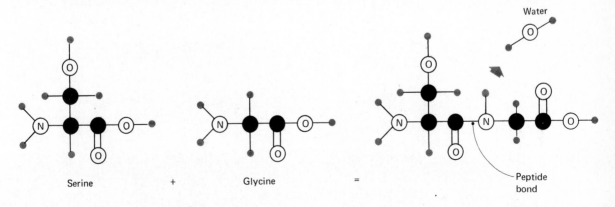

Serine   +   Glycine   =

Water

Peptide bond

FIGURE 20.3 The three-dimensional structure of a protein.

THE THREE-DIMENSIONAL STRUCTURE OF PROTEINS. A protein can consist of many hundreds of amino acids; the particular sequence of the amino acids specifies the nature of the protein. However, a protein molecule is not shaped like a long rod; it has a complex, three-dimensional structure. An example is shown in **FIGURE 20.3**.

Various parts of the protein chain are linked together by special attachments called *disulfide bonds*. (There are other kinds of bonds as well, but disulfide bonds are the strongest and apparently most important.) *Cysteine*, one of the amino acids, contains a sulfur atom, that normally has a hydrogen atom attached to it. If this hydrogen atom is removed from two different molecules of cysteine, the sulfur atoms are capable of joining together and forming a new double amino acid, called *cystine*. (You would think someone would have come up with better names than *cysteine* and *cystine*.) (See **FIGURE 20.4**.)

The disulfide bonds do not occur between cysteine molecules that are adjacent members of the chain. Instead, bridges are formed across loops in the chain, or even between one chain and another, in the case of complex proteins made up of more than one chain of amino acids. An example of a relatively simple protein (insulin) is shown in Figure 20.5. The black bars represent disulfide bonds; the letters are abbreviations for the various amino acids. (See **FIGURE 20.5**.)

The three-dimensional structure of a protein is of extreme importance; an enzyme that has been straightened out by chemically dissolving its disulfide bonds no longer acts as an enzyme. (The term for the straightening-out process, in fact, describes this loss of activity; the protein is said to be *denatured*.) An enzyme attaches only to substrates that are able to nestle into its three-dimensional conformation. Thus, enzymes act only on certain substrates. When the substrate and enzyme join, the enzyme apparently bends; in some cases this also causes the substrate to bend, exposing some part of it so that another molecule can now be attached (synthesis). In other cases, some portion of the substrate is exposed to the destructive effects of other molecules, as in the case of enzymes that facilitate *hydrolysis*

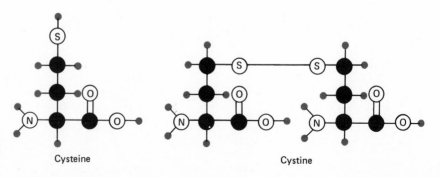

FIGURE 20.4 The disulfide bond.

Cysteine

Cystine

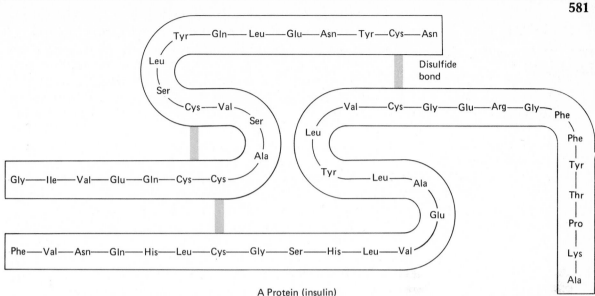

A Protein (insulin)

FIGURE 20.5 Disulfide bonds
between various locations
on the amino acid chains of a
protein. (Redrawn from Roller,
A. *Discovering the Basis of
Life*. Copyright 1974 by
McGraw-Hill Book Company,
New York.)

(dissolution by water) of their substrates. The important aspect of the three-dimensional structure of enzymes is that specificity for a given substrate is achieved, and the substrate is subsequently altered in a particular way.

The process of bending and folding appears to depend solely on the location of the cysteine molecules, as can be shown by the fact that a denatured protein can resume its original conformation (and enzymatic activity) if the denaturing chemicals are carefully removed from the solution. This process is shown schematically in **FIGURE 20.6.** Since this is the case, the process of protein synthesis entails only the assembly of the proper amino acids into the proper sequence. The three-dimensional structure of the protein and its enzymatic characteristics (if it is an enzyme rather than a structural protein) will automatically take care of themselves.

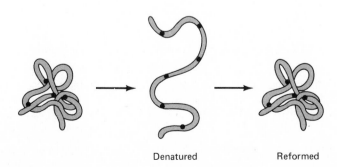

Denatured   Reformed

FIGURE 20.6   Denaturation
of a protein molecule by
dissolution of the disulfide
bonds.

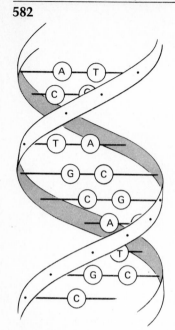

FIGURE 20.7 A molecule of deoxyribonucleic acid (DNA).

We have seen that proteins are essential for initiating long-term alterations in the properties of cells; they serve both enzymatic and structural roles. We have also seen that the nature of a protein is determined by its sequence of amino acids. Therefore, we must understand the process by which a particular protein is produced and also the mechanisms that initiate and terminate its production.

Protein Synthesis

THE STRUCTURE OF DNA. Since a protein is specified by a listing of its sequence of amino acids, there obviously must be a set of lists contained somewhere in the cell that directs the construction of each protein the cell can produce. These lists are found in the chromosomes. Each of our twenty-three pairs of chromosomes consists of a double-stranded helix (coil) of *deoxyribonucleic acid* (*DNA*). The important thing about DNA is not its helical structure, or the sugar molecule (2-deoxy-D-ribose) that serves as its backbone. What is important is the fact that DNA contains a set of four nucleotide bases, *adenine* (*A*), *guanine* (*G*), *cytosine* (*C*), and *thymine* (*T*). These nucleotide bases are arranged in pairs down the center of the DNA strand, linked together by an easily broken *hydrogen bond*. Note that nucleotide bases are complementary; A and T bond together, as do G and C. (See **FIGURE 20.7.**)

An Overview of Protein Synthesis. The synthesis of protein is accomplished by means of two processes. A portion of the DNA strand (a gene) contains a coded list of the amino acids that specify a particular protein. The information contained in this stretch of DNA is copied onto a strand of RNA (*ribonucleic acid*, which uses the sugar *ribose* instead of 2-deoxy-D-ribose). During this process, the two strands of DNA temporarily break apart. The RNA just assembled (called *messenger RNA*, or *mRNA*, since it conveys coded information from the DNA strand) then travels to the ribosome, where the proper amino acids are assembled into protein. (See **FIGURE 20.8.**)

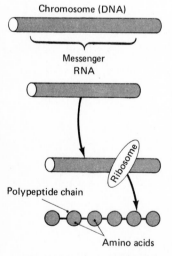

FIGURE 20.8 A schematic overview of the process of protein synthesis.

THE GENETIC CODE. What is the nature of the code? A set of painstaking experiments have shown that information on the DNA strands (and on RNA, also) is represented in three-letter words, the letters being represented by nucleotide bases. Thus, since there are four different letters (A, G, C, and T) sixty-four unique three-letter words can be formed. Since only twenty amino acids need to be specified, that means there are more than enough words in this language to encode a protein's sequence of amino acids. The codes (in terms of the base sequences of RNA, and not of DNA) are shown in Figure 20.9. Note that there is redundancy; a particular amino acid can be specified in more than one way. Also, there are special codes for *start* and *stop*, which serve as punctuation. The *start* and *stop* codes indicate the beginning and end of the protein chain. (See **FIGURE 20.9.**)

TRANSCRIPTION.   When protein synthesis is initiated, the strands of DNA separate, and a strand of RNA is produced. RNA is very similar to DNA, except that it consists of only one chain, and, as I already noted, its sugar is ribose. There is one other exception; one of the nucleotide bases of RNA is different. Thymine is replaced by *uracil*. So the letters used by RNA are A, G, C, and U.

Figure 20.10 gives an example of this process of RNA synthesis, which is called *transcription* because the code is copied onto the messenger RNA. Five *codons* are shown (that is what the three-letter words are called), specifying the following sequence of amino acids; methionine (*start*)—alanine—glycine—serine—(*stop*). (See **FIGURE 20.10.**)

Ala	GCU GCC GCA GCG	His	CAU CAC	Thr	ACU ACC ACA ACG
		Ile	AUU AUC AUA		
Arg	AGA AGG CGU CGC CGA CGG			Tyr	UAU UAC
				Try	UGG
		Leu	CUU CUC CUA CUG UUA UUG	Val	GUU GUC GUA
Asn	AAU AAC				
		Lys	AAA AAG	Val START	GUG
ASP	GAU GAC				
		Met START	AUG	STOP	UAA UAG UGA
Cys	UGU UGC	Phe	UUU UUC		
Glu	GAA GAG				
		Pro	CCU CCC CCA CCG		
Gln	CAA CAG				
Gly	GGU GGC GGA GGG	Ser	AGU AGC UCU UCC UCA UCG		

FIGURE 20.9   The genetic code. These sequences of bases on the RNA molecule specify corresponding amino acids.

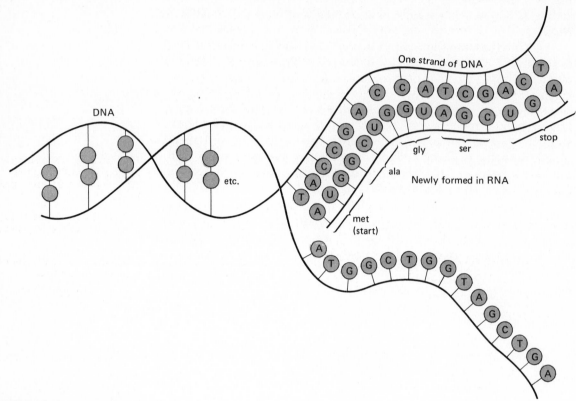

FIGURE 20.10 Transcription: The synthesis of messenger RNA from a portion of the DNA strand.

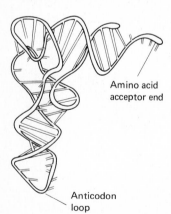

FIGURE 20.11 A molecule of transfer RNA.

TRANSLATION. The newly synthesized messenger RNA now travels to a ribosome, to which it attaches. The ribosome, consisting chiefly of protein, somehow facilitates the process that follows. Since the information that specifies the sequence of amino acids is contained in a series of three-letter words, there must be some mechanism that reads these words. The reading (or *translation*, as this process is called) is accomplished by another form of RNA called *transfer RNA*. This substance does not resemble a long coil, as messenger RNA does, but is folded and bent back upon itself. Transfer RNA has two important working sites: the *anticodon loop*, which "fits" the codon on the messenger RNA that specifies a particular amino acid, and an *amino acid acceptor end*, to which is attached that amino acid. (See **FIGURE 20.11**.)

The sequence of translation works this way: The ribosome attaches to the end of the messenger RNA, which signifies a *start* code. This attachment somehow exposes the first codon, to which a molecule of transfer RNA with the appropriate anticodon gets attached

For example, transfer RNA with the anticodon UAC attaches to the codon AUG, which specifies methionine and *start*. (See **FIGURE 20.12**)

The ribosome then moves down the strand of messenger RNA, exposing the next codon (GCU), which specifies alanine. The anticodon should be UCG; however, transfer RNA uses a variety of nucleotide bases. In this case, the codon contains *inosine*. The transfer RNA with the anticodon CGI has a molecule of alanine at its amino acid acceptor end. This molecule attaches to the second codon, its alanine attaches to the adjacent methionine, and the first molecule of transfer RNA drops off. This molecule, now amino acid–less, picks up another free amino acid and is ready to be used again. (See **FIGURE 20.13**.)

This process continues, the ribosome moving down the strand of messenger RNA and causing the assembly of the sequential amino acids until it gets to the *stop* codon, UGA, at which point it detaches. A new protein molecule has been produced. (See **FIGURE 20.14**.)

FIGURE 20.12   The beginning of translation: Production of a polypeptide from messenger RNA.

FIGURE 20.13   Translation: Attachment of the next amino acid.

FIGURE 20.14   Completion of the translation process.

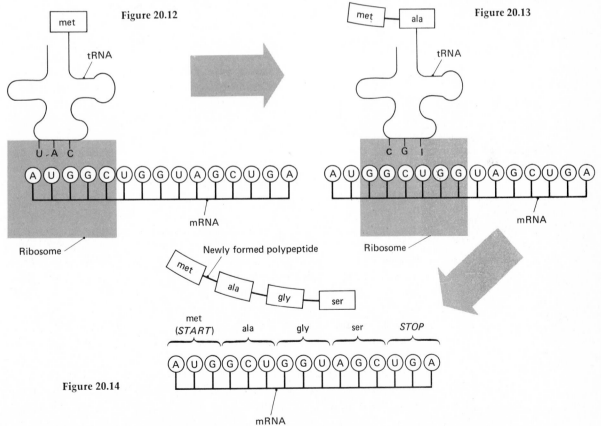

Figure 20.12

met
tRNA
U A C
A U G G C U G G U A G C U G A
mRNA
Ribosome

Figure 20.13

met   ala
tRNA
C G I
A U G G C U G G U A G C U G A
mRNA
Ribosome

Newly formed polypeptide
met
ala
gly
ser

met
(START)   ala   gly   ser   STOP
A U G G C U G G U A G C U G A
mRNA

Figure 20.14

Control of Protein Synthesis

We have seen how proteins are synthesized; the message along a particular region of DNA (a gene) is transcribed into messenger RNA, which goes to a ribosome. The ribosome moves along the strand of messenger RNA, permitting the assembly of the coded-for amino acids, with transfer RNA serving as an intermediary that brings the amino acids into position. The appropriate molecules of cysteine join together by means of disulfide bonds, and the protein adopts its active shape. The protein then goes out to do its stuff: to serve as a structural element or as an enzyme.

So far no control mechanism has been described. If all genes in a cell continuously produced messenger RNA, and thus synthesis of a protein, the situation would be chaotic. Too many different kinds of protein would be produced. In fact, a small proportion of the genes are active at any one time. All cells of the body (except for special ones like sperms, ova, and blood cells) have identical genetic material. Therefore, cells are not differentiated on the basis of DNA. A liver cell contains the system of genes that controls the synthesis of acetylcholine, for example. Similarly, a neuron contains all it needs to know about how to produce bile. And yet cells are specialized. They are all constructed from the same set of blueprints, and they all use these same blueprints to maintain their structure and to respond to changes in their environment. How can such an enormous variety of cells be constructed from a single set of plans, and how can these same plans be used to respond appropriately to a variety of different environmental stimuli?

AN OVERVIEW. The general answer to this question is quite clear: There are mechanisms that suppress those genes that are not needed by a particular type of cell. When a certain enzyme is needed, that gene is turned on (apparently by removing the source of suppression) and synthesis of messenger RNA, and ultimately protein, begins. The details of the way in which the genes are turned on and off are not at all clear. Enough is known, however, to sketch in a plausible link between neural activity (such as that which occurs during short-term memory) and protein synthesis (which would be necessary in order to produce structural changes of long-term memory). Even though more is known about the way in which protein synthesis is controlled in bacteria, I shall restrict my discussion to studies performed with mammalian cells. It is better to have an understanding of a more general scheme that is likely to be correct than to have a more detailed understanding of a process that may or may not apply to the mammalian brain.

HISTONE PROTEINS. According to a mechanism outlined by Stein, Stein, and Kleinsmith (1975), the regulation of protein synthesis is accomplished by two particular kinds of proteins that are attached to the strands of DNA. The first kind, the *histones*, turn the genes off. Histones, which are basic proteins with a positive charge, attach quite firmly to DNA (which is negatively charged). In this way the DNA is made more stable, apparently by tightening up the helix, thus making the nucleotide bases inside the strands less available for the process of RNA transcription. Histones are apparently nonspecific; there is not a particular kind of histone for each gene. One variety appears to work everywhere. Histones appear to be very stable and long-lived.

NONHISTONE PROTEINS. In contrast to the histones, there are many species of nonhistone proteins within the nucleus. Some of these proteins last for a very brief time, whereas others are as stable as DNA and the histones. The pattern of nonhistone proteins is very different for different types of cells; a graph of the amounts of proteins of various molecular weights is shown in Figure 20.15. Note that the patterns are quite different. (See **FIGURE 20.15.**)

Even for a given type of cell, variations are found in the types of nonhistone proteins that are produced. *Neuroblastoma cells* (nerve cancer cells) can be grown in a *tissue culture*—a glass dish containing the proper nutrients. These cells normally reproduce continuously, in a nondifferentiated form. However, they can be stimulated to differentiate, and they will then resemble normal neurons. Once they become differentiated, furthermore, they remain so. There ob-

FIGURE 20.15   The amount of histone and nonhistone proteins of various molecular weights in different types of cells. (From Stein, G. S., Stein, J. S., and Kleinsmith, L. J., Chromosomal proteins and gene regulation, *Scientific American*, 1975, 232, 46–57. Copyright © 1975 by Scientific American, Inc. All rights reserved.)

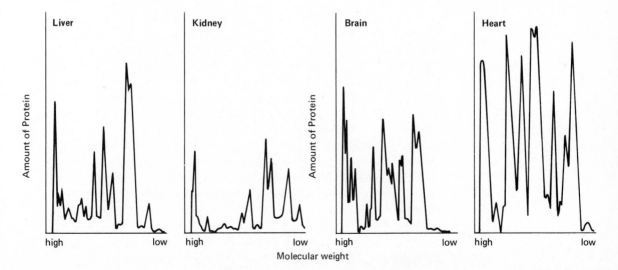

viously must be some change in their regulation of protein synthesis in order to produce and maintain these structural changes. Different nonhistone proteins appear to be produced by neuroblastoma cells in these two states; the nondifferentiated cells produce larger proteins at a faster rate.

These results, and those of other experiments, suggest that nonhistone proteins serve to reverse the inhibition of protein synthesis normally produced by histones. Moreover, a particular nonhistone protein appears to be specific for a particular part of the DNA strand. These proteins therefore do not serve as general facilitators; a given nonhistone protein turns on a particular gene (or perhaps a set of genes).

PHOSPHORYLATION OF NONHISTONE PROTEINS. Nonhistone proteins have a particular property that may serve as one of the links between external events and the control of protein synthesis; they are extensively *phosphorylated*. The addition of phosphate groups (*phosphorylation*) or their removal (*dephosphorylation*) alters the structural and functional properties of nonhistone proteins, and studies have shown that the ability of these molecules to induce RNA synthesis depends on their degree of phosphorylation. Since there are known mechanisms by which events outside the membrane of the cell can cause the phosphorylation of intracellular proteins, we have a highly plausible link between neural activity and changes in protein synthesis. I shall describe the nature of some of these mechanisms shortly, but first let us see how phosphorylation of a nonhistone protein might affect synthesis of RNA and, ultimately, of proteins.

A MODEL FOR CONTROL OF PROTEIN SYNTHESIS. Stein and his colleagues have presented the model shown in Figure 20.16. A strand of DNA (negatively charged) is shown with positively charged histones attached to it. These histones prevent transcription from occurring. A particular (dephosphorylated) nonhistone protein finds its place on the appropriate site; presumably the particular set of nonhistone proteins that cell has depends upon the type of cell it is. The portion of the DNA covered by this protein is still inactive. At a later time, however, some messenger causes the nonhistone protein to become phosphorylated. This makes the protein become more negatively charged, and the histone/nonhistone protein complex is repelled by the negative charge of the DNA strand. A portion of the chromosome is now available for the process of transcription of messenger RNA. (See **FIGURE 20.16.**)

This model may or may not be correct, but it is a good way to organize and remember these facts: (1) histones are general inhibitors of RNA synthesis, (2) nonhistone proteins are specific facilitators of RNA synthesis, (3) nonhistone proteins can bind to histone proteins, and (4) the degree of phosphorylation determines the activity of nonhistone proteins as inducers of RNA synthesis.

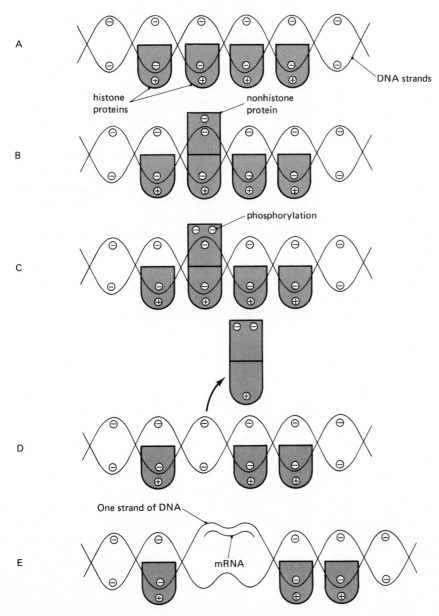

FIGURE 20.16 Control of RNA synthesis by phosphorylation of nonhistone protein. (From Stein, G. S., Stein, J. S., and Kleinsmith, L. J., Chromosomal proteins and gene regulation, *Scientific American*, 1975, *232*, 46–57. Copyright © 1975 by Scientific American, Inc. All rights reserved.)

The Role of Protein Synthesis in the Storage of Memory

How can external stimuli (most likely, synaptic events) lead to alterations in protein synthesis, and thus to structural changes? The most plausible way is by means of the *nucleotide cyclases* (these enzymes were mentioned earlier, in chapter 5). For example, there are receptor molecules in the membrane that are attached to enzymes such as *adenyl cyclase* (adenosine—or adenylic acid—is a nucleotide; hence the term nucleotide cyclase). The receptor site is on the outside of the membrane, while the enzyme is on the inside. When the appropriate extracellular substance (which can be a hormone or a neurotransmitter) is recognized by the receptor site, the enzyme inside the cell becomes active and causes *ATP (adenosine triphosphate)* to be converted into *cyclic AMP*. Cyclic AMP has the ability to phosphorylate proteins and thus to induce RNA synthesis if the appropriate nonhistone protein is involved. (See **FIGURE 20.17**.)

This process appears to be the way, for example, that trophic hormones of the anterior pituitary gland trigger hormone synthesis in the target cells (Sutherland, 1972). The sequence could go like this:

> Neural activity encoding STM → increases in extracellular transmitter substance (or other external chemical events, such as ionic changes) → activated nucleotide cyclase → cyclic nucleotide → phosphorylated nonhistone protein → synthesis of messenger RNA → protein synthesis → change in structure of cell → new properties of cell, contributing to the encoding of LTM.

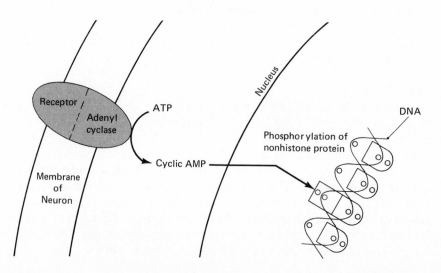

FIGURE 20.17 A schematic representation of the way in which extracellular chemicals can cause alterations in protein synthesis.

Entingh and his colleagues (Entingh, Dunn, Glassman, Wilson, Hogan, and Damstra, 1975) have presented a diagram that very nicely puts together these various steps and provides some details that I have not discussed, such as the possibility that phosphorylation of synaptic proteins may provide the basis for short-term memory; perhaps reverberation is "kept in one track," for example, by temporarily facilitating particular synaptic connections. The diagram also refers to experments that provide evidence for each of these hypothesized links. (See **FIGURE 20.18.**)

MACROMOLECULES AND MEMORY. I hope that the reasons for this long discussion of protein synthesis and its control are apparent to you. Unless you know how long-term physical changes are accomplished by a cell, you cannot hope to understand or to evaluate experimental evidence that purports to say something about the "biochemistry of memory." For example, knowing what you now do about RNA, would it seem reasonable to talk about it as a "memory molecule"? What would you think about this argument:

> The memory process requires that many bits of information be stored. DNA and RNA are complex molecules, each of which is made of a sequence of four different nucleotide bases. These sequences are millions of words long, and hence these molecules could encode the information stored in long-term memory.

Yes, indeed, these molecules are complex enough to store much information. Indeed, they do so. All the information that is needed to construct a human being is present in the nucleus of one cell. But there is not a shred of evidence to suggest that the sequence of DNA is altered as a result of experience, or that environmental events are represented in a particular sequence of bases in newly synthesized RNA. Different stimuli could indeed cause the induction of synthesis of different molecules of RNA by turning on different sets of genes, but that is another matter altogether.

A second criticism of the naive model I have put forth (so that I can shoot it down) is this: A molecule of messenger RNA does contain information, but that information is meaningful only insofar as it specifies the production of a particular protein. Otherwise, the sequence has no significance at all. An individual neuron does not learn a particular task. It does not store a memory. Memory can be stored only in a large and complex circuit, of which a single neuron is only one element. This means that the only meaningful change that can take place in an individual neuron is one that alters its relationship with its neighbors. After this change, it fires more easily (or less easily, or with a different pattern) in response to a given input. Or perhaps it makes new connections with other neurons, and thus

I. Resting state
(no input)

But cell is sensitive to electrolytes, hormones and metabolites.

I. Active state

Neurotransmitter from presynaptic cell attaches to post–synaptic membrane.

I. Reorganization state

Characteristics unknown.

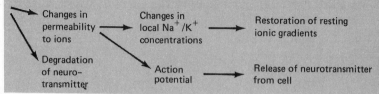

Active cellular processes engaged in maintenance of metabolic machinery

RNA synthesis → Protein synthesis → Enzymatic activities → Production of energy (ATP)
→ Regeneration of cell structure

Responses to general synaptic input

Changes in permeability to ions → Changes in local Na$^+$/K$^+$ concentrations → Restoration of resting ionic gradients

Degradation of neuro-transmitter

Action potential → Release of neurotransmitter from cell

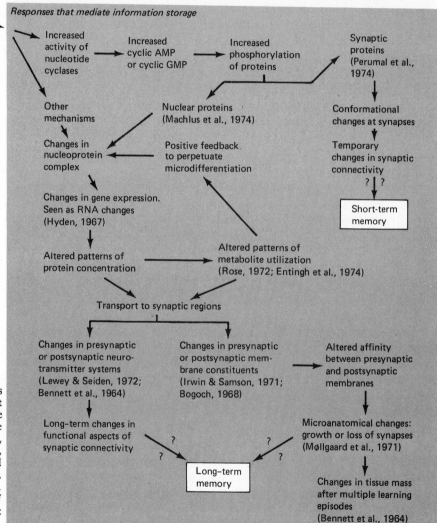

Responses that mediate information storage

Increased activity of nucleotide cyclases → Increased cyclic AMP or cyclic GMP → Increased phosphorylation of proteins → Synaptic proteins (Perumal et al., 1974)

Other mechanisms

Nuclear proteins (Machlus et al., 1974)

Conformational changes at synapses

Changes in nucleoprotein complex ← Positive feedback to perpetuate microdifferentiation

Temporary changes in synaptic connectivity
? ↓ ?

Changes in gene expression. Seen as RNA changes (Hyden, 1967)

Short-term memory

Altered patterns of protein concentration → Altered patterns of metabolite utilization (Rose, 1972; Entingh et al., 1974)

Transport to synaptic regions

Changes in presynaptic or postsynaptic neuro-transmitter systems (Lewey & Seiden, 1972; Bennett et al., 1964)

Changes in presynaptic or postsynaptic membrane constituents (Irwin & Samson, 1971; Bogoch, 1968)

Altered affinity between presynaptic and postsynaptic membranes

Long-term changes in functional aspects of synaptic connectivity

Long-term memory

Microanatomical changes: growth or loss of synapses (Møllgaard et al., 1971)

Changes in tissue mass after multiple learning episodes (Bennett et al., 1964)

FIGURE 20.18 Possible ways in which neurons might mediate memory. The references can be found in the bibliography. (From Entingh, D., Dunn, A., Glassman, E., Wilson, J. E., Hogan, E., and Damstra, T. In Gazzaniga, M. S., and Blakemore, C., editors, *Handbook of Psychobiology.* Copyright 1975 by Academic Press, New York.)

affects cells it did not previously synapse with. Or perhaps some of its terminals become inactive, so that it no longer affects some of its neighbors. The list of possibilities is limited only by a person's ingenuity and knowledge of the properties of neurons; unfortunately, however, we do not yet have the means to determine which of these possibilities actually occurs, and thus encodes memories.

NEURAL STIMULATION AND PHYSICAL CHANGE

Now it is time to see what we do know about the physical nature of memory. I shall consider each of the links in the chain from STM to morphological changes, and I shall review some representative studies that are relevant to these links. In particular, I shall review the effects of neural stimulation (or the learning process itself, to the degree that these events can be differentiated) on each of the steps in the process of neural change, starting at the end of the chain (the changes themselves) and working backward.

Neural Stimulation and Alterations in the Structure of Neurons

First of all, it should be made clear that neurons are indeed capable of altering their relationships with their neighbors. It is difficult to understand how induction of RNA synthesis can cause a change as complex as the growth of a new axonic process that finds its way to another cell and grows a new synapse there (which, of course, requires the cooperation of the second cell, for no synapse is functional without postsynaptic receptor sites and the appropriate membrane mechanisms for producing PSPs). This does happen, however, as is demonstrated during development, when a budding axon finds its way from one part of the nervous system to another. Synapses are made on the appropriate neurons or muscles, even though they may be far away. The genetic mechanisms that direct this growth during development could quite conceivably direct the establishment of similar connections later. The genes are there; they just have to be turned on.

Perhaps one of the ways they can be turned on is by the secretion of some substance by the neuron to which the new process is sent: we might call it a "come and get me" substance. For example, Raisman (1969) has shown that individual cells in the septum receive terminals from the hippocampus (via the fimbria) and from the hypothalamus (via the medial forebrain bundle). If the fimbria is destroyed, the terminals from the MFB axons will sprout and occupy the vacated synaptic sites. Similarly, MFB lesions will result in the

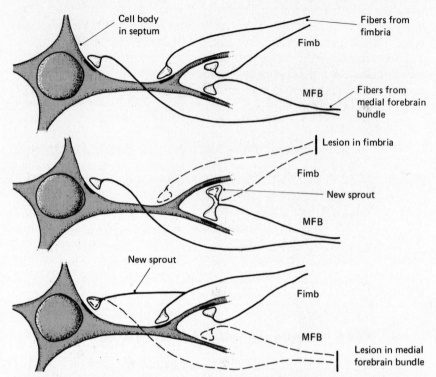

FIGURE 20.19 Sprouting of nerve terminals in the septum and attachment to new postsynaptic sites caused by degeneration of the fimbria or medial forebrain bundle. (From Raisman, G., *Brain Research*, 1969, 14, 25–48.)

sprouting of the axons from the fimbria and the establishment of new synapses on the soma, which does not normally receive terminals from these axons. These results are shown schematically in **FIGURE 20.19.**

This experiment indicates that neurons in the mature nervous system *can* establish new connections; whether the memory process involves similar kinds of changes has not yet been shown. However, Rosenzweig (1970) has reviewed evidence showing that environmental events can produce major alterations in the structure of cortical neurons. Whether these changes are a result of learning or some more general facilitation is not yet clear.

Rosenzweig and his colleagues divided litters of rats and placed the animals into two kinds of environments: enriched and impoverished. The enriched environment contained such things as running wheels, ladders, slides, and "toys" that could be manipulated. These objects were changed every day to maximize the variety of environmental stimuli and also, presumably, the memories that would be formed. The impoverished environments were plain cages in a dimly illuminated, quiet room.

The animals were sacrificed 80 days later and their brains were removed and analyzed. The brains of the rats from the enriched environment were found to be different from those of the impoverished group. The cortex was thicker, had a better capillary supply, and contained more acetylcholinesterase (and, therefore, probably more acetylcholine). There were also more glial cells. Even more significantly, Globus, Rosenzweig, Bennett, and Diamond (1973) found that the cortical neurons of rats raised in the enriched environment had a larger number of dendritic spines, which very strongly implies that there were more synapses on each cell.

The results may or may not be a consequence of learning. Perhaps an enriched environment produces some nonspecific effect. Whatever the nature of the intermediate steps might be, the results certainly show that environmental stimuli can affect the structure of the nervous system.

Neural Stimulation and Protein Synthesis

A number of studies have demonstrated that neural stimulation increases protein synthesis. A study by Wegener (1970) shows just how localized this effect can be. He removed the left eyes of a group of frogs and kept them in the dark for 10 days. The animals were then paralyzed with curare and given injections of radioactive histidine (an amino acid, and thus a constituent of protein). The frogs were divided into four groups. One group was exposed to diffuse light, the second saw a narrow vertical band of light, and the third saw two bands of light. The fourth group was kept in the dark. The stimuli were presented for 75 minutes. After time was allowed for protein synthesis to take place (and thus for the radioactive amino acid to be incorporated), the frogs were killed and fine-grain measurement was made of the radioactivity of various parts of the optic tectum.

The brains of frogs exposed to diffuse light contained radioactivity all over the optic tectum contralateral to the intact eye. Frogs kept in the dark showed the same amount of radioactivity in each hemisphere of the brain. The animals that saw the patterned light showed similar patterns of radioactivity on the optic tectum: a single wide band or two narrower bands, depending on the particular stimulus. These results suggest that visual input can alter the rate of protein synthesis in the cells that respond to the stimulus being presented.

METHODOLOGICAL PROBLEMS. We can draw fairly firm conclusions from the previous study because the pattern of stimulation was so nicely reflected in the pattern of radioactivity. Other studies that have attempted to compare the rates of protein synthesis in various parts of the brain have run into some serious methodological problems, as discussed by Entingh et al. (1975). For example, Hydén and Lange (1968) trained rats to learn to use their nonpreferred paw to reach for food. They then injected radioactive leucine (an amino acid) into the brain, and later measured the radioactivity (and hence, presumably, the rate of protein synthesis) in the hippocampus. They found that the rate of protein synthesis was increased, relative to control animals. However, the same authors (Hydén and Lange, 1972) later performed a similar experiment, this time injecting the radioactive leucine intraperitoneally, rather than intracerebrally. This time they observed a *decreased* rate of protein synthesis in the trained subjects. Two different methods of determining the rate of protein synthesis gave two completely different results. It is most likely that the results from the second study are more accurate, that reversal of hand preference *decreases* the amount of hippocampal protein synthesis.

Neural Stimulation and RNA Synthesis

Horn, Rose, and Bateson (1973) have described a series of experiments providing excellent biochemical evidence that neural stimulation produces changes in RNA synthesis. Their training method used the phenomenon of *imprinting.*

A young chick (or other *precocial* bird that must follow its mother around shortly after hatching) will become imprinted upon the first significant stimulus it sees. It will continue to follow that stimulus around—as if it were the chick's mother—whether that stimulus is a box or a toy train or even a human being. Usually the first thing the chick sees is its mother, so there are few problems in a natural setting.

Horn and his colleagues made use of this tendency to learn that is "wired into" young chicks. They presumed that such a significant learning experience, which clearly produces long-term memories for the stimulus, would be most likely to produce detectable physical changes. The newly hatched animals were injected with radioactive uracil (one of the nucleotide bases that make up RNA) and were exposed for varying amounts of time to a rotating, flashing light. The chicks were killed later, and estimates were made of the rate of RNA synthesis by measuring the radioactivity of RNA extracted from the animals' brains.

The results are seen in Figure 20.20. The curves represent the estimated amount of RNA produced in the roof of the brain at varying times after the onset of the stimulus. Experimental animals (upper line) saw a flashing light; control subjects (lower line) saw a steady light. (Chicks will not become imprinted to a steady light.) Note that RNA synthesis appeared to be selectively increased after 76 minutes of exposure to the flashing light. (See **FIGURE 20.20.**)

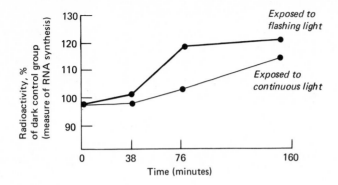

FIGURE 20. 20   Alterations in RNA synthesis in the roof of the brain (tectum) after exposure of a chick to a flashing or steady light. (From Horn, G., Rose, S. P. R., and Bateson, P. P. G., *Science*, 10 August 1973, *181*, 506–514. Copyright 1973 by the American Association for the Advancement of Science.)

If this were the only measure used to determine the rate of RNA synthesis, the results would not be conclusive (we shall see why, in a moment). However, some of Horn's colleagues (Haywood, Rose, and Bateson, 1970) also extracted, from the brain of chicks, an enzyme called *RNA polymerase*. Enzymes direct all kinds of biosynthetic events, and RNA synthesis is no exception. As we saw, nonhistone proteins remove histone proteins from DNA and thus expose a region that becomes active. Before RNA synthesis can begin, however, the enzyme RNA polymerase must be present to facilitate the process. Thus, if RNA synthesis in the brain were increased, one would expect to see an increase in RNA polymerase activity.

Indeed, this was found to be the case. A protein extract from the brains of the trained chicks was found to increase the rate of RNA synthesis *in vitro* (i.e., "in glass"—in a test tube containing purified cell-free DNA and the constituent nucleotide bases of RNA). Since the rate of RNA synthesis in such a case depends upon the amount of RNA polymerase present, we can conclude that there was more RNA polymerase activity in the brain of the chicks exposed to the flashing light. Therefore, there was also, apparently, a higher rate of RNA synthesis going on in the brain.

METHODOLOGICAL PROBLEMS.   Another study used a single measure of RNA synthesis, and the results of this study are consequently not conclusive. Shashoua (1970) attached plastic floats to goldfish, which made them float upside down. The change in buoyancy was small enough so that the fish could eventually overcome the force and swim right side up. After this "learning" situation the goldfish were killed and their brains were analyzed for RNA synthesis.

Shashoua injected radioactive *orotic acid* (a precursor of cytosine and uracil, two of the nucleotide bases of RNA) before training. After training he measured the relative amounts of radioactive *uridine* and *cytidine* in RNA extracted from the brain, using this measurement as an indication of new RNA synthesis. (Uridine and cytidine are uracil and cytosine with the attached sugar molecules that make up a part of the RNA molecule.) Shashoua noted increases in the ratio of uridine to cytidine. However, Baskin, Masiarz, and Agranoff (1972) found that a variety of stimuli (e.g., changes in the level of carbon dioxide of the water) would alter the uridine-to-cytidine ratio. They suggested that stimulation could alter the rate of conversion of cytidine to uridine (which normally occurs in cells) and thus make it impossible to determine whether, in fact, new RNA had been syntheszed.

Baskin, Masiarz, and Agranoff thus concluded Shashoua's results might be due to changes in conversion of one nucleotide to another, and not to alterations in RNA synthesis. The criticism applies not only to Shasoua's study, but to most studies that have been performed so far. Biochemical procedures that adequately control for these problems have only recently been developed, and very few studies have used these procedures.

Neural Stimulation and Phosphorylation of Nonhistone Proteins

As we saw earlier, RNA synthesis is apparently initiated by the phosphorylation of nonhistone proteins attached to DNA. Machlus, Wilson, and Glassman (1974) trained rats to avoid a shock by jumping from the grid floor onto a platform located at one end of the chamber. The authors measured the amount of radioactive phosphorus that became incorporated into nonhistone protein extracted from the rats' brain; thus, they obtained an estimate of the degree of protein phosphorylation. The results are shown in Figure 20.21. Note that the change is quite large (100 percent above the level obtained in control subjects) and is also quite brief, suggesting that a brief period of RNA synthesis is initiated, resulting in enough protein enzymes to initiate the needed physical changes. (See **FIGURE 20.21.**)

Machlus and his colleagues controlled for the artifacts that have plagued radioactive tracer studies; their biochemical results cannot be faulted (at least by present-day standards). They even used a direct measurement (the ratio of phosphorylated serine to non-phosphorylated serine), which did not entail the use of radioactive tracers, and obtained the same results. (Serine is an amino acid and is thus a constituent of protein.) Further analysis showed that not all nonhistone proteins were phosphorylated—only a specific subset. These results are consistent with the hypothesis that a selected set of genes was turned on by the experience.

Machlus, Entingh, Wilson, and Glassman (1974) obtained re-

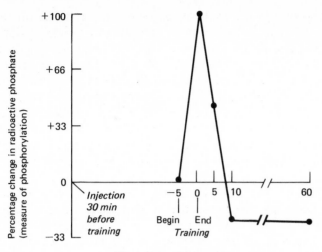

FIGURE 20.21 The amount of phosphorylated protein observed in the brain before and after training, in the study by Machlus et al. (1974). (From Entingh, D., Dunn, A., Glassman, E., Wilson, J. E., Hogan, E., and Damstra, T. In Gazzaniga, M. S., and Blakemore, C., editors, *Handbook of Psychobiology.* Copyright 1975 by Academic Press, New York.)

sults that suggest that the increased phosphorylation seen in the previous study was specific for learning itself. They trained rats in the previously described avoidance task, and used as controls rats that received inescapable shocks (a plastic barrier was placed in front of the platform). Mice were also trained in another apparatus. They were presented with the sound of a buzzer that signalled impending foot shock, and they eventually learned to jump to a platform when this buzzer sounded. Control mice received the buzzer-shock pairings but were not permitted to avoid the shock. None of the control groups showed increases in protein phosphorylation as compared with subjects that received no treatment at all, but remained in their home cages; the effect was seen only in the trained mice and rats. Furthermore, increased phosphorylation was seen when the previously trained rats were "reminded" of their experience by handling them or placing them in the apparatus. The control rats that had only been shocked did *not* show this increase. The results indicate that specific experiences produce phosphorylation of nonhistone proteins and thus, perhaps, induce RNA and protein synthesis. We cannot yet conclude what the nature of the experience is—whether it is the learning process itself or some specific form of stress-induced reaction.

Conclusions

There appears to be enough evidence to conclude that a link between neural activity and specific structural changes is at least plausible. The work of Hoffer, Siggins, Oliver, and Bloom (1971) and of Sutherland (1972) shows that norepinephrine exerts its postsynaptic effects via the adenyl cyclase–cyclic AMP mechanism, and that this mechanism is used by the cell to mediate the effects of polypeptide hormones (which do not cross the membrane) on protein synthesis by the cell. It is thus reasonable to suggest that the neurotransmitters themselves might initiate protein synthesis by similar means.

Other studies reviewed in this section have shown that neural stimulation can affect phosporylation of nonhistone proteins, and the synthesis of RNA and proteins. Finally, structural change in neurons (cortical thickness, number of dendritic spines) have been shown to be related to the animals' environment. Taken together, there is very good evidence for a link between the neural activity of STM and the physical changes necessary to produce LTM. Since a single learning experience probably produces a very slight change in a relatively small number of neurons, we are obviously a long way from locating the *particular* structural changes that encode long-term memories.

TREATMENTS THAT ALTER MECHANISMS PRODUCING PHYSICAL CHANGES

If long-term memory depends upon structural changes, then biochemical treatments that affect the mechanisms producing these changes should have an effect on the formation of memory. In this section I shall review some of the studies in which an attempt has been made to alter these mechanisms.

Inhibition of DNA Synthesis

Reinis (1972) has suggested that DNA synthesis is necessary for learning; DNA is a very stable molecule, and since long-term memories are themselves quite stable, new DNA might be produced, and thus encode these memories. There are arguments against this hypothesis, however. First, it appears that histone proteins, and some species of nonhistone proteins, are as stable as the DNA molecules themselves. Also, the fact that mouse neuroblastoma cells can be triggered to differentiate *permanently*, without any apparent alteration in the DNA itself, argues that permanent structural changes can be accomplished by means of alterations in the nuclear proteins alone. The suggestion that DNA changes must accompany learning argues for a novel mechanism in cellular machinery; lacking such evidence, it would appear to be more parsimonious to explain memory in terms of known cellular mechanisms.

The second argument against Reinis's hypothesis comes from a study by Casola, Lim, Davis, and Agranoff (1969). These investigators found that *cytosine arabinoside* (an inhibitor of DNA synthesis) does not impair the learning ability of goldfish. Thus, DNA synthesis does not appear to be involved in memory formation.

Inhibition of RNA or Protein Synthesis

Many experiments have been performed to determine whether synthesis of RNA and protein is necessary for the consolidation of memory. There are two problems inherent with all of these studies, however. First, no inhibitor has been found that affects *only* RNA or protein synthesis; other biochemical systems are also affected. Even if suppression of protein synthesis, for example, were the sole effect of a particular drug, we could not conclude that protein synthesis was necessary for the consolidation of memory if this drug did block memory. The biochemistry of neurons could be so upset by cessation of protein synthesis that the brain could not function normally; lack of consolidation could be a secondary, rather than a primary, effect of the halted protein synthesis. Thus, we cannot reach any firm conclusions about the necessity of protein synthesis for memory consolidation, even if we find this function impaired by these drugs.

The second problem is just the opposite. No drug used so far succeeds in *completely* inhibiting RNA or protein synthesis; the suppression is generally 80–95 percent complete. As a matter of fact, total suppression of RNA or protein synthesis would probably be lethal. If we fail to obtain amnesia after drug treatment, then it would be because enough protein synthesis could still take place to produce the necessary physical changes.

The results of the experiments carried out so far are just what might be expected given the problems with the available techniques: Some studies demonstrate amnesia, others do not, and still others show that the degree of amnesia depends upon the procedure used to train the subjects.

Actinomycin-D is an antibiotic drug that blocks the transcription of DNA into RNA. This drug produces up to 95 percent inhibition of protein synthesis. It was found this drug did not block the acquisition of a passive avoidance task (Barondes and Jarvik, 1964) or a maze-learning task (Cohen and Barondes, 1966) in mice. Retention, tested 4 hours later, was intact. The drug is highly toxic, so retention could not be tested on a longer-term basis. However, Agranoff, Davis, Casola, and Lim (1967) *did* obtain a consolidation deficit when actinomycin-D was injected into the brains of goldfish immediately after training. If the drug was administered 3 hours after training, no amnesia was seen. The reasons for the discrepancies between these experiments are not clear.

Protein synthesis has been experimentally disrupted by two drugs: *puromycin* and *cyclohexamide*. Puromycin is an antibiotic drug that disrupts protein synthesis by causing the growing polypeptides to break away from the ribosome prematurely. Studies that have investigated the effects of puromycin have been plagued with inconsistencies and results that are difficult to interpret. Puromycin injections appear to impair retention of a shock-avoidance task (learning to run toward one arm of a Y maze) in mice (Flexner, Flexner, and Stellar, 1963). Barondes and Cohen (1966) found that mice given puromycin 5 hours prior to training learned the task as well as did normal subjects, but did not retain the task 3 hours later; the consolidation process, but not STM, appeared to depend on protein synthesis. So far the results appear to be clear-cut. However, the following studies are more difficult to interpret. Flexner and Flexner (1967) found that the injection of a variety of substances (e.g., water, saline, and blood plasma) into the brain of the mice long after training "washes out" the effects of puromycin—the memory appears to return. The authors suggest that the effect is due to the removal of the short abnormal polypeptide chains previously produced by the administration of puromycin. These polypeptides presumably exert some suppressive effect on the brain. It is difficult, however, to imagine a chemical being "washed out" of the brain many weeks after puromycin treatment. If the injections really have a flushing effect on the extracellular fluid, one would imagine that the neural-glial relationships would be so disrupted as to produce widespread brain damage. If the peptides were still contained in the cytoplasm of the cells (and it is hard to imagine how they could get there, since polypeptides are much too large to migrate through the membrane), why should changes in the extracellular fluid affect the polypeptides within the cell? The only thing that can clearly be concluded is that the puromycin administration did not prevent the consolidation of memories.

There are also other inconsistencies in the effects of puromycin. Flexner and Flexner (1970) found that the performance of adrenalectomized animals was not affected by puromycin. If memory consolidation were being prevented by stopping protein synthesis, it is difficult to see why removal of the adrenal glands should allow the consolidation to take place. Furthermore, memories for appetitively motivated tasks (as opposed to those motivated by electrical shock) do not appear to be affected by puromycin (Ungerer, 1969).

Finally, intracranial injections of puromycin were found to produce abnormal electrical activity in the brain (Cohen, Ervin, and Barondes, 1966). Injections of Dilantin (an anticonvulsant) prevented the abnormal activity from occurring, and also prevented puromycin from producing amnesia. Thus, even if puromycin does produce amnesia (and the results are mixed), the mechanism by which it does so might have nothing to do with inhibition of protein synthesis.

The results of studies with *acetoxycyclohexamide* (AXM) are more consistent, but they are still not conclusive. Flexner and Flexner (1969) found that AXM did not affect memory for their shock-avoidance task. Barondes and Cohen (1967) used the same task, but they gave the animals less training. They found memory impairments in mice that had received AXM. Perhaps the less-than-complete inhibition of protein synthesis produced a less-than-complete inhibition of memory formation.

In another study, Barondes and Cohen (1968) used a task that is more difficult than the position habit used by Flexner and his colleagues. Mice were injected with AXM or saline, and 30 minutes later were trained to escape foot shock by running into the lighted arm of a T maze. All subjects learned the task, but the performance of the group that received AXM declined within a few hours. AXM did not affect the formation of STM, but it did appear to prevent (or severely retard) consolidation. (See **FIGURE 20.22.**)

It is impossible to say anything conclusive about these studies. Most investigators believe that protein synthesis is necessary for memory consolidation, but not because of the experimental evidence I have just described. Instead, this belief is sustained by our knowledge of the role that proteins play in the biochemistry of structural change. It is quite possible that we will never find a drug that effectively prevents consolidation by general suppression of protein synthesis. Per-

FIGURE 20.22 Acquisition and retention of a position habit of control subjects and of mice injected with AXM. (Redrawn from Barondes, S. H., and Cohen, H. D., *Nature*, 1968, *218*, 271–273.)

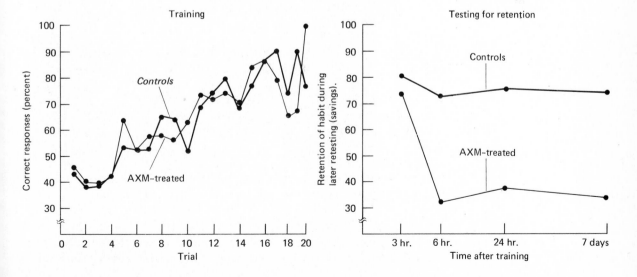

haps we will have to find out *which* proteins are involved in consolidation, and how they work, before we can prove that their selective inhibition can prevent short-term memories from becoming long-term ones. We may be in for a long wait.

Facilitation of RNA and Protein Synthesis

It would be wonderful if we could eat something that would make us smarter, or that would at least make us learn faster. We must remember, however, that the human brain has been evolving for many millions of years; thus, it does not seem reasonable that processes such as RNA and protein synthesis can be "improved upon" by drugs. (Certainly there are stimulants that can increase the rate of acquisition of a task, but these probably work by nonspecific means such as increased arousal—see Dawson and McGaugh, 1973, for a review.) The more we learn about the complex arrangements of biochemical systems within cells, and between them, the more crude our biochemical manipulations appear. Nature had a long time to select for chemicals that optimize the way things work.

A drug called *TCAP* (tricyanoaminopropene) has been reported to facilitate RNA and protein synthesis (Hydén and Egyhazi, 1962). Early reports (Schmidt and Davenport, 1967) found that this drug facilitates maze performance. However, later studies found that TCAP is an antithyroid drug that actually *impairs* learning (Gurowitz, Gross, and George, 1968; Davenport, 1970). In a review article, Jarvik (1972) notes that more caution should be used before publishing such "spectacular findings" as facilitation of learning.

Another drug (*magnesium pemoline*) was reported to facilitate both RNA synthesis and learning (Plotnikoff, 1966a, 1966b, 1967). However, Stein and Yellin (1967) found no effect of this drug on RNA or protein synthesis, and other studies (Bowman, 1966; Beach and Kimble, 1967) found that magnesium pemoline produced changes in activity and emotionality that would have accounted for the apparent facilitation in learning. It is safe to conclude that there is no good evidence yet for improvements in learning produced by facilitation of biosynthetic processes involved in physical change.

TRANSFER OF MEMORY

It would be nice to eat something to help us learn; it would be even more wonderful if we could eat something that would *make* us learn. I don't think this day will come, however. All the evidence we have so far suggests that memories are represented in *neural circuits*, not in *neurons*. You know what RNA is, and how it directs the production of specific proteins within the cell. At any one time there are countless species of RNA present in the brain. It would be an extraordinary event if the various kinds of RNA extracted from the brains of "trained animals" could find their various ways to the appropriate cells and initiate the right kinds of physical changes. Considering the fact that there is no evidence for the uptake of such large molecules through neural membranes, the transfer of memory by means of RNA injections would be especially surprising.

Nevertheless, experiments have successively obtained "transfer of learning" in rats. (Many studies have been done with *planaria*, a small flatworm. However, there is considerable disagreement as to whether planaria can even *learn*, so I shall not discuss these studies here.) Chapouthier (1973) reviewed these studies and noted that there seemed to be some features that characterized experiments that succeeded in obtaining interanimal transfer.

1. Crude extracts of RNA work best; experiments that used purified extracts generally did not succeed.
2. Larger doses are more likely to achieve positive results.
3. Transfer is usually not observed unless a sufficient amount of time is permitted to elapse after the injection before the recipient animal is tested.
4. The donors (trained animals) should be brought to a high level of performance and should be kept there for a few days before sacrificing them and preparing the extract.

The fact that crude extracts tend to work better than purified extracts of RNA suggests that it is some impurity, and not the RNA, that accomplished the "transfer" effect. In fact, Rosenblatt, Farrow, and Herblin (1966) found that *ribonuclease* (an enzyme that destroys RNA) did not block the effectiveness of their RNA extract. They concluded that the active factor was a polypeptide that was "contaminating" the extract.

Scotophobin

Ungar and his colleagues have identified some polypeptides that are capable of "transferring memory." Rats were shocked in the dark compartment of a two-chambered box, and learned to remain in the lighted side. Animals that received brain extracts spent more time in the lighted side than did controls (Ungar, Golvan, and Clark, 1968). The active ingredient was finally isolated and purified; it appears to be a polypeptide composed of fifteen amino acids (Ungar, Desiderio, and Parr, 1972).   The substance was named *scotophobin* (fear of dark).

As Smith (1974) has noted, there are methodological problems with these experiments, however, since Ungar and his colleagues did not provide a control group of mice that received noncontingent foot shock, that is, randomly presented shock in both compartments of the training apparatus.   It could be that "scotophobin" is a stress-related factor that would be produced by a variety of procedures—not just training to avoid the dark.   It could be that the chemical acts like a tranquilizer, reducing the fear produced when an animal is put into a novel situation.   Instead of hiding in the dark, the subjects now explore the lighted compartment of the apparatus.

Importance of Control Groups

Frank, Stein, and Rosen (1970) provided clear evidence for a non-specific form of transfer.   They subjected mice to several kinds of treatments.   One group received training in a shock-avoidance task. Another was placed in the training apparatus, but was not shocked. Animals in a third group were placed in a jar and were rolled about, receiving nonspecific stress (i.e., stress that was not related to per-formance of the avoidance task).   After these treatments, the mice were killed and extracts were made from the brain and liver.   (No one would suggest that the liver "learns" an avoidance task.)   Recip-ient mice were injected with the various extracts and were then trained in the shock-avoidance task.   Performance was facilitated by injections of extracts from either the trained or the stressed mice; as a matter of fact, the extracts from the mice that had been rolled in the jar worked the best.   Furthermore, liver extracts worked as well as did brain extracts.   Clearly, the stressed mice learned nothing about the avoidance task by being rolled in a jar.   This experiment shows us how treatments other than learning can cause the produc-tion of humoral factors that alter the performance of recipient sub-jects in ways that are clearly unrelated to learning.

The issue has not been resolved.   It has not yet been demon-strated to everyone's satisfaction that scotophobin really works (Gold-stein, Sheehan, and Goldstein, 1971, failed to obtain a facilitatory effect) and it is not known under what conditions scotophobin is produced.   If it is liberated only when animals are shocked in a lighted place and are allowed to escape to the dark, then one might argue that it mediates some sort of memory for this task.   If a variety of procedures can cause its release, then it would be viewed quite differ-ently.

Even those investigators who believe that specific information can be transferred by chemical means do not argue that we have to alter our notion of how the memory process works; they conceive of "chemical memory" as being an adjunct to memory encoded by structural change (Rosenblatt, 1967; Best, 1968; Ungar, 1968). If these chemicals are molecules the size of scotophobin, it is clear that they can directly affect the activity of neurons only by being recognized by receptor sites. Perhaps there are a number of neural circuits in an animal's brain that can be activated by specific neurochemicals, thus facilitating particular kinds of behaviors. It is difficult to imagine how the number of already-existing circuits could be as great as the number of experiences an animal could have, however.

Terkel and Rosenblatt's studies (cited in chapter 16) demonstrated, by means of chemical transfer, that there is a factor present in the bloodstream of rats at the time of parturition (the act of giving birth) that facilitates behaviors related to pup care. Furthermore, this factor does not appear to be any of the known hormones. These results suggest that even rather complex behaviors can be facilitated by chemical factors; it is not difficult to conceive of the existence of neurochemicals that will increase an animal's tendency to approach sources of light, or avoid them, or become more active, or remain relatively immobile.

CONCLUSIONS

In the last three chapters I have discussed evidence from a very small fraction of the experiments that have been performed in an attempt to discover something about the physiology of memory. I have concluded that memories (at least in the higher primates) are stored in association cortex related to the sensory modality through which the information is received. Complex memories requiring cross-modal interaction involve specific interconnections among these association areas of cortex. Short-term memories appear to be mediated by neural activity (perhaps reverberation), and long-term memories appear to consist of physical changes in neurons. The short-term memories appear to occupy approximately the same regions of cortex as the long-term memories into which they become consolidated.

Besides consolidation, there appears to be a process of cross-indexing or cataloging, which is disrupted by disturbances such as electroconvulsive shock and, in humans, bilateral damage to Papez's circuit. It appears likely, but not yet certain, that ECS disrupts both consolidation and cataloging.

Little is currently known about the nature of the physical

changes that mediate memory. The last chapter has been devoted to the process of cellular change, and an evaluation of the approaches that have been made so far to find out what memory really is. This chapter has therefore been more of a preparation to understand what future research will tell us than a summary of what we know about the physical basis of memory.

There are many problems I have not been able to address in these three chapters. For example, I have treated memory as if it consisted of simple associations, ignoring the fact that memories are organized in temporal sequences. A memory of an event that is retrieved resembles a movie more than a still photograph. What is the process that provides the time sequence of our memories? No one can say. And how does retrieval work? How is it that we can locate most memories so fast? Our total memory storage must run to many millions of bits of information, and yet we do not have to search through everything in order to find the representation of a particular experience stored there. Is there some sort of directory that contains a listing of memories along with their "addresses"? If so, we know nothing at all about the wherabouts of this directory or the way in which it works. It has been said that the more one studies a subject, the more one realizes one's ignorance. Of all the topics that I have covered in this book, none exemplifies this statement more than the memory process.

Afterword

In the preface I invited you to write to me so that we could discuss this book or issues raised (or not raised) here. I should like to extend this invitation again. My address is given in the preface. As I wrote this book, I had an invisible set of readers in mind; it would be very gratifying to hear from some of you.

SUGGESTED READINGS

BOHINSKI, R. C. *Modern Concepts in Biochemistry,* ed. 2. Boston: Allyn and Bacon, Inc., 1976.

ROLLER, A. *Discovering the Basis of Life.* New York: McGraw-Hill, 1974.

These books will provide more information about biochemistry and molecular biology; Bohinski's book is the more detailed of the two.

ENTINGH, D., DUNN, A., GLASSMAN, E., WILSON, J. E., HOGAN, E., and DAMSTRA, T. Biochemical approaches to the biology of memory. In *Handbook of Psychobiology,* edited by M. S. Gazzaniga and C. Blakemore. New York: Academic Press, 1975. This excellent chapter summarizes the biochemistry of memory and presents a critique of the research methods that have been employed.

CHAPOUTHIER, G. Behavioral studies of the molecular basis of memory. In *The Physiological Basis of Memory,* edited by J. A. Deutsch. New York: Academic Press, 1973.

JARVIK, M. E. Effects of chemical and physical treatments on learning and memory. *Annual Review of Psychology,* 1972, 23, 457–486.

These references discuss attempts to transfer memory by chemical means and to alter the memory process by physical and chemical means.

Glossary

Ablation: The intentional removal or destruction of portions of the central nervous system. Synonym: *brain lesion.*

Absorptive phase: The phase of metabolism during which nutrients are absorbed from the digestive system. Glucose and amino acids constitute the principal source of energy for cells during this phase. Stores of glycogen are increased and excess nutrients are stored in adipose tissue in the form of lipids.

Acetylcholine (ACh): A neurotransmitter found in the brain, spinal cord, ganglia of the autonomic nervous system, and postganglionic terminals of the parasympathetic division of the autonomic nervous system.

Acetylcholinesterase (AChE): The enzyme that destroys acetylcholine soon after it is liberated by the terminal buttons, thus terminating the postsynaptic potential.

ACh: See *acetylcholine.*

AChE: See *acetylcholinesterase.*

ACTH: See *adrenocorticotrophic hormone.*

Actin: Actin and *myosin* are the proteins that provide the physical basis for muscular contraction. See Figure 10.3.

Action potential: The brief electrical impulse that provides the basis for conduction of information along an axon. The action potential results from brief changes in membrane permeability to sodium and potassium ions. See Figure 3.11.

Activational effect: See *hormone.*

AD: See *androstenedione.*

Adenine: One of the nucleotide bases of RNA and DNA.

Adenohypophysis: See *pituitary gland.*

Adenosine triphosphate (ATP): A molecule of prime importance to cellular energy metabolism; the conversion of ATP to ADP liberates energy. ATP can also be converted to *cyclic AMP,* which serves as intermediate messenger in the production of postsynaptic potentials by some neurotransmitters, and in the mediation of the effects of protein hormones. See *adenyl cyclase* and Figure 5.10.

Adenyl cyclase: An enzyme that converts *ATP* to *cyclic AMP* when the receptor to which it is bound is stimulated by the appropriate substance. See *adenosine triphosphate* and Figure 5.10.

ADH: See *antidiuretic hormone.*

Adipose tissue: Fat tissue, composed of cells that can absorb nutrients from the blood and store them in the form of lipids during the *absorptive phase,* or release them in the form of fatty acids and keto acids during the *fasting phase.*

Adipsia: Complete lack of drinking; can be produced by lesions in the lateral hypothalamus.

Adrenocorticotrophic hormone (ACTH): A hormone produced and liberated by the anterior pituitary in response to ACTH releasing hormone, produced by the hypothalamus. ACTH stimulates the adrenal cortex to produce various corticosteroid hormones. ACTH also inhibits testosterone-dependent intermale aggression.

Affect (ăf′fĕct′): An emotional state of strong feelings, either positive or negative in nature.

Affective attack: A highly emotional attack of one animal upon another; can be elicited by electrical stimulation of certain regions of the brain. Contrasts with *quiet-biting attack.*

Agonist: Literally, a contestant. An agonistic drug facilitates the effects of a particular neurotransmitter on the postsynaptic cell. An agonistic muscle produces or facilitates a particular movement. Antonym: *antagonist*.

Aldosterone: A hormone of the adrenal cortex that causes the retention of sodium by the kidneys.

All-or-none law: Refers to the fact that once an action potential is triggered in an axon, it is propagated, without decrement, to the end of the fiber.

Alpha activity: Smooth electrical activity of 8 to 12 Hz, recorded from the brain. Alpha activity is generally associated with a state of relaxation.

Alpha motor neuron: A neuron whose cell body is located in the ventral horn of the spinal cord or in one of the motor nuclei of the cranial nerves. Stimulation of an alpha motor neuron results in contraction of the extrafusal muscle fibers upon which its terminal buttons synapse.

Amino acid: A molecule that contains both an amino group and a carboxyl group. Amino acids are linked together by peptide bonds and serve as the constituents of proteins.

Amino group: NH_2; two molecules of hydrogen attached to a molecule of nitrogen.

Aminostatic theory: The theory that hunger and satiety depend on the level of amino acids in the blood plasma, low levels being associated with hunger.

Amplifier: An electronic device that increases the amplitude of a small electrical signal.

AMPT: See *α-methyl-para-tyrosine*.

Amygdala: The term commonly used for the amygdaloid complex, a set of nuclei located in the base of the temporal lobe. The amygdala is a part of the limbic system.

Analgesia: Lack of sensitivity to pain.

Androgen: A male sex steroid hormone. *Testosterone* is the principal mammalian androgen.

Androgenization: The process initiated by exposure of the cells of a developing animal to androgens. Exposure to androgen causes embryonic sex organs to develop as male, and produces certain changes in the brain. See *hormone*.

Androstenedione (AD): An androgen secreted by adrenal cortex of both males and females.

Angiotensin: See *renin*.

Angiotensinogen: See *renin*.

Anion: See *ion*.

Antagonist: The muscle that produces a movement contrary or opposite to the one being described. An antagonistic drug opposes or inhibits the effects of a particular neurotransmitter on the postsynaptic cell.

Anterior: See Figure 6.1.

Anterior pituitary gland: See *pituitary gland*.

Anterior thalamus: A group of three thalamic nuclei that receive fibers from the mammillary bodies and project fibers to the *cingulate gyrus*, and thus comprise a portion of *Papez's circuit*.

Anterograde amnesia: See *posttraumatic amnesia*.

Anterograde degeneration: Rapid degeneration of an axon distal to its point of damage. See Figure 7.6.

Antidiuretic hormone (ADH): A hormone secreted by the posterior pituitary gland that causes the kidneys to excrete a more concentrated urine, thus retaining water in the body.

Antipsychotic drug: A drug that reduces or eliminates the symptoms of psychosis. Antischizophrenic drugs exert their effect by antagonizing dopaminergic synapses.

Aphagia: Complete lack of eating. Can be produced by lesion of the lateral hypothalamus.

Arachnoid: The middle layer of the *meninges*, between the outer *dura mater* and inner *pia mater*.

Arcuate fasciculus: A bundle of long association fibers that interconnect *Wernicke's area* on the left temporal lobe with *Broca's speech area* on the left frontal lobe. Damage to the arcuate fasciculus results in *conduction aphasia*.

Arcuate nucleus: The hypothalamic nucleus that contains the cell bodies of neurosecretory cells that produce the hypothalamic hormones.

Area postrema: A region of the medulla where the *blood-brain barrier* is weak. Systemic poisons can be detected there, and can initiate vomiting.

Arousal: A state of alertness characterized by relative pupillary dilation and *beta activity* of the EEG.

Astrocyte (astroglia): A glial cell that provides support and transmission of nutrients and waste products to and from neurons of the central nervous system. Astrocytes also participate in the formation of scar tissue after injury to the brain or spinal cord.

ATP: See *adenosine triphosphate.*

Auditory nerve: The auditory nerve has two principal branches. The *cochlear nerve* transmits auditory information and the *vestibular nerve* transmits information related to balance.

Autonomic nervous system (ANS): The portion of the peripheral nervous system that controls the body's vegetative function. The *sympathetic branch* mediates functions that accompany arousal, while the *parasympathetic branch* mediates functions that occur during a relaxed state.

Axoaxonic synapse: The synapse of a *terminal button* upon the axon of another neuron, near its terminals. These synapses mediate presynaptic inhibition.

Axodendritic synapse: The synapse of a *terminal button* of the axon of one cell upon the dendrite of another cell.

Axon: A thin elongated process of a neuron that can transmit action potentials toward its terminal buttons, which synapse on other neurons, gland cells, or muscle cells.

Axosomatic synapse: The synapse of a *terminal button* of the axon of one neuron upon the membrane of the soma, or cell body, of another neuron.

Baroreceptor: A special receptor that transduces changes in barometric pressure (chiefly within the heart or blood vessels) into neural activity.

Basilar artery: An artery found at the base of the brain, connecting the blood supplies of the *vertebral* and *carotid arteries.*

Basolateral group: The phylogenetically newer portion of the amygdaloid complex. See *amygdala.*

Beta activity: Irregular electrical activity of 13 to 30 Hz, recorded from the brain. Beta activity is generally associated with a state of arousal.

Bilateral: On both sides of the midline of the body.

Bipolar neuron: A neuron with only two processes—a dendritic process at one end and an axonal process at the other end. See Figure 2.6.

Blood-brain barrier: A barrier produced by the *astrocytes* and cells in the walls of the capillaries in the brain; this barrier permits passage of only certain substances.

Bregma: The junction of the sagittal and coronal sutures of the skull. It is often used as a reference point for stereotaxic brain surgery.

Broca's speech area: A region of frontal cortex, located at the base of the left precentral gyrus, that is necessary for normal speech production. Damage to this region results in *Broca's aphasia,* characterized by extreme difficulty in speech articulation.

Cable properties: Passive conduction of electrical current, in a decremental fashion, down the length of an axon, similar to the way in which electrical current traverses a submarine cable.

Cannula: A small metal tube that may be inserted into the brain to permit introduction of chemicals or removal of fluid for analysis.

Carboxyl group: COOH; two atoms of oxygen and one atom of hydrogen bound to a single atom of carbon.

Carotid artery: An artery, the branches of which serve the rostral portions of the brain.

Cation: See *ion.*

Caudal: See Figure 6.1.

Caudate nucleus: A telencephalic nucleus, one of the basal ganglia. The caudate nucleus is principally involved with inhibitory control of movement.

Central canal: The narrow tube, filled with cerebrospinal fluid, that runs through the length of the spinal cord.

Central gray of the tegmentum: Stimulation of this brain region may result in aggressive behavior and also can produce analgesia.

Cerebral aqueduct: A narrow tube interconnecting the third and fourth *ventricles* of the brain.

Cerebral cortex: The outermost layer of gray matter of the cerebral hemispheres.

Cerebrospinal fluid: A clear fluid, similar to blood plasma, that fills the ventricular system of the brain and spinal cord, and in which they float.

Cerveau isolé: A *mid-collicular transection;* a brainstem transection that results in a chronically comatose animal.

Chemoreceptor: A receptor that responds, by means of receptor potentials or neural impulses, to the presence of a particular chemical.

Choroid plexus: Highly vascular tissue that protrudes into the *ventricles* and produces *cerebrospinal fluid.*

Cingulate gyrus: A strip of limbic cortex lying along the lateral walls of the groove separating the cerebral hemispheres, just above the *corpus callosum.* See *Papez's circuit.*

Circumstriate belt: A region of visual association cortex; receives fibers from *striate cortex* and from the *superior colliculi,* and projects (in monkeys) to *inferotemporal cortex.*

CNS: Central nervous system; the brain and spinal cord.

Cochlea: The snail-shaped structure of the inner ear that contains the auditory transducing mechanisms.

Cochlear nerve: See *auditory nerve.*

Codon: The basic three-letter word of the genetic code. Each codon (represented by a sequence of three nucleotide bases on a strand of messenger RNA) specifies a particular amino acid that will be added to a *polypeptide* chain.

Commissure: A fiber bundle that interconnects corresponding regions on each side of the brain.

Conduction aphasia: Damage to the *arcuate fasciculus,* which interconnects *Wernicke's area* and *Broca's speech area,* results in the inability to repeat words that are heard, although they can usually be understood and responded to appropriately.

Cone: See *photoreceptor.*

Consolidation: The process by which *short-term memories* are converted into *long-term memories.*

Contralateral: Residing in the side of the body opposite to the reference point.

Convergence: See Figure 10.10.

Coolidge effect: The restorative effect of introducing a new female sex partner to a male that has apparently become "exhausted" by sexual activity.

Coronal section: See Figure 6.2.

Corpus callosum: The largest commissure of the brain, interconnecting the areas of association cortex on each side of the brain.

Corpus luteum: After ovulation, the ovarian follicle develops into a corpus luteum, and secretes estrogen and progesterone.

Correctional mechanism: In a regulatory process the correctional mechanism is that which is capable of changing the value of the system variable.

Corticomedial group: The phylogenetically older portion of the amygdaloid complex.

Cranial nerve: One of a set of twelve pairs of nerves that exit from the base of the brain.

Cranial nerve ganglion: See *ganglion.*

Cross section: See Figure 6.2.

CSF: See *cerebrospinal fluid.*

Cyclic AMP: See *adenyl cyclase.*

Cytoplasm: The viscous semiliquid substance contained in the interior of a cell.

D sleep: A period of desynchronized sleep, during which dreaming and rapid eye movement occur. Also called *REM sleep* (for the rapid eye movements) and *paradoxical sleep* for the fact that EEG activity resembles that of arousal.

Decremental conduction: Conduction of a subthreshold stimulus along an axon, according to its *cable properties.*

Decussation: Crossing of a fiber to the other side of the brain.

Delta activity: A regular synchronous electrical activity of approximately 3 to 5 Hz, recorded from the brain. Delta activity is generally associated with slow wave sleep (*S sleep*).

Dendrite: Treelike processes attached to the *soma* of a neuron, which receives *terminal buttons* from other neurons.

Dendritic spine: Small buds on the surface of a dendrite, on which synapse terminal buttons from other neurons.

2-Deoxy-D-glucose (2-DG): A sugar that interferes with the metabolism of glucose.

Deoxyribonucleic acid (DNA): A long complex macromolecule consisting of two interconnected helical strands. Strands of DNA, along with their associated proteins, constitute the chromosomes that contain the genetic information of the animal.

Depolarization: Reduction (toward zero) of the membrane potential of a cell from its normal resting potential of approximately −70 mV.

Desynchrony: Irregular electrical activity recorded from the brain, generally associated with periods of arousal. See *beta activity.*

Detector: In a regulatory process, a mechanism that signals when the system variable deviates from its set point.

2-DG: See *2-deoxy-D-glucose.*

Diabetes mellitus: A disease that results from insufficient production of *insulin,* thus causing, in an untreated state, a high level of blood glucose.

Differentiation: The process by which cells in a developing organism begin to develop differentially, into specialized organs.

Diffusion: Movement of molecules from regions of high concentration to regions of low concentration.

Disulfide bond: A chemical bond between the sulfur molecules of two molecules of cysteine. These bonds are chiefly responsible for the three-dimensional structures of proteins.

Divergence: See Figure 10.10.

DNA: See *deoxyribonucleic acid.*

Dorsal: See Figure 6.1.

Dorsal root: See *spinal root.*

Dorsal root ganglion: See *ganglion.*

Drive-inducing effect: The hypothesized effect of rewarding electrical stimulation of the brain that provides the drive that motivates the animal to seek further stimulation.

Duodenum: The portion of the small intestine immediately adjacent to the stomach.

Dura mater: The outermost layer of the three *meninges.*

ECS: See *electroconvulsive shock.*

EEG: See *electroencephalogram.*

Effector: A muscle or gland, or one of the active cells of these organs.

Electroconvulsive shock (ECS): A brief electrical shock, applied to the head, that results in electrical seizure and convulsions. Used therapeutically to alleviate severe depression, and experimentally (in animals) to study the *consolidation* process.

Electrode: A conductive medium (generally made of metal) that can be used to apply electrical stimulation or record electrical potentials.

Electroencephalogram (EEG): Electrical brain potentials recorded by placing *electrodes* on or in the scalp or on the surface of the brain.

Electrolyte: An aqueous solution of a material that ionizes—namely, a soluble acid, base, or salt.

Electromyogram: Electrical potential recorded from an electrode placed on or in a muscle.

Electrostatic pressure: The attractive force between atomic particles charged with opposite signs, or the repulsive force between atomic particles charged with the same sign.

Encéphale isolé: An animal whose central nervous system has been severed transversely between the brain and spinal cord, resulting in paralysis but possessing normal sleep-waking cycles.

Endocrine gland: A gland that liberates its secretions into the extracellular fluid around capillaries, and hence into the bloodstream.

Ependyma: The layer of tissue around blood vessels and on the interior walls of the ventricular system of the brain.

Epinephrine: A hormone, secreted by the adrenal medulla, that produces physiological effects characteristic of the sympathetic division of the *autonomic nervous system.*

EPSP: See *postsynaptic potential.*

Equilibrium: A balance of forces, during which a system is not changing.

Estrogen: A sex hormone that causes maturation of the female genitalia, growth of breast tissue, and development of other physical features characteristic of females. Estrogen is also necessary for normal sexual behavior of most mammals other than humans.

Estrous cycle: A cyclic change in the hormonal level and sexual receptivity of sub-primate mammals.

Estrus: That portion of the *estrous cycle* during which a female is sexually receptive.

Et al. (et alii): And others.

Evoked potential: A regular series of alterations in the slow electrical activity recorded from the central nervous system, produced by a sensory stimulus or an electrical shock to some part of the nervous system.

Excitatory postsynaptic potential: See *postsynaptic potential.*

Exocrine gland: A gland that liberates its secretions into a duct.

Extracellular thirst: See *volumetric thirst.*

Extrafusal muscle fiber: One of the muscle fibers that are responsible for the force exerted by a muscular contraction.

Extrapyramidal motor system: A complex system of structures in the brain, including the basal ganglia, pontine nuclei, cerebellum, parts of the reticular formation, and their connections with motor neurons of the spinal cord and cranial nerve nuclei.

Fascia: A sheet of fibrous connective tissue encasing a muscle.

Fasting phase: The phase of metabolism during which nutrients are not available from the digestive system. Glucose, amino acids, fatty acids, and keto acids are derived from glycogen, protein, and adipose tissue during this phase.

Fatty acid: A substance of importance to metabolism; during the fasting phase fats can be broken down to fatty acids, which can be metabolized by most cells of the body. The basic structure of a fatty acid (which may be saturated or unsaturated) is an alkyl group (CH_3) attached to a carboxyl group $(COOH)$.

Fimbria: A fiber bundle that runs along the lateral surface of the hippocampal complex, connecting this structure with other regions of the forebrain, especially the hypothalamus. The fibers of the fimbria become the *fornix* as they course rostrally from the hippocampal complex.

Fissure: A major groove in the surface of the brain. A smaller groove is called a *sulcus.*

Fistula: An artificial opening or tube into a normal cavity of the body. For example, a gastric fistula permits introduction of substances into the stomach, or their removal from it.

Follicle: A small secretory cavity. The ovarian follicle consists of epithelial cells surrounding an oocyte, which develops into an ovum.

Follicle-stimulating hormone: The hormone of the anterior pituitary gland that causes development of a follicle and maturation of its oocyte into an ovum.

Foramen: A normal passage that allows communication between two cavities of the body. The intervertebral foramen permits passage of the spinal nerves through the vertebral column. The foramina of Megendie and of Luschka permit the passage of CSF out of the fourth ventricle and into the subarachnoid space. The foramen of Monroe interconnects the lateral and third ventricles.

Forebrain: See Table 6.1

Fornix: See *fimbria.*

Fourth ventricle: See *ventricle.*

Fovea: The region of the retina that mediates the most acute vision of birds and higher mammals. Color-sensitive cones constitute the only type of photoreceptor found in the fovea.

Foveal prestriate area: A region of the *circumstriate belt* of visual association cortex, located adjacent to primary visual cortex, mediating foveal vision.

Frontal section: See Figure 6.2.

Fructose: Fruit sugar; a monosaccharide that can be used in metabolism. Since fructose cannot cross the blood-brain barrier, it cannot be utilized by the brain.

FSH: See *follicle-stimulating hormone.*

FTG: The *gigantocellular tegmental field* of the pons. Activity of neurons in this region appears to be important in the production of D sleep.

Gamete: A mature reproductive cell; a sperm or ovum.

Gamma motor neuron: A lower motor neuron whose terminal buttons synapse upon *intrafusal muscle fibers.*

Ganglion: A collection of neural cell bodies, covered with connective tissue, located outside the central nervous system. *Autonomic ganglia* contain the cell bodies of postganglionic neurons of the sympathetic and parasympathetic branches of the *autonomic nervous system.* *Dorsal root ganglia* (*spinal nerve ganglia*) contain cell bodies of afferent spinal nerve neurons. *Cranial nerve ganglia* contain cell bodies of afferent cranial nerve neurons. The *basal ganglia* include the *amygdala, caudate nucleus, globus pallidus,* and *putamen;* in this case the term *ganglion* is a misnomer, since the basal ganglia are actually brain nuclei.

Gene: The functional unit of the chromosome, which directs synthesis of one or more proteins.

Generator potential: A graded electrical potential produced by the transducing action of a specialized neuron that serves as a *receptor cell.*

Gestagen: A group of hormones (the progestins) that promote and support pregnancy.

Gigantocellular tegmental field: See *FTG.*

Glia: The supportive cells of the central nervous system—the *astroglia, oligodendroglia,* and *microglia.*

Gliosis: The process by which dead neurons are destroyed and replaced with glial cells.

Globus pallidus: One of the basal ganglia (see *ganglion*); an excitatory structure of the *extrapyramidal motor system.*

Glucagon: A pancreatic hormone that promotes the conversion of liver *glygogen* into *glucose.*

Glucocorticoid: One of a group of hormones of the adrenal cortex that are important in protein and carbohydrate metabolism, secreted especially in times of stress.

Glucoprivation: A state in which the cells of the body are deprived of glucose; can occur when injections of insulin lower the blood glucose level drastically.

Glucose: A simple sugar, of great importance in metabolism. Glucose and *keto acids* constitute the major source of energy for the brain.

Glucostatic theory: A theory that states that the level or availability of glucose in the blood determines whether an organism is hungry or sated.

Glycogen: A polysaccharide often referred to as animal starch. The hormone *glucagon* causes conversion of liver glycogen into glucose.

Glycogenolysis: The conversion of glycogen into glucose within a cell.

Gold thioglucose (GTG): A molecule consisting of glucose, to which are attached molecules of gold and sulfur. Administration of GTG results in brain damage, especially in the region of the *ventromedial nucleus of the hypothalamus (VMH).*

Golgi apparatus: A complex of parallel membranes in the cytoplasm of a cell that wraps the products of a secretory cell.

Golgi tendon organ: The receptive organ at the junction of the tendon and muscle that is sensitive to stretch.

Gonadotrophin: A hormone of the anterior pituitary gland that has a stimulating effect on cells of the gonads. See *follicle-stimulating hormone* and *luteinizing hormone.*

Graded potential: A slow electrical potential in a neuron or a receptor cell (generator potential, PSP, or receptor potential).

Gradient: A grade or slope; more typically, a change in the amount or concentration of a substance with distance or with time.

Growth hormone (GH; also called *somatotrophic hormone,* or *STH):* A hormone that is necessary for the normal growth of the body before adulthood; also causes the conversion of glycogen to glucose, and thus has an anti-insulin effect.

GTG: See *gold thioglucose.*

Guanine: One of the nucleotide bases of RNA and DNA.

Gyrus: A convolution of the cortex of the cerebral hemispheres, separated by *sulci* or *fissures.*

Hair cell: The receptive cell of the auditory or vestibular apparatus.

Hepatic portal system: The system of blood vessels that drains the capillaries of the digestive system, travels to the liver, and divides again into capillaries.

Hindbrain: See Table 6.1.

Hippocampus: A forebrain structure of the temporal lobe, constituting an important part of the *limbic system* and of *Papez's circuit.*

Histology: The microscopic study of tissues of the body.

Horizontal section: See Figure 6.2.

Hormone: A chemical substance liberated by an endocrine gland that has effects on target cells in other organs. *Organizational effects* of a hormone affect tissue differentiation and development; for example, androgens cause prenatal development of male genitalia. *Activational effects* of a hormone are those that occur in the fully developed organism; many of these depend upon the organism's prior exposure to the organizational effects of hormones.

6-Hydroxydopamine: A chemical that is selectively taken up by axons and terminals of noradrenergic or dopaminergic neurons and that acts as a poison, damaging or killing them.

Hyperphagia: Excessive intake of food.

Hyperpolarization: An increase in the membrane potential of a cell, relative to the normal resting potential. *Inhibitory postsynaptic potentials (IPSPs)* are hyperpolarizations.

Hypoglycemia: A low level of blood glucose.

Hypopolarization: See *depolarization.*

Hypothalamic hormone: A hormone produced by cells of the hypothalamus that affects the secretion and production of hormones of the anterior pituitary gland. The effects are excitatory in the case of *releasing hormones (releasing factors)* and inhibitory in the case of *inhibiting hormones (inhibiting factors).*

Hypothalamic-hypophyseal portal system: A system of blood vessels that connects capillaries of the hypothalamus with capillaries of the anterior pituitary gland. Hypothalamic hormones travel to the anterior pituitary gland by means of this system.

Hypovolemia: See *volumetric thirst.*

Immune system: The system by which the body protects itself from foreign proteins. In response to an infection the white blood cells produce antibodies that attack and destroy the foreign antigen.

Incus: One of the bones of the middle ear. See Figure 8.10.

Inferior: See Figure 6.1.

Inferior colliculi: Protrusions on top of the midbrain that relay auditory information to the medial geniculate nucleus.

Inferotemporal cortex: In monkeys, the highest level of visual association cortex, located on the inferior surface of the temporal lobe. The exact location of the homologus structure in humans is not known.

Inhibitory postsynaptic potential: See *postsynaptic potential.*

Insulin: A pancreatic hormone that facilitates entry of glucose and amino acids into the cell, facilitates conversion of glucose into glycogen, and facilitates production of fats in *adipose tissue.*

Integration: The process by which inhibitory and excitatory postsynaptic potentials summate and control the rate of firing of a neuron.

Intermediate horn (of gray matter of spinal cord): Location of the cell bodies of *preganglionic* neurons of the sympathetic branch of the autonomic nervous system and of the sacral portion of the parasympathetic branch.

Intrafusal muscle fiber: A muscle fiber that functions as a stretch receptor, arranged in parallel with the *extrafusal muscle fibers,* thus detecting muscle length.

Intragastric fistula: A tube that can be used to introduce substances into the stomach, or to remove substances from it.

Intraoral fistula: A tube that can be used to introduce substances into the mouth.

Intraperitoneal (IP): Pertaining to the peritoneal cavity, the space surrounding the abdominal organs.

Intromission: Insertion of one part into another, especially of a penis into a vagina.

Ion: A charged molecule; *cations* are negatively charged and *anions* are positively charged.

IP: See *intraperitoneal.*

Ipsilateral: Located on the same side of the body as the point of reference.

IPSP: See *postsynaptic potential.*

Isolated cortical slab: A region of cortex surgically separated from surrounding tissue but with a relatively intact blood supply.

Iso-osmotic: Equal in osmotic pressure.

Isotonic: Equal in osmotic pressure to the contents of a cell. A cell placed in an isotonic solution neither gains nor loses water.

Keto acid: An organic acid consisting of two hydrocarbon radicals attached to a carbonyl group (CO). Keto acids are produced from the breakdown of fats, and can be utilized by the brain.

Krebs cycle (citric acid cycle, tricarboxylic acid cycle): A series of chemical reactions that involve oxidation of pyruvate. The Krebs cycle takes place on the cristae of the mitochondria, and supplies the principal source of energy to the cell.

Lactate: Noun: a salt of lactic acid; produced when muscles metabolize glycogen in the absence of oxygen. Verb: to produce milk.

Latency: The time interval between an event and a succeeding event that is caused by it.

Lateral: See Figure 6.1.

Lateral geniculate nucleus: A group of cell bodies within the lateral geniculate body of the thalamus. It receives fibers from the retina and projects fibers to primary visual cortex.

Lateral hypothalamus (LH): A region of the hypothalamus that contains cell bodies and diffuse fiber systems. The *LH syndrome* that follows destruction of the lateral hypothalamus is characterized by a relative lack of spontaneous movement, *adipsia,* and *aphagia,* from which the animal at least partially recovers.

Lateral lemniscus: A band of fibers running rostrally through the medulla and pons, which carries fibers of the auditory system.

Lateral ventricle: See *ventricle.*

Lemniscal system: The somatosensory fibers of the lateral or trigeminal lemniscus, as contrasted with the extralemniscal system, a polysynaptic pathway that ascends through the reticular formation.

LH: See *lateral hypothalamus* or *luteinizing hormone.*

LH syndrome: See *lateral hypothalamus.*

Limbic system: A group of brain regions including the anterior thalamus, amygdala, hippocampus, limbic cortex, and parts of the hypothalamus, as well as their interconnecting fiber bundles.

Lipostatic theory: The theory that suggests that hunger and satiety depend on levels of lipids in the blood or stored in *adipose tissue.*

Locus coeruleus: A dark-colored group of cell bodies located near the rostral end of the floor of the fourth ventricle.

Long-term memory (LTM): Relatively stable memory as opposed to *short-term memory.*

Lower motor neuron: A neuron located in the *intermediate horn* or *ventral horn* of the gray matter of the spinal cord or in one of the motor nuclei of the cranial nerves, the axon of which synapses on muscle fibers.

LTM: See *long-term memory.*

Luteinizing hormone (LH): A hormone of the anterior pituitary gland that causes ovulation and development of the follicle into a *corpus luteum.*

Malleus: One of the bones of the middle ear. See Figure 8.10.

Mammillary body: A protrusion of the bottom of the brain at the posterior end of the hypothalamus, containing the medial and lateral mammillary nuclei.

Mannose: A simple sugar that may be metabolized by all cells of the body.

Massa intermedia: A bridge of tissue across the third ventricle that connects the right and left portions of the thalamus.

Medial: See Figure 6.1.

Medial dorsal nucleus (dorsomedial nucleus): A large nucleus of the thalamus that projects to prefrontal cortex and has connections with other thalamic nuclei and with the limbic system.

Medial forebrain bundle: A fiber bundle that runs in a rostral-caudal direction through the basal forebrain and lateral hypothalamus.

Medial geniculate nucleus: A group of cell bodies within the medial geniculate body of the thalamus; part of the auditory system.

Medial lemniscus: A fiber bundle that ascends rostrally through the *medulla* and *pons,* carrying fibers of the somatosensory system.

Medulla oblongata (usually *medulla*): The most caudal portion of the brain, immediately rostral to the spinal cord.

Meiosis: The process by which a cell divides to form *gametes* (sperms or ova).

Membrane: A structure consisting principally of lipid-like molecules that defines the outer boundaries of a cell, and also constitutes many of the cells organelles such as the Golgi apparatus.

Meninges (singular = *meninx):* The three layers of tissue that encase the central nervous system: the *dura mater, arachnoid,* and *pia mater.*

Mesencephalon: See Table 6.1.

Messenger ribonucleic acid: See *ribonucleic acid.*

Metabolism: The sum of all physical and chemical changes that take place in an organism, including all reactions that liberate energy. See *absorptive phase* and *fasting phase.*

Metencephalon: See Table 6.1.

α-Methyl-para-tyrosine: A substance that interferes with the activity of tyrosine hydroxylase and thus prevents the synthesis of dopamine and norepinephrine.

Microelectrode: A very fine electrode, generally used to record activity of individual neurons.

Microglia: See *glia.*

Microphonic: Electrical activity recorded from the *cochlea* that corresponds to the sound vibrations received at the oval window.

Midbrain: See Table 6.1.

Mid-collicular transection: See *cerveau isolé.*

Midline nuclei: Thalamic nuclei that lie near the midline of the brain.

Midpontine transection (also called midpontine pretrigeminal transection): A transection through the middle of the *pons* that produces an animal with ocular and electroencephalographic signs of wakefulness present most of the time.

Midsagittal plane: The plane that divides the body in two symmetrical halves through the midline.

Mirror focus (secondary epileptogenic focus): A region of neural tissue in the side of the brain opposite a primary irritative lesion that eventually becomes an epileptogenic focus, without showing any signs of physical damage.

Mitochondrion: A cell organelle in which the chemical reactions of the *Krebs cycle* take place.

Mitosis: Duplication and division of a somatic cell into a pair of daughter cells.

Modality: See *sensory modality.*

Monosynaptic stretch reflex: A reflex consisting of sensory ending of the intrafusal muscle fiber, its afferent fiber, synapsing upon an alpha motor neuron, and the efferent fiber of this neuron, synapsing on its *extrafusal muscle fibers* in the same muscle. When a muscle is quickly stretched, the monosynaptic stretch reflex causes it to contract.

Motor cortex: The precentral gyrus, which contains a considerable number of motor neurons.

Motor end plate: Region of the membrane of a muscle fiber upon which synapse terminal buttons of the efferent axon.

Motor neuron (motoneuron): A neuron, the stimulation of which results in contractions of muscle fibers.

Motor unit: A lower motor neuron and its associated muscle fibers.

mRNA: See *ribonucleic acid.*

Müllerian system: The embryonic precursors of the female internal sex organs.

Multipolar neuron: A neuron with a single axon and numerous dendritic processes originating from the somatic membrane.

Muscle spindle: A sense organ found in muscles; *intrafusal muscle fiber.*

Myelencephalon: See Table 6.1.

Myelin: A complex fat-like substance produced by the *oligodendroglia* in the central nervous system, and by the *Schwann cells* in the peripheral nervous system, that surrounds and insulates myelinated axons.

Myosin: *Actin* and *myosin* are the proteins that provide the physical basis for muscular contraction. See Figure 10.3.

Negative feedback: A process whereby the effect produced by an action serves to diminish or terminate that action. Regulatory systems are characterized by negative feedback loops.

Nephrectomy: The removal of the kidneys.

Nernst equation: $V = k \log \frac{[x_o]}{[x_i]}$; where V = membrane potential in volts, k = constant, the value of which is determined by physical conditions such as temperature and by the valence of ion x, $[x_o]$ = concentration, in millimoles per liter, of ion x outside the cell, and $[x_i]$ = concentration of ion x inside the cell.

Neurohypophysis: See *pituitary gland.*

Neuromuscular junction: The synapse between terminal buttons of an axon and a muscle fiber.

Neurosecretory cell: A neuron that secretes a hormone or hormone-like substance into the interstitial fluid.

Nigro-striatal bundle: A bundle of axons, originating in the *substantia nigra,* terminating in the neostriatum *(caudate nucleus* and *putamen).*

Nissl substance: Cytoplasmic material dyed by cell body stains (Nissl stains).

Node of Ranvier: A naked portion of a myelinated axon, between adjacent *oligodendroglia* or *Schwann cells.*

Nondecremental conduction: Conduction of an action potential in an all-or-none manner down an axon.

Norepinephrine: A neurotransmitter found in the brain and in the terminal buttons of postganglionic fibers of the sympathetic branch of the autonomic nervous system.

Nucleolus: An organelle within the nucleus of a cell that produces the ribosomes.

Nucleotide cyclase: An enzyme that causes the conversion of a triphosphate nucleotide (such as ATP) to a cyclic monophosphate nucleotide (such as cyclic AMP). See *adenyl cyclase.*

Nucleus: 1. The central portion of an atom. 2. A spherical structure, enclosed by membrane, located in the cytoplasm of most cells, and containing the chromosomes. 3. A histologically identifiable group of neural cell bodies in the central nervous system.

Olfactory bulb: The protrusion at the end of the olfactory nerve; receives input from the olfactory receptors.

Oligodendroglia: A type of glial cell in the central nervous system that form myelin sheaths.

Optic chiasm: A cross-shaped connection between the optic nerves, located below the base of the brain, just anterior to the pituitary gland.

Optic disk: See *optic nerve.*

Optic nerve: The second cranial nerve, carrying visual information from the retina to the brain. The *optic disk* is formed at the exit point of the fibers of the ganglion cells from the retina that form the optic nerve.

Organ of Corti: The receptor organ situated on the basilar membrane of the inner ear.

Organizational effect: See *hormone.*

Oscilloscope: A laboratory instrument capable of displaying a graph of voltage as a function time on the face of a cathode ray tube.

Osmometric thirst: Thirst produced by an increase in the osmotic pressure of the interstitial fluid relative to intracellular fluid, thus producing cellular dehydration.

Osmosis: Movement of ions through a semipermeable membrane, down their concentration gradient.

Oval window: An opening in the bone surrounding the *cochlea.* The base plate of the *stapes* presses against a membrane exposed by the oval window, and transmits sound vibrations into the fluid within the cochlea.

Oxytocin: A hormone of the posterior pituitary gland that strengthens uterine contractions and causes ejection of milk.

Papez's circuit: A neural circuit consisting of the mammillary bodies, anterior thalamus, cingulate cortex, hippocampus, and their interconnecting fibers.

Para-chlorophenylalanine (PCPA): A substance that blocks the action of the enzyme tryptophan hydroxylase and hence prevents synthesis of *serotonin* (5–HT).

Paradoxical sleep: See *D sleep.*

Parasympathetic division: See *autonomic nervous system.*

Paraventricular nucleus: A hypothalamic nucleus that contains cell bodies of neurons that produce oxytocin and transport it through their axons, to the posterior pituitary gland.

PCPA: See *para-chlorophenylalanine.*

Peptide bond: A bond between the amino group of one amino acid and the carboxyl group of its neighbor. Peptide bonds link amino acids to form *polypeptides* or *proteins.*

Permeability: The degree to which a membrane permits passage of a particular substance.

PGO spikes: Bursts of phasic electrical activity originating in the *pons,* followed by activity in the lateral geniculate and visual cortex; a characteristic of D sleep.

Phosphorylation: The addition of phosphate to a protein, thus altering its physical characteristics.

Photoreceptor: The receptive cell of the retina, which transduces photic energy into electrical potentials. *Cones* are maximally sensitive to one of three different wave lengths of light, and hence encode color vision, whereas all *rods* are maximally sensitive to light of the same wave length, and hence do not encode color vision.

Pia mater: The meningeal layer adjacent to the surface of the brain.

Pituitary glands: The "master endocrine" gland of the body, attached to the base of the brain. The *anterior pituitary gland (adenohypophysis)* secretes hormones in response to the hypothalamic hormones. The *posterior pituitary gland (neurohypophysis)* secretes oxytocin or antidiuretic hormone in response to stimulation from its neural input.

Plexus: A network formed by the junction of several adjacent nerves.

Polypeptide: A chain of amino acids joined together by peptide bonds. Proteins are long polypeptides.

Pons: The region of the brain rostral to the medulla and caudal to the midbrain.

Positive feedback: A process whereby the effect produced by an action serves to increase or prolong that action.

Posterior: See Figure 6.1.

Posterior pituitary gland: See *pituitary gland.*

Postganglionic: Referring to the neurons of the autonomic nervous system that synapse directly upon their target organ.

Postsynaptic: Referring to the cell upon which the terminal button synapses.

Postsynaptic potential: Alterations in the membrane potential of a postsynaptic neuron, produced by liberation of transmitter substance at the synapse. Excitatory postsynaptic potentials *(EPSPs)* are depolarizations and increase the probability of firing of the postsynaptic neuron. Inhibitory postsynaptic potentials *(IPSPs)* are hyperpolarizations, and decrease the probability of neural firing.

Posttraumatic amnesia (anterograde amnesia): Later amnesia for events that occur after some disturbance to the brain, such as head injury, electroconvulsive shock, or certain degenerative brain diseases.

Predatory attack: Attack of one animal directed at an individual of another species on which the attacking animal normally preys. When this behavior is elicited by electrical stimulation of the brain it is generally referred to as *quiet-biting attack.*

Preganglionic: Pertaining to the efferent neuron of the autonomic nervous system whose cell body is located in a cranial nerve nucleus or in the *intermediate horn* of the spinal gray matter, and whose terminal buttons synapse upon postganglionic neurons in the autonomic ganglia.

Preoptic area: An area of cell bodies (usually divided into the *lateral* and *medial preoptic areas*) just rostral to the hypothalamus. Some investigators refer to the preoptic area as a part of the hypothalamus, although embryologically they are derived from different tissue.

Presynaptic: Referring to a neuron that synapses upon another one, as opposed to *postsynaptic.*

Priming: A phenomenon often observed in studies that investigate the response of animals to rewarding brain stimulation. Priming refers to the fact that an animal that previously responded for brain stimulation will fail to do so until it is given a few "reminder shots" of brain stimulation.

Primordial: In embryology, refers to the undeveloped early form of an organ.

Probabilistic: Referring to the fact that although the exact time of occurrence of an event cannot be predicted, some statements may be made about the probability of its occurrence. For example, probabilistic statements can describe the decay of radioactive substance, but cannot predict when a particular atom will emit energy and change its state. Similarly, probabilistic statements about neural representation of information refer to the activity of groups of neurons, but not to the occurrence of an action potential in a single isolated neuron.

Projection: The efferent connection between neurons in one specific region of the brain and those in another region.

Prolactin: A hormone of the anterior pituitary gland, necessary for production of milk and (in some sub-primate mammals) development of a *corpus luteum.* (Occasionally called *luteotrophic hormone.*)

Protein: A long polypeptide that can serve in a structural capacity or as an enzyme.

Pulvinar: A region of the thalamus that receives fibers from, and projects fibers to, areas of visual cortex.

Putamen: One of the nuclei that constitute the basal ganglia. The putamen and *caudate nucleus* compose the neostriatum.

Pyramidal motor system: A system of long axons whose cell bodies reside in cortex, and whose terminals synapse upon neurons in motor nuclei of the cranial nerves and on interneurons or (in primates) lower motor neurons of the spinal cord.

Pyruvate: A substance produced by the breakdown of glycogen in the muscles, in the absence of oxygen.

Quiet-biting attack: See *predatory attack.*

Raphe: A region of the medulla situated along the midline, just dorsal to the aqueduct of Sylvius.

Receptive field: That portion of the visual field in which the presentation of visual stimuli will produce an alteration in the firing rate of a neuron.

Receptor: A specialized type of cell that transduces physical stimuli into slow, graded *receptor potentials.*

Receptor potential: A slow, graded electrical potential produced by a receptor in response to a physical stimulus. Receptor potentials alter the firing rate of neurons upon which the receptors synapse.

Receptor site: The region of the membrane of a cell that is sensitive to a particular chemical, such as a neurotransmitter or hormone. When the appropriate chemical stimulates a receptor site, changes take place in the membrane or within the cell.

Reflex: A stereotyped glandular secretion or movement produced as the direct result of a stimulus.

REM sleep: See *D sleep.*

Renin: Sympathetic stimulation of the kidney, or reduction of its blood flow, results in liberation of renin, a hormone that causes conversion of *angiotensinogen* in the blood into *angiotensin.* Angiotensin produces thirst, and also stimulates the adrenal cortex to produce *aldosterone,* a hormone that stimulates the kidney to retain sodium.

Reticular formation: A large network of neural tissue located in central regions of the brainstem, from the medulla to the diencephalon.

Retina: The neural tissue and photoreceptive cells located on the inner surface of the posterior portion of the eye.

Retrieval: The process by which memories stored in the brain can affect neural activity, and hence alter the animal's subsequent behavior.

Retrograde amnesia: Amnesia for events that preceded some disturbance to the brain, such as head injury or electroconvulsive shock.

Retrograde degeneration: Gradual degeneration of an injured axon from the point of injury back toward the *soma*, which itself often dies. See Figure 7.11.

Re-uptake: The re-entry of a transmitter substance just liberated by a terminal button back through its membrane, thus terminating the *postsynaptic potential* that is induced in the postsynaptic neuron.

Reverberation: Circulating electrical activity maintained in a closed loop of neurons, which might constitute the physical basis for short-term memory.

Ribonucleic acid: A complex macromolecule composed of a sequence of nucleotide bases attached to a sugar-phosphate backbone. *Messenger RNA (mRNA)* delivers genetic information from a portion of a chromosome to a ribosome, where the appropriate molecules of *transfer RNA (tRNA)* assemble the appropriate *amino acids* to produce the *polypeptide* coded for by the active portion of the chromosome.

RNA: See *ribonucleic acid.*

Rod: See *photoreceptor.*

Rostral: See Figure 6.1.

Round window: An opening in the bone surrounding the cochlea of the inner ear that permits vibrations to be transmitted, via the *oval window,* through the fluids and receptive tissue contained within the cochlea.

S sleep: Slow wave sleep, or synchronized sleep, as opposed to *D sleep.*

Sagittal section: See Figure 6.2.

Satellite cell: A cell that serves to support neurons of the peripheral nervous system, such as the *Schwann cell* that provides the *myelin sheath.*

Satiety: Cessation of hunger produced by adequate and available supplies of nutrients.

Schwann cell: A cell in the peripheral nervous system that is wrapped around a myelinated axon, providing one segment of its myelin sheath.

Scotoma: A region of blindness within an otherwise-normal visual field, produced by localized damage somewhere in the visual system.

Semicircular canal: One of the three ring-like structures of the vestibular apparatus that transduce changes in head rotation into neural activity.

Sensory coding: Representation of sensory events in the form of neural activity.

Sensory cortex: Regions of cortex whose primary input is from one of the sensory systems.

Sensory modality: A particular form of sensory input, such as vision, audition, or olfaction.

Sensory transduction: The process by which sensory stimuli are transduced into slow, graded *generator potentials* or *receptor potentials.*

Septum: A portion of the limbic system, lying between the walls of the anterior portions of the lateral ventricles.

Set point: The optimal value of the system variable in a regulatory mechanism. The set point for human body temperature, recorded orally, is approximately 37° C.

Short-term memory (STM): Immediate memory for sensory events that may or may not be consolidated into *long-term memory.*

Single unit: An individual neuron.

Smooth muscle: Non-striated muscle innervated by the autonomic nervous system, found in the walls of blood vessels, in sphincters, within the eye, in the digestive system, and around hair follicles.

Sodium-potassium pump: A metabolically active process in the cellular membrane that extrudes sodium and transports potassium into the cell.

Solitary nucleus: A nucleus in the medulla that receives input from the gustatory system and sensory information from the viscera.

Soma: A cell body or, more generally, the body.

Somatosenses: Bodily sensation; sensitivity to such stimuli as touch, pain, and temperature.

Somatosensory cortex: The postcentral gyrus, which receives many projection fibers from the somatosensory system.

Somatotrophic hormone (STH). See *growth hormone.*

Spinal root: A bundle of axons, surrounded by connective tissue, that occurs in pairs that fuse and form a spinal nerve. The *dorsal root* contains afferent fibers whereas the *ventral root* contains efferent fibers.

Spinal sympathetic ganglion: See *ganglion.*

Spiral ganglion: A group of small nodules located near the cochlea that contain the cell bodies of axons of the cochlear nerve.

Stapes: One of the bones of the inner ear. See Figure 8.10.

Steroid hormone: A hormone of low molecular weight, derived from cholesterol. Steroid hormones affect their target cells by attaching to receptors found within the nucleus.

Stria terminalis: A long fiber bundle that connects portions of the amygdala with the hypothalamus.

Striate cortex: Primary visual cortex.

Subarachnoid space: The fluid-filled space between the *arachnoid* and the *pia mater.*

Subcortical: Located within the brain, as opposed to being located on its cortical surface.

Substantia gelatinosa: The tip of the dorsal horn of the spinal cord gray matter.

Substantia nigra: A darkly stained region of the *pons,* which communicates with the neostriatum via the *nigro-striatal bundle.*

Sulcus: A groove in the surface of the cerebral hemisphere, smaller than a *fissure.*

Superior: See Figure 6.1.

Superior colliculi: Protrusions on top of the midbrain; part of the visual system.

Supraoptic nucleus: A hypothalamic nucleus that contains cell bodies of neurons that produce *antidiuretic hormone* and transport it through their axons to the posterior pituitary gland.

Sympathetic chain: See *ganglion.*

Sympathetic division: See *autonomic nervous system.*

Synapse: A junction between the terminal button of an axon and the membrane of another neuron.

Synaptic vesicle: A small, hollow beadlike structure found in terminal buttons. Synaptic vesicles contain transmitter substance.

Synchrony: High-voltage, low-frequency electroencephalographic activity, characteristic of *S sleep* or coma. During synchrony, neurons are presumably firing together in a regular fashion.

System variable: That which is regulated by a regulatory mechanism; for example, temperature in a heating system.

Target cell: The type of cell that is directly affected by a hormone or nerve fiber.

Tectum: The roof of the midbrain, comprising the *inferior* and the *superior colliculi.*

Tegmentum: The portion of the midbrain beneath the *tectum,* containing the red nucleus and nuclei of various cranial nerves.

Telencephalon: See Table 6.1.

Tentorium: The tentlike fold of *dura mater* that separates the occipital lobe from the cerebellum.

Terminal button: The rounded swelling at the distal end of an axonic process that synapses upon another neuron, muscle fiber, or gland cell.

Testosterone: The principle *androgen* found in males.

Third ventricle: See *ventricle.*

Threshold of excitation: The value of the membrane potential that must be reached in order to produce an action potential.

Thymine: One of the nucleotide bases found in DNA. In RNA this base is replaced by uracil.

Transduction: See *sensory transduction.*

Transfer ribonucleic acid (tRNA): See *ribonucleic acid.*

Transmitter substance: A chemical that is liberated by the terminal buttons of an axon, which produces an EPSP or an IPSP in the membrane of the postsynaptic cell.

Transverse section: See Figure 6.2.

Trigeminal lemniscus: A bundle of fibers running parallel to the medial lemniscus, which conveys afferent fibers from the trigeminal nerve to the thalamus.

tRNA: See *ribonucleic acid.*

Trophic hormone: A hormone of the anterior pituitary gland that affects the hormonal secretion of another endocrine gland.

Unipolar neuron: A neuron with a long, continuous fiber that has dendritic processes on one end and axonal processes and terminal buttons on the other. This fiber connects with the *soma* of the neuron by means of a single, short process.

Uracil: One of the nucleotide bases of RNA. See *thymine.*

Urea: The by-product of metabolism of amino acids, excreted in the urine.

Vagus nerve: The largest of the cranial nerves, conveying efferent fibers of the parasympathetic nervous system to organs of the thoracic and abdominal cavities. The vagus nerve also carries non-painful sensory fibers from these organs to the brain.

Vena cava: The principal vein draining the blood supply of the body to the right atrium. The inferior vena cava drains the lower portion of the body, whereas the superior vena cava drains the upper portion of the body.

Ventral: See Figure 6.1.

Ventral amygdalofugal pathway: The diffuse system of fibers connecting portions of the *amygdala* with various forebrain structures.

Ventral horn (of gray matter of spinal cord): Location of the cell bodies of *alpha* and *gamma motor neurons* of the spinal cord.

Ventral noradrenergic bundle: A system of noradrenergic fibers, running through the hypothalamus, connecting brainstem and forebrain regions.

Ventral posterior nucleus: The thalamic nucleus that projects to somatosensory cortex.

Ventral root: See *spinal root.*

Ventricle: One of the hollow spaces within the brain, filled with cerebrospinal fluid, including the *lateral, third,* and *fourth ventricles.*

Ventromedial nucleus of the hypothalamus (VMH): A large nucleus of the hypothalamus located near the walls of the third ventricle.

Vertebral artery: An artery, the branches of which serve the posterior regions of the brain and spinal cord.

Vestibular nerve: See *auditory nerve.*

VMH: See *ventromedial nucleus of the hypothalamus.*

Volumetric thirst (extracellular thirst): Thirst produced by *hypovolemia,* or reduction in the amount of extracellular fluid. Volumetric thirst is mediated by baroreceptors in the right atrium of the heart, and by reduced blood flow to the kidneys.

Wernicke's area: A region of auditory association cortex on the left temporal lobe of humans, which is important in comprehension of words and production of meaningful speech. *Wernicke's aphasia,* which occurs as a result of damage to this area, results in fluent, but meaningless, speech.

Wolffian system: The embryonic precursors of the male internal sex organs.

Bibliography

ADAMS, D. B. The activity of single cells in the mid-brain and hypothalamus of the cat during affective defense behavior. *Archives Italiennes de Biologie*, 1968, *106*, 243–269.

ADAMS, R. D. The anatomy of memory mechanisms in the human brain. In *The Pathology of Memory*, edited by G. A. Talland and N. C. Waugh. New York: Academic Press, 1969.

ADOLPH, E. F., BARKER, J. P., and HOY, P. A. Multiple factors in thirst. *American Journal of Physiology*, 1954, *178*, 538–562.

AFFANNI, J., MARCHIAFAVA, P. L., and ZERNICKI, B. Orientation reactions in the midpontine pretrigeminal cat. *Archives Italiennes de Biologie*, 1962, *100*, 297–304.

AGNEW, H. W., JR., WEBB, W. B., and WILLIAMS, R. L. The effects of stage four sleep deprivation. *Electroencephalography and Clinical Neurophysiology*, 1964, *17*, 68–70.

AGNEW, H. W., JR., WEBB, W. B., and WILLIAMS, R. L. Comparison of stage four and 1–REM sleep deprivation. *Perceptual and Motor Skills*, 1967, *24*, 851–858.

AGRANOFF, B. W., DAVIS, R. E., CASOLA, L., and LIM, R. Actinomycin D blocks formation of memory of shock avoidance in goldfish. *Science*, 1967, *158*, 1600–1601.

AKERT, K., KOELLA, W. P., and HESS, R., JR. Sleep produced by electrical stimulation of the thalamus. *American Journal of Physiology*, 1952, *168*, 260–267.

AKIL, H. Unpublished Ph.D. dissertation, UCLA, 1972.

AKIL, H., and MAYER, D. J. Antagonism of stimulation-produced analgesia by *p*-CPA, a serotonin synthesis inhibitor. *Brain Research*, 1972, *44*, 692–697.

AKIL, H., MAYER, D., and LIEBESKIND, J. C. Antagonism of stimulation-produced analgesia by Naloxone, a narcotic antagonist. *Science*, 1976, *191*, 961–962.

ALEKSEYEVA, T. T. Correlation of nervous and humoral factors in the development of sleep in non-disjointed twins. *Zhurnal Vysshei Nervnoi Beyatel'nosti Imeni I. P. Pavlova*, 1958, *8*, 835–844.

AMENOMORI, Y., CHEN, C. L., and MEITES, J. Serum prolactin levels in rats during different reproductive states. *Endocrinology*, 1970, *86*, 506–510.

AMOORE, J. E. *Molecular Basis of Odor*. Springfield, Ill.: Charles C Thomas, 1970.

ANAND, B. K., and BROBECK, J. R. Hypothalamic control of food intake in rats and cats. *Yale Journal of Biology and Medicine*, 1951, *24*, 123–140.

ANDÉN, N.-E., FUXE, K., HAMBERGER, B., and HÖKFELT, T. A quantitative study on the nigrostriatal dopamine neuron system in the rat. *Acta Physiologica Scandinavica*, 1966, *67*, 306–312.

ANDEN, N.-E., and STOCK, G. Effects of clozapine on the turnover of dopamine in the corpus striatum and in the limbic system. *Journal of Pharmacy and Pharmacology*, 1973, *25*, 346–348.

ANDERSEN, V. O., BUCHMANN, B., and LENNOX-BUCHTHAL, M. A. Single cortical units with narrow spectral sensitivity in monkey (*Cercocebus torquatus atys*). *Vision Research*, 1962, *2*, 295–307.

ANDERSSON, B. The effect of injections of hypertonic NaCl solutions in different parts of the hypothalamus of goats. *Acta Physiologica Scandinavica*, 1953, *28*, 188–201.

ANGELBORG, A. R., and ENGSTRÖM, H. The normal organ of Corti. In *Basic Mechanisms in Hearing*, edited by A. R. Møeller. New York: Academic Press, 1973.

ANGELERI, F., MARCHESI, G. F., and QUATTRINI, A. Effects of chronic thalamic lesions on the electrical activity of the neocortex and on sleep. *Archives Italiennes de Biologie*, 1969, *107*, 633–667.

ANGRIST, B., SATHANANTHAN, G., WILK, S., and GERSHON, S. Amphetamine psychosis: behavioural and biochemical aspects. *Journal of Psychiatric Research*, 1974, *11*, 13–24.

ANONYMOUS. Effects of sexual activity on beard growth in man. *Nature*, 1970, *226*, 867–870.

ANTELMAN, S. M., ROWLAND, N. E., and FISHER, A. E. Stress related recovery from lateral hypothalamic aphagia. *Brain Research*, 1976, 346–350.

ANTELMAN, S. M., SZECHTMAN, H., CHIN, P., and FISHER, A. D. Tail pinch–induced eating, gnawing and licking behavior in rats: Dependence on the nigrostriatal dopamine system. *Brain Research*, 1975, *99*, 319–377.

ARAI, Y., and GORSKY, R. A. Critical exposure time for androgenization of the rat hypothalamus determined by antiandrogen injection. *Proceedings of the Society*

625

for Experimental Biology and Medicine, 1968, *127*, 590–593.

AREES, A. E., VELTMAN, B. I., and MAYER, J. Hypothalamic blood flow following gold thioglucose–induced lesions. *Experimental Neurology*, 1969, *25*, 410–415.

ASANUMA, H., and ROSÉN, I. Topographical organization of cortical efferent zones projecting to distal forelimb muscles in monkey. *Experimental Brain Research*, 1972, *14*, 243–256.

ASCHOFF, J. C., CONRAD, B., and KORNHUBER, H. H. Acquired pendular nystagmus in multiple sclerosis. Proceedings of the Bárány Society. 1970, 127–132.

ASDOURIAN, D., STUTZ, R. M., and ROCKLIN, K. W. Effects of thalamic and limbic system lesions of self-stimulation. *Journal of Comparative and Physiological Psychology*, 1966, *61*, 468–472.

ASERINSKY, N. E., and KLEITMAN, N. Regularly occurring periods of eye motility and concomitant phenomena during sleep. *Science*, 1955, *118*, 273–274.

ASERINSKY, N. E., and KLEITMAN, N. Two types of ocular motility occurring in sleep. *Journal of Applied Physiology*, 1955, *8*, 1–10.

ASSCHER, A. W., and ANSON, S. G. A vascular permeability factor of renal origin. *Nature*, 1963, *198*, 1097–1099.

AZRIN, N. H. Aggression. Paper presented at the meeting of the American Psychological Association, Los Angeles, September, 1964.

AZRIN, N. H., HUTCHINSON, R. R., and McLAUGHLIN, R. The opportunity for aggression as an operant reinforcer during aversive stimulation. *Journal of the Experimental Analysis of Behavior*, 1965, *8*, 171–180.

BALAGURA, S., and HOEBEL, B. G. Self-stimulation of the lateral hypothalamus modified by insulin and glucagon. *Physiology and Behavior*, 1967, *2*, 337–340.

BALAGURA, S., and RALPH, T. The analgesic effect of electrical stimulation of the diencephalon and mesencephalon. *Brain Research*, 1973, *60*, 369–379.

BALASUBRAMANIAM, V., KANAKA, T. S., and RAMAMURTHI, B. Surgical treatment of hyperkinetic and behavior disorders. *International Surgery*, 1970, *54*, 18–23.

BALL, G. G. Electrical self-stimulation of the brain and sensory inhibition. *Psychonomic Science*, 1967, *8*, 489–490.

BALL, G. G., and ADAMS, D. W. Intracranial stimulation as an avoidance or escape response. *Psychonomic Science*, 1965, *3*, 39–40.

BARD, P. Studies in the cortical representation of somatic sensibility. *Harvey Lectures*, 1938, *33*, 143–169.

BARONDES, S. H., and COHEN, H. D. Puromycin effect on successive phases of memory storage. *Science*, 1966, *151*, 594–595.

BARONDES, S. H., and COHEN, H. D. Comparative effects of cyclohexamide and puromycin on cerebral protein synthesis and consolidation of memory in mice. *Brain Research*, 1967, *4*, 44–51.

BARONDES, S. H., and COHEN, H. D. Effect of acetoxycyclohexamide on learning and memory of a light-dark discrimination. *Nature*, 1968, *218*, 271–273.

BARONDES, S. H., and JARVIK, M. E. The influence of actinomycin D on brain RNA synthesis and on memory. *Journal of Neurochemistry*, 1964, *11*, 187–195.

BARRACLOUGH, C. A. Hormones and development. Modifications in the CNS regulation of reproduction after exposure of prepuberal rats to steroid hormones. *Recent Progress in Hormone Research*, 1966, *22*, 503–539.

BASKIN, F., MASIARZ, F. R., and AGRANOFF, B. W. Effect of various stresses on the incorporation of (^{3}H) orotic acid into goldfish brain RNA. *Brain Research*, 1972, *39*, 151–162.

BATINI, C., MORUZZI, G., PALESTINI, M., ROSSI, G. F., and ZANCHETTI, A. Persistent patterns of wakefulness in the pretrigeminal midpontine preparation. *Science*, 1958, *128*, 30–32.

BATINI, C., MORUZZI, G., PALESTINI, M., ROSSI, G. F., and ZANCHETTI, A. Effects of complete pontine transections on the sleep-wakefulness rhythm: the midpontine pretrigeminal preparation. *Archives Italiennes de Biologie*, 1959, *97*, 1–12.

BATINI, C., PALESTINI, M., ROSSI, G. F., and ZANCHETTI, A. EEG activation patterns in the midpontine pretrigeminal cat following sensory deafferentation. *Archives Italiennes de Biologie*, 1959, *97*, 26–32.

BATSEL, H. L. Electroencephalographic synchronization and desynchronization in the chronic "cerveau isolé" of the dog. *Electroencephalography and Clinical Neurophysiology*, 1960, *12*, 421–430.

BATSEL, H. L. Spontaneous desynchronization in the chronic cat "cerveau isolé." *Archives Italiennes de Biologie*, 1964, *102*, 547–566.

BAZETT, H. C., McGLONE, B., WILLIAMS, R. G., and LUFKIN, H. M. Sensation. I. Depth, distribution, and probable identification in the prepuce of sensory end-organs concerned in sensations of temperature and touch; thermometric conductivity. *Archives of Neurology and Psychiatry* (Chicago), 1932, *27*, 489–517.

BEACH, F. Effects of injury to the cerebral cortex upon sexually receptive behavior in the female cat. *Psychosomatic Medicine*, 1944, *6*, 40–55.

BEACH, F. Cerebral and hormonal control of reflexive mechanisms involved in copulatory behavior. *Physiological Review*, 1967, *47*, 289–316.

BEACH, F. Factors involved in the control of mounting behavior by female animals. In *Reproduction and Sexual Behavior*, edited by M. Diamond. Bloomington: University of Indiana Press, 1968.

BEACH, F. A., and WILSON, J. R. Effects of prolactin, progesterone, and estrogen on reactions of nonpregnant rats to foster young. *Psychological Reports*, 1963, *13*, 231–239.

BEACH, G., and KIMBLE, D. P. Activity and responsibility

in rats after magnesium pemoline injections. *Science,* 1967, *155,* 698–701.

BEALER, S. L., and SMITH, D. V. Multiple sensitivity to chemical stimuli in human taste papillae. *Physiology and Behavior,* 1975, *14,* 795–800.

BEAMER, W., BERMANT, G., and CLEGG, M. Copulatory behavior of the ram, *Ovis aries* II: Factors affecting copulatory satiation. *Animal Behaviour,* 1969, *17,* 706–711.

BEATTY, W. W., and SCHWARTZBAUM, J. S. Commonality and specificity of behavioral dysfunctions following septal and hippocampal lesions in rats. *Journal of Comparative and Physiological Psychology,* 1968, *66,* 60–68.

BEECHER, H. K. *Measurement of Subjective Responses: Quantitative Effects of Drugs.* New York: Oxford University Press, 1959.

BEEMAN, E. A. The effect of male hormone on aggressive behavior in mice. *Physiological Zoology,* 1947, *20,* 373–405.

BEIDLER, L. M. Physiological properties of mammalian taste receptors. In *Taste and Smell in Vertebrates,* edited by G. E. W. Wolstenholme. London: J. & A. Churchill, 1970.

BELLOWS, R. T. Time factors in water drinking in dogs. *American Journal of Physiology,* 1939, *125,* 87–97.

BENNETT, E. L., DIAMOND, M. C., KRECH, D., and ROSENZWEIG, M. R. Chemical and anatomical plasticity of brain. *Science,* 1964, *146,* 610–619.

BERKUN, M. M., KESSEN, M. L., and MILLER, N. E. Hunger-reducing effects of food by stomach fistula versus food by mouth measured by a consummatory response. *Journal of Comparative and Physiological Psychology,* 1952, *45,* 550–554.

BERLUCCHI, G., MAFFEI, L., MORUZZI, G., and STRATA, P. EEG and behavioral effects elicited by cooling of medulla and pons. *Archives Italiennes de Biologie,* 1964, *102,* 372–392.

BERMAN, A. L. *The Brain Stem of the Cat.* Madison: University of Wisconsin Press, 1968.

BERMANT, G. Response latencies of female rats during sexual intercourse. *Science,* 1961a, *133,* 1771–1773.

BERMANT, G. Regulation of sexual contact by female rats. Unpublished Ph.D. dissertation, Harvard University, 1961b. Cited by Bermant and Davidson (1974).

BERMANT, G., and DAVIDSON, J. M. *Biological Bases of Sexual Behavior.* New York: Harper & Row, 1974.

BERMANT, G., and TAYLOR, L. Interactive effects of experience and olfactory bulb lesions in male rat copulation. *Physiology and Behavior,* 1969, *4,* 13–18.

BERMANT, G., and WESTBROOK, W. Peripheral factors in the regulation of sexual contact by female rats. *Journal of Comparative and Physiological Psychology,* 1966, *61,* 244–250.

BERNARD, C. *Leçons de Physiologie Expérimentale Ap-* *pliquée à la Médicine Faites au Collège de France.* Vol. 2. Paris: Bailliere, 1856.

BEST, R. M. Encoding of memory in the neuron. *Psychological Reports,* 1968, *22,* 107–115.

BISHOP, G. H. Responses to electrical stimulation of single sensory units of skin. *Journal of Neurophysiology,* 1943, *6,* 361–382.

BLANK, M., ALTMAN, D., and BRIDGER, W. H. Cross-modal transfer of form discrimination in preschool children. *Psychonomic Science,* 1968, *10,* 51–52.

BLASS, E. M., and EPSTEIN, A. N. A lateral preoptic osmosensitive zone for thirst. *Journal of Comparative and Physiological Psychology,* 1971, *76,* 378–394.

BLASS, E. M., and KRALY, F. S. Medial forebrain bundle lesions: Specific loss of feeding to decrease glucose utilization in rats. *Journal of Comparative and Physiological Psychology,* 1974, *86,* 679–692.

BLASS, E. M., NUSSBAUM, A. I., and HANSON, D. G. Septal hyperdipsia—specific enhancement of drinking to angiotensin in rats. *Journal of Comparative and Physiological Psychology,* 1974, *87,* 422–439.

BLEULER, E. *Dementia Praecox or the Group of Schizophrenias.* New York: International University Press, 1950.

BLUMER, D. Hypersexual episodes in temporal lobe epilepsy. *American Journal of Psychiatry,* 1970, *126,* 1099–1106.

BOGEN, J. E., FISHER, E. D., and VOGEL, P. J. Cerebral commissurotomy: A second case report. *Journal of the American Medical Association,* 1965, *194,* 1328–1329.

BOGOCH, S. *The Biochemistry of Memory with an Inquiry into the Function of the Brain Mucoids.* New York: Oxford University Press, 1968.

BOLLES, R. C. *Theory of Motivation.* New York: Harper & Row, 1967.

BONVALLET, M., and ALLEN, M. B., JR. Prolonged spontaneous and evoked reticular activation following discrete bulbar lesions. *Electroencephalography and Clinical Neurophysiology,* 1963, *15,* 969–988.

BONVALLET, M., and SIGG, B. Etude électrophysiologique des afférences vagales au neveau de leur pénétration dans le bulbe. *Journal of Physiology* (Paris), 1958, *50,* 63–74.

BOWER, G. H., and MILLER, N. E. Rewarding and punishing effects from stimulating the same place in the rat's brain. *Journal of Comparative and Physiological Psychology,* 1958, *51,* 669–674.

BOWMAN, R. E. Magnesium pemoline and behavior. *Science,* 1966, *153,* 902.

BRADY, J. V., and NAUTA, W. J. H. Subcortical mechanisms in emotional behavior: affective changes following septal forebrain lesions in the albino rat. *Journal of Comparative and Physiological Psychology,* 1953, *46,* 339–346.

BRECHER, G., and WAXLER, S. Obesity in albino mice due to single injections of goldthioglucose. *Proceed-*

ings of the Society for Experimental Biology and Medicine, 1949, 70, 498.

BREGER, L., HUNTER, I., and LANE, R. W. The effects of stress on dreams. *Psychological Issues Monograph Number 27*. New York: International University Press, 1971.

BREMER, F. L'activité cérébrale au cours du sommeil et de la narcose. Contribution à l'étude du mécanisme du sommeil. *Bulletin de l'Academie Royale de Belgique*, 1937, 4, 68–86.

BREMER, F. Preoptic hypnogenic focus and mesencephalic reticular formation. *Brain Research*, 1970, 21, 132–134.

BRION, S. Korsakoff's syndrome: Clinico-anatomical and physiopathological considerations. In *The Pathology of Memory*, edited by N. C. Waugh. New York: Academic Press, 1969.

BROBECK, J. R., TEPPERMAN, J., and LONG, C. N. H. Effects of experimental obesity upon carbohydrate metabolism. *Yale Journal of Biology and Medicine*, 1943, 15, 893–904.

BROOKS, D., and BIZZI, E. Brain stem electrical activity during sleep. *Archives Italiennes de Biologie*, 1963, 101, 648–665.

BROOKS, V. B., and STONEY, S. D., JR. Motor mechanisms: The role of the pyramidal system in motor control. *Annual Review of Physiology*, 1971, 33, 337–392.

BROWN, T. S., ROSVOLD, H. E., and MISHKIN, M. Olfactory discrimination after temporal lobe lesions in monkeys. *Journal of Comparative and Physiological Psychology*, 1963, 56, 190–195.

BUDDINGTON, R. W., KING, F. A., and ROBERTS, L. Emotionality and conditioned avoidance responding in the squirrel monkey following septal injury. *Psychonomic Science*, 1967, 8, 195–196.

BUGGY, J., FISHER, A. E., HOFFMAN, W. E., JOHNSON, A. K., and PHILLIPS, M. I. Ventricular obstruction: Effect on drinking induced by intracranial injection of angiotensin. *Science*, 1975, 190, 72–74.

BULLOCK, N. P., and NEW, M. I. Testosterone and cortisol concentration in spermatic, adrenal and systemic venous blood in adult male guinea pigs. *Endocrinology*, 1971, 88, 523–526.

BURNS, B. D. *The Mammalian Cerebral Cortex*. London: Arnold, 1958.

CAFFYN, Z. E. Y. Early vascular changes in the brain of the mouse after injections of goldthioglucose and bipiperidyl mustard. *Journal of Pathology*, 1972, 106, 49–56.

CAGGIULA, A. R. Shock-elicited copulation and aggression in male rats. *Journal of Comparative and Physiological Psychology*, 1972, 83, 393–407.

CAMPBELL, C. S., and DAVIS, J. D. Licking rate of rats is reduced by intraduodenal and intraportal glucose infusion. *Physiology and Behavior*, 1974a, 12, 357–365.

CAMPBELL, C. S., and DAVIS, J. D. Peripheral control of food intake: Interaction between test diet and post-ingestive chemoreception. *Physiology and Behavior*, 1974b, 12, 377–384.

CANNON, W. B. The James-Lange theory of emotions: A critical examination and an alternative. *American Journal of Psychology*, 1927, 39, 106–124.

CANNON, W. B., and WASHBURN, A. L. An explanation of hunger. *American Journal of Physiology*, 1912, 29, 444–454.

CARLSON, A. J. *The Control of Hunger in Health and Disease*. Chicago: University of Chicago Press, 1916.

CARLSON, N. R., and THOMAS, G. J. Maternal behavior of mice with limbic lesions. *Journal of Comparative and Physiological Psychology*, 1968, 66, 731–737.

CARROLL, D., LEWIS, S. A., and OSWALD, I. Effects of barbiturates on dream content. *Nature*, 1969, 223, 865–866.

CARTWRIGHT, R. D., GORE, S., and WEINER, L. Paper presented at the meeting of the Association for the Psychophysiological Study of Sleep. San Diego, 1973. Cited by Greenberg and Pearlman, 1974.

CASOLA, L., LIM, R., DAVIS, R. E., and AGRANOFF, B. W. Behavioral and biochemical effects of intracranial injection of cytosine arabinoside in goldfish. *Proceedings of the National Academy of Science*, 1969, 60, 1389–1395.

CASTALDO, V., and SHEVRIN, H. Different effect of an auditory stimulus as a function of rapid eye movement and non-rapid eye movement sleep. *Journal of Nervous and Mental Diseases*, 1970, 150, 195–200.

CERLETTI, U. Electroshock therapy. In *The Great Psychodynamic Therapies in Psychiatry*, edited by F. Marti-Ibanez, A. M. Sackler, M. D. Sackler, and R. R. Sackler. New York: Hoeber-Harper, 1956.

CERLETTI, U., and BINI, L. Electric shock treatment. *Bollettino ed Atti della Accademia Medica di Roma*, 1938, 64, 36.

CHAPOUTHIER, G. Behavioral studies of the molecular basis of memory. In *The Physiological Basis of Memory*, edited by J. A. Deutsch. New York: Academic Press, 1973.

CHOROVER, S. L., and SCHILLER, P. H. Short-term retrograde amnesia in rats. *Journal of Comparative and Physiological Psychology*, 1965, 59, 73–78.

CHOW, K. L. Effects of local electrographic after discharge on visual learning and retention in monkey. *Journal of Neurophysiology*, 1961, 24, 391–400.

CLEMENS, L. G. Influence of prenatal litter composition on mounting behavior of female rats. *American Zoologist*, 1971, 11, 617–618.

CLEMENS, L. G., WALLEN, K., and GORSKI, R. Mating behavior: Facilitation in the female cat after cortical application of potassium chloride. *Science*, 1967, 157, 1208–1209.

CLEMENTE, C. D., and CHASE, M. H. Neurological substrates of aggressive behavior. *Annual Review of Physiology*, 1973, 35, 329–356.

CLEMENTE, C. D., STERMAN, M. B., and WYRWICKA, W. Forebrain inhibitory mechanisms: Conditioning of basal forebrain induced EEG synchronization and sleep. *Experimental Neurology*, 1963, 7, 404–417.

COHEN, H. D., and BARONDES, S. H. Further studies of learning and memory after intracerebral actinomycin D. *Journal of Neurochemistry*, 1966, 13, 207–211.

COHEN, H. D., ERVIN, F., and BARONDES, S. H. Puromycin and cyclohexamide: Differential effects on hippocampal electrical activity. *Science*, 1966, 154, 1557–1558.

COMARR, A. E. Sexual function among patients with spinal cord injury. *Urologia Internationalis*, 1970, 25, 134–168.

CONNER, R. L., and LEVINE, S. Hormonal influences on aggressive behaviour. In *Aggressive Behaviour*, edited by S. Garattini and E. B. Sigg. New York: Wiley, 1969.

COONS, E. E., and CRUCE, J. A. F. Lateral hypothalamus: Food and current intensity in maintaining self-stimulation of hunger. *Science*, 1968, 159, 1117–1119.

COONS, E. E., and MILLER, N. E. Conflict vs. consolidation of memory traces to explain "retrograde amnesia" produced by ECS. *Journal of Comparative and Physiological Psychology*, 1960, 53, 524–531.

COWEY, A., and WEISKRANTZ, L. Demonstration of cross-modal matching in rhesus monkeys, *Macaca mulatta*. *Neuropsychologia*, 1975, 13, 117–120.

CRAGG, B. G. Centrifugal fibers to retina and olfactory bulb, and composition of supraoptic commissures in rabbit. *Experimental Neurology*, 1962, 5, 406–427.

CRAMER, H., RUDOLPH, J., CONSBRUCH, U., and KENDEL, K. On the effects of metatonin on sleep and behavior in man. *Advances in Biochemical Psychopharmacology*, 1974, 11, 187–191.

CRONHOLM, B. Post-ECT amnesias. In *The Pathology of Memory*, edited by G. A. Talland and N. C. Waugh. New York: Academic Press, 1969.

DAVENPORT, J. W. Cretinism in rats: Enduring behavioral deficit induced by tricyanoaminopropene. *Science*, 1970, 167, 1007–1009.

DAVENPORT, R. K., ROGERS, L. M., and RUSSELL, I. S. Cross-modal perception in apes: Altered visual cues and delay. *Neuropsychologia*, 1975, 13, 229–235.

DAVIDSON, J. M. Activation of male rats' sexual behavior by intracerebral implantation of androgen. *Endocrinology*, 1966a, 79, 783–794.

DAVIDSON, J. M. Characteristics of sex behavior in male rats following castration. *Animal Behaviour*, 1966b, 14, 266–272.

DAVIS, J. M. A two-factor theory of schizophrenia. *Journal of Psychiatric Research*, 1974, 11, 25–30.

DAVSON, H. *The Physiology of the Eye*, ed. 3. New York: Academic Press, 1972.

DAW, N. W. Colour-coded ganglion cells in the gold-fish retina: Extension of their receptive fields by means of new stimuli. *Journal of Physiology (London)*, 1968, 197, 567–592.

DAWSON, R. G., and McGAUGH, J. L. Drug facilitation of learning and memory. In *The Physiological Basis of Memory*, edited by J. A. Deutsch. New York: Academic Press, 1973.

DEBONS, A. F., KRIMSKY, I., and FROM, A. A direct action of insulin on the hypothalamic satiety center. *American Journal of Physiology*, 1970, 219, 938–942.

DEBONS, A. F., and LIKUSKI, H. J. Gold thioglucose damage to the satiety center: Inhibition in diabetes. *American Journal of Physiology*, 1968, 214, 652–658.

DELGADO, J. M. R. *Physical Control of the Mind*. New York: Harper & Row, 1969.

DELONG, M. Motor functions of the basal ganglia: Single-unit activity during movement. In *The Neurosciences: Third Study Program*, edited by F. O. Schmitt and F. G. Worden. Cambridge: MIT Press, 1974.

DEMENT, W. The effect of dream deprivation. *Science*, 1960, 131, 1705–1707.

DEMENT, W. C. *Some Must Watch While Some Must Sleep*. San Francisco: W. H. Freeman & Company, 1972.

DEMENT, W., FERGUSON, F., COHEN, H., and BARCHAS, J. Nonchemical methods and data using a biochemical model: The REM quanta. In *Psychochemical Research in Man*, edited by A. J. Mandell and M. P. Mandell. New York: Academic Press, 1969.

DEMENT, W. C. Dream recall and eye movement during sleep in schizophrenics and normals. *Journal of Nervous and Mental Disease*, 1955, 122, 263–269.

DEMENT, W. C., and KLEITMAN, N. The relation of eye movements during sleep to dream activity: An objective method for the study of dreaming. *Journal of Experimental Psychology*, 1957, 53, 339–346.

DEMENT, W., MITLER, M., and HENRIKSEN, S. Sleep changes during chronic administration of parachlorophenylalanine. *Revue Canadienne de Biologie*, 1972, 31, 239–246.

DEMENT, W., and WOLPERT, E. Relation of eye movements, body motility, and external stimuli to dream content. *Journal of Experimental Psychology*, 1958, 55, 543–553.

DENNY-BROWN, D. The general principles of motor integration. In *Handbook of Physiology. Section I: Neurophysiology*, edited by J. Field, H. W. Magoun, and V. E. Hall. Washington: American Physiological Society, 1960.

DESIRAJU, T., BANERJEE, M. G., and ANAND, B. K. Activity of single neurons in the hypothalamic feeding centers: Effect of 2-deoxy-D-glucose. *Physiology and Behavior*, 1968, 3, 757–760.

DeSISTO, M. J., and ZWEIG, M. Differentiation of hypothalamic feeding and killing. *Physiological Psychology*, 1974, 2, 67–70.

DEUTSCH, J. A., and DiCARA, L. Hunger and extinction in intracranial self-stimulation. *Journal of Comparative and Physiological Psychology*, 1967, *63*, 344–347.

DEUTSCH, J. A., and HOWARTH, C. I. Some tests of a theory of intracranial self-stimulation. *Psychological Review*, 1963, *70*, 444–460.

DE VALOIS, R. L. Behavioral and electrophysiological studies of primate vision. In *Contributions to Sensory Physiology*, Vol. 1, edited by W. D. Neff. New York: Academic Press, 1965.

DE VALOIS, R. L., ABRAMOV, I., and JACOBS, G. H. Analysis of response patterns of LGN cells. *Journal of the Optical Society of America*, 1966, *56*, 966–977.

DEWEY, W. L., SNYDER, J. W., HARRIS, L. S., and HOWES, J. F. The effects of narcotics and narcotic antagonists on the tail-flick response in spinal mice. *Journal of Pharmacy and Pharmacology.* 1969, *21*, 548–550.

DIAMOND, I. T., and NEFF, W. D. Ablation of temporal cortex and discrimination of auditory patterns. *Journal of Neurophysiology*, 1957, *20*, 300–315.

DiCARA, L., BRAUN, J., and PAPPAS, B. Classical conditioning and instrumental learning of cardiac and gastrointestinal response following removal of neocortex in the rat. *Journal of Comparative and Physiological Psychology*, 1970, *73*, 208–216.

DOBELLE, W. H., MLADEJOVSKY, M. G., and GIRVIN, J. P. Artificial vision for the blind: Electrical stimulation of visual cortex offers hope for a functional prosthesis. *Science*, 1974, *183*, 440–444.

DOETSCH, G. S., GANCHROW, J. J., NELSON, L. M., and ERICKSON, R. D. Information processing in the taste system of the rat. In *Olfaction and Taste III. Proceedings of the Third International Symposium*, edited by C. Pfaffman. New York: Rockefeller University Press, 1969.

DOUGLAS, R. J. The hippocampus and behavior. *Psychological Bulletin*, 1967, *67*, 416–422.

DOWLING, J. E., and BOYCOTT, B. B. Organization of the primate retina: Electron microscopy. *Proceedings of the Royal Society of London*, 1966, Series B, *166*, 80–111.

DOWNER, J. L. deC. Interhemispheric integration in the visual system. In *Interhemispheric Relations and Cerebral Dominance*, edited by V. B. Mountcastle. Baltimore: Johns Hopkins University Press, 1962.

DUA, S., and MacLEAN, P. D. Location for penile erection in medial frontal lobe. *American Journal of Physiology*, 1964, *207*, 1425–1434.

DUNCAN, C. P. The retroactive effect of electroshock on learning. *Journal of Comparative and Physiological Psychology*, 1949, *42*, 32–44.

DZENDOLET, E. A. A structure common to sweet-evoking compounds. *Perception and Psychophysics*, 1968, *3*, 65–68.

EDWARDS, D. A. Mice: Fighting by neonatally androgenized females. *Science*, 1968, *161*, 1027–1028.

EGGER, M. D., and FLYNN, J. P. Effect of electrical stimulation of the amygdala on hypothalamically elicited attack behavior in cats. *Journal of Neurophysiology*, 1963, *26*, 705–720.

EGGER, M. D., and FLYNN, J. P. Further studies on the effects of amygdaloid stimulation and ablation on hypothalamically elicited attack behavior in cats. In *Progress in Brain Research*, Vol. 27, edited by W. R. Adey and T. Tokizane. Amsterdam: Elsevier, 1967.

EINSTEIN, E. R. Basic protein of myelin and its role in experimental allergic encephalomyelitis and multiple sclerosis. In *Handbook of Neurochemistry*, Vol. 7, edited by A. Lajtha. New York: Plenum Press, 1972.

ELDRED, E., and BUCHWALD, J. Central nervous system: Motor mechanisms. *Annual Review of Physiology*, 1967, *29*, 573–606.

ELDREDGE, D. H., and MILLER, J. D. Physiology of hearing. *Annual Review of Physiology*, 1971, *33*, 281–310.

ELLISON, G. D. and FLYNN, J. P. Organized aggressive behavior in cats after surgical isolation of the hypothalamus. *Archives Italiennes de Biologie*, 1968, *106*, 1–20.

EL-WAKIL, F. W. Unpublished master's thesis. University of Massachusetts, 1975.

ENGSTRÖM, H. ADES, H. W., and HAWKINS, J. E. Cellular pattern, nerve structures, and fluid spaces of the organ of Corti. In *Contributions to Sensory Physiology*, edited by W. D. Neff. New York: Academic Press, 1965.

ENTINGH, D. J., DAMSTRA-ENTINGH, T., DUNN, A., WILSON, J. E., and GLASSMAN, E. Brain uridine monophosphate: Reduced incorporation of uridine during avoidance learning. *Brain Research*, 1974, *70*, 131–138.

ENTINGH, D., DUNN, A., GLASSMAN, E., WILSON, J. E., HOGAN, E., and DAMSTRA, T. Biochemical approaches to the biology of memory. In *Handbook of Psychobiology*, edited by M. S. Gazzaniga and C. Blakemore. New York: Academic Press, 1975.

EPSTEIN, A. N., FITZSIMONS, J. T., and ROLLS, B. J. Drinking induced by injection of angiotensin into the brain of the rat. *Journal of Physiology (London)*, 1970, *210*, 457–474.

EPSTEIN, A. N., and TEITELBAUM, P. Severe and persistent deficits in thirst produced by lateral hypothalamic damage. In *Thirst: Proceedings of the First International Symposium on Thirst in the Regulation of Body Water*, edited by M. J. Wayner. Oxford: Pergamon, 1964.

EPSTEIN, A. N., and TEITELBAUM, P. Specific loss of the hypoglycemic control of feeding in recovered lateral rats. *American Journal of Physiology*, 1967, *213*, 1159–1167.

ETHOLM, B. Evoked responses in the inferior colliculus, medial geniculate body, and auditory cortex by single and double clicks in cats. *Acta Oto-Laryngologica (Stockholm)*, 1969, *67*, 319–325.

ETTINGER, G. Cross-modal transfer of training in monkeys. *Behaviour*, 1960, *16*, 56–65.

EVARTS, E. V. Relation of discharge frequency to conduction velocity in pyramidal tract neurons. *Journal of Neurophysiology*, 1965, 28, 215–228.

EVARTS, E. V. Discussion of O. Pompeiano. The neurophysiological mechanisms of the postural and motor events during desynchronized sleep. *Research Publications of the Association for Research on Nervous and Mental Disorders*, 1968a, 45, 450.

EVARTS, E. V. Relation of pyramidal tract activity to force exerted during voluntary movement. *Journal of Neurophysiology*, 1968b, 31, 14–27.

EVARTS, E. V. Activity of pyramidal tract neurons during postural fixation. *Journal of Neurophysiology*, 1969, 32, 375–385.

EVARTS, E. V. Sensorimotor cortex activity associated with movements triggered by visual as compared to somesthetic inputs. In *The Neurosciences: Third Study Program*, edited by F. O. Schmitt and F. G. Worder. Cambridge: MIT Press, 1974.

EVERETT, J. W., and NICHOLS, D. C. The timing of ovulatory release of gonadotropin induced by estrogen in pseudopregnant and diestrous cyclic rats. *Anatomical Record*, 1968, 160, 346.

EVERITT, B. J., and HERBERT, J. Adrenal glands and sexual receptivity in Rhesus female monkeys. *Nature*, 1969, 222, 1065–1066.

EXLEY, D., GELLERT, R. J., HARRIS, G. W., and NADLER, R. D. The site of action of "chlormadinone acetate" (6-chloro-Δ^6-dehydro-17-α-acetoxyprogesterone) in blocking ovulation in the mated rabbit. *Journal of Physiology (London)*, 1968, 195, 697–714.

FALCK, B., HILLARP, N.-Å., THIEME, G., and TORP, A. Fluorescence of catechol amines and related compounds condensed with formaldehyde. *Journal of Histochemistry and Cytochemistry*, 1962, 10, 348–364.

FENCL, V., KOSKI, G., and PAPPENHEIMER, J. R. Factors in cerebrospinal fluid from goats that affect sleep and activity in rats. *Journal of Physiology (London)*, 1971, 216, 565–589.

FETZ, E. E. Personal communication. Cited by A. L. Towe, 1973.

FEX, J. Neural excitatory processes of the inner ear. In *Handbook of Sensory Physiology*, Vol. 5, *Auditory System*, edited by H. H. Kornhuber. Berlin: Springer-Verlag, 1972.

FEX, J. Neuropharmacology and potentials of the inner ear. In *Basic Mechanisms in Hearing*, edited by A. R. Møller. New York: Academic Press, 1973.

FIBIGER, H. C., ZIS, A. P., and McGEER, E. G. Feeding and drinking deficits after 6-hydroxydopamine administration in the rat: Similarities to the lateral hypothalamic syndrome. *Brain Research*, 1973, 55, 135–148.

FINERTY, J. C. Parabiosis in physiological studies. *Physiological Review*, 1952, 32, 277–302.

FISHBEIN, W. Disruptive effects of rapid eye movement sleep deprivation on long-term memory. *Physiology and Behavior*, 1971, 6, 279–282.

FISHBEIN, W., McGAUGH, J. L., and SWARZ, J. R. Retrograde amnesia: Electroconvulsive shock effects after termination of rapid eye movement sleep deprivation. *Science*, 1971, 172, 80–82.

FISHER, C. Dreaming and sexuality. In *Psychoanalysis: A General Psychology*, edited by L. Lowenstein, M. Newman, M. M. Schur, and A. Solnit. New York: International University Press, 1966.

FISHER, C., BYRNE, J. EDWARDS, A., and KAHN, E. A psychophysiological study of nightmares. *Journal of the American Psychoanalytic Association*, 1970, 18, 747–782.

FISHER, C., GROSS, J., and ZUCH, J. Cycle of penile erection synchronous with dreaming (REM) sleep. Preliminary report. *Archives of General Psychiatry*, 1965, 12, 29–45.

FITZSIMONS, J. T. Drinking by rats depleted of body fluid without increase in osmotic pressure. *Journal of Physiology (London)*, 1961, 159, 297–309.

FITZSIMONS, J. T. The physiology of thirst: A review of the extraneural aspects of the mechanisms of drinking. In *Progress in Physiological Psychology*, Vol. 4, edited by E. Stellar and J. M. Sprague. New York: Academic Press, 1971.

FITZSIMONS, J. T., and LE MAGNEN, J. Eating as a regulatory control of drinking in the rat. *Journal of Comparative and Physiological Psychology*, 1969, 67, 273–283.

FITZSIMONS, J. T., and SIMONS, B. J. The effect on drinking in the rat of intravenous infusion of angiotensin, given alone or in combination with other stimuli of thirst. *Journal of Physiology (London)*, 1969, 203, 45–57.

FLEMING, A., and ROSENBLATT, J. S. Olfactory regulation of maternal behavior in rats: I. Olfactory bulbectomy in experienced and inexperienced females. *Journal of Comparative and Physiological Psychology*, 1974a, 86, 221–232.

FLEMING, A., and ROSENBLATT, J. S. Olfactory regulation of maternal behavior in rats: II. Effects of peripherally induced anosmia and lesions of the lateral olfactory tract in pup-induced virgins. *Journal of Comparative and Physiological Psychology*, 1974b, 86, 233–246.

FLEMING, D. G. Food intake studies of parabiotic rats. *Annals of the New York Academy of Science*, 1969, 157, 985–1002.

FLEXNER, J. B., and FLEXNER, L. B. Restoration of memory lost after treatment with puromycin. *Proceedings of the National Academy of Science*, 1967, 57, 1651–1654.

FLEXNER, J. B., and FLEXNER, L. B. Further observations on restoration of memory lost after treatment with puromycin. *Yale Journal Biology and Medicine*, 1969, 42, 235–240.

FLEXNER, J. B., and FLEXNER, L. B. Adrenalectomy and suppression of memory by puromycin. *Proceedings of the National Academy of Science*, 1970, 66, 48–52.

FLEXNER, J. B., FLEXNER, L. B., and STELLAR, E. Memory

in mice as affected by intracerebral puromycin. *Science*, 1963, *141*, 57–59.

FLOCK, Å. Transducing mechanisms in the lateral line canal organ receptors. *Cold Spring Harbor Symposia on Quantitative Biology*, 1965, *30*, 133–146.

FLYNN, J., VANEGAS, H., FOOTE, W., and EDWARDS, S. Neural mechanisms involved in a cat's attack on a rat. In *The Neural Control of Behavior*, edited by R. F. Whalen, M. Thompson, M. Verzeano, and N. Weinberger. New York: Academic Press, 1970.

FOSTER, R. S., JENDEN, D. J., and LOMAX, P. A comparison of the pharmacological effects of morphine and N-methyl-morphine. *Journal of Pharmacology and Experimental Therapeutics*, 1967, *157*, 185–195.

FOULKES, D. Dream reports from different stages of sleep. *Journal of Abnormal and Social Psychology*, 1962, *65*, 14–25.

FRANK, B., STEIN, D. G., and ROSEN, J. Interanimal "memory" transfer: Results from brain and liver homogenates. *Science*, 1970, *169*, 399–402.

FREDERICSON, E. The effects of food deprivation upon competitive and spontaneous combat in C57 black mice. *Journal of Psychology*, 1950, *29*, 89–100.

FREEMON, F. R. *Sleep Research: A Critical Review.* Springfield, Ill.: Charles C Thomas, 1972.

FRIEDMAN, M. I., and BRUNO, J. P. Exchange of water during lactation. *Science*, 1976, *191*, 409–410.

FRIEDMAN, M. I., ROWLAND, N., SALLER, C. F., and STRICKER, E. M. Homeostasis during hypoglycemia: Central control of adrenal secretion and peripheral control of feeding. *Science*, 1976, (in press).

FRIEDMAN, M. I., and STRICKER, E. M. The physiological psychology of hunger: A physiological perspective. *Psychological Review*, 1976, (in press).

FROHMAN, L. A., and BERNARDIS, L. L. Growth hormone and insulin levels in weanling rats with ventromedial hypothalamic lesions. *Endocrinology*, 1968, *82*, 1125–1132.

FROHMAN, L. A., and BERNARDIS, L. L. Effects of hypothalamic stimulation on plasma glucose, insulin, and glucagon levels. *American Journal of Physiology*, 1971, *221*, 1596–1603.

FROHMAN, L. A., GOLDMAN, J. K., and BERNARDIS, L. L. Metabolism of intravenously injected ^{14}C-glucose in weanling rats with hypothalamic obesity. *Metabolism*, 1972, *21*, 799–805.

FROMMER, G. P. Gustatory afferent responses in the thalamus. In *Physiological and Behavioral Aspects of Taste*, edited by M. R. Kare and B. P. Halpern. Chicago: University of Chicago Press, 1961.

FUJIMORI, M., and HIMWICH, H. E. Electroencephalographic analyses of amphetamine and its methoxy derivatives with reference to their sites of EEG alerting in the rabbit brain. *International Journal of Neuropharmacology*, 1969, *8*, 601–615.

FUORTES, M. G. F. Electric activity of cells in the eye of Limulus. *American Journal of Ophthalmology*, 1958, *46*, 210–223.

FUXE, K., NYSTRÖM, M., TOVI, M., SMITH, R., and ÖGREN, S. -O. Central catecholamine neurons, behavior and neuroleptic drugs: An analysis to understand the involvement of catecholamines in schizophrenia. *Journal of Psychiatric Research*, 1974, *11*, 151–162.

GALLISTEL, C. R. The incentive of brain stimulation reward. *Journal of Comparative and Physiological Psychology*, 1969, *69*, 713–721.

GALLISTEL, C. R. Self-stimulation: The neurophysiology of reward and motivation. In *The Physiological Basis of Memory*, edited by J. A. Deutsch. New York: Academic Press, 1973.

GALLISTEL, C. R., STELLAR., J. R., and BUBIS, E. Parametric analysis of brain stimulation reward in the rat: I. The transient process and the memory-containing process. *Journal of Comparative and Physiological Psychology*, 1974, *87*, 848–859.

GANDELMAN, R., ZARROW, M. X., DENENBERG, V. H., and MYERS, M. Olfactory bulb removal eliminates maternal behavior in the mouse. *Science*, 1971, *171*, 210–211.

GARCIA, J., ERVIN, F. R., YORKE, C. H., and KOELLING, R. A. Conditioning with delayed vitamin injections. *Science*, 1967, *155*, 716–718.

GARCIA, J., GREEN, K. F., and McGOWAN, B. K. X-ray as an olfactory stimulus. In *Taste and Olfaction*, edited by C. Pfaffman. New York: Rockefeller University Press, 1969.

GARCIA, J., KIMMELDORF, D. J., and HUNT, E. L. The use of ionizing radiation as a motivating stimulus. *Psychological Review*, 1961, *68*, 383–385.

GARCIA, J., KIMMELDORF, D. J., and KOELLING, R. A. Conditioned aversion to saccharin resulting from exposure to gamma radiation. *Science*, 1955, *122*, 157–158.

GARCIA, J., and KOELLING, R. A. Relation of cue to consequence in avoidance learning. *Psychonomic Science*, 1966, *4*, 123–124.

GARDNER, R. A., and GARDNER, B. T. Teaching sign language to a chimpanzee. *Science*, 1969, *165*, 664–672.

GAZZANIGA, M. F. *The Bisected Brain.* New York: Appleton, 1970.

GENOVESI, U., MORUZZI, G., PALESTINI, M., ROSSI, G. F., and ZANCHETTI, A. EEG and behavioral patterns following lesions of the mesencephalic reticular formation in chronic cats with implanted electrodes. *Abstracts of Communications of the Twentieth International Physiology Congress*, Bruxelles, 1956, 335–336.

GESCHWIND, N. Disconnexion syndromes in animals and man. *Brain*, 1965, *88*, 237–294, 585–644.

GESCHWIND, N. Language and the brain. *Scientific American*, 1972, *226*, 76–83.

GESCHWIND, N. The apraxias: Neural mechanisms of

disorders of learned movement. *American Scientist,* 1975, *63,* 188–195.

GESCHWIND, N., QUADFASEL, F. A., and SEGARRA, J. M. Isolation of the speech area. *Neuropsychologia,* 1968, *6,* 327–340.

GIACHETTI, I., MACLEOD, P., and LE MAGNEN, J. Influence des états de faim et de satieté sur les réponses du bulbe olfactif chez le rat. *Journal de Physiologie (Paris),* 1970, *62* (Supplement 2), 280–281.

GIBSON, A., BAKER, J., STEIN, J., and GLICKSTEIN, M. Visual cells in the pons: Locus and properties. *Federation Proceedings,* 1974, *33,* 433P.

GIBSON, W. E., REID, L. D., SAKAI, M., and PORTER, P. B. Intracranial reinforcement compared with sugar-water reinforcement. *Science,* 1965, *148,* 1357–1359.

GILMAN, A. The relation between blood osmotic pressure, fluid distribution and voluntary water intake. *American Journal of Physiology,* 1937, *120,* 323–328.

GIRDEN, E., METTLER, F. A., FINCH, G., and CULLER, E. Conditioned responses in a decorticate dog to acoustic, thermal, and tactile stimulation. *Journal of Comparative Psychology,* 1936, *27,* 367–385.

GLENDENNING, K. K. Effects of septal and amygdaloid lesions on social behavior of the cat. *Journal of Comparative and Physiological Psychology,* 1972, *80,* 199–207.

GLICKSTEIN, M., KING, R. A., and STEIN, J. F. The visual input to neurones in N. pontis. *Journal of Physiology (London),* 1971, *218,* 79P.

GLICKSTEIN, M., and STEIN, J. F. Electrical activation of visual neurones in nucleus pontis in the cat. *Journal of Physiology (London),* 1973, *229,* 28P.

GLOBUS, A., ROSENZWEIG, M. R., BENNETT, E. L., and DIAMOND, M. C. Effects of differential experience on dendritic spine counts in rat cerebral cortex. *Journal of Comparative and Physiological Psychology,* 1973, *82,* 175–181.

GODDARD, G. V. Development of epileptic seizures through brain stimulation at low intensity. *Nature,* 1967, *214,* 1020–1021.

GOLD, R. M. Hypothalamic obesity: The myth of the ventromedial nucleus. *Science,* 1973, *182,* 488–490.

GOLD R. M. Anodal electrolytic brain lesions: How current and electrode metal influence lesion size and hyperphagiosity. *Physiology and Behavior,* 1975, *14,* 625–632.

GOLDBERG, J. M., and FERNANDEZ, C. Vestibular mechanisms. *Annual Review of Physiology,* 1975, *37,* 129–162.

GOLDSTEIN, A., SHEEHAN, P., and GOLDSTEIN, J. Unsuccessful attempts to transfer morphine tolerance and passive avoidance by brain extracts. *Nature,* 1971, *223,* 126–129.

GOLDSTEIN, M. Discussion. *Journal of Psychiatric Research,* 1974, *11,* 219.

GOLDSTEIN, M. H., HALL, J. L., and BUTTERFIELD, B. O.

Single-unit activity in the primary auditory cortex of unanesthesized cats. *Journal of the Acoustical Society of America,* 1968, *43,* 444–455.

GOODENOUGH, D. R., SHAPIRO, A., HOLDEN, M., and STEINSCHRIBER, L. A comparison of "dreamers" and "nondreamers": Eye movements, electroencephalograms, and the recall of dreams. *Journal of Abnormal and Social Psychology,* 1959, *59,* 295–302.

GOODMAN, E., JANSEN, P., and DEWSBURY, D. Midbrain reticular formation lesions: Habituation to stimulation and copulatory behavior in male rats. *Physiology and Behavior,* 1971, *6,* 151–156.

GORSKI, R. A. Gonadal hormones and the perinatal development of neuroendocrine function. In *Frontiers in Neuroendocrinology,* edited by L. Martini and W. F. Ganong. New York: Oxford University Press, 1971.

GOTSICK, J. E., and MARSHALL, R. C. Time course of the septal rage syndrome. *Physiology and Behavior,* 1972, *9,* 685–687.

GOURAS, P. Identification of cone mechanisms in monkey ganglion cells. *Journal of Physiology (London),* 1968, *199,* 533–548.

GOURAS, P., and KRÜGER, J. Similarities of color properties of neurons in areas 17, 18, and V4 of monkey cortex. Paper presented at the Seventh International Neurobiology Meeting, Göttingen, September, 1975.

GOY, R. W. Experimental control of psychosexuality. In *A Discussion of the Determination of Sex,* edited by G. W. Harris and R. G. Edwards. London: *Philosophical Transactions of the Royal Society,* Series B, Vol. 259, 1970.

GOY, R. W., and PHOENIX, C. Hypothalamic regulation of female sexual behavior: Establishment of behavioral oestrus in spayed guinea pigs following hypothalamic lesions. *Journal of Reproduction and Fertility,* 1963, *5,* 23–40.

GOY, R. W., PHOENIX, C. H., and YOUNG, W. C. A critical period for the suppression of behavioral receptivity in adult female rats by early treatment with androgen. *Anatomical Record,* 1962, *142,* 307.

GRADY, K. L., PHOENIX, C. H., and YOUNG, W. C. Role of the developing rat testis in differentiation of the neural tissues mediating mating behavior. *Journal of Comparative and Physiological Psychology,* 1965, *59,* 176–182.

GRANT, E. C. G., and MEARS, E. Mental effects of oral contraceptives. *Lancet,* 1967, *2,* 945–946.

GREEN, J., CLEMENTE, C., and DEGROOT, J. Rhinencephalic lesions and behavior in cats. *Journal of Comparative Neurology,* 1957, *108,* 505–545.

GREENBERG, R., MAYER, R., BROOK, R., PEARLMAN, C., and HARTMANN, E. Sleep and dreaming in patients with post-alcoholic Korsakoff's disease. *Archives of General Psychiatry,* 1968, *18,* 203–209.

GREENBERG, R., and PEARLMAN, C. Cutting the REM nerve: An approach to the adaptive role of REM sleep. *Perspectives in Biology and Medicine*, 1974, 17, 513–521.

GREENBERG, R., PEARLMAN, C., FINGAR, R., KANTROWITZ, J., and KAWLICHE, S. The effects of dream deprivation: Implications for a theory of the psychological function of dreaming. *British Journal of Medical Psychology*, 1970, 43, 1–11.

GREENBERG, R., PILLARD, R., and PEARLMAN, C. The effect of dream (stage REM) deprivation on adaptation to stress. *Psychosomatic Medicine*, 1972, 34, 257–262.

GREISER, C., GREENBERG, R., and HARRISON, R. H. The adaptive function of sleep: The differential effects of sleep and dreaming on recall. *Journal of Abnormal Psychology*, 1972, 80, 280–286.

GROSS, C. G. Inferotemporal cortex and vision. In *Progress in Physiological Psychology*, edited by E. Stellar and J. M. Sprague. New York: Academic Press, 1973.

GROSS, C. G., COWEY, A., and MANNING, F. J. Further analysis of visual discrimination deficits following foveal prestriate and inferotemporal lesions in rhesus monkeys. *Journal of Comparative and Physiological Psychology*, 1971, 76, 1–7.

GROSS, C. G., ROCHA-MIRANDA, C. E., and BENDER, D. B. Visual properties of neurons in inferotemporal cortex of the macaque. *Journal of Neurophysiology*, 1972, 35, 96–111.

GROSS, M. D. Violence associated with organic brain disease. In *Dynamics of Violence*, edited by J. Fawcett. Chicago: American Medical Association, 1971.

GROSSMAN, S. P. Neurophysiologic aspects: Extra-hypothalamic factors in the regulation of food intake. *Advances in Psychosomatic Medicine*, 1972, 7, 49–72.

GULEVICH, G., DEMENT, W. C., and JOHNSON, L. Psychiatric and EEG observations on a case of prolonged (264 hours) wakefulness. *Archives of General Psychiatry*, 1966, 15, 29–35.

GUMULKA, W., SAMANIN, R., VALZELLI, L., and CONSOLO, S. Behavioural and biochemical effects following the stimulation of the nucleus raphis dorsalis on rats. *Journal of Neurochemistry*, 1971, 18, 533–534.

GUROWITZ, E. M., GROSS, D. A., and GEORGE, R. Effects of TCAP on passive avoidance learning in rats. *Psychonomic Science*, 1968, 12, 293–294.

HAGINS, W. A., PENN, R. D., YOSHIKAMI, S. Dark current and photocurrent in retinal rods. *Journal of Biophysics*, 1970, 10, 380–410.

HALASZ, B. Endocrine function of hypothalamic islands. *Proceedings of the Third International Congress of Endocrinology, Mexico City, 1968.* New York: Excerpta Medica Foundation, 1969.

HAMMOND, P. H., MERTON, P. A., and SUTTON, G. G. Nervous gradation of muscular contraction. *British Medical Bulletin*, 1956, 12, 214–218.

HAMMOND, W. A. *Sleep and Its Derangements.* Philadelphia: Lippincott, 1883.

HANKINS, W. G., GARCIA, J., and RUSINIAK, K. W. Dissociation of odor and taste in baitshyness. *Behavioral Biology*, 1973, 8, 407–419.

HARDING, C. F., and LESCHNER, A. I. The effects of adrenalectomy on the aggressiveness of differently housed mice. *Physiology and Behavior*, 1972, 8, 437–440.

HARLOW, H. F. Recovery of pattern discrimination in monkeys following unilateral occipital lobectomy. *Journal of Comparative Psychology*, 1939, 27, 467–489.

HARLOW, H. F. *Learning to Love.* New York: Ballantine, 1973.

HARPER, A. E. Effects of dietary protein content and amino acid pattern on food intake and preference. In *Handbook of Physiology*, Vol. 1, edited by C. F. Code and W. Heidel. Washington, D.C.: American Physiological Society, 1967.

HARRIS, G. W., and JACOBSOHN, D. Functional grafts of the anterior pituitary gland. *Proceedings of the Royal Society, London*, Series B, 1951–1952, 139, 263–276.

HARRIS, G. W., and LEVINE, S. Sexual differentiation of the brain and its experimental control. *Journal of Physiology*, 1965, 181, 379–400.

HARRIS, G. W., and MICHAEL, R. P. The activation of sexual behavior by hypothalamic implants of oestrogen. *Journal of Physiology* (London), 1964, 171, 275–301.

HART, B. Sexual reflexes and mating behavior in the male dog. *Journal of Comparative and Physiological Psychology*, 1967a, 66, 388–399.

HART, B. Testosterone regulation of sexual reflexes in spinal rats. *Science*, 1967b, 155, 1283–1284.

HART, B. Alteration of quantitative aspects of sexual reflexes in spinal male dogs. *Journal of Comparative and Physiological Psychology*, 1968, 66, 726–730.

HART, B. Gonadal hormones and sexual reflexes in the female rat. *Hormones and Behavior*, 1969, 1, 65–71.

HART, B. Mating behavior in the female dog and the effects of estrogen on sexual reflexes. *Hormones and Behavior*, 1970, 1, 93–104.

HARTLINE, H. K., and RATLIFF, F. Spatial inhibitory influences in the eye of the *Limulus*, and the mutual interaction of receptor units. *Journal of General Physiology*, 1958, 41, 1049–1066.

HARTMAN, E. *The Biology of Dreaming.* Springfield, Ill.: Charles C Thomas, 1967.

HARTMANN, E. L. *The Functions of Sleep.* New Haven: Yale University Press, 1973.

HATTON, G. I. Nucleus circularis: Is it an osmoreceptor in the brain? *Brain Research Bulletin*, 1976, 1, 123–131.

HAWKINS, J. E. Cytoarchitectural basis of cochlear transducer, *Cold Springs Harbor Symposium on Quantitative Biology*, 1965, 30, 147–157.

HAYWOOD, J., ROSE, S. P. R., and BATESON, P. P. G. Effects of an imprinting procedure on RNA polymerase activity in chick brain. *Nature*, 1970, 228, 373–374.

HEATH, R. G. Pleasure response of human subjects to direct stimulation of the brain: Physiologic and psychodynamic consideration. In *The Role of Pleasure in Behavior*, edited by R. G. Heath. New York: Harper & Row, 1964.

HEATH, R. G., and MICKLE, W. A. Evaluation of seven years' experience with depth electrode studies in human patients. In *Electrical Studies on the Unanesthetized Brain*, edited by E. R. Ramey and D. S. O'Doherty. New York: Paul B. Hoeber, 1960.

HEFFNER, R., and MASTERSON, B. Variation in form of the pyramidal tract and its relationship to digital dexterity. *Brain, Behavior, and Evolution*, 1975, 12, 161–200.

HEIMER, L., and LARSSON, K. Drastic changes in the mating behavior of male rats following lesions in the junction of diencephalon and mesencephalon. *Experientia*, 1964, 20, 460–461.

HEIMER, L., and LARSSON, K. Impairment of mating behavior in male rats following lesions in the preoptic-anterior hypothalamic continuum. *Brain Research*, 1966/1967, 3, 248–263.

HENRICKSEN, S., DEMENT, W., and BARCHAS, J. The role of serotonin in the regulation of a phasic event of rapid eye movement sleep: The ponto-geniculo-occipital wave. *Advances in Biochemical Psychopharmacology*, 1974, 11, 169–179.

HENSEL, H. Thermoreceptors. *Annual Review of Physiology*, 1974, 36, 233–249.

HENSEL, H., and KENSHALO, D. R. Warm receptors in the nasal region of cats. *Journal of Physiology (London)*, 1969, 204, 99–112.

HERBERG, L. Seminal ejaculation following positively reinforcing electrical stimulation of the rat hypothalamus. *Journal of Comparative and Physiological Psychology*, 1963, 56, 679–685.

HERNANDEZ-PEON, R., O'FLAHERTY, J. J., and MAZZUCHELLI-O'FLAHERTY, A. L. Sleep and other behavioral effects induced by acetylocholine stimulation of basal temporal cortex and striate structures. *Brain Research*, 1967, 4, 243–267.

HERVEY, G. R. The effects of lesions in the hypothalamus in parabiotic rats. *Journal of Physiology (London)*, 1959, 145, 336–352.

HERZ, A., ALBUS, K., METYŠ, J., SCHUBERT, P., and TESCHEMACHER, H. On the central sites for the antinociceptive action of morphine and fentanyl. *Neuropharmacology*, 1970, 9, 539–551.

HESS, W. R. Das Schlafsyndrom als Folge dienzephaler Reizung. *Helvetica Physiologica et Pharmacologica Acta*, 1944, 2, 305–344.

HETHERINGTON, A. W., and RANSON, S. W. Experimental hypothalamohypophyseal obesity in the rat. *Proceedings of the Society for Experimental Biology and Medicine*, 1939, 41, 465–466.

HEUSER, J. E., and REESE, T. S. Evidence for recycling of synaptic vesicle membrane during transmitter release at the frog neuromuscular function. *Journal of Cell Biology*, 1973, 57, 315–344.

HIERONS, R., and SAUNDERS, M. Impotence in patients with temporal lobe lesions. *Lancet*, 1966, 2, 761–764.

HILTON, S. M., and ZBROZYNA, A. W. Amygdaloid region for defense reactions and its afferent pathway to the brain stem. *Journal of Physiology (London)*, 1963, 165, 160–173.

HIRSCH, H. V. B., and SPINELLI, D. N. Visual experience modifies distribution of horizontally and vertically oriented receptive fields in cats. *Science*, 1970, 168, 869–871.

HIRSCH, H. V. B., and SPINELLI, D. N. Modification of the distribution of receptive field orientation in cats by selective visual exposure during development. *Experimental Brain Research*, 1971, 13, 509–527.

HITT, J. C., HENDRICKS, S. E., GINSBERG, S. I., and LEWIS, J. H. Disruption of male, but not female, sexual behavior in rats by medial forebrain bundle lesions. *Journal of Comparative and Physiological Psychology*, 1970, 73, 377–384.

HOBSON, J. A., McCARLEY, R. W., and WYZINSKI, P. W. Sleep cycle oscillation: Reciprocal discharge by two brainstem neuronal groups. *Science*, 1975, 189, 55–58.

HOEBEL, B. G. Inhibition and disinhibition of self-stimulation and feeding: Hypothalamic control and post-ingestional factors. *Journal of Comparative and Physiological Psychology*, 1968, 66, 89–100.

HOEBEL, B. G., and TEITELBAUM, P. Weight regulation in normal and hypothalamic hyperphagic rats. *Journal of Comparative and Physiological Psychology*, 1966, 61, 189–193.

HOFFER, B. J., SIGGINS, G. R., OLIVER, A. P., and BLOOM, F. E. Cyclic AMP mediation of norepinephrine inhibition in rat cerebellar cortex: A unique class of synaptic response. *Annals of the New York Academy of Science*, 1971, 185, 531–549.

HOLMES, G. The cerebellum of man. *Brain*, 1939, 62, 21–30.

HORN, G., ROSE, S. P. R., and BATESON, P. P. G. Experience and plasticity in the central nervous system. *Science*, 1973, 181, 506–514.

HOROVITZ, A. P., PIALA, J. J., HIGH, J. P., BURKE, J. C., and LEAF, R. C. Effects of drugs on the mouse-killing (muricide) test and its relationships to amygdaloid function. *International Journal of Neuropharmacology*, 1966, 5, 405–411.

HOSTETTER, G. Hippocampal lesions in rats weaken the retrograde amnesia effect of ECS. *Journal of Comparative and Physiological Psychology*, 1968, 66, 349–353.

HOWARTH, C. I., and DEUTSCH, J. A. Drive decay: The cause of fast "extinction" of habits learned for brain stimulation. *Science*, 1962, 137, 35–36.

HUBEL, D. H., and WIESEL, T. N. Receptive fields and functional architecture in two nonstriate visual areas (18 and 19) of the cat. *Journal of Neurophysiology,* 1965, *28,* 229–289.

HUGHES, J., SMITH, T. W., KOSTERLITZ, H. W., FOTHERGILL, L. A., MORGAN, B. A., and MORRIS, H. R. Identification of two related pentapeptides from the brain with potent opiate agonist activity. *Nature,* 1975, *258,* 577–579.

HUNSICKER, J. P., and REID, L. D. "Priming effect" in conventionally reinforced rats. *Journal of Comparative and Physiological Psychology,* 1974, 87, 618–621.

HUNSPERGER, R. In *The Sleeping Brain,* edited by M. H. Chase. Los Angeles: Brain Information Service/Brain Research Institute, UCLA, 1972.

HUNTER, R., LOGUE, V., and MCMENEMY, W. H. Temporal lobe epilepsy supervening on longstanding transvestitism and fetishism. *Epilepsia,* 1963, *4,* 60–65.

HUTCHINSON, R. R., and RENFREW, J. W. Stalking attack and eating behavior elicited from the same sites in the hypothalamus. *Journal of Comparative and Physiological Psychology,* 1966, *61,* 300–367.

HYDÉN, H. Biochemical changes accompanying learning. In *The Neurosciences: Second Study Program,* edited by G. C. Quarton, T. Melnechuk, and F. O. Schmitt. New York: Rockefeller University Press, 1967.

HYDÉN, H., and EGYHAZI, E. Nuclear RNA changes in nerve cells during a learning experiment in rats. *Proceedings of the National Academy of Science,* 1962, *48,* 1366–1372.

HYDÉN, H., and LANGE, P. W. Protein synthesis in the hippocampal pyramidal cells of rats during a behavioral test. *Science,* 1968, *159,* 1370–1373.

HYDÉN, H., and LANGE, P. W. Protein changes in different brain areas as a function of intermittent training. *Proceedings of the National Academy of Science,* 1972, *69,* 1980–1984.

ILLIS, L. Changes in spinal cord synapses and a possible explanation for spinal shock. *Experimental Neurology,* 1963, *8,* 328–335.

INGELFINGER, F. J. The late effects of total and subtotal gastrectomy. *New England Journal of Medicine,* 1944, *231,* 321–327.

INGRAM, W. R., BARRIS, R. W., and RANSON, S. W. Catalepsy. An experimental study. *Archives of Neurology and Psychiatry (Chicago),* 1936, *35,* 1175–1197.

IRWIN, L. N. and SAMSON, F. E. Content and turnover of gangliosides in rat brain following behavioral stimulation. *Journal of Neurochemistry,* 1971, *18,* 203–211.

ISAACSON, R. L. *The Limbic System.* New York: Plenum Press, 1974.

JANOWITZ, H. D., and GROSSMAN, M. I. Some factors affecting the food intake of normal dogs and dogs with esophagostomy and gastric fistula. *American Journal of Physiology,* 1949b, *159,* 143–148.

JANOWITZ, H. D., HANSON, M. E., and GROSSMAN, M. I. Effects of intravenously administered glusoce on food intake in the dog. *American Journal of Physiology,* 1949, *156,* 87–91.

JANOWITZ, H. D., and HOLLANDER, F. Effect of prolonged intragastric feeding on oral ingestion. *Federation Proceedings,* 1953, *12,* 72.

JARVIK, M. E. Effects of chemical and physical treatments on learning and memory. *Annual Review of Psychology,* 1972, *23,* 457–486.

JOHN, E. R. *Mechanisms of Memory.* New York: Academic Press, 1967.

JOHN, E. R. Switchboard versus statistical theories of learning and memory. *Science,* 1972, *177,* 850–864.

JOHN, E. R., and KLEINMAN, D. "Stimulus generalization" between differentiated visual, auditory, and central stimuli. *Journal of Neurophysiology,* 1975, *38,* 1015–1034.

JOHNSON, A. K. Localization of angiotensin in sensitive areas for thirst within the rat brain. Paper presented at the meeting of the Eastern Psychological Association, Boston, April, 1972.

JOHNSON, A. K. Personal communication, 1976.

JOHNSTON, P. J., and DAVIDSON, J. M. Intracerebral androgens and sexual behavior in the male rat. *Hormones and Behavior,* 1972, *3,* 345–357.

JONES, B. Catecholamine-containing neurons in the brain stem of the cat and their role in waking. Unpublished master's thesis. Lyon: Tixier, 1969. Cited by Jouvet, 1972.

JONES, B. E., BOBILLIER, P., and JOUVET, M. Effets de la destruction des neurones contenant des catécholamines du mésencéphale sur le cycle veille-sommeils du chat. *Comptes Rendus de la Société de Biologie, Paris,* 1969, *163,* 176–180.

JONES, B. P., MOSKOWITZ, H. R., and BUTTERS, N. Olfactory discrimination in alcoholic Korsakoff patients. *Neuropsychologia,* 1975, *13,* 173–179.

JOST, A. Embryonic sexual differentiation. In *Hermaphroditism, Genital Anomalies and Related Endocrine Disorders,* edited by A. Jost, H. W. Jones, and W. W. Scott. Baltimore: Williams & Wilkins, 1958.

JOST, A., JONES, H. W., and SCOTT, W. W., editors. *Hermaphroditism, Genital Anomalies and Related Endocrine Disorders,* ed. 2. Baltimore: Williams & Wilkins, 1969.

JOUVET, M. Recherches sur les structures nerveuses et les mécanismes responsables des différentes phases du sommeil physiologique. *Archives Italiennes de Biologie,* 1962, *100,* 125–206.

JOUVET, M. Insomnia and decrease of cerebral 5-hydroxy-tryptamine after destruction of the raphé system in the cat. *Advances in Pharmacology,* 1968, *6,* 265–279.

JOUVET, M. The role of monoamines and acetylcholine-containing neurons in the regulation of the sleep-waking cycle. *Ergebnisse der Physiologie*, 1972, *64*, 166–307.

JOUVET, M., MICHEL, F., and MOUNIER, D. Comparative study of the "paradoxical phase" of sleep in cat and man (abstract). *Electroencephalography and Clinical Neurophysiology*, 1960, *12*, 937.

JOUVET, M., and RENAULT, J. Insomnie persistante après lésions des noyaux du raphé chez le chat. *Comptes Rendus Dendus de la Société de Biologie et de ses Filiales*, 1966, *160*, 1461–1465.

JOY, M. D., and LOWE, R. D. Evidence for a medullary site of action in the cardiovascular response to angiotensin II. *Journal of Physiology (London)*, 1970, *206*, 41P–42P.

JOY, R., and PRINZ, P. The effect of sleep alerting environments upon the acquisition and retention of a conditioned avoidance response in the rat. *Physiology and Behavior*, 1969, *4*, 809–814.

KALES, A., HEUSER, G., JACOBSON, A., KALES, J. D., HANLEY, J., ZWEIZIG, J. R., and PAULSON, M. J. All-night sleep patterns in hypothyroid patients, before and after treatment. *Journal of Clinical Endocrinology*, 1967, *27*, 1593–1599.

KALES, A., HOEDEMAKER, F. S., JACOBSON, A., KALES, J. D., PAULSON, M. J., and WILSON, T. E. Mentation during sleep: REM and NREM recall reports. *Perceptual and Motor Skills*, 1967, *24*, 555–560.

KALRA, S. P., and SAWYER, C. H. Blockade of copulation-induced ovulation in the rat by anterior hypothalamic deafferentation. *Endocrinology*, 1970, 87, 1124–1128.

KANE, F. J. Psychiatric reaction to oral contraceptives. *American Journal of Obstetrics and Gynecology*, 1968, *102*, 1053–1063.

KAPATOS, G., and GOLD, R. M. Evidence for ascending noradrenergic mediation of hypothalamic hyperphagia. *Pharmacology, Biochemistry, and Behavior*, 1973, *1*, 81–87.

KARLI, P. The Norway rat's killing response to the white mouse. *Behavior*, 1956, *10*, 81–103.

KASSIL, V. G., UGOLEV, A. M., and CHERNIGOVSKII, V. N. Regulation of selection and consumption of food and metabolism. *Progress in Physiological Sciences*, 1970, *1*, 387–404.

KATSUKI, Y. Neural mechanism of auditory sensation in cats. In *Sensory Communication*, edited by W. A. Rosenblith. Cambridge: MIT Press, 1961.

KEELE, C. A. Measurement of responses to chemically induced pain. In *Touch, Heat, and Pain*, edited by A. V. S. deReuck and J. Knight. Boston: Little, Brown, 1966.

KENT, E., and GROSSMAN, S. P. Evidence for a conflict interpretation of anomalous effects of rewarding brain stimulation. *Journal of Comparative and Physiological Psychology*, 1969, *69*, 381–390.

KIANG, N. Y.-S. Discharge patterns of single fibers in the cat's auditory nerve. Cambridge: MIT Press, 1965.

KIM, Y. K., and UMBACH, W. Combined stereotaxic lesions for treatment of behavior disorders and severe pain. Paper presented at the Third World Congress of Psychosurgery, Cambridge, England, 1972. Cited by Valenstein, 1973.

KIMBLE, D. P., ROGERS, L., and HENDRICKSON, C. W. Hippocampal lesions disrupt maternal, not sexual, behavior in the albino rat. *Journal of Comparative and Physiological Psychology*, 1967, *63*, 401–407.

KINCL, F. A., and MAQUEO, M. Prevention by progesterone of steroid-induced sterility in neonatal male and female rats. *Endocrinology*, 1965, 77, 859–862.

KING, C. D. 5-Hydroxytryptamine and sleep in the cat: A brief overview. *Advances in Biochemical Psychopharmacology*, 1974, *11*, 211–216.

KING, D., and JEWETT, R. E., The effects of alpha methyltyrosine on sleep and brain norepinephrine in the cat. *Journal of Pharmacology and Experimental Therapeutics*, 1971, *177*, 188–194.

KISSILEFF, H. R. Unpublished data cited by J. Le Magnen, Advances in studies on the physiological control and regulation of food intake. In *Progress in Physiological Psychology*, Vol. 4, edited by E. Stellar and J. M. Sprague. New York: Academic Press, 1971.

KLEITMAN, N. *Sleep and Wakefulness*, ed. 2. Chicago: University of Chicago Press, 1963.

KLING, A., LANCASTER, J., and BENITONE, J. Amygdalectomy in the free-ranging vervet (*Cercopithecus althiops*). *Journal of Psychiatric Research*, 1970, *7*, 191–199.

KLÜVER, H., and BUCY, P. C. Preliminary analysis of functions of the temporal lobes in monkeys. *Archives of Neurology and Psychiatry*, Chicago, 1939, *42*, 979–1000.

KOELLA, W. P. Serotonin—A hypnogenic transmitter and an antiawakening agent. *Advances in Biochemical Psychopharmacology*, 1974, *11*, 181–186.

KOLÁŘSKÝ, A., FREUND, K., MACHEK, J., and POLÁK, O. Male sexual deviation. Association with early temporal lobe damage. *Archives of General Psychiatry*, 1967, *17*, 735–743.

KOMISARUK B. R. Paper presented at the First World Congress on Pain, Florence, Italy, 1975. Cited by Liebeskind and Giesler (1976).

KORNHUBER, H. H. Cerebral cortex, cerebellum, and basal ganglia: An introduction to their motor functions. In *The Neurosciences: Third Study Program*, edited by F. O. Schmitt and F. G. Worden. Cambridge: MIT Press, 1974.

KORSAKOFF, S. S. Étude médico-psychologique sur une forme des maladies de la mémoire. *Revue de Philosophie*, 1889, *28*, 501–530.

KOSLOW, S. H. 5-Methoxytryptamine: A possible central nervous system transmitter. *Advances in Biochemical Psychopharmacology*, 1974, *11*, 95–100.

KOVNER, R., and STAMM, J. S. Disruption of short-term

visual memory by electrical stimulation of inferotemporal cortex in the monkey. *Journal of Comparative and Physiological Psychology*, 1972, *81*, 163–172.

KRASNE, F. B. General disruption resulting from electrical stimulus of ventromedial hypothalamus. *Science*, 1962, *138*, 822–823.

KRIECKHAUS, E. E., and WOLF, G. Acquisition of sodium by rats: Interaction of innate mechanisms and latent learning. *Journal of Comparative and Physiological Psychology*, 1968, *65*, 197–201.

KUFFLER, S. W. Discharge patterns and functional organization of mammalian retina. *Journal of Neurophysiology*, 1953, *16*, 37–68.

KUHAR., M. J., PERT, C. B., and SNYDER, S. H. Regional distribution of opiate receptor binding in human and monkey brain. *Nature*, 1973, *245*, 447–450.

LARSON, J. D., and FOULKES, W. D. Electromyogram suppression during sleep, dream recall, and orientation time. *Psychophysiology*, 1969, *5*, 548–555.

LARSSON, K. Mating behavior in male rats after cerebral cortex ablation: II. Effects of lesions in the frontal lobes compared to lesions in the posterior half of the hemispheres. *Journal of Experimental Zoology*, 1964, *155*, 203–214.

LASHLEY, K. Studies of cerebral function in learning: XI. The behavior of the rat in latch-box situations. *Comparative Psychology Monograph*, 1935, *11* (2), 5–40.

LASHLEY, K. S. The mechanism of vision: XVI. The functioning of small remnants of the visual cortex. *Journal of Comparative Neurology*, 1939, *70*, 45–67.

LASHLEY, K. S. Studies of cerebral function in learning: XII. Loss of the maze habit after occipital lesions in blind rats. *Journal of Comparative Neurology*, 1943, *79*, 431–462.

LASHLEY, K. In search of the engram. *Society of Experimental Biology*, 1950, Symposium 4, 454–482.

LAW, D. T., and Meagher, W. Hypothalamic lesions and sexual behavior in the female rat. *Science*, 1958, *128*, 1626–1627.

LAWRENCE, D. H., and MASON, W. A. Intake and weight adjustments in rats to change in feeding schedule. *Journal of Comparative and Physiological Psychology*, 1955, *48*, 43–46.

LAWRENCE, J. E. S. Science and sentiment: Overview of research on crowding and human behavior. *Psychological Bulletin*, 1974, *81*, 712–720.

LECONTE, P., HENNEVIN, E., and BLOCH, V. Increase in paradoxical sleep following learning in the rat: Correlation with level of conditioning. *Brain Research*, 1972, *42*, 552–553.

LEE, J. R., and FENNESSY, M. R. The relationship between morphine analgesia and the levels of biogenic amines in the mouse brain. *European Journal of Pharmacology*, 1970, *12*, 65–70.

LEGRENDE, R., and PIÉRON, H. Recherches sur le besoin de sommeil consécutif a une veille prolongés. *Zietschrift fuer Allgemeine Physiologie*, 1913, *14*, 235–362.

LE MAGNEN, J. Hyperphagie provoquée chez le rat blanc par altération du mécanisme de satiété périphérique. *Comptes Rendus des Séances de la Société de Biologie*, 1956, *150*, 32.

LE MAGNEN, J. Advances in studies on the physiological control and regulation of food intake. In *Progress in Physiological Psychology*, Vol. 4, edited by E. Stellar and J. M. Sprague. New York: Academic Press, 1971.

LE MAGNEN, J., and TALLEN, S. La periodicité spontanée de la prise d'aliments ad libitum du rat blanc. *Journal of Physiology*, (Paris), 1966, *58*, 323–349.

LERNER, A. B., CASE, J. D., TAKAHASHI, Y., LEE, T. H., and MORI, W. Isolation of melatonin, the pineal gland factor that lightens melanocytes. *Journal of the American Chemical Society*, 1958, *80*, 2587.

LESHNER, A. I., WALKER, W. A., JOHNSON, A. E., KELLING, J. S., KREISLER, S. J., and SVARE, B. B. Pituitary adrenocortical activity and intermale aggressiveness in isolated mice. *Physiology and Behavior*, 1973, *11*, 705–711.

LETTVIN, J. Y., and GESTELAND, R. C. Speculations on smell. *Cold Spring Harbor Symposium*, 1965, *30*, 217–225.

LETTVIN, J. Y., MATURANA, H. R., McCULLOCK, W. S., and PITTS, W. H. What the frog's eye tells the frog's brain. *Proceedings of the Institute of Radio Engineers*, 1959, *47*, 1940–1951.

LEWIN, I., and GOMBOSH, D. Increase in REM time as a function of the need for divergent thinking. Report to the First European Congress of Sleep Research, 1972, Basil, Switzerland.

LEWIS, D. J., MISANIN, J. R., and MILLER, R. R. Recovery of memory following amnesia. *Nature*, 1968, *220*, 704–705.

LEWY, A. J., and SEIDEN, L. S. Operant behavior changes norepinephrine metabolism in rat brain. *Science*, 1972, *175*, 454–455.

LICKLIDER, J. C. R. Three auditory theories. In *Psychology: A Study of a Science*, Vol. I, edited by I. S. Koch. New York: McGraw-Hill, 1959.

LIEBELT, R. A., BORDELON, C. B., and LIEBELT, A. G. The adipose tissue system and food intake. In *Progress in Physiological Psychology*, edited by E. Stellar and J. M. Sprague. New York: Academic Press, 1973.

LIEBESKIND, J. C., and GIESLER, G. J., JR. Evidence pertaining to an endogenous mechanism of pain inhibition in the central nervous system. In *Sensory Functions of the Skin in Primates, with Special Reference to Man*, edited by Y. Zotterman. Oxford: Pergamon Press, 1976.

LIEBESKIND, J. C., GUILBAUD, G., BESSON, J. -M., and OLIVERAS, J. -L. Analgesia from electrical stimulation of the periaqueductal gray matter in the cat: Behavioral observations and inhibitory effects on spinal cord interneurons. *Brain Research*, 1973, *50*, 441–446.

LINDEN, E. R., BERN, D., and FISHBEIN, W. Retrograde amnesia: Prolonging the fixation phase of memory consolidation by paradoxical sleep deprivation. *Physiology and Behavior*, 1975, *14*, 409–415.

LINDSLEY, D. B., SCHREINER, L. H., KNOWLES, W. B., and MAGOUN, H. W. Behavioral and EEG changes following chronic brain stem lesions in the cat. *Electroencephalography and Clinical Neurophysiology*, 1950, *2*, 483–498.

LISK, R. D. Diencephalic placement of estradiol and sexual receptivity in the female rat. *American Journal of Physiology*, 1962, *203*, 493–496.

LISK, R. D. Neural localization for androgen activation of copulatory behavior in the rat. *Endocrinology*, 1967, *80*, 754–761.

LISK, R. D., PRETLOW, R. A., and FRIEDMAN, S. Hormonal stimulation necessary for elicitation of maternal nest-building in the mouse (*Mus musculus*). *Animal Behaviour*, 1969, *17*, 730–737.

LIVETT, B. G. Histochemical visualization of adrenergic neurones, peripherally and in the central nervous system. *British Medical Bulletin*, 1973, *29*, 93–99.

LLOYD, D. P. C. The spinal mechanism of the pyramidal system in cats. *Journal of Neurophysiology*, 1941, *4*, 525–546.

LOEWENSTEIN, W. R., and MENDELSON, M. Components of receptor adaptation in a Pacinian corpuscle. *Journal of Physiology (London)*, 1965, *177*, 377–397.

LOEWENSTEIN, W. R., and RATHKAMP, R. The sites for mechano-electric conversion in a Pacinian corpuscle. *Journal of General Physiology*, 1958, *41*, 1245–1265.

LORENS, S. A. Effect of lesions in the central nervous system on lateral hypothalamic self-stimulation in the rat. *Journal of Comparative and Physiological Psychology*, 1966, *62*, 256–262.

LOTT, D. F., and FUCHS, S. S. Failure to induce retrieving by sensitization or the injection of prolactin. *Journal of Comparative and Physiological Psychology*, 1962, *55*, 1111–1113.

LUBAR, J. F., BOYCE, B. A., and SCHAEFER, C. S. Etiology of polydipsia and polyuria in rats with septal lesions. *Physiology and Behavior*, 1968, *3*, 289–292.

LUCERO, M. A. Lengthening of REM sleep duration consecutive to learning in the rat. *Brain Research*, 1970, *20*, 319–322.

LURIA, A. R. The functional organization of the brain. *Scientific American*, 1970, *222*, 66–79.

MacDONNELL, M. F., and FLYNN, J. P. Control of sensory fields by stimulation of hypothalamus. *Science*, 1966, *152*, 1406–1408.

MACHLUS, B., ENTINGH, D., WILSON, J. E., and GLASSMAN, E. Brain phosphoproteins: The effect of various behaviors and reminding experiences on the incorporation of radioactive phosphate into nuclear proteins. *Behavioral Biology*, 1974, *10*, 63–73.

MACHLUS, B., WILSON, J. E., and GLASSMAN, E. Brain phosphoproteins: The effect of short experiences on the phosphorylation of nuclear proteins of rat brain. *Behavioral Biology*, 1974, *10*, 43–62.

MacKAY, E. M., CALLOWAY, J. W., and BARNES, R. H. Hyperalimentation in normal animals produced by protamine insulin. *Journal of Nutrition*, 1940, *20*, 59–66.

MacLEAN, P. D., and DELGADO, J. M. R. Electrical and chemical stimulation of frontotemporal portion of limbic system in the waking animal. *Electroencephalography and Clinical Neurophysiology*, 1953, *5*, 91–100.

MacLEAN, P. D., DENNISTON, R. H., and DUA, S. Further studies on cerebral representation of penile erection: Caudal thalamus, midbrain, and pons. *Journal of Neurophysiology*, 1963, *26*, 273–293.

MacLEAN, P. D., DUA, S., and DENNISTON, R. H. Cerebral localization for scratching and seminal discharge. *Archives of Neurology*, 1963, *9*, 485–497.

MacLEAN, P. D., and PLOOG, D. W. Cerebral representation of penile erection. *Journal of Neurophysiology* 1962, *25*, 29–55.

MAFFEI, L., MORUZZI, G., and RIZZOLATTI, G. Influence of sleep and wakefulness on the response of lateral geniculate units to sinewave photic stimulation. *Archives Italiennes de Biologie*, 1965, *103*, 596–608.

MAGNES, J., MORUZZI, G., and POMPEIANO, O. Synchronization of the EEG produced by low-frequency electrical stimulation of the region of the solitary tract. *Archives Italiennes de Biologie*, 1961, *99*, 33–67.

MAGNI, F., MORUZZI, G., ROSSI, G. F., and ZANCHETTI, A. EEG arousal following inactivation of the lower brain stem by selective injection of barbiturate into the vetebral circulation. *Archives Italiennes de Biologie*, 1959, *97*, 33–46.

MARANTZ, R., and RECHTSCHAFFEN, A. Effect of alpha-methyltyrosine on sleep in the rat. *Perceptual and Motor Skills*, 1967, *25*, 805–808.

MARCZYNSKI, T. J., YAMAGUCHI, N., LING, G. M., and GRODZINSKA, L. Sleep induced by the administration of melatonin (5-methoxy-N-acetyltryptamine) to hypothalamus in unrestrained cats. *Experientia*, 1964, *20*, 435–437.

MARGULES, D. L. Noradrenergic rather than serotonergic basis of reward in the dorsal tegmentum. *Journal of Comparative and Physiological Psychology*, 1969, *67*, 32–35.

MARK, V. H., and ERVIN, F. R. *Violence and the Brain.* New York: Harper & Row, 1970.

MARK, V. H., ERVIN, F. R., and YAKOVLEV, P. I. The treatment of pain by stereotaxic methods. *Confina Neurologica*, 1962, *22*, 238–245.

MARK, V. H., SWEET, W. H., and ERVIN, F. R. The effect of amygdalectomy on violent behavior in patients with temporal lobe epilepsy. In *Psychosurgery*, edited by E. Hitchcock, L. Laitinen, and K. Vaernet. Springfield, Ill.: Charles C Thomas, 1972.

MARKS, W. B., DOBELLE, W. H., and MACNICHOL, E. F. Viscual pigments of single primate cones. *Science*, 1964, *143*, 1181–1183.

MARTINEZ, C., and BITTNER, J. J. A non-hypophyseal sex difference in estrous behavior of mice bearing pituitary grafts. *Proceedings of the Society for Experimental Biology and Medicine*, 1956, *91*, 506–509.

MAYER, D. J., and LIEBESKIND, J. C. Pain reduction by focal electrical stimulation of the brain: An anatomical and behavioral analysis. *Brain Research*, 1974, *68*, 73–93.

MAYER, J. Regulation of energy intake and the body weight: The glucostatic theory and the lipostatic hypothesis. *Annals of the New York Academy of Science*, 1955, *63*, 15–43.

MAYER, J., and MARSHALL, N. B. Specificity of gold-thioglucose for ventromedial hypothalamic lesions and obesity. *Nature*, 1956, *178*, 1399–1400.

MCCARLEY, R. W., and Hobson, J. A. Discharge patterns of cat brain stem neurons during desynchronized sleep. *Journal of Neurophysiology*, 1975a, 38, 751–766.

MCCARLEY, R. W., and HOBSON, J. A. Neouronal excitability modulation over the sleep cycle: A structural and mathematical modal. *Science*, 1975b, *189*, 58–60.

MCGAUGH, J. L., and HERZ, M. J. *Memory Consolidation*. San Francisco: Albion, 1972.

MCGINTY, D. J. Effects of prolonged isolation and subsequent enrichment of sleep patterns in kittens. *Electroencephalography and Clinical Neurophysiology*, 1969, *26*, 332–337.

MCGINTY, D., EPSTEIN, A. N., and TEITELBAUM, P. The contribution of oropharyngeal sensations to hypothalamic hyperphagia. *Animal Behaviour*, 1965, *13*, 413–418.

MCGINTY, D. J., HARPER, R. M., and FAIRBANKS, M. K. Neuronal unit activity and the control of sleep states. In *Advances in Sleep Research*, edited by E. D. Weitzman. Flushing, New York: Spectrum Publications, 1974.

MCGINTY, D. J., and STERMAN, M. B. Sleep suppression after basal forebrain lesions in the cat. *Science*, 1968, *160*, 1253–1255.

MCKENNA, T., MCCARLEY, R. W., AMATRUDA, T., BLACK, D., and HOBSON, J. A. Effects of carbachol at pontine sites yielding long duration desynchronized sleep episodes. In *Sleep Research*, Vol. 3. Los Angeles: Brain Information Service/Brain Research Institute, UCLA, 1974, p. 39.

MELLINKOFF, S. M., FRANKLAND, M., BOYLE, D., and GREIPEL, M. Relation between serum amino acid concentration and fluctuations in appetite. *Journal of Applied Physiology*, 1956, *8*, 535–538.

MELZACK, R., and WALL, P. D. Pain mechanisms: A new theory. *Science*, 1965, *150*, 971–979.

MENDELSON, J. Lateral hypothalamic stimulation in satiated rats: The rewarding effects of self-induced drinking. *Science*, 1967, *157*, 1077–1079.

MEYER, D. R. Acceses to engrams. *American Psychologist*, 1972, *27*, 124–133.

MICHAEL, R. P., KEVERNE, E. B., and BONSALL, R. W. Pheromones: Isolation of male sex attractants from a female primate. *Science*, 1971, *172*, 946–966.

MILLER, G. A., and TAYLOR, W. G. The perception of repeated bursts of noise. *Journal of the Acoustical Society of America*, 1948, *20*, 171–182.

MILLER, N. E., BAILEY, C. J., and STEVENSON, J. A. F. Decreased hunger but increased food intake resulting from hypothalamic lesions. *Science*, 1950, *112*, 256–259.

MILLER, R. R., and SPRINGER, A. D. Amnesia, consolidation, and retrieval. *Psychological Review*, 1973, *80*, 69–70.

MILNER, B. Memory disturbance after bilateral hippocampal lesions. In Milner, P., and Glickman, S., *Cognitive Processes and the Brain*. Princeton: Van Nostrand, 1965.

MILNER, B. Memory and the temporal regions of the brain. In *Biology of Memory*, edited by K. H. Pribram and D. E. Broadbent. New York: Academic Press, 1970.

MILNER, B., BRANCH, C., and RASMUSSEN, T. Evidence for bilateral speech representation in some non-right-handers. *Transactions of the American Neurological Association*, 1966, *91*, 306–308.

MILNER, B., CORKIN, S., and TEUBER, H. -L. Further analysis of the hippocampal amnesic syndrome: 14-year follow-up study of H. M. *Neuropsychologia*, 1968, *6*, 317–338.

MISELIS, R. R., and EPSTEIN, A. N. Feeding induced by 2-deoxy-D-glucose injections into the lateral ventricle of the rat. *The Physiologist*, 1970, *13*, 262.

MISHKIN, M. Visual mechanisms beyond the striate cortex. In *Frontiers in Physiological Psychology*, edited by R. W. Russell. New York: Academic Press, 1966.

MITCHELL, C. L., and KAELBER, W. W. Unilateral vs. bilateral medial thalamic lesions and reactivity to noxious stimuli. *Archives of Neurology*, 1967, *17*, 653–660.

MITCHELL, W., FALCONER, M. A., and HILL, D. Epilepsy with fetishism relieved by temporal lobectomy. *Lancet*, 1954, *2*, 626–630.

MOGENSON, G. J. Hypothalamic limbic mechanisms in the control of water intake. In *The Neuropsychology of Thirst: New Findings and Advances in Concepts*, edited by A. N. Epstein, H. R. Kissileff, and E. Stellar. Washington: Winston, 1973.

MØLLGAARD, K., DIAMOND, M. C., BENNETT, E. L., ROSENZWEIG, M. R., and LINDNER, B. Quantitative synaptic changes with differential experience in rat brain. *International Journal of Neuroscience*, 1971, *2*, 113–128.

MOLTZ, H., LUBIN, M., LEON, M., and NUMAN, M. Hormonal induction of maternal behavior in the ovariectomized nulliparous rat. *Physiology and Behavior*, 1970, *5*, 1373–1377.

MOLTZ, H., ROBBINS, D., and PARKS, M. Caesarian delivery and maternal behavior of primiparous and multiparous rats. *Journal of Comparative and Physiological Psychology*, 1966, *61*, 455–460.

MONCRIEFF, R. W. Olfactory adaptation and odour likeness. *Journal of Physiology (London)*, 1956, *133*, 301–316.

MONEY, J. Components of eroticism in man: Cognitional rehearsals. In *Recent Advances in Biological Psychiatry*, edited by J. Wortis. New York: Grune and Stratton, 1960a.

MONEY, J. Phantom orgasm in the dreams of paraplegic men and women. *Archives of General Psychiatry*, 1960b, *3*, 373–382.

MONEY, J., and EHRHARDT, A. A. *Man and Woman, Boy and Girl*. Baltimore: The Johns Hopkins University Press, 1972.

MONNIER, M., and HÖSLI, L. Dialysis of sleep and waking factors in blood of rabbit. *Science*, 1964, *146*, 796–798.

MONNIER, M., and HÖSLI, L. Humoral regulation of sleep and wakefulness by hypnogenic and activating dialysable factors. *Progress in Brain Research*, 1965, *18*, 118–123.

MONNIER, M., KOLLER, T., and GRABER, S. Humoral influences of induced sleep and arousal upon electrical brain activity of animals with crossed circulation. *Experimental Neurology*, 1963, *8*, 264–277.

MOOK, D. G. Oral and postingestional determinants of the intake of various solutions in rats with esophageal fistulas. *Journal of Comparative and Physiological Psychology*, 1963, *56*, 645–659.

MOORE, R. Y. Effects of some rhinencephalic lesions on retention of conditioned avoidance behavior in cats. *Journal of Comparative and Physiological Psychology*, 1964, *53*, 540–548.

MORGAN, C. T., and MORGAN, J. D. Studies in hunger: II. The relation of gastric denervation and dietary sugar to the effect of insulin upon food intake in the rat. *Journal of General Psychology*, 1940, *57*, 153–163.

MORGANE, J. P. Alterations in feeding and drinking of rats with lesions in the globi pallidi. *American Journal of Physiology*, 1961, *201*, 420–428.

MORISON, R. S., and DEMPSEY, E. W. A study of thalamo-cortical relations. *American Journal of Physiology*, 1942, *135*, 281–292.

MORRELL, F. Physiology and histochemistry of the mirror focus. In *Basic Mechanisms of the Epilepsies*, edited by H. H. Jasper, A. A. Ward, and A. Pope. Boston: Little, Brown, 1969.

MORUZZI, G. The sleep-waking cycle. *Ergebnisse der Physiologie*, 1972, *64*, 1–165.

MORUZZI, G., and MAGOUN, H. W. Brain stem reticular formation and activation of the EEG. *Electroencephalography and Clinical Neurophysiology*, 1949, *1*, 455–473.

MOTOKAWA, K., TAIRA, N., and OKUDA, J. Spectral responses of single units in the primate cortex. *Tohoku Journal of Experimental Medicine*, 1962, *78*, 320–337.

MOUNT, G. B., and HOEBEL, B. G. Lateral hypothalamic reward decreased by intragastric feeding: Self-determined "threshold" technique. *Psychonomic Science*, 1967, *9*, 265–266.

MOUNTCASTLE, V. B. The problem of sensing and the neural coding of sensory events. In *The Neurosciences*, edited by G. Quarton, T. Melnechuk, and F. O. Schmitt. New York: Rockefeller University Press, 1967.

MOUNTCASTLE, V. B., and POWELL, T. P. S. Neural mechanisms subserving cutaneous sensibility, with special reference to the role of afferent inhibition in sensory perception and discrimination. *Bulletin of the Johns Hopkins Hospital*, 1959, *105*, 201–232.

MOYER, K. E. Kinds of aggression and their physiological basis. *Communications in Behavioral Biology*, 1968, *2*, 65–87.

MOZELL, M. M. Evidence for a chromatographic model of olfaction. *Journal of General Physiology*, 1970, *55*, 46–63.

MURRAY, R. G., and MURRAY, A. The anatomy and ultrastructure of taste endings. In *Taste and Smell in Vertebrates*, edited by G. E. W. Wolstenholme and J. Knight. London: J. & A. Churchill, 1970.

NACHMAN, M. Taste preference for sodium salts by adrenalectomized rats. *Journal of Comparative and Physiological Psychology*, 1962, *55*, 1124–1129.

NACHMAN, M. Learned aversion to the taste of lithium chloride and generalization to other salts. *Journal of Comparative and Physiological Psychology*, 1963, *56*, 343–349.

NADLER, R. D. Masculinization of female rats by intracranial implantation of androgen in infancy. *Journal of Comparative and Physiological Psychology*, 1968, *66*, 157–167.

NAFE, J. P., and WAGONER, K. S. The nature of pressure adaptation. *Journal of General Psychology*, 1941, *25*, 323–351.

NAKAO, H. Emotional behavior produced by hypothalamic stimulation. *American Journal of Physiology*, 1958, *194*, 411–418.

NAPOLI, A. M., and GERALL, A. A. Effects of estrogen and antiestrogen on reproductive function in neonatally androgenized female rats. *Endocrinology*, 1970, *87*, 1330–1337.

NAQUET, R., DENAVIT, M., and ALBE-FESSARD, D. Comparison entre le rôle du subthalamus et celui des différentes structures bulbomésencephaliques dans le maintien de la vigilance. *Electroencephalography and Clinical Neurophysiology*, 1966, *20*, 149–164.

NARABAYASHI, H. Stereotaxic amygdalectomy. In *The Neurobiology of the Amygdala*, edited by B. E. Eleftheriou. New York: Plenum Press, 1972.

NARABAYASHI, H., NAGAO, T., SAITO, Y., YOSHIDA, M., and NAGAHATA, M. Stereotaxic amygdalotomy for behavior disorders. *Archives of Neurology*, 1963, *9*, 1–16.

NATHAN, P. W., and RUDGE, P. Testing the gate-control theory of pain in man. *Journal of Neurology, Neurosurgery, and Psychiatry*, 1974, *37*, 1366–1372.

NAUTA, W. J. H. Hypothalamic regulation of sleep in rats. Experimental study. *Journal of Neurophysiology*, 1946, *9*, 285–316.

NICOLAÏDIS, S. Résponses des unités osmosensibles hypothalamiques aux stimulations salienes et aqueuses de la langue. *Comptés Rendus Hebdomadaires des Séances de l'Academie des Sciences. Series C*, 1968, *267*, 2352–2355.

NIIJIMA, A. Afferent impulse discharge from glucoreceptors in the liver of the guinea pig. *Annals of the New York Academy of Science*, 1969, *157*, 690–700.

NOIROT, E. Selective priming of maternal responses by auditory and olfactory cues from mouse pups. *Developmental Psychobiology*, 1970, *2*, 273–276.

NOIROT, E. Ultrasounds and maternal behavior in small rodents. *Developmental Psychobiology*, 1972, *5*, 371–387.

NOVIN, D., SANDERSON, J. D., and VANDERWEELE, D. A. The effect of isotonic glucose on eating as a function of feeding condition and infusion site. *Physiology and Behavior*, 1974, *13*, 3–7.

NOVIN, D., VANDERWEELE, D. A., and REZEK, M. Hepatic-portal 2-deoxy-D-glucose infusion causes eating: Evidence for peripheral glucoreceptors. *Science*, 1973, *181*, 858–860.

NUMAN, M. Medial preoptic area and maternal behavior in the female rat. *Journal of Comparative and Physiological Psychology*, 1974, *87*, 746–759.

OAKLEY, K., and TOATES, F. M. The passage of food through the gut of rats and its uptake of fluid. *Psychonomic Science*, 1969, *16*, 225–226.

O'BRIEN, J. H., and FOX, S. S. Single-cell activity in cat motor cortex: II. Functional characteristics of the cell related to conditioning changes. *Journal of Neurophysiology*, 1969, *32*, 285–296.

O'KELLY, L. I. The psychophysiology of motivation. *Annual Review of Psychology*, 1963, *14*, 57–92.

OLDS, J. Commentary. In *Brain Stimulation and Motivation*, edited by E. S. Valenstein. Glenview, Ill.: Scott, Foresman, 1973.

OLDS, J., ALLAN, W. S., and BRIESE, E. Differentiation of hypothalamic drive and reward centers. *American Journal of Physiology*, 1971, *221*, 368–375.

OLDS, J., and MILNER, P. Positive reinforcement produced by electrical stimulation of septal area and other regions of rat brain. *Journal of Comparative and Physiological Psychology*, 1954, *47*, 419–427.

OLDS, M. E., and OLDS, J. Effects of lesions in medial forebrain bundle on self-stimulation behavior. *American Journal of Physiology*, 1969, *217*, 1253–1264.

OLSON, L. Post-mortem fluorescence histochemistry of monoaminergic neuron systems in the human brain: A new approach in the search for a neuropathology of schizophrenia. *Journal of Psychiatric Research*, 1974, *11*, 199–204.

ORBACH, J., MILNER, B., and RASMUSSEN, T. Learning and retention in monkeys after amygdala-hippocampus resection. *Archives of Neurology*, 1960, *3*, 230–251.

OSWALD, I. Drugs and sleep. *Pharmacological Reviews*, 1968, *20*, 272–303.

OVER, R., and MACKINTOSH, N. J. Cross-modal transfer of intensity discrimination by rats. *Nature*, 1969, *224*, 917–918.

PANDYA, D. N., and KUYPERS, H. G. J. M. Corticocortical connections in the rhesus monkey. *Brain Research*, 1969, *13*, 13–36.

PANKSEPP, J. Drugs and stimulus-bound attack. *Physiology and Behavior*, 1971a, *6*, 317–320.

PANKSEPP, J. Aggression elicited by electrical stimulation of the hypothalamus in albino rats. *Physiology and Behavior*, 1971b, *6*, 321–329.

PANKSEPP, J., and TROWILL, J. A. Intraoral self-injection: I. Effects of delay of reinforcement on resistance to extinction and implications for self-stimulation. *Psychonomic Science*, 1967a, *9*, 405–406.

PANKSEPP, J., and TROWILL, J. A. Intraoral self-injection: II. The simulation of self-stimulation phenomena with a conventional reward. *Psychonomic Science*, 1967b, *9*, 407–408.

PARMEGGIANI, P. L. Telencephalo-diencephalic aspects of sleep mechanisms. *Brain Research*, 1968, *7*, 350–359.

PASIK, P., PASIK, T., and SCHILDER, P. Extrageniculostriate vision in the monkey: Discrimination of luminous flux-equated figures. *Experimental Neurology*, 1969, *23*, 421–437.

PAUKER, S. G. Grand-rounds whiplash. *New England Journal of Medicine*, 1970, *283*, 600–601.

PAUL, L., MILEY, W. M., and BAENNINGER, R. Mouse killing by rats: Roles of hunger and thirst in its initiation and maintenance. *Journal of Comparative and Physiological Psychology*, 1971, *76*, 242–249.

PAVLOV, I. P. "Innere Hemmung" der bedingten Reflexe und der Schlaf—ein und derselbe Prozeß. *Skandinavisches Archiv für Physiologie*, 1923, *44*, 42–58.

PAXINOS, G., and BINDRA, D. Hypothalamic knife cuts: Effects on eating, drinking, irritability, aggression, and copulation in the male rat. *Journal of Comparative and Physiological Psychology*, 1972, *79*, 219–229.

PAXINOS, G., and BINDRA, D. Hypothalamic and midbrain neural pathways involved in eating, drinking, irritability, aggression, and copulation in rats. *Journal of Comparative and Physiological Psychology*, 1973, *82*, 1–14.

PEARLMAN, C. Latent learning impaired by REM sleep deprivation. *Psychonomic Science*, 1971, *25*, 135–136.

PEARLMAN, C. REM sleep deprivation impairs latent extinction in rats. *Physiology and Behavior*, 1973, *11*, 233–237.

PEARLMAN, C. A., JR., and GREENBERG, R. Posttrial REM sleep: A critical period for consolidation of shuttlebox avoidance. *Animal Learning and Behavior*, 1973, *1*, 49–51.

PECK, J. W. Discussion: Thirst(s) resulting from bodily water imbalances. In *The Neuropsychology of Thirst: New Findings and Advances in Concepts*, edited by A. N. Epstein, H. R. Kissileff, and E. Stellar. Washington: Winston, 1973.

PECK, J. W., and NOVIN, D. Evidence that osmoreceptors mediating drinking in rabbits are in the lateral preoptic region. *Journal of Comparative and Physiological Psychology*, 1971, *74*, 134–147.

PENFIELD, W., and JASPER, H. *Epilepsy and the Functional Anatomy of the Human Brain*. Boston: Little, Brown, 1954.

PENFIELD, W., and MILNER, B. Memory deficit produced by bilateral lesions in the hippocampal zone. *American Medical Association Archives of Neurological Psychiatry*, 1958, *79*, 475–497.

PERKEL, D. H., and BULLOCK, T. H. Neural coding. *Neuroscience Research Progress Bulletin*, 1968, *6*, 221–347.

PERRY, T. L., HANSEN, S., and KLOSTER, M. Huntington's chorea: Deficiency of δ-aminobutyric acid in brain. *New England Journal of Medicine*, 1973, *288*, 337–342.

PERT, C. B., SNOWMAN, A. M., and SNYDER, S. H. Localization of opiate receptor binding in presynaptic membranes of rat brain. *Brain Research*, 1974, *70*, 184–188.

PERUMAL, R. Phosphorylation of synaptosomal proteins from mammalian brain during short-term behavioral experiences. Doctoral dissertation, University of North Carolina, Chapel Hill. Ann Arbor, Mich.: University Microfilms, 1973. No. 73–26, 227.

PETRIDES, M., and IVERSEN, S. D. Cross-modal matching and the primate frontal cortex. *Science*, 1976, *192*, 1023–1024.

PFAFF, D. W. Luteinizing hormone–releasing factor potentiates lordosis behavior in hypophysectomized female rats. *Science*, 1973, *182*, 1148–1149.

PFEIFFER, C. A. Sexual differences of the hypophysis and their determination by the gonads. *American Journal of Anatomy*, 1936, *58*, 195–226.

PIÉRON, H. *Le Problème Physiologique du Sommeil*. Paris: Masson, 1913.

PLOTNIKOFF, N. Magnesium pemoline: Enhancement of memory after electroconvulsive shock in rats. *Life Sciences*, 1966a, *5*, 1495–1498.

PLOTNIKOFF, N. Magnesium pemoline: Enhancement of learning and memory of a conditioned avoidance response. *Science*, 1966b, *151*, 703–704.

PLOTNIKOFF, N. Pemoline and magnesium hydroxide: Memory consolidation following acquisition trials. *Psychonomic Science*, 1967, *9*, 141–142.

POLC, P., and MONNIER, M. An activating mechanism in the ponto-bulbar raphe system of the rabbit. *Journal of Pharmacology and Experimental Therapeutics*, 1966, *154*, 64–73.

POMPEIANO, O., and SWETT, J. E. EEG and behavioral manifestations of sleep induced by cutaneous nerve stimulation in normal cats. *Archives Italiennes de Biologie*, 1962, *100*, 311–342.

POMPEIANO, O., and SWETT, J. E. Actions of graded cutaneous and muscular afferent volleys on brain stem units in the decerebrate cerebellectomized cats. *Archives Italiennes de Biologie*, 1963, *101*, 552–583.

POWERS, B., and VALENSTEIN, E. S. Sexual receptivity: Facilitation by medial preoptic lesions in female rats. *Science*, 1972, *175*, 1003–1005.

POWERS, J. B. Hormonal control of sexual receptivity during the estrous cycle of the rat. *Physiology and Behavior*, 1970, *5*, 831–835.

POWLEY, T. L., and KEESEY, R. E. Relationship of body weight to the lateral hypothalamic feeding syndrome. *Journal of Comparative and Physiological Psychology*, 1970, *70*, 25–36.

POWLEY, T. L., and OPSAHL, C. A. Ventromedial hypothalamic obesity abolished by subdiaphragmatic vagotomy. *American Journal of Physiology*, 1974, *226*, 25–33.

PRIBRAM, K. H. *Languages of the Brain*. Englewood Cliffs, N.J.: Prentice-Hall, 1971.

PRISKO, L. H. Short-term memory in focal cerebral damage. Unpublished Ph.D. dissertation. McGill University, 1963.

PUJOL, J. F., BUGUET, A., FROMENT, J. L., JONES, B., and JOUVET, M. The central metabolism of serotonin in the cat during insomnia: A neurophysiological and biochemical study after P-chlorophenylalanine or destruction of the raphe system. *Brain Research*, 1971, *29*, 195–212.

QUARTERMAIN, D., and WEBSTER, D. Extinction following intracranial reward: The effect of delay between acquisition and extinction. *Science*, 1968, *159*, 1259–1260.

RADO, S. Hedonic self-regulation of the organisms. In *The Role of Pleasure in Behavior*, edited by R. G. Heath. New York: Harper & Row, 1964.

RAISMAN, G. Neuronal plasticity in the septal nuclei of the adult rat. *Brain Research*, 1969, *14*, 25–48.

RAYBIN, J. B., and DETRE, T. P. Sleep disorder and symptomatology among medical and nursing students. *Comprehensive Psychiatry*, 1969, *10*, 452–467.

RECHTSCHAFFEN, A., and KALES, A., editors. *A Manual*

of Standardized Terminology, Techniques and Scoring System for Sleep Stages of Human Subjects. Washington: Public Health Service, United States Government Printing Office, 1968.

RECHTSCHAFFEN, A., VOGEL, G., and SHAIKUN, G. Interrelatedness of mental activity during sleep. *Archives of General Psychiatry*, 1963, 9, 536–547.

RECHTSCHAFFEN, A., WOLPERT, E. A., DEMENT, W. C., MITCHELL, S. A., and FISHER, C. Nocturnal sleep of narcoleptics. *Electroencephalography and Clinical Neurophysiology*, 1963, 15, 599–609.

REED, D. J., and WOODBURY, D. M. Effects of hypertonic urea on cerebrospinal fluid pressure and brain volume. *Journal of Physiology (London)*, 1962, 164, 252–264.

REINIS, S. Autoradiographic study of ^{3}H-thymidine incorporation into brain DNA during learning. *Physiological Chemistry and Physics*, 1972, 4, 391–397.

RIDDLE, O., LAHR, E. L., and BATES, R. W. The role of hormones in the initiation of maternal behavior in rats. *American Journal of Physiology*, 1942, 137, 299–317.

RINGLE, D. A., and HERNDON, B. L. Plasma dialysates from sleep deprived rabbits and their effect on the electrocorticogram of rats. *Pflügers Archives*, 1968, 303, 344–349.

ROBBINS, M. J., and MEYER, D. R. Motivational control of retrograde amnesia. *Journal of Experimental Psychology*, 1970, 84, 220–225.

ROBERTS, W. W. Rapid escape learning without avoidance learning motivated by hypothalamic stimulation in cats. *Journal of Comparative and Physiological Psychology*, 1958a, 51, 391–399.

ROBERTS, W. W. Both rewarding and punishing effects from stimulation of posterior hypothalamus of cat with same electrode at same intensity. *Journal of Comparative and Physiological Psychology*, 1958b, 51, 400–407.

ROBERTS, W. W., and KIESS, H. O. Motivational properties of hypothalamic aggression in cats. *Journal of Comparative and Physiological Psychology*, 1964, 58, 187–193.

ROBERTS, W. W., and ROBINSON, T. C. L. Relaxation and sleep induced by warming of preoptic region and anterior hypothalamus in cats. *Experimental Neurology*, 1969, 25, 282–294.

ROBERTS, W. W., STEINBERG, M. L., and MEANS, L. W. Hypothalamic mechanisms for sexual, aggressive, and other motivational behaviors in the opossum, *Didelphis virginiana. Journal of Comparative and Physiological Psychology*, 1967, 64, 1–15.

ROBINS, R. B., and BOYD, T. E. The fundamental rhythm of the Heidenhain pouch movements and their reflex modifications. *American Journal of Physiology*, 1923, 67, 166–172.

RODGERS, W. L. Specificity of specific hungers. *Journal of Comparative and Physiological Psychology*, 1967, 64, 49–58.

RODIECK, R. W., and STONE, J. Response of cat retinal ganglion cells to moving visual patterns. *Journal of Neurophysiology*, 1965a, 28, 819–832.

RODIECK, R. W., and STONE, J. Analysis of receptive fields of cat retinal ganglion cells. *Journal of Neurophysiology*, 1965b, 28, 833–849.

ROEDER, F., and MÜLLER, D. The stereotaxic treatment of paedophilic homosexuality. *German Medical Monthly (English Language Monthly)*, 1969, 14, 265–271.

ROEDER, F., ORTHNER, H., and MÜLLER, D. The stereotaxic treatment of pedophilic homosexuality and other sexual deviations. In *Psychosurgery*, edited by E. Hitchcock, L. Laitinen, and K. Vaernet. Springfield, Ill.: Charles C Thomas, 1972.

ROFFWARG, H. P., DEMENT, W. C., MUZIO, J. N., and FISHER, C. Dream imagery: Relationship to rapid eye movements of sleep. *Archives of General Psychiatry*, 1962, 7, 235–258.

ROITBAK, A. I. Electrical phenomena in the cerebral cortex during the extinction of orientation and conditioned reflexes. *Electroencephalography and Clinical Neurophysiology*, 1960, *Supplement 13*, 91–100.

ROSE, J. E., BRUGGE, J. F., ANDERSON, D. J., and HIND, J. E. Phase-locked response to low-frequency tones in single auditory nerve fibers of the squirrel monkey. *Journal of Neurophysiology*, 1967, 30, 769–793.

ROSE, R. M., BOURNE, P. G., POE, R. O., MOUGEY, E. H., COLLINS, D. R., and MASON, J. W. Androgen responses to stress: II. Excretion of testosterone, epitestosterone, androsterone, and etiocholanolone during basic combat training and under threat of attack. *Psychosomatic Medicine*, 1969, 31, 418–436.

ROSÉN, I., and ASANUMA, H. Peripheral inputs to the forelimb area of the monkey motor cortex: Input-output relations. *Experimental Brain Research*, 1972, 14, 257–273.

ROSENBLATT, F. Recent work on theoretical models of biological memory. In *Computer and Information Sciences*, Vol. 2, edited by J. Tou. New York: Academic Press, 1967.

ROSENBLATT, F., FARROW, J. T., and HERBLIN, W. F. Transfer of conditioned responses from trained rats to untrained rats by means of a brain extract. *Nature*, 1966, 209, 46–48.

ROSENBLATT, J. S. The development of maternal responsiveness in the rat. *Journal of Orthopsychiatry*, 1969, 39, 36–56.

ROSENFELD, J. P., and KOWATCH, R. Differential effect of morphine on central versus peripheral nociception. *Brain Research*, 1975, 88, 181–185.

ROSENZWEIG, M. R. Evidence for anatomical and chemical changes in the brain during primary learning. In *Biology of Memory*, edited by K. H. Pribram and D. E. Broadbent. New York: Academic Press, 1970.

ROSS, J., CLAYBOUGH, C., CLEMENS, L. G., and GORSKI,

R. A. Short latency induction of estrous behavior with intra-cerebral gonadal hormones in ovariecto-mized rats. *Endocrinology*, 1971, *81*, 32–38.

ROUTTENBERG, A., and LINDY, J. Effects of the avail-ability of rewarding septal and hypothalamic stimula-tion on bar pressing for food under conditions of de-privation. *Journal of Comparative and Psysiological Psychology*, 1965, *60*, 158–161.

ROWLAND, N. E., and ANTELMAN, S. M. Stress-induced hyperphagia and obesity in rats: A possible model for understanding human obesity. *Science*, 1976, *191*, 310–312.

ROZIN, P. Specific aversions and neophobia as a con-sequence of vitamin deficiency and/or poisoning in half-wild and domestic rats. *Journal of Comparative and Physiological Psychology*, 1968, *66*, 82–88.

RUSSEK, M. Hepatic receptors and the neurophysiolog-ical mechanisms controlling feeding behavior. In *Neurosciences Research*, Vol. 4, edited by S. Ehren-preis. New York: Academic Press, 1971.

RUSSELL, W. R., and NATHAN, P. W. Traumatic amnesia. *Brain*, 1946, *69*, 280–300.

SAMANIN, R., and BERNASCONI, S. Effects of intraven-tricularly injected 6-OH dopamine or midbrain raphe lesion on morphine analgesia in rats. *Psychopharma-cologia (Berlin)*, 1972, *25*, 175–182.

SAR, M., and STUMPF, W. E. Neurons of the hypothal-amus concentrate (³H) progesterone or its metabolites. *Science*, 1973, *182*, 1266–1268.

SASANUMA, S. Kana and kanji processing in Japanese aphasics. *Brain and Language*, 1975, *2*, 369–383.

SAUNDERS, J. C. Cochlear nucleus and auditory cortex correlates of a click stimulus-intensity discrimination in cats. *Journal of Comparative and Physiological Psychology*, 1970, *72*, 8–16.

SCHACHTER, S. Cognitive effects on bodily functioning: Studies of obesity and eating. In *Neurophysiology and Emotion*, edited by D. C. Glass. New York: Rockefeller University Press, 1967.

SCHACHTER, S. Some extraordinary facts about obese humans and rats. *The American Psychologist*, 1971, *26*, 129–144.

SCHALLY, A. V., REDDING, T. W., LUCIEN, H. W., and MEYER, J. Enterogastrone inhibits eating by fasted mice. *Science*, 1967, *157*, 210–211.

SCHEIBEL, M. E., and SCHEIBEL, A. B. On circuit patterns of the brain stem reticular core. *Annals of the New York Academy of Science*, 1961, *89*, 857–865.

SCHILDER, P., PASIK, P., and PASIK, T. Extrageniculate vision in the monkey: III. Circle vs. triangle and "red" vs. "green" discrimination. *Experimental Brain Research*, 1972, *14*, 436–448.

SCHMIDT, M. J., and DAVENPORT, J. W. TCAP: Facilita-tion of learning in hypothyroid rats. *Psychonomic Science*, 1967, *7*, 185–186.

SCHMITT, M. Influences of hepatic portal receptors on

hypothalamic feeding and satiety centers. *American Journal of Physiology*, 1973, *225*, 1089–1095.

SCHNEDORF, J. F., and IVY, A. C. An examination of the hypnotoxin theory of sleep. *American Journal of Physiology*, 1939, *125*, 491–505.

SCHNEIDER, A. M., TYLER, J., and JINICH, D. Recovery from retrograde amnesia: A learning process. *Science*, 1974, *184*, 87–88.

SCHREINER, L., and KLING, A. Rhinencephalon and be-havior. *American Journal of Physiology*, 1956, *184*, 486–490.

SCOVILLE, W. B. The limbic lobe in man. *Journal of Neurosurgery*, 1954, *11*, 64–66.

SCOVILLE, W. B., and MILNER, B. Loss of recent memory after bilateral hippocampal lesions. *Journal of Neu-rology, Neurosurgery, and Psychiatry*, 1957, *20*, 11–21.

SELIGMAN, M. E. On the generality of the laws of learning. *Psychological Review*, 1970, 77, 406–418.

SEM-JACOBSEN, C. W. *Depth-electrographic Stimulation of the Human Brain and Behavior*. Springfield, Ill.: Charles C Thomas, 1968.

SENOH, S., CREVELING, C. R., UDENFRIEND, S., and WITKOP, B. Chemical, enzymic, and metabolic studies on the mechanism of oxidation of dopamine. *Journal of the American Chemical Society*, 1959, *81*. 6236–6240.

SETTLAGE, P. H. The effect of occipital lesions on visually-guided behavior in the monkey. I: Influence of the lesions on final capacities in a variety of problem situations. *Journal of Comparative Psychol-ogy*, 1939, *27*, 93–131.

SEWARD, J. P., UYEDA, A. A., and OLDS, J. Resistance to extinction following cranial self-stimulation. *Journal of Comparative and Physiological Psychology*, 1959, *52*, 294–299.

SHALLICE, T., and WARRINGTON, E. K. Word recognition in a phonemic dyslexic patient. *Quarterly Journal of Experimental Psychology*, 1975, *27*, 187–199.

SHARMA, K. N., and NASSET, E. S. Electrical activity in mesenteric nerves after perfusion of gut lumen. *Amer-ican Journal of Physiology*, 1962, *202*, 725–730.

SHASHOUA, V. E. RNA metabolism in goldfish brain during acquisition of new behavior patterns. *Pro-ceedings of the National Academy of Science*, 1970, *65*, 160–167.

SHERRINGTON, C. S. Experiments on the value of vas-cular and visceral factors for the genesis of emotion. *Proceedings of the Royal Society (London), Series B*, 1900, *66*, 390–403.

SHIFFRIN, R. M. Information persistence in short-term memory. *Journal of Experimental Psychology*, 1973, *100*, 39–49.

SIDMAN, M., STODDARD, L. T., and MOHR, J. P. Some additional quantitative observations of immediate memory in a patient with bilateral hippocampal lesions. *Neuropsychologia*, 1968, *6*, 245–254.

SIGG, E. B., DAY, C., and COLOMBO, C. Endocrine factors in isolation induced aggressiveness in rodents. *Endocrinology*, 1966, 78, 679–684.

SIMPSON, B. A., and IVERSEN, S. D. Effects of substantia nigra lesions on the locomotor and stereotype responses to amphetamine. *Nature*, 1971, 230, 30–32.

SIMPSON, J. B., and ROUTTENBERG, A. Subfornical organ lesions reduce intravenous angiotensin–induced drinking. *Brain Research*, 1975, 88, 154–161.

SINCLAIR, D. C. *Cutaneous Sensation*. London: Oxford University Press, 1967.

SINGER, J. Hypothalamic control of male and female sexual behavior in female rats. *Journal of Comparative and Physiological Psychology*, 1968, 66, 738–742.

SITARAM, N., WYATT, R. J., DAWSON, S., and GILLIN, J. C. REM sleep induction by physostigmine infusion during sleep. *Science*, 1976, 191, 1281–1283.

SLOTNICK, B. M. Disturbances of maternal behavior in the rat following lesions of the cingulate cortex. *Behaviour*, 1967, 29, 204–236.

SLOTNICK, B. M., and McMULLEN, M. F. Intraspecific fighting in albino mice with septal forebrain lesions. *Physiology and Behavior*, 1972, 8, 333–337.

SLOTNICK, B. M., McMULLEN, M. F., and FLEISCHER, S. Changes in emotionality following destruction of the septal area in albino mice. *Brain, Behavior, and Evolution*, 1974, 8, 241–252.

SLOTNICK, B. M., and NIGROSH, B. J. Maternal behavior of mice with cingulate, cortical, amygdala, or septal lesions. *Journal of Comparative and Physiological Psychology*, 1975, 88, 118–127.

SMITH, G. P., and EPSTEIN, A. N. Increased feeding in response to decreased glucose utilization in the rat and monkey. *American Journal of Physiology*, 1969, 217, 1083–1087.

SMITH, L. T. Interanimal transfer. *Psychological Bulletin*, 1974, 81, 1078–1095.

SNOWDON, C. T. Motivation, regulation and the control of meal parameters with oral and intragastric feeding. *Journal of Comparative and Physiological Psychology*, 1969, 69, 91–100.

SNYDER, S. H. *Madness and the Brain*. New York: McGraw-Hill, 1974.

SOLOMON, P. Insomnia. *New England Journal of Medicine*, 1956, 255, 755–760.

SONDEREGGER, T. B. Intracranial stimulation and maternal behavior. *Proceedings of the Seventy-eighth Annual American Psychological Association Convention*, 1970.

SPINELLI, D. N. Receptive field organization of ganglion cells in the cat's retina. *Experimental Neurology*, 1967, 19, 291–315.

SPINELLI, D. N., and BARRETT, T. W. Visual receptive field organization of single units in the cat's visual cortex. *Experimental Neurology*, 1969, 24, 76–98.

SPINELLI, D. N., HIRSCH, H. V. B., PHELPS, R. W., and

METZLER, J. Visual experience as a determinant of the response characteristics of cortical receptive fields in cats. *Experimental Brain Research*, 1972, 15, 289–304.

SPINELLI, D. N., PRIBRAM, K. H., and WEINGARTEN, M. Centrifugal optic nerve responses evoked by auditory and somatic stimulation. *Experimental Neurology*, 1965, 12, 303–319.

SPOENDLIN, H. The innervation of the cochlear receptor. In *Basic Mechanisms in Hearing*, edited by A. R. Møeller. New York: Academic Press, 1973.

SPOENDLIN, H., LICHTENSTEIGER, W. The adrenergic innervation of the labyrinth. *Acta Oto-Laryngology*, 1966, 61, 423–434.

SQUIRE, L. R. Stable impairment in remote memory following electroconvulsive therapy. *Neurophychologia*, 1974, 13, 51–58.

STEBBINS, W. C., MILLER, J. M., JOHNSSON, L. -G., and HAWKINS, J. E. Ototoxic hearing loss and cochlear pathology in the monkey. *Annals of Otology, Rhinology, and Laryngology*, 1969, 78, 1007–1026.

STEFFENS, A. B. Influence of reversible obesity on eating behavior, blood glucose, and insulin in the rat. *American Journal of Physiology*, 1975, 228, 1738–1744.

STEIN, G. S., STEIN, J. S., and KLEINSMITH, L. J. Chromosomal proteins and gene regulation. *Scientific American*, 1975, 232, 46–57.

STEIN, H. H., and YELLIN, T. O. Pemoline and magnesium hydroxide: Lack of effect on RNA and protein synthesis. *Science*, 1967, 157, 96–97.

STEIN, L., BELLUZZI, J. D., RITTER, S., and WISE, C. D. Self-stimulation reward pathways: Norepinephrine vs. dopamine. *Journal of Psychiatric Research*, 1974, 11, 115–124.

STEIN, L., and WISE, C. D. Release of norepinephrine from hypothalamus and amygdala by rewarding medial forebrain stimulation and amphetamine. *Journal of Comparative and Physiological Psychology*, 1969, 67, 189–198.

STEIN, L. and WISE, D. Possible etiology of schizophrenia: Progressive damage to the noradrenergic reward system by 6-hydroxydopamine. *Science*, 1971, 171, 1032–1036.

STEINHAUSEN, W. Ueber den experimentallen Nachweis der Ablenkung der Cupula terminalis in der intakten Bogengangsampulle des Labyrinths bei der thermischen und adäquaten rotatorischen Reizung. *Zeitschrift für hals-, nasen- und ohrenheilkunde*, 1931, 29, 211–216.

STELLAR, J. R., and GALLISTEL, C. R. Runway performances of rats for brain-stimulation or food reward. Effects of hunger and priming. *Journal of Comparative and Physiological Psychology*, 1975, 89, 590–599.

STERMAN, M. B. Comment in *The Sleeping Brain*, edited by M. H. Chase. Los Angeles: Brain Information Service/Brain Research Institute, UCLA, 1972.

STERMAN, M. B., and CLEMENTE, C. D. Forebrain inhibitory mechanisms: Cortical synchronization induced by basal forebrain stimulation. *Experimental Neurology*, 1962a, *6*, 91–102.

STERMAN, M. B., and CLEMENTE, C. D. Forebrain inhibitory mechanisms: Sleep patterns induced by basal forebrain stimulation in the behaving cat. *Experimental Neurology*, 1962b, *6*, 103–117.

STERN, J. M., and EISENFELD, A. J. Distribution and metabolism of ^{3}H-testosterone in castrated male rats: Effects of cyproterone, progesterone and unlabeled testosterone. *Endocrinology*, 1971, *88*, 1117–1125.

STERNBACH, R. A. *Pain: A Psychophysiological Analysis.* New York: Academic Press, 1968.

STETSON, R. H. The hair follicle and the sense of pressure. *Psychological Review Monographs*, 1923, *32*, 1–17.

STEVENS, S. S., and NEWMAN, E. B. Localization of actual sources of sound. *American Journal of Psychology*, 1936, *48*, 297–306.

STOSSEL, T. P. The forgotten aspect of medical education. *Pharos*, 1970, *33*, 16–18.

STRICKER, E. M. Osmoregulation and volume regulation in rats: Inhibition of hypovolemic thirst by water. *American Journal of Physiology*, 1969, *217*, 98–105.

STRICKER, E. M. Thirst, sodium appetite, and complementary physiological contributions to the regulation of intravascular fluid volume. In *The Neuropsychology of Thirst: New Findings and Advances in Concepts*, edited by A. N. Epstein, H. R. Kissileff, and E. Stellar. Washington: Winston, 1973.

STRICKER, E. M., FRIEDMAN, M. I., and ZIGMOND, M. J. Glucoregulatory feeding by rats after intraventricular 6-hydroxydopamine or lateral hypothalamic lesions. *Science*, 1975, *189*, 895–897.

STRICKER, E. M., and WOLF, G. The effects of hypovolemia on drinking in rats with lateral hypothalamic damage. *Proceedings of the Society for Experimental Biology and Medicine*, 1967, *124*, 816–820.

SUTHERLAND, E. Studies on the mechanism of hormone action. *Science*, 1972, *177*, 401–408.

SWANSON, H. H. Determination of the sex role in hamsters by the action of sex hormones in infancy. In *The Influence of Hormones on the Nervous System*, edited by D. H. Ford. New York: S. Karger, 1971.

SWEET, W. H. Participant in brain stimulation in behaving subjects. Neurosciences Research Program Workshop, 1966.

SWETT, C. P., and HOBSON, J. A. The effects of posterior hypothalamic lesions on behavioral and electrographic manifestations of sleep and waking in cats. *Archives Italiennes de Biologie*, 1968, *106*, 283–293.

SZENTAGOTHAI, J., FLERKO, B., MESS, B., and HALASZ, B. *Hypothalamic Regulation of the Anterior Pituitary.* Budapest: Hungarian Academy of Science Press, 1965.

TALBOT, W. H., DARIAN-SMITH, I., KORNHUBER, H. H., and MOUNTCASTLE, V. B. The sense of flutter-vibration: Comparison of the human capacity with response patterns of mechanoreceptive afferents from the monkey's hand. *Journal of Neurophysiology*, 1968, *31*, 301–334.

TEITELBAUM, P. The encephalization of hunger. In *Progress in Physiological Psychology*, Vol. 4, edited by E. Stellar and J. M. Sprague. New York: Academic Press, 1971.

TEITELBAUM, P., and CYTAWA, J. Spreading depression and recovery from lateral hypothalamic damage. *Science*, 1965, *147*, 61–63.

TEITELBAUM, P., and EPSTEIN, A. N. The lateral hypothalamic syndrome: Recovery of feeding and drinking after lateral hypothalamic lesions. *Psychological Review*, 1962, *69*, 74–90.

TEITELBAUM, P., and STELLAR, E. Recovery from the failure to eat produced by hypothalamic lesions. *Science*, 1954, *120*, 894–895.

TERENIUS, L., and WAHLSTRÖM, A. Morphine-like ligand for opiate receptors in human CSF. *Life Sciences*, 1975, *16*, 1759–1764.

TERKEL, J. Aspects of maternal behavior in the rat with special reference to humoral factors underlying maternal behavior at parturition. Unpublished Ph.D. dissertation. Rutgers University, 1970.

TERKEL, J. A. Chronic, cross-transfusion technique in freely behaving rats by use of a single heart catheter. *Journal of Applied Physiology*, 1972, *33*, 519–522.

TERKEL, J., and ROSENBLATT, J. S. Maternal behavior induced by maternal blood plasma injected into virgin rats. *Journal of Comparative and Physiological Psychology*, 1968, *65*, 479–482.

THOMAS, G. J., HOSTETTER, G., and BARKER, D. J. Behavior functions of the limbic system. In *Progress in Physiological Psychology*, Vol. 2, edited by E. Stellar and J. M. Sprague. New York: Academic Press, 1968.

TOMITA, T., KANEKO, A., MURAKAMI, M., and PAUTLER, E. Spectral response curves of single cones in carp. *Vision Research*, 1967, *7*, 519–531.

TONNDORF, J., and KHANNA, S. M. Submicroscopic displacement amplitudes of the tympanic membrane (cat) measured by a laser interferometer. *Journal of the Acoustical Society of America*, 1968, *44*, 1546–1554.

TOWE, A. L. Motor cortex and the pyramidal system. In *Efferent Organization and the Integration of Behavior*, edited by J. D. Maser. New York: Academic Press, 1973.

TOWE, A. L., and ZIMMERMAN. Unpublished observations. Cited by Towe, 1973.

TROWILL, J. A., PANKSEPP, J., and GANDELMAN, R. An incentive model of rewarding brain stimulation. *Psychological Review*, 1969, *76*, 264–281.

TSANG, Y. The function of the visual areas of the cortex of the rat in the learning and retention of the

647

maze. *Comparative Psychology Monographs*, 1934, *10*, 1–56.

Tsou, K., and Jang, C. S. Studies on the site of analgesia action of morphine by intracerebral microinjection. *Scientia Sinica*, 1964, *13*, 1099–1109.

Tunturi, A. R. A difference in the representation of auditory signals for the left and right ears in the isofrequency contours of right middle ectosylvian auditory cortex in the dog. *American Journal of Physiology*, 1952, *168*, 712–727.

Ungar, G. Learned fear transferred by a brain peptide. *Federation Proceedings*, 1968, *27*, 223.

Ungar, G., Desiderio, D. M., and Parr, W. Isolation and synthesis of a specific-behavior-inducing peptide. *Nature*, 1972, *238*, 198–202.

Ungar, G., Galvan, L., and Clark, R. H. Chemical transfer of learned fear. *Nature*, 1968, *217*, 1259–1261.

Ungerer, A. Effets comparés de la puromycine et de *Datura stramonium* sur la rétention d'un apprentissage instrumental chez la souris. *Comptes Rendus Academie Sciences, Serie D*, 1969, *269*, 910–913.

Ungerstedt, U. Stereotaxic mapping of the monoamine pathways in the rat. *Acta Physiologica Scandinavica*, 1971, *367*, 1–48.

Ungerstedt, U., and Ljungberg, T. Central dopamine neurons and sensory processing. *Journal of Psychiatric Research*, 1974, *11*, 149–150.

Ursin, H., and Kaada, B. R. Functional localization within the amygdaloid complex in the cat. *Electroencephalography and Clinical Neurology*, 1960, *12*, 1–20.

Uttal, W. R. *The Psychobiology of Sensory Coding.* New York: Harper & Row, 1973.

Vallbo, Å. B. Muscle spindle response at the onset of isometric voluntary contractions in man: Time differences between fusimotor and skeletomotor effects. *Journal of Physiology (London)*, 1971, *218*, 405–431.

Valenstein, E. S. The anatomical locus of reinforcement. In *Progress in Physiological Psychology*, edited by E. Stellar and J. M. Sprague. New York: Academic Press, 1966.

Valenstein, E. S. *Brain Control.* New York: Wiley, 1973.

Valenstein, E. S., and Beer, B. Continuous opportunity for reinforcing brain stimulation. *Journal of the Experimental Analysis of Behavior*, 1964, *7*, 183–184.

Valenstein, E. S., Cox, V. C., and Kakolewski, J. W. Polydipsia elicited by the synergistic action of a saccharin and glucose solution. *Science*, 1967, *157*, 552–554.

Valenstein, E. S., and Valenstein, T. Interaction of pontine and negative reinforcing neural systems. *Science*, 1964, *145*, 1456–1458.

Van Dis, H., and Larsson, K. Induction of sexual arousal in the castrated male rat by intracranial stimulation. *Physiology and Behavior*, 1971, *6*, 85–86.

Van Hoesen, G., Vogt, B., Pandya, D. N., and McKenna, T. M. Compound stimulus discrimination following periarcuate ablations in the rhesus monkey. *Bulletin of the Psychonomic Society*, 1974, *4(4A)*, 255.

van Meter, W. G., and Ayala, G. F. EEG effect of intracarotid or intravertebral arterial administration of *d*-amphetamine in rabbits with basilar artery ligation. *Electroencephalography and Clinical Neurophysiology*, 161, *13*, 382–384.

Verney, E. B. The antidiuretic hormone and the factors which determine its release. *Proceedings of the Royal Society (London), Series B*, 1947, *135*, 25–106.

Verzeano, J., Laufer, M., Spear, S., and McDonald, S. The activity of neuronal networks in the thalamus of the monkey. In *Biology of Memory*, edited by K. H. Pribram and D. E. Broadbent. New York: Academic Press, 1970.

Verzeano, J., and Negishi, K. Neuronal activity in cortical and thalamic networks: A study with multiple electrodes. *Journal of General Physiology*, 1960, *43*, (6, part 2), 177–195.

Vilberg, T. R., and Beatty, W. W. Behavioral changes following VMH lesions in rats with controlled insulin levels. *Pharmacology, Biochemistry, and Behavior*, 1975, *3*, 377–384.

Voci, V. E., and Carlson, N. R. Enhancement of maternal behavior and nest behavior following systemic and diencephalic administration of prolactin and progesterone in the mouse. *Journal of Comparative and Physiological Psychology*, 1973, *83*, 388–393.

Volicer, L., and Lowe, C. G. Penetration of angiotensin II into the brain. *Neuopharmacology*, 1971, *10*, 631–636.

von Békésy, G. The vibration of the cochlear partition in anatomical preparations and in the models of the inner ear. *Journal of the Acoustical Society of America*, 1949a, *21*, 233–245.

von Békésy, G. On the resonance curve and the decay period at various points on the cochlear partition. *Journal of the Acoustical Society of America*, 1949b, *21*, 245–254.

von Békésy, G. Sweetness produced electrically on the tongue and its relation to taste theories. *Journal of Applied Physiology*, 1964, *19*, 1105–1113.

von Meduna, L. General discussion of the cardiazol therapy. *American Journal of Psychiatry (Supplement)*, 1938, *94*, 40–50.

Wade, G. N., Harding, C. F., and Feder, H. H. Neural uptake of (1,2-^{3}H) progesterone in ovariectomized rats, guinea pigs and hamsters: Correlation with species differences in behavioral responsiveness. *Brain Research*, 1973, *61*, 357–367.

Wald, G. Molecular basis of visual excitation. *Science*, 1968, *162*, 230–239.

Walker, W. A., and Leschner, A. I. The role of the

adrenals in aggression. *American Zoologist*, 1972, *12*, 652.

WALL, P. D., and SWEET, W. H. Temporary abolition of pain in man. *Science*, 1967, *155*, 108–109.

WALLACH, H., NEWMAN, E. B., and ROSENZWEIG, M. R. The precedence effect in sound localization. *American Journal of Psychology*, 1949, *62*, 315–336.

WARD, A. A. The cingular gyrus: Area 24. *Journal of Neurophysiology*, 1948, *11*, 13–23.

WARD, I. Prenatal stress feminizes and demasculinizes the behavior of males. *Science*, 1972, *175*, 82–84.

WARD, OJEMAN, and CALVIN. Personal communication cited by Towe, 1973.

WARRINGTON E. K., and SHALLICE, T. Neuropsychological evidence of visual storage in short-term memory tasks. *Quarterly Journal of Experimental Psychology*, 1972, *24*, 30–40.

WARRINGTON, E. K., and TAYLOR, A. M. Immediate memory for faces: Long- or short-term memory? *Quarterly Journal of Experimental Psychology*, 1973, *25*, 316–322.

WARRINGTON, E., and WEISKRANTZ, L. New method of testing long-term retention with special reference to amnesic patients. *Nature*, 1968, *217*, 972–974.

WAXENBERG, S. E., DRELLICH, M. G., and SUTHERLAND, A. M. The role of hormones in human behavior: I. Changes in female sexuality after adrenalectomy. *Journal of Clinical Endocrinology and Metabolism*, 1959, *19*, 193–202.

WEBB, W. B. Paper presented at a symposium of the First International Congress of the Association for the Psychophysiological Study of Sleep, 1971, Bruges, Belgium.

WEGENER, G. Autoradiographische Untersuchungen über gesteigerte proteinsynthese in tectum opticum von Fröschen nach opticher Reizung. *Experimental Brain Research*, 1970, *10*, 363–379.

WEISKRANTZ, L., and COWEY, A. Cross-modal matching in the rhesus monkey using a single pair of stimuli. *Neuropsychologia*, 1975, *13*, 257–261.

WEISKRANTZ, L., and MISHKIN, M. Effects of temporal and frontal cortical lesions on auditory discrimination in monkey. *Brain*, 1958, *81*, 406–414.

WEISKRANTZ, L., WARRINGTON, E. K., SANDERS, M. D., and MARSHALL, J. Visual capacity in the hemianopic field following a restricted occipital ablation. *Brain*, 1974, *97*, 709–728.

WERSÄLL, J., FLOCK, Å., and LUNDQUIST, P. Structural basis for directional sensitivity in cochlear and vestibular sensory receptors. *Cold Spring Harbor Symposia on Quantitative Biology*, 1965, *30*, 115–132.

WETZEL, M. C. Self-stimulation aftereffects and runway performance in the rat. *Journal of Comparative and Physiological Psychology*, 1963, *56*, 673–678.

WETZEL, M. C. Self-stimulation anatomy: Data needs. *Brain Research*, 1968, *10*, 287–296.

WEVER, E. G., *Theory of Hearing*. New York: Wiley, 1949.

WEVER, E. G., and BRAY, C. W. Present possibilities for auditory theory. *Psychology Review*, 1930, *37*, 365–380.

WHALEN, R. E. Hormone induced changes in the organization of sexual behavior in the male rat. *Journal of Comparative and Physiological Psychology*, 1964, *57*, 175–182.

WHALEN, R. E., NEUBAUER, B. L., and GORYALKA, B. B. Potassium chloride–induced lordosis behavior in rats is mediated by the adrenal glands. *Science*, 1975, *187*, 857–858.

WHALEN, R. F., THOMPSON, R. F., VERZEANO, M., and WEINBERGER, N. M., editors. *The Neural Control of Behavior*. New York: Academic Press, 1970.

WHITEHORN, D., and BURGESS, P. R. Changes in polarization of central branches of myelinated mechanoreceptor and nociceptor fibers during noxious and innocuous stimulation of the skin. *Journal of Neurophysiology*, 1973, *36*, 226–237.

WHITFIELD, I. C., and EVANS, E. F. Responses of auditory cortical neurons to stimuli of changing frequency. *Journal of Neurophysiology*, 1965, *28*, 655–672.

WICKELGREN, W. A. The long and the short of memory. *Psychological Bulletin*, 1973, *80*, 425–438.

WIESNER, B. P., and SHEARD, N. *Maternal Behaviour in the Rat*. London: Oliver and Body, 1933.

WILSKA, A. Eine Methode zur Bestimmung der Horschwellenamplituden der Tromenfells bei verscheideden Frequenzen. *Skandinavisches Archiv für Physiologie*, 1935, *72*, 161–165.

WILSON, M. Effects of circumscribed cortical lesions upon somesthetic and visual discrimination in the monkey. *Journal of Comparative and Physiological Psychology*, 1957, *50*, 630–635.

WILSON, M. Further analysis of intersensory facilitation of learning sets in monkeys. *Perceptual and Motor Skills*, 1964, *13*, 917–920.

WISE, C. D., BADEN, M. M., and STEIN, L. Post-mortem measurement of enzymes in human brain: Evidence of a central noradrenergic deficit in schizophrenia. *Journal of Psychiatric Research*, 1974, *11*, 185–198.

WISE, C. D., and STEIN, L. Dopamine-β-hydroxylase deficits in the brains of schizophrenic patients. *Science*, 1973, *181*, 344–347.

WOLPERT, E. A. Studies in psychophysiology of dreams. II: An electromyographic study of dreaming. *Archives of General Psychiatry*, 1960, *2*, 231–241.

WOLSTENCROFT, J. H. Reticulospinal neurones. *Journal of Physiology (London)*, 1964, *174*, 91–99.

WOODWORTH, R. S., and SHERRINGTON, C. S. A pseudaffective reflex and its spinal path. *Journal of Physiology*, 1904, *31*, 234–243.

WYRWICKA, W., and DOBRZECKA, C. Relationship between feeding and satiation centers of the hypothalamus. *Science*, 1960, *131*, 805–806.

YEHLE, A. L., and WARD, J. P. Cross-modal transfer of a specific discrimination in the rabbit. *Psychonomic Science*, 1969, *16*, 269–270.

YOKOYAMA, A., HALASZ, B., and SAWYER, C. H. Effect of hypothalamic deafferentation on lactation in rats. *Proceedings of the Society for Experimental Biology and Medicine*, 1967, *125*, 623–626.

YOUNG, R. W. Visual cells. *Scientific American*, 1970, *223(4)*, 80–91.

YOUNG, W. C. The hormones and mating behavior. In *Sex and Internal Secretions*, ed. 3, edited by W. C. Young. Baltimore: Williams & Wilkins, 1961.

YUNGER, L. M., HARVEY, J. A., and LORENS, S. A. Dissociation of the analgesic and rewarding effects of brain stimulation in the rat. *Physiology and Behavior*, 1973, *10*, 909–913.

ZEIGLER, H. P., and KARTEN, H. S. Central trigeminal structures and the lateral hypothalamus syndrome in the rat. *Science*, 1974, *186*, 636–637.

Name Index

Subject Index